A Critical Woman

Barbara Wootton (then Barbara Adam), c.1914 (GCPP Wootton)

A CRITICAL WOMAN

Barbara Wootton, Social Science and
Public Policy in the Twentieth Century

ANN OAKLEY

BLOOMSBURY ACADEMIC

First published in 2011 by

Bloomsbury Academic
an imprint of Bloomsbury Publishing Plc
36 Soho Square, London W1D 3QY, UK
and
175 Fifth Avenue, New York, NY 10010, USA

CIP records for this book are available from the
British Library and the Library of Congress

ISBN (hardback) 978-1-84966-468-4
ISBN (ebook) 978-1-84966-470-7

This book is produced using paper that is made from wood grown in managed, sustainable forests.
It is natural, renewable and recyclable. The logging and manufacturing processes conform to the
environmental regulations of the country of origin.

Printed and bound in Great Britain by the MPG Books Group, Bodmin, Cornwall

Cover designer: Sharon Cluett
Cover photograph: Barbara Wootton at 80 (Bridget Trotter)

www.bloomsburyacademic.com

For Vera

Contents

List of Illustrations

Note: *The author and publishers would like to thank those shown in square brackets [ ] in the list below for their kind permission to reproduce photographs. (GCPP Wootton refers to Girton College Personal Papers, Barbara Wootton, and GCPP Cam refers to Girton College Personal Papers, Helen Maud Cam.)*

Plates appearing between pages 266 and 267

Federal Union meeting, 1940 [Federal Trust]

Barbara Wootton in the House of Lords for her Life Peerage, 1958 [Press Association]

Barbara and High Barn, Abinger, Surrey, 1960s: house and garden and with donkeys [Vera Seal]; inside High Barn [Getty Images]

Barbara Kyle, taken by Sir George F. Pollock, The Westcott Art Centre, Surrey [GCPP Wootton]

Barbara Kyle, Barbara Wootton and Ann Monie on the terrace of High Barn, early 1960s [Ann Monie]

Barbara Wootton with Liberian delegation, 1963 [Crown copyright, issued for the British Information Services by the Central Office of Information, London]

Barbara Wootton at the 20th international training course in Tokyo, Japan, 1969, United Nations Asia and Far East Institute for the Prevention of Crime and the Treatment of Offenders [GCPP Wootton]

Honorary degrees: Essex, 1975 [University of Essex]; Southampton, 1971 [*Southern Daily Echo*]; Warwick, 1972 [GCPP Wootton]; York, 1966 [*Yorkshire Post Newspapers*]; Bath, 1968 [University of Bath]

Barbara Wootton at 67, taken by Walter Bird [© National Portrait Gallery, London, 1964]

Barbara Wootton at 80, [Peter Johns/ Guardian News & Media Ltd, 1977]

'Any Questions?', 1974, taken by Geoff Ellis of Abergavenny [GCPP Wootton]

On the tenth anniversary of Horizon Holidays [GCPP Wootton]

Barbara Wootton's 80th birthday party, with James Callaghan and others, and with James Callaghan and Gordon Brunton [GCPP Wootton]

Barbara in China [GCPP Wootton]

Vera Seal, mid-1980s [Vera Seal]

Foreword

This is the story of the life of a remarkable woman. It is superbly well told. It is extraordinarily well researched. It is a magnificent intellectual biography. It is also an engaging account of a long life lived to the full but tinged with sadness in its lack of fulfilment in certain deeply private and personal senses. It begins with a conundrum: Why is Barbara Wootton not widely remembered today, given her manifest achievements in so many spheres? In asking this question Ann Oakley never quite finds the answer, but she certainly convinces me that Barbara Wootton deserves a greater place in the history of Britain in the twentieth century than she has been given.

Few people are better qualified to write this biography. Ann Oakley has worked for many years in social research and public policy, and, like Barbara Wootton, has written both autobiography and fiction as well as publishing widely in her academic field. Coincidentally, twenty years ago, soon after Barbara Wootton's death, I considered writing her biography myself. However, I realized that I probably did not have the time to do it justice. I may also have been influenced by Jim Callaghan who, when I consulted him about it, said he thought perhaps she was not a 'big enough figure'. Most people who read this fascinating book will come to a different conclusion. Barbara Wootton was a 'big figure'. However, she did not fit into any conventional box. She was neither a politician nor a conventional academic, nor a head of an important institution. She could not easily be compared to the great women reformers before her – the Florence Nightingales, Elizabeth Frys or Eleanor Rathbones – who espoused a single issue and gave that issue their lives. The causes she fought for were many and varied, so her energies were spread rather than concentrated. To me this makes her more interesting and more remarkable. But because her contributions were so widely diverse, it is harder to define her and, therefore, easier to forget her.

Barbara Wootton was a public intellectual who applied her searching intellect to many of the important questions which faced Britain from the 1930s to 1980s. She did so from the perspective of a social scientist, having abandoned classics for economics as a student at Cambridge. She had no time for social or economic theory or, indeed, for disciplinary labels of any kind. Instead she wished to use the techniques of empirical social science research to identify evidence-based solutions to policy problems. She was a thinker who wanted to improve the world, not just to define it. The books she wrote were critical and iconoclastic, and they did not endear her to many of her more conventional colleagues in the social sciences. Her output was prodigious; yet her research and writing were only part of the contribution that she made.

In her early career she was a leading figure in adult education, running Morley College and then Extra-Mural Studies in London, and working with the Workers' Educational Association. She sat as a Magistrate on the Juvenile Bench for over forty years. She was the first woman life peer in the House of Lords, playing a leading part in its legislative work for more than twenty-five years. She sat on four Royal Commissions and many other government committees. She was a successful and sought after broadcaster, appearing regularly on programmes such as 'The Brains Trust' and 'Any Questions'. As her international reputation grew, she lectured in many parts of the world on a wide range of subjects.

To achieve all this required drive, energy, courage and self-sacrifice. Her achievements must also have demanded good organization in how she used her time and the support of people who she could persuade that what she believed in deserved their loyalty and help. She worked outside the conventional structures of academic departments or political parties. This gave her the freedom to range widely and to be forthright, and to say what she wanted without compromise. Had she been born half a century later she would have been a splendid head of a centre-left think tank focused on reform and finding solutions to the social problems which face us.

Sharing her political values, her commitment to social reforms and her engagement with the application of social science to the search for rational solutions to policy issues, I found it easy to identify with her and to admire her. Many readers of this book will undoubtedly feel, as I do, that it would have been a pleasure and a privilege to know this woman. To have been in her company would certainly have been challenging: she clearly did not tolerate fools and was probably sometimes intimidating. However, to have obtained her respect must have been rewarding.

She was not blessed with good fortune in her personal life. Her childhood appears to have been relatively happy: she enjoyed a close relationship with her two brothers and adored her nanny whose devotion to her lasted a lifetime. Yet she lost her father at an early age and suffered from her mother's coldness and overweening ambition that her daughter should succeed as a classicist. Marriage at twenty might have provided an escape. But tragically Jack Wootton was killed at Passchendaele less than six weeks after she married him. She did not marry again for another eighteen years. Her second husband was a taxi driver, a student at the adult education classes she organized, later becoming a Labour Party education officer. She and George Wright had a number of happy years together, but eventually she left him. A close female friend with whom she then lived died of cancer. But Barbara Wootton was no victim: she was committed to life and to the causes in which she believed; she enjoyed many important friendships with interesting men and women of the period, and she made the most of the varied opportunities that came her way for visiting other countries and learning about other cultures.

She had no children. Although apparently she did not dwell on it, she did express regret that she did not become a mother. It is perhaps a paradox that in spite of this she spent much of her working life fighting for a better deal for children in trouble. It is another paradox, and Ann Oakley reflects on this, that in spite of being the first woman to reach a variety of positions in public life, she appears not to have been much interested in questions of gender.

The last years of her long life were lonely but made infinitely better than they might have been by the loving support of Vera Seal to whom this book is dedicated. In doing so, Ann Oakley has recognized the generous and selfless care that women often give to others. Barbara Wootton's life was enriched by her friends in the absence of a family and no more so than by Vera Seal.

Tessa Blackstone

Acknowledgements

Researching and writing a book such as this generates a long list of debts. My primary debt is to Vera Seal, to whom this book is dedicated. As Barbara Wootton's longtime friend, colleague, personal assistant, carer and manager of her literary estate, Vera gave the project a very warm welcome when I first approached her in October 2007. She has provided me with an enormous amount of valuable material – lists of people to contact, letters, papers, photographs, mementoes, and many hours of memories of Barbara. Her commitment to the book and her friendship have sustained me through the inevitable hardships of writing, and have enabled me to benefit from many other kindnesses, including a Charles de Mills rose, luscious swiss chard plants and a marvellous unpatented design for a squirrel-proof bird-feeder. Vera has read several drafts of the book and her meticulous comments have contributed not only to the story but to remedying my deficient habits of grammar and punctuation. Without her help, my task in writing *A Critical Woman* would have been even more daunting than it has been. I hope she feels the final product repays the effort she has put into it.

Vera Seal worked with Kate Perry, the College Archivist, in the Library at Girton College, Cambridge, to place a collection of Barbara Wootton's Papers there after Barbara's death. It would have taken me far longer to find my way round those papers and the other valuable assets of the Girton Library without Kate's help and interest. I remember with particular fondness her determination one day to find the room Barbara lived in when she first taught at Girton in 1920, and our mutual delight in locating this particular room with a view. Kate's successor as Girton Archivist, Hannah Westall, has continued this tradition of help in supplying references and scanning in photographs for reproduction.

I am grateful for the help of staff in many other archives and libraries, and (where relevant) for permission to quote from material thus accessed. The list includes Bedford Central Library; Bethlem Royal Hospital, Archives and Museums; Birmingham District Probate Registry Office; the British Association for Adoption and Fostering; the British Library; the British Library of Political and Economic Science (the papers of William Beveridge, Duncan Burn and Lena Jeger); the Cambridgeshire Association for Local History; the Charity Commission; the Christian Science Archives; the Churchill Archives Centre, Churchill College, Cambridge (William Haley's Papers); the City of Westminster Archives Centre; the Cunard Archives at the University of Liverpool; the Dartington Hall Trust Archives; Emmanuel College, Cambridge, Archives; the Hull History Centre; the Institute of Advanced Legal Studies, London; the London Borough of Camden Local Studies and Archive Centre; the London Borough of Hammersmith and Fulham Archives and Local History Centre; the London Cremation Company; London Metropolitan University (the TUC Archives); the Magistrates' Association; the National Archives at Kew; the National Portrait Gallery; Nuffield College, Oxford (G.D.H. Cole's papers); Milton Keynes Local Studies and Family History Library; *New Humanist Magazine*; the Parliamentary Archives, Houses of Parliament; the People's History Museum, Manchester; Queen Mary, University of London (Westfield College Archives); Royal Holloway, University of London (Bedford College Archives); Ruskin College, Oxford; St Albans Library; Senate House Library, University of London, Special Collections; the Stephen Perse Foundation; Trinity College, Cambridge; Trinity College, Oxford; the University of Southampton, Archives, Manuscripts and Special Collections (Neil Kensington Adam's papers); the University of Sussex (Kingsley Martin Archives); and Wheaton College, USA, Special Collections (Malcolm Muggeridge Archives). My apologies if there are any inadvertent omissions from this list.

For permission to use photographs and to quote from interviews, letters, and archives, I have done my best to contact the relevant people; I apologize to any whom I have failed to trace.

Special thanks for providing information or researching particular aspects of Barbara Wootton's life and work are due to Anna Baghiani at the Société Jersiaise and Val Nelson at the Jersey Museum in St Helier, Jersey, for help with genealogical research; Dorothy Baker, guide to Goddards at the Landmark Trust, for information about Barbara Wootton's Surrey home; Helen Bruce at the University of Adelaide in Australia, for retrieving correspondence related to Barbara Wootton's Australian visit; Shirley Corke, for material on the Farrer family and the history of Abinger; Paul Cox, for information about Barbara's maternal grandmother; Stefan Dickers at the Bishopsgate Institute, and Naomi Phillips and David Pollock of the British Humanist Association, for providing information and material on Barbara's association with the humanist movement; Sue Donnelly at the British Library of Political and Economic Science, for responding to queries about Barbara Wootton and George Wright's student records; Catharine Hanlon at the Stephen Perse Foundation, for researching Barbara's schooldays; Trish Hayes at the BBC Written Archives Centre, for locating Barbara's media performances; Bill Hetherington at the Peace Pledge Union, for information on conscientious objectors; Bridget Howlett at the London Metropolitan Archives, for uncovering material about George Wright's connection with the London County Council; Karen Johnson at the National Library of Australia in Canberra, for access to the correspondence between Barbara Wootton and John Barry; Lisa Kerrigan and Kathleen Dickson at the British Film Institute, for providing transcripts and arranging viewings of Barbara's television appearances; Tammy Little, for retrieving a copy of one of Barbara's early publications; Bill Luckin, for details of Barbara's work as a road safety campaigner; Patricia McGuire, King's College, Cambridge, for copies of letters relating to Barbara Wootton in the papers of Noel Annan; Nicholas Morgan, the executor of Barbara Wootton's will, for information on contracts and bequests; Jacques Oberson in the United Nations Library, Geneva, for details of Barbara's attendance at the World Economic Conference; Sue Slack at the Cambridgeshire Collection, Cambridge Central Library, for tracking down material relating to the Adam family, Barbara Wootton's first wedding and Adela Adam's work for the suffrage movement; Mary Turner and Kathy Atherton of the Dorking Local History Group, for information about Abinger; Mike Weaver at the Working Class Movement Library in Salford, for providing a copy of Barbara's pamphlet on *Taxation Under Capitalism*; and staff at the Women's Library at London Metropolitan University, for permission to transcribe fully Brian Harrison's interview with Barbara Wootton. For information about, and permission to refer to, Barbara Wootton's correspondence with HRH Prince Philip, Duke of Edinburgh, I am grateful to His Royal Highness and Dame Anne Griffiths. I am indebted to Sergio Graziosi in the Social Science Research Unit at the Institute of Education in London, for translating material in Italian drawn on in Chapter 9 and for invaluable computing support.

To the following who have given me with great goodwill valuable information, access to unpublished material, and/or the benefit of their personal memories and appreciations of Barbara Wootton's life and work, I record my particular thanks: David Adams; Jessica Adams; Mimi, Lady Adamson; Ann Ashford; David Ashford; Professor Tony Atkinson; Paul Barker; Professor Philip Bean; Professor Maxine Berg; Keith Bilton; John Bird; Sir Louis Blom-Cooper, QC; Audrey Bradley; Don Bradley; Sir Gordon Brunton; Alan Bryant; Anne Bryant;

Margaret Clark; Brenda Collison; Baroness Jean Corston; Andy Croft; Professor David Donnison; Professor David Downes; Professor Gavin Drewry; Frank Field, MP; Professor Jean Floud; Sir John Ford; Kate Fox; Tony Gould; Diana Grassie; Professor A.H. Halsey; David Jacobs; Lord Neil Kinnock; Nellie, Lady McGregor; Ross McGregor; Ann Monie; Professor J.N. Morris; Professor Terry Morris; Diane Munday; Professor Michael Newman; Rachel Pierce; Professor Robert Pinker; Dorothy Runnicles; Freda Russell; Professor Sir Michael Rutter; Madeleine Simms; Professor Peter Townsend; Bridget Trotter; Professor Nigel Walker; Malcolm Wicks, MP; and John Melville Williams, QC. For information about Arthur Adam, my thanks to Sue Collins, Rob Dean, Barry Foulds, Professor Jeffrey O'Riordan, Anthony Payne and Jonathan Payne, and to Elliott Lushaba and Nombulelo Lushaba. Gavin Thomas and Rollo Prendergast were generous with access to their genealogical websites, which saved me much time filling in gaps in Barbara Wootton's family history; my thanks also to Dr Gavin Thomas, for the reference to the Mark Pattison connection and for help with Barbara's family tree. Without Professor Alberto Castelli's valuable knowledge of Italian federalism, my understanding of Barbara Wootton's work in the 1930s would have been incomplete. Professor Philip Graham's connection with the Perse School enabled me to find out more about Hubert Wootton. Thanks also to Christopher Clarke, Private Secretary to the Lord Speaker, for clarifying the circumstances of Barbara Wootton's departure from the House of Lords; to Dr Hera Cook, for drawing my attention to the Barbara Wootton interview in the Kingsley Martin Archive; to Professor Graham Crow, not only for correcting my use of the word 'only', but for several references to material relating to Barbara Wootton's work; to Dr Lesley Hall, for various archival pointers, and especially for information about Barbara Wootton's connection with the Abortion Law Reform Association; to Dr Yvonne Johnson, for sharing her expertise about Barbara Wootton's role in social work education; to Professor Hilary Land, for her paper updating Barbara Wootton's zoological comparison of professorial salaries; to Dr Shawne Miksa, for sharing information about Barbara Kyle; to Terence O'Kelly, for supplying a photograph of Barbara's house; to Stephen Pickles of the Institute of Education Library, for discussions about Barbara Kyle's work; to Tom Rivers, for advice about legal issues; and to members of the Social Work History Network, for recollections of Barbara's role in the education of social workers. For accompanying me on various expeditions to research Barbara Wootton's family background, and for technical help, I am indebted to Penrose Robertson. The conversations I have had about Barbara Wootton and about biography-writing with Tony Gould have inspired and encouraged me. I am grateful to Professor J.W. Winter for our profoundly educational journey round the Historial de la Grande Guerre, Péronne, and the Somme Battlefields in France. Dr Robin Oakley's support and help in a multitude of ways is greatly appreciated, and not at all taken for granted (as he sometimes suspects). Tabitha Oakley-Brown's help with various papers and her interest in Barbara Wootton have energized and impressed me.

In piecing together the account in *A Critical Woman* of the many places reached by Barbara Wootton's life and work, I have been enormously helped by the indefatigable researches of Anne Ingold at the Social Science Research Unit. I grew to rely on her tendency to wander down all sorts of potentially promising side-alleys, and to talk so persuasively to total strangers. I know she thinks we need another five years to gather a complete record, but I hope this interim account will do.

For financial support, I would like to thank the Nuffield Foundation. The Foundation's commitment to the project, and especially the interest and wisdom of its Deputy Director, Dr Sharon Witherspoon, have greatly eased my journey through Barbara Wootton's life and work, as well as supplying important information about both Barbara Wootton's and Barbara Kyle's links with the Foundation. Thanks also to the Titmuss-Meinhardt Fund at the London School of Economics and to the Institute of Education, for additional support. To my agent, Rachel Calder, my thanks for seeing me and my project through difficult times, and to Caroline Wintersgill and Frances Pinter at Bloomsbury Academic, for believing in it – and to Caroline (and to David Owen) for coming up with the title *A Critical Woman*. I would also like to thank Matthew Hough for once again performing his beautifully critical and efficient copy-editing services.

A number of people have been kind enough to read particular chapters of the book: Professor Tony Atkinson, Professor Philip Bean, Sir Louis Blom-Cooper, Professor Alberto Castelli, Felicity Cave, Professor Sir Iain Chalmers, Professor David Donnison, Professor A.H. Halsey, Professor Terry Morris, Professor Robert Pinker, Professor Sir Michael Rutter and Professor J. W. Winter. I am grateful for their time and for their comments. Aside from Vera Seal, some colleagues, friends and family, and people who knew Barbara Wootton have also read and commented on the entire manuscript; for these sterling services, which have resulted in the removal of many embarrassing howlers and errors, I would like to thank Ann Ashford, Professor Jennifer Coates, Professor Graham Crow, Dame Karen Dunnell, Tony Gould, Anne Ingold, Dr Robin Oakley, Penrose Robertson and Dr James Thomas. It is customary to say that none of the people whom one thanks in a book of this kind is responsible for its contents. That is, of course, true. Biographies require decisions about inclusion and omission, and about interpretation and evaluation which must ultimately be the biographer's responsibility. I have done my best not to misrepresent anything in this account of Barbara Wootton's life and work, but there are bound to be places where expert eyes will notice that I have missed something or not got it quite right. For this, I offer my apologies.

I fear that my family and close friends have suffered from having to share me with Barbara Wootton for too long. I am grateful for their patience, forbearance, love and support.

Ann Oakley
February 2011

Barbara Wootton's Family Tree (Abridged)

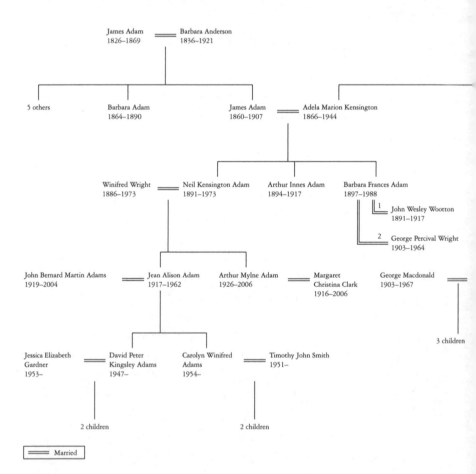

James Adam
1826–1869 ═══ Barbara Anderson
1836–1921

5 others

Barbara Adam
1864–1890

James Adam
1860–1907 ═══ Adela Marion Kensington
1866–1944

Winifred Wright
1886–1973 ═══ Neil Kensington Adam
1891–1973

Arthur Innes Adam
1894–1917

Barbara Frances Adam
1897–1988
 └ 1 John Wesley Wootton
        1891–1917
   2 George Percival Wright
        1903–1964

John Bernard Martin Adams
1919–2004 ═══ Jean Alison Adam
1917–1962

Arthur Mylne Adam
1926–2006 ═══ Margaret
Christina Clark
1916–2006

George Macdonald
1903–1967 ═══

3 children

Jessica Elizabeth
Gardner
1953– ═══ David Peter
Kingsley Adams
1947–

Carolyn Winifred
Adams
1954– ═══ Timothy John Smith
1951–

2 children

2 children

═══ Married

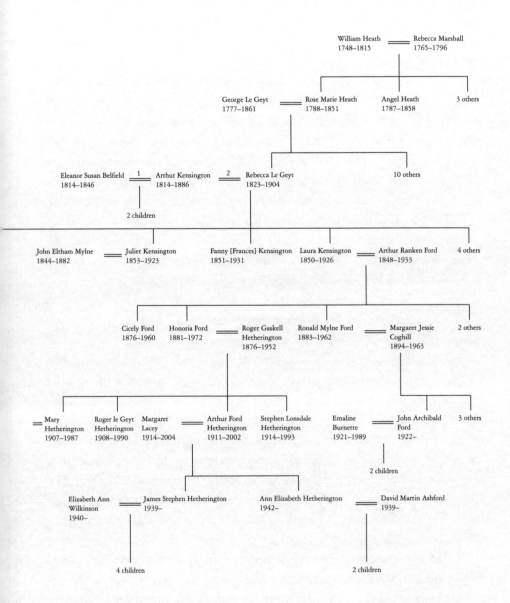

Writing a Life of Barbara Wootton

Barbara Wootton's work and life are remembered by only a few people today. Her name is not one that conjures up a notable record of public achievement, even though this was the nature of her work, in her lifetime, which spanned the greater part of the twentieth century (1897–1988). Her name is, for example, the answer to the following questions: Who first suggested community service as an alternative to imprisonment in Britain? Who chaired a commission on drugs policy which recommended fundamental changes in the law in 1968? Who succeeded in getting the Bill to abolish capital punishment through the House of Lords and on to the statute book in 1965? Who set up a campaign to persuade the Government of the time to adopt the principles of the 1942 Beveridge Report and establish the welfare state? Who was the first woman to give University lectures in Cambridge in 1921, be a member of a national policy commission in 1924, go as a delegate to a League of Nations World Conference in 1927, work in the House of Lords as a life peer in 1958, and become Deputy Speaker there in 1965? Who campaigned in Parliament to abolish corporal punishment in schools, legalize assisted dying and abortion, change the laws about who could marry whom, protect the environment, curtail the unrestricted development of airports and motorways, and treat crime on the roads as equal in severity to crime in other places? Who was the first Chair of the Countryside Commission? Who was a founder member of the Campaign for Nuclear Disarmament, the British Humanist Association, the British Sociological Association and the first modern movement for human rights? Whose contributions to the movement for a federation of countries committed to world peace underpinned the development of the European Community? Who wrote the first sustained critique in English of the deficits of traditional economic theory, provided the first framework for understanding how what people earn is determined as much by social as by economic factors, and participated in a famous and influential debate about the benefits of centralized economic planning versus those of free-market capitalism? Who put forward new theories about the role of intent and of punishment in the criminal justice system? Who took the first systematic look at theories about the causes of anti-social behaviour in young people, challenged the tendency of professionals to assume the role of expert, and helped to establish a new critique of medicalization as a damaging process which strips us of our autonomy and moral responsibility? Who was the first academic and policy activist to argue seriously that policies designed to promote human welfare must be based on sound scientific evidence, and that social research, as a significant endeavour feeding the policy process, ought to concern itself with systematic understandings of human behaviour?

This biography begins with a paradox: that such a tremendous record of achievement should be so forgotten. It is the first full-length account of Barbara Wootton's life and work.[1] People's posthumous reputations are a notoriously poor guide to the nature of their living contributions. It is thus sometimes the self-appointed task of biographers to rescue people from unjustified anonymity – from what historian E.P. Thompson called 'the enormous condescension of posterity'.[2] But that was not my original motive for researching and writing *A Critical Woman*. As a social scientist, I had used Barbara Wootton's work, particularly her book *The Social Foundations of Wage Policy*, which I read as an economics student in the early 1960s, and her *Social Science and Social Pathology*, which came into its own when I was trying, in the early 1990s, to establish a culture within social research of systematic evidence reviews. Through her publications, I had developed a deep respect for her intellect and her rationality, and for the way in which she harnessed these to the dissection and treatment of social problems; I was impressed by her constant, reasoned refusal to be taken in by grand theory or professional arrogance. She believed that people are the experts on their own lives. She did not believe that long words and technical vocabularies are aids to understanding. Along with this – and entirely consistent with it – was her passion for democracy and for social and economic equality. She was too radical to act as the spokesperson of any one political party. Her thinking, and her contributions to social science and to public policy, were lateral and diverse: she crossed boundaries, and re-crossed them, argued that they should not exist, and thus perpetually and valuably provoked people into reassessing their own positions.

My fascination with her mind and its impact on social science and public policy led me to want to know more about the person and her work. There was a personal connection too: my father, Professor Richard Titmuss, was a colleague of Barbara Wootton's when she headed a social studies department at the University of London in the 1950s. I recall her coming to dinner in our house in London, and I remember being taken to see her in her house in the country, where she lived with two donkeys. I did not warm to her; she had rather a formidable presence and to a child (I was thirteen) she did not seem easily approachable. Fifty years passed between that meeting and the time I decided I wanted to write a biography of her. Much, obviously, had happened during that half-century, to her, to me and to the society in which we lived. The greater part of her achievements came after the mid-1950s. I went on to study economics, like her, and then discover social science, again like her. Many years further on, and in the course of trying to map the development of one branch of social science – what was then called 'medical sociology' – I came across an account by Margot Jefferys, a sociologist who worked with Barbara Wootton at Bedford College in London during the early 1950s. Margot also knew my father, in the shadow of whose quite considerable reputation I had grown up. Describing Barbara as 'iconoclastic, clear-minded and coldly witty', Margot went on to make an observation which burnt a small hole in my brain: Barbara Wootton's reputation, she said, was so much less than Richard Titmuss's, yet 'she was a more brilliant social analyst than he'.[3] This remark made me think hard about the circumstances which allow some people's achievements to be noticed, and others not. For anyone who has pondered the mysteries of gender, this is hardly a new question. It was one I took with me through the process of writing *A Critical Woman*.

My sense, as a thirteen-year-old, of Barbara Wootton as not an easily approachable person, proved to be an early warning of my task as a biographer. The material records a person leaves behind are a footprint of character as well as the way life was lived. Barbara Wootton was a private person – she did not talk easily about her emotions and her private life. She also did not care much for history. Her concerns were for the present, and about how the present can be helped by learning from the past. These traits of character are reflected in the fact that she made no provision for her literary estate, she made no plans about where her papers would be lodged after her death, and she left a very partial record of her life. Without the careful guidance of Vera Seal, Barbara's longtime colleague, friend and personal assistant, there might well have been no Barbara Wootton archives at all; as it is, the 237 files of papers, newspaper cuttings, correspondence and photographs in the library of Girton College, Cambridge, are as notable for what they do not contain as for what they do. According to Barbara's solicitor, much was destroyed in her lifetime.[4] For example, there are no diaries in the Girton archives, and relatively few personal letters; there is no correspondence with her parents, or with either of her husbands. This suggests that she did not entertain the possibility that someone might want to write her biography. When asked once how she wanted to be remembered, she said she did not particularly want to be remembered at all, but, if she were, it should be 'as a person who tried hard for what she thought were good causes. And what I hope other people will think are good causes, and there will still be people who think they're good causes even when I'm dead and gone.'[5]

There is no need to read undue modesty into this statement: Barbara Wootton was an intensely pragmatic and realistic person, and the sentiments she expressed here follow the course of a life that really did have the promotion of 'good causes' at its centre. Perhaps she was ambivalent about being the subject of a biography – her reputation for clear thinking co-exists with a much less obvious talent for ambivalence. But it *was* something she did seriously consider. When she got to know the writer Tony Gould in the last years of her life, she asked him to write her biography. In 1985, he decided to agree. He wrote to Penguin Books to ask whether they would commission a volume in their series *Lives of Modern Women*, but their answer was no: they had a full set of titles already, and were worried about Barbara Wootton's appeal to an American audience.[6] She herself wrote an account of the first seventy years of her life, *In a World I Never Made,* published in 1967, but this is a judicious selection from the available material, and it does not cover the twenty years of activity that were still to come. Several reviewers of the book noted that the silences and gaps in it spoke volumes. There is also a sense in the autobiography, for anyone at all familiar with Barbara Wootton's work and life, of a manufactured story; of an account that has been tailored in various ways to fit with a particular interpretation. This is an inevitable feature of autobiographies, as it is also, to some extent, but differently, of biographies.

There is no such thing as an authentic story of someone's life. There are stories about lives, which can be authenticated in various ways, but the life-writer who pursues the phantasm of truth has given herself or himself an impossible task. To any social researcher, this is a familiar difficulty. Our strategies for building a knowledge base about the workings of the social world rest on two conflicting obligations: to reflect that world in as accurate a way as possible; and to respect all the different perspectives and positions that contribute to it. Although biography is an evidence-based enterprise, there are inevitably choices to be made between different versions of 'the facts'. 'Biography is not *the* representation but the re-making, not the reconstruction but the construction, in written form of a life.'[7] The interpretive act, or series of acts, through which lives are constructed involves a process which is very like the 'triangulation' used by qualitative social researchers. You take one account and put it next to another, and then the next one; you look at the context and consider what makes the most sense.

The data relating to Barbara Wootton's life that I collected and drew on to examine in this way began with the Girton College Archives, and her published writings and other public outputs. Between 1919, when she emerged from her Classics and economics studies at Girton College, until two years before she died aged ninety-one in 1988, there is an unbroken record of policy and academic work and publications. Barbara Wootton was a communicator as well as a parliamentarian and a policy analyst and a magistrate and a professor of social studies and a baroness and an economist and all the other things she was; perhaps, above all else, she was a communicator. She wrote enormously, though also in a very precisely guided way, about all the subjects in which she was interested; her main audiences were not academic ones, but policy and practice circles, and the public whose lives were affected by whatever was at issue. She wrote for daily and Sunday newspapers, for journals such as *Adult Education, Agenda, Common Sense, The Freethinker, The Highway, New Society, The Political Quarterly,* the *Probation Journal,* and *Social Service,* as well as for more standard outlets such as *The Economic Journal, The British Journal of Psychiatry, The British Journal of Sociology* and the *British Medical Journal.* She was a broadcaster and, for a time, what was known as a 'television personality': 'the Baroness who married a taxi-driver', who went on 'The Brains Trust', and 'Any Questions?', and 'Question Time', and 'Man Alive', and 'Your Witness' and 'Panorama' and 'Tonight', and entertained them all with her sage witticisms and down-to-earth commonsense. I read almost all her writings, and listened to or watched some of her media appearances, but I did not read all the 1,792 contributions she made to House of Lords debates – had I done so, this book is unlikely ever to have materialized. Beyond Barbara Wootton's own outputs, I searched other people's archives; I read the social, economic and political literature of the period; I interrogated biographies and autobiographies relating to people she knew and worked with; and, most importantly, I was fortunate to be able to interview and talk informally to some of the people who knew her. The result of all this was an enormous quantity of material: the 'raw data' – messy, unclassified and sometimes unclassifiable, contradictory on occasion, often repetitive. Of course it has proved impossible to include everything in the book; my file of 'things to put in somewhere' remains substantial. I was also making new discoveries until the last minute – for example, about Barbara Wootton's contentious record as a road safety campaigner, and about her efforts in the 1940s to increase government investment in social science research – and I have no doubt that more time would have yielded more such treasures. This book, like Barbara Wootton's life, has the status of a work in progress. Nonetheless, I hope it gives the main areas of her work the space they deserve.

As I collected all this material, I became increasingly conscious of a contradiction between its volume, on the one hand, and the difficulty of accessing the private side of Barbara Wootton's life, on the other. The woman seemed constantly to disappear underneath the piles of what she did. I kept removing the layers, so that she saw the daylight again, but she still seemed determined to hide. People talk about 'writing a biography', yet it is not the writing that is the journey, but the researching and the data-collecting and the sifting of data that come first. A good portion of the work that goes into writing a biography is filing: imposing some system of order on the assembled material, so that what is faintly remembered, completely forgotten, or looked for again can be found. Although there is a literature on life-writing, there are very few 'how to do it' guides; the housework of biography, like other forms of housework, is not much spoken about. But the process of collecting and organizing the data is what yields the picture round which the biography is written. This was how I discovered what I did not know at the beginning – just *how much* Barbara Wootton did to shape public policy, and to leave a heritage of writing and analysis which is so remarkable a foundation for what is today known as 'evidence-based' or 'evidence-informed' public policy. I often joked to friends and colleagues over the period when I was researching and writing *A Critical Woman* that I would never have embarked on it had I realized how much ground there was to cover.

There are many challenges in trying to write a narrative about someone's life.[8] The relationship between biographers and their subjects is one of them. If the biographer likes the subject too much, there is the danger of uncritical hagiography. The biographer reads too much into her or his subject, making her or him too much the centre of attention and action, and through a kind of 'vicarious egocentrism', there is liable to be an excess of apology and defence.[9] Ambivalence or dislike can lead to other forms of one-sided interpretation. Although biographers sometimes change their minds about their subjects in the course of writing about them – dislike turns to like, regard to disaffection, and unanticipated discoveries may upset originally held interpretations – I feel much the same about Barbara Wootton at the end of writing *A Critical Woman* as I did at the outset. In the writing of a biography, there is a very concrete sense of a dialogue with one's subject, of the sparking of arguments, of the testing of insights, of *opposition*. Barbara Wootton has been very good at this, so I have her to thank for maintaining the level of my interest in her. At the end, I still admire her, and I remain overawed by the amount and importance of what she achieved. But she has also retained her capacity to irritate me – not just because of her absolutely impeccable logic and punctilious attention to detail and the way she gets everything right, but because sometimes, when she succumbs to normal human fallibility and gets things wrong, she appears to have difficulty in recognizing and admitting this.

As well as what biographers may think or feel about their subjects, there is the problem of identification. The biographer may identify with the subject, which is itself a danger, though some form of identification is probably a necessary element in biography, because if you do not get lost in someone's life, you are unlikely to find an authentic story to write about. I have spent more than three years living with Barbara Wootton, and at times have felt as though I have begun to think and speak like her. If I did not sympathize with her values and her outlook and her interests in the first place, this temporary merging of identity would, of course, never have happened. I cannot rule out the possible result that there is too much of me in *A Critical Woman*; but I prefer to think that here is simply a good match between biographer and subject: two women, with similar academic and policy interests, though with different social backgrounds and separated by half a century.

In other respects, Barbara Wootton and Ann Oakley are very different kinds of people. Barbara Wootton enjoyed the networking, ceremonies and accolades of the public policy world; she had an unsatisfying, at times tragic, personal life; she had no close family; and she did not call herself a feminist. In these ways, I, as her biographer, do not share her experiences or her inclinations. She might not agree with the emphasis I have placed on what happened to women in her lifetime in this story about her life. But to me, the transformation in the lives of women that occurred during the major part of the twentieth century, and to which Barbara Wootton's own role contributed, is a key part of the context in which she worked and had an impact. A relative of hers expressed the view that she would want, above all, to be remembered for her intellectual work.[10] *A Critical Woman* sets out to be an intellectual biography: principally an account of how Barbara Wootton's thought and philosophy evolved through the various stages of her life and was reflected in what she said, wrote and did. But the mind is part of the body and the body belongs to a social order. 'Neither the life of an individual nor the history of a society can be understood without understanding both.'[11] Thus, I have also tried to set the story of her life within its context; particularly in a life such as hers, which was so much occupied with the problem of the individual *in* society, the interplay between the personal and the public, the effect of one on the other, is a constantly running theatre, not only of the imagination, but of the real way in which the lives of human beings construct the social world.

The choices I made in writing this story about the life and work of Barbara Wootton have had certain consequences for the format of the book. While it does, on the whole, follow the chronology of her life, there are some exceptions. Chapter 1 begins with her entry into the House of Lords as the first woman life peer. Socialist readers may be irritated by this, but the invasion of this most patriarchal and undemocratic structure, finally, by women, and the attendant nonsenses about dress and ceremony and toilets and so forth, seemed to me too good to miss as a starting point. The narratives in chapters 2 and 3 about her birth, family, early life and education are more standard biographical stratagems. Chapter 4 is about Jack Wootton, the man whom she married at the age of twenty and spent thirty-six hours with before he was killed in the Battle of Passchendaele in the First World War. Jack Wootton took up a small proportion of Barbara Wootton's life in a material sense; emotionally, however, he was an epic and eponymic presence throughout all of it. His death removed her from the normal world of wifehood and motherhood. It also pressured her to forge an independent life for herself away from her family, at a time when for most women this only happened with marriage. Chapters 5 and 6 describe this process of separation from her family, and her first encounters with the world of paid work in the academic setting of Cambridge and the political world of London. In Chapter 7 we meet another side of Barbara Wootton: her hidden life as a fiction-writer, played out during the same period as her exploration of the Soviet experiment in central economic planning, which had a substantial impact on her own economic thinking, and on the contribution she made to economic debates and Labour Party policy. Chapter 8 is like Chapter 4: an interlude, devoted to a husband. Of course, husbands were much more than interludes in Barbara Wootton's life, but they were not constantly present as intellectual partners – Jack because he died, and George Wright, whom she married in 1935 when she was thirty-eight, because he was a very different kind of man altogether. Chapter 9 takes up the theme of her work for a federal union of nations opposed to war, a movement which would eventually lead to closer relations between Britain and other European countries; and returns to her lifelong preoccupation with how to combine democracy with centralized planning: she thought you could, but others considered the principles of free-market capitalism far too sacred to expose to the flagellations of a bossy centralized State. Chapter 10 carries the title of Barbara's major critique of neoclassical economics, *Lament for Economics*, and is about her writings and thought on economics, and her move away from the label of a professional economist. Chapters 11 and 12 follow the path of her career as an academic social scientist, her book *Testament for Social Science*, and that first trail-blazing analysis of the scientific, or rather unscientific, basis of criminology, *Social Science and Social Pathology*. Chapter 13 is another interlude about a new phase in her life: the move to a house in Surrey away from London and George Wright with a new companion, a woman. I have devoted Chapter 14 to the area of Barbara Wootton's life in which her name is most remembered: crime and penal policy. By the time we get to Chapter 15, we are back at the beginning, with Baroness Wootton of Abinger in the House of Lords; and we stay there for Chapter 16 when she holds onto her role in the House of Lords, and to life, before dying in her ninety-second year in a Surrey nursing home. The final chapter, Chapter 17, attempts to sum up her achievements and her impact: The World She Never Made of the 1967 autobiography has become The World She Definitely Did Help to Make. But how is it, and why is it, that the world appears largely to have forgotten what she did; and – a much more general question – what might this forgetting tell us about our habits of regarding only certain types of lives as worth remembering?

Biography, like all genres, has its conventions, and I have taken a particular position on some of them in A Critical Woman. Firstly, there are endnotes, indicated by superscripts in the text, and quite a lot of them. The endnotes, mostly very short, are there for people who are interested in my sources, and/or who are surprised by some of the statements I make; otherwise they should be ignored. There is no comprehensive bibliography of Barbara Wootton's work in A Critical Woman; that has been reserved for a website (http://www.barbarawootton.co.uk). The interested reader will also find there examples of her work and some of her media appearances. Secondly, all biographers have to decide what to call their subjects: I call Barbara either 'Barbara Wootton' or 'Barbara'. My decision to call her 'Barbara' has the effect sometimes of making the relationship between us seem too intimate, which is unfortunate, and not intended. (I can hear her arguing with me about this.) According to several of her friends I interviewed, she did prefer being called just 'Barbara', and, after becoming a baroness in 1958, she announced her intention of not using the title.[12] However, she could get quite shirty at times with people she did not know well who left off her title, or who got it wrong. Equally irritating to her were misspellings of the surname which she carried with her for the seventy-one years after Jack Wootton's death: there was, she protested, something that amounted to an 'international conspiracy' to rob her of one 'T' or one 'O' or both;[13] the effect of losing one 'T' was worst because it made her name look mean and unbalanced.[14]

One great challenge about biographical life-writing is the one I have left until last, because it is in many ways the most difficult. The standard Victorian 'testimonial-to-a-great-life' tradition of biography made a very clear separation between public and private aspects of a person's life. The convention was that the public story could be told, but the private one should not be; it was irrelevant, essentially separate. This division has now been worn down by the more modern view (one promoted by feminists particularly) that the personal is political: how someone's private life is lived is an essential part of the public story. It is not only relevant, but likely to be illuminating. Well-known figures such as the economist Maynard Keynes and the social reformer Eleanor Rathbone (both of whom Barbara Wootton knew), have been subjected to both treatments: Robert Skidelsky's mammoth three volume biography of Keynes included Keynes' homosexuality, in contrast to the previous version by Roy Harrod, which left it out; Eleanor Rathbone's more than forty-year-long relationship with Elizabeth Macadam is present in Susan Pedersen's account of her life, but excised from that by Mary Stocks. Barbara Wootton was married twice, and for two periods in her life she lived with two women. She was clearly very close to one of these women; her first live-in female relationship, in the 1920s and early 1930s, was probably more a matter of practical convenience, though there was also a long-term friendship. But her second female domestic partner was someone with whom she obviously enjoyed a considerable emotional and intellectual intimacy. Having considered the evidence, I do not think there was a physical intimacy as well – at least not in the sexual sense. Barbara Wootton was seen by all her friends as indisputably heterosexual, and one nice anecdote relayed by one of them – it is nice because it introduces a note of frivolity into an otherwise unfalteringly serious life – was that she would never miss an episode of the detective drama 'Perry Mason' on television because she really fancied the character of private investigator Paul Drake who was played by the darkly handsome William Hopper.[15]

Actually, I do not even think whether or not Barbara Wootton had a physical relationship with any female partner is a very interesting question; it seems to me very much a prurient enquiry thrown up by a culture obsessed by sexual matters. What is interesting, and important, is how one life meshes with another; the ways in which social interaction, at the personal level, shapes people's lives and thus the difference they make, or do not make, to the world.

There sits on my desk as I write this a small solid brass ornament inscribed with the name 'Barbara' on a tiny plate at the front. It is probably an inkwell; there is a little pole at the side for a writing implement. When you lift the lid of the pot in the centre, the faded blue-and-white insignia of the House of Lords blinks at you from the bottom. The act of lifting the lid causes a tune to be played; the item is dual-purpose, both a musical box and an aide to writing. But the lid reveals another surprise: embedded in its underside is what looks remarkably like an amethyst engagement ring. This ornament is in my possession because Vera Seal gave it to me: 'You should have something of Barbara's', she said. Barbara had it because an unknown admirer gave it to her. The identity of the admirer remains unknown and, on the whole, I have resisted the temptation to try to find out who it was.

More puzzling to me, and more worthy of puzzle, is the fate of Barbara Wootton's potential destiny as a mother. I refer to this at several points in the book. She never, to my knowledge, had a child. But she made no secret of her regret that she did not become a mother. She was probably pregnant once or twice; why did she not give birth? Why did she leave money to an adoption charity in her will? Were her feelings about thwarted motherhood behind her awkward position in the debates which led up to the 1967 Abortion Act? I do not feel I have got to the bottom of this. But perhaps Barbara did not want me to. Even from the most prying eyes of the most searching biographer some secrets should remain hidden, because this saves us from the danger of falling into that illusory trap of the one true story.

1

Ladies of the House

Nineteen-fifty-eight was the year suffragette Christabel Pankhurst died; the Campaign for Nuclear Disarmament and Barbie dolls were born; Britain got its first motorway; instant noodles went on sale for the first time; and the musical *My Fair Lady* opened in London's Drury Lane. Alan Sillitoe published his novel *Saturday Night and Sunday Morning*, and economist J.K. Galbraith his less fictitious *The Affluent Society*. Growing ethnic diversity on Britain's streets began to challenge traditional notions of Britishness, and the ban on portraying homosexuality on the stage was lifted. On the world's stage, Egypt and Syria became the United Arab Republic; Sputnik 2 disintegrated in space; there was a military coup in Algeria and a revolution in Iraq; and Britain and Iceland started to argue about who had rights to empty the North Atlantic of fish. In July 1958, one of the oldest political institutions in the world received a dramatic shock to its constitution when the Life Peerages Act admitted both non-hereditary peers and women to Britain's Upper House for the first time. The House of Lords became a House of Lords and Ladies, although it was never officially renamed, because that would have meant another long-drawn out battle to drag Britain into the modern age.

The Life Peerages Act was not the first notable public event in Barbara Wootton's life, but it is one of those with which her name is most associated. She was the first woman to be created a Baroness under the terms of the Act. Women over thirty got the vote in 1918, but eligibility for the Upper House did not automatically follow enfranchisement in Britain, as it did in Australia, Austria, Belgium, Czechoslovakia, Denmark, Germany, Iceland, the Irish Free State, the Netherlands, New Zealand, Poland, Sweden and the USA; for this reason, Britain was unable to sign up to the United Nations Convention of Human Rights in 1953. Women in Britain could inherit titles, although they did so much less frequently than men, but they were not allowed to use these to gain entry to the House of Lords. Two-chamber political systems are common in democracies, with the second chamber having some function of watching over the constitution and revising legislation. The problem with Britain's two chambers is that they go back a long way – more than 500 years – and an institution full of dukes, marquesses, earls, viscounts and barons, who have inherited their titles through no merit of their own, is fundamentally difficult to fit into a modern parliamentary democracy. This is one reason why it took women, whose public political roles are exemplars *par excellence* of the modern age, such a long time to get in. Gender got mixed up with the issue of constitutional reform; most people who wanted to do something about the House of Lords did not want to do anything about women.[1]

Prime Minister William Gladstone once famously remarked that admitting women to the House of Lords would be disastrous, since most of the peers would die of shock and the women thus admitted would die of boredom.[2] 'The main point is that many of us do not want women in this House. We do not want to sit beside them on these Benches, nor do we want to meet them in the Library. This is a House of men,' said the Earl of Glasgow in 1957.[3] There were centuries of excuses. Women would be too bossy, too distracting, too frivolous; they would have bees of various kinds in their bonnets which would buzz far too loudly. Following the 1919 Sex Discrimination (Removal) Act, which stated that women should not be disqualified either by sex or by marriage from the exercise of any public function, Margaret Mackworth, Viscountess Rhondda, who had inherited a title from her father, argued that these public functions must surely include the ability to contribute to the work of the House of Lords. A decision in her favour was overturned by the Lord Chancellor, Viscount Birkenhead, an unrepentant anti-feminist, who argued unpleasantly that 'physiologically' women such as her were merely acting 'as a conduit pipe through which the blood of distinguished men may pass from one generation to another'.[4] When the House of Lords itself finally passed a motion in 1949 to admit women, the possibility of equality fell foul of the Labour Government's antipathy to it as an unreformed establishment institution. Socialist politician Jennie Lee spoke for many when she said that she was 'no more in favour of ladies being Members of the House of Lords than men, because I do not believe in the House of Lords'.[5] Jennie Lee would later eat her words when she herself accepted a life peerage in 1970, and Barbara Wootton would encourage her to do so: 'There seems not the slightest prospect that the House will be abolished, as it ought to be,' counselled Barbara, 'but while it survives, I really don't think it ought to be an exclusive Tory platform'.[6]

Barbara Wootton was another word-eater. 'It is not...enough to abolish the House of Lords,' she had announced in her trenchant *End Social Inequality,* published in 1941. 'If we are serious about democracy, it is necessary also to abolish the Lords.'[7] What all political parties had to recognize was that, by the 1950s, poor attendance and an ageing population had made the House of Lords an ineffective tool for any type of government.[8] Many peers never turned up, and some of those who did fell asleep as soon as they got there.[9] A solution to this problem was the introduction of selected younger members who would be more likely to stay awake.

Schemes for reforming the House of Lords had been intermittent since the 1830s, and private members' Bills seeking to create life peerages were introduced in 1869, 1888, 1907, 1929, 1935 and 1953. The 1911 Parliament Act had expressed an intention to 'substitute for the House of Lords as it at present exists a Second Chamber constituted on a popular instead of hereditary basis', though nothing was subsequently done to bring this about. The final push came with Harold Macmillan's Conservative Government in 1957. Predictably, however, this did not bring the sexist nature of the debate to an end; when the Bill that became the Life Peerages Act was being discussed, Earl Ferrers likened women in politics to the action of acid on metal, corroding the purity of masculine authority,[10] and the Earl of Home observed that 'taking women into a Parliamentary embrace would seem to be only a modest extension of the normal functions and privileges of a Peer'.[11]

Barbara Wootton was sixty-one when the Prime Minister, Harold Macmillan, wrote to her to say that he wished to submit her name to the Queen 'with a recommendation that Her Majesty may be graciously pleased to approve that the dignity of a Barony of the United Kingdom for life be conferred upon you'.[12] All the new members of the House were to be known as 'baronesses' or 'barons'. Barbara Wootton's elevation to a feudal title came at the instigation of Frank Pakenham, Lord Longford, who prompted Labour politician Hugh Gaitskell, then Leader of the Opposition, to suggest her name.[13] Gaitskell and Longford had been close friends as undergraduates at Oxford.[14] Longford's complicated political career had begun in the Conservative Party; converted to socialism by his wife, he converted her to Catholicism and was famous for the moral stand he took on such issues as gay rights and prison reform; he and Barbara Wootton would have much to do with one another in subsequent debates in the House. Longford had been 'right-hand man' to William Beveridge in the latter's landmark welfare state Report, an enterprise in which Baroness-Wootton-to-be had also shared.

Gaitskell put Barbara Wootton on the list of the first life peers not because she was a woman, but because she was the cleverest left-wing person he and his advisors knew.[15] Hers was one of fourteen names – ten men and four women – on the first list of life peers. Six of the men were, or had been, MPs; one was a trade unionist, one a colonial Governor, one an academic, and one a prominent member of the Church of Scotland. In *The Times* announcement, the photographs of the four women were placed above those of the men: Dame Katherine Elliot, Lady Ravensdale, Dowager Lady Reading, and plain 'Mrs Wootton'. All the new recruits had brief biographies appended to their names. Both Katharine Elliot and Stella Reading were described as 'the widow of …'; Irene Ravensdale, the unmarried one, was attached instead to her father, 'the elder daughter of the late Lord Curzon'. Barbara's began 'Mrs. Barbara Frances Wootton (Mrs. Wright), who was educated at…'[16] Her surnames were a cause of confusion throughout her life. In 1958, she was still married to her second husband, George Wright, but 'Wootton', the name of her first husband, was the one she always used. The confusion is neatly marked in her Writ of Summons to Parliament, which is addressed 'To Our right trusty and well beloved Barbara Frances Wright of Abinger Common in Our County of Surrey' and ends with the name 'Barbara Frances Baroness Wootton of Abinger'.[17]

For most of her life, Barbara Wootton had worked as an academic. She was tired of the small-mindedness and seclusion from real life issues of university life, and with considerable experience behind her of public service, and a fierce conviction that the point of being alive is to try to improve public welfare, she was looking for something else to do. Her background was rather different from that of her three titled female co-entrants, and she was the only one of the four to be chosen after consultation with the Leader of the Opposition. But there were also some striking similarities between the four new Ladies of the House: all four had been born within nine years of one another; all had been brought up by nannies (as was customary among the British upper classes at the time); all had a reputation for being fearlessly outspoken; all were childless; one had never married, and three were widows. One of several ways in which Barbara embarrassed House of Lords' officials was by having her second husband, George Wright, still alive. George was very proud of her achievement; accordingly, he claimed the title of 'peeress', and requested the traditional right exercised by the spouses of peers to sit in a special part of the House. This raised the demon of 'facilities'. If George joined the other wives, he would have to use their lavatory, and as that could not be allowed, he was given a special place in the front row of the Distinguished Strangers' Gallery instead.[18]

Lavatories, titles and clothes were all formidable problems – details which rapidly became of absorbing interest to the press. A special Sub-Committee of the House of Lords' Offices Committee was set up to consider the 'facilities' issue. *The Times* thought the creation of a 'Life Peeresses' room at Westminster worthy of its political correspondent's attention; the room was decorated and furnished in what the Ministry of Works described as 'a more feminine style', with 'light neutral shades' on the walls and printed linen curtains. There was a red carpet and 'attractive seats' with 'bright loose covers'; small tables and a mirror were provided.[19] The toilet, 'a sort of mahogany throne with blue roses on the bowl', had to be seen to be believed.[20] On the door hung a sign announcing 'Life Peeresses', but, as Barbara's George had proved, a peeress is the wife of a peer. Barbara was much exercised about this, writing to Viscount Hailsham as Leader of the House of Lords and to the Lord Great Chamberlain on behalf of herself and her three female colleagues in an effort to get the sign changed to 'Women Life Peers'. 'The point may seem a small one,' she conceded, 'but the reasons for the request are both practical and a matter of principle. The principle involved arises from the fact that our peerages have been personally conferred on us and are not derived from our husbands.'[21] The sign was eventually changed to 'Women Peers', but the new label was enclosed in inverted commas, as though the sign-writer could not quite believe it.

And then there was the little matter of the clothes. Should the new Ladies of the House, like the old Lords, wear robes on ceremonial occasions? 'I don't know what the situation would be if a new peer or peeress refused to wear them,' admitted Sir George Bellew, Garter King of Arms, somewhat desperately, 'It has never happened.'[22] Robes were expensive; perhaps the ladies could hire them – it would cost only £8 a day.[23] Barbara Wootton, who hoped to avoid the whole robes issue, agreed that this would be an excellent idea. The traditional robes of a baron, dating from the fifteenth century, are made of scarlet wool, trimmed with bars of ermine and gold oak leaf lace, though these days the ermine is miniver – rabbit fur – painted with black dots, which is cheaper. Baronesses, as well as barons, could wear such robes, but there was a further problem to be resolved: the hat. During the introductory ceremony new peers had to undergo, it was customary for the hat to be raised three times, but this would savage the ladies' hair-dos. A special tricorne hat, resembling that worn by women naval officers, was thus designed by robemakers Ede & Ravenscroft. This consisted of lightweight black velour with a gold lace rosette on the side – a tiny, sensational rosette, 'the feminine touch'[24] – and its wearers were allowed to keep the hat on throughout the ceremony. The hat business entertained the journalists: 'Women First to Join Lords: Keep Hats On' and 'The Ladies Join the Lords as Though Born to It: Revolution Kept under Hat'.[25] The possibility that women might also want to wear ordinary hats during the ordinary business of the House also had to be allowed for, and since the constitution barred peers from wearing hats while speaking, this was yet another custom that had to be changed.

Of the four women who would wear this negotiated regalia, Barbara was the first to be 'gazetted' with the title Baroness Wootton of Abinger in 'letters patent' dated 8 August 1958. She was in the first batch of life peers to be introduced, the second woman, after Lady Reading. Stella Reading and Barbara had already

crossed paths in their capacity as Governors of the BBC. The main feature of this
first meeting recalled by Barbara had also involved the inconvenience of having
to provide conveniences for token women. When she first went to Broadcasting
House in 1950 to meet Sir William Haley, the then Director-General, Barbara had
been handed a Yale key marked 'women's toilet'. This facility she shared with Stella
Reading as the only other woman member. The nailbrush in the toilet was chained
to the basin, and the two women wondered which of them was the target of this
precaution.[26] Such privations would, for Stella Reading, have stood out as unusual
in an otherwise well-resourced life. She shared with another of the new ladies,
Irene Ravensdale, an imperial Indian connection: her father had been a member of
the British Foreign Service, and director of the tobacco monopoly of the Ottoman
empire, and the unmarried Stella had served as secretary to the wife of the Viceroy
to India, Rufus Isaacs, Marquess of Reading. When the Viceroy's wife died, Stella
had married him after a decent interval, thus acquiring the title 'Marchioness of
Reading', although this did not stop her from a considerable record of achievement –
most notably, the founding of the Women's Voluntary Service.

Proceedings on 21 October when the first new peers were introduced went
smoothly. The House was packed and awake. In a ceremony almost unchanged
since the seventeenth century, the peers followed a procession led by Black Rod
and the other officials in their sparkling ceremonial wear, bowed to the throne,
then knelt at the Woolsack while their Writs of Summons to Parliament were
read out. True to her word, Barbara Wootton wore borrowed robes – those of
Lord Catto, one time Governor of the Bank of England, at the suggestion of the
mechanic who serviced her car in rural Surrey, who had observed that Lord Catto,
a neighbour, not being well, would probably not need his robes on this occasion.[27]
Lady Reading hesitated slightly when taking the oath of allegiance. As she added
her signature to the great Book of Peers, 'a solemn hush' filled the House, followed
by a 'long, warm murmur of applause'.[28] Then came the first of the commotions
Barbara Wootton would cause their Lordships: looking 'greatly interested in what
was happening to her, though less than overwhelmed with awe',[29] she waved the
bible aside and tried to give it to the clerk, who refused to take it.[30] Then she
declared in firm tones her conscientious objection to anything other than a simple
affirmation of allegiance to the Queen.[31] Each new peer had to have two sponsors
from among existing peers. Barbara's were Lord Longford and Lord Burden –
Tom Burden, a socialist friend from Barbara's days in the Workers' Educational
Association. An archive photograph shows the three of them, in descending order
of height, Barbara with strangely angled feet looking rather on her guard between
the two avuncular men. As the senior sponsor, Lord Longford remembered waiting

uneasily while a search took place at the Clerk's table for the alternative wording required for the making of an affirmation. Two old Tories on the bench opposite wondered out loud (one of them was somewhat deaf) what accounted for the hold up: 'She doesn't believe in God.' 'Why the Devil not?'[32] But, after that, Barbara did her three bows, the kneeling and all the rest of it, 'like a good girl'.[33]

Once in the House, the four women life peers became part of an expanding brigade of Ladies whose levels of energy more than matched those of buzzing bees, and certainly exceeded the political activity of the sleepy or absentee Lords. According to the calculations undertaken by academics Gavin Drewry and Jenny Brock in their study of women in the House of Lords in 1980, sixty-five per cent of women life peers compared with forty per cent of male life peers had attended half or more of the House's sessions in the previous year.[34] At a Fawcett Society party in honour of the four new Ladies of the House, Stella Reading called the House of Lords a 'delicious place to be in. People move so slowly. Nobody runs down passages; nobody uses used envelopes; nobody does anything for himself if he can ask a gentleman with a gold chain to do it for him.' Irene Ravensdale wondered what her father, a swaggering adulterous aristocrat,[35] would have said, given that he had been so violently opposed to the suffrage movement.[36] She continued the insect analogy others had used by comparing the Lords with 'a drowsy lot of flies in a very hot room' among which women like herself might be regarded as 'an excited bluebottle coming to disturb their sleep'.[37] Katharine Elliot, the daughter of a baronet and the half-sister of Prime Minister Asquith's wife,[38] spoke more conservatively about the extreme kindness of their Lordships. Barbara, typically, had her eye on the future: 'There are strongholds that have not yet been breached,' she declared firmly. 'We look forward to a far greater distinction than entry into the House of Lords, and that is entry for women into the Athenaeum Club.'[39] This was not an achievement she would see in her lifetime: the Athenaeum did not agree to embrace women until 2002.

As Melanie Phillips mentioned in her book about women at Westminster, one of Barbara's elderly Conservative colleagues in the House of Lords once remarked, 'Barbara Wootton is quite brilliant, you know, even though she's frightfully left-wing, but she's a bit odd. She married a taxi driver, you know. Wasn't that an extraordinary thing to do?'[40] It was possibly one of the least extraordinary things Barbara ever did, and it certainly seems somewhat less extraordinary than her decision to enter the House of Lords. Ambivalence about its pomp and circumstance has been a common aspect of the general regard in which the House has been held, and ambivalence was a thread running through the new Baroness Wootton's life. But she was also attuned to evidence, and the evidence she encountered once in the House was that here was an establishment where, perversely, women could be, and were, treated as equals – more so than in The Other Place (parliamentary terminology for the House of Commons). Interviewed by *The Observer* in 1977, Barbara observed that she had never been anywhere else where the men had treated her more as an equal, except, she added, 'for that Longford, who always makes some fatuous remark about one's dress or hairstyle'.[41]

Breaching the masculine citadel of the House of Lords was an element in women's long battle to be treated as citizens. When Stella Reading and Barbara Wootton swayed through the House that day in October 1958 in their scarlet and gold regalia flanked, preceded and followed by men, their presence symbolized a very particular version of modernity. The 1950s were an ultra-conservative decade for women: the militancy of the suffragettes had been swallowed up in women's massive mobilization as substitute male labourers during the First World War, and the token concession of the over-thirties vote in 1918; the traditional family, with women at its centre, underpinned all programmes of post-war reconstruction, giving most women no option but to accede gracefully and become iconic housewives, wives and mothers. Simone de Beauvoir had published her now classic *The Second Sex* in France in 1949, less than four years after French women obtained the vote, but her arguments about masculine society creating restrictive roles for women took years to permeate other languages and cultures. In the 1950s, the Anglo-American world was dominated by pseudo-psychoanalytic views of the widespread neurosis inflicted by women's refusal to be happy housewives at home.[42] Day nurseries were closed, and experts pronounced on the importance of mothers to children's socialization.[43] The sinister idea that proper mothering would prevent all social problems was one that Barbara Wootton tackled in her own *Social Science and Social Pathology*, finished around the same time as she entered the House of Lords. Like the notion of 'the teenager', that of 'the working mother' arrived in the 1950s to signify the displacement and panic of changing family arrangements. Women, of course, had always worked, but their equal participation with men in the world of paid work outside the home has always been another matter. Post-war, the ideology was that women had simply acquired a new role – they had two, whereas men had one.[44]

The widespread conservative turn away from a feminist agenda which occurred in many countries after the Second World War affected popular culture, fashion, political propaganda and social science alike. The American harbinger of discontent, Betty Friedan's *The Feminine Mystique*, which revealed the unhappy truth behind the happy housewife ideal, would not be published until 1963, and the new wave of feminism did not begin its tidal sweep of patriarchal sands until the late 1960s.

All the countries in which the new women's movement arose could point to similar patterns of discrimination: the legal exclusion of women from public functions persisted; their incursion into formal male politics had been paltry; reproductive freedom remained a mirage; and women in the labour force worked mainly in unskilled jobs for half or two-thirds of the equivalent male wage.[45] Much of this discrimination persists today. Even some of the more apparently trivial themes in women's induction to the House of Lords have been raised to the status of serious subjects for study. The problems the women peers had with their lavatory provision continued well into the 1970s, and there is now a respectable body of research and political campaigning on the topic of 'urination discrimination'. This is most notably a place in which women experience the restrictions of both biology and culture, being allocated about half the public toilets provided for men, despite spending twice as much time in them, for physiological reasons.[46]

None of the four new baronesses had experienced the ordinary problems of women's two roles. It is doubtful whether three of them would have earned their new passports to ennoblement without the connections they had to men; again, there is nothing very extraordinary about this. Writing of the four names, *The Daily Telegraph* noted, 'The list makes history – without unduly disturbing it'.[47] Barbara Wootton was the exceptional new Lady of the House. She was the only one to have got there under her own steam, commented *The Observer*, calling her (incorrectly) '"Professor" Wootton'. She was likely to be the most vigorous of the new creations: 'A tall, handsome woman of sixty with a formidable deep voice and a subtle mock-serious wit, she sometimes gives the impression of a stern masculine character', but fortunately she also exudes a 'natural feminine warmth'.[48] 'To the ordinary thinking woman like myself,' wrote one admirer, Mrs Margaret Rees, to Barbara on reading of her life peerage, 'it will be a great satisfaction to know that matters which concern women, child welfare & subjects which the male members can never understand properly, will be left in your capable hands .... My politics are not yours,' she went on honestly, 'but there are so many things needing attention today, which need commonsense, plain speaking & understanding. May God Bless & guide you during your life & so help to uplift women on to the same equality as man, in all walks of life.'[49]

2

A Cat Called Plato

Cambridge in 1897, the year of Barbara Wootton's birth, was a small rural town in which the trappings of modern life were arriving slowly; few homes had electricity, coal was used for cooking, and middle-class houses listened to the hissing of the old unshaded gas-burners. Cattle were still driven to the weekly market, and retired Newmarket racehorses drew hansom cabs with bells. The town was the place where farmers and small traders from villages as much as fifteen miles away brought their goods to sell; but it was also the home of The University. The University was the business of Barbara's parents, James and Adela Adam, both classical scholars, both devoted to the study of earlier civilizations, and both determined to wrestle from such study habits that would mould the childhoods and characters of their three children: Neil, Arthur and Barbara. Barbara enjoyed her brothers, who were six and three years older than her; she made slaves of them whenever she could and later concluded that this type of family pattern yielded a most useful training in the development of feminine wiles.[1]

She was named 'Barbara Frances' after a favourite aunt on each side of the family. These two sides provided contrasting inheritances. James Adam's origins lay in the austere soil of Aberdeenshire, where his family had been farmers for generations; Adela was the daughter of a well-off family based originally in the Channel island of Jersey, where her ancestors had played important roles in island politics since the thirteenth century. Most of what we know about Barbara Wootton's childhood comes from her own autobiographical account, published when she was seventy, and from the records assembled by Adela, following the premature deaths of her husband at the age of forty-seven and of her younger son, Arthur, at the age of twenty-two. It seems clear that, for Adela, the men in the family were the most important figures.

The year after James Adam died, Adela published a fifty-five page memoir of his life. The memoir was the Preface to a volume he had not finished called *The Religious Teachers of Greece*, and which she finished for him. In the memoir, she describes the hamlet of Kinmuck, in the parish of Keithhall, where the Adam family came from: 'To the north and east the country is very bare and featureless: nothing is to be seen but an expanse of rolling hillside, divided with pitiless regularity by "dykes" (stone walls) into fields of grass, oats, or "neeps" (turnips) ... for miles around there is an absence of any collection of houses compact enough to be called a village.'[2] Into this uncompromising landscape, Barbara's father, James Adam, was born on 7 April 1860, the second child and only son of a family of seven. His father, also called James (like *his* father before him), worked first as a farm-servant but 'had ambitions beyond his calling' and was given to studying Latin while following the plough. James Adam senior went away in his twenties to learn the art of village trading, and on his return started a small grocer's shop in Kinmuck. This prospered, providing a sound base for his marriage, at the age of thirty-one, to the twenty-one-year-old daughter of another farming family in the nearby parish of Clatt. Barbara Anderson, Barbara Wootton's paternal grandmother, was the youngest of ten: in a popular tradition, the boys went to school, but the girls did not, and this family was so poor that all the children were sent away to earn their own living as soon as they were able to work.

After the birth of James Adam junior, Barbara Wootton's father, the family moved to bigger premises in Kinmuck: a good-sized shop, a house and a large garden, and a smaller house with a tailor's workshop. James Adam senior was determined that his children should have the best education possible. He got together with a few local farmers and built a small schoolhouse. They hired a schoolmistress whose upkeep, James, with his canny business sense, subsidized by taking her in as a boarder at the low rate of five shillings a week. He bought maps for the school and was in every way 'a leading man in the neighbourhood'.[3] Unfortunately for the neighbourhood and for his family, he died at forty-three in a local epidemic of typhoid fever. His widow carried on the shop business with splendid determination for a further thirty-seven years, retiring at the age of seventy. Her exceptional efforts ensured a successful start in life for James and his five sisters – Barbara, Mary, Jeanie, Jessie and Isabella (one sister had died in infancy). Mrs Adam had special ambitions for her only son. At ten, he went to the parish school of Keithhall, a mile away, marching off every morning with a flask of milk and a piece of bread and syrup. A school inspector there was heard to remark, 'That's a boy who'll go far',[4] but the rough boys gave him a hard time, so at twelve he was sent with his elder sister to live with an aunt in Aberdeen, where he attended a more congenial school. James and this sister, Barbara, after whom Barbara Wootton was named, must have had a special relationship on account of being sent away together, but, as the only boy in a family of girls, he was much adored by all of them.[5] It was at school in Aberdeen that James Adam discovered the capacity for academic excellence which would drive him for the rest of his life. He particularly fell in love with Greek: 'The letters looked so nice,' he would say.[6] From time to time he helped in the family shop, reading his books in between customers, as his father had while out ploughing, and his mother therefore determined that he should go to university. He won a bursary to the University of Aberdeen, where he studied, not only Greek and Latin, but mathematics, zoology, geology, English, physics, logic and metaphysics 'according to the system of that day',[7] adding Sanskrit and German, just for his own satisfaction.

By this time, the pattern of mood swings between exhilaration and depression which marked Barbara Wootton's father's adult life had become established. At nineteen, he wrote to his sister back in Kinmuck, 'With my weighty head burdened with care and anxiety as to what I am to do when I leave College, and wretched discomfort and corroding disgust and general debility and what not, I'm afraid I'm going to sink .... I think it is all very good to boast about the pleasures and nobilities of knowledge and all that, but where is the practical use of it all?'[8] This question was one his daughter, Barbara, would ask in her turn, but her answer would be different from his. James Adam thought about becoming a country parson, because the peace of the countryside seemed so attractive when he was under such stress, or perhaps a bishop, but his tutors at Aberdeen thought he should go to Cambridge, and so, in the end, did he. With first class classical Honours and an array of prizes from Aberdeen, and no less than three scholarships (necessary for financial reasons), he proceeded to Cambridge in 1880 at the age of twenty. There he enjoyed the food and the architecture, but, like many others, not the climate: 'A stranger would think it fairyland; but if he had to attend morning-chapel in these freezing mornings he would very soon change his opinion ... this low-lying place – not a hill is visible all round ... seems very congenial to frost. So it is to rain.'[9] James Adam was the best classical scholar of his year, and he talked endlessly with his friends of religion, Platonism, philosophy and poetry: it was all about ideas, not, according to Adela's account, about feelings, or about the practical elements of life. He did, however, have a playful side; he enjoyed the company of friends' children, and he learnt to waltz. Then, at twenty-four, with a second brilliant degree under his belt, he was offered the post of Junior Fellow at Emmanuel College, a smallish institution that had just embarked on a growth spurt towards becoming one of the wealthiest of all the Cambridge colleges. The new Fellow looked young for his age, with his pink-and-white complexion and fair hair, and his slight figure; he was simply dressed, and very Scottish in appearance, manner and accent. He lectured on Plato, Cicero and Pindar, Aristotle's *Ethics* and the Greek Lyric Poets, and rapidly became a most entertaining performer, learning how to insert humorous anecdotes in appropriate places, and communicating to his students, above all, how classical study could be

(despite his earlier doubts) such *fun*. In 1903, when the Classical Tripos was altered
to emphasize the importance of classical philosophy, the lecture hall was hardly big
enough to hold all those who came to hear James Adam's thoughts on Plato and
Aristotle.[10] He formed a close friendship with the classical scholar and orientalist,
Robert Alexander Neil, of Pembroke College, another ex-Aberdonian, after whom
he would name his first son. The two men lunched together every Sunday for sixteen
years until Robert Neil died, their lunches continuing irrespective of anything else
that was going on, including James's marriage to Adela Marion Kensington.

James and Adela met in 1885 when he added the task of lecturing to the young
ladies of Girton College to his duties at Emmanuel College. Girton at the time was
still fighting for equality with the Cambridge men's colleges, and it was an effort
for the College to provide any kind of parallel education. James was rather worried
about meeting the young ladies, but in the event he found them very industrious
'even when they are not clever'.[11] However, one or two *were* clever, and one of
these was Adela. She was in her first year as a student at Girton, having come from
Bedford College, her first experience of formal education at the age of sixteen.
Under the tutelage of James and others at Girton, she gained two first classes and
a special distinction in philosophy in the Classical Tripos examination. This success
did not result in a degree, however, as women were not allowed to have degrees
at Cambridge then – an absurdity from which her daughter, Barbara, would
also suffer. By this time, Adela and James were in regular correspondence. He
contrived with a couple of his Cambridge friends to join her and her sister, Juliet,
in Greece at Easter, 1890. The party embarked on a trip through the Peloponnesus
and to Delphi and Thebes. James sat with the driver of the carriage practising his
modern Greek, and the other four sat inside. They ate oranges, read Herodotus
and discussed the Platonic theory of education. When they reached the middle
of Arcadia, James proposed marriage to Adela. 'This is the day that J. Adam
and A.M. Kensington were engaged to be married,' wrote James in his diary on
30 April 1890. Hers for the same day recorded only that the two of them 'walked
up a hill'.[12] According to family legend, the hill was the Parthenon.[13]

He was thirty, she was twenty-four. They were married the following summer
at St Mary's, the parish church in Paddington, with Adela's mother, Rebecca
Kensington, and her niece, Cicely Ford, as witnesses, and James's friend, Robert
Neil, as best man. After the wedding, James and Adela had to go straight to
Kinmuck, as his favourite sister Barbara had sadly just died of tuberculosis aged
twenty-six. James registered her death the day after his wedding. The newly-weds
returned to Cambridge where they took a furnished house owned by Millicent
Fawcett of suffragist fame.[14] Soon, however, they moved to St Giles' House,

Chesterton Lane, a large semi-detached establishment conveniently and pleasantly situated in a street facing the River Cam, with the agreeable aspect of Jesus Green on the other side. Here, Barbara and her two brothers were born: Neil on 5 November 1891, Arthur on 25 April 1894, and Barbara on 14 April 1897, three proficiently-spaced offspring who were expected to meet their parents' high expectations for them without too much trouble.

A photograph of Adela about this time shows her as an attractive young woman with a straight-backed Victorian posture, a high forehead, and a level, no-nonsense expression. This was definitely a woman with whom you would not wish to tangle. She came from an even larger family than her husband: born in 1866, she was the tenth child of Arthur Kensington, and the eighth of Rebecca. Arthur, whose occupation was described on Adela's birth certificate as 'gentleman', was first married to a woman called Eleanor Belfield, who bore him two sons, Edgar and Theodore, before dying of typhoid fever. Arthur was the son of a banker, John Pooley Kensington of Lime Grove, Putney, who went bankrupt when his firm, Kensington and Company of Lombard Street, collapsed.[15] In her autobiography, Barbara says of her maternal grandfather that he 'had something to do with banking in the days before this had become the giant joint-stock enterprise that it is now'.[16] He was certainly sufficiently well-off to maintain ten children and homes in both Jersey and England. Jersey was an attractive place to live due to the absence of taxes and duties, as all the nineteenth-century guide books were at pains to point out.[17] For a time in the late 1830s and early 1840s, Arthur Kensington was also a fellow of Trinity College, Oxford, where he had earlier taken a degree in mathematics. For two years, he lectured to Trinity undergraduates on classical literature and philosophy. He also served as a most efficient Dean, leaving for his successors twelve practical 'rules', which included providing information to all new students about chapel and exercise regulations, locking the garden gate at 10.30 pm in summer, and never omitting to send 'for men if they have done anything wrong'.[18] The rules governing College appointments at the time did not allow Fellows to marry, which is probably why Arthur resigned from his Trinity post sometime in the early 1840s.[19]

Arthur's second marriage, in 1848, was to Rebecca Le Geyt, Barbara Wootton's maternal grandmother. The name 'Le Geyt' takes us back to a long line of distinguished Jersey ancestors, a history that is recorded as early as 1274.[20] In 2008 there were still eleven Le Geyts listed in the Jersey telephone directory; in 1891, the year after Rebecca's daughter, Adela, married James Adam, there were forty-seven. Barbara may not have known a great deal about her Jersey ancestry, or she may not have been very interested in it, but she knew enough to remark many years later (in 1981, when she was eighty-four) to her friend Sir William Haley, ex-Director-General of the BBC, that a portrait of one of her ancestors hung on the walls of Elizabeth Castle in St Helier. Haley, brought up in Jersey himself, was pleased to know this, and remarked that, 'It is still a good Jersey name ... When I was a child our family doctor was a Le Geyt'.[21]

The said portrait may actually never have decorated the walls of Elizabeth Castle, an unappetising building stuck on a rock which can be reached from the Jersey mainland only at high water. In 2009, Charles William Le Geyt (1733–1827), Barbara Wootton's great-great-great uncle, resplendent in his red, gold and blue regimentary Captain's uniform, gazed out with a piercing blue-eyed clarity, not unlike Barbara's own, from the walls of the Jersey Museum in St Helier. Charles William distinguished himself when young quelling a riot in Bristol, and leading his regiment most successfully at the battle of Minden in Germany in 1759 during the Seven Years' War.[22] What most Jersey residents knew Charles William Le Geyt best for, however, was his energetic defence of their rights to stand up against the autocrats who governed them. Jersey was run by a few rich old Norman-French landowning families, whose habits of intermarriage ensured a concentration of surnames, interests and inherited power.[23] In 1769, the island had its own little revolution with themes not dissimilar from those that sparked the more famous American and French ones: the impotence of the poor under a despotic political system; and the imposition on their labour of duties and revenues which reduced them literally to starvation. Charles William Le Geyt was on the side of the islanders, several hundreds of whom gathered in St Helier to protest and request a reasonable list of rights.[24] A few years later, his political skills were even more famously deployed in resisting a new set of Acts which proposed duties, not favoured by many islanders, on 'wines and liquors'. They got up another petition and dispatched Charles William with it to London, where he won the argument. On his return, he was hailed as a champion: bonfires were lit in the town and on the sands, and the cries 'Vive Le Geyt!' and 'Le Geyt for ever!' 'resounded everywhere throughout the country'.[25]

Although the face of Charles William Le Geyt looks at us today from the walls of the Jersey Museum, the portrait of his wife, Elisabeth, daughter of 'the notorious pamphleteer' John Shebbeare, whose extravagant political writings *Letters to the People of England* (1755–8) landed him in Newgate prison,[26] is hidden in an inland storeroom, along with a lithograph of a sour-looking man with an elaborate mane of dark hair. The dour figure is another of Barbara's ancestors, Philippe Le Geyt (1635–1716), who was a judge and a lawyer, educated in Caen and Paris, and the author of careful and important works on Jersey law which are together known as the 'Code Le Geyt', and which are still used in Jersey today whenever it is necessary to understand the background of Norman customary law.[27]

Adela's childhood and the experiences of the Kensington and Le Geyt families were populated by multiple aunts, uncles and cousins. George and Rose Marie Le Geyt, Adela's maternal grandparents, had a child every year or every other year from 1813 to 1833, except for one four-year gap (perhaps a miscarriage). In such families, children were often dispatched to live with other relatives for a while. When she was fifteen, Barbara's grandmother, Rebecca Le Geyt, was living in Devon, together with her younger sister, Frances Maria, in the home of her aunt, her mother's sister, the memorably named Angel Heath, and it was from Angel Heath's home that Rebecca married Arthur Kensington. Angel was something of a 'kin-keeper' in this family, recording a dense four-page memoir of her parents which was printed in a private publication in 1882. *Heathiana*,[28] as it is called, packages affectionately, though a little chaotically, many details of this branch of the family history. It includes the delightful story of Rose Marie and her parentage, which has the ingredients of all the best family tales: huge and unmanageable passion in a wild landscape ending in ultimate tragedy. Today George and Rose Marie Le Geyt rest in a solid ivy-covered tomb in St Helier's Green Street cemetery. The Le Geyt tomb is imposing, standing on its own, away from the simpler leaning gravestones of other less well-to-do families. Barbara must surely have been taken here as a child, on one of her visits to Jersey. In 1861, when George died, the family was living at 55 Colomberie, in a house big enough to accommodate four adults and two servants. The house was rented by the Le Geyts, not owned, and they seem to have moved around St Helier a fair amount; as the years pass, the servants disappear from the Census records, and at least one of the St Helier Le Geyt descendants ends up in penury.[29]

Adela Marion Kensington, Barbara's mother, and the daughter of a Le Geyt, was born near Hyde Park in London. Of *her* seven brothers and sisters, Laura (1850–1926) was the only other London birth; Arthur Hayes (1859–1886) and Harry Rawlins (1861–1890) were both born in Devon; Fanny (Frances, 1851–1931) was born in Hastings, and three children – Alfred (1855–1918), Juliet (1853–1923) and Gertrude Rose (1856–1899) – were born in Jersey. The house in St Helier where Alfred and Gertrude were born is still standing: a long squat building with eight windows and a slate roof, now divided into flats, and facing a pub and a corner shop. The geographical distribution of births suggests a close extended family with branches in both Jersey and England, though based mainly in England. In her autobiography, Barbara calls it 'a cultivated, reasonably prosperous, but not rich, middle-class family'.[30] Of her seven maternal aunts and uncles, it was two in particular, Aunt Fanny and Aunt Juliet, who played the most important roles in Barbara's life. Adela was closest to her sister, Fanny, who was fifteen years her senior;

and the obituary Adela wrote on Fanny's death is the closest we have to an account of her own childhood.[31] The family was based in London with long sojourns in Devon (at the home of Angel Heath) and Jersey. The girls did not go to school, but engaged in quite wide reading: Virgil, Homer and other Greek texts; *Pride and Prejudice, Tales of the Alhambra*, Charles Lamb's *Letters*, and the *Waverley* novels; and *Beauty and the Beast* in French. They did a lot of English-French translations. Laura and Fanny went to French and to German classes for a time, but two girls were the most the family could afford to pay for. The eldest ones became Sunday school teachers. Their father took them to see Shakespeare, and they would always read the play first. In Devon they enjoyed three donkeys, and consuming quantities of wild fruit.

As a child, Barbara benefited from the resource of these multiple kinships. She recalled family holidays in the summer spent with various combinations of aunts, uncles and cousins 'in some country rectory rented for the purpose while the incumbent was on holiday'.[32] The holidays were not always in Britain; in 1905 they went to France, to look at the Loire chateaux and at Christmas the following year (this was something of a special event), they travelled with two aunts and two cousins to Morocco on S.S. *Sweena* of the Forwood Line. Long holidays, in which extended families gathered together and enjoyed each other's company, were a common upper-middle-class habit at the time, and seem uniformly remembered by the young as delightful.[33] The houses rented by the Adams were always chosen carefully by Aunt Juliet, and they had to have a study for James, who did most of his writing during the summer vacations. Barbara remembered the large hampers packed with his books that had to accompany them.'He liked to stir up children to a high pitch of excitement, and would then suddenly decamp to his work,' recalled Adela. They used a system of 'danger signals': 'One handkerchief was hung out from the window, and another outside the door: while these were visible (usually about eight hours a day), no sound must be heard.'[34] Despite this discipline, Barbara and her brothers enjoyed considerable freedom in these summer interludes to swim or explore the countryside instead of reciting Greek verbs. The atmosphere at home the rest of the time was quite unrelenting: Adela took the view that 'the irregular verbs and similar monstrosities of Greek and Latin' were best learnt by the very young, instead of nursery rhymes that did no-one any good at all. Even the cat was called Plato.[35] Ann Ashford, the great grand-daughter of Adela's oldest sister Laura, remembers how Adela's childrearing habits were disapproved of by other members of the family: Adela was regarded as 'this incredible intellectual snob' and as much too harsh in refusing her children any playtime whatsoever.[36] While Adela's banishment of childish amusements was probably unusual, in university households at the time the emphasis on Greek and Latin was not: writer Rosamund

Essex read Latin and Greek before she could spell English;[37] the Postgate children (one of whom, Raymond, later became famous as the editor of the *Good Food Guide*, while the other, Margaret, was a well-known socialist writer and wife of the political theorist and historian G.D.H. Cole) had to speak Latin at dinner on Sundays, under the stern eye of their father, a Classics don at Trinity. Any failure on their part to find the Latin equivalents for 'roast beef and Yorkshire pudding' resulted in hunger.[38]

When James Adam became Senior Tutor at Emmanuel College, the family moved into a spacious house in the College grounds with their three children and four servants (an average number for the period). This was the first generation of married dons in Oxbridge; the rule under which Arthur Kensington had to resign his Fellowship at Trinity in order to marry was not changed in Cambridge until 1878. The Adam family was therefore an early specimen of a new breed – what the economist J.M. Keynes called 'the first age of married society in Cambridge'.[39] Brought up, like Barbara, in such a family, Keynes recalled the propensity of the first married dons to choose as wives students at the women's colleges, a habit which infused the domestic atmosphere with the added spice of an intellectual bond. Among such 'a peculiar self-conscious and very talented élite', the Adams were, apparently, 'a legend'.[40] Their new Cambridge home, Emmanuel House, was ornate and matronly, a brooding red-brick three-storied and bay-windowed edifice looking out over a paddock where the undergraduates played tennis in summer; an enormous horse-chestnut tree swept the second-floor windows of the house. There was a large fish pond, home to a colony of Mallard ducks, and a little wooden bridge which led to an uncultivated island, where a pair of breeding swans generated an annual display of fluffy cygnets. James Adam enjoyed nightly walks around the gardens, watching the moonlight and the yellow light of the College windows captured in the pond, and admiring the symmetrical elegance of the Emmanuel front court crowned with its Christopher Wren chapel. His depressions continued – the rapid alternations from horrible misery to vitality and back again. Adela put it down to his inability to relax, to his habit of driving himself too hard. In 1902, when Barbara was five, he published his two-volume edition of Plato's *Republic* which became a classic undergraduate text in every English-speaking country in the world. This was preceded by translations of other Platonic dialogues: *Apology*, *Crito, Protagoras* and *Euthyphro* (the latter, jointly with Adela). In 1902 also, he achieved the honour of being nominated Gifford Lecturer at Aberdeen, choosing as his subject 'The Religious Teachers of Greece', and delivering the lectures in 1904 and 1905; these are the lectures that Adela would later edit for him.

The reality of James Adam's world was that of masculine classical scholarship. It was a closed world, allowing few concessions to any reality other than that spoken by the classical Greek and Roman philosophers. His own philosophy, which very much shaped his children's childhoods, distinguished a 'liberal' from a 'professional' education: while the aim of the former was to develop mental and moral qualities, the latter merely enabled people to earn their living. A liberal education, which means the study of classical literature and life, implied the power of intellectual sympathy, the faculty of 'entering into another man's thoughts', but it was also most importantly about the training of a man's will and character.[41] James Adam regarded the study of Greek as an essential element in a university education, and at Cambridge he resisted all attempts to make it optional.[42]

Barbara was an obedient daughter; by the age of ten she had been reading the New Testament proficiently in Greek aloud to her father on Sunday evenings for some time. Among the few photographs remaining of her childhood, there is one of her in a white dress and curls aged about two or three with her hand raised and her finger pointed as though expounding a lecture. In a second, she is a few years older with longer hair tied neatly in a bow; and she sits on one leg with a large book open on her lap; she has obviously been told to smile at the camera. Barbara was fond of her father, and she saw his playful, as well as his austere, side, but they had relatively little contact: 'Every morning he used to come into the nursery and issue a warning to each of us three children to try to keep clear of whatever at the moment was thought to be our besetting fault; but this was a cheerful, almost jovial, performance.' He was, she said, a brilliant teacher, warm-hearted towards his pupils, even if sometimes over-critical, and any success she herself had enjoyed in public speaking she was sure must have come from these qualities of his.[43]

Her relationship with her mother was much more complex. 'Mother', she said, 'was an extremely intellectual woman, as well as what is what is commonly called a strong character'. She was known as 'the Boss', and Barbara was in no doubt that Adela ran her husband and the marriage.[44] She was also formidably accomplished: a first-rate classical scholar, Adela spoke French, German and Italian well; she was a distinguished pianist, she played in an orchestra in her Girton student days at a time when it was thought 'scarcely proper' for a woman to do so,[45] and for many years she sang in the Cambridge University Musical Society (which she could not abide being called 'CUMS'[46]). Her politics were what most people today would regard as an odd mixture of radicalism and conservatism, though it was not odd at the time, when 'votes for women' attracted the commitment of women across the political spectrum. Conservative associations as well as socialist ones spawned Women's Franchise associations, and Adela was on the Executive Committee of the Cambridge branch. She was a 'fervent feminist'[47] about the suffrage, and about women's rights to an equal education. She was active in the Cambridge branch of the National Union of Women's Suffrage Societies, sitting on the platform with speakers such as the notable suffragist Clara Rackham, who proclaimed: 'We are tired of always working for men and through men. We want to work as voters, side by side with men.'[48]

Clara Rackham remembered, soon after her move to Cambridge in 1901, being called on by Adela who told her she was the secretary of a small Women's Suffrage Society: the subscription was a shilling a year. Would Mrs Rackham care to join? The members campaigned for women police officers and for women magistrates; they started schools for delicate and for sub-normal children, and a women's luncheon club.[49] Florence Keynes, mother of J.M. Keynes, pursued changing the law so women could stand for election to the local town council; she herself became the first woman councillor in Cambridge and one of the first woman magistrates.[50] Much effort was put into penal reform, which would become one of Barbara Wootton's abiding interests. As a child Barbara recalled women gathering in their drawing room, she supposed to agitate for the vote, and to pass resolutions for their MPs and so forth, though all in a very ladylike manner.[51] But Adela was not afraid of speaking out: in 1917, she was the leading signatory of a letter in the local Cambridge press headed 'Women's Suffrage' protesting about the Electoral Reform Committee's assent to the continued disenfranchisement of women. The position of British women vis-à-vis the franchise was worse than that prevailing in many countries of the Empire.[52] But in other respects, Barbara's mother was a 'very traditional Anglican',[53] a 'high-and-dry conservative'.[54] She despaired at the invention of Old Age Pensions, and found the stamping of insurance cards for her servants really too much. Barbara was especially incensed by her mother's treatment of the servants; for example, when Adela thought she had discovered that they were smoking cigarettes, she threatened to cut their wages. Barbara's passion for social equality was ignited by these domestic politics, which provided an intimate and early acquaintance with the evidence of class discrimination.

Whenever Barbara spoke about her mother in later life, she defined their relationship as difficult: 'I never felt any affection for my mother. She wanted to achieve through her children';[55] 'I was no lover of my own family … I had a very hostile relationship with my mother';[56] 'My earliest recollection – it's a sad thing to say it, I know – is tiptoeing past the door she was in so as not to be called in. I *detested* my mother, and if I have modelled myself, I *have* modelled myself…I've modelled myself by reaction *against*. I've tried not to get like her.'[57] Interviewed by MP Ann Clwyd in 1983, Barbara described Adela as 'a great slave-driver intellectually': 'I found her very pressing. What are you reading? What are you reading next? It was like that.'[58] Barbara was driven to reading books way beyond the interests and competence appropriate to her age. Yet perhaps, despite herself, she did slightly have her mother in mind as a role model when she declared at the age of ten that she wanted to be 'an organizing female with a briefcase'.[59]

Adela taught all her children at home, the boys until they were ten, Barbara until she was thirteen. Neil and Arthur went on to a small preparatory school and then, with scholarships, to boarding school, Winchester. Barbara was dispatched to a drawing class, which she hated; to a 'formidable Alsatian lady' for French and German; to a class in Swedish gymnastics; and to a dancing class. She liked and was good at both of the last two. The dancing class was run by a 'Miss Ratcliffe', and it was the same class as had been attended by little Gwen Darwin, Charles Darwin's granddaughter, and several of Gwen's cousins; but, whereas Gwen hid under the nursery table and prayed for Miss Ratcliffe's death,[60] Barbara liked Miss Ratcliffe so much she attended the class for fourteen years.[61]

Barbara and Gwen shared two experiences which were common among girls of their class at the time: between them and the world (including their parents) stood the ever-present figure of a nanny. Of course she stood there for boys as well, but boys went to school, and girls did not; so the other thing that Barbara and Gwen had in common was a burning desire to be *allowed* to go to school. Barbara wanted to go to boarding school, like her brothers, and any childish faith she had in the Almighty was sorely tested because she knelt down and prayed for this every time she went to the lavatory, but it never happened – perhaps, she later wondered, because the Almighty did not consider the lavatory a fitting place for such requests.[62]

Barbara's nanny, Elizabeth Haynes, came to the Adam household from another élite academic household – that of the future economist John Maynard Keynes. Mrs Keynes and Mrs Adam probably shared information about reliable domestic staff at their women's suffrage meetings. Barbara remembered her nanny taking her to see the Keynes' cook, Jenny, with whom she maintained a friendship, and the latter berating 'Mr Maynard' for his lazy habits (staying in bed until all hours).[63] This was Barbara's first impression of a man whose ideas about economics would transform the management of capitalist economic systems, and would have considerable resonance with her own.[64] In later life, she was fond of attributing the commonalities in the Keynes and Wootton philosophies of economics to their shared nannying.[65]

Elizabeth Haynes joined the Adam household when Neil was a month old and she stayed for fifty years. Although no letters from Adela are preserved in Barbara's Girton College Archives, there are ninety-five from her nanny. In later life, Barbara made no secret of the fact that the 'mutual devotion' between herself and her nanny largely compensated for the lack of affection she felt for her mother.[66] Barbara and Neil both supported their nanny financially in her old age, and Barbara sustained a regular correspondence with her, and visited her often until she died at ninety-one. She was always known as 'The Pie', though no-one could remember why. The Pie was born in 1868 (so she was twenty-three when she joined the Adam household), the daughter of a Huntingdonshire farm labourer and his wife, Ebenezer and Margaret Haynes, the only one of their ten children who never married. She went into service young, to a family in Bedford, followed by the Keynes' household, and then to the Adams to provide for Barbara and her brothers the kind of steadfast warmth and ordinary kindness that it seems was lacking from their parents. A photograph shows The Pie, a pretty young woman, dressed in the starched white apron and cap of a nanny, looking tenderly down into the face of a baby, who was, perhaps, Barbara. The Pie expected high standards of behaviour from her charges, was a devout Baptist and went about her business singing hymns. She made dresses and chair-covers, and, despite having no education to speak of, wrote admirably clear and direct English. From time to time she would take offence at something that had been said or done, and would be virtually silent for two or three days; these and other episodes of temporary rejection at The Pie's hand afforded Barbara an experience of trauma which she claimed stood her in good stead in her later work as a juvenile court magistrate.[67]

Barbara called The Pie 'a remarkable specimen of that remarkable but now nearly extinct race'.[68] The habit of handing the daily care of one's children over to a paid servant who lived in the house but came from a very different echelon of society is peculiarly British: 'a unique and curious way of bringing up children'.[69] The central character of Winston Churchill's only novel, *Savrola*, is still tended by his nanny in her old age: Savrola comments: 'It is a strange thing, the love of these women. Perhaps it is the only disinterested affection in the world.'[70] Churchill himself enjoyed such affection from his nanny, Nanny Everest, until she died when he was twenty, and for all those years she was effectively his carer, his confidante, and his friend. Gwen Darwin, who shared the experience of Barbara's dancing-class teacher, observed of her nanny that: 'I can never remember being bathed by my mother, or even having my hair brushed by her, and I should not at all have liked if she had done anything of the kind. We did not feel it was her place to do such things'.[71] Social reformer Eva Hubback, born eleven years before Barbara, was closer to her nanny than to her parents: this nanny stayed with the family for thirty-two years, but, unlike The Pie, she preferred the two boys in her charge.[72]

There is no sign of such a preference in the records that exist of Barbara's relationship with The Pie. The warmth of those ninety-five letters burns out of the direct but difficult-to-decipher handwriting like a living flame: 'My Own Dear,' writes The Pie to the fifty-seven-year-old Barbara, from her hospital bed in May 1954, 'Your letter was brought to me today while I was having my dinner ....

My word you do have a busy time what with one thing & another. But I believe you enjoy a good deal of it … I do congratulate you on your lift up but I think you deserve it.'[73] The letters are infused with unwavering affection: Barbara is called 'Missie', so most of the letters begin 'My Own Dear Missie'. But the style is also very proper: there is much attention to detail – what Barbara is doing; the clothes she is buying; the mentions of her achievements The Pie has read in the newspapers; the socks The Pie is knitting for Barbara's second husband; the state of the weather; the temperaments of the staff in the hospital and in the nursing home which Barbara's kindness, and that of 'Mr Neil' – he is always called 'Mr Neil' – has made possible. Among all this detail are flashes of emotion. As she grows older, The Pie thinks about the old days a lot. 'I did love looking after you all three very much when you were little & we I think had a happy time.'[74]

Despite The Pie's devoted care, Barbara said she did not enjoy her childhood.[75] This was also despite the beauty and ease of Cambridge, which was then a good place to be a child in: a town small enough for children to know well, with a colourful street market and many open spaces; 'Coe Fen still wild, with no great road running across it. The water ran sluggishly through it; water beetles danced endlessly in the sun on the river's surface; a child could lose himself there quietly for a whole day through.'[76] There was the charm of the Backs and the Bridges, the huge weeping willows, the sun shining through the great windows of King's College Chapel.[77] What did seep into Barbara Wootton's soul was the East Anglian countryside: 'the flat loneliness, the delicate light and the wide skies of the fen country'.[78] Perhaps she played down in her remembrances the easy pleasure that is often obtained from being one of several siblings. Her brothers were clever and industrious as she was, but also thoughtful and humorous companions. One of Adela's letters (in James Adam's Emmanuel College papers) recalls the eight-year-old Barbara being much occupied, together with her brother Neil, 'with glass-blowing at the Balfour laboratory, & extensive carpentering & photographic works'.[79] One day Barbara lay down on the nursery floor and proposed to Neil and Arthur that the three of them should invent their own language as a protection from adult interference; they should pronounce all words as though they were spelt backwards; recalling this years later, she noted that 'backslang' was also a habit of the 'criminal classes'.[80] The three of them became very proficient at backslang, finding ways round the more awful tongue-twisters, and realising that 'dog' backwards would be no good, so their knowledge of Latin came in handy ('sinac'). They carried this proficiency into adulthood. Arthur, who died in the First World War, used some of this language in his letters to his family, and Neil and Barbara were both able to carry on a conversation in it for the rest of their adult lives.

There is little record of Neil's relationship with the sister who was six years younger than him, but, after Arthur died in the war, Adela put together a memoir based
on Arthur's letters. In 1904, aged ten, he wrote, with childish honesty, 'Barbara is
getting on well with her Two Scale Studies. She plays the first one quite nicely but
she does not play the second so well.' Later, he observed rather pompously that,
'We are doing William and Mary now in our history. Sometimes Barbara forgets
the most important things and remembers the things of lesser importance. But
that is by no means always the case. In fact, I think she is making a lot of progress
and I am quite satisfied with her.'[81] According to Adela, Barbara remembered
vividly the pains he took to teach her the big towns of England on the nursery floor
in Emmanuel House, which was the scene of most indoor occupations. Adela must
have been proud of Arthur when she found a self-congratulatory missive he had
written to the twelve-year-old Barbara about her progress in Greek: 'You appear to
be becoming an advanced scholar in the Greek tongue, as you quote Greek in your
letter to Mother which I saw yesterday: still I have no doubt you are yet ignorant
of when you may use [certain letters], which interesting facts are to be discovered
in my notes on Homeric Grammar taken from the information imparted to me by
Frank Carter Esq. M.A. I should also think you may be unaware of the principles of
Stem Variation and Root Gradation.'[82] This was an intensely and highly traditional
hothouse atmosphere, one in which the language of learning and communication
was emblematic of exactly those devotions and differences which turned Barbara
Wootton into one of the most important social scientists of the twentieth century.

The particular constellation of pleasures and difficulties that made up the Adam
children's childhoods was unalterably affected when their father died suddenly
at the age of forty-seven. Barbara was ten, the boys thirteen and sixteen. James
had been depressed again, and afraid that his mental power was failing; the only
thing that cheered him up was listening to little Barbara reading the Bible in
Greek. In the summer of 1907, he gave his last lecture of the season at Cambridge,
and set off to see his mother in Scotland, planning to join Adela, the children
and the extended family in North Wales later. While in Scotland, he consulted
a doctor about what he thought 'a slight local complaint' unconnected with his
depression and insomnia, and general mental misery. Carcinoma of the rectum was
diagnosed; he went into hospital for an operation, but died four hours later with
Adela at his side. For the young Barbara, this was the first of a series of deaths that
would introduce her to the notion, which possessed her for the rest of her life, that
absolutely nothing could ever be counted on, that whatever comfort and certainty
you thought you had was always liable to crumble away at a moment's notice.

3

Alma Mater

James Adam's death at the early age of forty-seven left Barbara's mother, Adela, the family breadwinner with three children under sixteen. There was also a new home to find. Emmanuel House belonged to Emmanuel College, and it was needed for the next incumbent of James Adam's post as Senior Tutor. Sometime between November 1907 and February 1908 – only weeks after James's death[1] – the family moved to a house on the edge of town. Number twenty-one (later renumbered twenty-nine) Barton Road lies on what is today a busy road leading from Barton village into the centre of Cambridge. Barbara described it as, 'a tall, ugly house with a basement and three stories above'.[2] Although its fussy red-brick façade lacked aesthetic appeal, it hid capacious accommodation. Barbara inhabited a bedroom with The Pie on the top floor of the house, a location that fuelled the fears she had throughout her childhood of some great conflagration that would end everything forever. It was usual then for middle-class girls to sleep either with nannies or mothers until well into their teens or later; writer Naomi Mitchison, born the same year as Barbara, slept in her mother's bedroom while an undergraduate at Oxford,[3] and Lynda Grier, born in 1880, shared a room with her mother until she was a forty-year-old Professor of Economics.[4]

As Gwen Raverat put it in her book about her own Cambridge childhood, 'For nearly seventy years, the English middle classes were locked up in a great fortress of unreality and pretence; and no one who has not been brought up inside the fortress can guess how thick the walls were, or how little of the sky outside could be seen through the loopholes'.[5] In the years between her father's death and the end of the First World War, these walls largely protected Barbara from the world outside upper-middle-class Cambridge. But the sky outside was full of dark clouds: the massing clouds of war and death. Before she was twenty, death at home and death abroad would rob Barbara of three more of the people to whom she was closest. These encounters with mortality left legendary scars, and helped to precipitate a tendency to depression and self-containment which lasted her entire life. But it was also during these years that Barbara rehearsed her parents' particular dream for her – that she would become a first-rate classical scholar. The story played out during this process encapsulates many of the central motifs of the evolution of women's education in Britain.

After the death of her husband, Adela expanded her own teaching duties by adding sessions at two other women's colleges – Newnham in Cambridge, where for some years she was Director of Studies in Classics, and Bedford in London, where for a term she replaced the Greek lecturer – to her duties at Girton, where she had been teaching Classics for seventeen years; and she went on educating Barbara at home. Middle- and upper-class families at the time, even those who could have afforded to send their daughters to school, believed that keeping them at home was much better suited to the female role in society.[6] Aristocratic parents boasted that, 'We do not send our daughters away to school', and a particular theory abounded 'that day schools for girls were Bad'.[7] In Cambridge, Margaret Cole, four years older than Barbara, went to a little private school run by Mrs Berry, wife of a don at King's, with her two brothers, mornings only.[8] Somewhat strangely, Naomi Mitchison, another daughter of academic parents, attended a boys' school, the Dragon School in Oxford (it took the occasional girl) with her brother, but was pulled out and confined to the care of a governess at home when she reached puberty.[9] The long-lived doctrine of men's and women's separate spheres carried with it the sociobiology of female inferiority, according to which women's main function was reproduction, and anything that interfered with this – which was more or less everything else, and certainly education – had to be regarded with grave suspicion.

The routine of Adela's lessons every morning (Adela must have been *very* busy), and listening to her recitation of Walter Scott novels on Sundays, was unvarying and not very enlivening for someone with Barbara's appetite for learning. In the school holidays, with two boisterous brothers around, life was a good deal more exciting; they played bicycle polo in the back garden, and there were interesting guests at lunch. And then the Almighty seemed to have been half-listening to Barbara's lavatorial prayers, or Adela felt she could not carry Barbara's education further, or the supply of local children to be taught alongside Barbara dried up – the reason did not matter very much: the point was that Barbara was allowed to go to school for the first time. At the age of thirteen a new world opened up. Adela's choice for her daughter was the Perse School for girls, an institution with a respectable history as an offshoot of the much better known Perse School for boys, which had been founded in 1618 on a Cambridge site belonging to the Augustinian Friars: the site was given the name it still has today – Free School Lane. The girls' version of the Perse School opened its doors in January 1881, with twenty-eight pupils.[10] It came, like many others, in the aftermath of the mounting attention given by campaigning women to the appalling neglect of girls' and women's education. In 1867, the Report of the Schools Inquiry Commission had identified the cardinal faults of existing educational provision for girls as: 'Want of thoroughness and foundation; slovenliness and showy superficiality; inattention to rudiments; undue time given to accomplishments, and these not taught intelligently or in any scientific manner; want of organisation'.[11] The girls' high school movement, of which the Perse School was a part, was very much about providing real intellectual training for middle-class girls, not simply 'finishing' them as decorative embellishments, or equipping them to be the mothers and helpers of men. The strength of the movement was reinforced by the increasingly recognized reality of the unmarried middle-class woman who needed to earn her own living.[12]

The curriculum of 'Perse Girls' (as it was known) when Barbara went included 'Christian religious education'; geography; history; English grammar, composition and literature; Latin, French and German; 'one or more branches of Natural Science'; mathematics; needlework; 'Domestic Economy and Laws of Health'; drawing; music; and 'Drill, or other physical exercises'.[13] In its early decades, the school was not highly regarded by Cambridge parents.[14] An unfavourable report by the Board of Education in 1907 persuaded the school's managers that a new young headmistress was needed with the focus necessary to improve academic standards. One of those who made this decision was Barbara's own mother, Adela. She had been co-opted as a Perse Girls' School manager representing Girton College in 1907, and she went on to become Honorary Secretary of the Perse Governors for twenty-four years until her death in 1944. In the first twenty years of her service to the school, Adela managed to attend eighty-two out of ninety-two Governors' meetings; no wonder the Governors wanted to place on record their 'high appreciation' of her 'valuable services'.[15] Surprisingly, since she was otherwise a cautious mother, Adela took a risk in sending Barbara to Perse Girls; not only were there questions about academic standards, but numbers were falling: from 217 in 1904, the school roll had dropped to 146 in 1908.[16] Perhaps Adela was confident that things would improve, or perhaps she wanted to convince other parents that Perse Girls was a worthy place, or perhaps she got reduced fees for Barbara, which helped with her straitened financial circumstances. The new headmistress was one Bertha Lucy Kennett, a Girton-trained mathematician. She was paid partly on a capitation basis – a basic salary of two hundred pounds a year plus additions calculated according to the number and age of her pupils. Whether it was this scheme that worked, or Miss Kennett's brilliant teaching and advanced administrative ability, by 1911, the year after Barbara joined, the school inspectors reported an improvement in standards, and the Perse School for Girls was added to the list of those designated as 'efficient' by the Board of Education.[17]

But did Barbara know, and if she did know would she have cared, about any of this? 'Equipped with my unbecoming school hat with its black and blue ribbon and the school crest of a pelican plucking its breast for its young, I embarked, full of joyful anticipations upon my new life.'[18] So efficient had been Adela's own education of her, that Barbara was placed in a form ahead of her age; she began to learn science, and to play netball and tennis, and she acquired a lifelong distaste for Shakespeare. She was a diligent student, repeatedly winning prizes in Classics, Greek and English Literature; playing a leading part in the Perse Girls' School Debating Society; and helping to found its Literary Club. She took her school certificate in the summer of 1913: Latin, Greek, elementary mathematics (with algebra and geometry), German, English, and Scripture. Her proficiency as a well-behaved student was evidenced by the reference Bertha Lucy Kennett wrote for her:

> My colleagues on the Staff and I have been greatly impressed by her powers of mind and character. Miss Adam is an exceedingly able student who could scarcely fail to do brilliantly at any subject in which she might elect to specialize. She possesses, moreover, the perseverance and steadiness of aim not always associated with brilliancy of intellect. I desire, as Headmistress, to pay a special tribute to Miss Adam's helpful influence in School. Her loyalty to the School, her reliability and her unselfish acceptance of her responsibility as a member of the Upper Sixth Form have been beyond praise.[19]

Most importantly, Barbara was very happy at Perse Girls.[20] The school offered her the opportunity to make friends. In her autobiography, she singled out two for different reasons. The first, Dorothy Russell, was one of those all-round stars who cause epidemics of envy among their fellows: she was Secretary of the Natural Science Club; winner of the Science prize; Vice-President of the Debating Club; Captain of the first netball team; editor of the school magazine; and Head Girl. At the age of fourteen, when Barbara first met her, Dorothy had decided to become a doctor, and to specialize in research. This was remarkable at a time when medicine had only just begun to entertain the idea of women doctors, and also because Dorothy did not have the advantage of a resourceful and supportive family – she had been orphaned at the age of eight and sent from Australia to live with her aunt and uncle in a mournful rectory outside Cambridge. When Dorothy Russell left Girton, she entered the London Hospital in 1919, the year after women were first admitted as medical students, and she went on to become Professor of Morbid Anatomy there, write a textbook on brain tumours, and acquire an international reputation in pathology and neuropathology. Not the least remarkable fact about her was that she charged two friends after her death to make it known that all her life she had suffered from epilepsy; such a disability was therefore no bar to achievement in professional life.[21] Barbara's second close friend at Perse Girls, Helen Grant, another 'exceptionally gifted and beautiful girl', was not so fortunate. She complained of internal pains one day at school, which Barbara and Dorothy assumed must be appendicitis, but after two operations performed at home (as they were in those days), she died of cancer at the age of fifteen. Barbara saw her, in a scene of 'deep serenity'[22] a few days before she died.

Barbara's reaction to adolescence included the voracious reading of poetry, and books on religion and mysticism. Several poems published in *The Persean Magazine* – 'To the Moon on a Cloudy Night', 'Soul-Wanderings' and 'The Orphan' – testify to Barbara's absorption in matters of the soul.[23] On her seventeenth birthday, she announced her intention of 'putting her hair up', an artifice of femininity customary at the time; Adela considered it too soon, but Barbara did it anyway. During this period after James Adam's death, Adela was occupied, not only with her own extended teaching engagements, but with tidying up for publication his unpublished lectures and essays, and promoting his ideas about the value of a classical education in her own papers and publications, although rather stretching the point beyond where James would have taken it, in recommending that Classics students should broaden their interests to study the links between the classical texts and more modern European literature.[24] Her work shows that she was a considerable scholar in her own right, but her ambitions outstripped her circumstances. In 1920, Adela applied for the Cassel Fellowship at Girton with a major programme of research and writing, which included a history of the expansion of studies at the University of Cambridge since 1850, the links between classical literature and medieval Italian comedy, and a non-technical handbook on classical metres. Although the Council awarded her the Fellowship, she never had enough time to finish these projects.[25] But the links with Europe were already made in practice; in the autumn of 1909, the family went to Austria, where Barbara (aged twelve) proved herself an excellent walker, managing twenty miles a day, and proving her superiority to Neil and Arthur by knowing a fair amount of German.[26] In the long hot summer of 1911, they went to Jersey, where they saw the portrait of their ancestor Charles William Le Geyt. Aunts Juliet and Fanny took them to Italy, to the Dolomites and then to Venice, Verona and Florence. The Pie was not allowed to come on these foreign holidays, which Barbara minded, though whether The Pie did or not, we do not know. At home, the house in Barton Road was enlivened by boarders (presumably taken in for the money), and Barbara was

much impressed by one in particular, Rosalind Mendl, an especially beautiful
young woman who scorned Barbara's childish clothes and introduced her to the
world of alcoholic parties.[27] According to a later correspondence with Margaret
Cole,[28] Rosalind was actually Vera Rosalind Mendel, a student of medieval and
modern languages at Girton just before Barbara in 1913–6. She later married the
poet, book designer and founder of the Nonesuch Press, Francis Meynell, but the
zest for life she displayed in Barton Road eventually evaporated: after leading a
colourful life with Francis and various other men, she committed suicide during
the Second World War.[29]

Aunts, and especially maiden aunts (a 'most admirable species'[30]) were a feature of
many Victorian and Edwardian childhoods. The two who featured most in Barbara's
childhood, her mother's sisters, Fanny Kensington and Juliet Mylne, helped not
just with holidays but with many other aspects of the Adam family life. They were
both women of character and public accomplishment with strong connections to
the movement for women's education, and they must have been convincing models
of energy and public service for the young Barbara. Aunt Juliet had been married
briefly at the age of twenty-eight to a well-off barrister, John Eltham Mylne, who
had the misfortune to die less than a year after their marriage. Like so many of those
attached to the Adam/Kensington family, Mylne was a great protagonist in the field
of women's education. As Honorary Secretary of an organization called the Ladies'
Educational Association, he had helped to open the doors of London University
to women in 1878, a full forty-two and seventy years before the same landmarks
in Oxford and Cambridge respectively.[31] The Ladies' Educational Association – of
which there were branches in Manchester, Liverpool, Leeds, London, Sheffield and
Newcastle – sponsored external courses of lectures given by university staff for
'ladies' over seventeen barred from university admission.[32] Mylne's other service to the
Adam/Kensington family was his premature death, which left Aunt Juliet a widow
of considerable independent means. Barbara tells the story of Mylne's death in her
autobiography: he died supposedly of consumption, although the family suspected
he might have been killed by the cure to which he was subjected – a sea voyage to
Australia. The cure was prescribed by a fashionable London physician, Sir Andrew
Clark, a man of somewhat peculiar clinical habits – when he could not diagnose an
illness, he would follow a patient home and study their 'moral surroundings'.[33] In fact,
John Eltham Mylne's death certificate specifies 'Phthisis pulmonalis [tuberculosis]
several years' as the cause of death, so exposure to the oceanic elements probably did
not have the dramatic effect imagined by the family. His will, a lengthy seven-page
document worthy of a barrister, bequeathed his young widow a substantial amount
of money and other material assets – wines, liquors, linen, watches, jewellery, books

and pictures. When Juliet herself died in 1923, she left money to Adela and to both Barbara and Neil. Barbara's portion provided an income of £100 a year which her socialist principles forced her to give away, although she never disposed of the capital.[34] More of Mylne's wealth was to come Barbara's way after Adela's own death. Aunt Juliet never remarried, but she was a JP, a Poor Law Guardian, Chairman of the Paddington Board of Guardians, an Alderman of the Metropolitan Borough of Paddington, an active member of the Women's Local Government Society, and one of the first women elected as a Fellow of the Royal Geographical Society in 1892.[35] She, Fanny and Adela were all great travellers.

Barbara's favourite aunt, Fanny – she is Fanny on her birth certificate, but she also used the name Frances – was the liveliest of the trio. In the 1870s, when in her early twenties, she did voluntary social work in London (a common occupation for upper-middle-class women at the time) and otherwise led a jolly social life with dances, theatricals, picnics and cruises in a friend's yacht.[36] She became Secretary to England's first institution of higher education for women, Bedford College, a place where her niece Barbara would eventually become a professor. During this period, she featured in a somewhat salacious story about a relationship between a married ageing Oxford scholar called Mark Pattison, and a young woman, Meta Bradley. Pattison was an ordained priest and rector of Lincoln College, Oxford. An 'emotionally castrated man',[37] he married late in life a woman who was said to refuse him sex. On the plus side, he played a role in organizing lectures for women in the 1870s when Oxford was still resistant to the idea. But he is remembered most vividly for being an inveterate womanizer, enjoying the company of young women, and especially that of Meta and Meta's constant companion, Fanny Kensington, whom for a while he picked as a possible ideal companion. It is a strange semi-erotic Victorian drama in which the outlines of what actually happened cannot really be determined. The final perversity is that Pattison had the misfortune to be treated by the same doctor as had sent John Eltham Mylne on his last fatal voyage; in Pattison's case, when the local doctor said there was not a ghost of a chance of his getting better, Sir Andrew Clark advised a trip to Colorado.[38]

Adela was therefore not alone in managing her household: she had her sisters Juliet and Fanny to help her. They would have participated in plans for Barbara's future. It was decided that she would leave school in 1914, spend a few months in Germany living with a family to improve her German, and then apply for entry to Girton College as a Classics scholar in October 1915. The middle part of this plan was doomed, in view of what happened to the world in the summer of 1914. On the day Britain declared war, Barbara was staying with Dorothy Russell in the countryside outside Cambridge. On her way home, she met crowds cheering in the streets.

'Little though the word "war" conveyed to me at this stage,' she observed in her autobiography, 'I knew enough to recognize that theirs was an emotion that I would never share.'[39] By this time, her brothers Neil and Arthur were both at university. Neil, at Trinity College, Cambridge, had acquired a double first in natural sciences, and was established on his path to becoming a distinguished physical chemist and a world leader in quantitative surface chemistry.[40] Arthur had entered Balliol College, Oxford, with the Senior Balliol Classical Scholarship, much, presumably, to Adela's joy. He had given a very able speech in the Union in favour of women's suffrage, but had also become acutely aware of social inequality and interested in 'socialist schemes of betterment'. Like many male students, he served in the Officer Training Corps which, when War broke out, inquired whether 'in the event of a general mobilization', he would be interested in a Commission. Once he had overcome the obstacle of his poor eyesight by finding a doctor prepared to test him in his spectacles, Arthur joined the 1st Battalion of the Cambridgeshire Regiment. During the early months of the War, the Battalion was stationed in Suffolk and Cambridgeshire. By April 1915, Arthur was writing to a friend in France, 'The voice of Oxford, as is inevitable, grows fainter as the clouds fall deeper. Surely warfare is a damnable business, and it gets worse'.[41] In mid-June, Adela and Barbara met Arthur on the Fleam Dyke in Lincolnshire, 'marvellously beautiful with summer flowers', and at home in Cambridge he played Bach preludes and sang Italian songs – like Adela, he was a very accomplished musician. After dark, and despite the War, he engaged in his favourite habit of running up and down the Barton Road, a ghostly figure in a white jersey and shorts accompanied by Barbara on a bicycle.[42]

Barbara's other brother, Neil, escaped the terrors to which Arthur was exposed by being a scientist whose services to his country were judged more useful at home than in the trenches. After starting some biochemistry research on muscle protein, he was posted to the Royal Naval Air Service at Farnborough, later at Kingsnorth, in Kent, where he was put to work on the construction of non-rigid airships.[43] For a short time, the general gloom and doom of war was relieved when Neil fell in love with a mathematician colleague at Kingsnorth, Winifred Wright. They were married in London in June 1916. Arthur, now in France, was unable to get leave to attend the wedding, so he ate his piece of the wedding cake in the mud and stench of the trenches. Soon after his marriage, Neil had what was called in those days 'a nervous breakdown'; the reasons probably had something to do with guilt about not being on active service in the War, and he was also without work.[44] He and Winifred, who was now pregnant with their first child, returned to live in Barton Road. Neil was very depressed, and Winifred and Adela did not get on – Adela was beastly to her, and The Pie was violently prejudiced against

the new mother and her methods of childrearing. Baby Jean was born in Barton
Road in May 1917. Barbara remembered it as a harrowing time, with all of them
wrapped in anxiety about Arthur's fate in France, about what was wrong with
Neil, and why baby Jean was so difficult; Barbara acted as mediator, through it all
continuing, diligently like the dutiful daughter she was still trying to be, to perfect
her knowledge of dead languages.[45]

On quiet nights in Cambridge, the distant rumble of guns in Belgium and
France could be heard. The War was confidently expected to be short and sharp.
Then it became clear that it would not be over by Christmas; men began to be
killed, 'really killed so that we would never see them again';[46] long columns of the
dead and wounded began to appear daily in *The Times*.[47] Barbara did volunteer
office work in a military hospital and then helped in a military canteen, and it
seemed increasingly absurd to her that she should be spending her time studying
dead civilizations, when the only living civilization she knew was crashing about
her ears. So she pleaded with Adela to be allowed to study economics, or at least
history. A compromise of sorts was reached. Barbara would attend some lectures
in economics while preparing for her classical scholarship at Girton; she would
then read Classics for three years, following this with a year's study in economics.
The restrained account of these negotiations in Barbara's autobiography belies
what was probably an awful row, since it challenged the heart of Adela's view of
Barbara's future life. Barbara was destined for a career in the moribund, but safe,
world of classical literature and scholarship – that world which James Adam had
believed so essential a form of both intellectual and moral training.

The new, negotiated plan once in place, Barbara lost no time in making it work;
she went to see the Director of Economics at Newnham College, Lynda Grier – she
who still shared a room with her mother – and Grier set her to read the works of
Alfred Marshall. Barbara read and annotated every line of Marshall's *The Economics
of Industry* and his much bigger *Principles of Economics*, so immensely relieved to have
escaped Greek and Latin that she ignored any further irrelevancies to the problems
of civilization this new subject might have contained.[48]

Barbara left her economics books temporarily behind and went to Girton in
October 1915, armed with a Classics scholarship. Arthur came home from France
for a week, and they spent much companionable time together. One afternoon
he poured out his concerns to her about the prevalence of venereal disease among
the men under his command; familiar from his letters with the blood and squalor
of trench warfare, this was something Barbara had never considered. But they
also talked of other things. She was his little sister, and he had watched over her
babyhood and her early attempts at learning, and now he was finding how much

they had in common in terms of attitudes to war, and what one ought to do with one's life. Later he would write to her from France: 'I think you know that I want some day to go and live in a poor part of London, and see what it is all really like; and I have prayed that it might happen, and that you would possibly be able to come too; and if this war ever stops whilst I am alive (which I have come to doubt very much), perhaps it may yet; but at least, if I am killed, I will now have mentioned the idea to you'.[49]

Barbara Adam joined fifty-five other new students who entered Girton in 1915. She left no account of her own induction into Girton life, but Lily Baron, a medical student, who arrived at about the same time, wrote her recollections of arriving at Girton:

> I travelled up by train sedately clad in a tweed costume, the skirt carefully covering my calves, a felt hat and kid gloves. In my trunk I had another hat, my best one, and a pair of white gloves for wearing on Sundays when I went calling. I also had a dinner dress – I adored it – to wear during the week for Hall, and a ball dress for Saturday dances in College, where, despite the absence of men (except those officially engaged to students), the evening was a formal one … At Girton, in my day, there were strict rules of protocol. You had to wait to be addressed by a student senior to you; the use of Christian names was forbidden unless the person had 'propped' – that is, proposed. The magic formula 'May I prop?' gave you permission to use the Christian name, and how honoured you as a fresher felt if a third-year student 'propped' to you. … We were not admitted as members of the University and any lecturer could refuse us permission to attend his course. I used to attend some chemistry lectures where the front two rows were filled by women from Girton and Newnham. Each morning the Professor sternly said 'Good Morning, Gentlemen!'.[50]

Like the Perse School for Girls, Girton College has a starred entry in the history of women's education. It owed its existence to Emily Davies – dainty, small, obstinate and highly conventional, rather like Queen Victoria, and possessed of considerable administrative and networking skills, a woman utterly intransigent in the pursuit of her vision of a New Jerusalem for women.[51] Her New Jerusalem was about allowing women exactly the same access to the same education as men; she rejected completely the other idea, fashionable at the time, that women needed a separate education: it was even proposed at one stage that Oxford and Cambridge should together sponsor a special women's university.[52] Girton College also had the status of an Adam/Kensington family institution; it was a home from home. Adela maintained a connection with Girton from 1882 until her death in 1944: first as a student, then, after 1890, as a lecturer and/or governor, and Honorary Treasurer of a Fund set up in 1912 in memory of Frances Buss to help poor students.[53] Her sister Fanny trod the same path as Adela from Bedford College in London to Girton in Cambridge, though in a different capacity. At Bedford College, Fanny worked as Secretary and then, in 1882, Emily Davies recruited her for the equivalent post at Girton, which she kept for fifteen years: 'Pre-twentieth century students recall with admiration the letters and handwriting of Frances Kensington, and her tactful sympathy in interviews'.[54] For part of her time at Girton, Fanny was also Bursar, and then a member of the Executive Committee and a Governor, and, with Adela, she was a trustee of the Frances Buss Loan Fund.

Emily Davies believed that women's capacity to enjoy these new freedoms required a protected existence. For all her radical views – perhaps because of them – she considered that women students should be kept away from the distractions of the men. When it moved from its original location in a rented house in Hitchin, the College was sited in Girton village, a safe two-and-a-half miles outside Cambridge. The students' journeys into Cambridge were carefully arranged and monitored, with special horse cabs provided, and a space called the Girton Waiting Rooms in central Cambridge where they could safely pass time between lectures. In the 1880s, when Adela Kensington was an undergraduate, two of her fellow students kept their own horses, and another two scandalized the Mistress by riding on a double tricycle.[55] When bicycles became more of a general habit, Girtonians were allowed to ride only halfway, with the cabs taking them the rest.[56] Most of the Girton girls' socializing occurred within the College, and twice a year big evening parties were hosted; there was dancing in the Stanley Library, beautifully illuminated by the candles in brass candlesticks the students brought from their rooms (these were pre-electric days) which were set on the tops of the bookcases; candle grease on dresses was regarded as the distinctive mark of a Girtonian.[57] Although Girton was part of the University, like the other early women's colleges it was also a world apart, and deliberately kept so in order to conform to the mores of the time. It is a theme repeated in novels of the period: for example, Judith Earle, the innocent, home-educated central character of Rosamond Lehmann's novel *Dusty Answer*, arriving at Cambridge in 1918, senses a society of values and behaviour which is completely beyond her knowledge and experience.[58] Another of Emily Davies's precepts, for which generations of Girtonians must have been thankful (especially those used to sharing bedrooms with nannies or mothers), followed Virginia Woolf's dictum that every woman should have a room of her own. This emphasis inevitably produced economies in other areas: although Girton was built in red-brick Gothic in imitation of the men's colleges, shortage of money meant that it was some time before a quadrangle actually materialized. The grounds were not landscaped at first, and, since women were not allowed to be seen playing sports outdoors, in winter they had to exercise inside in the gymnasium or run up and down the fortunately very lengthy corridors.[59] Girton had its own swimming pool, built as part of a large new extension in 1899–1902, and in the early 1900s the College Swimming Club had a healthy membership. It organized annual water polo matches, which were played (rather incredibly) by girls in long flowing white dresses.[60]

Barbara lived in Girton for her first two years. According to Dora Russell, then Dora Black, who went there in 1912, three years before Barbara, the routine still resembled that of a boarding school.[61] Facilities were quite primitive: the oil lamps and the earth closets and 'the secret activities of the night-soil men' were not replaced until after the War.[62] College servants, known as gyps, filled the students' coal scuttles and made their beds and cleaned their rooms every day except Sundays. Lily Baron recalled that many of the Girton young ladies were domestically ignorant, never having had to do for themselves things such as lighting a fire, boiling an egg, or even, in the case of one student, washing one's own hair. The life of the gyps was remembered by one of them, Gladys Crane, as hard but happy. They were assigned their own corridors, and had nine stoves and nine rooms to do before breakfast by candlelight. They wore blue print dresses and white aprons in the morning, black dresses and white aprons in the afternoon, and big white aprons when waiting in hall at night, where there was a constant danger of slipping and dropping something on the highly polished wooden floor.[63] In the evenings, they took small jugs of milk to the students' rooms:

> If someone asked you to "jug" that evening (by a written invitation) you went along to your hostess's room armed with your jug of milk. There other guests would have assembled, and there, before the fireplace, would be a row of jugs, and we drank hot chocolate during the winter evenings, and coffee when it got warmer. Over a blazing coal fire, the party-giver toasted crumpets on a brass fork, and everybody talked themselves hoarse till a warning cry rang out: "SILENCE HOURS Please".[64]

A pivotal strategy for protecting women from the misogynies of the outside world, still in place when Barbara was a student there, was the chaperone system. Men had uncontrollable passions, and women therefore had to avoid ever being alone in male company.[65] No men could be invited to one's room in College, and no outside visits involving men could be made without a chaperone. Known locally as 'dragons', chaperones were either staff or retired ladies (for whom the system provided a small but reliable income).[66] Most young women took the chaperone system for granted; tactful 'chaps' who stayed quietly in the corner were preferred,[67] and sympathetic staff, such as the medieval historian Eileen Power, who were willing to make a brief formal entry and then exit, were much in demand.[68] A common strategy for subverting the system was just to say that whatever man one wanted to see was a cousin: 'It was remarkable how many university men were cousins of women undergraduates'.[69] Like their social interaction, the bodies of the women students were confined: in bone corsets with tight back lacings and long skirts, and gloves and hats outside the College.[70] Margaret Cole, who went to Girton four years before Barbara, recalled being rebuked because she went cycling without a hat.[71]

Barbara's academic record at Girton was impeccable, and included the Agnata Butler prize in 1917 and the Therese Montefiore prize in 1919. But she did manage some fun, too. Girton had a Debating Society, a Fire Brigade, a Women's Suffrage Club, clubs for tennis, hockey, lacrosse, cricket and swimming, a Society for the Study of Little Known Literature and something called the Spontaneous Speaking Society. Barbara's name crops up in the records of the first two of these. In 1916, for instance, she proposed the motion at the Girton Debating Society, 'That it is a good thing for society that people are afraid of being peculiar'. It is not entirely clear what this meant, but Barbara opposed Cubism as being socially undesirable and deemed the desire for peculiarity the result of conceit or the wish to attract attention. Afterwards, 'B.F. Adam' was congratulated on 'the remarkable fluency with which she can speak, using notes only'.[72] The initials 'B.F.' – Bloody Fool – were something Barbara always held against her parents.[73] A couple of years later, she is down as speaking about public schools, and arguing, with the logic for which she would later become famous, that the so-called evils of the Public School system were not necessarily a consequence of this, any more than the dandelions on the Girton tennis courts were a consequence of the higher education of women.[74] In 1915–7, her name appears as one of three Sub-Captains of Corps II of the Girton College Fire Brigade. This outfit came into being in 1879 after some nearby haystacks went up in flames (a large part of the grounds was rented out to local farmers to raise money). In its heyday, the Girton Fire Brigade was a prestigious society with rigorous discipline, energetic, well-attended weekly practices, and its own song, set to the music of 'John Peel'. There was a Head Captain, and a corps for each corridor, with its own Captain and Sub-Captain, and training from Captain Shaw and his men from the London Fire Brigade. Though a wise precaution, in view of all those students wandering around in the dark with candles, and obviously also a great deal of fun, it was only ever called out once, to a fire in Girton village, on the first day of the Easter vacation in 1918.[75] Those members of the fire brigade who were still in College, plus several gyps, dragged eighteen leaky hoses across ploughed fields and prickly hedges – it was an 'epoch-making occasion' – but was Barbara there?

Girton struggled, and so did women at Cambridge, for many years: it was a history of small numbers, slow gains, multiple setbacks and severe financial constraints.[76] As late as 1940, a history of Cambridge noted that hostility to the women's colleges was still almost universal. The University was to be congratulated on having the strength of mind to exclude women from full membership: 'The most serious indictment of the women students, apart from the fearsomeness of the women which those students nearly always become unless they marry quickly and forget it all, is the complete pointlessness of their being there'.[77] Cambridge University would not let women take the examinations set for men, then it would not allow them to do so on the same terms, then it was not prepared to acknowledge that the women had been successful and should have degrees. The most famous of these refusals to admit women was in the year of Barbara's birth, 1897. The door was closed, and not even half opened until 1923 when women were allowed to attend lectures by right and not simply as a privilege. They had to wait until 1926 before they could be appointed to university posts, and until 1948 to become full members of the University. All these points Barbara noted in her autobiography, but without rancour, for women at the time did not on the whole expect to be treated fairly. Adela might not have agreed with her daughter's interpretation on this point.

It is hard to imagine now how it felt to be a young woman of seventeen poised on the edge of so many new horizons for women, but stopped in your tracks by the horror of war. Despite their exposure to the brave new world of women's higher education, for Barbara and many of her contemporaries, the world also seemed to have come to an end. Naomi Mitchison, born in 1897 like Barbara, went to study science at St Anne's College, Oxford: 'It appeared, up to 1914, that one could foresee one's whole life. One would grow up, marry, have children ... live ... with a house and servants and punctual meals, and nothing would ever change. Presumably 1914 was the last year when young people thought like that.'[78] The social dynamics of the University were deeply affected by the young men's absence at the War. Women considerably outnumbered men at lectures. On a practical level, Girton responded to the War by instituting economies such as growing vegetables in the College grounds and giving over the orchard to pigs; sweeping up leaves, digging potatoes, earthing up celery, and tying carrots and onions into bundles took the place of afternoon walks and sports. Students were encouraged to work together in the library rather than in their own rooms to save coal. They walked the cold corridors with their sparse rations of bread, margarine and sugar.[79] At the beginning of Barbara's second year, in 1916, the first-year students entertained wounded soldiers. About thirty soldiers came on a bitterly cold day for a 'plentiful tea of sandwiches, sausage rolls and cake':

All the First Year helped to wait on them, and some sat at the tables and talked to them. There was also music at intervals, chiefly trios, by violin, 'cello and piano. Tea finished up with crackers, and then all the soldiers sat round in arm-chairs and smoked ... There were songs and a recitation, and also a toy symphony, which seemed to amuse them very much. Some of the men performed themselves, which part of the programme probably pleased them most. They were able to stay about two hours and a half, and when they were at last obliged to go at 5.30, the hostesses and the guests cheered one another lustily, and both seemed quite satisfied that they had spent a successful afternoon.[80]

The unreality of the Girton teas for wounded soldiers must have impressed itself on Barbara when the unimaginable (what had always been imagined, because so ultimately feared) actually happened. Her brother Arthur had been in France, with spells of leave, since June 1915. On 1 July 1916, the Battle of the Somme was launched; during the four-and-half months it lasted, some 1,120,000 men, 420,000 of them British, became casualties of war – killed, wounded, taken prisoner, or missing in action; the advance of seven miles that was accomplished by the British and their allies cost 1.4 casualties for every inch.[81] A major new offensive, the British Army's final attempt to force a breakthrough, began on 15 September, with the battle of Flers-Courcelette. Eleven divisions attacked over a ten-mile front. On the night of September 15–16, a party from 'A Company' of Arthur's battalion was sent to bomb a German post on the left bank of the river Ancre. The second-in-command, Lieutenant Shaw, was to do the bombing, and Arthur was to stay near the portable bridge which they had thrown across the river, and wait with a covering party for Shaw's return. Shaw and his party were unable to carry out their mission and Arthur ordered them all to retire. The two officers followed the men towards their trenches. Then, for some reason, Shaw and Arthur turned back, and both were wounded. The adjutant, Captain Sir Guy Butlin, went out with a stretcher and bearers to rescue them. He found Shaw, who was lying close under the German wire, about twenty yards behind Arthur, bound up his wounds, sent back one man for help and was then hit himself, as was the remaining bearer, who was just able to crawl back. 'Heroic efforts' were made all night long to rescue the three officers, but they were never found. Shaw turned up in hospital, where he died later that month. But no evidence was ever found of what happened to Arthur Adam and Guy Butlin.[82]

Arthur, aged twenty-two, is recorded as having died on 16 September, although it was not until eleven months later that *The Times* reported that he had officially been declared killed.[83] According to Barbara's autobiography, several years later a grave was found marked with Arthur's name. His official memorial lies today with 1,423 others in the War Cemetery in the village of Achiet-le-Grand, nineteen kilometres south of Arras. The cemetery, like all of those that pepper the now quiet but suspiciously uneven chalk uplands of northern France, was constructed after the Armistice when hundreds of graves were moved from the battlefields around Achiet. Arthur's is the last in a row, by a wall, under a large old tree; there are rows and rows of pure white graves cast from the same uniform marble, evenly spaced, geometrically planted with flowering shrubs. In the spring, red roses and purple aubretia are in bloom, and the entrance to the cemetery is draped in white wisteria; the only sounds, apart from that of the man mowing between the graves, is the ringing of the church bell and legendary birdsong. There is a manufactured realism to these cemeteries. The order on the ground is not necessarily matched by order underneath. Many bodies were in bits and the bits are buried in a mass grave. That is what war does: it breaks people and societies up.

'Awake and Sing ye that Dwell in Dust' is inscribed on the front of Arthur's grave, no doubt chosen by Adela, who with his death had lost her favourite child, and who entered a prolonged period of mourning for him: 'She could talk about nothing else but him for years, and Neil and Barbara were forgotten'. Arthur was a genius and a saint; by comparison Neil and Barbara were both second-class citizens.[84] In the immediate aftermath of Arthur's death, Adela was preoccupied with the fact that the War Office, the Red Cross, and the other agencies trying to trace him referred to him as 'Lieutenant Adam', whereas he had in fact been Acting Captain. The impact on the family included Great Aunt Margaret reputedly dropping down dead with shock.[85] Adela wrote an effusively affectionate book about him: *Arthur Innes Adam 1894–1916*. The book is mainly based on the letters he wrote to her, but it also contains her memories and her pride at his achievements. You can see why she loved him so much: he used colons in his essays before he was six, and when he went to the front he took with him the Greek Testament, *The Iliad,* Virgil, Plato's *Republic* and *The Shaving of Shagpat*, a fantasy novel by George Meredith. The fair hair and complexion of his childhood never left him; 'his men' called him 'Parson Snowy' on account of his tendency to exhortations and his flaxen head.[86]

Minus a brother, Barbara went back into residence at Girton at the beginning of October. But her life had already changed in another way: she had met Jack Wootton.

4

Jack

Barbara Adam assumed her adult persona as Barbara Wootton on 5 September 1917 at the age of twenty. She remained Barbara Wootton for the rest of her life – for the thirty-six days of her marriage to Jack Wootton, and for the whole of the seventy years and three months that she lived after it. She was one of a generation of women whose pathways into marriage and domesticity were permanently altered, disrupted or blocked by war. The scars of war appear not only on the bodies of soldiers, but on the demographics of countries and cultures, in the personal and collective memories of citizens. *This* war, the one that accelerated Barbara Adam's marriage, was not only the war to end all wars – the 'Great' War – but an international conflict that sharpened the edges of history, moving people into a new age with different customs and habits, cutting them loose from their anchors in traditional ways of living. And this was particularly so for women.

'Tall and dark and handsome in a rather melancholy-looking sort of way', Jack Wootton was a friend of Barbara's brother, Neil, at Trinity College, Cambridge. Barbara is somewhat coy in her autobiography: among all the comings and goings of her brothers' friends in the house in Barton Road in the early years of the War, 'the visits of Jack Wootton began to acquire a special significance'.[1] When she first noticed Jack, and he presumably her, she was still living at home, awaiting her entry to Girton, and occupied with the economics books of which her mother disapproved. Jack, six years older, had already collected his first class history degree and had been awarded a research studentship for a further year's study at Cambridge. We know little about Jack's interests, beliefs, motivations or emotions. At Trinity College, he was noted for being an outstanding scholar, a member of a none-too-serious formal debating society named after a Dutch brothel and a stuffed bird – the Magpie and Stump[2] – and a good athlete: he was President of the Trinity Athletic Club.[3] There are close associations between sport and war in the ideology of masculinity – hundreds of football games were played daily in the army's base camps and even some in the trenches; the Battle of the Somme began with an infantryman kicking a football into no man's land.[4] In Edwardian culture, the duties of 'a Cambridge man' included not only athleticism but the obligation to fight for one's nation. The University Officer Training Corps, which dragged many young men like Jack Wootton and Arthur Adam into the awful realities of war, was a main outlet and expression of this 'élite masculinity'.[5] In 1910, the year Jack went to Cambridge, one in three male undergraduates belonged to the Cambridge University Officer Training Corps; it organized drills, parades, lectures on military strategy, shooting exercises, summer camps, and an annual military tournament against Oxford. When war was declared in 1914, the Cambridge headquarters was crowded with young men eager to apply for commissions; by the time conscription was introduced at the beginning of 1916, seventy-five per cent of male students at Cambridge had already joined up.[6]

But there was nothing particularly élite about Jack Wootton's origins. The house where he was born survives today in a run-down area of Nottingham, a large industrial city in the East Midlands with a reputation based on the legend of Robin Hood and alarmingly high modern crime figures. Jack Wootton's birthplace lives on as a shabby red-brick house, large, with five front windows and an uneven privet hedge, and it overlooks a cemetery where grey graves stand at awkward angles, leaning in or out of the earth. There are no flowers anywhere; the people in the earth have been forgotten, like Jack Wootton. A little further down the street, also facing the cemetery, is the house where Jack's father was born. Many working-class families did not move far in those days. The Woottons worked in Nottingham's most famous industry – lace-making, an occupation descended from the manufacture of hosiery, popularized by the Victorian taste for prudery and privacy, and facilitated by the invention of machines that replaced the tradition of hand-knitting, although, as late as 1910, it was still 'a familiar sight in the side streets of Nottingham to see women sitting at the open door on a warm summer's day drawing, clipping, and scalloping lace'.[7] In the centre of the city today there is an area called the Lace Market, now given over to aspiring shops, restaurants and bars, where some of the original flat-fronted many-windowed tenement buildings still stand, the buildings that housed the lace-workers and the products of their labour. In the 1901 Census, Jack's father, Arthur Wootton, is described as a 'lace curtain manufacturer' and as an 'employer' rather than a 'worker', suggesting a degree of prosperity that paid for the large house by the cemetery and the large family that inhabited it. When the 1901 Census was taken, Jack was ten, and his brothers Tom and Hubert were fourteen and seventeen. Nearest to him in age was Annie, eleven: the other two girls, Grace and Ethel, were nineteen and twenty. Their mother, Julia, must have had her hands full, with no living-in servants, unlike Adela, Barbara's mother, in Cambridge, who had four to help her with half the number of children.

Jack's full name was John Wesley Wootton, after the founder of Methodism, a religious movement which attempted a revival of Christian worship by reaching out to those on the fringes of society, contesting the corruptions of the established clergy, and focusing on Bible study and a 'methodical' way of life. The Woottons were committed members of a local Wesleyan chapel, and Jack's brother, Tom, was a lay preacher. Arthur and Julia Wootton believed in education, which accounts for their children's social mobility, and they believed in *equal* education for all their children. Like his brothers, Jack went to Nottingham High School; the Wootton girls went to the girls' version. Both Hubert and Annie became teachers. Annie was on the staff of Nottingham Girls' High School, while Hubert provided another link with the world of Cambridge by becoming head of the boys' Perse School. 'A tall austere figure, unapproachable, unpredictable', and given to dogmatic assertion, he introduced a telephone, school dinners and a ruthless system of rules in the School; moreover, his phenomenal rudeness did not make him popular.[8] The remaining three siblings – Tom, Grace and Ethel – devoted themselves to the family business. They were a close-knit family. When Barbara first visited their home in Nottingham, she was shown the mark on the wall where Jack had thrown his dinner in a fit of rage at one of his brothers. All the Wootton siblings were prone to hot tempers.[9]

Early in the war, Jack was commissioned through the University Officer Training Corps in the Suffolk Regiment ('The Cambs Suffolk'). This was closely associated with the Cambridgeshire Regiment in which Barbara's brother, Arthur, served. Now she had got to know Jack, and fallen under the spell of those dark eyes, Barbara worried that she would be the last to know if he were injured; like many women of her class, she took to scrutinizing the daily list of casualties in *The Times*. Jack's Battalion, the 11th, left England and crossed to France in early January 1916. For a time the men enjoyed reasonably comfortable quarters in French farmhouses, good food, and the pretty orchards and streams of Northern France.[10] 'The men are as happy as sandboys', declared one officer, 'the country is exactly like the fens near Cambridge'.[11] They helped the local farmers, driving pigs and filling dung-carts. The Battalion fought in the trenches in Armentières in February, sustaining its first casualties; by mid-March they had accomplished three tours in the front line and had been congratulated on this by the Brigade Commander.[12] On 5 May, they went by train to Calais and then to Amiens, where they walked in drizzling rain on the straight road to Albert, part of a movement of thousands of men to Picardy in preparation for the Battle of the Somme. By the

end of June, they were headquartered in Bécourt Chateau, near the village of La
Boisselle, only a thousand yards from the German trenches. The land round the
chateau was a riot of wild flowers, flooded with the song of nightingales during
the hours of darkness.[13] The first day of the Battle of the Somme, 1 July, was a
clear sunny morning. At 5 a.m. the 11th Battalion followed the 10th Lincolns
out of Bécourt Wood into 'an inferno of blood, smoke and iron'.[14] Each attacking
company formed a line, with the men two to three yards apart, four lines in all,
fifty to a hundred yards behind one another. The men walked slowly in straight
lines across no man's land into the German front line. Private W.J. Senescall in
Jack's battalion described how it went:

> The long line of men came forward, rifles at the port as ordered. Now Gerry started.
> His machine guns let fly. Down they all went. I could see them dropping one after
> the other as the gun swept along them. The officer went down at exactly the same
> time as the man behind him. Another minute or so and another wave came forward.
> Gerry was ready this time and this lot did not get as far as the others ... Then during
> the afternoon Gerry started shelling no man's land in a zig zag fashion to kill the rest
> of us off. As each shell landed they gave a burst of machine gun fire over where it fell,
> to catch anyone who should jump up ... A very large shell fell some yards to my left.
> With all the bits and pieces flying up was a body. The legs had been blown off right
> to the crutch ... It sailed up and towards me. I can still see the deadpan look on his
> face under the tin hat, which was still held on by the chin strap.[15]

The outcome of the battle was decided by 8 a.m., but throughout the day further
rushes were attempted by survivors, many of whom were instantly burnt to death
by German flame-throwers. Jack Wootton was one of 120,000 men who 'went
over the top' along the thirteen-mile front of what was afterwards known as the
Battle of Albert. But to Barbara's relief and delight, he escaped with 'a splendid
wound'[16] – in other words, a small wound that took a long time to heal. A shell
fragment had severed the Achilles tendon in one of his heels, and it kept him safe
in England for fourteen months.

Many years later, a man who described himself as Captain Wootton's servant,
a 'Mr H. Allgood', wrote to Barbara on reading her autobiography to tell her
more about what happened to Jack that day: 'We were going forward in rows.
One row was leaving too large gaps, Captain shouts, Fill those gaps up. Soon after
that I heard his voice. I looked back, he was on the ground, I went back & took
off his boots, saw a hole through his ankle. He said, You will have to go, Allgood.
I hope I shall see you again.' Allgood got a bullet in his neck, but he was back at
the front three months later. 'The next time I saw Captain Wootton was when he

was in command of a Labour Battalion. He came to ask me to go with him as his servant again but I was not allowed to go. I would have liked that.'[17]

Jack had been lucky: of the 750 men of the 11th Battalion who climbed out of their trenches early in the morning of 1 July 1916, 196 were dead before the end of the day, most within thirty minutes of the opening assault, and many of the 495 who were injured died of their wounds. Of his fifteen fellow officers in the 11th Battalion, seven others were wounded, four were killed and two were registered as missing.[18] On hearing the news of Jack's own splendid wound, his mother immediately telegraphed Barbara's mother, although nothing had officially been said at this stage about the growing attachment between the two young people. Some time later, Jack upset Barbara greatly by confessing that a letter proposing marriage had been in his pocket the day he was wounded: did he not have the imagination to understand, she asked furiously, how she might have felt if proposed to posthumously?[19] The dust settled, and the family holiday that summer in Wiltshire included Jack, and Barbara's first experience of working for wages – they all went hop-picking. Then, in October, Barbara returned to Girton, and Jack to Nottingham, a semblance of ordinary life. In November he visited, but obviously was not quite courageous enough to broach the issue of marriage, so it was only after he had gone that Barbara finally received a letter proposing they get engaged. Adela was happy, though adamant that this must not interfere with Barbara's degree: the future was uncertain, and women ought to be able to earn their own living. Neil was happy: Jack was one of his closest friends, and perhaps his absorption into the family might soften the loss of Arthur. The Pie was not happy, not because she disliked Jack, but because no-one would be good enough for her 'Own Dear Missie'. Jack bought Barbara an engagement ring, an opal set in a cluster of rowan berries, and Barbara became one of a small band of Girtonians who had 'a fiancé with a ring'. The young couple's good luck continued when Jack was posted to an Officer Training Corps actually in Cambridge. He could now visit Barbara regularly, although only according to the Girton protocol which required no more than one visit a fortnight and a note each time requesting permission from the Mistress of the College. Even in cases of allowable visits from men (fathers, brothers, *married* uncles, fiancés with rings, but the young man in question had to be acknowledged by the student's parents), unchaperoned entertainment was still not allowed.[20]

For around six months, Barbara and Jack saw each other regularly in Cambridge under these carefully supervised conditions, and then Jack was declared fit for active service and ordered to rejoin his regiment in France. Adela, to her credit, as Barbara acknowledged,[21] suggested that this meant they should bring the marriage forward.

If Jack were injured, Barbara would then be able to go to him. The young couple were easily persuaded, although Barbara notes that Jack may have had 'some conscientious worries about the remoter future' (she does not say what these were). He thought that after the War he might seek an academic job in a Commonwealth university, and they both liked the idea of eventually producing 'a considerable family'.[22] The wedding was announced in *The Times* on 21 August 1917: 'The marriage of Captain John Wesley Wootton, the Suffolk Regiment, youngest son of Mr. and Mrs. Arthur Wootton, 137, Foxhall-road, Nottingham, and Barbara Frances, only daughter of the late Dr. James Adam of Emmanuel College, Cambridge, and Mrs. Adam, 21, Barton-road, Cambridge, will take place at St. Mark's, Barton-road, Cambridge, on Wednesday, September 5, at 2. All friends will be welcome at the church.' Barbara did not have far to go; St Mark's, an undistinguished red-brick building, was in the same street as the Adam household. Despite the haste with which the ceremony was arranged, Adela made sure that everything was done properly. Her musical taste ruled out the popular Mendelssohn Wedding March; Barbara entered the church instead to the Bach Cantata *Sleepers Wake* played by the Girton Organ Scholar, Miss I. G. Bonnett. Adela gave Barbara away and second cousins Mary and Arthur Hetherington, aged ten and six respectively, the grandchildren of Adela's sister Laura, acted as bridesmaid and page. The best man was Arthur Ritchie, a friend of Neil's, later to be a Professor of Logic and Metaphysics, and the author of a key philosophical work on the scientific method.[23] The bride wore a long white dress and a veil; in the wedding photograph published in the local newspaper, she looks feminine and almost demure, her arm through the much taller and handsome uniformed Captain's. Barbara is smiling, Jack is not. They were both victims of misprints, 'Barham Frances' rather than 'Barbara Frances', and 'Captain Wooton' with a missing 't', both of which, if her irritation at such errors in later life is anything to go by, probably annoyed Barbara greatly.[24]

They thought they were going to have two weeks' honeymoon in Norfolk, but the day before the wedding Jack got a telegram ordering him to leave London early on 7 September. The honeymoon was cancelled, and a friend found a low white farmhouse in a village called Haslingfield, in the flat fen country a few miles from Cambridge, where they could go for their wedding night. So there they went, in the autumn sunshine, 'with the last of the corn stooks standing in the fields'. Looking back, Barbara thought both of them very young for their ages (twenty and twenty-six), with little conception of what they were doing and little idea of what they were committing themselves to.[25] They were both virgins; it would not have occurred to them to be anything else.[26] Writer Naomi Mitchison, the same age as Barbara, and marrying her Dick the year before Barbara married Jack, recalled a general expectation that men and women would 'keep themselves' for their future spouses; there were plenty of virgin soldiers around.[27] The day after the wedding, Barbara and Jack took the train to London and stayed at the Rubens Hotel so as to be near the station for Jack's early departure. 'I saw him off from Victoria along with a train-load of other cannon fodder.'[28] The term 'cannon-fodder' was his, not hers.[29]

It is hard to appreciate how she must have felt, how the constant imagining and reality of violent death must have infused the very emotion of love. Margaret Cole called it, 'this narrow margin between vigorous life and muddy and gangrenous death'.[30] The future together Barbara and Jack envisaged was a precarious thing, and they both knew it. When Jack rejoined his regiment, the men were stationed in Péronne, on the banks of the Somme. In October they moved to the neighbourhood of Langemarck and Poelcappelle to take part in the Ypres-Passchendaele action. The 11th Battalion was responsible for filling shell holes and otherwise repairing the roads in the forward area close to the front line. It was a horribly unpleasant task, carried out under constant shell- and machine-gun fire. The German painter and war realist Otto Dix famously described the trenches with a barrage of nouns: 'lice, rats, barbed wire, fleas, shells, bombs, underground caves, corpses, blood, liquor, mice, cats, artillery, filth, bullets, mortars, fire, steel'.[31] Trench warfare meant living with the dead, with bodies and bits of bodies stacked up in untidy piles. On 9 October, the attack on Poelcappelle was launched, but only minor advances were secured at the cost of 13,000 casualties for the Allies.[32] Everything was worse in the bad weather conditions. Most of the Battle of Passchendaele took place on swampy reclaimed marshland; sometimes the soldiers simply drowned in mud. Jack Wootton did not drown; he was shot through the eye while repairing the roads. He was one of fifty men in his Battalion to be killed in this way. He died on a French ambulance train somewhere in either France or Belgium forty-eight hours later.[33]

The individuality of loss is muted by statistics: between 1914 and 1918, half Jack's Battalion died,[34] some 722,785 British men, one in eight of those who set out to fight;[35] altogether thirteen million people were killed in the War.[36] It was 'industrialized slaughter',[37] a war of 'staggering carnage'.[38] But the young Mrs Wootton, who received the official telegram announcing her husband's death, was unaware of these statistics; she had lost her husband of five weeks, the man with whom she had planned to spend the rest of her life. A corner of the telegram was torn; she became unreasonably obsessed with this trivial detail, just as her mother, Adela, had complained at the War Office's description of her beloved son Arthur as a 'Lieutenant' instead of a 'Captain'. Eventually Jack's blood-stained kit was 'punctiliously' returned to Barbara.[39] Inflicting 'the terrible smell of mud and blood' directly on grieving relatives was common practice.[40]

Jack Wootton was, according to an officer in the 9th Battalion Northumberland Fusiliers, a 'most conscientious and hard-working officer' who was well liked by all the members of his Company.[41] An officer in Jack's Battalion wrote to Barbara after hearing her on the radio in December 1958 to tell her that he used to feel Jack's men would follow him anywhere. This correspondent, C. Lloyd Morgan, had taught Jack history at school and had known Jack's family well; his daughter had taught at Nottingham Girls' High School with Annie Wootton. He and his wife well remembered a Sunday lunch at Barbara's home in 1914, when the Battalion had been training at Cambridge. 'You were there, with your mother and, I think, both of your brothers and Jack. Not far short of a half-century ago. We wonder what has happened to your brothers.'[42]

After Jack's death, Barbara stayed at Barton Road with Adela, Neil, Winifred, baby Jean and The Pie, but she resumed her Classics studies at Girton. Dora Russell, Barbara's contemporary there, remembers 'vividly seeing her blank, shut-in face'.[43] By the time Barbara wrote her own autobiography half a century later, she had evolved an organized presentation of Jack's death and its meaning: it was one of four deaths of people close to her (father, school-friend, brother, husband), all before her twenty-first birthday. 'In ten years I had learned little about life, much about death.' She was clear, but not over-dramatic about the psychological consequences. 'I do not think that anyone can live through such experiences without some significant and permanent marks remaining. Had these years been different, I am sure that I should have been different too, even to-day. But at least I entered upon my adult life with a realistic sense of the impermanence of earthly relationships.'[44]

John Wesley Wootton's grave is in the Longuenesse Souvenir Cemetery in the southern outskirts of St Omer in France. The road that passes the cemetery is busy, the route to an Auchan supermarket, a McDonalds, a Citroën garage; a nearby restaurant is called L'Envoi. Christ on a blue cross faces the local cemetery which abuts the military one; in the military cemetery, the white graves and manicured lawns follow the standard pattern, exactly like the cemetery where Arthur Adam is commemorated, a few miles away. In the Longuenesse Cemetery, a path divides the 2,874 First World War graves from the 403 of the Second; Jack is 54th from the right in row 119. He shares his tombstone with a twenty-year-old Lance Corporal from the Yorkshire Regiment, J.W. Holmes, who died the same day. A red rose is planted in front of the grave. At the bottom are inscribed the words: 'These are they which came out of great tribulation'. This passage from the Bible (Revelation 7:14) continues, 'they have washed their robes and made them white in the blood of the Lamb'.

Did Barbara choose these words, or was it Adela? In 1984, when Barbara was eighty-seven, MP Ann Clwyd asked her how she remembered Jack, and what his death meant to her. Barbara said she remembered him most as a strong-minded person, and that his death had been 'completely shattering'. The scar it had left was 'a total mistrust of life'.[45] It was one reason that it took her eighteen years to marry again. But she was not much given to psychological speculation. As she explained in her autobiography, she was brought up with the attitude that one did not succumb to emotion or wallow in unhappiness: 'Whatever happened, one was expected to go ahead and make the best of whatever the next job might be'.[46] This was a markedly different response from the one spelt out in that iconic First World War text, the book that William Haley, editor of *The Times* and a man who would later become a close friend of Barbara's, called 'the war book of the Women of England':[47] Vera Brittain's *Testament of Youth*. There were many parallels between Barbara Wootton's and Vera Brittain's lives. They were born within a year of one another, and experienced solid middle-class upbringings; Vera became a student at Oxford, Barbara at Cambridge; they both lost brothers and lovers to the War. Vera's brother, Edward, acquired a splendid wound on the first day of the Battle of the Somme, like Jack Wootton, and his convalescence was nearly as long as Jack's; like Jack, he was killed shortly after returning to the front the following year. Roland Leighton, Vera's fiancé, was her brother's friend, just as Jack was Barbara's brother Neil's. Roland Leighton was killed in December 1915 when Vera was twenty-one. He had been out in the moonlight inspecting the barbed wire at the front of a trench when he was shot in the stomach by a German sniper.[48]

It was this action, one that served no military purpose and was utterly devoid of heroism, that provoked Vera Brittain's memoir. *Testament of Youth* was a mixture, as Brittain acknowledged, of fiction and fact, although much of its power emanated from its almost universal acclamation as fact.[49] The book, subtitled 'An Autobiographical Study of the Years 1900–1925', was first published in 1933, and it rapidly became, and remained, a bestseller; reprinted by Virago in 1978, and boosted by a BBC Television five-part dramatization in 1979, sales by the mid-1990s had reached three-quarters of a million.[50] *Testament* offered itself as a testimony of women about *their* War, and in so doing confirmed a dominant legend of the War – the sacrificed generation, the tremendous wastage of ideals.[51] But the book upset some, including Barbara, for what they read as its self-centred and self-indulgent rendering of women's war experiences. Vera Brittain treated herself as special, but loss and grief were the ordinary experiences of millions of women: war losses touched virtually every household in the country.

The First World War and its deaths gave rise to a literature of grief, anger and despair at the barbarity and insanity of war, and to litanies about 'the lost generation'.[52] This gentle phrase belies the reality, which is that those who were lost were killed, because, after all, the main business of war is not dying but killing.[53] The War converted many, including Vera Brittain and Barbara Wootton, to pacifism. 'It's one's future, not one's past, that they really hide, those graves in France,' says one of the young women in Vera Brittain's much less successful novel *The Dark Tide*, written well before *Testament of Youth*, in 1922.[54] There is no evidence that Barbara ever visited her hidden future in the St Omer Cemetery, or evidence that she did not – other than her wish to close the door on the past and carry on. But she could hardly have avoided seeing Jack's name on the roll of honour borne by the now badly-weathered war memorial which stands at the front of St Mark's Church in Barton Road, Cambridge, the same church in which they had been married. Jack's is the last of fifty-one names, and Arthur Adam's is the second: Barbara's experience of grief nearly spanned the alphabet.

So twenty-year-old Barbara Wootton, widowed after five weeks of marriage, had to make sense of life without Jack. Along with the invocation 'the lost generation' went another, that of 'Surplus Women', the generation of women who expected to marry but found themselves deprived through the slaughter of the First World War of adequate numbers of possible mates. The War killed fifteen per cent of British men under 29; the 1921 Census showed a gap of a million-and–three-quarters between the numbers of males and females.[55] This indicated 'a seismic effect' of the War on marriage rates. Most of the effect was confined to the upper and middle classes where War deaths had been concentrated, because the poor physical state of many industrial workers had saved them from active service.[56] One consequence was more intermingling of the classes, as upper- and middle-class women married 'down'; this is what Barbara Wootton was herself perceived to have done when she married for the second time in 1935. But the inter-war years were also years when spinsterhood became a real choice. Some professions required women to resign on marriage, which was a reason why ambitious women might not marry in the first place. Feminism combined with demographics to make women's financial independence increasingly plausible. Surplus Women gave birth to the New Woman who eschewed traditional feminine pathways, thus providing a focus for male anxiety and castigation of the politics of female freedom, although neither the idea of being surplus to requirements nor the notion of womanhood reinvented was actually quite new.

The story of what happened to Barbara Wootton combines both these themes: her life, forever scarred by the killing of Jack Wootton, became one of unbroken female achievement. It was hard at first – well, it probably went on being hard, but she rarely commented later on the difficulties. In the months following Jack's death, life in Barton Road began to get easier as her remaining brother's mental health improved. The pages of *The Girton Review* for that term and the next two make little mention of Barbara, though she was awarded a £20 Classics scholarship, and she remained one of the 'consuls' of the Classical Club. In May 1918, she was due to take the Part I examination of her Classics Tripos. Thereby hung a considerable tale which did not please her mother. A week or two before the examination was due to begin, Barbara, who was never normally ill, developed raging tonsillitis. Adela wandered restlessly from room to room, eaten up with anxiety about her daughter's potential imminent failure to prove herself as a brilliant Classics scholar. Letters flew back and forth between Adela and Girton and the University of Cambridge Local Examinations and Lectures Syndicate. The examination was relocated to Barbara's bedroom. 'I am to fetch the paper,' wrote Adela to the Mistress of Girton on 15 May, 'and Lizzie [The Pie] will be allowed to take it to Syndicate Buildings.' Adela would also take the doctor's certificate to the Guildhall. She changed the time of her Plato class to the afternoon to make these arrangements possible. Then she reported that, 'The little girl' – rather an odd designation, given Barbara's status as a twenty-one-year-old war widow – 'finished both her papers to-day in spite of her troubles. She has a slight temperature, 99 1/2'.[57] Four days later the little girl's temperature had risen to 102.6, and the doctor considered she might not be able to take any more papers.[58] In her autobiography, Barbara spelt out what Adela may or may not have suspected: she pleaded with the doctor to certify her as ill so she would not have to continue with the examination. The result was what was known in peculiar Oxbridge parlance as an 'aegrotat' (Latin, literally 's/he is ill') degree. This is an honours degree awarded on the assumption that the candidate, if well, would at least have passed, but it lacks the crucial classification into first class, second class etc, and so it deprived Adela of the ability to claim her daughter as a first-class Classics scholar. By the time she published her autobiography, half a century later, Barbara acknowledged that the whole business had been a conscious and deliberate act of revenge on her part: 'revenge for the Greek verbs on my lovely summer holidays, revenge for years of being exhibited as the clever daughter, revenge for a world which could value my distinction as a classical scholar above the extra hours that Jack and I might have had together'.[59]

When the Armistice was declared on 11 November 1918, the bell of Girton College chapel rang, like many across the land, and the flag went up over the tower. A notice was put up in the Reading Room: 'Students may smoke in their own rooms after dinner.'[60] Many of those who were in Cambridge at the time attended a thanksgiving service in the dim candlelight of King's College Chapel. After dinner in Hall, Girtonians toasted the King, the Navy, the Army, and the future League of Nations, and then retired for their own chapel service which ended with Kipling's *Recessional*, with the refrain, 'Lest We Forget'.[61] There was never any danger of Mrs J.W. Wootton doing that. For decades, Barbara kept in touch with Jack's family: with Tom, who ran the family business; with Ethel, who ran the Nottingham household; and with Annie, the teacher at Nottingham Girls' High School. 'Always uses her first husband's name', someone has written on the form Barbara filled in for *The Girton Register* in 1973. Barbara herself, then aged seventy-six and widowed for the second time, wrote on the form '(Mrs) WOOTTON, otherwise WRIGHT [her second husband's surname] (not ADAM)'.[62] She called herself Wootton for the rest of her life, although nowhere publicly did she ever comment on the reason why. Perhaps the inquisitive reporters just did not ask the right question: 'I presume that one takes a title. I wish still to be known as Barbara Wootton', she told *The Evening Times* when she was made a peer forty-one years after Jack died.[63] Did she love Jack Wootton for the rest of her life? If so, was it the man himself she loved, a man whom she had only just started really to get to know, or was it what his disappearance from her life symbolized: the enormous and pointless waste of life occasioned by man's folly towards man; the urgent need for human beings to create the meanings of their lives out of what exists here on earth? And/or was holding on to the Wootton name a way of keeping in touch with that parallel life of wifehood and motherhood his death stole from her? Whatever shaped her decision to remain Barbara Wootton, Jack stayed around. Fifteen years after he first gave it to her, Barbara thought she had lost Jack's ring in a hotel bathroom, and was so distressed that she managed to remember the name of its designer, who made her a replica which she wore for the rest of her life. Then, a few years before she died, Barbara's faithful colleague and friend, Vera Seal, found the original 'in a drawer with all kinds of rubbish and stuff', and Barbara told Vera to wear it, so she did. They both wore Jack's ring. Vera even did the gardening wearing it. As Barbara's mind declined, one day when they were out visiting friends, Barbara unhappily accused Vera of stealing it.[64] Stealing Jack's ring was something that mattered very much, even at a distance of more than seventy years. And the photograph of Jack, unsmiling in his military uniform, with his clipped moustache and his dark brooding eyes, looked down from her bedside as she died.

5

Cambridge Distinctions

The First World War changed the world and Barbara Wootton's life. For women in general, it proved a combustious mixture of liberation and repression. It issued in a modern age of revamped social habits in which traditional forms of exploitation – of one social class by another, of women by men – emerged from their cultural hiding places and began openly to be challenged. Over these quiet and unquiet revolutions hovered the mass reality of death and bereavement. People were immersed in the paradox that something as terrible as a war that killed millions could also be a unique cultural moment offering up new possibilities for personal transformation and social change.

Some changes happened more suddenly than others. Economically, the War had a major destabilizing effect; it had cost Britain thirteen per cent of its national wealth, and immense war debts to the USA permanently transformed the country's economic position.[1] Higher wages and people's willingness to pay for goods and services that had been in short supply led to a rise of over a hundred per cent in the cost of living; the decline of traditional industries combined with other dislocations produced the creeping growth of mass unemployment.[2] 'With national indebtedness mounting up, the birth rate at its lowest, the death rate at its highest, unemployment increasing day by day, one wonders when the crash will come,' wrote Beatrice Webb morbidly, but presciently, in her diary for March 1919.[3] Across the land, fortune-telling became hugely popular.[4] The December 1918 election returned a victory for the Coalition Government with its ambitious programme of reconstruction. It also, importantly, transformed the Labour Party into the official opposition for the first time.

During the War, women's work had become more and more essential, and this included increasing demand for the services of university-educated women. 'Past students of the women's colleges, beginning as scrubbers in hospitals or waitresses in canteens, were found to be valuable as scientific investigators, chemists, clerks in government offices, or teachers in boys' schools.'[5] Suffrage for women arrived in

1918, over half a century since it had first been proposed in the British Parliament. Women had been 'given' the vote 'rather like a chocolate is given to a child who has behaved unexpectedly well under trying circumstances'.[6] This treat was reserved for women over thirty on the presumption that they would be less given to radicalism than younger women, and also disinclined to register, for surely many women of that age would not want openly to admit to it?[7] But what was given with one hand was taken away with the other. By the autumn of 1919, nearly three-quarters of a million women had lost their jobs, and by 1921 the percentage of women in the labour force had fallen below its 1911 level.[8] 'It was back to the kitchen sink for bus conductors, insurance clerks, landgirls and electricians alike.'[9] The problem of finding jobs for former servicemen forced the government to create 'the dole' – originally an out-of-work donation for discharged soldiers – but there was no such provision for unemployed women.[10]

A series of changes in the law allowed women to claim their status as morally responsible persons for the first time. For example, the 1920 Larceny Act disposed of the rule that a woman living with her husband could not be accused of stealing from him; and the 1925 Criminal Justice Act abolished the presumption that a woman who committed a crime in her husband's presence could do so only because he made her. But, at the same time, doors that had been opened were slammed shut: Barbara's friend from school and university, Dorothy Russell, left Girton to study medicine at the London Hospital Medical College in 1919 when it decided to admit women students, but this decision was rescinded in 1922.[11] The Sex Disqualification (Removal) Act of 1919 theoretically enabled women to exercise most public functions, judicial offices and professions, and to serve as jurors. Years later, Barbara Wootton reflected that she and other young women at the time had mistakenly believed that the Act had meant what it said.[12] And looking back on it all in 1982 at the age of eighty-five, she observed that young women would be staggered to realize how recent were the gains on which a new feminist movement could build.[13]

As Barbara returned to her studies at Girton in the autumn of 1918, she had other things on her mind. The disgrace of her *aegrotat* degree confirmed the pre-war agreement she had reached with her mother – that, after three years of Classics, if she still disliked the subject, she could change to economics. Jack's death was the final blow to any interest in extinct civilizations she might once have pretended. Margaret Cole, who read Classics at Girton from 1911 to 1914, observed that, 'if you have leisure to think about Roman society and Greek society, it is improbable that your thinking will stop there'.[14] Vera Brittain, back in Oxford after her fiancé's death, gave up English in favour of History for similar reasons – the preference for a subject that might offer a greater chance of yielding an understanding of the modern world.[15] Girton awarded Barbara a fourth-year College Scholarship of £20, and she put away her Classics texts forever. Out came the economics books she had read in the fallow time between leaving school and entering Girton: the enlivening *World of Labour* by G.D.H. Cole, and the works of Alfred Marshall. Marshall dominated Cambridge economics for many years, inheriting the Chair of Political Economy from Henry Fawcett, the husband of suffragist Millicent Fawcett, from whom Barbara's newly-married parents had rented a house. Keynes called Marshall 'the father of economic science' as it existed in England in the 1920s;[16] it was Marshall's combination of mathematical approaches and acknowledgement of complex human motives for economic behaviour that produced the enduring term 'neoclassical economics'.[17] This structure of thought was one which Barbara would later dissect and decisively reject. As a new economics student, she must have realized that Marshall's vehement opposition to women's participation in university work was not to his credit. He conducted a long-drawn out private war against it, believing that women's characters would be damaged if they lectured to male audiences, and that the feminization of the University would cause immediate degeneration.[18] Married himself to an economist, Mary Paley (one of Newnham College's first five students), Marshall relegated her to a subordinate role as wife and assistant, even reissuing under his own name the book, *The Economics of Industry,* that had originally been *her* book. In a life merged with Alfred's, Mary Paley Marshall suffered from her husband's belief, referred to with sensitive outrage by Keynes in his obituary of Mary, 'that there was nothing useful to be made of women's intellects'.[19]

Cambridge University's only concession to the enhanced public contribution of women during the War was to allow them, from 1916, and initially as a War emergency measure only, to sit for the first and second M.B. (Bachelor of Medicine) examinations in order to speed up the process of qualifying as doctors. Otherwise, the University tried very hard to stand still or even to walk backwards. There was an organized campaign by Cambridge women, including Adela Adam, to remove the many absurdities of women's position: the fact that their attendance at lectures was up to the 'courtesy' of the individual lecturer, not a right; they could sit for university examinations but not be awarded degrees; they were eligible for only five of the 145 available university scholarships, studentships and prizes; staff of the two women's colleges could take no part in decisions about syllabuses and examinations; and women staff and students were admitted to the University Library only on the same terms as the general public. A syndicate appointed by the University, reporting in May 1920, reflected Marshallian conservatism in iterating a litany of ambivalence and prejudice – for example, that it was not desirable for women to become full members of the University since they lacked originality and the capacity for high standards of scholarship, and were capable of routine work only. All three proposals put to the Senate in December – to admit women as equal members, to establish a separate university for them, and to let them in under restricted conditions – were decisively rejected.[20] When Girton's founder, Emily Davies, died in 1921, the position of women at Cambridge was (with the exception of the M.B. examinations) exactly as it had been in 1881.

But Cambridge was not exempt from other changes in the position of women and gender relations. Many of the old taboos had worn thin: 'Smoking, swearing, and playing tennis in shorts became inalienable feminine rights';[21] short skirts, originally a war economy measure, lived on; and the 'pull-over', the first gender-neutral garment, was born. Some of the women dons even acquired sports cars.[22] A quarter of the male students who went off to fight never came back, and those that did were older and less inclined to put up with traditional protocols separating the sexes.[23] Chaperones as a breed died out and dance clubs and love poems flourished. In the Michaelmas Term of 1918, Girton held the first dance to which men could be invited. It was a good time to be poor and intellectual, as Oliver Postgate, Margaret Cole's nephew, remembered his parents' lives in the 1920s: there were still servants to be had; motor cars were arriving; wine and chickens were cheap; and there were ideals – love, life and liberty were all new and all their own invention.[24] Life for middle-class young women lapsed into fun as a relief from the seriousness of war: '"Ain't we got fun?" was a line in a popular song,' recalled writer Ethel Mannin. 'It was a sardonic song, to be sure, but still we liked it, we sang it, we danced to it, kicking up our heels.'[25] The big towns nurtured dancing, jazz, cocktail parties and nightclubs. Seaside holidays overwhelmed towns such as Great Yarmouth and Clacton; Sunday picnics in cars deprived the churches of their custom; commercial flying started, albeit slowly, at only 100 miles an hour; and the first wireless broadcasts by the Marconi company entertained people with weather forecasts and time signals.[26]

Barbara Wootton's raw widowhood fostered a temporary immunity to these social and technical revolutions. She threw herself into her work, and the pastimes she chose were more serious ones. Although, after Jack's death, she never returned to live in Girton College, she did take part in various College Debating Society debates with motions such as 'Strikes are essential to progress', 'Modern inventions do not tend to increase human happiness', and 'The party system is unnecessary'; she opposed the first two and spoke in favour of the third.[27] It must have been with a real sense of pride that she achieved the outcome recorded in *The Girton Review* for the May Term of 1919: 'B.F. Wootton' had 'passed with special distinction' the Economics Tripos Part II, Class I: 'This distinction has not been conferred on any man or woman candidate before, since the foundation of the Economics Tripos', announced *The Review* with a blast of collegiate pride.[28] Female economics students generally did well at Cambridge. At Newnham in 1908, Eva Spielman, later the social reformer Eva Hubback, had gained a first class in Part II of the Economics Tripos, as had Lynda Grier, and both had achieved higher honours than any of the men reading economics in that year.[29] After her own success, Girton awarded Barbara a J.E. Cairnes Scholarship (for £60) and the Therese Montefiore prize (worth 'about £66'[30]). She hoped her distinctive first in the Economics Tripos would make up for her mother's disappointment at the *aegrotat* episode, although there is little sign that this happened. Dorothy Russell unkindly, but perhaps truthfully, observed that Adela, 'an unmaternal and undomesticated woman whose whole heart and soul seemed bound to the chariot wheel of academic life' would never relinquish the loss of the vicarious glory of her daughter's abandoned first in Classics.[31] But of course daughter, like mother, left Cambridge without being entitled to put the letters 'B.A.' after her name.

What to do next, after Cambridge? The inhospitality of Cambridge towards women, particularly in economics, suggested the alternative of a more sympathetic and democratic institution, the London School of Economics (LSE).[32] In this path, Barbara followed other eminent students, such as Alice Clark, Ellen McArthur, Lilian Knowles, Ivy Pinchbeck and Eileen Power. She secured a research scholarship there, although the LSE today has no record of Barbara's sojourn as a postgraduate student,[33] perhaps because it was one of the few enterprises in her life that came to nothing. She was vague about what she wanted to research, and the 'eminent economist' appointed as her supervisor was even vaguer about his obligations to her. No-one at the LSE, she said, ever tried to find out what had happened to her.[34] By the summer of 1921, Barbara had resigned her scholarship, and so had another Girtonian, a Miss Welsby, who had gone to the LSE at the same time, although nothing was officially said about the reasons why either of these young women had chosen to desert their new academic home.[35]

Before she abandoned the LSE, Barbara had taken on part-time teaching duties at another institution with a significant place in the history of women's education. Westfield College in north London had been opened in 1882, four years after the progressive London University first admitted women. Its founder, Constance Maynard, had herself been one of Girton's first students in 1872. She was a devout proponent of education for women, religious, overworked and lonely, and given to complex relationships with favoured students and colleagues.[36] Her ambition had been to establish a small residential college for women in London, which would be like the early Oxbridge women's colleges, but would be run on avowedly

Christian principles and would provide a protected environment affordable by the kind of middle-class parents whose means would not stretch to Oxbridge. In 1891, Westfield College moved to a site on the south-west corner of Hampstead Heath, whose 'bracing air' provided the students with most of their leisure-time entertainment. (They did also venture as far as the shops in Golders Green, but central London was out of bounds.)

The Westfield College staff were young, the first generation of university-educated women, and they taught traditionally female subjects, such as art, history, Greek and Latin, but also stretched the boundaries by adding mathematics and botany and, then, economics. Nearly a quarter of the regular tuition was given by visiting lecturers, in a system of 'piecemeal teaching arrangements',[37] and it was under this scheme that Barbara Wootton joined the staff. By that time, Maynard had retired, and Westfield's Principal was Bertha Surtees Phillpotts, another ex-Girtonian, a cousin of the better known Sophia Jex-Blake, one of the first woman doctors, and aunt of Katharine Jex-Blake who had been Mistress and Director of Studies in Classics at Girton when Barbara had studied there. Phillpotts was a 'brilliant scholar',[38] 'absolutely charming',[39] and evidently an extraordinary woman: she was the first woman to enter the male realm of Scandinavian studies as a specialist in Icelandic literature, and she much impressed the Icelanders with her journeys across their harsh landscape, especially in 1909 when she wore out several pairs of shoes, clocking up 500 miles.[40] When Phillpotts first went to Westfield, she offered a prize for the best entry in an examination testing students on their first-hand knowledge of Hampstead Heath,[41] but, more seriously, it was under her leadership that Westfield became an official part of London University, with a grant from the London County Council; salaries were raised to university levels and staff became eligible for the university pension scheme. After her spell at Westfield, Phillpotts returned to Cambridge as Mistress of Girton and later as Director of Scandinavian Studies. It was a closed circle, this world of the first university women; most of them knew, or were related to, one another.

Like other institutions for women's higher education, Westfield College experienced a considerable rise in demand after the War. In 1919, when Barbara Wootton became a part-time Visiting Lecturer, there were 110 students, and much needed extensions to the buildings were in progress. The student intake reflected Maynard's original aspirations for an affordable education: of the thirty-three students entering the year Barbara went, only three had fathers of independent means; other fathers included a commercial traveller; a manufacturer of sports goods; managers of a building society and a steel and tinplate factory; a mill cashier; a lighterman; a tailor; and a book-keeper. Some of the students Barbara taught were close to her in age: six of the thirty-three were the same age or older.[42] Her lectures, 'Elementary Principles of Economics', one per week, were part of a two-year Citizenship Diploma Course intended to provide a broad educational base for social work 'and also to fit those who may not intend to become professional workers to gain a knowledge of the foundations of modern life and to take their part in civic affairs'.[43] The majority of Westfield graduates went into charity work or became teachers. 'What I put into my Westfield lectures, I now tremble to think', wrote Barbara forty-eight years later. Most of the students were not aiming to be professional social workers but were young 'do-gooders' with independent means and leisure, who 'came in their cars and their pearls and their elegant clothes to hear what I and others had to say; and I for my part dutifully tried to teach them what I had myself been taught, and not to be put off by the fact that they appeared to be so much more sophisticated and worldly-wise than I was myself'.[44] This admission in her autobiography drew a sarcastic letter from one ex-student, Eileen Wicksteed: 'Dear Lady Wootton, Ever since, dripping with pearls and in my elegant clothes and car, I attended your lectures at Westfield College, I have followed your subsequent career with interest'. She wished to point out that at the time she had owned no pearls and had walked everywhere, and had been puzzled when Barbara noted of her essay that 'for her age' (more or less the same as Barbara's) she had 'an unusually wide vocabulary'.[45]

Westfield College provided Barbara with lodgings, which she used for part of the week, returning to Barton Road in Cambridge for the rest of it. Although she took her teaching duties in London seriously, there was little intellectual stimulation. The job was clearly just a filler. She was rescued from it when, in 1920, Girton invited her back to become Director of Studies in Economics. It was an invitation she felt she could not refuse. No alternative full-time job had presented itself, and she had not come up with any other ideas about what to do.[46] The model of enforced and unhappy spinsterhood for bereaved war widows such as Barbara dominated the cultural imagery of the time. It robbed women in this position of an alternative reality: that they might anyway, in the presence of new freedoms for women, actually have chosen to do something with their lives other than (or as well as) marriage and motherhood.[47] One problem was that there were very limited opportunities for women in the 1920s. The good posts were reserved for the men who had survived the War, and great persistence was required to negotiate this obstacle.[48]

The complexity of the financial terms Girton proposed definitely merited someone with expertise in economics. The College offered Barbara a salary made up of four components: first a '£40 Directing Fee for ten or more students, or for less than ten students, £3.3.0 for the first student and £1.1.0 for each additional student'; second, a 'guarantee for teaching' fee of £120; thirdly, a 'retaining fee' of

£40 rising by increments of £5 a year to £120; and fourthly, board and lodging throughout the year.[49] Quite what this added up to financially is not clear, but Barbara regarded herself as well-paid by the standards of the time.[50] As Dora Russell, who also became a junior don at Girton in 1918, noted, a small income did not matter so much when combined with the perks of free accommodation and subsidized board at the College.[51] The College Council formally appointed Barbara in June 1920; her reply to the letter announcing this was delayed owing to her 'absence touring the rivers of England in a canoe'.[52] Experiencing the peace of the English countryside from the perspective of its waterways was a favourite escape for Barbara during this period. She went with a friend, Diana Rhodes, and they took no tent or other protection from the weather, preferring to sleep in the cramped canoe, and enjoying many incidents involving water rats, weirs and irate swans.[53]

In the process of memory people use to construct a linear story of their lives, there are often episodes or events which acquire emblematic status. One such in Barbara Wootton's life was her experience of being asked to lecture outside Girton to other university undergraduates in Part II of the Economics Tripos. 'People don't any longer believe the stories (though they are true) of what used to be,' she said of this. 'We all know the days when we couldn't take our degrees perhaps, but stories of things like the first lectures that I ever gave in Cambridge when the Economics Board, who were unusually progressive, asked me if I would give some compulsory lectures – lectures for compulsory subjects for the Economics Tripos, and very nervously I said "Yes", and the General Board of Studies said – "We can't prevent this person from lecturing, but since she is not a Member of the University we cannot advertise her lectures in the University Reporter" ... Well now, things are very different today, nobody believes this; I sometimes wonder if I made it up myself.'[54] *The Cambridge University Reporter* for 12 January 1921 listed under 'Lectures proposed by the Special Board for Economics and Politics' a series by a Mr Henderson on 'Economic Functions of Government'. A footnote added, 'This course will be delivered during the Lent term by Mrs Wootton in the Girton Lecture Room, St Edward's Passage, on Tuesdays and Saturdays at 9'.[55] Barbara did not remember feeling any resentment at the time: 'I suppose women in my position were so accustomed to what we would now regard as outrageous insults that we took them as all in a day's work'.[56] However, her disguise as Mr Henderson was cited as quite 'disgraceful' by the famous Keynes in the case he put against the humbug of the Cambridge opposition to women: it was disgraceful, he said, that Barbara Wootton's name appeared only in a footnote to the lecture list, and that the male teachers were debarred from electing their women colleagues to Boards of Studies, 'however useful we may deem the assistance of particular individuals to be'.[57] Hubert Henderson, the kindly liberal economist who lent his name to the arrangement whereby Mrs Wootton was permitted to render her assistance, was a brilliant lecturer on his own account, and author of a famous textbook on *Supply and Demand*; he subsequently led a distinguished career as an Oxbridge academic and as economics advisor to various governments.[58]

It was the first time a woman had given university lectures at Cambridge. Barbara was only twenty-four, and her sole previous experience of teaching had been the do-gooders at Westfield. When she first started giving the Cambridge lectures, she was terribly nervous. She wore a green suit she had made herself. 'The skirt had an elastic band round the waist and I was so worried that it might break, that I made two skirts and wore one on top of the other.'[59] Perhaps the experience of lecturing to men altered her character forever, as Alfred Marshall predicted. The economist Austin Robinson took the Economics Tripos in 1922 (having, like Barbara, deserted Classics) and he sat at her feet when she gave the lectures; he was grateful to her for helping him to defeat in the Tripos one of his examiners 'who, I understand, wrote the paper on that subject – a young London School of Economics Lecturer called Hugh Dalton'[60] – a man who would subsequently become a leading Labour politician and a friend of Barbara's. Robinson was lectured to by many clever economists of that generation – Keynes, Arthur Pigou, Dennis Robertson, Frederick Lavington, Gerald Shove, Hubert Henderson himself – but Barbara was the best of the lot: 'Tall, smartly turned out, and always immensely audible and clear'. Only later did Robinson realize she was exactly the same age as himself, and that it must have been quite a challenge lecturing to an audience mostly made up of men who were her exact contemporaries or older.[61] Unlike them, and all male lecturers, Mrs Wootton did not wear an academic gown when she lectured; she was not entitled to, being a woman with no official degree.[62] Another of Barbara's students, Kingsley Martin, the future editor of the *New Statesman*, remembered her 'as a slim, dark, intense woman' when he arrived in Cambridge as an undergraduate in 1919. 'She had the reputation of being a first-rate classical scholar.' He admitted to finding her 'extremely attractive' but was too immature and too interested in other things to do anything about it – one gains the sense of a mutually missed opportunity here.[63] They thought of her as a war widow, and she was much respected. It was probably around this time that the liquid-eyed, long-haired (though the hair is arranged 'up') photographs of Barbara give way to the much more serviceable ones. In all the photographs, she is a strikingly handsome woman, but in none of them is she smiling.

The other thing Kingsley Martin remembered was Barbara's close involvement in Cambridge socialist politics through the University Labour Club. She remembered this as the chief source of her intellectual stimulation at the time. The Cambridge socialists met and argued and enjoyed one another's company, and not incidentally designed the future. There were the Cambridge dons Maurice Dobb and R.B. Braithwaite, scientists Pat Blackett and J.D. Bernal, and Kingsley Martin. It was through the University Labour Club that Barbara first met Beatrice and Sidney Webb at a country house in Sussex in the company of Kingsley Martin, Bertrand and Dora Russell, Harold and Frida Laski, Eileen Power and others. Barbara heard heated arguments about Guild socialism, and about events in China and Japan, and she listened to Bertrand Russell accusing Beatrice Webb of only liking the Japanese because they were efficient and sanitary, and of disliking the Chinese because they had no urinals at their railway stations.[64]

Giving lectures disguised as Hubert Henderson proved to have hidden advantages. Because Barbara was not a member of the University, the fees that students had to pay for the course could not go to her College, which was the normal arrangement. Instead she was told to bill all the students individually (except the first, who was quaintly always treated as a 'free sample'). She waited until the second lecture to assess how much money she might earn from this source, and, when most of the first considerable audience reappeared, she went to the shop round the corner and bought her first typewriter.[65] It would be nice to think that it was on this machine that she typed her first full-length academic paper, 'Classical Principles and Modern Views of Labour', which appeared in *The Economic Journal* in March 1920,[66] a month before her twenty-third birthday, but the timing is wrong – the paper came before the typewriter. This first academic publication was a dense fourteen-page engagement with the implications of the clause contained in the 1919 Versailles Peace Treaty stipulating that 'labour should not be regarded merely as a commodity or article of commerce'.[67] Barbara argued that the only way in which this could happen was through the introduction of socialism, which would organize the labour of human beings on moral principles very different from the profit motive underscoring capitalism. She doubted whether the authors of the phrase which headed the Labour Charter of the Peace Treaty had adequately realized what a 'radical reconstruction of industry' their dictum implied.[68] Margaret Cole called it 'cloud-cuckooland economics'.[69]

The style of Barbara's early papers was designed to appeal to a conventional academic audience, and they lacked the accessibility of her later writings on economics. At this stage in her life, she was still concerned to impress other economists with her ability in the subject, and the path of her later detachment from the unreal world of neoclassical economics was only beginning to loom mistily ahead. In 1921, she gave a paper at the British Association Meeting in Edinburgh in the prestigious company of names such as William Beveridge, Josiah Stamp, and Edwin Cannan. Lynda Grier, the economist whose advice Barbara had taken on the reading of economics texts, talked about vocational training and the labour of women; Barbara's paper had the impressively long title of 'Self-supporting Industries; An Inquiry Into the Principle of Regulating Wages and Provision against Unemployment in Accordance with Industrial Capacity'.[70] The reviews of economics books she was commissioned to write for *The Economic Journal* by Keynes, its editor from 1911 to 1944, address the interests of academic economists too, although signs of the older Barbara's irritation with misprints and, more seriously, with the extreme tendency of many economists to dress up common-sense as 'laws' of this and that, do become increasingly evident.[71] Her objection to the reverence for Marshallian economics and other outdated pre-war treatises begins to emerge: students of economics, she declared in a review of one 1920 economics textbook, are unfortunately apt 'to assume with sublime academicism that the conditions described in these volumes are as eternal as the principles predicated of them … The economist is rightly sensitive to the charge of unreality'.[72] Another early article gives rein to a rather impenetrable set of reflections about the moral values of contemporary civilization in relation to 'the theistic hypothesis'. 'Is Progress an Illusion?' was published in *The Hibbert Journal* – a quarterly review of religion, theology and philosophy – in 1920.[73] It is a very clever piece, laced with Greek and Latin quotations (a sense of Adela's approbation lurks in the background), and it is quite impossible to tell from it whether the author, a 'Mrs J.W. Wootton', is or is not a believer. She would later acknowledge in her autobiography that these were the years in which she disposed of religion, became to all intents and purposes a pacifist, and developed an analytical and political rejection of the class system.

Despite the unfriendly treatment of women at Cambridge, life as a lecturer at Girton was very comfortable. Barbara had no domestic responsibilities, and the bath water was always hot. She was lucky enough to be given the most attractive set of rooms in the College, with a 'charming polygonal window seat overlooking the garden'.[74] Nestled in the Girton archives is a watercolour sketch of Barbara's sitting-room, probably painted by the historian Helen Maud Cam, who became a Fellow at Girton in 1921.[75] The painting shows part of the window, the tall trees outside, and a cushioned window seat in front, with a small table and a vase of tulips. The exterior view is hardly altered today, though the window seat has become an extension of a modern desk, the columns and architraves in front of the window have been repainted yellow, and the curtains have also changed their colour.

When not engaged in nervously teaching male undergraduates, Barbara took some part in the non-academic life of the College. In the Lent term of 1921, she followed a performance by staff for the students of Molière's *Les Femmes Savantes* given by the Modern Languages Club with another amusing entertainment in aid of the Imperial War Relief Fund.[76] However, the emotional devastation of Jack's death restrained her. She recommended life as a don in an Oxbridge women's college as one of the 'most sheltered lives' available to an unmarried woman.[77] The trouble was, Barbara did not really want to be sheltered. The Girton job did not occupy all her time, a fact she admitted to the College Secretary when negotiating her resignation. It was not where her heart lay. Her heart lay in the real world of socialist public policy.[78] She may also have felt that she needed to leave Cambridge in order to separate herself from her family, particularly her mother. When Barbara's appointment to Girton had been announced in *The Girton Review*, the news was followed in its pages by a piece entitled 'Women at Cambridge' by Adela Adam.[79] Barbara needed to become a woman *not* at Cambridge, and the socialist fervour which now increasingly gripped her drove her to seek more appropriate and overtly democratic outlets in London: extra-mural classes, the Workers' Educational Association and other such bodies. After a day thus spent she would return on the last train to Cambridge, exhausted but far more satisfied than after a day in the comfortable life of a Cambridge don.[80]

6

Real Work

A major restructuring of party politics in Britain was one of many unanticipated consequences of the First World War. During the 1920s, the political and the economic landscape altered, and it was these reconfigurations which opened up opportunities for Mrs Wootton, Cambridge University's undercover economics lecturer, to step out of the academic shadows onto the brighter light of the public policy stage.

The 1920s were a Jekyll and Hyde era: a time for bright young things, 'short-skirted flappers ... and young men with Valentino haircuts ... playing noisy ukuleles in the dickey seats of open touring cars';[1] but the other face of this gay abandon was extreme poverty, misery and industrial unrest. Lloyd George, Liberal Prime Minister since 1916, had marked his symbolic promise to the nation by establishing a Ministry of Reconstruction in 1917. Out of the chaos and ruins of war, a new Britain would be created, a far better home for everyone, not just for heroes. His leadership of the Coalition Government of Liberals and Conservatives transformed the political scene for the Labour Party, making possible its first spell of national government in 1924; a longer one followed in 1929–1931. Political parties, citizens and all sorts of associations and pressure groups struggled to understand and control the economic instability that mirrored the shifts in political platforms: a boom in 1919–20, and an 'economic blizzard' in 1929–32.[2] Economic expertise, such as that which Barbara Wootton had acquired in Cambridge, was much in demand. The War had left Britain, like many other nations, in an economic mess. Her traditional heavy industries suffered from antiquated methods, most of her raw material needed to be imported, and her traditional European customers were too poor to buy. In this desperate situation, organized labour had a pivotal role. Labour had a definite presence on the party political scene, and the old symbiosis of the unions and the Labour Party was weakening, so that the Trades Union Congress (TUC) was free to develop the industrial side of its work. The problem was the lack of a single body to co-ordinate industrial action.

This serious deficit was highlighted in 1919 by a wave of strikes by the police, army, miners, printers and transport workers. In 1921, a TUC General Council charged with the co-ordination of industrial action was created, and out of the same mood of reorganization a new Research and Information Department was born. Although the term 'labour research' could be interpreted in different ways – research into subjects of importance to Labour, or research designed to prove the Labour case[3] – both the Labour Party and the trade union movement needed access to evidence. They needed to know what was going on in order to decide strategy. Since duplication of effort would be wasteful, why not combine the efforts of both organizations in a Joint Research Department?

Barbara Wootton, restless in the confines of academia, spotted the advertisement in *The Daily Herald* for two Research Workers in the new Research and Information Department of the General Council of the Trades Union Congress and the Labour Party Executive Committee, to give it its full name. The Department would be housed in Eccleston Square in London, where the TUC and the Labour Party occupied adjoining premises. Its staff would be drawn mainly from existing Labour Party appointments, but there would be two new research posts and a typist.[4] Walter Milne-Bailey, who had worked as a research officer for the Union of Post Office Workers, was appointed to the first research post, and Barbara Wootton to the second. She was interviewed by the 'affable and booming'[5] Labour politician Hugh Dalton, whom she had helped with his (unsuccessful) candidacy in a Cambridge Parliamentary by-election. Dalton wanted her to get the job, but he complained after the interview that she had nearly ruined it with her 'apparently cold-blooded and pompous intellectualism'. Asked why she had applied for the post, Barbara attributed it to 'a multitude of converging considerations'. It undoubtedly was: the consideration of the need to escape Cambridge; to earn a living; and to bury the personal tragedies of the War. Dalton, however, told her she should have referred instead to her desire to do something about 'the unbearable injustices of our social system'.[6] This would hardly have been disingenuous.

Extricating herself from Girton was not easy. She was responsible for her Girton students until the end of the 1921–1922 academic year. Two days after her interview with Dalton, Barbara wrote with disarming honesty to the Girton College secretary, Miss Clover, about her dilemma: 'I have come increasingly to feel that the centre of my interest is in the Labour Movement rather than in University Work; and while the opportunity which I have had of acting as Director of Studies in Economics at Girton has been of great value to me, I had come to the conclusion some months ago that I should seek a post at the end of the current academic year in which I should be able to devote my services completely to this movement'.[7] She told Miss Clover that the new post involved exactly the kind of work to which she felt most strongly drawn, and such openings were rare. The Department wanted her to start immediately. They would, however, be prepared for her to begin on a part-time basis, so she proposed working half-time in London and half-time for Girton until the end of May, when she would resign her Girton post. Perhaps unwisely, she offered the justification that Girton, being so small, had never occupied the whole of her time. However, the Girton Council did accept her proposal. Although many grieved Barbara's departure from Cambridge, they also recognized that what Girton lost, the country won.[8] Her emancipation from Girton bore similarities with another, the previous year, achieved by economic historian Eileen Power, who escaped Girton, which she likened to a medieval nunnery, for the much more utilitarian LSE.[9] The plain fact was that for women like these, a university that sheltered women at the same as discriminating against them put impossible limits on their aspirations and abilities to use their talents.

Barbara took some 'rather squalid lodgings' in Ebury Street near Eccleston Square, so she could walk to work. Her new boss was Arthur Greenwood, later deputy leader of the Labour Party, a member of Churchill's War Cabinet, and the main architect of the idea of a Joint Research Department.[10] She found him both charming and exasperating: 'He had absolutely no idea of forward planning or method: everything had to be done in a hurry at the last minute'.[11] Greenwood had been invited to leave the civil service and set up the Joint Research Department by Arthur Henderson, a politician whose dedication to reorganizing the Labour Party into an effective governmental machine earned him the nickname 'Uncle Arthur'.[12] The new Department was small, much smaller than Girton College. The two colleagues with whom Barbara worked most closely were Milne-Bailey and the Secretary, Cecil Delisle Burns. Between them, Greenwood, Milne-Bailey and Barbara were supposed to cover 'every field of knowledge which could possibly be of concern to the Labour Party or the Trades Union Congress'. She recalled writing 'endless memoranda' and answering 'innumerable questions on all manner of subjects'.[13] During 1924, the work involved completing an inquiry into conditions in the shipbuilding industry; preparing additional material for the Colwyn Committee on National Debt and Taxation; drawing up a memorandum for the General Council on the effects on workers' health of using pneumatic tools; collating material on agricultural conditions and prices; proceeding with work on a Wages Index; and adopting a new method of keeping parliamentary voting records – all at the same time as investigating a proposed Summer School, and undertaking 'the usual amount of work' in the form of 'enquiries, reviews etc'.[14] Anthony Greenwood, Arthur Greenwood's son, met Barbara around the time she started working in the Joint Research Department: 'a young war widow, very strikingly good-looking with pale blue eyes which I have always remembered'. He never forgot hearing his father speak of her great ability and her unique contribution towards enabling the Party to match up intellectually with the other two.[15] These were absolutely crucial days for the Labour Party, and they would not have been at all the same without Barbara Wootton.

One of her first tasks in Eccleston Square was to write a critical review of the social credit theories of Major Douglas. Douglas, a Cambridge-trained civil engineer, had developed an economic philosophy which redefined democracy as the power of consumers to establish the policy of production by exercising their monetary vote.[16] Economist Joan Robinson called Douglas 'a crank' who believed it could 'all be done with a fountain pen'.[17] Douglas's was a complicated theory, wrapped up in religious sentiment, and, although some trade unionists took to it, the Labour Party leadership did not. They wanted an argued case to support their dislike of it. Barbara did not find this difficult. The fact that her memorandum drew negative comments from Sidney Webb, who chaired the Departmental Committee on behalf of the Labour Party Executive, did not even dishearten her – she was just so pleased to be working for the Labour Movement at last.[18] Soon after she joined the Department, Barbara added to her work the role of Secretary to the Committee on Agriculture and Rural Problems. She often took work home. It was an odd experience after academic life. Staff worked office hours, and 'at 5.30 on the dot, in mid-sentence even, some people would stop what they were doing and go home'. However, she enjoyed the variety and the evident practical importance of the job. She liked preparing wage claims and dealing with a bus conductor who walked in and asked for help with his income tax. What she *dis*liked was election time. 'We would have to write notes for candidates and sometimes we would go along to evening meetings and listen to what they did with those notes. It put me off for ever wanting to be a Parliamentary candidate. So phoney.'[19]

In 1926 came the General Strike. On the first morning of the strike, Barbara arrived at the office ready for anything: she was asked to go out and buy a map. The country's transport systems were paralysed, but no substitute communications could be improvised as the office had no map of England and Wales. This lack of preparedness was odd, as the strike had been brewing for some time. Unemployment was high – throughout the 1920s the numbers of insured unemployed were never below a million, and they rose to an unprecedented two and a half million by December 1930.[20] For many of those in work, wage cuts were threatened. Housing was in short supply. Where was the reconstructed Britain its citizens had been promised? The dissatisfactions of the coal-miners, exposed to pit closures, withdrawal of the government subsidy, and lower wages for the same hours, spearheaded the strike. For nine days there was an extraordinary display of peacefully withdrawn labour, then the unions capitulated, recognizing that the Government had the power to hold out a lot longer than they could. Barbara's colleague, Milne-Bailey, wrote an account of the strike which shows the level of violence lurking just beneath the surface: troops with the freedom to use any force necessary stationed in working-class areas; and even Royal Navy battleships and destroyers positioned in the Clyde, the Tyne and the Mersey just in case of trouble.[21]

Barbara's other contribution to the strike was to carry messages to and from strike headquarters, and drive members of the TUC General Council around in her car. On one occasion, she offered a ride to the Labour politician Ernest Bevin, who refused, having seen the size of her car – he accepted a lift from one of her colleagues who had a bigger one.[22] Many years later Margaret Cole reminded Barbara of this insult, and that the trade unionist Will Thorne, a much larger man, agreed to ride in *her* car.[23] These were the days of small cars – the first days. The increase in the annual car tax to £1 per unit of horsepower in 1921, combined with the introduction of assembly line production techniques, produced a boom in more affordable small cars,[24] and ushered in the era of mass motoring. Barbara bought her first car in 1924, an open, two-cylinder Rover. Between 1919 and 1924, when she first became a motorist, car registrations in Britain more than quadrupled.[25] Car manufacturers targeted female motorists with light saloons adorned with silver flower vases and special compartments for a shopping diary.[26] Britain's lanes were full of motorists learning how to drive in vehicles whose capacity to go far exceeded their capacity to stop. Barbara's own first purchase, made by cashing in her Girton pension policy, was more like a wild animal than a civilized machine. Matters improved with the introduction of front wheel brakes in 1925. Unsurprisingly, Barbara was afraid of her car for quite a long time.[27]

Motoring added spice to Barbara Wootton's life during a period when she was still raw from the emotional shock of Jack's death. The paragraphs in her autobiography which refer to her psychological state during these years are parsimonious: there were times of emotional disturbance; at best, she was a 'somewhat depressed character'; and she would hardly have 'enlivened any man's breakfast table'.[28] Yes, there were men she was attracted to, and men who were attracted to her, but there was little overlap between these categories. Perhaps the bereaved heroine of a contemporary novel by Irene Rathbone, *We That Were Young*, described something akin to what Barbara Wootton felt: 'The curious thing about misery was the way it rose and fell. Sometimes you felt quite ordinary. You read books; you shopped; the world seemed normal and pleasant. And suddenly, out of the four corners as it were, misery came, and swamped you. You could do nothing about it. You just sat there at the heart of it ... People said: "Time will heal," but you didn't want time to heal – or rather you didn't want it to heal at the price of remembrance. The one thing you were terrified of was numb forgetfulness. Suffering was atrocious; it was not a thing to be sentimentally hugged; but if it was the inevitable accompaniment of remembrance you would keep it.'[29]

The year of the car brought another very considerable diversion for Barbara: her appointment as the only woman to the Colwyn Committee on National Debt and Taxation. The question of the national debt dominated post-war politics, and this Committee was purportedly a condition of the King appointing the first Labour Government.[30] The National Debt was a subject which had already incensed Barbara Wootton, both as economist and as someone who had personally suffered loss through the national habit of expensive militarism. In 'Where Your Money Goes: What Every Woman Ought to Know', a delightful piece published in *Good Housekeeping* in 1922, Barbara advised the women of Britain that they should concern themselves with national as well as domestic housekeeping. One of the most striking observations to be made about the former was that most of the money people paid in income tax went on warfare – both current expenditure on 'the fighting services' and on servicing the debt for past warfare. 'Where Your Money Goes' is an early example of the diversified and accessible writing in which Barbara specialized. Her piece nestles comfortably in the same pages as suffragist Millicent Fawcett on women voters, and domestic advice on 'Adjustment and Care of the Corset'.[31]

The newspaper headlines announcing Barbara's membership of the Colwyn Committee were effusive and selective, stressing her youth, scholarship and gender: 'Woman's Sudden Fame: Mrs Wootton's Crowded 26 Years';[32] 'Debt Committee: Brilliant Woman Scholar';[33] 'Romance of a Girton Girl: Only Woman on the Debt Committee – War Widow: Too Young to Receive a Vote'.[34] 'Young and slim, with quantities of soft brown hair surmounting a soft-complexioned face,' began the piece in *The Daily Chronicle,* 'Mrs Barbara Wootton ... does not fulfil the old-fashioned idea of an expert on economic and financial subjects.'[35] 'Her grave demeanour,' declared *The Daily News,* 'hides a sense of humour. Her blue eyes twinkled at the suggestion that bank directors and captains of industry would get a shock at the prospect of sitting in conference on high finance with a girl young enough to be a daughter of any one of them.'[36] *The Manchester Guardian* regarded the appointment as proof of the value of Barbara's work as an expert economist rather than as a woman.[37] *The Evening Standard* reporter found her 'pale-faced, wearing rimless eye-glasses, and with her hair very plainly dressed', sitting at a table in a paper-littered room on the top floor of 33 Eccleston Square.[38] By then, Barbara was clearly irritated by the more salacious aspects of the press interest. 'I am not going to tell you my hobbies or games,' she snapped at the journalist from *The Daily News*. 'It is quite irrelevant to the question whether I eat chocolates before breakfast or smoke cigarettes afterwards. The only relevant matter is to what extent I am fitted for the work I am going to undertake.'[39]

She was so fitted, and she was undoubtedly in very exalted company. Lord Colwyn, the Committee's Chairman, was director of several railway companies and a previous chair of a Royal Commission on Income Tax. There were two directors of the Bank of England, a City banker, a leading chartered accountant, another railways director, two members of the TUC, the conservative politician Sir Arthur Balfour, the economists J.A. Hobson (who later resigned and was replaced by Fred Hall) and J.B. Lees-Smith, and 'the eminent authority on taxation and statistics', Sir Josiah Stamp,[40] with whom Barbara had already shared a conference platform when she had given a paper with a long-winded title at a British Association meeting in 1921. The Women's Freedom League told Labour's first Prime Minister Ramsay MacDonald that Barbara Wootton's appointment to the Committee was a sign of progress for women.[41] The Committee's brief was to 'consider and report on the National Debt and on the incidence of existing taxation, with special reference to their effect on trade, industry, employment and national credit'.[42] The reason for its existence was the economic aftermath of the War which had left many industrial nations, including Britain, with enormous debts, the mere servicing (let alone repayment) of which was almost beyond their means. Such debts also, of course, constrained 'social' expenditure on housing, education, health, pensions and so forth – those very areas critical to post-war reconstruction plans. The Colwyn Committee came on the heels of another Committee on National Expenditure set up by Lloyd George and chaired by Sir Eric Geddes, a businessman who, unusually, favoured statistical analysis as a key business strategy. His Committee, which gave rise to a much-used phrase 'the Geddes axe', argued for public economy and retrenchment in public expenditure of £87 million out of a total projected spend of around £528 million.[43] The Government agreed to the figure of £52 million, which meant a forty one per cent reduction in defence and a twelve per cent reduction in social spending on education, health, housing, pensions and unemployment.[44]

The scale of Britain's financial problem was huge. At the end of March 1926, the national debt amounted to £7,615,916,000. Nearly the whole of this was the result of expenditure in the First World War, and most of the remainder was left over from earlier wars.[45] Interest payments on the debt were running at about a million pounds for every working day.[46] One seventh of the debt was external – owed to other countries, with ninety per cent due to the USA. This was payable

in instalments starting with $23,000,000 in December 1923 and ending with
$175,000,000 in December 1984.[47] The TUC and Labour argument – with which
Barbara Wootton and some other members of the Colwyn Committee agreed – was
that servicing the war debt was essentially an issue of social justice, since paying for
it meant (as the Geddes axe had demonstrated) cutting social expenditure, and thus
depriving the working classes of the 'amenities and necessities of civilized life'.[48] In
addition, about one-third of the internal debt was owed to rich individuals, which
imposed a continuing transfer of purchasing power from taxpayers to debt-holders,
further aggravating social injustice. As a Labour Party pamphlet baldly put it, 'The
workers, including the young men who fought in the war, are, in effect, saddled
with a tribute to those who were lucky enough to have money to lend, including
wealthy men who were too old to be called upon to fight'.[49]

The problem was how to pay for the national debt and create a more comfortable
and equitable society at the same time. It was a problem that divided the members
of the Colwyn Committee. The result was two reports: a weighty Majority Report
signed by eight members of the Committee; and a much shorter and more incisive
Minority Report signed by Barbara Wootton and three other members, although
one of these, Fred Hall, added a reservation about his unhappiness that the Minority
group's recommendations did not place more emphasis on taxing earned income.
We know from a draft in Barbara's handwriting in her Colwyn Committee papers,
which are lodged in the TUC Archives at London Metropolitan University,[50] that
she wrote every word of the Minority Report – contrary to the assertion, made by
one historian of fiscal policy, that she only 'claimed' to have done so.[51]

The need to pay for the War after it was over led many countries to consider
radical proposals. Although income tax had been rising in Britain – five-fold in the
years between 1913 and 1919[52] – the main tax paid by the working classes was
indirect, taking the form of duties on tobacco, beer, entertainment, food and other
basic goods and services. The authors of the Minority Report objected in principle
to indirect taxation as necessarily regressive, and they recommended its abolition.
An even more explosive suggestion was the inheritance tax scheme proposed by
the Italian economist Eugenio Rignano.[53] In the Rignano plan, immediate and
more remote forms of inheritance would be distinguished by a modest tax on the
former and a much heavier tax on the latter. Hugh Dalton was one of many on the
Left in Britain who promoted Rignano's ideas. He also favoured another radical
approach to disposing of the national debt – a one-off tax on wealth, a 'capital
levy'. The Labour Party's own capital levy proposal, laid out in a 1922 pamphlet,
Labour and the War Debt, set the tax at five per cent for wealth of £5,000–£6,000,
rising to thirty-five per cent for £30,000–£50,000, and to sixty per cent for figures

above £1,000,000.[54] As Barbara's colleague in the Research Department, Delisle Burns, pointed out, this idea of a capital levy which made the Carlton Club shudder and caused some Liberals to wonder whether they might not after all be Tories, was hardly new: it could be traced back to the thirteenth century when the English King Edward 1, in conflict with his Welsh counterpart, had raised a war loan and then taxed his wealthy subjects to pay it back.[55] In 1820, the political economist David Ricardo had also established a precedent in suggesting a one-time tax on property as a solution to the debt incurred by the Napoleonic Wars.[56] With unashamed deviousness, Barbara wrote to Dalton in confidence in advance of his giving evidence to the Colwyn Committee to ensure that he would fully address various arguments against the capital levy favoured by some Committee members; his wife Ruth obligingly sent Barbara a draft of what he would say.[57] The Minority Report of the Colwyn Committee recommended incorporating the Rignano approach into the British system of death duties, and a special tax on investment income, and it took a much more favourable view than the Majority Report of the capital levy. It concluded that introducing such a levy would be 'a wise and practicable measure'; it would mean both an immediate reduction in the national debt and an increase in economic equality.[58] But a capital levy would take a long time to implement, would require the co-operation of the banks, and would have the fundamental drawback, which the signatories of the Majority Report saw as insurmountable, that the owners of capital would dislike and resist it.

How to deal with the enormous debts incurred as a result of engaging in war, and how to design a workable tax system which would generate enough government income to finance post-war reconstruction, preoccupied British policy-makers throughout the 1920s and 1930s. This was not simply a matter of fiscal calculations, but of powerful rhetoric and ideology: arguments about the nature of the national debt and about the differential class impact of different forms of taxes were used by political parties to shape their own identities.[59] The idea of paying off the debt once and for all with a levy on wealth, which was initially regarded by the Treasury, the Inland Revenue and the Chancellor as pragmatic and sensible, became a menacing socialist plot once those on the Left had enfolded it in the language of class opposition. A tax on wealth – like the rising power of the trade unions, the extension of the franchise, and declining standards of public behaviour – signified a seismic and worrying shift in the class system. In these circumstances, it is not surprising that the Majority Report was a highly conservative document. Not only did it dismiss as impracticable and as 'highly injurious' to social and industrial life any kind of tax on accumulated wealth, but it argued that the existing burden of taxation was 'less crushing than is frequently represented'.[60] Keynes did not mince words in calling the Report 'a vindication of the British System of Taxation as it now is'.[61] Several years later, Barbara commented cynically of the history of the national debt that, 'There can, indeed, be few chapters of economic history more completely devoid of progress ... In two hundred and fifty years we have neither invented any significant new method of dealing with the Debt nor shown any growth in the persistence with which we are prepared to apply old methods.'[62] Her Minority Report disappeared virtually without trace, except that its suggestions about a more steeply graduated and differentiated income tax, together with a surtax on unearned income above £500 a year, were absorbed into official Labour Party policy.[63]

The Colwyn Committee was a considerable drain on Barbara's time: between early 1924 and late 1926, there were forty-eight sittings, most lasting an entire day, and the Committee took written and oral evidence from sixty-two witnesses, including representatives of the Stock Exchange, banks, chambers of commerce, chartered accountants, insurance brokers, trade unions, the Women's Co-operative Guild, the British Association for the Advancement of Science, the National Farmers' Union and the legal profession. There were also, of course, the opinions of leading economists to consider, not forgetting those of women witnesses 'representing the householder'; at the Committee's first meeting, Barbara, as the token woman, was asked 'to advise as to suitable names'.[64] Throughout the Committee's work, she enjoyed the analytical powers of Josiah Stamp and the benign attention of Lord Colwyn, who on one occasion offered her two tickets for Wimbledon, which she declined on the grounds that she could not be absent from the office during the day. He then hinted that, if the fare to Wimbledon were the real obstacle, he would be only too happy to provide it.[65]

The positive effect on her confidence and career in public life of taking part in the Colwyn Committee helped Barbara to think about whether it might be time to move on from her backroom career in party politics. There were some concrete grounds for dissatisfaction with the Joint Research Department job. The brilliant young economist, Barbara Wootton, knew that the level of her pay was 'meagre'. When Jack Wootton died, she had turned down the widow's pension to which she was entitled because she could see no justification for a young, able-bodied and childless woman being subsidized at the taxpayer's expense.[66] She and her colleagues at the Research Department, Milne-Bailey and Delisle Burns, wrote to the Joint Finance Sub-Committee asking for their rates of pay to be revised in order to bring these into line with the rates paid for comparable work in other Departments. Sidney Webb investigated the matter, and as a consequence the maximum salaries (achievable by annual increments) for Milne-Bailey and Barbara were raised to the same ceiling as for Delisle Burns.[67] But Barbara was still paid less than Milne-Bailey, despite the fact that they were doing the same work. Two women members drew this differentiation to the attention of the Labour Party Executive Committee, making the dastardly suggestion that the salary gap might be on account of sex.[68] Fortunately for the Department, Burns left for a job at the LSE and when, eventually, Barbara also decided to depart, their posts were not filled because of 'financial stringency'.[69]

There was little possibility of advancement in Eccleston Square. Not only did the men hold all the higher posts and the women the lower ones, but in the end there was something eminently dissatisfying about never being recognized as speaking for oneself. While important and busy people cannot be expected to write all the documents for which they are responsible, Civil Service anonymity, Barbara decided, can be a farce. She approved of the suggestion made by Milne-Bailey that at the annual fair organized by the London Labour Party, all the material on sale should be autographed by its *real* authors.[70] But her spell in Eccleston Square did bring some benefits. The job provided the rationale for a decisive break from the claustrophobic atmosphere of Cambridge. She made new friends, including Hugh and Ruth Dalton, for whom she became an important source of gossip about internal Labour politics. Hugh Dalton, himself the subject of considerable gossip about his ambiguous sexuality, apparently much admired Barbara's ankles.[71] She saw a good deal of Beatrice and Sidney Webb, who regularly included her in the informal lunches they gave for people active in the Labour Movement. 'The lunch was always substantial, but the talk not particularly lively, unless Bernard Shaw was present,' Barbara noted.[72]

Barbara's exposure to real work for the Labour movement introduced her to an important friendship, a woman with whom she would live for eleven years until she married again in 1935. Mary Leonora Simeon (Leo, as she was known) was six years older than Barbara. She was a colleague in the Joint Research Department, in charge of the clerical staff there (on a salary considerably more meagre than Barbara's[73]), but she had an impressive social pedigree. The Simeons were a family of wealthy landowners, baronets and MPs. Leo's father, Lionel Barrington Simeon, had been Under-Secretary to the Government of the North-West Provinces in India, and responsible for building a difficult road through the Himalayas. Her grandfather, Sir John Simeon, had been a friend of the poet Tennyson – Tennyson inscribed parts of his famous poem 'Maud' in the Simeons' Isle of Wight home, Swainston Manor, and another short poem ('In the Garden at Swainston') when Sir John died prematurely in 1870.[74] The TUC reports, which record the activities of Leo and Barbara in the Joint Research Department, also contain the name of the fourth baronet, Sir John Stephen Barrington Simeon, who was Liberal Unionist MP for Southampton. A less conventional family connection through Leo's mother was with the Awdry family, which produced Wilbert Vere Awdry, creator of that popular star of children's books, *Thomas the Tank Engine*. This exotic background meant that Leo Simeon was independently wealthy: when she died in 1969, nineteen years before Barbara, she left her socialist friend a significant bequest of Marks & Spencer shares.[75]

The only possible photograph of Leo in Barbara's Girton College papers shows her as a conservatively dressed middle-aged woman with bobbed dark hair and glasses. Barbara and Leo first shared a tiny flat in St John's Wood, and then a more spacious one in Hampstead. Hampstead Hill Gardens occupies a wide crescent on a hill rising up above Hampstead Heath; number twenty-five is a large white-painted early Victorian house divided into four flats, of which Barbara and Leo inhabited the one on the ground floor. While their addresses can be traced, there is no record of the texture of their relationship. It was not at all uncommon at that time for the newly emancipated cohort of single women to set up home together: Vera Brittain shared a series of homes with her writer friend Winifred Holtby; Geraldine Aves, Barbara's contemporary at Cambridge, a magisterial woman later known for her pivotal role in organizing the personal social services and social work training, went to live with Nancy Rackstraw, an LSE social science graduate a decade older than her; and there are countless other examples.[76] Such arrangements were eminently practical; the accompanying relationships often emotionally intimate. Leo and Barbara shared, as well as a flat, their early car-driving adventures, and holidays, chiefly in Norway, and Leo was soon introduced to The Pie, who called her 'Miss Leo'. One indication of enduring services performed is hidden in the Preface to Barbara's *Freedom Under Planning*, published in 1945. Barbara thanked five people for their help, and Leonora Simeon is there 'for making an impossible manuscript into a clean typescript'.[77] Apart from such duties, and her work in the Joint Research Department, Leo was also active in the Workers' Educational Association; she appears in library catalogues in connection with the work of the Hadow Committee which produced a series of reports in the period from 1923 to 1933 on Britain's educational system.[78] Her name is attached to two WEA publications[79] relating to the most famous of the Hadow reports, *The Education of the Adolescent*, which proposed a basic division between primary and secondary education with a break at eleven, and also suggested raising the school-leaving age to fifteen.[80]

Leonora Simeon shared Barbara Wootton's involvement in the local Labour Party. It was through this route that Barbara embarked on an interest that would absorb her for the next forty-four years: the Party put her name forward as a potential magistrate, and the Lord Chancellor accepted its suggestion. This was yet another first – not the first woman magistrate – a mark of achievement that belonged to Ada Summers, a local philanthropic worker in Cheshire who had taken up the office seven years earlier in 1919[81] – but the first and only woman to become a magistrate at an age at which as a woman she was ineligible to vote. Many people recognized that the magistracy needed new, younger, female blood. Becoming a magistrate was an experience which taught Barbara much about the workings of the criminal justice system and about the circumstances that nourish anti-social behaviour; most importantly, it moulded the central intellectual passion of her life – that public policy should be built on evidence as to what actually works in promoting welfare.

The magistracy work was part-time, and it did not pay the bills. From her viewpoint in Eccleston Square, and unimpressed by the Labour Party's façade of equality, after four years in the job, Barbara scoured the newspapers for an escape. Eventually she applied for a post in which the rate of pay was still different for men and women, but there was at least no secrecy about it. Morley College in south London had the advantage that it resonated very well with her growing interest in adult education. The College's constitution committed it to 'the advanced study by men and women belonging to the working classes of subjects of knowledge not directly connected with or applied to any handicraft, trade or business'.[82] It had started out sharing premises with the 'Old Vic' theatre, where its classes were held back-stage and in the dressing-rooms.[83] The College needed a new principal. When Barbara applied, Morley College had about a thousand part-time students of assorted ages. Barbara borrowed one of Leo's hats for the interview, which blew off as she crossed Westminster Bridge, but she got the job.[84] The Appointments Committee felt they had faced a difficult choice. They had eventually overcome, in the Vice-Chairman's words, 'Their fear of her tender years and golden curls' and had voted unanimously for Barbara Wootton.[85] A former principal, Mary Sheepshanks, noted that Barbara's strong Labour sympathies would fit comfortably with the college ethos.[86]

Perhaps Barbara would have been less enthusiastic had she known what would be involved in sorting out Morley College. She and a secretary were the only full-time posts – the rest of the staff were part-time, fee-based lecturers. The College's records were in a state of chaos; the retiring head, Clare Brennand, had moved abroad for the sake of her health; and soon the secretary developed pneumonia and, within a month, he was dead.[87] Many of the part-time lecturers had been there for years and did a poor job of stimulating the students. With surprisingly few qualms, Barbara sacked 'a considerable proportion' of them.[88] Then she enlisted her friends to give lectures: Kingsley Martin on 'English Ideas of the Nineteenth Century', May Wallas on 'French Life, Literature and History'; and Barbara herself provided a series on 'Problems of the Wage Earner'. R.H. Tawney and Sir Josiah Stamp were persuaded to deliver free public lectures to enhance the standing of the College.[89] She abolished individual College examinations, cut drastically the amount of time devoted to commercial subjects, established bursaries for foreign travel and Summer School attendances, and – most importantly – tackled the large debt of £3,000 consequent on recent building operations. The core of Morley College was an elegant but cramped eighteenth-century townhouse. A new block containing a gymnasium, a refreshment room, a hall and a laboratory had been added. Barbara solved the College's debt problem a great deal more easily than that of the national debt: she did a deal with the London County Council whereby they paid the College an extra £700 a year for three years in return for permission to run a day continuation school in the new building. Then, meeting Lady Astor at a reception, she was open about the College's difficulties. Nancy Astor was a wealthy American, the first woman MP, famous for her politically uncomfortable views and wit – 'I married beneath me; all women do' is one of those ascribed to her.[90] After Barbara had shared Morley College's problems with her at the social event, Lady Astor retired for a few moments and returned to press into Barbara's hands a cheque for a further £750.[91]

The new Principal also had to get her head round the complex London County Council (LCC) regulations – the LCC was the College's main funder – which prescribed different rates of pay for different classes; she quickly realized that the goal was to present as many classes as possible in the highest fee-earning categories. Since the College offered many attractive social activities, some students enrolled in the easiest and cheapest classes just to get access to these. One student had apparently taken the same elementary botany class for eighteen years.[92] In order to sort out the mess and do her new job properly, Barbara's physical presence was required during most of the College's opening hours, which included every evening until 10 p.m. or 10.30 p.m. When William Beveridge wrote to suggest an evening meeting in early 1926 at the LSE to discuss 'one or two things' of undoubted importance to them both, Barbara regretted that she was unable to be free *any* evening.[93] In February 1927, when she had been in the job just over a year, the College had an open day and Barbara was interviewed by a journalist from *The Manchester Guardian*. He or she referred to Barbara as a 'brilliant young economist' (as many at the time did) and she referred the journalist to some of the facts about Morley students: the range in their ages (from seventeen to seventy-seven), and in their occupations: clerks of every kind; dressmakers; shop assistants; transport workers; printers; policemen (with an obscure penchant for the French classes); a few taxi-drivers and engineers; and teachers, who displayed a fondness for the choir and orchestra. Barbara advertised the purpose of the College: 'rational enjoyment'. The journalist was taken on a tour, and admired the library with its 6,000 books; the gymnasium, where a class of 'business girls' was preparing a public display; the large new hall which hosted the madrigal circle; and a laboratory, enormously popular as more and more people wanted to find out about the wireless and electricity.[94]

The following spring, the growing fame of Morley College's fourth Principal was boosted by a completely unexpected and flattering invitation to attend the League of Nations' first World Economic Conference in Geneva. There had been eighteen months of preparation for this event, which was widely regarded by those inside and outside the League as holding the key to future world economic security. The human and economic costs of the First World War, and the huge dislocations of the inter-war years, inspired many visions of a new internationalism which would be achieved through a rational use of science and economics. The League of Nations was the cradle of many such hopes, particularly for disarmament and the future avoidance of international conflict. Although the subsequent verdict of history would be that, in this most important goal, the League failed,[95] it did achieve important successes in social and humanitarian fields. For a while it seemed that its economic programme would lead the way: the Economic Organization headquarters in Geneva were viewed by many hopefuls as the repository of an economic policy to save the world.[96] The 194 delegates and 226 experts from fifty countries [97] who took part in the first World Economic Conference in Geneva in May 1927 spent their time listening to persuasive speeches in favour of freer trade: the argument that the main obstacles to economic revival were the hindrances to the free flow between countries of labour, capital and goods, and that these should therefore be removed. The Final Report of the Conference recommended the abolition of tariffs and other long-established barriers to free trade. It and the Conference were acclaimed as great successes,[98] but unhappily the draft convention for the Abolition of Import and Export Prohibitions, the Conference's 'supreme achievement', was ratified by only seventeen of the eighteen states needed to put the recommendations into force.[99] The League's economic proposals met the same fate as the far more important idea that human beings should stop fighting one another: in each case, the enemy was nationalism. Freer trade meant *other* countries reducing tariffs, not one's own; disarmament and the abandonment of territorial aggression were always policies that *other* nations should adopt.

Conferences of this kind were normally only attended by delegates nominated by the governments of member states – eminent politicians, Ministers, businessmen and so forth. Where were the women? The original Covenant of the League in 1919 had omitted them entirely, but protest by international women's organizations had resulted in the insertion of Article 7 requiring that all positions connected with the League should be open equally to both sexes. 'Perpetual vigilance' had been needed to ensure that this happened, and the women's organizations had set up a Standing Committee precisely for this purpose; it was this Committee that nominated Barbara Wootton.[100] She was one of four women delegates at the Conference. The others were the Dutch feminist economist and politician E.C. van Dorp; Dr Marie-Elisabeth Lüders, a member of the German Reichstag; and Emmy (or Emmi) Freundlich, the first woman to occupy a ministerial post in Austria.[101]

Barbara counted her invitation to Geneva an important mark of recognition as a woman and as an economist. In a letter to the Secretary-General of the League, she asked for clarification about who would fund the cost of her visit: the League itself, the British Government, or the Women's Societies?[102] The Government refused to pay her the expenses which were automatic for the male delegates. The Women's International League came to Barbara's rescue and raised enough to cover her essential expenses, although she had to stay in a cheap hostel rather than in the expensive hotels frequented by the other delegates. By way of protest, she refused to equip herself with the evening gown required for some of the formal social events. However, this story of second-class citizenship had a happy ending, as at the last minute the British Government relented and issued a cheque which could be cashed only by dint of a Geneva bank staying open an extra quarter of an hour – an unheard of concession. With the proceeds, Barbara booked a sleeper on the train home, and she and Leo had a nice holiday in Norway.[103] Back in London, Barbara dutifully did her part in publicizing the World Economic Conference's achievement (getting people from different countries to say the same thing in different ways), speaking at an event arranged by the Standing Joint Committee of Industrial Women's Organizations in London in July, and at another three-day conference held in the Guildhall in December.[104] Unhappily for the women's organizations, however, the achievement of getting a few women to take part in these discussions was overridden by the failure of the second World Economic Conference six years later to nominate any: 'Again no woman!' shouted the suffragist magazine *The Vote* – and one of the male delegates, J.H. Thomas, then added insult to injury with his suggestion that the best way to cure unemployment was to remove women from the labour force altogether.[105]

The job at Morley College was only the second for which Barbara had formally applied. In 1927, when she had been there less than eighteen months, she was offered without interview a new post: that of Director of Studies for the University of London's Extra-Mural Department. This was a newly-created position, firmly grounded in the movement for increasing access to university-level education, and thus instantly attractive to Barbara, whose (by now considerable) experience of giving and receiving education had instilled in her the belief that it should be a right and not a privilege. The new job could almost have been tailor-made for her, and in a way it was. It was an instance of that 'multitude of converging considerations' for which she had been reprimanded by Dalton: a position that badly needed her organizational and academic talents, just as she needed to feel she was doing something of real practical utility, and would be publicly recognized for so doing. In the eight years since she had taken her final degree examinations at Cambridge, she had tried four jobs, and none of them had been quite right. A mark of the rightness of this one was that she did it for seventeen years.

The idea of universities reaching out into the communities from which their full-time students would not normally be drawn had its roots in late Victorian liberalism, and there were strong associations with the movements for both working-class and women's education.[106] The first university extension lectures were given on astronomy by James Stuart, 'the father of university extension' in Cambridge in 1867 to audiences recruited by the North of England Council for the Higher Education of Women. A London movement for university extension launched its first programme of classes on political economy, history, political philosophy, electricity and magnetism and astronomy (clearly a popular subject) in 1876. The first female lecturer was a Mrs Sophie Bryant, a young widow who gave a course on 'moral ideals' (though she was a mathematician by training). The students of these early classes included manual workers – shipbuilders, boiler-makers, dock labourers – as well as clerks and elementary schoolteachers.[107] Then, in the early 1900s, two closely connected things happened to the university extension movement: the Workers' Educational Association (WEA) and the tutorial class. Albert Mansbridge, who founded the WEA in 1903, had himself once taken a university extension course ('The Chemistry of Everyday Life'); he could see that the movement was failing to attract many working-class people, and so came up with the idea of classes for no more than thirty or forty people based on the university model, and offering a more intimate context for learning than the traditional large-audience lecture.[108] An alliance between the WEA and the universities was, he believed, critical to the success of this idea. The original tutorial classes scheme was developed at Oxford and it committed groups of

adults to attend for three years during the winter months weekly classes, held
mostly in the evenings or on Saturdays, following courses of study worked out by
them and a tutor of their choice.[109] Other universities followed the Oxford model.
The first three tutorial classes in London took place at Toynbee Hall (a university
settlement in the East End of London which provided education and social welfare
programmes of various kinds) in 1900–1 on the totally non-contentious topics of
the dissolution of the monasteries, Tennyson, and combustion and oxidation.[110] By
the end of the First World War, London housed twenty-one tutorial classes with a
much wider range of topics: for example, the poet T.S. Eliot talked about literature,
and Barbara's Joint Research Department Colleague, Delisle Burns, lectured on
reconstruction.[111] The buzzword 'reconstruction' gave the extra-mural tutorial class
system an important stimulus, featuring in a blueprint for an integrated system
of publicly-funded post-school education issued by Lloyd George's Ministry of
Reconstruction. Although the Report was a victim of conservative economies and
was never adopted, its impassioned critique of those social and educational structures
which institutionalized inequality inspired many important inter-war initiatives.[112]

The young Barbara Adam may well have met Albert Mansbridge when he visited
Girton College to talk about the aims and methods of the WEA in her first term
there.[113] The origins of the post she was offered twelve years later lay in London
tutorial classes outgrowing the administrative structure – the London Society for
the Extension of University Teaching, later the Board to Promote the Extension of
University Teaching – into which they had been born. The increase in classes and
numbers of students brought an ever-expanding challenge of maintaining standards.
The plan for a full-time academic organizer was first hatched by H.P. Smith, a keen
young socialist who was secretary to the London District of the WEA. His idea
was that a full-time university staff member should be recruited to co-ordinate all
extra-mural work: to act as guide and organizer; find and vet new tutors (most of
whom did the work as a sideline and had other positions in universities); arrange
locations and timetables; and supervise the all-important series of annual residential
Summer Schools.[114] In 1922, G.D.H. Cole was appointed as staff tutor to fill this
role. He entirely lived up to Smith's aspirations, exhibiting 'all the qualities of an
electric eel'.[115] Cole started advanced tutorial classes so that students who had
completed three years' work could move on to more advanced study; he set up
'training groups' providing instruction in teaching methods and research so that
students could become teachers themselves; he founded a Tutors' Association, wrote
a *Tutors' Manual* and started a journal, the *Tutors' Bulletin*. He also found the time
to fight and win a battle with the University when it proposed to sack a married
woman tutor who had gone off with one of her students.[116] Eventually Cole penned

a memorandum to argue for the appointment of a proper Director of Studies. He may have had himself in mind, but when Senate passed a resolution to put his plan into action it recommended that the post be offered to Barbara Wootton. This notion was greeted with some consternation among the London tutors, who wanted the post to be advertised as widely as possible. It was Margaret Cole who wrote to the Joint Committee of the University responsible for tutorial classes to say this, which suggests, perhaps, an element of marital collusion.[117] However, no-one seems to have been particularly unhappy when Barbara took the post, after considerable misgivings, mostly about leaving Morley College in the lurch after less than two years. It helped in making the decision that the salary was higher, and there was no associated condition, as there had been at Morley College, that any female post-holder would have to resign on marriage. The prospect of a second marriage, ten years on from Jack's death, was one Barbara obviously entertained.

She was embarrassed about her short stay at Morley, but the College Council was sympathetic. It understood that the new post was one for which she had 'unique qualifications of aptitude, experience and sympathy', and did not question the wisdom of her decision to exploit the wider opportunities of the new appointment. She had done a splendid job for the College in a short time and they appreciated it.[118] Moreover, they were fortunate in finding another extremely capable ex-Cambridge economics graduate to replace her. Like Barbara Wootton, Eva Hubback had lost her husband to the War but, unlike Barbara, she had three young children to support. For many years, Eva would continue Barbara Wootton's good work in promoting the intellectual and artistic profile of Morley College.[119]

Barbara began the London extra-mural job in June 1927, almost immediately after her return from Geneva, although she continued to give some economics classes at Morley until the late 1930s. A measure of her new task is contained in the 'Tutorial Classes Statistical Abstract' for the academic session 1928–29, her second year. Fifty-three classes ran that year across Greater London. A total of 1,199 students were enrolled, although only 643 effectively attended. Barbara herself taught a third-year economics class in Westminster, and an advanced class in St Pancras on 'Control of Industry', and she was about to start another there on the 'History of Socialistic Thought'. Other tutors on the list included C.E.M. Joad, a philandering philosopher who had been expelled from the Fabian Society for sexual misbehaviour at a Summer School; Mrs. A. Blanco-White, whose reputation as one of H.G. Wells' many mistresses unfairly exceeded her reputation as a writer and political activist; and W. Milne-Bailey, Barbara's colleague from the Joint Research Department.[120] Barbara's main memory of these years was one of 'waiting in cold, dark and rain at eleven o'clock at night in deserted and ill-lit suburban railway stations for trains that did not come'.[121] Tutors often found themselves in dirty offices with broken gas fires hired for the evening from the local trades council, or in schoolrooms full of tiny desks equipped with dreadful lighting – it being assumed that children would only be there in daylight hours.[122] One of Barbara's predecessor's classes was held in a room sandwiched between a group rehearsing a Gilbert and Sullivan opera, and army recruits learning to play the drum, with only glass partitions dividing these opposed activities.[123]

She had a secretary and two staff tutors to help her with a considerable and diverse workload: the endless business of finding suitable premises, and dealing with other material matters; the delicate task of choosing the right tutors; and the sometimes impossible, but essential, need to monitor standards. Much time was given over to details: for example, 'Mrs G.D.H. Cole's' request for a map 'in connection with her course on Social History of the World' – a large wall map, preferably showing Europe, Asia and Africa; the request was referred to a committee and the sum of £2.10s allocated for the purpose.[124] With respect to the choice of tutors, a little brown notebook in the University of London Archives contains some of Barbara's observations. It is a very telling little book. 'Elias, Norbert, D.Phil … Breslau, Works in Sociol. at LSE'; 'Eysenck H.J., Young refugee … degree U.C. (?Ist) psych … No teaching yet. Too young except in emergency'; 'Gellhorn, Peter, Music qualifications v. high, Specialty int. opera. Young, vital, talks too much. Shd be tried at Toynbee only'; 'Meyer, Ernst H., MA Heidelberg, Music and Sociology … Farfetched pseudo-Marxism. Not suitable'; 'Turner, Marie. Out of wk Classical School mistress. Seeks new line. Hopeless.'[125] Elias, Eysenck, Gellhorn, and many other names in the little brown book subsequently became very well-known in their own fields.

As always, Barbara Wootton applied her sharp analytic powers to her new occupation. She faced its weaknesses, as well as its strengths. Academic standards could not be the same in extra-mural as in intra-mural classes, since students in the former picked their own tutors and classes without being selected or graded in any way. In tutorial classes, the measure of success was quantitative (the number of students recruited and the amount of grant money received from the Board of Education) rather than qualitative (the standard of the work achieved). Many students embarked on adult education for a reason – occupational and financial advance or sociability – rather than for its own sake. So tutors often had to make up for their students' deficiencies in schooling, teaching grammar and logic at the same time as the substantive topic.[126] The doctor and politician Charles Hill (later Lord Hill of Luton) was hired in the mid-1920s as a tutor for classes in biology at Morley College and in Hampstead:

I was a young man of twenty one who had shown no outstanding enthusiasm for education, and here were middle-aged men and women, voluntarily attending weekly classes in serious subjects ... A stockbroker's clerk, a bricklayer, an upholsterer were typical of the regulars at Hampstead. This was truly seeking after knowledge for its own sake ... Though essays were difficult to extract from many of them, the questions these adult students asked left one in no doubt as to their intelligent interest in what they heard.

Hill remembers being inspected by Barbara in her role as Director of Tutorial Classes; she 'dropped in from time to time to see how one managed'. 'One of the ablest women of her generation', he knew enough of her academic triumphs to be slightly scared of her.[127] The problems Hill noted with his biology class are echoed many times in the reports Barbara turned in: her own class of students doing 'Control of Industry' in St Pancras, for instance, were pleasant, eager people, and three or four of them did a good deal of reading, but the results were always disappointing. 'The others never got beyond facile generalizations based on personal experience.'[128] An uneasy ambivalence lay at the core of the very idea of the University extra-mural tutorial class: a clash between the liberal values of scholarship and the very disparate ambitions and capacities of extra-mural students.

The years from 1922 to 1932 were extremely busy and diversified ones for Barbara. When her appointment to the Colwyn Committee received its avalanche of press interest, the *Everywoman* reporter recorded some of her subject's other extra-curricular activities: Barbara was a part-time lecturer in Social Economics at Bedford College; she was engaged in presenting 'the results of original researches to the world through papers read to the British Association'; she was the London correspondent of an organ called the *Volkszeitung für das Vogtland* (a local newspaper for an area of Germany and Czechoslovakia); and she was a member of the Central and London executives of the WEA, a member of their London Joint Committee and, from 1923 to 1925, editor of the WEA journal *The Highway*, transforming it into a more influential academic product.[129]

Throughout the decade after Barbara left Cambridge, there was also a flood of reviewing: books on economics, and on social subjects, a cluster of books about women workers and family policy, and Cole's *The Next Ten Years in British Social and Economic Policy* – a political tract containing the interesting idea of tackling unemployment through a National Labour Corps of voluntary recruits from the unemployed who would occupy themselves by rehabilitating shabby housing and generally cleaning up the country. Unfortunately, Mr Cole provided few details of how such an 'exceedingly complicated experiment' might work.[130] G.B. Shaw's *The Intelligent Woman's Guide to Socialism and Capitalism* was also treated to the scrutiny of Barbara's critical eye: 'Mr. Bernard Shaw has gallantly credited the intelligent woman with a large measure of assiduity, leisure, and money beyond what, on his own showing, she is likely to have'.[131]

During this period, some of Barbara's own leisure was devoted to a cause that would later occupy much more of it: the promotion of world peace. In 1924 she spoke on 'Economic Problems of Peace and International Collaboration' at an International Democratic Congress for Peace in London presided over by the peace campaigner and later Labour MP Norman Angell. The subtext of the Congress was soliciting the collaboration of Germany and admitting the limitations of the Versailles Peace Treaty. The Pope and the Archbishop of Canterbury both sent goodwill messages.[132] She wrote a paper on 'Banking, Credit and Currency' for *The Book of the Labour Party*,[133] and a careful but also passionate analysis of 'The Costs of Unemployment' for *The Labour Magazine*.[134] The unequal impact of unemployment on women did not escape her; her short paper 'Unemployment Amongst Women', in the suffragist publication *Woman's Year Book*, noted that female unemployment was particularly high in 'masculine' sectors which had welcomed women in wartime and were now trying to get rid of them; there was no proper unemployment benefit for women, many of whom consequently had to fall back on poor relief.[135] On 10 November 1926, *The Manchester Guardian* reported the presence of about forty young women in two poster parades outside the Houses of Parliament. On one of the posters was inscribed the legend: 'Gentlemen Prefer Blondes, but Blondes Prefer the Vote'. The young women were members of the Young Suffragist movement, and Barbara was their President. The police ordered the parades to disperse. When one of the young suffragists visited Scotland Yard to find out why, she was told that their posters had exceeded the allowable size, regulations decreed that no woman was permitted to hold up a poster; any poster carried by a woman must be slung from the shoulders; and any poster-carrying woman would be questioned by the police and must give her name and address. None of these requirements applied to men.[136]

Barbara's public activities, especially those connected with the Labour movement, expanded. In 1928, she was one of two Labour trustees appointed to select candidates for travelling scholarships endowed under the will of Sir Arthur Acland to foster international research on labour and co-operative problems.[137] The same year, her name joined others in what was 'almost a definitive list of the good, the great and the promising of progressive opinion of the time' in the appeal and manifesto which gave birth to a new journal, *The Political Quarterly*.[138] She started to become a regular broadcaster, giving an intriguing series of talks for students on 'Some Modern Utopias' in 1929.[139] She covered both well-known utopias

(Samuel Butler, William Morris, H.G. Wells) and *Freeland*, a rather less known description of a practical utopia constructed on sound business principles created by the German economist Theodor Hertzka.[140] This branching out into utopian fiction signalled an aspect of Barbara's character that remained well-hidden most of the time. It surfaced at the Independent Labour Party Summer School in 1926, where she not only talked about nationalizing the banks, but took part in G.D.H. Cole's comic opera about the General Strike. The opera and the Summer School were staged at the magnificent Easton Lodge in Essex, the home of the notorious Daisy, 'the Red' Countess of Warwick, who attempted to make up for a life of extravagant wealth and exuberant liaisons (including one with the Prince of Wales) by converting to socialism and offering her entire estate to the Labour Party, the TUC and London Zoo, in that order. Only the TUC was interested, but after the 1926 General Strike the running costs of Easton Lodge could not be afforded.[141] Cole's opera, *The Striker Stricken*, was written in a white-hot mood in forty-eight hours to the music of Gilbert and Sullivan (perhaps absorbed by Cole through the walls of that tutorial class) and *Hymns Ancient and Modern*. In an apocalyptic third act, St Peter opens the gates of heaven to Karl Marx, the miners and their allies. This creation was certainly libellous and was never published, although it did go on tour in the Durham coalfields and elsewhere from time to time.[142] Other stars of the 1926 production were C.E.M. Joad, John Strachey (the Labour politician and writer), and Margaret Cole (who played Lady Astor). One imagines that they all had a great deal of much-deserved fun.[143] The spring of 1930 saw Barbara's first trip to the United States to attend an adult education conference in Chicago, where she was most affected by the lakeside slums.[144] But she did not make this trip on the *Queen Mary*, as she said in her autobiography – an error picked up by an assiduous reader in Edinburgh who pointed out that the maiden voyage of the *Queen Mary* was not until 1934.[145]

Given this enormous industry, it was small wonder that some of the press then and later wondered what she did in any of the spare time she probably did not have. The photographs of the period display her as an unsmiling and incurably serious young woman with cropped hair in 1920s style, wearing sombre clothes and either sitting at a desk or staring out from under a tightly fitted low-brimmed hat. Sometimes she is wearing glasses, sometimes not. But what one sees is a woman young in years with an experience and determination of much greater maturity. She would make use of as many opportunities that presented themselves as possible; and she would not waver from her conviction that vision, reason and hard work would make the world a more congenial and more equitable place.

7

Fact and Fiction

Radical politics are fertilised by catastrophe, and the catastrophes of the 1930s gave birth, outside Russia as well as inside it, to the 'Red Decade'.[1] In many countries, the decade began with widespread economic recession and ended with a second world war. The cataclysmic Wall Street crash of 1929 highlighted the vulnerability of capitalist monetary systems. Was this the end of capitalism? In an attempt to answer this question, British left-wing politics developed an unprecedented sense of cohesion and radicalism: the conceptual landscape shifted to a perception of an essential struggle between socialism and 'capitalist-imperialism', which, for many on the Left, could no longer credibly be fought with the old-fashioned tactics of gradualism.[2] Events at home, and even more abroad – fascism and nationalist aggression in Germany, Spain, Italy, and Japan, particularly – roused intellectuals, writers and artists to a new political seriousness about failures of the economic and social system. In 1938, Virginia Woolf's outspoken *Three Guineas* laid out the connections between nationalism, fascism, capitalism and patriarchy. Significantly, Woolf did not offer her devastating thesis as an academic text, but as a fictional reply to fictional letters requesting donations to worthy causes. *Three Guineas* was illustrative of another important aspect of the tenor of the decade: for those whose business was ideas, it was not only a dismal, but a radicalizing and inspirational time. People believed all sorts of things, and then changed their minds. Facts hid behind fictions. Sometimes it was difficult to tell the difference between them.

The single most important metaphor of the decade was the journey: the journey across countries and political systems; across classes, nations and genders; from public to private; from past to future; from one form of writing to another.[3] Between 1932 and 1936, Barbara Wootton published her first three books: two were presented as fiction, and one was fact, although its business was disentangling fact from fiction. *Plan or No Plan,* published in 1934, was a 'magisterial'[4] analysis of the advantages and disadvantages of planned and unplanned economies. The book is a systematic comparison of capitalism, a method of economic organization based on price variations in 'free' markets, with a planned economy driven by the very different model of abolishing the profit motive and the expropriation of workers' labour this entails. Like much of the economic and political literature of the 1930s, *Plan or No Plan* was provoked by the 'experiment' of the Soviet Union which, following the 1917 Revolution, had embarked on what would more usually be considered the stuff of utopian (or dystopian) fiction. What were the truths about the Soviet experiment? What lessons might these have for societies which were unlikely to follow the Soviet example in violently disposing of their capitalist regimes? Barbara's only published novel, *London's Burning,* was written immediately after she finished *Plan or No Plan.* Theodore Frinton, the 'hero' of *London's Burning* (although, as the novel unfolds, his actions are seen to be far from heroic), is a benevolent capitalist confronted with an uprising organized by the International Unemployed Workers' League. In the novel, the structural weaknesses of capitalism undermine the British tradition of cosy liberalism, just as they do in *Plan or No Plan.*

Her first book was different: *Twos and Threes,* a volume of short stories, bears hardly a hint of these political issues. Barbara's job as Director of Studies for London University's Extra-Mural Department gave her free time during the day. *Twos and Threes* was written in the Hampstead flat she shared with Leo Simeon and published in 1933, when Barbara was thirty-six. It marked, she said, the end of an emotional phase in her life, but it did not have any particular success, and it was soon pulped to make paper for other more saleable works.[5] For a biographer, the six stories in *Twos and Threes* form a tantalizing harvest. They are all about relationships between men and women, and probably reflect aspects of Barbara's own experiences – not because art mirrors life in any direct way, but because all our creative productions, whether artistic or academic, are rooted in our own locations in the social world. 'If it's any good it's your own experience every time, whatever strange form it may take; for the essence of sympathy is simply discovering your own experience in somebody else', as one of the characters in one of her stories remarks.[6]

In her autobiography, Barbara does admit that the second of the six stories in *Twos and Threes,* 'The Morning After', captures some of the atmosphere of a relationship she had with a character whose name she does not give us: he is 'J.T.' in the autobiography, Geoffrey in the story. When the autobiography was published, Barbara's brother Neil wrote to her and asked her who J.T. was.[7] Her reply, if there was one, is not in Neil's archives in Southampton. According to the non-fictional account, Barbara and the real J.T. were given to travelling in the stormy years of their relationship (the late 1920s) through Normandy and Brittany on foot, drinking calvados, and eating French bread and camembert by the roadside. He was a 'highly neurotic character with a passion for everything French, especially Flaubert'. They were 'deeply attached' to one another despite (or because of) the fact that he was the only person she knew intimately with whom she perpetually quarrelled.[8]

In J.T.'s fictional representation as Geoffrey the same is true: the story is about the disputed end of a relationship between Geoffrey and his woman friend, Nora. Geoffrey and Nora are in France, in a small hotel. Geoffrey's response to imminent closure is to be much occupied with timetables; Nora's is to agonize about fault, and responsibility, and the inability of learning from one's mistakes or from other people's sensible advice. He suggests having one more tomorrow together; she, taken aback, agrees. On the morning after this decision, they walk in the French sunlight and watch a kingfisher and remember all their delightful times together: 'So they had walked day after day in the spring when primroses smiled everywhere in the hedgerows and the orchards were in blossom. So they had walked in the first laughing days of love when there was nothing that would not shape itself to their liking.'[9] Nora cries with a morbid passion that she wants to 'Damn the world with its Eastern incidents and oppressed minorities ... Damn it, Geoff! I only wanted to be me ... Why did we have to be conscripted with the rest? Conscripted into this blasted civilization and robbed of our birthright of simplicity?' Geoffrey tells her that she has got it wrong: 'Complexities, relations, problems – these are your daily bread and the only food you can stomach; and only the world you pretend to despise can feed you with them. You're no conscript, Nora! You're the readiest volunteer that ever wore the livery of civilisation – the civilisation that gives you your tangles, your situations, your subtle miseries of emotion.'[10] After these *cris du coeur*, which have a ring of non-fictional truth about them, Geoffrey and Nora take a room in a dingy hotel and go to bed. 'They were animals, came together, and were satisfied. They were man and woman, separate, discordant, alone.'[11] The next day they go to the station, where Nora is to see Geoffrey off on a train, the final end of the affair. 'God,' says Nora, in another disturbing reminder of Barbara's own past, 'if only there was a war and I could be seeing you off to be killed.'[12] But the train never comes, because Geoffrey's watch is six minutes late.

Other points in these stories also touch the authenticity of Barbara's own non-fictional life. There are the middle-class academic pretensions ridiculed in 'The Happy Animal'; normally, says Francis, one of the two men in the story, 'there's only one right name for anything. Why should there be more? ... you can write off three-quarters or seven-eighths of the present literary output, which simply consists of using the long and complicated names and the fantastic images instead of the simple direct ones.'[13] His wife interpolates another bit of Woottonesque commonsense at the end of the story: 'No one who'd ever tossed a load of hay would have [the] patience to sit through ten minutes of the muck that's been talked round this table tonight'.[14] In 'Turning Sixty', a rather sad story about a retired, widowed Colonel who makes a ridiculous play for a younger woman, the relationship with his daughter is tenderly and convincingly portrayed. In 'One Thursday', the fourth story, a young married couple, Denys and Molly, lead a daily life of relentless boredom. He is a civil servant, she a housewife. Every day he goes on the same train to the office and she thinks about whether they might have chops for supper. Going out one evening to the local cinema to see a Harold Lloyd film, they see, but hardly notice, a 'subdued-looking woman' who is on her way to post a letter. The woman has no interest in the pictures, which she considers vulgar, but she watches Denys and Molly going into the cinema: 'They were young, they were married, they were going out together, and until they were forgotten she hated them'.[15] The statement is insufferably sad. Had the War not robbed her of Jack, Barbara Wootton might herself have been rooted, like Denys and Molly, in safe domesticity.

The remaining two stories feature triadic relationships (the 'Threes' of the title): two men and a woman in 'Odd Man Out', and two women and a man in 'So This is Adultery', a rather unsatisfactory tale which ends with a sudden suicide through a window. The main plot in 'Odd Man Out' is set in Norway, one of Barbara's favourite holiday destinations. She went there often with Leo, and would go there with George, her second husband, on their honeymoon in 1935, and also later with Barbara Kyle, in the second great female friendship of her life. In the story, the descriptions of Norway, entered on a boat, are satisfyingly lyrical: 'The last stages, when the fjord narrowed, made you feel as though you were taking the clothes off your soul. You shed layer after layer till there was nothing left at all except stillness and colour. It was just blue below and blue above and dark green walls on each side... suddenly we came round a bend and there was the head of the fjord; green valley, white wooden village, and the busy landing-stage running out into the sea.'[16]

The stories in *Twos and Threes* are competent diversions on the themes of gender, generation and class. Some elements jar – such as the suicide in 'So This is Adultery', the Colonel's break from habit in 'Turning Sixty', and the monochrome conversations in 'The Happy Animal'. But the characters are convincing, recognizable creatures from the world of the 1930s, and not all, by any means, came from Barbara's own circle. The book feels like an experiment. These were highly experimental times in literature, art, manners and politics. They were times when politicians, artists and intellectuals of all kinds were watching and noting the greatest experiment of the twentieth century – the building of a workers' state in the Union of Soviet Socialist Republics. 'I use the term "experiment" advisedly,' noted Barbara in her *Plan or*

No Plan, 'for during the whole period the Soviet regime has shown, and still shows, a power of trying out new and bold ventures, and of discarding lines of policy that prove unsuccessful, which is one of its most conspicuous points of contrast with the Western world.'[17] She may have been somewhat mistaken in believing that systematic trial-and-error was the motif of the Soviet regime, but she was not alone in regarding the establishment in Russia of a centrally planned and managed economy as promising both a technical and moral solution to the mess in which Britain and other Western countries were then floundering.

Russia at the start of the twentieth century was still largely feudal: peasants made up eighty per cent of the population, there was little developed industry and no legal political parties or central elected parliament. The First World War exposed and increased the vulnerability of the old Tsarist regime. The economic machine had virtually shut down, and army and civil population alike were threatened with famine. In February 1917, a popular revolution led by women demanding bread disposed of the autocracy and produced a Russian Provisional Government; in October, a radical socialist network of Soviets (workers' councils) and the Bolshevik party, led by Lenin, overthrew the Provisional Government and created the conditions for a Union of Soviet Socialist Republics.[18] After the Revolution, in the 1920s, came Lenin's brainchild, the New Economic Policy, 'market socialism': communism plus a limited private sector. After Lenin's death, and the rise of Stalin as General Secretary of the Communist Party, a programme of state-run Five-Year Plans established the ambitious goals of rapid industrialization and the collectivization of agriculture, to be achieved through the mechanism of a State General Planning Commission, Gosplan. But the importance of events in the USSR for many in Europe and North America was not only (or even chiefly) what was *actually* happening there, but what people *imagined* might be happening.[19] Whatever else it was, Soviet Russia was the antithesis of the failing capitalist system. However, the Soviet experiment represented more than the economic expedients devised to drag a feudal society into the twentieth century; it symbolized a brave new world in which technology and rationality would be applied to social development in a process of levelling that should bestow on all citizens equal rights to the same reasonable standard of living. 'Russophilia' mobilized a desire for order that had been lost in the economic and social chaos of the inter-war years in Britain.[20]

The term 'fellow-traveller' – meaning someone who sympathized with communist ideas without being a Party member – first came into use in the 1930s.[21] Membership of the Communist Party in Britain burgeoned during this period: from 1,356 in 1930 to 15,570 in 1938.[22] The many Western fellow-travellers who thought and wrote about and visited Russia were sons and daughters of the Enlightenment, believers in the doctrine of progress. Most were neither communists nor revolutionaries, but pilgrims and sightseers disillusioned with the failure of their own society to create liberty and equality out of the stuff of laissez-faire and (often un)enlightened self-interest.[23] Russia was 'the hope of the world,' declared Fabian socialist Margaret Cole: 'not merely had the Russians expropriated kings, priests, and capitalists ... their new State was boldly introducing most of the reforms which Socialists had been vainly demanding for generations'.[24] 'We were all interested, one way or another, in Soviet Russia,' wrote journalist Kingsley Martin.[25] And so they went to find out. Kingsley Martin went in 1932 with cartoonist David Low. They visited Leningrad, Moscow, Nizhni-Novgorod, Rostov, Kharkov, Kiev and the Dnieper Dam; they travelled down the Volga by boat. When they came back, they produced a book, *Low's Russian Sketchbook*, which was banned in the Soviet Union because Martin's text did not acknowledge the existence of a utopian state – though Low's cartoons made fun of 'the professional anti-Communist' who interpreted every delay before a meal and every mechanical failure (there were many of both) as proof that Communism was breaking down.[26]

The journeys of inspection made by left-wing intellectuals to Russia started early. Two visitors – Arthur Ransome, author of *Swallows and Amazons*, and war correspondent for *The Daily News* – and M. Philips Price, war correspondent for *The Manchester Guardian* – were actually witnesses of the October Revolution.[27] The outspoken writer and socialist, H.G. Wells, went early enough (in 1919) to have a long conversation with Lenin himself, and to arrive at the view that only Lenin could save Russia from anarchy.[28] By the time of Wells' later visit in 1934 (which changed his mind), encounters with Lenin in his deceased form had become an obligatory part of the tourist experience, here described by politician and economist Hugh Dalton, who went with a Fabian party in 1932: 'We descended into a deep chamber .... All marble within, mostly a dark, speckled grey, but with a pink pediment .... There was strip lighting, a soft golden yellow, behind clouded glass. The central figure, Lenin, lay beneath a glass case, his head on a blood-red pillow, his hands resting on black and purple drapery.'[29] Bertrand and Dora Russell – philosopher and mathematician, and writer, socialist and feminist campaigner respectively – went to Russia in 1920 with 'a delegation of Labour men and women'.[30] Bertrand recoiled from what he called a 'glib and narrow philosophy';[31] Dora was most interested in what the Bolshevik Revolution would do for the position of women. The list of voyagers glittered with the names of well-known political writers, poets, novelists and other artists – and scientists as well, for the rejection of religion and the espousal of technocratic planning were in tune with the ideology of science.[32] The technical side of these pilgrimages was eased by the formation in Russia of the All-Union Society for Cultural Relations with Foreign Countries (VOKS) in 1925 and the State travel company, Intourist, in 1929.

Barbara Wootton believed that you should never speculate without empirical data. The year, 1932, in which she went to uncover the facts behind the legends about the Soviet experiment, was a peak for curious British visitors. By this time, Labour politics in Britain were in obvious trouble. In August 1931, the working-class politician and first Labour Prime Minister Ramsay MacDonald committed what many on the Left read as a betrayal of Labour politics when he jettisoned most of his Cabinet, and formed a 'National' government. After the election, Oswald Mosley and a group of independents defected, the latter to form the Independent Labour Party (ILP). The more intellectual members of this group split off to form the Socialist League, which, unlike the ILP, maintained a connection with the centre Labour party. The ILP moved dramatically to the Left, justifying its position at least partly with reference to its very favourable views of the Soviet Union.[33] As alignments shifted in this unstable kaleidoscope, many in Britain developed a deep-seated disillusionment with party politics, that 'grand old party game' into which the two elder parties seemed by this time to have enticed Labour.[34] The second Labour Government, in 1929–31, had failed to deal effectively with the growing financial and social crisis. Anyone with left-wing sympathies could see that the politics of gradualism deployed in the first two Labour Governments had not worked, and they had not worked because capitalism itself was rotten; socialism could not be embedded in any capitalist state. The whole debate captured the public imagination. Political literature and books about contemporary history encroached on sales of fiction and biography.[35] In 1936, politics and literature came together in the hugely successful Left Book Club, which dispatched monthly reading matter, bound in characteristic orange paper, to members for a small fee. The club's services to socialism extended to organizing Russian language classes and arranging Russian tours.

'A pilgrimage to the Mecca of the equalitarian state led by a few Fabians, all well over seventy years of age, will bring about the world's salvation!' exclaimed Beatrice Webb excitedly, and rather incredibly, as she set off with Sidney in May 1932 on the expedition that would produce their mammoth 1,007-page *Soviet Communism: A New Civilisation?*, first published in 1935.[36] The Webbs travelled by Russian steamer, seventy-four-year-old Beatrice complaining about the lack of chamber pots and hot water bottles; they arrived in Leningrad to a royal welcome, infused by their reputation as the authors of a key revolutionary work, *The History of Trade Unionism*, translated into Russian by no less a person than Lenin himself. Any hesitation suggested by the question mark in the title of their book was overcome in the book's second edition, when the question mark disappeared (it was also omitted from the Russian translation[37]), as the Webbs decided that developments in the two years since the first edition merely confirmed the practicability of the Russian approach to the total abolition of 'private profit-making'.[38] Encouraged by cheap trade union editions, their 'leviathan of fellow-travelling' had sold nearly 40,000 copies by 1939.[39] *Soviet Communism* was presented as 'a comprehensive description of the entire social order of the USSR', 'an objective view'.[40] In it, the Webbs drew repeatedly, usually in extensive footnotes, on Barbara's own *Plan or No Plan*, which they deemed 'able', 'the most serious of the economic examinations of the Plan', and 'the most complete analysis yet made'.[41] In fact, the Webbs, like many visitors to Russia, already knew what they thought before they went. 'What attracts us in Soviet Russia, and it is useless to deny that we are prejudiced in its favour', observed Beatrice in her diary in January 1932, 'is that its constitution, on the one hand, bears out our *Constitution of a Socialist Commonwealth*, and, on the other, supplies a soul to that conception of government ... We don't quite like that soul; but still it seems to do the job.'[42] It was this 'loyalty to their vision' that induced the Webbs to take at face value most of what the official Soviet authorities told them.[43]

It is not quite clear who went with whom in that summer of 1932. The New Fabian Research Bureau (NFRB), a radical offshoot of Fabianism set up by Margaret Cole's husband, G.D.H. Cole, in 1931, organized one deputation of 'experts': economist and social historian H.L. Beales; Margaret Cole; Hugh Dalton; engineer Graeme Haldane; film-maker Rudolph Messel; Dick and Naomi Mitchison, Labour politician and writer respectively; farmer John Morgan; politician and supporter of women's suffrage, F.W. Pethick-Lawrence; writer and historian (and brother of Margaret Cole) Raymond Postgate; Communist lawyer D.N. Pritt; and architect Geoffrey Ridley. The NFRB party took a Russian boat to Leningrad and thence travelled to Moscow. They spent some four to six weeks in Russia, some going as far as Saratov on the Volga and Magnitogorsk in the Urals. Like the Webbs, most of the NFRB visitors rejoiced in seeing what they wanted to see: 'the "spirit of the Revolution", the sense of collective purpose and planning so notably lacking in Europe and America in 1932'.[44] Doubtless they were also shown what their hosts wanted them to see, for example, the Trekhgornaya (Three Hills) cotton mill, a cradle of the 1917 Revolution. 'The many sleeping-places built over the looms, where the weavers had slept before the revolution, many of them having no homes, were still to be seen, although not in use; and the mansion of the former owner, just across the road, had been turned into a crèche for the weavers' babies'.[45]

Barbara is not mentioned as a member of the Fabian party, and in her autobiography she refers to going with 'a group of well-mixed educationalists, drawn from practically every type of English school or college, and including at least one clergyman'.[46]

Among them was the teacher and writer Edward Upward, who had recently converted to Communism, and who later recorded some of his experiences in the autobiographical trilogy *The Spiral Ascent*. Barbara's group of explorers travelled by train, third class, from Ostend to Leningrad, in spartan conditions. From Leningrad, they took the 'well-worn tourist route' to Moscow and the Ukraine. 'Travel in Russia in those days was a good deal rougher than it is now,' she recalled, 'and we sometimes had to make train journeys of more than twelve hours without any provision for refreshment other than occasional stops for tea. Forewarned of this I had come equipped with several tins of almonds and raisins ... This made me very popular with our fellow-travellers.'[47] (Barbara was using the term in a literal sense.) They were shown Parks of Culture and Rest, schools, clinics and factories – the latter were obligatory for all tourists – but she earned herself black marks by declaring that she was not interested in machinery; she had come to Russia to see living conditions. The focus of her interest is clear from the forty-five tiny black and white photos tucked away in her Girton College Archives: rows of unsmiling children sitting in classrooms; men drawing water; people queuing with shopping bags. Barbara herself stands in a long pale coat and glasses in a posed and rather misty snap of her delegation. Everywhere they went, they were presented with 'before-and-after' contrasts: 'Before the Revolution only x per cent of the children were in school: now the figure was x + y ... Just as grace is said before dinner at formal functions in this country, so every headmaster, every factory manager or hospital superintendent had to deliver himself of his ritual lecture, before anything else could be done.'[48] The group had difficulty getting to see collective farms, being fobbed off with excuses about impassable roads and melting snow. When they said there was nothing else they wished to see, so they would have to leave Russia forthwith, they won the argument.

Barbara gives no motive for her trip, other than observing that people were interested in Russia because in the West, 'the lunatic expedient of reducing everybody's income and spending', meant that public policy (aside from in wartime) had 'never been more abysmally stupid'.[49] This was the era before Keynes had shattered conventional economic thinking with his proposal that increased spending is the only sensible way out of a recession. Barbara Wootton was one of forty-one economists, including Keynes himself, who signed a letter to *The Times* in July 1932, putting forward the kernel of this approach.[50] The increased government spending they advocated was a form of state intervention, but discussion of the relationship between planning and state intervention was not at this time very far advanced. It is said that the idea of economic planning as a strategy for British government originated in 1930 with Oswald Mosley, who tried unsuccessfully to get it on the political agenda.[51] During the 1930s, planning became a central plank in Labour's refurbished socialist ideology, although 'romantic' ideas of what it meant continued to be bolstered by uncritical Russophilia.[52] By the time Barbara came to write *Plan or No Plan*, discussions of planning embraced, not only the Russian experiment, but the growing fascist threat in Europe, from corporatist state planning in Mussolini's Italy, to German National Socialism.

Everybody, it seems, wrote a book when they came back from their Soviet journeys. 'Of the writing of books about modern Russia there is no end,' complained Ethel Mannin, who wrote another one.[53] Among the early visitors, Ransome produced *Six Weeks in Russia in 1919*, Price, *My Reminiscences of the Russian Revolution* (1921), Wells, *Russia in the Shadows* (1920), and Russell, *The Practice and Theory of Bolshevism* (1920). Disposing of the Webbs' treatise as 'the most preposterous book ever written about Soviet Russia',[54] historian A.J.P. Taylor recommended instead Malcolm Muggeridge's *Winter in Moscow* (1934). The product of the NFRB journey, *Twelve Studies in Soviet Russia,* was a mixed bag, veering between Pritt's uncritical adulation of the Soviet justice system, and Morgan's sad honesty about the victims of the Soviet agricultural policy. 'I looked for tractors at work. Camels passed. Old women sat on the platforms of reapers as old-fashioned as one can find anywhere, drawing the swathes into little heaps that dotted a landscape at times as wide as an English county. Here and there horse-drawn wagons loaded and unloaded the tail-ends of a hay crop, spoilt with rain. But scarcely a tractor anywhere to be seen; not at work on the land, anyway.'[55] The Five-Year Plan was all very well, but it did not allow for droughts and freak weather, nor, most importantly for the intractability of the Russian peasant, who had enjoyed free access to land in the years immediately following the revolution, and was unwilling to be told what to do.

Her visit made a great impression on Barbara, though she did not follow the Webbs in buying the Soviet success wholesale: she found 'depressingly childish ... the black and white mentality, the reluctance to recognize shades of goodness or badness or of success or failure, the kindergarten children singing songs about achieving Five-year Plans in four, the inability to admit the existence of, or to talk over, the real problems of the present'.[56] She was not quite so balanced in the piece she wrote for the WEA magazine *The Highway* in December 1932, celebrating there for a different readership the 'extraordinary unity and consistency of Soviet ideas in every field',[57] and so getting a stern ticking-off from the Marxist economist Edgar Hardcastle: 'Mrs Wootton ... knows little of Russia, not very much about capitalism .... and understands nothing at all of Marx'.[58] But what she did understand was the value to a society of citizens sharing a common purpose, and that there was not much difference between communists and capitalists in their esteem of hard work and material output. As the Webbs had appreciated in their many footnotes, her *Plan or*

No Plan took the Russian experiment and subjected it to the piercing analytic gaze which would come to be recognized as her trademark. Of the book's six chapters, the first two examine the nature of an unplanned economy and the Russian planned economy respectively; the next two the achievements and possibilities of unplanned and planned economies; in the last two chapters she asks, What next?, and finishes by considering the conditions of successful economic planning. At this point in her intellectual life, Barbara is still an economist, but she has developed an impatience with theory for its own sake; thus, she finds it delightful to be able to refer all those philosophical contentions about capitalism versus socialism which abound at the time to the concrete example of a real socialist society. Can socialism create full employment and abolish poverty? Let us look and see. How effective is the price mechanism in allocating scarce resources? What are the other consequences of allowing prices to set who gets what and what is produced by whom? How does central planning as practised by the Soviets compare with this? What disadvantages does it have? Again, we must take a hard look at the facts of the case.

Plan or No Plan draws on Barbara's own experience, not only of her sojourn in Soviet Russia, but of capitalism. For instance, ten years before, when she was working for the TUC and the Labour Party, one of her tasks was to handle some of the schemes produced by local authorities for creating employment and improving amenities. One such scheme involved cutting a canal across Scotland, converting the Severn tides into electricity, building roads and bridges, and planting hundreds of trees. It is difficult to believe, comments Barbara, that such projects would be among those 'the need of which would have first struck a visitor from another planet who had been asked to look over our economic system and suggest enterprises which he thought might usefully be set on foot to meet genuine public needs'.[59] Surely such a visitor, after touring our cities, would argue for plans to create thousands of extra pairs of boots, more milk, underwear, pots and pans, and chairs and tables, and houses. In other words, a planned economy can make choices which are in the interests of *most* of the people, choices which aim at the goal of providing *everyone* with jobs and a decent standard of living. The rhetoric of capitalism giving us what we want ignores the reality that it makes us want what we are given.[60] Planning is about ethics, as well as economics. Buried in the middle of *Plan or No Plan* is a statement of Barbara's central belief that the ethical objections to capitalism are more powerful than any others: 'the system is guilty of grave and widespread and continuous injustice, such as is degrading to those who suffer, and tormenting to any decent-minded person who prospers, under it'.[61] Since the evidence is that the Russians are 'enormously much nearer' to economic equality than any industrial capitalist country, their approach must have much to recommend it.[62]

Barbara's scrutiny of fact versus fiction in the new civilization of communism left her with some substantive criticisms. For example, the Russians seemed to have no monetary policy as such, so there was a danger of the Government issuing more and more money to support its industrial and employment goals, and this would lead to an uncomfortable price inflation. As to lessons for Britain, it was a matter, she considered, of accommodating the model of central planning to a very different social structure and political system, a goal that did, indeed, call for a more gradualist approach. But there was nothing gradualist about her proposal that Britain imitate Russia by setting up a Planning Commission, a public body which would enjoy nation-wide authority. Key to Barbara's argument here was her starting point that, 'There is no part of their job which Parliaments do worse than their economic work, and no department of affairs in which the theory of democratic control is further removed from actual practice'.[63] *Plan or No Plan* was 'a strident demand for insulating planning from politics',[64] a call for economic policy to be separated off from the game of party politics, and given the stability and consistency that only a body of non-partisan evidence-minded experts could impart. Unlike its Russian prototype, the British Planning Commission should be composed of expert members appointed by Parliament, and their duties would be both to initiate, and to execute and monitor, economic policy.

Plan or No Plan made a distinctive contribution to the vast literature of the period on the Soviet experiment. It stood out from the rest for being a judicious attempt to disentangle fact from fiction: to separate out political, economic, social and ethical questions; to define terms; and to interrogate and weigh the evidence. The book prefigured Barbara's later analysis of the shortcomings of economics as a method for analysing social systems. It was a step on the path of her journey away from economics to the more broadly-based platform of a social scientist, or a scientist of social studies, as she would probably have preferred to put it. It distinguished itself for the absence of emotion and passion; what Barbara was passionate about was the *method* of considering the facts, and arriving at a judgement, but all such procedures throughout her life were informed by a very clear notion of the supremacy of moral values in determining the ends to which plans of all kinds should be geared.

When academic Jenifer Hart joined the newly formed British Communist Party to explore 'an English brand of communism which would be humane and not involve a bloody revolution', her decision was partly influenced by Barbara's *Plan or No Plan*. She thought the book provided 'a thorough, balanced, undoctrinaire analysis of the achievements and possibilities of planned as contrasted with unplanned economies ... I was particularly impressed by her belief that the authorities in a planned economy could eliminate our kind of unemployment if they wanted to.'[65]

But, since planning and Russia were topics which aroused strong opinion, *Plan or No Plan* was variously regarded at the time as exaggerating or minimizing the achievements of Soviet planning. One reviewer deemed it the 'Intelligent Socialist's Guide to Economics', considering it 'quite brilliant', 'a magnificent fight' on 'difficult ground', 'the Soviet experiment's first subjection to purely economic reasoning'.[66] Another praised 'Miss Wootton' for raising the controversy to a more intelligent plane: 'It is not that she has said anything new to economists, but rather that she has said with clarity and no little felicity of style what has heretofore lain imbedded in a jargon which the layman finds insupportable'.[67] *The Political Quarterly* reviewer tackled *Plan or No Plan* along with a book on *Reconstruction* by the young Tory MP (and future Prime Minister) Harold Macmillan: Mrs Wootton's book, he opined, possessed 'the rare qualifications of being entirely readable by the layman and wide in scope, while none the less managing to examine with great impartiality the causes underlying all the major economic problems of today'. And the book was good value for money (only 5s) – an approbation that would surely please any economist author.[68] Somewhat more critical was a University of Chicago reviewer who argued that the book's 'readable sprightly style' concealed unsound economic reasoning, but even he, after six pages along these lines, decided that the most serious statement he had to make was that 'it is really an extraordinarily good book'.[69] George Halm at the University of Würzburg also found it 'exceedingly interesting' but unrealistic on the role of the price mechanism, which was essential even in a planned economy and would not work in the absence of private property.[70] The lack of a worked-out economic theory for the socialist state equivalent to the equilibrium theory of free enterprise beloved among capitalist economists, was a serious problem, but the criticism was not quite merited, as Barbara herself showed in the attention she gave around the same time to a book called *The Russian Financial System* by the young Cambridge economist William Reddaway. Reddaway's exposition went some way towards elucidating the questions of principle raised by the use of money in a planned socialized economy; she liked his book.[71]

In her autobiography, Barbara records the question with which she ended *Plan or No Plan*: whether we should rejoice or despair in the fact that successful economic planning is more likely to be inhibited by failures of the human will than by anything else. 'No sooner had I finished this book,' she says, 'than I was seized with a desire to answer myself.'[72] National Socialism was on the rise in Germany, and Oswald Mosley's blackshirts were disrupting the streets of Britain. Could rationality really prevail against such forces of evil? Her answer took the form of a novel called *London's Burning*, with the subtitle 'A Novel for the Decline and Fall of the Liberal Age'.

Theodore Frinton, a man in his fifties, is Personnel Manager of Watson's World Wide Biscuits, a factory located on an industrial estate rising out of Hackney Marshes. He has a wife and a frivolous twenty-something daughter, Kitty, who is living at home without gainful employment, as was the custom of the day. The Frintons live in Barlow, a village not far from Cambridge, distinguished by its fine elms and by a church whose size is quite out of proportion to the religious zeal of the Barlow villagers. The Frintons live lives of regulated middle-class simplicity, lives made up of 'happy, trivial things'.[73] Theodore goes to the office during the week and reads the papers at weekends; Mrs Frinton manages their domestic affairs and Kitty enjoys her dalliance with Dick, who sells motor cars, and is regarded by her parents as not good enough for her. There is a maid called Milly from a Durham mining village who thinks the Frintons speak like radio announcers.

Theodore is a benevolent capitalist: he contributes to many good causes; at Watson's he has set up a Works Council and provided other important fringe benefits, including sports pitches and a heated swimming pool. The cosiness of his professional life overlaps with that of his domestic one, but into both the declining economy interpolates its counterpoint of misery: unemployment, bankruptcy and '(not very voluntary) Voluntary Liquidations'.[74] Theodore must get rid of five hundred staff by the end of the month. Into his office comes Rose Salmon, aged twenty-one, from the packing department, to warn Theodore that there will be trouble on a grand scale if his plan goes through. Rose helps to organize the International Unemployed Workers' League (IUWL). In a scene of studied ambiguity, she suggests to Theodore that the two of them might come to an understanding which would involve Theodore becoming better acquainted with the 'over-developed breasts'[75] she hangs over his desk, and would also result in her keeping her job and the IUWL not causing Theodore any further bother.

His disposition – to ignore these signs of changing times and hope they will simply go away – fights against the contrary evidence of mass demonstrations and marches accompanied by mounted police. That evening he is to preside at a meeting of another League, the League of National Service, a somewhat sinister outfit to which members devote ten per cent of their incomes to various schemes designed to promote 'National Well-being'. At the meeting, most of his attention is taken by Rose Salmon, whom he spots in the audience sucking sweets and ranting with her friends about the League, and by a literary member of the National Committee, a Miss Hester Lomax, who has intelligent grey eyes, elegant ankles and a melodious voice. He walks home with Hester, who invites in him for a drink, but, faithful to the Barlow idyll, he declines.

The 31st of October is to be a day of national demonstrations, October being a good month for revolutions. As the demonstrators assemble on the marshes below the Watson Biscuit Works, Kitty turns up in her father's office and with her usual mindless frivolity asks him to buy her a car. The demonstrators burst through the factory gates, smash glass, call for a general strike, and resist Theodore's attempts to negotiate. In the ensuing fracas, biscuits and biscuit tins are hurled through the air and a fire is started which cannot be put out, since Rose Salmon and her friends have thrown all the fire extinguishers out of the window. There is an explosion and Watson's Biscuits is reduced to a pile of debris. As these dramas unfold, Kitty returns to her boyfriend in London. The pair of them go to the cinema and afterwards walk though streets replete with crashed cars, broken shop windows, and dozens of bodies dead or dying; the statue of Eros in Piccadilly Circus is decked out with underwear from the department store Swan and Edgar's. Kitty misses her train and stays the night with Dick. The inevitable happens. 'How can we wait?' pleads Dick. 'I might be shot.' He promises her there is no chance of pregnancy – it never happens the first time.[76]

After the conflagration at Watson's, Theodore feels relief: he is no longer responsible for property and for making decisions. He puts on a smart suit and goes to a party in Bloomsbury, where he waits in vain for Hester Lomax to turn up. In the novel's last scene, we are back in Barlow on a Saturday afternoon, though now there are no papers to read – a national strike has paralysed the country – and Milly, the maid, has developed a new insolence. Theodore, looking at her, perceives that the familiar world crashing down around him prefaces what is to her the creation of something altogether new and good. The Frintons try to reimmerse themselves in trivia: the chimney that needs sweeping, and the dog's skin condition. Mrs Frinton tells a story about a girl in the village who has got herself pregnant. Kitty is upset. A letter arrives telling Theodore of Hester Lomax's death in the street fighting. It is then that he realizes he had loved Hester, that he should have been her lover, and that there is something despicable and claustrophobic about his cosy middle-class life. But this is the life he has to live.

Looking back on *London's Burning* thirty years later, Barbara saw it as a dated political tract, redeemed only by the chance it gave her to write about the East Anglian countryside she loved.[77] She did this very well. Take, for example, Theodore Frinton's drive through the villages on a lovely golden day: 'Ten, twenty, thirty, the familiar miles went by – past Buntingford where from week to week the hurdles of the cattle-market stood under the roadside trees; over the switchback stretch to Puckeridge, where in May the white hawthorn rose and fell with the dips of the road; across the Lea at Ware, where horse-drawn barges still floated along their painted ways; on and on, past meadow and ploughland, spreading, clean and spacious, under a generous sky'.[78] Buntingford is a real village, the site of many WEA Summer Schools Barbara attended. Theodore Frinton is, even, Barbara herself. He is a man after her own heart – a man with a classical education who riles against common misuse of the English language, a man who knows 'that the great thing to remember is that one must deal always with the obvious – or rather deal in terms of simple primary things'.[79]

Barbara admitted the affinity between herself and Theodore Frinton in a later correspondence with the writer and poet (and then part-time WEA tutor), Andy Croft. In 1981, Croft wrote to Barbara in connection with a study he was doing of British fiction in the 1930s. *London's Burning* was one of the most interesting novels he had read: why did she write it? Did she have any particular literary models in mind? Was Theodore intended as a satirical figure? How did the novel sell, and how was it reviewed?[80] By then, age had worn down Barbara's ability to engage in dialogues with strangers about the past, and her response was not sympathetic: 'Even if I had the time (which I haven't) I could not possibly answer all your questions ... because (as you may some day yourself discover) at the age of eighty-four one simply does not remember details of one's work and objectives forty-six years ago.' It did not help that Croft misspelt her name.[81] According to the writer Tony Gould, a friend of Barbara's, she wrote her novel 'just to see if she could do it'.[82] She did not answer Croft's question about reviews, but there were at least two – in *The Manchester Guardian* and *The Sydney Morning Herald*. The first gave a rather ambivalent appraisal. On the one hand, Mrs Wootton evidently has 'a graphic and incisive pen' and a shrewd eye for the idiosyncrasies of her characters, but only the 'futile flapper Kitty' and Dick, the 'ineffectual motor salesman', really come to life: unlike the curate's egg, Mrs. Wootton's novel is excellent in all its parts, but 'as a whole there is something unsatisfying about it'.[83] The Australian reviewer decided that *London's Burning* was a very readable novel: the author had wisely kept to material she could handle, and the result was a credible and logical narrative with a good level of human interest.[84] In the early 1980s Barbara raised the issue of republication with Croft, and also with Gould. Both Virago and Penguin were approached, but neither was interested. Inside Tony Gould's copy of *London's Burning*, is tucked a rejection letter addressed to him from Carmen Calil at the feminist publishing house Virago: 'Three of us have now read "London's Burning": I wish any of the three of us had liked it enough to want to publish it. Whilst we all found good things in it, we honestly do not see that it would be successfully re-published now .... Can you think of something tactful to say though to Baroness Wootton whom I much admire on every other front!'[85]

Croft's study was published in 1990: *Red Letter Days: British Fiction in the 1930s.*[86] Barbara was not aware at the time she wrote it that her novel belonged to a whole genre of politicized literary writing, a manifestation in art of the shift to the Left that was happening in politics during the Red Decade. Her novel's dystopian narrative, occupying 'a liminal space between history and fiction, between reformist ideology and revolutionary politics',[87] classifies it with some 300 novels published in the 1930s that were exemplars of the new socialist literary culture. Many of these were 'future-fictions' – imaginative speculations on the utopian or dystopian forms that might arise from the real chaos and disintegration of contemporary social conditions. During this period, the format of utopian fiction changes its colour, becoming not simply the depiction of societies outside history, but the creation of 'believable characters confronted with the problem of how to create and live in an often ironically "ideal" society while still retaining their humanity'.[88] The violent demonstrations described by Barbara in 1936 which confronted Theodore Frinton on the Hackney Marshes in 1940 were her future prophecy about the presence of fascism in Britain. Herein lies, however, one of the puzzles of the novel – perhaps a consequence of Barbara's immaturity as a fiction-writer: the claims she makes in her autobiography of *London's Burning*'s status as an anti-fascist novel hardly seem supported by the events with which Frinton has to deal. Rose Salmon and her colleagues are, surely, just aggrieved workers – well, not 'just', but certainly justifiably, given that many were about to be sacked. Benevolent capitalism creates a violence of its own.

But, if *London's Burning* is to be classed as an anti-fascist novel, it is in good company: Terence Greenidge's *Philip and the Dictator* (1938), Storm Jameson's *In the Second Year* (1936), Naomi Mitchison's *We Have Been Warned* (1935) and Montagu Slater's *Haunting Europe* (1934) are better known examples. Orwell's *Animal Farm* has come to be emblematic of the Red Decade's literary preoccupation with political futures, though it was not published in England until 1945 (publishers did not like its anti-Soviet stance). And when it comes to the business of people experimenting with 'fantastic' novels, Barbara was also in distinguished company: Fenner Brockway, Malcolm Muggeridge, Eric Linklater, C.S. Forester, Harold Nicolson, Herbert Read, C.P. Snow, Hilaire Belloc and Stephen King-Hall were all prominent public figures who wrote at least one futuristic novel. Even Beatrice Webb nearly managed it: in her thirties, the same age as Barbara was when she penned her fiction, Beatrice was overcome by what she called 'the vulgar wish to write a novel'. Perhaps Barbara Wootton would have echoed Beatrice Webb's words: 'There is intense attractiveness' she reflected, 'in the comparative ease of descriptive writing. Compare it with work in which movements of commodities, percentages, depreciations, averages and all the ugly horrors of commercial facts are in the dominant place.'[89] The novel Beatrice was contemplating was to be a utopian one, *Looking Forward*, but she was seduced by Sidney into writing *The History of Trade Unionism* instead. Five years later the utopian novel had been renamed *Sixty Years Hence*, but again Beatrice was deflected.[90]

The Red Decade was a time for women's literary voices to be heard, but, in much subsequent literary criticism and history, they come through weakly, if at all.[91] Katharine Burdekin's *Swastika Night*, which was published in 1937, was reissued in 1940 by the Left Book Club as one of its rare ventures into fiction. *Swastika Night* is a feminist dystopia set in Nazi Germany seven centuries forward in time; the descendants of Hitler's Nazis have taken over and women are reduced to their biological function. The novel prefigures many other more modern versions of this disturbing fate, for example, Margaret Atwood's, *The Handmaid's Tale* (1985), which takes as its context the totalitarian dictatorship of post-nuclear America. Burdekin shared Virginia Woolf's understanding of fascism and war as central discourses of masculinity. This was a perspective which Barbara Wootton never overtly entertained; nothing particularly dramatic related to their gender position (except perhaps the suicide in the short story 'So This is Adultery') happens to any of the female characters in her fiction. The representation of gender (like that of class) in *Twos and Threes* and *London's Burning* is conventional, even stereotypical: men are men and women are women, and the sense that this is why they have difficulty relating, and why femininity and masculinity may have different impacts on the social system, is never made explicit.

The crisis of European civilization, combined with the thirties' metaphor of the journey, also produced an immense growth in travel writing, much of which toyed with the Russian theme.[92] Of course, returning intellectuals accompanied their own serious reflections with entertaining side-notes about travelling. The journey, painstakingly and exotically described, spiced up the political text at a time when few people travelled beyond their own communities and countries. It was amusing to record what the roads were like, how the trains were prone to sudden derailing, and the reception given by local peasant women selling milk and eggs and apples and tomatoes at stations the trains passed through. Charlotte Haldane, the first British woman war correspondent to visit Russia, went on behalf of the *Daily Sketch* at a time when the War Office had a rule that no women were allowed at the front. She inveigled her way to the Red Army front and wrote a book about this and the lives of the Russian people at war with Germany: *Russian Newsreel* (1942).[93] The same year, scientist Marie Curie's daughter, Eve, a war correspondent for New York and London newspapers, charted a journey through the Near East and Russia to Asia and back to the USA. 'On the road to Volokolamsk I had seen girls in uniform sitting in the open, on gun carriers coming back from the front. I knew that there were still other women in Russia – famous ones – leading a real warrior's life, such as Major Valentine Grisodobova, a well-known flyer whose job it was to take bombers over the enemy lines, to wound and to kill Germans.' Stalin was calling these women 'Heroines of the Soviet Union'; the Germans called them 'Nachthexen' (night witches).[94]

'The confusion of thought over Russia arises from the fact that almost everything you read about it, both for and against, is true,' pronounced writer Ethel Mannin.[95] Certainly, the division of views about the Soviet experiment among British politicians and intellectuals on the Labour Left during the 1930s, the different conclusions they drew from the material available, including the evidence of their own eyes, had a paralytic effect. Its legacy was the lack of a single convincing political programme which could rescue Britain from the dismal excesses of the decade.[96] Confusion jostled with betrayal, a major theme of 1930s literature: the pain of betrayal, of broken promises and expectations, runs through narratives of both individuals and societies.[97] Although Barbara Wootton's view of Russia was appreciated as objective in a way that the Webbs' was not, the British fascination with Russia tended to be weighted on the side of fiction. Communism might be an ideology of equality, but, pulling the veil of fiction aside, Stalin was a dictator. Adherence to his Five-Year Plans caused multiple deprivations. Everyday life for the Soviet citizen was a matter of endemic police surveillance, webs of bureaucratic red tape, and endless queues. Moscow was the show city, but most Soviet towns lacked roads, public transport and sewerage, and public spaces were dangerous;[98] millions died during the Stalinist regime of famine, for counter-revolutionary offences, or through banishment to camps and forced expatriation.[99]

In the light of these contrasts between imagined utopias and real dystopias, Barbara Wootton should perhaps be commended for the 'counsels of restraint and moderation'[100] she offered in Plan or No Plan. In favour of central planning – no-one interested in the facts could not be – she found the notion of violent revolution repugnant on rational grounds. Violence bred more violence; the chances of failure were too high; and revolution involved a suspension of the normal framework of everyday life which would cause all aspects of the system to break down. In the end, the scientist in her won over the novelist and over the imaginer of possible futures. At the end of the penultimate chapter in Plan or No Plan, she speaks directly, and prophetically, given that her words were written five years before the second world war of the century started:

Neither do I offer apology for having sketched no Utopia, but merely indicated what appear to be the better among alternative possibilities of which none is perfect. For to do otherwise is to ignore both the plainest lessons of human history and the nature of human material. In neither is there ground to suppose that imperfect humanity will evolve perfect social and economic institutions. Yet even within the degrees of partial accomplishment that are open to us lie opportunities of choice, upon which possibilities of happiness or misery for nameless millions depend. We may already be set on courses which lead straight to disaster: disaster from which few perhaps will survive, and which will blot out, even for those few, all hope of the simple pleasures and interests which are the most satisfying substance of ordinary human lives. Such disaster is avoidable. Courses can be changed, and at human will. Because we cannot step straight into Utopia is no ground for despising the limited step, the partial reform, the measure which makes things not perfect, but better than they were before.[101]

8

George

Barbara Frances Wootton married George Percival Wright on 5 July 1935. If she stood beside him meekly in a white dress, as she had for Jack Wootton on that doomed September day in Cambridge eighteen years before, there is no record of it. George was her second marriage, and this marriage was different. Everything about it was different. Barbara was six years older than George, and they had been teacher and student. Her privileged background was matched by his disadvantaged one. Whereas Jack and she had met in the cloistered spaces of Cambridge, her courtship with George was conducted in the much freer and distinctly socialist arena of the adult education movement. When they married, Beatrice Webb wrote to congratulate Barbara on taking a partner in research (there was perhaps a little projection here), and to discuss the matter of a wedding gift. Beatrice used to give her nieces teasets, but apparently people no longer drank tea: 'they all drink cocktails, and I don't know how to give you a cocktail set, so I'll give you some money'. With the money Barbara bought a rug. But nobody, observed Barbara with respect to the 'partner in research' phrase, would have called George that.[1] Left-wing students at the LSE dispatched a wedding telegram commenting warmly on 'a union of theory and practice'.[2] What it was exactly a union of remains in large part a matter of conjecture. There are no private papers left which record the history of the relationship. George, an elusive character in his lifetime, has bequeathed few traces of either his public or private life. There are photographs in the archives: photographs of George smiling, of George smoking, of George reading, of George posturing on holiday beaches; photographs of convivial times with friends; but there are remarkably few photographs of George and Barbara together. Two that have survived portray a couple standing slightly apart on a Corsican beach, courtesy of Barbara's friend Vladimir Raitz, who founded the package holiday; George's lean muscular body is next to Barbara's somewhat more rounded one; the sea shows through the space between them, George's feet are rooted confrontationally in the sand, and on the back are inscribed the words 'an argument'. George scandalized their friends with this swimming costume which 'revealed rather more than it concealed to the point where people's eyebrows raised'.[3] In a more discrete view, the two of them stand side by side, shoulders touching, in a sunlit English garden. She wears the white dress and clutches a book. He, in rumpled shirt and shorts, faces the camera with a defiant manly look.

How did they meet? Who was George? Why did Barbara enter this unlikely union? There are differing accounts of their first meeting: at a Summer School in 1934;[4] at the WEA Centre in Fulham.[5] Throughout the period from the early 1920s to the late 1930s, Barbara maintained an active WEA connection: she was on the District Executive Committee of the London branch; she chaired the WEA Advisory Board responsible for appointing WEA tutors and also visited WEA classes on its behalf; from around 1930 she represented the London District on the Central Executive of the WEA and was a member of its Finance and General Purposes Committee;[6] as editor of the WEA journal *The Highway* for several years, she was responsible for overseeing the development of WEA policy.[7] In one of these WEA capacities, she might well have visited the WEA Centre in Fulham to which George Wright was attached and encountered him there. According to her autobiography, they first met properly at a Summer School somewhere in the English countryside in the late 1920s or early 1930s. 'I have many happy memories of these months in Herts or Hants or Sussex, with their blend of stimulating company and golden harvest fields,' she wrote. 'Students came and went, mostly staying one or two weeks at a time, and amongst those who came most regularly, stayed longest and was most popular was one of the name of George Wright. Blond and vivacious, with considerable histrionic gifts, and a marvellous repertoire of near-extinct Cockney songs, George was very attractive to the opposite sex, and more than one of his fellow students was disposed to fall in love with him. So was I.'[8] In the photographs of these Summer Schools, George looks rakish with his shorts and patterned jersey; Barbara has developed shorts herself, but she still looks bookish and composed. One of the many who wrote to her when the autobiography was published was Alec Linton, who had met George at a Summer School in Buntingford during the War (that very Buntingford the hero of Barbara's novel *London's Burning* passed through on his way to work). A photograph of George smoking and reading in a deckchair at Buntingford in 1942 has survived in the archives. 'I was so impressed with his friendly and kind attitude to everybody,' Alec Linton reported. 'One night at a dance I well remember pointing out to George that none of the students were asking the staff girls of the village to dance with them and as I am not a dancer, George went over to the girls and gave them a dance or two.'[9]

It was one of the most pleasurable of Barbara's obligations as Director of the University of London's Extra-Mural Department, to take charge during August of a residential programme of lectures and entertainment for adult students returning to education. This tradition of the Summer School had become an established part of the adult education movement by 1900; the first in London happened at Eton College in 1914, and was attended by a fishmonger, a needlewoman, two tailors, two joiners, and five clerks, among others.[10] In 1925 eight centres across England and Wales provided Summer Schools for 774 students, figures which had become twelve and 1,423 respectively by 1935.[11] Margaret Cole called Summer Schools 'that peculiarly Anglo-Saxon combination of holiday-making, sociability and more-or-less intellectual effort'.[12] Their ostensible purpose was to enable tutorial class students to carry their studies further than was possible under ordinary class conditions, 'and to meet and exchange ideas with their fellow students and tutors under delightful conditions'.[13] The emphasis on delight is evident in the brochures for the London Tutorial Class Summer Schools, which depict the various country houses where the Schools were held, and advertise the leisure opportunities available: the brochure for the 1934 School, for example, offers four tennis courts, a pool, a cricket pitch, a gym, rooms for 'socials and dancing', rambles and tournaments. The balance between fun and work was always a slight tension in the proceedings. Some students did treat Summer Schools as a cheap summer holiday, and it was certainly the case that many workers had to use their annual holiday to attend them, which was why the holiday aspect was deliberately made attractive, but, on the other hand, students' minds were there to be stretched. Some came for the full four weeks, others for three or two or one. The fees were a modest £2 and 5 shillings (in 1934), and many were paid by trade unions or the WEA. Students worked on their own in the mornings, saw their tutors three or four times a week, and attended lectures 'on topics of general interest'.[14] At the 1934 Summer School, the twenty lectures provided included Barbara Wootton on 'Social Class and Social Equality', 'The Place of Dogma in the Modern World', 'First Lessons from the Soviet Experiment' and 'A Bird's Eye View of Contemporary Economic Trends and Policies'. Other offerings were 'Is Town Life Fatal to Poetry?' (Miss H.M. Matthews), 'Red Vienna' (R.M.M. Stewart), 'Laughter' (Mrs E. Collie-Radford), and sociologist David Glass on 'The Development of Modern Japan' and 'The Future of the Town'. Special lectures were given by two visiting speakers: Dr Ulrich Mayer on 'Why Democracy in Germany has Failed' and Dr Nikolaus Pevsner on 'William Morris'. Mr J.R. Williams gave a piano recital.[15]

The practical arrangements for these annual events, for which Barbara was responsible, were extremely taxing. Visits of inspection had to be made to schools and other places, and there were doubts about the standard of accommodation, whether linen would be provided, or vegetarian meals served. They needed a big house, comfortably furnished, with grounds and leisure facilities. In 1931, she triumphed in finding Stratton Park, a splendid originally Elizabethan manor house with a 170-acre park and formally landscaped gardens. William Cobbett's *Rural Rides* called it a 'large and very beautiful estate' with a very fine oakwood.[16] The estate had passed from the dukes of Bedford through the Baring banking dynasty to a Miss James who ran it as a girls' school.[17] Stratton Park housed the annual University of London Tutorial Class Summer School for seven years. It sits on the front of the Summer School brochure as a large solid white house with an Italianate portico at the front, a backdrop of trees and manicured lawns. The place was so comfortable and the food so good that an HM Inspector suspected that the meal he ate there on his visit had been specially staged for his benefit.[18] Unfortunately, later the food deteriorated and Barbara was advised to hire a housekeeper and cook from the King's College of Household and Social Science.[19]

George Wright was one of fifty-four students who attended the 1934 Stratton Park Summer School. The romance between the thirty-seven-year-old tutorial class director and the dashing thirty-one-year-old student would undoubtedly have caused much non-intellectual gossip, but it was not their first meeting. George had taken part in the Stratton Park Summer School since 1931. We know this because he declared his allegiance to the place at a joint Tutorial Class and WEA Conference held in February 1935, a few months before he married Barbara. She was there at the same conference, giving a 'lantern lecture', and the topic of moving the Summer School from Stratton Park to a seaside resort, which some students favoured, was aired. George, representing the Fulham WEA branch at the Conference, expressed the view that it would be difficult, if not impossible, to find a more suitable place; he would like it to stay there.[20] Stratton Park occupied a special place in their relationship.

The name 'George Wright' first crops up in the Minutes of the Tutorial Classes Committee in 1933 when he is recorded as having been successful in obtaining one of the two adult scholarships awarded by the Council in that year.[21] The scholarship scheme started in 1932 with the purpose of allowing selected London Tutorial Class students to progress to further study, either full- or part-time, by taking a University of London Diploma. It was a way into a university course for people who had missed out on formal schooling. The procedure was for students to apply and be interviewed by Barbara, who made recommendations to the Tutorial Classes Committee, although the final decision about admission rested with the school or college concerned.[22] Thus, George would have had his suitability for further study scrutinized by Barbara in 1932, and he would have been an established Tutorial Class student by then, perhaps even taking one of her classes. In the 1929–30 session, she was teaching the 'History of Socialistic Thought' and 'Control of Industry', and in 1930–1 'Democracy in Politics and Industry', all in St Pancras; in 1931–2 her classes included 'British Social Policy and Finance' in Lambeth and 'Economics' in Harrow.[23] George and she had a spirited exchange about the working of the scholarship scheme at the February 1935 Conference, when George said he thought the one-year scholarship (which he had had) should be abolished in favour of the two-year one, and that arrangements should be made to ensure that students were found suitable positions at the end of their course. He was, perhaps, making a personal comment here. Barbara's riposte was to suggest that students could take evening courses, to which George replied that many working-class students finished work too late for this to be possible.[24] He did complete his own diploma, which was in Economics and Social Science at the LSE, a popular choice among scholarship students.

George Percival Wright was born in Fulham in 1903, to a long-established working-class family. His father, Thomas, was a journeyman baker. There were five sons: Thomas, Alfred, George, Frederick and Herbert, and one daughter, Winnie. All the sons, except Frederick, worked in the family taxi-cab firm. Frederick became a baker, like his father, and worked for J. Lyons at Cadby Hall, eventually being promoted to General Foreman of the Sponge Cake Department.[25] He met his wife Florence (Florrie) there, in the French pastry department; Florrie and Barbara got on well and stayed in touch for many years. In the 1901 Census, the Wright family is living in Tabor Road, Fulham, but George was born two streets away two years later in Southerton Road. By the next Census in 1911 the Wrights are three-quarters of a mile south in Prothero Road, a short street at an angle off Dawes Road, today an unprepossessing, traffic-dense route leading from Hammersmith to Fulham. They shared the Prothero Road house, from where they ran their taxi business, with another family; it must have been cramped in a two-storey house with no inside toilet. The whole of George's life was lived in this same square mile or so of south-west London, nestled in a loop of the Thames between Putney and Chelsea. By the time he was born, Fulham had lost its rural character; nearby Hammersmith Broadway had become a major transport hub, with the extension of the London Underground and connecting railways; and featureless streets of terraced houses provided cramped homes for large working-class families. Today the house in Southerton Street where George was born is run down, with rubbish and broken-into meters in the front, whereas the Tabor Road house is gentrified, with a smart red door and a blue pot of flowers on the window-sill.

George and his siblings went to local schools. Frederick, the baker, left school at fourteen, so George probably did as well. It seems that George got up to the usual sort of trouble for working-class boys; discussing her work as a magistrate on a television programme, 'The War Against Crime' in the 1960s, Barbara revealed that, at the age of nine or ten, he had been a juvenile delinquent.[26] Her comments provoked a headline in *The Daily Mirror*, 'When my husband was a delinquent, by Baroness'.[27] There were two things that marked George out from the rest of his family and his background: his physical appearance; and his drive to rise up in the world. George was 'a very good-looking chap'.[28] Everybody who met him noticed this, and it was a feature of which George himself was not unaware. Brenda Collison, George's niece, daughter of Frederick and Florrie, remembers: 'Uncle George always looked immaculate. He was casually dressed, but immaculate. He would remind me of somebody like Noel Coward. And he had these amazing bushy eyebrows. He reminded me of an actor. To me, he was glamorous.' To her, he was a star. As a child, she absolutely idolized this glamorous uncle, who was interested in her schooling and the psychology of her family, and who took her and her brother John for rides on their bikes in Richmond Park, after which the children would be bought lemonade while George had his half-pint in the pub. 'I remember Uncle George as being apart from the rest of us ... he was the only one in the family who bettered himself.'[29]

'Taxi-cab driver' was George's occupation on the marriage certificate, but at some point in his twenties he had discovered the WEA, and thereafter he had taken advantage of this route for bettering himself. The WEA was born the same year as George, in 1903; its founder, Albert Mansbridge, had a somewhat romantic vision of education (no educated man could do harm to his community, education was an instrument for social justice[30]), but Mansbridge's efforts did bring together the co-operative movement, the trade unions, and the patronage of universities such as Oxford in a genuine alliance of workers and intellectuals. This alliance had the solid underlying political purpose of educating those who would serve the growing Labour movement. Socialism and education went hand in hand. Any rational (educated) analysis of social and economic issues must surely yield the conclusion that capitalism is inefficient and unfair.[31] This diagnosis was immensely congenial to Barbara Wootton, whose own involvement in adult education was underpinned by a commitment to a moral need for equality. But there was, according to her, another fundamental concern here: the problem of modern industrial work, which is so unsatisfying that it cannot possibly form the basis of people's life interests. The job is just something to be done in order to live; living means a productive use of leisure time. Workers want education, but on their terms; most of them know incomparably more than they easily convey and most academics know incomparably less. It was a radical point of view which she was not afraid of declaring, including at a Conference of the Industrial Welfare Society in Oxford in 1927, before George entered her life.[32] He was not a writer or a public figure, so there was no danger of his upsetting audiences with such sentiments, but they must surely have endeared Barbara to him. When he died it was said of him at his memorial service that he had no patience with cant of any kind and would have sympathized with William Morris's testy remark: 'I don't need to read Karl Marx in order to know that this society has to be changed'.[33]

The reading of Karl Marx was something that happened in Barbara's tutorial classes, although the Tutorial Classes Committee kept a watchful eye on the line that tutors were taking; in 1936–7, she was instructed to enquire carefully into the precise scope of a proposed Westminster class on 'Marxism and Modern Thought'.[34] The topic of Marxism was a heated one for the adult education movement in Britain, some regarding its espousal as essential to working-class activism, and others seeing it as antipathetic to the important goal of integrating working-class students into a national culture.[35] This argument was part of a much wider one about how socialist the new Labour Party ought to, or could, be, in order to fit itself for effective long-running government.[36] Barbara herself was focused on the business of expecting conventional academic standards of people with little previous exposure to formal education, an expectation which her experience running tutorial classes was leading her increasingly to criticize. As she explained, in March 1935, to another Conference on the Teaching of Economics in Adult Classes, chaired by G.D.H. Cole, there were three issues: often working-class adult students had great difficulty producing written work; they had to be dissuaded from simply trotting out their own views; and academics had to lose a few of their own pretensions. 'We have no right to be teaching Economics to working-class people unless (1) the people who come to our classes get the sense that really valuable results can be got by the thinking process; and (2) the students also get the impression that unsolved problems remain of which *nobody* has got the whole solution yet'.[37] By the time she elaborated on this view in the journal *Adult Education* in 1937, she had made some 500 visits to different University of London tutorial classes, and had seen some 2,000 examples of written work. Her piece entitled 'A Plea for Constructive Teaching' took the side of the extra-mural students whose concern was to derive something useful from their exposure to academic education against the conventional Socratic tradition of the university – that very tradition her own parents had upheld which combined scepticism with contempt for applying knowledge to any practical uses. Was this not, she asked, and did students not perceive it as, a case of 'sheer intellectual immorality'? She suggested that all tutorial classes should operate with a kind of 'standing order' which would require them to end with the question: if I was the person who had to act in this matter, what is the best answer my knowledge and insight would suggest? It was in this sense that teaching ought always to be constructive.[38]

Albert Mansbridge feared a middle-class takeover of the WEA, and available statistics do suggest a decline in the proportion of students from working-class backgrounds after the 1930s. But when George Wright first became involved, around one in three WEA students were manual workers like himself.[39] When George went to the LSE in 1933, he still drove a taxi for a living. This gave the press much cause for celebration, as they spotted the headline-creating conjunction of well-known lady academic and unknown uneducated consort. *The Manchester Guardian* picked up the impending marriage in its 'Court and Personal' section on 26 March 1935: 'Mrs. Barbara Wootton, Director of Studies for Tutorial Classes at the University of London, is to marry Mr. George Wright, a Fulham taxi-cab driver'. Asked about his future plans, George said, "'I shall probably just carry on as I am for a while"'.[40] *The Daily Herald* tracked him down to the cabmen's shelter near Brompton Oratory, featuring the alliance on its front page: 'Economist to Wed Taxicab Driver'.[41] In *The Daily Mail* and *The Daily Mirror* Barbara was photographed wearing a curious little hat and looking definitely not amused next to the headlines 'Woman Finance Expert to Marry Taxi-Driver'[42] and 'Woman Chief of Varsity to Wed Taxi-man'.[43] The *Mirror* journalist patently had fun with George, whom he described as 'a good-looking fair-haired young man'. George told him that Mrs Wootton had been a great help to him in his studies 'clarifying many points which might otherwise have proved intricate'. By the time she met George, Barbara had a considerable public profile as an academic, a policy pundit and a broadcaster. She had two books published and a long list of articles. Women like her were rare at the time. 'Speak the name Barbara Wootton,' commented a journalist in 1967, 'and a good many people will say: "Isn't that the brilliant economist on 'The Brains Trust' who married a taxi-driver?"'[44] 'Don who married taxi driver'[45] became a legend whose power was only superseded by the even greater shock to class-ridden Britain of the first woman peer having such a personage as a husband. In 1958, the new Baroness Wootton was asked for a photo of herself and George standing 'beside his taxi' (the taxi that he had hardly been near except as a passenger for twenty years) outside the House of Lords.[46] Long after George's death, Barbara was haunted by the designation 'Cabbie's widow'.[47]

George Wright and Barbara Wootton decided to marry after the 1934 Summer School at Stratton Park. They spent a few days together at Mundesley on the East Norfolk coast playing tennis and bar billiards; the September sun shone for

them out of cloudless skies. Back in London, they tried to keep the engagement a
secret, but a well-meaning friend announced it at a students' social gathering, and
thereafter they were besieged by the press. Barbara stayed in her flat in Hampstead,
and George tried unsuccessfully to deflect the journalists by riding round London
on a bus, but he got caught when he went home in the evening to Fulham, despite
the strategy of entering through a neighbour's house and climbing over the garden
wall. At the height of the press interest, Barbara's mother, Adela, ate her lunch in
the market place in the centre of Cambridge to show her refusal to be affected by
this kind of prurient publicity.[48] One reviewer of Barbara's autobiography had a
particular reason for remembering the media attention attracted by the Wootton-
Wright marriage:

> The three of us emerged from a meeting in the City one evening and George said
> gaily to Mrs Wootton (who had her car) 'Are you going to give me a ride?'. Such
> a request had not occurred to me, but I quickly thought 'I've much more right to
> a lift than he has; I've known her longer, we have worked in the same office, and,
> moreover, she will be practically passing my door'. Mrs Wootton unhesitatingly
> invited me to get in beside her, and George sat behind us, leaning forward and
> spreading his arms over our shoulders. Only a short time after this incident I heard
> (indeed, the world heard) that they had married each other. The shock of this
> unsuspected news, plus the embarrassing realisation that I had unwittingly 'played
> gooseberry', embedded the incident in my memory for all time.[49]

They did, however, manage to keep the date of the wedding secret. It took place
in the registry office in Fulham with Barbara's brother Neil and Leo Simeon as
witnesses, and afterwards Barbara and George lunched in the restaurant attached
to the London County Council school for cooks and waiters, where you could get
an excellent lunch for 2s 6d, 'prepared by chefs of the future and served by young
waiters under training'.[50] Then they played a game of tennis on the municipal courts
in Fulham. Barbara secured a sabbatical from her University of London Summer
School obligations, and they treated themselves to a honeymoon in Barbara's
favourite Norway, in Ulvik on the spectacular Hardanger fjord. Unhappily, after a
week George fell ill and Barbara was convinced he had diphtheria and would die
and disappear from her life, just as Jack Wootton had done.[51] But George recovered
and they returned from Norway to a flat Barbara had found for them in Fulham.
It was on the top floor of a block in a garden where tenants were allowed their
own plots to cultivate, thereby saving the landlords the cost of upkeep. Number
eighty-four Napier Court, though technically in Fulham, was in a smart area
close to the river with trees and greenery and landscaped gardens. Close by was a

private members' club, with a Georgian clubhouse and forty-two acres of grounds, where the English upper-middle classes played croquet and sipped gin and tonic. A public park backing onto this provided tennis courts and a pleasant open space. Solid red-brick mansion blocks sat comfortably between the road and the river, where today the Thames cycle path will take you to Kingston in one direction and Hammersmith in the other. Within earshot of the flat, trains rumble over the embankment to Putney Bridge Station, but the aeroplanes on their low flight paths to and from Heathrow would have been absent in George and Barbara's day. A concrete 1960s block now stands in place of the original Napier Court. Their flat, on the top floor, had a balcony, and a view of open green space, so important to Barbara, and when they took it they were unaware that in a few years' time living in a top-floor flat in London would be a risky enterprise; in the event, and much to their surprise, the flat was not bombed. The first record of Barbara living in Napier Court is with Leo Simeon,[52] so some delicate relationship-manoeuvring may have needed to be done; intriguingly, the second woman Barbara would live with, after her years with George were over, later also moved to Napier Court.

After their marriage, and perhaps helped by it, George reduced the time he devoted to the taxi business and increased his activities in adult education and in Labour politics. It was probably through the local Labour Party in Fulham that he met Morgan Phillips, who in 1944 began a seventeen-year stint as National Secretary of the Labour Party. Morgan Phillips and George became close friends. Like George, Phillips had a working-class background – he was the son of a Welsh coal-miner, and had started out working in the pits himself. His route to prominence in the Labour Party was accomplished through trade unionism, work as an agent for the West Fulham Labour Party and the post of Propaganda Officer at Transport House.[53] However, George's friendship with Phillips did not guarantee professional support; years later, on at least one occasion, Phillips was overtly critical of George's work as Education Officer at Transport House. (George had silly ideas about training and used unnecessary words to express them.)[54] It is rumoured that George supported Phillips' work for the Labour movement by reverting to his original occupation and driving him around.[55]

Another of George's socialist alignments was with a fictional character called Henry Dubb. George penned a regular column 'full of warm beer and arguments in public bars' under the title 'Adventures of Henry Dubb' in a new Socialist weekly called *Forward*.[56] Henry Dubb is the iconic class-unconscious proletarian, the 'good, working man' of the capitalist imagination. He is the working man who does not see the corrupt social system behind the manifold capitalist illusions of his everyday life, and whose resilient lack of awareness lands him in all sorts of scrapes which are excuses for the more correctly politicized to make fun of him.[57] Henry Dubb was created by the American cartoonist Ryan Walker. During the 1920s especially, the class politics of laughter generated by radical cartoonists such as Walker had a didactic as well as an entertaining function: Henry Dubb and his like were active forces in spreading socialist ideologies and goals.[58] *Forward* had reprinted the first Henry Dubb cartoon series, but the character also turned up in other newspapers, such as *The Daily Herald*. In the reincarnation penned by George Wright, the by-line was 'the life and times of an ordinary bloke', and Henry Dubb appeared as a rather dour manual worker with a penchant for the ladies and propping up the bar in his local, The Queen's Legs. There were columns about the Annual General Meeting of the Floodtyde Labour Party, getting 'the NHS into focus' (Henry visits 'Pupils, the Opticians') and a catchy account of a local by-election: Henry drove a van around with a loudspeaker operated by a Lady DeNaquer, who was 'easy on the eyes ... and a Fabian'.[59] Henry Dubb meant different things to different people. R.H. Tawney, staunch supporter of the WEA, defined him in a footnote to an essay on 'Christianity and the Social Revolution', published in 1935: 'H.D.: the civilian equivalent of P.B.I. or poor bloody infantry, i.e. the common, courageous, good-hearted, patient, proletarian fool, whose epic is contained in the well-known lines, "We go to work to earn cash to buy the bread to get the strength to go to work to earn the cash," etc ... I seem to remember,' goes on Tawney, 'an occasion on which a telegram addressed to Henry Dubb, Labour Party Conference, was duly delivered at the correct sea-side resort. The statement that, on the chairman inviting the addressee to claim it, four-fifths of the comrades sprang to their feet, is, however an exaggeration.'[60]

Forward was originally a Scottish publication, the voice of the Glasgow Independent Labour Party. It was converted into an English national weekly by a group around the journalist and newspaper editor Francis Williams (later to be a colleague of Barbara's on the Board of the BBC and in the House of Lords). The move to bring *Forward* down south was galvanized by the need for a strategy to influence developments in Labour politics, and specifically to address the problem of false consciousness among the working classes. Persuading the working man and his wife (Henry Dubb's was called Henrietta) to support socialism was critical in these years when the Labour Party was still in its infancy as the main political alternative to Conservative Government. Francis Williams edited *Forward* and its assistant editor was John Harris (later Lord Harris of Greenwich) who became Hugh Gaitskell's personal assistant; the paper and its contributors were agents in an internal Labour Party fight between the Gaitskellites who wanted to 'modernize' the constitution by making it less socialist and the 'Bevanites' who were determined to keep it that way.[61]

George Wright's escape from taxi-driving was furthered when he became active in local government. He was a member of the London County Council (LCC), representing Islington in north London from 1946 to 1952, and thereafter an Alderman.[62] The creation of the LCC in 1889 marked the birth of the idea of London as one great city, and provided an outlet for the energies of 'public-minded men and women' like George who wanted to do something practical to improve living conditions and opportunities in their local areas.[63] The year before George and Barbara got married saw the first Labour-controlled LCC, with a strong Fabian component, including Sidney Webb; most appropriately, in the summer of their marriage, the LCC took a national lead in removing the so-called 'marriage bar' – the provision whereby professional women were compelled to resign their posts on marriage. At its inception, the LCC consisted of 118 Councillors, elected for three years, and nineteen Aldermen selected by the Councillors and serving for six years; the numbers varied according to a formula which took account of the number of London MPs. In the early decades, governing London was arduous work – on average, Councillors needed to commit four days a week; those who were also Committee Chairs even longer.[64] It seems unlikely that George was as devoted as this, but in the 1940s he did perform various roles for the LCC: Vice-Chairman of the Parks Committee, 1947–8; Chairman of the Restaurants and Catering Committee, 1948–50; and LCC representative on the Joint Committee of Governors of the Bethlem and Maudsley Hospitals, 1948–51.[65] According to Barbara, his political ambitions went beyond local politics, and several times he attempted to get a parliamentary seat, but was never adopted.[66] In the early 1950s, he took a paid job for the Labour Party at Transport House as Education Officer. He was made redundant from the Transport House job in 1961, 'an action which evoked protests from many members', according to George's obituary in The Sunday Telegraph.[67] But whatever George did in these various capacities never attracted public attention the way his wife's activities did. As comments after he died phrased it, 'George was not a leader and never thought of himself as a leader';[68] his main interests remained in local government affairs, and what he enjoyed most of all was lively talk with others who shared his passion for Labour causes.[69]

It is a heartening memento to George's role in her life that Barbara declared, when interviewed at the age of eighty-one by a local newspaper journalist, that of all her years the happiest were the first five of this second marriage.[70] From their base in Napier Court, Barbara and George fitted in a lot of travelling before the outbreak of the Second World War. They sailed three times to New York: the first time in July 1936, they went for two months on the splendidly new Queen Mary; this was their first voyage on that ship, a voyage which had been misremembered by

Barbara in her autobiography as having taken place six years earlier. The passenger lists record their personal details: 'five foot nine inches, of fair complexion, fair hair with grey eyes' (him); 'five foot seven inches, of fair complexion, brown hair with blue eyes' (her).[71] They went to the USA again in 1937 and in 1938 on the *Transylvania*. These journeys enabled them to enjoy holidays in California and Mexico, among other places, although the ostensible purpose was always Barbara's work. In 1936 she attended a conference in Virginia on 'War Debts and the Future of the League of Nations',[72] and she was a Chatham House delegate at another conference of the Institute of Pacific Relations in Yosemite National Park in California.[73] The Tutorial Classes Committee had to be consulted about these invitations, because they would mean her missing the annual Summer School; Barbara put her case most persuasively (and successfully), citing the useful contacts she would make and the fact that she would be bound to learn much of value to her tutorial class work.[74] It helped that the previous year she had instituted a system whereby she and her two staff tutors had leave of absence from Summer School duties one year in six. But the 1936 absence came on top of her first year off, the summer of her marriage to George; interestingly, the private reason for absence, the conjoining of the Director of Tutorial Classes with a Tutorial Class student, does not feature at all in the official Minutes.

In Barbara's memory of the 1930s, there is the extra-mural work, the continuation of a long list of government committees – adult education, workmen's compensation – and this 'rather absorbing personal life'. It occupied a lot of time, she told an interviewer in 1971. 'Private affairs don't do much good to public affairs'.[75] Her and George's escapades generated several amusing stories, which were repeated by Barbara on many occasions subsequently. On one of their arrivals in New York, George was examined for venereal disease and Barbara for head lice: 'The odd thing was that it apparently never occurred to anybody that the risks might have been reversed'.[76] The travel to Mexico was financed from the proceeds of a lecturing trip, and thereby hangs another tale, again retold by Barbara several times, including when she spoke in 1962 at the Golden Jubilee dinner of the Cambridge branch of the National Council of Women. Having recited a number of the disadvantages that still accrue to being a woman, Barbara noted that it occasionally works to one's advantage:

I recall one occasion when I was fortunate enough to give some rather well paid lectures in the United States, and my husband came with me, and went on the razzle, and when we had finished, we went, as you always have to do, to get an income tax clearance. And we sat down side by side, and all the conversation was naturally addressed to the man of the party. They looked at his papers and said, 'Oh, you've been here on vacation?' 'Yes', says George. 'Have you had a good time?' 'Yes', says George, with mounting enthusiasm. 'Don't suppose you've earned any money?' 'No,' says George, with absolute truth. I thought, I don't expect to be spoken to but if they would just say, 'Did your wife earn any money?' I will own up, but, if I am the furniture, the furniture I will be. This is thirty years ago, and in my house to this day there is what in those days was considered an outsize refrigerator, which I bought, I am delighted to say, with the money which is entirely owing to the Bureau of the Internal Revenue of the United States of America. And it is still going – and to complete the story, the lectures which provided this were in honour of Anna Howard Shaw, a very well known American feminist – so the whole thing matches very well.[77]

Her American lectures on social and economic conditions in England were spread out over five weeks – a not inconsiderable assignment that probably did justify a refrigerator – and again she had to get official permission from her employers at the University of London, a complicated business that involved the recalculation of the entire annual leave system, as well as consent for her to receive payment from the American University (the $2,000 that paid for the prized refrigerator).[78]

The conventional stereotypes of the Revenue authorities reversed their actual roles: Barbara was the main breadwinner, George the person whose less remunerative occupation varied according to circumstances. When they went to New York in 1936, he gave his occupation as 'teacher'; in 1937 as 'taxi driver'.[79] Convention would have dictated that Barbara should have taken the surname 'Wright' after her marriage to George, and it seems that she did have a passport in that name.[80] In the 1938 transatlantic passenger lists she appears as 'Barbara Frances-wright', but on the *Queen Mary* list in 1936 she reinvokes her maiden name and becomes 'Barbara Frances-Wright Adam'.[81] One imagines the two of them having fun with names. She must, at any rate, have made it clear to George that she was not going to change her name. By the time of their marriage, 'Wootton' had been her surname for nearly half her life; it was the name she worked and wrote under and was known by, and her irremediable loyalty to Jack outweighed any displeasure she might cause George by continuing to use it. Actually, all the evidence points to George being extremely proud of Barbara. He enjoyed rather than envied her achievements. He greeted her successes with generosity and genuine pleasure, and he was particularly pleased to become 'the first male peeress in the world'.[82] He would neither have been surprised nor displeased by the headlines of his obituary notices: 'Lady Wootton's husband dies';[83] 'Baroness Wootton's husband dies';[84] 'Life peeress's husband dies'.[85]

At thirty-eight when she married George, Barbara could still have had children. It seems that she wanted to, but that George was reluctant to be tied down.

He 'set his face resolutely against' their having a child, and Barbara was forced to accept that 'the price of insistence would be too high'.[86] She told a friend in later years that she did not think George was responsible enough to be a father.[87] It would have generated great stress; her being the main breadwinner was another problem. There is some mystery about the cost of Barbara's insistence, however. According to the politician Frank Field, in a piece he wrote for *The Independent*, Barbara had a termination at some point in her relationship with George.[88] The publication of this claim (along with other remarks Frank made about Barbara's socialism and her yellow hair) angered some of those closest to Barbara, most notably her long-term friend and colleague, Vera Seal, politician Lena Jeger, and O.R. McGregor, another close academic colleague and friend.[89] These allegations and counter-allegations are part of a general mystery about Barbara's reproductive history. Both Vera in a letter (never published) to *The Independent Magazine* in 1988,[90] and McGregor in the Preface he wrote in 1992 to a posthumous collection of Barbara's writings, referred to 'the lifelong sadness' of the early miscarriage she had after marrying Jack: 'Throughout her life this loss remained her keenest bitterness'.[91] What is clear is that Barbara did not have children, with or without George, and that she regretted this.

Children would have complicated things, since this second marriage, though possessed of real strengths, also had a seam of weakness running through it. What had attracted Barbara to George also attracted other women. Women fell for his face, his body, his conversation, his conviviality, his humour, his generosity; and he fell for them, one after another. George liked women, and they liked him. When he lectured to thirty-five of them at a Regional Women's Summer School for the East Midlands Labour Party in 1953, many wrote to say how much they had appreciated 'the vigorous discussion that George had stimulated'; the influence he had wielded would cover a wide area.[92] But when he was not thus engaged in (intellectually) stimulating women, much of the time, with Barbara busy at her job, and writing, and her committee work, and then away lecturing herself, he was lonely. His old haunts and the Wright family home in Fulham were only a mile or so away, so it was natural to go back, and reinstate himself in the pub with his brothers and old and new friends, drinking warm beer, maybe under the guise of collecting material for Henry Dubb's latest exploits. In her autobiography, Barbara is up front and civilized about the problem of George's infidelities: 'From the earliest days of our marriage he had always found it necessary to have what I can only call a secondary wife round the corner. These relationships were not in any way casual affairs. All these secondary wives – at least all whom I knew – were unmarried, intelligent, sensible girls, nice-looking without being devastatingly glamorous.'[93] George's reluctance to break up his home with Barbara on their account was well understood by his family. His niece Brenda recalls her mother, Florrie's, intervention on one occasion: 'My mother knew. I remember her saying to somebody, she told me, "I said to this lady 'He's never going to leave Barbara, he will never leave Barbara, he thinks the world of her, so you're wasting your life. You should go off and make your own.'" And she did.' After the Second World War, in the late 1940s and early 1950s, the Wrights used to have holidays on the south coast with Florrie's two brothers, who ran a couple of little guest houses by the sea. One of the brothers had a very attractive young wife 'and I can remember being down there, we were all down there together, and I used to watch these two, if we went out anywhere these two would always be in a corner talking... what's going on over there? "You know what your Uncle George is." He just loved the ladies. And it would take some special sort of woman to tolerate that.'[94]

Barbara, of course, *was* a special sort of woman, and as a social scientist she read this situation as a perfectly acceptable custom entrenched in many areas of the world – polygamy.[95] As it was acceptable there, so she decided to regard it as perfectly acceptable to her in Fulham. After all, she was in the limelight and George was not, and she was very busy and George was not quite so busy, and so he had every reason for finding a way to amuse himself. She was even quite friendly with several of the secondary wives. More of a problem was the social disapproval occasioned by George's behaviour. A society which called itself monogamous could be deeply censorious of those who were not, especially perhaps when the alternative that had been established was some kind of *modus vivendi* which worked, at least on some level. There was, after all, nothing sacred about the monogamous family, nothing intrinsically wonderful about it. Barbara did not adore the family or consider family life a life of bliss, as she confided to the audience for a Channel 4 'Face the Press' programme many years later.[96] What one had to contend with was a façade of glorification: 'This contemporary idealization of the monogamous family is itself a remarkable social phenomenon,' she wrote when she and George divided their domestic lives in 1955, noting that the statistics now showed that marriage had become a feeble obstacle to both pre- and extra-marital intercourse.[97] George and she were merely part of a trend.

As the years passed in Napier Court, traditional arguments about how a household should be run surfaced and added a further complication to the structural weaknesses of their marriage. The only rational conclusion was that Barbara should leave George's domestic life and become a secondary wife herself. Her flight from Napier Court to Abinger in Surrey, the subject of a later chapter, came after twenty-one years of marriage, took several years to accomplish, and

Barbara Wootton's parents,
Adela Kensington and James Adam

Elizabeth Haynes, 'The Pie', Barbara's nanny

Barbara as a child, c. 1900

Barbara as a child, c. 1903

Barbara Adam, c.1916

Her brothers, Arthur Innes Adam
and Neil Kensington Adam

John Wesley ('Jack') Wootton

The wedding of Barbara Adam
and John Wesley Wootton,
5 September 1917

Barbara Wootton, c. 1924

Barbara's room in Girton College, Cambridge
(painted by Helen Maud Cam in the early 1920s)

Russia, 1932: photographs from Barbara Wootton's journey
(BW in bottom photograph near the top, right of the centre, wearing glasses)

George Percival Wright, mid-1940s

George Wright and Barbara Wootton, c. 1937

A Summer School gathering, early 1930s

George Wright and Barbara Wootton, early 1950s, in Calvi, Corsica ('An Argument')

caused much unhappiness. When Barbara was asked, at the age of eighty, to explain her relationship with George, this is what she said:

> He was one of my students, and a very unusual character. He had great social gifts and considerable intellectual powers. But, when he was born, the good fairies did not give him just that little bit of extra self-discipline that would have made him go a long way. There was a very strong, indestructible bond between him and myself. As for the taxi-driver/lecturer business, George was described after his death, by one of his best friends, as behaving as though the classless society already existed. So he did. I would say more than that. When he did so, other people responded accordingly.[98]

When Barbara moved out of Napier Court in the mid-1950s, George returned to the Wright family haunts in Fulham. His younger brother Herbert, who looked after the maintenance of the taxis, had a flat above a shop opposite the garage in Bishops Road, and George went to live there, running a little secretarial business. Soon he was joined by a woman called Joan. The secretarial business was his downfall – or at least the ostensible reason for his being sacked by Transport House. 'The Private Enterprise of Lady Wootton's Husband', read *The Daily Mail* headline in January 1961, reproducing the myth that the baroness who married the taxi-driver was still with him. George complained that Transport House had not given him enough work to do, so he had quietly set up a new occupation on the side, and Transport House complained about the new occupation, especially when George circulated them and other Labour organizations with promotional material offering shorthand, typing and duplicating services.[99] According to niece Brenda, George and his friends were all heavy smokers and drinkers – down the pub a couple of nights a week and on both weekend days. 'I know there was one occasion when he'd been out for a night, he had a lovely bicycle, a Raleigh bicycle, and he was riding home on his bicycle and he said, "I was riding along and this lamp-post jumped out and hit me in the face".'[100] In these post-Napier Court years, George seems to have somewhat gone to pieces. Nellie McGregor, the wife of O.R. McGregor, remembers visiting the 'shoddy' flat in Fulham in the late 1950s or early 1960s: 'Terrible place to go to, because George really was a drinker, and he was making his own home brews and you went into this flat, and the corridor where you went in just had rows and rows of buckets with fermenting stuff in'.[101] His family could not understand why he had behaved so badly that Barbara chose to leave him. As Brenda Collison put it, 'This is the selfishness of men, isn't it? I mean he knew that she knew and he wouldn't stop ... Uncle George, I feel, didn't value what he had ... I think he was a very sad man. I think he knew that he'd played it wrong.'[102]

After they stopped living together, Barbara continued to support George financially – including backing his secretarial business – and her extreme loyalty to George impressed her friends.[103] She was reluctant to admit their separation publicly. As late as 1961, six years after the break, in a resumé for a visit to Australia, she presented the marriage as an ongoing affair.[104] Barbara's old nanny, The Pie, went on knitting socks for George, and asking Barbara to bring more wool, long after the separation, and it looks from the correspondence as though no-one was actually ever brave enough to tell The Pie that Barbara's husband had not left Napier Court with her to live in the country. George and Barbara never divorced. It seems that neither wanted to. Whether it was a successful marriage or not depends on your definition of both 'success' and 'marriage'. As Terry Morris, writer of Barbara's obituary in *The British Journal of Sociology*, aptly observed, it is difficult to judge success 'when so much about the institution of marriage is cloaked in half-blind denials of realities'.[105] George and Barbara were certainly not blind to any of the realities of their marriage. They never denied their deep-rooted commitment to one another, and, in their indestructible bond of friendship (itself no mean feat), they shared a vision of a just society in which those differences between them on which others so repetitively commented would neither matter nor exist.

9

Planning for Peace

The crises of the 1930s produced two great debates: one about the role of centralized planning in mitigating the miseries of capitalism, and the other about how to avoid war. The thought and political activity that went into these debates laid the foundations for the post-war welfare state in Britain and also for the wider European Community. Barbara Wootton was a leading figure in both these arenas. Of all her public activities, these in the 1930s are probably the least well known. The links between her work for world peace and for a planned socialist economy and society have mostly escaped comment. Yet, for her, they were aspects of the same vision. How could you have justice and liberty without freedom from violence; what did democracy mean if the elected governors did not protect the vulnerable, and promote equal rights to life's necessities and opportunities; and how could these goals be achieved other than by organized planning which transcended the narrow limits of nationalistic sentiment?

'What is wrong at the moment, I believe,' she wrote in 1939, 'is that some of our established institutions no longer fit the realities and the wishes of our time.' The two key institutions were those of the nation-state and of war. International politics was 'a monstrous chess game of "national interests"'; between the nation-state and war there was a 'devilish interaction', so that killing people and being killed to defend national sovereignty had become a mindless reflex.[1] Since capitalist nations seemed especially prone to the disease of war, one could even argue that capitalism and war were directly related, although Barbara herself would not say this. Instead she pointed out that, as there had been wars long before capitalism, the main cause of war must lie in the absence of any kind of effective international machinery to prevent it.[2]

The Federal Union was born in Bloomsbury, in an office at 44 Gordon Square, on 14 September 1938, around a barrel of beer. Its midwives were three young men – Charles Kimber, Patrick Ransome and Derek Rawnsley. Kimber and Rawnsley had been at Eton and Oxford together, and both worked in the public relations department of the oil company Shell, although Rawnsley, a perpetually restless character, had left in order to set up his own business, School Prints Ltd, supplying art reproductions to schools. Before that, he had made history by flying solo in a Tiger Moth from Australia to Oxford.[3] Charles Kimber was equally known for his eccentricity; at various stages in his life, he ran a market garden in Devon and a pub in Oxfordshire, and enjoyed an adulterous union with a writer with whom he lived in a covered lifeboat in Port Meadow, Oxford.[4] When Prime Minister Chamberlain returned from Munich in September 1938, declaring to cheering crowds at Croydon Airport that he had averted war, Kimber, sharing the depression of many at this strategy of appeasement, joined Rawnsley in Gordon Square to set up a new organization campaigning for a federation of nations committed to world peace. The term 'federation' was introduced to them by their friend, Patrick Ransome, a journalist with a degree in international law. Barbara remembers the 'oddly assorted trio' in her autobiography: 'Patrick Ransome, a life-long cripple, unable to move from his wheelchair .... the most intellectually sophisticated ... Derek Rawnsley ... the wildest of the three ... and both were quite unlike the gentle, idealistic, incurably amateurish and entirely lovable, Charles Kimber'.[5] The three men drafted a pamphlet entitled *Federal Union* and sent it to their friends, some sixty or seventy of whom endorsed its aims, and who put up money to have it printed and distributed. Kimber searched through *Who's Who,* identifying four hundred public figures with an interest in international affairs; the pamphlet and a handwritten letter were then posted to each of these (with the local post office protesting at the consequent burden on its services). The response to the mailout was 'astonishing'.[6] At a meeting in Gordon Square in April 1939, a panel of advisers was recruited: Lionel Curtis, founder of Chatham House (the Royal Institute of International Affairs); Kingsley Martin, editor of the *New Statesman*; politician and diplomat and guilty drafter of the failed Versailles Treaty, Lord Lothian; Wickham Steed, ex-editor of *The Times*; and Barbara Wootton.

Barbara probably came to Kimber's attention because she was Secretary to an outfit called 'Study Groups on Reconstruction' at Chatham House. This elitist organization, which occupied an elegant privately donated house in St James's Square, had been set up by Lionel Curtis in 1920 'to collect, examine, and distribute information on imperial and foreign, political, economic and social problems'.[7] It was an attempt to translate the old-fashioned imperialism of Dominion into a new doctrine of internationalism, with the British Commonwealth of nations as an exemplar of international co-operation. Barbara was the TUC representative on the Chatham House Council in 1940–1. In her experience, the place resembled 'a miniature Foreign Office', and so was not much to her taste. When the bombing of London started, she was put on firewatching duties there; staff were instructed that *for this purpose* the bosses and the porters and the women who did most of the work in between were to regard themselves as equals, an instruction she found to be an apt comment on the normal pattern of hierarchy.[8] The Australian economic historian Keith Hancock, an expert on the British Commonwealth, was also involved with Chatham House, and he replied to Kimber's letter as an emissary of a group there interested in federalist ideas. Hancock's own peroration on the political troubles of the time, *Argument of Empire* (1943), must have pleased Barbara, with its focus on the three targets of welfare, freedom and peace.

The Federal Union's new panel of advisers wrote to friends and sympathizers for signatories to a statement about the urgent need to replace national sovereignty with an alternative ideology. Among the thirty-five they recruited were many divergent stars: the Archbishop of York, the Bishop of Chichester, Lord Astor, Lancelot Hogben, Julian Huxley, Storm Jameson, Ramsay Muir, Sir John Orr, J.B. Priestley, Lady Rhondda, Seebohm Rowntree, Arnold Toynbee, and Ralph Vaughan Williams. The statement of aims they signed subscribed to a belief in 'a Federal Union of free peoples under a common government elected by and responsible to the people for their common affairs ... as a first step towards democratic self-government for the prevention of war, the creation of prosperity and the preservation and promotion of individual liberty'.[9] Barbara Wootton's contribution to Federal Union was significant from the start.[10] At the outbreak of War in September 1939, she was one of those elected to form a Council which would determine the policy of the Federal Union during the conflict. The Council decided to use any appropriate means to work towards 'securing the inclusion in statements of war aims or peace proposals of an announcement of readiness' on the part of any country to embrace the motives and strategies of federal union;[11] it also launched a mass membership campaign. By June 1940, membership of the Federal Union had reached 12,000 and there were 253 local branches organizing meetings; an international committee had been formed with contacts in Belgium, France, the Netherlands and Switzerland.[12] The movement was supported by leading newspapers – *The Times, The Guardian,* the *New Statesman* and *Time and Tide* (of which Lady Rhondda was the editor). The idea of federalism – for Europe or a wider international geography – gained currency in the early months of the War, as many people understood that Britain was no longer a fortress, but a vulnerable, inadequately defended island off the landmass of Europe. The seriously contemplated possibility of invasion was met with equally serious plans: for example, the diplomat and politician, Harold Nicolson, and his wife, Vita Sackville-West, were not alone in persuading a friendly doctor to give them a poison pill with which they would be able to escape potential torture and humiliation.[13]

The headmaster of Dartington Hall School, W.B. Curry, was a passionate early proponent of Federal Union. A lifelong pacifist, he was a believer in progressive education as a necessary step to a saner human society. Barbara's friendship with him was one of the 'most treasured incidental consequences' of the considerable time and energy she devoted to the Federal Union movement during these years.[14] Curry wrote *The Case for Federal Union*, which was published as a Penguin Special in December 1939, and sold more than 100,000 copies in six months.[15] He invited Barbara down to Dartington Hall in April 1940 to give a talk. 'What am I to do?' she responded. 'I have a firm rule that I will not speak on anything for anybody outside London.'[16] She was just too busy with the Federal Union work and trying to maintain tutorial classes in the exigencies of wartime conditions. In this, her main daytime job – though it also occupied many of her evenings – her activities included promoting a 'tutorial version of history' which emphasized the increasingly deleterious effects of capitalism on the working classes, an approach rapidly spreading to adult education classes throughout the country.[17] She was involved in other initiatives whose aim was the use of education as a political tool for spreading liberal-democratic values. The Association for Education in Citizenship was formed in 1934, with the industrialist and politician, Ernest Simon, and social reformer Eva Hubback as its leading lights, and Barbara Wootton as a member of its Council. Its rationale was the promotion of direct citizenship education in schools to counter the threat of totalitarianism.[18] Nonetheless, Barbara did accede to Curry's invitation, and the audience at Dartington Hall was treated to a version of the tract about socialism and federation she was preparing for the Federal Union.

People in power were uncomfortable about these goings-on. A question was asked in the House of Commons about whether Barbara Wootton as a member of the Council of Federal Union was actually being paid by His Majesty's Government for her work as economic adviser to the Chatham House Reconstruction Committee; she was not.[19] Curry's Penguin Special was regarded in certain circles as so scurrilous that another parliamentary question was raised about its bad effect on public morale, in view of which it should quite possibly be suppressed.[20] His book was addressed 'not to politicians or learned professors of political science' but to 'John Citizen (or Fritz, or Alphonse – it doesn't really matter)'. Curry's was an impassioned attack on the evils of national sentiment as a method for protecting individual freedom. This freedom, he argued, must be 'a very queer thing. It compels us to do without things we want in order to spend vast sums on armaments that we don't want. It causes us to throttle each other's trade and to impede each other's travel. From time to time it causes us all to be conscripted and thus lose our freedom altogether. Finally it gives rise to periodic outbreaks of mass mutual homicide during which millions lose not merely their freedom but their lives.'[21] The practical proposals for reducing nationalism through federation included at the end of Curry's book were taken from another bestseller, American journalist Charles Streit's *Union Now*. Streit used the model of the United States of America to propose a similar arrangement for fourteen countries: Australia, Belgium, Canada, Denmark, Finland, France, Ireland, the Netherlands, New Zealand, Norway, South Africa, Sweden, Switzerland and the UK. These countries, along with USA, were, he argued, the 'founder democracies' and culturally interconnected; they governed nearly half mankind; conducted two-thirds of world trade; and owned nearly all the world's gold and banked wealth. Such a federation, though limited, would do as a beginning of a 'Great Republic' which would eventually spread round the earth, so that everyone would be 'a citizen of it, a citizen of a disarmed world enjoying free world trade, a world money and a world communications system'.[22]

The language was visionary and emotional. But the notion of a Federal Union, however constituted, attracted the serious attention of many in this period. Most famously Clement Attlee, the British Labour politician and post-war Prime Minister, declared: 'Europe must federate or perish'.[23] A new and more dynamic structure was needed to replace the League of Nations, which had been set up after the First World War, and which had miserably failed to guarantee peace. It had done so, many argued, because it was based on that very sentiment of nationalism which led to war. The economist in Barbara saw what perhaps other people did not: 'In many fields – in economic fields especially – you will find policies in State hands which appear to be economic in intention, but which are really much more designed to promote politico-nationalist ends. Tariffs, currency manipulations, prohibitions of migration, often have more a political than an economic basis … They are a form of economic planning conceived only in the interests of a particular state and which emphasize before the mind of every citizen the separateness of one state from another.'[24] The pursuance of nationalism would not only lead to more killing and dying, she argued, but would threaten people's ordinary standard of living. The columns of her piece 'Do the British Need Their Empire?' published in the journal *Common Sense* in December 1941, were arranged round a cartoon of her face – clear-eyed, square-jawed, determined. She was determined to point out what she anticipated would be some of the most important lessons of the War for Britain: that we would lose our foreign investments; that, if Britain and other countries practised extreme economic nationalism after the War – erecting 'a *cordon sanitaire* against everybody else's goods, as though they were infected with the plague' – then the British people would be thrown back on their own inadequate resources. It was time to learn the moral of the contrast between the economics of war and the

economics of peace: that, in wartime, the planners ensure a more or less equitable
(and sometimes free) distribution of the necessities of life, whereas, in peacetime,
we have yet to see that this is what we ought to do. 'When all is said,' she enquired
with her customary logic, 'what *is* the objection to distributing milk or sugar or
bread or butter or oranges on the same principle that we already distribute gas
masks and domestic air-raid shelters?'[25] One of the major attractions of federalism
for her was the possibility of central economic planning 'up to the Russian level'.[26]

Barbara aired her views about the relationship between socialism and federation
in a well-publicized debate held jointly by the Socialist Party and the Federal Union
at the Conway Hall in London in May 1940, just before Britain settled down to
total war. Ronald Mackay (solicitor, Labour MP, campaigner on internationalist
issues and, later, Vice-President of the European Parliamentary Union) chaired
the debate, and her adversary described himself as 'Mr E. Hardy'. This was Edgar
Hardcastle, a Marxist economist and a founder member of the Socialist Party of
Great Britain. Barbara began by defining what she meant by Socialism: a Socialist
is a person who thinks that the world's economic resources should be used and so
organized to provide a good living for everyone in the world; someone who puts
equality high in the scale of social values, 'who not only thinks that ordinary people
ought to have enough, but also thinks that other people, also ordinary, ought not
to have too much'; a Socialist believes that we are very unlikely to get equality and
an equitable distribution of the world's resources without collective ownership and
collective organization; and a Socialist is someone who abhors the class system as
getting in the way of these ends. The definition does not end there, however, as
a true Socialist cannot want these things for the people of one nation alone. True
socialism is international: 'All Socialists are ashamed of themselves when they are
not internationalists, and all Socialists…will blush to the roots of their hair if they
lay themselves open to the charge of being called National Socialists'.[27] However –
and Barbara emphasized this point – federalism is *not* socialism. To a socialist,
Federal Union is like the engine on a train: a device for getting somewhere – to a
socialist society; but the engine is not itself the place we want to go.

Barbara's stance on socialism and federation entered the pages of the *Fabian
Quarterly* in the summer of 1940 in another confrontation, this time with Denis
Pritt, the lawyer who had been expelled from the Labour Party for his pro-
communist views.[28] Her own socialism had strong roots in the Fabian tradition of
gradualism. Many Fabians were committed to the principle of European unity.[29]
The idea of a united Europe was an organizing platform for many left-wing
intellectuals during this period, who saw it, not only as a method for preventing
war, but as a strategy that would combat a trio of evils: fascism, communism

and British imperialism.[30] Barbara's position on the relationship between federal and socialist ideals was elaborated in the tract which she had tried out on the Dartington Hall audience, *Socialism and Federation,* published by the Federal Union in 1941. Her definition of federalism entailed:

> the establishment over more than one previously independent state of a supra-national government with strictly limited functions. Those functions may be ranged in a sort of priority as follows: first is the rock-bottom minimum, without which a federation is not a federation, namely federal control of armed forces and of foreign policy. Next come powers which a large body of federalist opinion wishes to see federalized, but the lack of which would not actually destroy the distinctively federal character of a supra-national state. These are control of tariffs and other trade restrictions, control of migration and of currency, and administration of any dependent territories ... Finally, comes a third group of powers, such as the right to initiate public works and operate public utilities, and to enforce standards in working conditions and social services.[31]

Whether or not these latter powers ought to be included, she admitted, depended on the attitudes of different types of federalists themselves. Although anything was possible, a Western European federation looked most likely. Reading these words, one has a real sense of the person sitting there, head in hands, desperate to communicate and convince: 'twice in half a century socialists have seen the social progress of years shattered in a single night. Twice in half a century they have seen money desperately needed for the homes and health of the people diverted to the hideous business of war. So long as we have to carry burdens of this magnitude, so long shall we have, not socialist prosperity and equality, but poverty, malnutrition and colossal waste both of human and material resources.'[32] These are the reasons why socialism and federation are complementary parts of the same whole.

Barbara was a leading speaker at the first Federal Union rallies in London. One admirer remembered her standing very demurely at the first Annual Conference of the Federal Union in February 1940 in the Queen's Hall, London (one of the last events before it was bombed), and replying with a simple 'Yes' to the question 'Do you really believe all this rubbish?'[33] She signed a letter to *The Manchester Guardian* in November 1939 with nineteen other notables (the psychologist Cyril Burt, Bill Curry, Lynda Grier – the Cambridge economist who had helped her with her Girton studies – economic historian Eileen Power, H.G. Wells and Ralph Vaughan Williams among them). The letter was headed 'Manifesto by Leading Educationalists' and it urged all educationalists to demand from the Government an unequivocal statement of commitment to the goals of Federal Union.[34]

One (then) leading educationalist was William Beveridge. Before he achieved his most famous legacy of the Beveridge Report which gave Britain the blueprint for its welfare state, Beveridge was, with Barbara Wootton, an acknowledged ideologue of the Federal Union. Patrick Ransome, one of the original Federal Union trio, had known Beveridge when he was a student at University College, Oxford, where Beveridge was then Master, and he remembered Beveridge saying to him 'If there's a war, come and see me'. Beveridge laid out his own ideas in his pamphlet *Peace by Federation* for a collaboration between the British Dominions and Europe (excluding Russia, but possibly including the USA).[35] We do not know when Barbara Wootton and William Beveridge first met, but they knew each other by 1926, when he had identified topics of common interest and she was unable to find the time from her job at Morley College to meet him. By 1935 she knew him well enough to ask for his help in getting her name suggested (unsuccessfully) as 'the woman member' of the new Unemployment Assistance Board.[36] In 1937 she enlisted his help in securing funding for a student working on Soviet economics and planning who had been forced to leave Russia;[37] wearing a different hat, she later wrote to beg him to renew his annual subscription to the WEA.[38]

Beveridge's plans about how Federal Union might develop as an organization led to an Executive Committee, chaired by Barbara, to supervize the Union's day-to-day affairs. It was under her leadership that the Union focused down on the practical proposal that the most manageable arrangement for post-war federation would be Britain, France and Germany, plus some of the smaller European democracies.[39] But much of her intellectual work for the Union was done in her key role for the Union's research wing, another of the ever-inventive Beveridge's initiatives. The Federal Union Research Institute, set up in March 1940, yielded the suitable acronym of FURI. FURI was chaired by Beveridge, with Ransome as the Secretary, and Barbara as a member of its Economic Research Committee.[40] The first event organized by the Committee was a conference on economic aspects of federation held at University College, Oxford, in the autumn of 1939. Barbara participated, and she wrote the report. The conference agreed on the aim of complete freedom of trade and migration, together with unification of the currency, federal control of legal tender and inter-state payments, and a federally controlled bank. This should prevent 'divisions of economic interest from coinciding with national boundaries, and so help to destroy the economic basis of nationalism'. Participants understood that the degree of unification to be proposed would depend on public sentiment.[41]

While it succeeded in swaying the opinions of 'John Citizen' with its tide of meetings and propaganda, as an organization Federal Union developed financial difficulties because of its rapid expansion. Barbara, as Chair, was 'flabbergasted' when debts of several thousand pounds were uncovered.[42] Since the Union had never been incorporated as a limited company, these debts were the responsibility of individual members. Incorporation was hurriedly arranged and Barbara became one of seven directors. Members sold icecreams on Hampstead Heath one August bank holiday to raise money. Partial recovery was achieved, but disputes broke out, and by the end of the War, Rawnsley, who had gone into the Royal Air Force, had been killed in a flying accident, and both Kimber and Ransome had resigned. After the War, the rumbling divisions between proponents of world government, European unity and Atlantic union, respectively, came to the surface, although the organization continues today as the Federal Trust, a non-partisan think-tank devoted to education and information. Barbara herself left the Federal Union in September 1944 when the short-term goal of European federation, rather than the more 'utopian' aim of world federation, was voted in. She was always in favour of utopianism, discerningly noting that the term 'utopian' tended to be applied to all studies that extended beyond the limited assumptions of contemporary power politics.[43]

In 1946, Harold Laski, Chairman of the Labour Party, proclaimed, 'We cannot rest content until we have a genuine World Government expressing, through the direct choice of peoples, in a parliament responsible to them, the will of the common folk, instead of being dependent, like the United Nations, upon the sovereign wills of nation states which express, in all vital matters, the purposes of their ruling classes and subordinate to those purposes the interests of the common peoples'.[44] The idea of world government was espoused by many politicians in the years immediately after the War.[45] This was one sign that the Federal Union's influence on world politics had been very much greater than its power. In their book about its history, John Mayne and Richard Pinder observe that it was the first 'avowedly popular federalist movement in Europe'; its intellectual contribution was recognized and used by continental federalists whose influence helped shape the European Community; on the Atlantic front, it provided the basic ideas which led to the formation of the Organization for Economic Co-operation and Development; it helped to shape and articulate pressure for the reform of the United Nations and for an international peacekeeping force; and today it continues to promote the much-needed message that 'unfettered national sovereignty is outdated and a barrier to peace'.[46] On the back of the enthusiasm for the idea of international federation generated by the Federal Union, Jean Monnet, who would later be celebrated as the father of the European Community, put the idea of Anglo-French union to the British War Cabinet, which approved it, making its historic offer of union to France. Monnet was one of those eclectic individuals whose activities spanned many different sectors, from being Deputy Secretary General of the League of Nations, to running the family cognac business, becoming an international financier, and advising the Chinese on the reorganization of their railway system. However, he was not a federalist in the sense that word held for the thousands of Federal Union activists in Britain. It was the thinking of these federalists, especially those who worked for FURI, which gave force and conviction to the design of post-war European integration. The successful campaign for membership of the European Economic Community in the early 1970s was led by federalists, and they played an important role in the 1975 referendum.[47]

The European Union had a godfather as well as a father.[48] The Italian political theorist, Altiero Spinelli, spent sixteen years as a political prisoner under Mussolini, the last four of these on the island of Ventotene off the coast of Italy between Rome and Naples. A professional revolutionary, he was imprisoned for his anti-fascist activities in the Italian Communist Party, but he left the Party six years before his release in 1943, and became, instead, a proponent of federalism, convinced that particular ideologies, such as communism and liberalism, all in their own ways feed the aggressive narcissism of nation-states.[49] Ventotene was a 'revolutionary hothouse',[50] home to around a thousand political prisoners. Its link to the mainland was a twice-weekly supply boat on which political material could be illicitly shipped in and out. Some of this reached Spinelli via an economics professor, Luigi Einaudi, whose own views about national sovereignty had been heavily influenced by three British writers – William Beveridge, Walter Layton, editor of *The Economist* (Einaudi was a financial correspondent for the journal), and Barbara Wootton. Einaudi sent Spinelli some of their publications, which Spinelli assessed as 'first class'. Informed by this reading, the 'Ventotene Manifesto', *Towards a Free and United Europe,* was drafted in 1941 and delivered by boat to the mainland written on cigarette papers and concealed in the false bottom of a tin box. This manifesto positioned European federation as the first and necessary stage to world federation; the aim was to tie European countries so intimately together that they would no longer be able to go to war with one another. The Ventotene Manifesto was circulated through the Italian Resistance, becoming the basic document of the European Federalist Movement.[51] After his release from Ventotene, Spinelli travelled to Milan where he established the Movimento Federalista Europeo (MFE). MFE published clandestinely eight issues of a newsletter *L'Unità Europea*; four of these carried reprints of articles by Beveridge, Layton and Wootton. When the war finished, the MFE persuaded all the Italian political parties, except the Communists, to include federalism in their programmes. Membership of the MFE spread to France. Spinelli eventually became a member of the European Parliament in 1976. He and Jean Monnet were both forceful characters, but held rather different views. After Monnet's death in 1979, it was Spinelli's position which directly influenced the Maastricht Treaty;[52] the main building of the European Parliament in Brussels is named after him.

Thus, by a roundabout route entailing a conjunction of historical accidents, political subterfuge, risk-taking, revolutionary passion, and boxes with false bottoms, the focused clarity of Barbara Wootton's thought helped to shape the political contours of modern Europe. How much of this history did Barbara herself know? Probably not very much. Her influence on the Italian federalist movement has mainly been explored by the Italian historian of ideas, Alberto Castelli, whose publications on this did not begin to appear until 2001. Barbara would, of course, have known about the Italian translation of her *Socialism and Federation*, which appeared in 1945,[53] and a publishing house run by Einaudi's son translated her *Freedom Under Planning* into Italian in 1947.[54] In the Italian literature, much more recognition is given than in British or American commentaries to the singularity of her contribution, especially in the area of economic thinking. Castelli's 'I Socialisti Britannici e l'idea di "Popolo Europeo"' ('British Socialists and the idea of a "People's Europe"') identifies Beveridge, Ronald Mackay and Barbara Wootton as the only three thinkers who get close to the central notion of European unity – the indissolubility of peace and democratically elected government.[55] While the Federal Union literature produced in Britain has been almost completely forgotten here, it continues to be highly regarded by continental scholars, especially in Italy, where they consider it to be the foundation of the modern European federalist movement.[56] The range of political positions adopted by federalists, and the oscillation between idealism and realism in their politics, succeeded in paralyzing many British scholars.[57]

Both socialism and peace can be construed as matters of basic human rights. Barbara Wootton fought metaphorically for these on various fronts. The year her *Socialism and Federation* was published also saw a slim volume by Barbara called *End Social Inequality: A Programme for Ordinary People*. This was one of seventeen pamphlets edited by her friend, the journalist Francis Williams, later Lord Francis-Williams. The series, under the title *The Democratic Order*, was devoted to an elaboration of different aspects of what was by now widely called post-war 'reconstruction'. The focus of *End Social Inequality* is on the 'hard, real facts' of class, which must be faced to bring such a society into being.[58] Class differences, Barbara argued, are made up of two related structures: 'opportunity-class' and 'social-' or 'snob-class'. The most fundamental aspect of opportunity-class is the opportunity to go on living, but, as Richard Titmuss had shown in *Poverty and Population* (his book, published in 1938, which documented the relationship between environmental factors and preventable death), premature mortality strikes most at those who are already disadvantaged. 'Snob-class' inflicts the further insult of differentiated social prestige: manual work has low social status; people of different social statuses are not expected to mix together socially. But, in Britain, the true problem is not the consciousness of class but *un*consciousness about it. *End Social Inequality* contains some of Barbara's most acute and memorable observations: for example, 'public life is administered by people who, quite literarily, know next to nothing, at first hand, about the life of the public. And these people are not even conscious of their own ignorance.'[59]

These were years which spawned one radical organization after another. The Federation of Progressive Societies and Individuals (FPSI) – which some joked stood for the Federation for the Promotion of Sexual Intercourse[60] – had its origins in a breakaway group from the Rational Press Association. The dissidents were led by the philosopher and renowned womanizer Cyril Joad, who had taught some of Barbara's London tutorial classes. Joad's letter to *The Manchester Guardian* announcing the formation of the FPSI explained its rationale: the existence throughout England of many small groups of 'advanced' persons who were politically impotent because of their isolation. The FPSI had a catholic list of aims: central economic planning; the abolition of national armaments; access to birth control; the abolition of censorship; the preservation of rural England; and the rescue of Sundays 'from the dead hand of the nineteenth century'.[61] It was a group of what the outspoken author, socialist and pacifist H.G. Wells called 'open conspirators to change the world'.[62] Barbara helped to found the FPSI, becoming one of its Vice-Presidents and, later, its President. The FPSI was a pressure group to which she devoted some time, writing in its mouthpiece, *Plan*, speaking on an FPSI platform at Conway Hall in London, and signing letters to newspapers about issues such as the unwarranted imprisonment of two members of the National Unemployed Workers' Movement.[63] A national organization of this kind was partly an attempt to re-affirm a humanist socialism as the basis of Labour politics at a time when the British Labour Party was in disarray following its major defeat in the 1931 General Election.[64]

H.G. Wells reappeared on the stage with Barbara Wootton when he launched a new version of an old campaign for a Universal Declaration of the Rights of Man.[65] In September 1939, *The Times* hosted a series of letters reframing the aims of the War in terms of rights. Wells set out ten principles intrinsic to the 'rights of man' which he had assembled 'in conjunction with a few friends', and which he hoped would set the discussion of the aims of the War on a new and more constructive footing. The 'few friends' were a small group of socialists, writers, teachers and lawyers, including the peace campaigner and writer, Norman Angell, J.B. Priestley, A.A. Milne (who was said to motor up from the proximity of Pooh Corner to make his contribution[66]), Viscount Sankey (the first Labour Lord Chancellor), G.B. Shaw and Barbara Wootton. Barbara had first got to know Wells as a result of the tribute she had paid to 'the masterly sanity' of his writings in the Preface to her *Lament for Economics* (her attack on neoclassical economics, discussed in the next chapter). Wells had responded by inviting her to his home in Regent's Park for 'many a Sunday evening flowing with vodka and conversation'.[67] What Wells and his friends put together was the first modern Declaration of Human Rights. Men – the androcentrism of the old language did not shift in this new version – had rights to nourishment, housing, covering, medical care, employment and education sufficient to promote health, ensure effective citizenship and realize individual potential; they and their property were entitled to legal protection and to protection from 'secret dossiers'; free movement around the world should be guaranteed, as well as the right to buy anything that is for sale; they should not be imprisoned for more than three weeks without being charged, and not for more than three months without a public trial; all forms of bodily assault should be outlawed, along with non-consensual sterilization and imprisonment in infectious, verminous or otherwise insanitary conditions; they should not be forcibly fed, and they had the right to starve themselves if they wanted; no drugs should be given without knowledge or consent; and these rights should be established in a formal legal code; since they incorporated all previous declarations of human rights, they should stand as 'the fundamental law for mankind throughout the whole world'.[68]

Wells called for a broad public debate on the issue. Details of the Declaration were sent to over 300 newspapers in 48 different countries.[69] In Britain, *The Daily Herald*, the left-wing newspaper, made a page a day available for a month for a discussion of the draft declaration. 'HISTORIC CHALLENGE TO CIVILISATION' ran the advertisement for the series everyone ought to read on a 'modern Magna Charta' [sic] written by 'many of the foremost thinkers of the day'. The names included Clement Attlee, Sir Arthur Greenwood (Barbara's old boss at Transport House), J.B. Priestley, G.B. Shaw, Cyril Joad, the Liberal MP Sir Richard Acland (inventor of the 'Common Wealth' movement, which supported Federal Union), various religious notables, the chairman of the TUC, socialist and peace activist Ritchie Calder (who was secretary of the Declaration's Drafting Committee), and scientists J.B.S. Haldane and Lancelot Hogben.[70] The newspaper's headlines were stirring: 'You are the Heir to the Earth's Wealth', 'End the Death Penalty', 'Leave Creeds Out'. Towards the end of the month, women were allowed to put their particular case. This included a representation from an Indian Women's Organization: 'Urge include women by changing title ... into Declaration of Human Rights'.[71] The title was not changed. *The Rights of Man* was issued as a Penguin Special, and translated into thirty languages. The British Foreign Office translated it into German and dropped it on the Nazis as they advanced through France. The Nazis probably did not read it, but Wells sent it to his friend President Roosevelt, to Gandhi and Nehru (all of whom responded to him with reactions), and to Jan Christian Smuts, the South African Prime Minister, who later drafted the preamble to the United Nations Charter.[72] Roosevelt drew on the efforts of Wells and his friends in his famous 'For Freedom' speech in January 1942, which set the aims of the War in the framework of human rights, and the four essential freedoms of speech and religion, and from hunger and fear.[73] But it was Eleanor Roosevelt who, after her husband's death, finally accomplished the transition from 'men's' to 'human' rights in her work with the United Nations. This led to the signing of the Universal Declaration of Human Rights in December 1948, which in turn laid down the framework of international human rights as it exists today. The European Convention of Human Rights was made enforceable in British courts by the Human Rights Act of 2000.

The work of Wells and his friends was among the first in English to substitute the language of enforceable social rights for the pre-modern lexicon of 'natural' rights. Although their role has been largely forgotten, these people were 'the true progenitors of the modern human rights movement'.[74] The contribution Barbara Wootton made to the political values of modern democracies is evident when one traces these particular histories of the federal and human rights movements. She combined, and saw no essential disjunction between, searching intellectual analyses and the kind of practical networking, dissemination and political negotiation that turned these analyses into tools for action. This approach to the shaping of public policy, with the ultimate goal of creating a more equal, just, and peaceable society, was one she followed throughout her life.

At the outbreak of the Second World War, Barbara was forty-two and George Wright was thirty-six. The story she tells in her autobiography is that he registered as a conscientious objector and was deployed first in agricultural work, and then in civil defence as an ambulance driver, while her own work as a magistrate exempted her from being called up. George and she had a 'daily woman', a Mrs Brown, the same age as Barbara; Mrs Brown was also let off on the grounds that her services were necessary to the Wootton-Wright household.[75] However, a somewhat more complicated story lies behind Barbara's telling of it. George was not registered for National Service until the spring of 1941, and his conscientious objection would probably have been heard by a local tribunal in the summer. But neither Barbara nor Mrs Brown, as ageing women, came within the purview of the National Service (Armed Forces) Act of 1939; an extension to that Act in 1941 applied only to women aged between twenty and thirty. What did apply to Mrs Wright and Mrs Brown was the Registration for Employment Order of 1941, according to which the Ministry of Labour and National Service had the power to require whole classes of people to register at their local employment exchanges, not with a view to call-up into the armed forces, but as part of an attempt to monitor the types of labour power available for civilian employment directed to the war effort. Women of Barbara's cohort were included in this scheme sometime in 1943. She would have been interviewed by a man from the Ministry, a National Service Officer, who probably decided on the spot that her work as a magistrate was of sufficient use, and so the monitoring authorities would no longer need to bother with the labour of Barbara Wootton, which could therefore go on being deployed as she chose in her own effort to avoid not only personal involvement in the War, but the involvement of all human beings in all wars.[76]

George and Barbara did help as volunteers with the ambitious and premature scheme – a good example of centralized planning – for evacuating children out of London. Their group of children came from the East End of London and was transported to Aylesbury in Buckinghamshire. The children were 'shrewd, entertaining, bored and intermittently troublesome'; their hosts 'bewildered, well-meaning and outraged',[77] but it all worked reasonably well. In this early phase of the evacuation, more than a million children and adults were moved in four days, a figure which included three-quarters of a million children who went without their parents.[78] Very quickly complaints were fed back to the Ministry of Health and local authorities: rough language, bad behaviour, bedwetting, headlice, dirty bodies and clothes. Britain's two nations were encountering each other at close quarters for the first time.[79] At County Hall in London, Geraldine Aves, an almost exact contemporary of Barbara's at Cambridge, was organizer of the evacuation schemes, and therefore on the receiving end of many of these laments. The evacuation of children, and the needs of those made homeless because of the War, created a new public awareness of the vast range of deprivation and social need existing in Britain's unequal society. Public services were mainly restricted to those provided under the Poor Law. Britain needed a welfare state.

When Barbara and George returned from their month-long efforts to settle troublesome children in rural England, they were surprised to find their flat in Fulham still intact. During the six years of the War, the ceilings collapsed, but not a single pane of glass was shattered. People in 'essential' occupations had no choice but to go on living in London. The blackout was the one real inconvenience – hence the old lady who said that the good thing about the Blitz, when it came, was that it took your mind off the blackout. It was during this period that bored soldiers in camps demanded social and political reading matter, and talk of Federal Union escalated, though it seemed to some, including Kingsley Martin, about as far off as Mount Everest from the South Downs.[80] Steeped in the ideological and economic meaning of warfare and the need for revolution, Barbara Wootton and George Wright found their own escape in the Chiltern Hills in Oxfordshire, where they enjoyed weekend retreats in a pub in a village called Fingest. The communist physicist J.D. Bernal lived opposite the pub with one of his 'wives', an entertaining and artistic woman called Margaret Gardiner, and their 'most undisciplined' small son Martin (later a distinguished and highly disciplined sinologist), so there was much stimulating conversation to be had.[81]

She mentions it only in passing in her autobiography, so presumably it was not an important experience in her life, but at the end of 1938 Barbara followed her success as the token woman on the Colwyn Committee with membership of her first Royal Commission, on financial compensation for injured or sick workers. The TUC had long been agitating for reform of the law on payment to workers who were injured in the course of their employment. The machinery for compensation was complex, litigation was often costly and lengthy, the awards paltry, and the people who made the most profit were the insurance companies. Most basic of all, existing legislation did not guarantee compensation, because employers did not have to insure against accidents or provide a fund from which compensation could be paid. The State needed to take this out of the hands of insurance companies and, through a levy on companies, ensure that all workers had the right to compensation in the event of injury or death.[82] The remit of the Royal Commission on Workmen's Compensation was to inquire into, and report on, the operation and effects of the existing system and the scope of the relevant law, and to examine how this related to others for helping the unemployed or incapacitated. Sir Hector Hetherington, Principal and Vice-Chancellor of the University of Glasgow, agreed to chair it. Barbara was one of fifteen other members, one of only two women and thus no longer quite the token woman she had been on the Colwyn Committee in 1927. The work of the Royal Commission on Workmen's Compensation was disrupted by the War; although a report was published in December 1944,[83] its findings were largely amalgamated with those of its much bigger sibling, the Beveridge Committee on Social Insurance.

If the notion of planning had been used with different political meanings in the early 1930s, by the end of the decade it had become so fashionable that it was in danger of meaning both everything and nothing. 'A flood of literature on social planning pours continually from the presses,' observed Aldous Huxley in 1937. 'Every "advanced" thinker has his favourite scheme, and even quite ordinary people have caught the infection. Planning is now in fashion. Some kind of deliberate planning is necessary. But which kind and how much?'[84] The rhetoric and policy of planning were a response to the economic and political crises of the years between the two world wars, but it was the experience of the Second World War that led to the widespread acceptance of the need for central direction of the economy to avoid the kinds of instability that helped to produce war.[85] The product was a new national consensus about the need for a programme of economic reconstruction.[86] The publication in 1936 of Keynes' *The General Theory of Employment, Interest and Money* provided some elements of the rationale needed to support the general approach of planning. Firstly, Keynes demonstrated that the way out of economic crises was not to reduce public spending and investment but to increase it. Secondly, it followed that this goal would not be accomplished by the chaos of markets left to themselves, but required instead some degree of centralized planning. Like Beveridge, Keynes was not a socialist radical, but a liberal; his analysis of the workings of capitalism led to a re-conceptualization of the Government's role as requiring intervention in the interests of improving efficiency, and in order to save both individualism and the principles of a market-based economic system.[87]

In 1934, the BBC had run a series of weekly broadcasts under the heading 'Poverty in Plenty' (later printed as a book, *The Burden of Plenty?*[88]). Contributors to the series included Keynes and Wootton. Her piece was called 'The Necessity of Planning',[89] and its premise was a paradox: economic systems which depend on markets regulated by price are both so simple (because nobody plans them) and so complicated (because every sale is the product of so many separate contracts and decisions) that it is surprising they work at all. These arguments drew on an article she had published a little earlier in the WEA journal *The Highway* which proffered the entertaining metaphor of capitalism as a recurring digestive disorder. We are hungry and greedy for more wealth; we get it; and then are sick. Growth is followed by recession; prices fall too low for producers and rise too high for consumers. 'Not merely is there poverty in plenty … there is poverty *because* of plenty.'[90]

Among the most central goals of planning was the maintenance of high levels of employment. The security and income provided by jobs help to protect the individual from poverty and need, and the economy from the escalating dangers of under-consumption. William Beveridge, emerging from the blaze of notoriety that greeted his Social Insurance Report of 1942, found himself sidelined in the post-war reconstruction programme as a man more given to brilliant ideas than practical plans. In 1943 he decided to pursue the all-important subject of full employment policy with a privately financed inquiry, and he enjoined a number of 'technical' experts, including Barbara Wootton, E.F. Schumacher (later famous for his book on economics and environmentalism *Small is Beautiful*), Joan Robinson,

Elspeth Mair (his step-daughter), and Frank Pakenham (who had been his research assistant, later Lord Longford) to help him work out the details.[91] The results of this Beveridge inquiry were published as *Full Employment in a Free Society*. The report proposed a level of central budgeting and direction of labour resources which went far beyond that then contemplated by government; it built directly on the new economic models, linking Keynesian economics with a general strategy for post-war social policy.[92] Although Beveridge wrote the report, it depended heavily on the ideas of the economists in the group, including Barbara Wootton's persuasive analysis which helped to change his mind about Keynes.[93]

Barbara's own views about full employment were laid out in a Fabian pamphlet published in 1943. She began with the paradox that war generates full employment, so the important question is whether full employment is possible 'otherwise than as a consequence of mutual slaughter'. Let us consider then, she proposes, what it is that happens in wartime that effectively ensures full employment. First of all, the Government obliges most of us to work in the war effort; secondly, no fuss is made about the cost of this; thirdly, much of the output is given away free: 'The soldier ... does not actually own his own rifle; but, equally, he does not buy it. The question whether he can afford it has nothing to do with whether he gets it'; fourthly, the State controls labour and capital markets; fifthly, there is a change in attitudes: 'No more black looks at the married woman, the old age pensioner, or the refugee ... The woman no longer steals the man's job; she releases him for the war effort.' In peacetime, a small wave of unemployment can quickly become a big one, because people and governments stop spending money. In wartime, this does not happen because there is no dependence on 'the moods, hopes, fears and calculations of profit-seeking investors'. Thus, the common analogy between the Chancellor of the Exchequer and the prudent housewife is false: the former, unlike the latter, needs to spend what he does not have. 'The straight road to full employment is a comprehensive and considered plan of public outlay.'[94] This is straightforward Keynesianism. But some of Barbara's other suggestions in *Full Employment* are not: for example, the notion that the Government should be committed to providing everyone with a minimum diet, thus killing the two birds of feeding the nation and creating jobs in the food trades with one stone. The double attack on unemployment and poverty has much to recommend it as a peacetime policy: 'the mind recoils from a doctrine that it is economically sound to give bombs away to people who don't want them, and unsound to give buns to people who do'.[95]

Barbara Wootton's contribution to the debate about planning took place in a broader intellectual context: that of the efforts of a group of socialist economists centred on Evan Durbin, an LSE economist and later a Labour MP, and the politician and economist, Hugh Gaitskell, to fashion a new type of socialist economics for a post-war Labour Government. The work of this group has been charted in detail by Elizabeth Durbin, Evan Durbin's daughter, herself an economist, in her book *New Jerusalems: The Labour Party and the Economics of Democratic Socialism*.[96] In 1934–5, Durbin and Gaitskell convened a small group of economists and politicians to discuss the Labour Party's future programme, and to develop resolutions which they put to the Party (most of which were unanimously adopted). Barbara was a member of this group. She was also a contributor to the work of the New Fabian Research Bureau (NFRB) which had been set up in 1931 by G.D.H. Cole out of frustration with the failure of the Fabian Society to come up with any new ideas to confront the contemporary social and economic crisis. Barbara chaired the NFRB's Taxation Committee which convinced the Labour Party of the merits of a Keynesian managed economy. The Committee's publication, *Taxation Under Capitalism: Effects on Social Services*, of which Barbara is the first author, is a clear exposition of the purposes and history of taxation, and of the differential class effects of different types of taxes; its central question – whether large-scale investment in the social services can be adequately financed through existing systems of taxation – leads inexorably to the answer that it cannot, as the necessary taxes would impose too large a burden on the private functions of saving and enterprise, which consequently need to become public functions. Once the country's economic activities are in public hands, taxation becomes simply part of the apparatus for distributing the nation's wealth. Socialized industries pay their surplus to the State, which uses it for the public good.[97] There is, nonetheless, the possibility of a 'real' conflict between economic planning and personal freedom. The balance between the two is one to be negotiated, to be determined on rational and empirical grounds. Barbara is credited with being the first to raise the full implications for the Labour Party of this issue.[98] She also foresaw the adaptation of capitalism to accommodate a considerable degree of state planning that happened in many Western democracies after the Second World War.[99]

One platform of disagreement during these years involved Barbara personally: she engaged in an infamous debate with the Austrian neoclassical economist, Frederick Hayek, about the relationship between centralized economic planning, and freedom and individual rights. Hayek had been a member of the FURI group and Barbara had travelled with him, Beveridge, Ransome and Robbins to Paris in April 1940, to confer with French counterparts on a plan to federate France, Britain and a democratic post-war Germany. The journey was bumpy, leaving Barbara with 'an endearing mental picture of Beveridge with a cloth cap drawn well over his forehead plunged into the depths of airsick gloom'.[100] Like many others, including Barbara, Hayek's determination to work for peace had been formed directly by his experiences in the

First World War. But unlike Barbara's husband and brother, Hayek had survived his active participation in the War, and had gone on to study law, political science, psychology and economics at the University of Vienna, where he gained a reputation as a theoretical economist. In 1931, he was recruited by Lionel Robbins for a Chair at the LSE. He is much less well known for his work in the economics department there than as the author of a highly contentious book called *The Road to Serfdom*, which was published in 1944, and which provided Barbara Wootton with a case against planning that could not be allowed to pass unchallenged.[101]

The Road to Serfdom began life as a memorandum to Beveridge, then Director of the LSE, disputing the popular claim that fascism represented the dying scream of a failing capitalist system.[102] Hayek's view was that centralized planning, or state intervention, was a form of totalitarianism that would unavoidably deprive people of their freedom. The best guarantee of freedom was competition, and, thus, the only kind of planning that could be countenanced was planning to make competition as efficient as possible. Contemporary difficulties with the capitalist system were merely due to inefficiencies in the system, which could be remedied; socialists (or collectivists, Hayek considered the two one and the same) were misguided in believing that directed economies were compatible with the preservation of individual liberty. There were three essential points in Hayek's case: firstly, that the most efficient form of regulation in complex industrial systems was the price mechanism; secondly, that no form of centralized planning could match the success of the market in achieving this; and, thirdly, that the inevitable economic failure of centralized planning would have the further disastrous consequence of disposing both of free markets and of individual freedom. Although Hayek and Wootton shared an interest in a federalist Europe as a means of preventing war, the attraction for Hayek was in the abolition of trade barriers and tariffs, whereas Barbara saw it as a mechanism for achieving socialist political goals.

Hayek was a life-long opponent of socialism. His book was enormously influential. It was read by, and responded to, by many. For instance, Winston Churchill's enthusiasm for it was reflected in his ill-fated 1945 election campaign, and he won no respect from Labour leaders for rehashing Hayek's specious arguments.[103] In the 1980s and 1990s, the book enjoyed a new spate of attention as among the favoured writings of conservative leaders in the UK and the USA. Thatcher took to heart Hayek's arguments about the evils of state planning,[104] and some of Ronald Reagan's economic advisers were friends of Hayek's, and shared the same anti-planning views.[105] Among academic reviewers at the time, *The Road to Serfdom* got a predominantly hostile reception. Many saw the book as damaging polemic: 'the most sinister offence against democracy to emerge ... for many decades'.[106] Hayek sent the proofs of his book to Barbara Wootton; her response, *Freedom Under Planning,* was published in 1945. While many of the responses to Hayek's book had pointed out the failures of logic and convincing reference to real world examples which characterized his case, it was Barbara who provided the most reasoned and carefully argued objections. *Freedom Under Planning* was received as 'a highly significant contribution to one of the most important debates of our time';[107] 'the most cautious and candid defence of planning that has so far appeared';[108] 'an essay ... written with diverting whimsy and often with philosophical penetration';[109] and a 'keenly reasoned, closely organized, and concisely stated' compendium of effective arguments against Hayek's extreme conclusions.[110] After reading it, the 'somewhat soporific effect on capitalistically inclined readers' of Hayek's tome would undoubtedly be shaken off.[111] Both *The Observer* and *The Manchester Guardian* used medical analogies to describe Barbara Wootton's treatment of the problem; she was 'a first-class surgeon' in her excision of unwarranted matter,[112] and 'a doctor for fevered subjects', in providing 'a cooling draught of pure facts' for the raised temperatures of the planning debate.[113]

The problem with Hayek's book, as some of its reviewers noted, was that his 'cynical and confused appeals' were not directed to reason at all, but to 'fear and distrust'.[114] *The Road to Serfdom* was an anti-rational text; Barbara, a specialist in rational thinking, was therefore bound to find it wanting. Central to *her* case was that one may 'philosophize endlessly about freedom', but in ordinary daily life it is *freedoms* that people want – civil, cultural, political and economic freedoms; it is therefore necessary to consider the impact of planning, conceived as 'the conscious and deliberate choice of economic priorities by some public authority',[115] on these different varieties of freedom, and to do so by drawing on the evidence of how different societies have deployed centralized planning and how their citizens have been affected by this. Only then can we reach sensible conclusions about whether planning really interferes with liberty – the central plank in the anti-planners' case. Barbara's own conclusion, drawn after eight chapters considering the relationship between planning and different varieties of freedom, was that,

> there is nothing in the conscious planning of economic priorities which is inherently incompatible with the freedoms which mean most to the contemporary Englishman or American. Civil liberties are quite unaffected. We can, if we wish, deliberately plan so as to give the fullest possible scope for the pursuit by individuals and social groups of cultural ends which are in no way state determined ... Planning need not even be the death-warrant of all private enterprise; and it is certainly not the passport of political dictatorship ... A happy and fruitful marriage between freedom and planning can, in short be arranged.[116]

In the Preface to the book, Barbara thanked her husband George for 'daily experience in the marriage of freedom and planning', perhaps subtly acknowledging that the lived experience of such unions could be a little more tricky than the theory suggested.[117]

Barbara's confrontation with Hayek's case against planning was notable for the amicable terms in which it was conducted. 'Intellectual controversy on serious practical and political issues is not always conducted in an atmosphere of personal goodwill,' she observed. 'It is on that account the greater pleasure to express here my appreciation and reciprocation of the unchanging friendliness of Professor Hayek's attitude.'[118] Hayek did not see it quite like that. Looking back on their exchanges many years later, he commented on the 'curious experience' he had had with Barbara Wootton. 'She said, "You know, I wanted to point out some of these problems you have pointed out, but now that you have so exaggerated it I must turn against you".'[119] In a nicely Woottonesque note, her final thanks in the Preface to *Freedom Under Planning* were to the staff of the Fulham Public Library, 'whose helpfulness, freedom from red tape and relentless struggle against the book famine are a magnificent demonstration of the standards of elasticity and efficiency attainable in the public services'.[120]

The Wootton-Hayek conversation about planning and freedom pushed forward the integration of Keynesian ideas with the progressive political mood that came to dominate Britain at the close of the Second World War. Neither the Keynesian mixed economy nor the Beveridgian welfare state – the 'managed economy' and society paradigm – would have been possible without the ideological groundwork of open discussion to which Barbara made a major contribution.[121] What she provided was the application of cool logic and the scientific method she so consistently championed to the highly emotional characterization of the state-as-dictator that inspired *The Road to Serfdom* and other contemporary anti-planning writings. It is impossible to read the intellectual and political history of the 1930s and 1940s without being impressed by the overlapping membership of the different circles participating in the debates and decisions which produced post-war Britain. Perhaps the most bizarre evidence of the interactions between different cultural networks is a letter published in *The Manchester Guardian* addressed to Hitler, then Chancellor of Germany, in 1934.[122] Its point was to request the release of Ernst Torgler, a well-known German Communist Party member, who had been arrested following a fire in the German Parliament in 1933 which was viewed by the Nazis as a communist plot against them. Torgler was charged with arson and treason. Barbara Wootton's name is there among the signatories appealing to Hitler, along with a catalogue of some of the most famous and argumentative figures of the time: Norman Angell,

Ernest Bevin, Vera Brittain, C. Delisle Burns, E.M. Forster, Winifred Holtby, Julian Huxley, Storm Jameson, C.E.M. Joad, John Middleton Murry, Emmeline and F.W. Pethick-Lawrence, Eleanor Rathbone, Seebohm Rowntree, Bertrand Russell, Siegfried Sasson, H.G. Wells, and 'the Wolves' (Leonard and Virginia) – among them.

The number and range of activities and networks with which Barbara Wootton engaged during this period is legion. It could, of course, be argued that she was just a woman who had a finger in a very large number of pies. It was a habit of the time to sign letters with one's friends; to invent and join campaigns; to name and re-name movements. But we are left with one simple point: she was there, and she made a difference. By the time Barbara published her autobiography more than twenty years later, complaining in its title about the world she never made, it is possible that she was in part observing that the world had forgotten how much she actually *had* made it.

10

Lament for Economics

Norbert Elias, born in the same year (1897) as Barbara Wootton, was a European sociologist most remembered today for his two-volume work on social attitudes and manners, *The Civilizing Process*. Elias fled Nazi Germany in 1933 and spent part of the War in internment camps in Liverpool and the Isle of Man. After the War, Barbara Wootton was one of those who facilitated his entry into British academia, initially through enlisting his help as a tutor for the London University extra-mural classes she was running.[1] Elias's autobiographical *Notes on a Lifetime*, published in 1984, begins by recalling how at a symposium of English sociologists held in the 1950s, Barbara had addressed the assembled sociologists, who were debating the strengths and weaknesses of contemporary sociology. She was somewhat bitter about something – Elias does not specify what. 'And none of you are proper sociologists,' he recalled her shouting, 'Look around you. You and you and you, none of you has ever studied sociology! You've all come in from somewhere else!'[2]

Sociology was a relatively new subject at the time, and poorly institutionalized, so it was bound to be the case that many of those who called themselves sociologists had 'come in from somewhere else'. Elias himself had started in medicine. Barbara Wootton had been trained in Classics, and then in Cambridge economics. She called herself an economist for many years. It was as an economist that she had lectured in Cambridge and then in London, startled the media by joining the Colwyn Committee on National Debt and Taxation in 1924, attended the League of Nations Conference in 1927, worked with William Beveridge on economic policy, and published many of her early works. But, during the 1920s and 1930s, there was a growing dissonance between her disciplinary allegiance to the language and theories of economics, and her desire to see academic expertise yoked to the practical promotion of human welfare. This dissonance broke out in the fever of the closely argued 322-page critique of conventional economics she published in 1938, *Lament for Economics*. It is a biting and intensely logical, but also in places humorous and personal, work. At the time when she wrote it, Barbara Wootton was regarded in public circles as 'a distinguished economist',[3] but the book marked the official end of this career and the beginning of her identification with the ranks of those who had come in from the cold to the relative warmth of sociology.

Lament for Economics takes the economics and economists of the time to task for a number of critical failings. Its target is 'neoclassical' economics, a term introduced by Thorstein Veblen in 1900 to distinguish the English tradition of economics under Alfred Marshall from other European schools of thought. The central features of neoclassical economics (often also called 'mainstream' economics) are a focus on markets, prices, and outputs, and the supposition that everyone acts independently to maximize their own self-interest. This was the approach that Barbara had learnt at Cambridge. *Lament for Economics* criticizes the neoclassical tradition on five main grounds: for being of no practical use; for being unintelligible to 'the plain man';[4] for being riddled with, and weakened by, internal dispute; in its resolution to ignore reality; and for being at heart no more than an elaborate system of apologetics for capitalism. This formidable list of allegations appears in the first chapter of *Lament* which is appropriately called 'The Indictment'. It is not a polite book. Economists 'feed on their own tails by busying themselves with the analysis of imaginary worlds which they have themselves invented';[5] they specialize in 'umbilical contemplation' rather than the methods of science;[6] their inability to interpret concrete situations usefully is reminiscent of the behaviour of reptiles before they become extinct;[7] and, in their addiction to outdated Victorian models, these 'paid sycophants of capitalism' 'live in a sort of perpetual regression ... like old people who are unable to let go the world of their childhood'.[8] It was this chapter of *Lament* that housed one of Barbara's most famed remarks, recycled by Winston Churchill[9] among many others, that 'Wherever six economists are gathered, there are seven opinions'.[10]

Such accusations need reinforcing with argument and evidence, and this Barbara does in four chapters concerned with how economic theory relates to the real world; its non-status as a science; its veiled function as a defence of capitalism; and its fatal over-dependence on the notion of the atomized individual. Much of what is transacted under the heading of economics is simply a study of market processes: the business of buying and selling, of demand and supply, of price and value. Moreover, most economists assume that people's behaviour in market economies is always strictly rational, that it is always geared to maximizing personal utility and satisfaction; that individuals always behave rationally as independent units, and the markets in which they so behave are places of 'perfect' competition. Left sufficiently to itself, the free play of market forces – the old doctrine of *laissez-faire* – will produce a state of equilibrium in which supply equals demand, and this is a condition that will benefit everyone equally. However, if economics is about the ordinary business of life, the attainment of the 'material requisites of being' to quote Marshall's *Principles of Economics*, which Barbara Wootton had first read as a girl before anyone allowed her to study the subject properly, then it is clear that it *ought* to be about more than the kind of market system currently prevailing in countries such as Britain and the USA, and it *ought* to allow for the irrational behaviour of the real world. Features such as tradition and nepotism and gross inequalities of capital and power underlie how labour and commodities are *actually* valued and exchanged for money.

The quarrels of *Lament* with the shortcomings of economic orthodoxy did not come out of nowhere. The notion of economics being about more than public markets had been aired for many years, and notables such as William Beveridge, in his departing address as Director of the LSE in 1937, were complaining that controversies in economic theory very rarely referred to empirical evidence.[11] It was clear even to the layperson in the 1930s that the famous default equilibrium of the industrial economies idolized by the neoclassical economists was repeatedly failing to materialize. The economists' main suggested remedy – the lowering of wages – made neither political nor social sense. All this would be put right, eventually, by the Keynesian revolution. Like Barbara Wootton, or perhaps she like him – after all, they had shared the same nanny in childhood – Keynes understood that the world is not made up of isolated units, independently motivated, but by interlocking networks and institutional structures. These operate within a framework bounded not by rationality, but by uncertainty. It is because people do *not* know the consequences of their actions that things happen to the economy, not because they do. Barbara Wootton regarded Keynes' illuminations as couched in unnecessarily complex language,[12] but she must surely have chuckled at some of his remarks about the absurdities of the neoclassicists, for example, that they 'resemble Euclidean geometers in a non-Euclidean world who, discovering that in experience straight lines apparently parallel often meet, rebuke the lines for not keeping straight'.[13]

Barbara's contemporary Cambridge economist, Joan Robinson, once remarked that, 'The purpose of studying economics is not to acquire a set of ready-made answers to economic questions, but to learn how to avoid being deceived by economists'.[14] *Lament* exorcizes this deception. However, one of the criticisms that can fairly be levelled at it is that its focus is narrowly on a particular school of English economists. This is a point made vociferously by some of the book's reviewers, who noted Barbara Wootton's disregard of the way economists outside England (particularly in Belgium, Sweden and Australia) did grapple with real world problems.[15] Barbara also paid insufficient attention to institutional economics in the USA, a distinctively different approach from the neoclassical one, and one which put forward similar arguments to hers: that the social and power relations embedded in institutional structures, not markets, are the main regulators of the economy.[16]

Lament was specifically targeted at the LSE school of economists, particularly at Frederick Hayek, whose opposition to socialist planning had provoked Barbara's *Freedom Under Planning*, and Lionel Robbins, arch-champion of neoclassical economics. The title of Chapter 3 of *Lament*, 'The Nature and Insignificance of Economic Science', is a play on Robbins' much-acclaimed text, *An Essay on the Nature and Significance of Economic Science*, published in 1932 and already in a reprint of its second edition by 1937. Robbins' *Essay* is best known for its still-used definition of economics as 'the science which studies human behaviour as a relationship between ends and scarce means which have alternative uses'.[17] This definition fitted very well with the rational choice model of economics, and with an approach that defended theory against the erosions of empiricism. Robbins and others regarded economics as a science because they considered it distinguished between means and ends – economists were properly only concerned with the latter – and because it was a system of logical deduction from first principles. Its basic propositions, deductions from 'simple assumptions reflecting very elementary facts of general experience' are 'on all fours', argued Robbins in his book, with the propositions of the other sciences.[18] Barbara Wootton disagreed. She could not see in the practices of most economists anything that resembled science. Did they examine their theories by close and accurate observation of phenomena? Did they develop hypotheses from observable facts? Did they test generalizations before proclaiming them? No, the only contribution of the real observable world to their treatises was in suggesting the hypothesis whose hypothetical consequences would then be elucidated without any empirical reference. The belief that important truths can be discovered merely by thinking is not what science is about. Some of this critique also applied to sociology, but economics suffered from an additional failure in that it did not acknowledge that the mechanisms of a capitalist market economy are limited in time and place. Neoclassical or mainstream economics, the target of Barbara's attack, was not about human experience in general but about some human experiences in particular: 'If the "science" is dumb except in relation to the conditions of the Western world in the seventeenth to twentieth centuries,' she noted, 'then it does seem to be an odd sort of a science indeed'.[19]

The elision between what is and what ought to be is the next problem. Why, after all, should economizing – making a little go as far as possible, the basic precept of economics – be preserved in aspic as commendable, 'rational', behaviour? How does such a theory connect with the observable fact that human beings live in societies whose complex networks and levels of influence affect their behaviour, so as to render the notion of the atomized individual simply another redundant abstraction? When we look at people's real experiences of markets, what do we see? Contrary to the idea that people are always selfishly maximizing their own satisfaction, economic decisions can have many other motives. Most importantly, we know what these motives are only through empirical study, by asking about them. In studying market behaviour, we must examine from their own subjective standpoints how both producers and consumers behave. In the case of consumers, for example, the business of selecting between scores of varieties of the same product is extremely arduous, and one which it is difficult to conduct intelligently: 'As a purchasers of jams, for example,' observed Barbara, domestically, 'I am quite incapable of deciding for myself which varieties are made of fruit and which of synthetic substitutes, nor do I even know, at all accurately, how far the substitutes are, on the one hand, actively pernicious, or on the other hand, just as good as the commodity which they replace'.[20] She is making a very important point here. The neoclassical case rests on the assumption that people know what they are doing, economically – that, after all, is the essence of rationality. But consumer choice is often, and increasingly, uninformed, because of the complexity of markets and of products, and it cannot therefore be deemed reasoned choice. The claim that markets faithfully direct resources into producing only those things that are really wanted is manifestly absurd.

Facts about the *dis*satisfactions experienced by many people living in politically unequal industrial systems impressed Barbara much more than the abstract elegance of economists' invented theories. Towards the end of *Lament*, she formulates the key problem: the important thing is 'to know what kind of enquiries are likely to be fruitful in terms of social welfare'. What she recommends is a programme in which economic analysis is applied to the imperfect market economies that do exist; there is sufficient empirical study of social situations and trends; and the focus is on the sorts of social and economic goals that will promote human welfare. She wants to know about the social structure and about the circumstances in which people live, and she suggests that there should be a regular body of investigators charged with just this task. She wants to find out about human needs, from the various standpoints of all who have them. She considers it important to establish whether people want freedom of choice, and how their opinions and choices may be conditioned by influences such as politically vested interests or advertising and other media persuasion. All this would mean redefining economists as students of social welfare.[21] And this in turn would mean economists' direct involvement in questions about the ultimate aims of public policy, and in particular their obligation to take seriously the observable fact that England, nominally a democratic country, was depriving many citizens of the wealth and opportunities afforded to some. In short, Barbara Wootton's *Lament for Economics* leads with an iron logic to the conclusion that all economists should become more like her. It was perhaps one of the intellectual tragedies of her life that this did not happen.

The book could be seen as a justification of her own move away from economics, and this would certainly explain one aspect of its impact, which on the development of economics was zero. It is not mentioned in histories of economic thought or methodology,[22] and it is strangely missing from biographies of her professional contemporaries, such as Keynes and Beveridge.[23] Reviews at the time in the popular press were enthusiastic, regarding it as a decisive exposé of the flaws inherent in all economics.[24] *The Times* reviewer deemed it, 'vigorous, witty and outspoken',[25] and *The Manchester Guardian* called it a 'sprightly onslaught' designed to strip economists of 'their last rags of self-respect'.[26] In Australia, *The Argus* observed that nothing was more satisfying for women than being able to say that men had made a mess of it, and that was what Mrs Wootton said.[27] Academic opinion was much more mixed. The American reviews were most charitable: the book was amusing, 'spirited', 'gossipy', although somewhat too personal: in one sentence on page 190 the pronoun 'I' was used seven times.[28] On the other hand, the reviewer at the University of North Carolina could not quarrel with *Lament*'s 'commendable keenness, fairness, and humility'.[29] A Pennsylvanian economist considered her case interesting and thought-provoking, although would not her conception of economics as the study of social welfare turn all of them into sociologists, which would be a mistake?[30]

Lament was used in some contemporary American discussions of the relationship between theory and applied subjects in economics teaching.[31] Unsurprisingly, the most negative responses came from the British economists who had been the main focus of her criticism. A long review by L.M. Fraser from Aberdeen commended 'Mrs Wootton' for reminding him and his colleagues to pay more attention to the concrete problems of economic life, but she went too far. She gave into emotion and prejudice and spoiled perfectly sound arguments with 'absurd over-statement'.[32] Roy Harrod, Oxford economist and friend and biographer of Keynes, did not quite say this in his Presidential Address to the British Association in Cambridge the year *Lament* came out, but he did refer to 'Mrs. Wootton's jeremiad': 'While her case against too grandiose claims for our subject is unassailable,' he pronounced, 'I am confident that a circumspect statement of its achievement and utility would be proof against her shafts'.[33] Harrod's reference to *Lament* may have had something to do with Keynes, who had corresponded with Harrod about his plans for this address, and had warned him off the subject he had selected – the scope and method of economics – as being too 'serious and academic' for an occasion that would get a lot of press attention. 'Couldn't you give the whole thing rather a different twist,' Keynes had asked, 'dealing, for example, with such matters as Barbara Wootton has handled I gather (I have not yet read the book) in her *Lament for Economics*, though I hope yours would be a Laurel for economics.'[34]

What explains the treatment Barbara Wootton's *Lament for Economics* received, and why it has disappeared virtually without trace? The timing of the book was appalling, published eighteen months before the Second World War. *Lament* is unashamedly a plea for the empirical grounding of academic work and an argument for understanding all human interactions in their social context. But neoclassical economics in the 1930s was attentive to neither of these orientations. It had evolved as a specialist theoretical subject with an internal technical language and a fixed model of self-interested economic behaviour. English economists acted in their own interests by creating closed professional networks promoting this or that theoretical school. One function of Robbins' work, for example, was to establish the LSE school as different from, and superior to, the Cambridge economists, who took a more lenient and practical view of economics under the influence, still, of that great master, Alfred Marshall, of 'welfare economics' as professed by those such as Pigou, and now of the policy-oriented work, set to bring about a revolution in economic thinking, of John Maynard Keynes. Just as Barbara Wootton was not interested in these intra-professional conflicts, those who engaged in them were not interested in her. Perhaps they also could not find the time for her 'doggedly empiricist' philosophy of science.[35] Had *Lament* been attached to more formal articulations of the then fashionable logical positivism of A.J. Ayer and the Vienna Circle, such as Terence Hutchinson's *The Significance and Basic Postulates of Economic Theory*, published the same year as *Lament*, it might have done as well in being regarded as essential reading for economics students decades later. Barbara Wootton's impatience with theory, and with the pretensions and preoccupations of the academic world, did her no service with her professional colleagues. *Lament*'s marginalization was aided by her absence from the debating platform of economic theory, unlike, for example, that generation's other famous British female economist, Joan Robinson, whose work was much better known because she engaged with American theorists such as Samuelson and Solow and with those abstract arguments about monopolistic competition much loved by professional economists at the time.[36] Barbara's independence from any particular school of thought was a strength, but also a weakness when it came to maximizing the utility of her own work. And it allowed it easily to become the victim of a general historical tendency among academics to ignore the contributions of women. Her *Lament* entered a field in which the names of significant key economics thinkers had already faded from the collective institutional memory – Clara Elizabeth Collet, Charlotte Perkins Gilman, Rosa Luxemburg and many others;[37] a field in which classic texts of economic history written by women such as Alice Clark, Ivy Pinchbeck and Eileen Power also tended to be sidelined or ignored.[38] Joan Robinson's critical commentary on the formalism and scientism of neoclassical economics, for example, although acknowledged as valid by many in the profession at the time, was subsequently largely ignored.[39]

More surprising in a way than *Lament*'s absence from standard histories of economics, is its neglect in another corpus of literature: more recent radical critiques of neoclassical economics. An avalanche of works published since the 1980s crucifies mainstream theory for its 'religious' defence of market theory in the face of easily observable evidence that neither markets nor people nor economic systems behave like that: books with such titles as *Debunking Economics* (Keen), *The Death of Economics* (Ormerod), *The Rhetoric of Economics* (McCloskey), *The Vices of Economists* (McCloskey), *Counting for Nothing* (Waring), *Whole Life Economics* (Brandt), *Beyond Economic Man* (Ferber and Nelson), and *Towards a Gendered Political Economy* (Cook and others). As the latter titles suggest, a core element of this newer criticism is the masculinity of mainstream economic theory: the corporate fantasy of that autonomous mechanical being, Rational Economic Man, and the astonishing neglect of what is statistically the most important work in the world, the unpaid domestic labour of women, which inconveniently (for the orthodox economic theorists) lies outside the market-place. These considerations of gender highlight the function of mainstream economics as a justificatory system for a hierarchical power-driven status quo, and in this they add to the other objections: economic theories are signally bad at predicting anything;[40] co-operative rather than atomistic behaviour is common;[41] important social and environmental values and costs are ignored;[42] the texts of economists are replete with metaphors and rhetoric rather than science;[43] the objectivity of economics is hugely exaggerated and misleading, and its narrow frame of reference a superb example of *ir*rationality.[44] Much modern economics said one female critic in 1996 – whose standpoint is interesting because she worked as a male professional economist for many decades – is about as useful as the games of small boys in a sandbox.[45]

In an account of Barbara Wootton's *Lament*, and how it has most lamentably been ignored,[46] Australian economist J.E. King ends with a modern quotation from a completely different source – the complaints of disaffected economics students at France's leading higher education institution, l'Ecole Normale Supérieure.

In 2000, they wrote an 'open letter' to their teachers and other authorities about the endemic failure of economics to address real world problems:

> We wish to escape from imaginary worlds! Most of us have chosen to study economics so as to acquire a deep understanding of the economic phenomena with which the citizens of today are confronted. But the teaching that is offered, that is to say for the most part neoclassical theory or approaches derived from it, does not generally answer this expectation... No matter how rigorous from a formalistic point of view or tight its statistical fit, any "economic law" or theorem needs always to be assessed for its relevancy and validity regarding the context and type of situation to which it is applied.[47]

In the light of this modern lament, the 'Woottonian image of economics' seems remarkably fresh still.[48]

She may have stopped regarding herself as an economist, but Barbara Wootton did not leave the subject alone, and her writings contributed to the propagation of Keynesian ideas during the 1940s. And then in her second major book on economics, *The Social Foundations of Wage Policy*, published seventeen years after *Lament*, she achieved a text which had a much greater longevity and influence. While *Social Foundations* continues her conversation with the neoclassical economists, it does so from a position much more decisively outside their territory. The word 'social' is in the title. As well as being a critique, the book is also a pioneering analysis and a proposal for a new approach to wage determination.

Its starting point is memorable, especially for all those economics students who were grappling with the verbose and abstract theories which made up much of their degree work. *Social Foundations* begins with a visit to Whipsnade Zoo just before the Second World War. Barbara picks up a brochure full of interesting facts and figures, from which she learns that the big elephant which gives rides to children earns exactly the same salary – £600 a year – as she does as Director of Tutorial Classes for the University of London. 'I found myself wondering what other occupations stood upon the same rung of the ladder as the elephant and myself, which would be above us, and which below, and why.'[49] This train of thought led to fundamental reflections about the social and economic forces shaping the valuations attached to different kinds of work. Such reflections were intensified by her membership of an Arbitration Tribunal charged with making decisions about Civil Service salaries. How, she asked, could any such decisions sensibly be made without a framework of principles about how they *ought* to be made? As she had pronounced in *Lament for Economics*, the decisions made by markets are imperfect, often unfair and frequently appallingly random. When the new Professor of Social Policy, Hilary Land, gave her inaugural address under the title 'What are Wages For?' at Royal Holloway and Bedford New College thirty-five years after *Social Foundations* was published, she updated Barbara Wootton's comparison between the earnings of the two types of mammals – elephants and professors. According to the Keeper of Mammals at the Royal Zoological Society in 1990, elephants were no longer employed to give rides to children, having been replaced by camels, but on the basis of camels' earnings there was now a substantial differential between animals and professors – it was considerably more profitable to be an animal than a professor.[50]

Social Foundations mixes research, critique and prescription in a typically Woottonian mode. Having stated the problem and asked why some people, or animals, earn more than others, Barbara looks again at mainstream economics – here, at classical wage theory – for an answer. Her first quotation is the first sentence of a book suitably called *The Theory of Wages*, written in 1932 by J.R. Hicks, an expert in the microeconomics of consumer behaviour. For him it is simple: there is nothing special about wages. They are the price of labour, and so, like all prices, they are determined by the factors of supply and demand, and so, like all problems in economics, they demand those abstract models which postulate a world of pure acquisition and pure competition. Classical wage theory, argues Barbara, is always conservative, in that it justifies an existing situation by explaining an imaginary one, but it also cannot explain existing patterns of wage differentials – or similarities, as in the case of the elephant and the university professor. How does one account for the fact that in October 1951, a male non-graduate teacher at the start of his career earned £411 a year in London, about the same as a Civil Service executive officer with six years' service, a male staff nurse in a general hospital with seven, a prison officer with six, and a fireman with four?[51] What, in any case, determines why some people earn *wages* while others earn *salaries*? And it is surely curious that the whole subject of personal income is shrouded in secrecy: a man's 'private economic parts' resemble other private parts in the powerful social taboo to which they are subject. Interestingly, secrecy is correlated with social status. It is much easier to find out what the lowest- than the highest-paid earn; a particularly telling demonstration of this for Barbara was one office where the salary slips of the monthly-paid staff arrived in sealed envelopes, while those of the weekly-paid were left open for all to see.[52] Once one moves away from the neoclassical economist's obsession with monetary value, it also becomes clear that there are different ways of rewarding people for their labour – free uniforms or lunches, extra holidays, and, at the other end of the scale, substantial bonuses, including lump sum additions to pensions. As a key source of economic inequality, these sorts of benefits were beginning to be investigated by Barbara's colleague at the University of London, Richard Titmuss, in the 1950s, though his book on income distribution, published in 1962, curiously makes no reference to her work.[53]

The main canon of the argument in *Social Foundations* is that social factors — the standing of particular occupations, the valuing of some types of labour and some kinds of labourers above others — operate together with market forces to shape what people are paid, and these social factors are commonly excluded from the economist's range of vision. For example, classical wage theory stipulates that working hours and remuneration are related, so that those who work longest will be paid more. But is this actually what happens? Barbara computed figures for weekly hours and rates for the lowest grade of adult male workers in 86 industries in London over the period 1945–51, and from these she calculated the correlation coefficients. The result was an inverse relationship between hours and income: shorter working hours are more profitable. The key factor here is prestige: long hours and low pay go together because both signify low class status.[54] The realities of human social life also hold the key to how wage and salary rates are decided. There are three main mechanisms for this — collective bargaining, statutory regulation and arbitration tribunals, such as the one that, along with the elephant, set Barbara Wootton off on her enquiry. A feature of all three is the use made of moral justifications, such as this job, or this worker, is worth more than another one. Such justifications appeal to social categorizations of value which lie beyond the currency of economic theory. And a point about these — which leads directly to the final chapter of her argument — is that they are made in a vacuum: there is no established and accepted framework of principles within which wages and salaries can be adjusted fairly in relation to one another. Should the principle be movements in the cost of living, or changes in the general level of wages? Should there be a comparison between similar employments? Or should it be a matter of redressing some of the historical anachronisms and inequities resulting from 'the accumulated deposit laid down by a rich mixture of economic and social forces' which is what the contemporary wage and salary structure of Britain amounts to?[55]

The first step in formulating a rational wages policy is bringing the whole subject out of the cupboard as a proper topic of political debate. Personal incomes may be regarded as personal, but the *distribution* of income is a public issue, and hence politicians, who are responsible for public policy, must engage with it. A compelling observation made much later by another economist was that, as a subject, income distribution has been treated with general disdain by professional economists: it has never been a mainstream interest.[56] Over the period since she last lamented economics, Barbara Wootton noted in *Social Foundations* a growing silence on the subject of egalitarian ideals. This was connected with changes in the trade union movement – in the 1950s less a defence of underprivileged manual workers than a professionalized bureaucracy representing a range of sectional interests – and with changes in the Labour Party, which had become more independent of the unions, and had thus acquired a broader and less socialist base. Both these were changes to be deprecated on the explicitly political ground that gross economic inequalities are an offence to human dignity. Her suggestions as to how to make future wage policy more rational are also designed to make it more just: for Barbara Wootton, throughout her life, these two terms were intimately related. The only rational society is one that affords the same opportunities to all its citizens, and the appeal of equality lies precisely in its appeal to reason. To put it the other way round, one could say that it is *un*reasonable to deny opportunities to some in order to heap them on the shoulders of those who already have them.

As with *Lament*, the immediate reception of *Social Foundations* found economists of different persuasions disagreeing about whether her analysis of the shortcomings of critical wage theory was 'remarkably lucid'[57] or demonstrated a rather weak comprehension,[58] whether it yielded 'perceptive answers'[59] or disappointed because of its outspokenly reformist slant.[60] J.R. Hicks, whose wage theory Barbara had taken as emblematic of the deficiencies displayed by all orthodox economic reasoning applied to wages, responded with a paper oppositely titled '*Economic* foundations of wage policy'.[61] It was the political orientation of economists as much as their technical approaches which set the tone of their responses to *Social Foundations*. The LSE reviewer, Henry Phelps Brown – a man after Barbara Wootton's own heart as he was also a fiction-writer[62] – found the issue of wage differentials 'not a useful object of negotiation or policy'.[63] What was anathema to many economists – the consideration of social influences on people's relative earnings – was applauded by other readers who praised the book as 'lucid, penetrating and timely'.[64] *The Political Quarterly* – a journal Barbara herself had helped to found – appreciated most of all its socialist devotion to equality: she had always excelled in the puncturing of humbug, but in this book she had also advanced a rational policy of equality in incomes 'that is of the utmost importance to socialists today'.[65]

Barbara continued to advertise the arguments of *Social Foundations* in a variety of formats, for example in a talk for a 'London Calling Asia' radio programme in 1958,[66] and in her Eleanor Rathbone Memorial Lecture, 'Remuneration in a Welfare State', given at the University of Liverpool in 1961. Eleanor Rathbone's work for the status and rights of women and financial benefits for families (a good use, noted Barbara, of the considerable financial fortune Rathbone had inherited from her own family) had led her, like Barbara, to the conclusion that the price of welfare was eternal vigilance. But was it not, inquired Barbara, perpetually astonishing that a so-called 'welfare state' should so consistently refuse to take responsibility for equal justice in relation to the incomes of its citizens? In this lecture, as in other places,[67] Barbara criticized the practice of trade union collective bargaining which had, she said, the effect of maintaining rather than challenging existing differentials, as well as causing price inflation: 'The collective bargain can I think justly be described as the last stronghold of complete *laissez-faire*'.[68] It was an extraordinary tactic for any true socialist to support. Her wrath about this hardened over the years: in 1980 (at the age of eighty-three) we find her in a discussion series issued together with colleagues by the Low Pay Unit reviewing the years of 'smash and grab' interspersed with periods of 'hastily improvised and temporary "incomes policies"' and concluding that the result has been neither social justice nor economic sense. Pay settlements are far too important to be left to the parties concerned; the public interest demands that they must be controlled.[69] By this time, she was given to such 'kite-flying ideas'[70] as that nobody should earn more than eight times as much as anybody else and inherited fortunes should be taxed out of existence within three generations. Such a programme, which materialized as a Fabian tract *In Pursuit of Equality*,[71] enlivened the dullness of much left-wing thinking in the 1970s.

Barbara Wootton was forty-one when she wrote *Lament*, fifty-eight when *Social Foundations* was published, and seventy-seven at the time of her third major excursion into the territory of professional economists. Her *Incomes Policy: An Inquest and a Proposal* continues with the theme of *Social Foundations*, and is an attempt to come up with a practical solution to the problem of the 'smash and grab' ethos whereby incomes are determined on the basis of who shouts loudest and with the most social power. It had given Barbara much satisfaction to write 'I told you so' in the Preface to the second edition of *Social Foundations*, which was issued three years before *Incomes Policy*.[72] The trends that she had analysed in the book's first edition had continued fast and furiously: the crisis of escalating inflation and unemployment, epidemic wage demands, and labour deficiencies in the public services, which she had prophesied, had all come to pass, taking her fellow economists by surprise: 'It seems that what the Baroness thought a long while ago, the rest of us may get round to seeing tomorrow', as a commentator in *New Society* observed.[73] In fact, the first edition of *Social Foundations* 'probably did more than any other private effort to stimulate discussion of the wage-policy problem'.[74]

Incomes Policy is a short book, and, although described in the Preface as a 'non-specialist essay for non-specialists',[75] it reads very much as a technical exposition of an idea, and one which makes few concessions to the non-specialist reader. It is written against a background of disillusionment with the efforts of Labour and

Conservative Governments in Britain between 1966 and 1972 to establish some sort of anti-inflationary control over incomes and prices. All their proposals, points out Barbara Wootton, were based on voluntarism, and most of the time 'income' meant only 'wages' – it did not cover salaries, or business income, or profits, or benefits in kind, and, despite Labour flourishes in the direction of equity, they did nothing to establish a framework of principles that would achieve this. 'Death from short-sightedness'[76] was her verdict. In *Incomes Policy* she put forward the idea of an Income Gains Tax (IGT). This built on the proposals she and her colleagues on the Colwyn Committee on National Debt and Taxation had examined in the 1920s for increasing taxation and using the tax system as a mechanism for greater economic equality. An IGT would be administered by the Inland Revenue and levied on personal incomes according to a graduated scale; smaller incomes would be allowed higher tax-free gains than larger incomes, and there would be a hundred per cent tax rate on any increase above prescribed maximum percentages in any financial year. Such a tax would mirror the already existing capital gains tax, but would tie allowable increases in personal incomes to increases in domestic output. In that sense, earnings would reflect efficiencies in the economy. But a second principle would also be built in – that of social justice: larger IGT-free exemptions would be allowed for the lowest earners. The proposed IGT would therefore have an exceptional combination of goals: it would be anti-inflationary at the same time as reducing economic inequality.

Barbara first articulated her ideas about an IGT in 'Why Not a Tax on Income Rises?', an article in *The Observer* in 1970. Among the other revolutionary suggestions she put forward was the proposal that manual workers should enjoy the same system of annual increments as was customary in professional employment.[77] There had been considerable interest during the 1970s in tax-based incomes policies both in Britain and in the USA, where they were even briefly floated as a proposal by the White House in 1977.[78] *Incomes Policy* spells out how a British version of the tax would work, and how exemptions to it and exceptional cases would be handled. Barbara was at pains to emphasize the main point, which is that the primary objective of an IGT is to ensure that 'nobody, not wage-earner, not shopkeeper, not industrial tycoon, not speculator in houses or raw materials or currency or anything else' should be able to enrich himself from inflation so as to have an interest in perpetuating and accelerating it.[79] Her effort in working out the scheme for an IGT was largely wasted, however. The idea did not catch on politically. In this, it shared a similar fate with the tax-based incomes policy proposed by American economists;[80] such proposals simply posed too much of a threat to established wealth and power structures. But Barbara also felt the dice were stacked against her personally. First of all, she had taken the wrong decision in deserting her usual publisher (Allen & Unwin) for a new one (Davis-Poynter), who had done a poor job and achieved very low sales for *Incomes Policy*. To Peter Townsend, whom she felt was among those who did not properly appreciate her book, she wrote to complain of the 'miserable publicity' that attended its publication.[81] But much more fundamentally, she was not the right person to get her ideas across. She was not a 'Friedman' or a 'Kaldor'. She was not a mainstream economist, and, like Joan Robinson, she did not belong to the charmed circle of men who ran professional economics.[82] However, it was probably some small consolation to her that J.K. Galbraith, whose work she much admired, read *Incomes Policy* 'with great interest'.[83]

Barbara Wootton never completely accomplished the transition from economist to sociologist. She disliked disciplinary labels: 'The important thing ... is not the nomenclature applied to particular branches of study, or the enforcement of a law of trespass between experts in different fields,' she said in *Lament for Economics*.[84] The important thing is to dedicate oneself to an egalitarian, happiness-maximizing public policy, and to employ whatever disciplinary tools are useful. She was reluctant to call herself a sociologist because the field of social studies (which she *would* admit to) was not an 'ology' like others, and she continued to select economic matters to write about, even economic aspects of institutions such as the family.[85] It was completely in line with her practical orientation to policy that she contributed to various national commissions on wages and pay over the period when she was emancipating herself from the strictures of professional economics. Her influence is obviously present in the conclusions of the Royal Commission on Civil Service Pay and Conditions, of which she was a member in 1953–5. The Commission's Report recommended that equal pay for men and women should be phased in over six years for most grades, and also instituted the principle that Civil Service pay should be comparable with that of others doing broadly similar work outside the Service.[86] One offshoot of this exercise was a separate investigation into the pay of postal workers, to which Barbara also contributed. The Union of Post Office Workers was demanding a substantial pay increase and had refused the normal negotiating machinery. The Committee on the Pay of Postmen's Report, issued in 1964, recommended more systematic comparisons with other work requiring similar skills, but was not conciliatory enough to prevent industrial action.[87] Barbara was not a member of the 1946 Royal Commission on Equal Pay, but, with eight other economists (Hubert Henderson and Joan Robinson among them), she wrote a signature Appendix to the Minutes of Evidence,[88] a radical essay on applied economics.[89] More than most other issues related to the wage and salary structure, the ethics of the gender gap pulled against the neoclassicists' argument that economic efficiency demanded a freely competitive market. Here was a direct contradiction between ethics and efficiency.

Thirty years after *Lament* was published, Barbara referred in a letter to *The Times* to 'the far-off days when I was trained as an economist (a title which a liking for commonsense has since caused me to renounce)'. She never lost her ability to offer incisively-worded solutions to economic problems. Talking about the financial crisis of the late 1960s in the same letter, for instance, she referred to the Russian habit of shooting speculators – a practice she did *not* recommend – and went on to ask the enduringly relevant rhetorical question, 'Is it not time that some steps were taken to put a stop to the activities of those who, in the irresponsible pursuit of private gain, periodically wreck the currencies upon whose stability ordinary citizens rely?'[90] In another letter to the same newspaper, written when she was eighty-three, she complained that control of the monetary supply was pointless unless there was also control of where it went to: 'A monetarist without an incomes policy is like a man with one leg. He can only hop and stumble … before long, without his other leg, he is bound to fall flat on his face'.[91] This letter elicited a response from a Dr K.V. Roberts, who had an alternative idea that everyone should be paid a basic rate and above that they should be able to earn in the free market.[92] Barbara did not like this idea, but she did wholeheartedly support the notion, and had advocated it herself many times, that every citizen should receive a share of the national income without any kind of means test or expectation of work to be done. Such a situation, which was already enshrined as a principle in child benefits and pensions, would be enormously attractive in saving the cost of all the bureaucratic organization involved in assessing people's entitlements to benefits.[93] She continued to engage with economic ideas and to promulgate her carefully worked out scheme for an IGT, and she also watched what was happening to professional economics. There were regular reviews of economics books for the journal *New Society,* remarkable for their no-nonsense tones: who on earth would read, she complained in 1978, aged eighty-one, the 658 pages of Rostow's *The World Economy,* and how many slaves had he used to write it?[94] When slightly younger, in 1975, she was pleased to read and review for the *Journal of Social Policy* two books written by formidably important men with radical economic ideas: the American economist Galbraith, who had admired her *Incomes Policy*, and the Swedish economist and politician Gunnar Myrdal. Both had Establishment reputations, and were listened to by those in government, yet both 'with one voice' condemned 'the work of contemporary economists in academic, business and government circles as being largely rubbish'.[95] The onslaughts in both the books she was reviewing – Galbraith's *Economics and the Public Purpose*, and Myrdal's *Against the Stream: Critical Essays on Economics* – were explicitly directed against what they called 'neo-classical economics'. But was the prefix correct, she wondered? There was nothing new about it. It all sounded too much like what she had read for her own *Lament for Economics* forty years before.

In the year of this déjà vu, 1975, she accepted an invitation to give a prestigious lecture at the LSE. Her chosen subject was the future of the British economy. The stance she adopted was one ascribed to her by the Conservative Prime Minister Edward Heath – that of 'heartless prophet'. The lecture was an occasion for looking both backwards and forwards. We all know that capitalism can work, she said, at least in the sense of turning out vast quantities of commodities, many of them of 'doubtful utility and frequently directed to the wrong addresses',[96] but it works only if the two main groups involved in it behave properly: the workers must work, and for wages that maintain demand but do not over-inflate costs; and the businessmen must organize production, make profits, and reinvest these so further production is possible. But neither side was actually behaving very well: the workers were striking or threatening to strike for inflationary pay increases, and the businessmen were refusing to invest – only in their case it was not called striking, but 'loss of confidence'. Capitalism was breaking down. It was astonishing, when you thought about it, as she obviously had, over many years, and through many fashions in economic analysis, that complex economic systems so wholly reliant on private enterprise should ever have worked at all. Indeed, capitalism had collapsed completely in some places. The speed of change was startling, and she wanted to draw her audience's attention to this in a personal note: 'I was myself grown-up and married before there was a single communist state in the world; yet I have lived to see not far short of one-third of the world's population relying for its daily bread on a fully socialized economy'.[97] Britain needed an economy which served the public interest. The radical Baroness proposed a three-point programme which would have come as no surprise to any of those who had read *Lament for Economics*, or *The Social Foundations of Wage Policy*, or *Incomes Policy*: more public ownership of industry; an effective incomes policy; and the abolition of poverty. Having gone through the main outline of what needed to be done, and identified various hopeful signs, she ended on a note whose optimism we now know to have been misplaced: 'I cannot conceive that we shall turn back on the road on which we have begun to travel and that at the end of this century, this country will still be floundering in the crumbling chaos of decaying capitalism, still fighting inflation and unemployment, and staggering from one financial crisis to the next; and still leaving the distribution of income to the law of the jungle'.[98]

11

Testament for Social Science

When the sociologist T.H. Marshall gave his inaugural lecture as a Professor of Social Institutions at the London School of Economics in 1946, the whole tenor of his text was to defend sociology as a serious subject. The defence was necessary. As Barbara Wootton pointed out in her autobiography, 'The social sciences are indeed not much older than I am myself.'[1] Marshall's metaphor was that of sociology as a 'poor lady' standing at the crossroads wondering which road to take. There was the journey of theoretical sociology through the realm of abstraction – what Marshall called the 'path to the stars'; and then there was the passionate empiricist, driven to collect more and more facts without quite knowing why. This latter 'path to the sands' was equally a mistake. No wonder the poor lady hesitated.[2] By the time of Marshall's lecture, Barbara had already made some of her own choices, and she had had others made for her. Starting out as a classical scholar, she had migrated to economics and discovered the limitations of that subject as a practical study of the real world, so the road ahead for her was clear: she needed to turn herself into a more broadly based social scientist instead. But she would take neither of Marshall's paths. *Her* social science was to be informed by important social questions and moulded by the need to find answers from the material of people's lives and experiences.

Barbara Wootton's journey from Classics to social science did not follow a linear, rational pattern. She herself always said she never thought of her work as a 'career' in the sense of a chosen ladder which led her determinedly from one place to another: 'There was never a time when I sat down and thought what shall I do to earn money?'[3] 'I don't at all feel as if I had shaped my life, but rather that it has just happened to me.'[4] In 1944, when she was forty-seven, she had a quarter of a century of work in education, political activity and public service behind her. The second world war of her lifetime had not been so personally disastrous for her as the first, but she recalled it (a little strangely, perhaps, in view of the significant agitations for peace and human rights which she had helped to command), as a depressingly fallow period, 'a semi-conscious interlude between one phase of life and the next'. She remembered 'looking at some women in a bus queue, and thinking to myself, "Those must be women in their forties. What can it feel like to be a woman in her forties? This is a decade that I don't ever seem to have had"'.[5] She was still a formidably good-looking woman, dressed in a secure middle-class style – from the London store Debenham and Freebody's, according to friends.[6] She had a husband, but marriage was not conventionally demanding as it was then for most women. She did not have to cook or wash or clean for George – not only because of the famous Mrs Brown whose wartime duties were composed of relieving JP Mrs Wootton of hers – but because, as early as 1947, Barbara held the modern view that, when man and wife are both working, their domestic responsibilities should be the same. Men already did quite a lot of washing up, she noted with approval, and some could occasionally be glimpsed pushing prams in which toddlers clutched the family ration books; but real domestic equality would take a long time to come. It would be a gradual revolution, if only because men would not stop exploiting their wives until their mothers stopped spoiling *them*.[7] (There are perhaps echoes here of Barbara's own childhood experiences as a girl with two brothers.)

On the eve of a new era of Labour Government and the much-acclaimed welfare state, Barbara was in many ways at the height of her powers. She was in no doubt that social science had an important role to play in designing this new society that would maximize welfare for *all* its citizens, and she was poised to be one of its principal actors. But where did Barbara Wootton really belong? The cloistered corridors of Girton College had not proved a suitable institutional home; research for the TUC and the Labour Party had been disappointingly, but unsurprisingly, subject to the constraints of party politics; and adult education, both at Morley College and for the wider University of London, had made use of her very considerable talents as a teacher and an organizer, but had not supplied a base for the kind of research she knew ought to be done (and which she wanted to do). The struggling social investigator inside Barbara is evident in two small pieces of work she undertook with her adult education students in the early years of the Second World War. In the first, they designed a study of the contemporary class structure, with a questionnaire for fellow-students which asked about family occupational history, political allegiances, schooling and employment.[8] The inquirers particularly wanted to know what the terms 'working class' and 'ruling class' then meant. This project, conducted in the difficult circumstances of the bombing of London in 1940, involved much usefully disciplined thinking about how to define social class, and yielded a fascinating table detailing the backgrounds of current politicians, civil servants, judges and magistrates, which included information on which clubs they belonged to and at what annual cost.[9] The second outcome of Barbara's empirical enquiries with her students was called 'Chaos in the Social Services', and was the forerunner of many subsequent more ambitious descriptions of how the social services work – or not. Most of the students who helped with it were professional social workers, and they must surely have been horrified to find so many anomalies and contradictions in the cash benefits available to citizens. For example, it was financially better for a man to be injured in an air raid than by an explosion at work, although for young men this rule was inverted; and health insurance enjoyed 'the ignominious distinction' of putting 'a premium on sin' by paying less to married than to single women.[10] All this, and much other, chaos, had been inherited from the old poor law, and it was up to William Beveridge in his eagerly awaited Report to tidy it up.

William Beveridge did just that. 'So full of meat, yet so appetizingly written, and with a record of sales which would hearten any established novelist – the Beveridge Report is a grand piece of work', wrote Barbara approvingly in February 1943, two months after the launch of the famous *Report on Social Insurance and Allied Services*.[11] Beveridge's early years had been spent in India, firmly within the embrace of unprogressive English colonial society, and he had arrived, like Barbara, via the study of Classics at Oxbridge, at an appreciation of the considerably greater challenges that were to be found for men and women of energy and commitment among modern cultures. In 1919, he took his conviction that empirical research and observation lay at the heart of social science's role in solving social problems to the LSE, where he became Director. His Social Insurance Report provided the Government with a Plan for Social Security which was not only visionary but workable, and its publication, as Barbara Wootton intimated in her review, transformed him from an obscure academic figure into a national hero. Within two weeks of the Report's publication, nineteen out of twenty people had heard of it;[12] Pathé News flashed pictures of Beveridge, 'looking prophetically white-haired and benign'[13] into every cinema in the land. Frank Pakenham, Lord Longford, recalled going into his local newsagent the morning the Report came out and asking for a morning paper; they were all sold out. '"It's that Sir William Beveridge," explained the shopkeeper. "He's going to abolish want".'[14]

'A revolutionary moment in the world's history is a time for revolutions, not for patching,' explained the benign white-haired man as a guiding principle for all his recommendations.[15] Beveridge's remit, to 'tidy up' existing schemes of social insurance and related services and make recommendations, particularly about the inter-relationships between these multiple schemes, had been interpreted as widely as it could possibly have been. His Plan for Social Security was part of a broad social policy programme, an element in a much-needed attack on the five 'giant evils' of physical Want, Disease, Ignorance, Squalor, and Idleness. The Beveridge vision was of a society in which the capitalist spirit would, significantly, still be nurtured: security against the five evils could, and should, be 'combined with freedom and enterprise and responsibility of the individual for his own life'.[16]

Barbara liked the Beveridge Report because what it proposed was precisely the simplification of the sorts of anomalies she and her students had found. She liked the Plan for its universalism – no longer would we suffer the distinction of the insured and the uninsured classes: the principle was that everyone would pay the same weekly national insurance contribution, and, in return, state benefits would be available to meet the needs of the sick, the unemployed, retired or widowed. Since the rich would not be exempt, this, following characteristically sharp Woottonesque logic, had the advantage of 'saving anyone the bother of finding out whether you are rich or not'. Further, the Beveridge Plan took the eminently practical and wise view that the benefits available for those who cannot earn (for whatever reason) must be enough to live on. But the Beveridge Report's conventionally sexist treatment of married women did not escape Barbara's keen eye.[17] Perhaps, also, what people did not quite realize – and this Barbara pointed out in a Forces Educational Broadcast in the summer of 1946 – was that Beveridge's Plan had a history. It was not quite his own invention. Germany had introduced compulsory insurance against sickness in 1884, long before Lloyd George's National Insurance Act of 1911 in Britain, on which the Beveridge Plan was built, had initiated compulsory health insurance for wage-earners. The New Zealanders were also pioneers in introducing a Social Security Act in 1938 which covered all the same principles as the Beveridge Plan on a very generous scale. 'I don't think that there is much doubt', declared Barbara, 'that some of the Beveridge ideas come from over there. I hope that Lord Beveridge won't mind if we say that his plan is a bit of a mongrel.' She softened the blow by adding, 'Mongrels, by the way, are sometimes said to be intelligent'.[18]

Intelligent mongrels do not, however, necessarily spur governments into action. The wartime Coalition Government considered not publishing the Report, and the House of Commons debate was lukewarm in its appreciation. 'What has happened to the Beveridge Report?' demanded Barbara Wootton in an article in *The Political Quarterly* in the autumn of 1943.[19] 'It is dreadful how the public has gone cold about the Beveridge Report', she wrote to its author in 1944.[20] Beveridge shared her desperation, convinced that his plan needed to be put into effect before the end of the War, and that the Government would have to be leant on for this to happen.[21] To this end, a campaigning body, the Social Security League, was formed in the summer of 1943. Barbara Wootton was its Chairman, and the magazine publisher Edward Hulton was its Treasurer; Beveridge later agreed to be President. Barbara, Hulton and the League's Secretary, Joan Simeon

Clarke, wrote to *The Manchester Guardian* explaining the aims of the League: to 'press for swift action' by further publicizing the details of the Report and urging the Government to respect 'the popular desire for immediate legislation'.[22] They held a party to celebrate the new initiative: 'Socially secure in Mr. Edward Hulton's Mayfair house and free from want on an anonymous donor's chicken sandwiches and claret-cup', indelicately observed *The Manchester Guardian*, guests listened to Beveridge, recently returned from his foreign travels, enthusing about international support (in North and Latin America) for the principles of his plan.[23]

For those, like Barbara Wootton, who had lived through the inter-war years and had struggled to imagine a better organized, more peaceful and just society, Labour's landslide victory in the 1945 election must have seemed the entry to a promised land. It is the habit of warfare to generate radical politics, and these particular manifestations grew from the seed of the 'planned society' which policy advocates such as Barbara Wootton had persistently contended in the 1930s, and which the circumstances of the Second World War had made a matter of national necessity. And so the new Labour Government *was* the promised land, in many ways. Prime Minister Attlee rapidly set about the business of reconstruction, with Barbara's friend Hugh Dalton at his right hand as Chancellor of the Exchequer. The King's speech that year straightforwardly listed public ownership of industry, a comprehensive scheme of social insurance and a national health service among the new administration's immediate goals. The Bank of England, the Coal Industry, Inland Transport, Civil Aviation, and Cable and Wireless communication all came under public control in 1946; Electricity and Gas followed in 1947–8. The 1946 Housing Act established the principle of housing as a public rather than a private problem, and the Town and Country Planning Act of 1947 created order out of chaos by cutting the number of agencies involved in planning from 1,441 to 145.[24] The right to education was extended to secondary school level, and universities entered a welcome phase of expansion, aided by increased Government grants to the tune of two-thirds of their budgets in 1951.[25] With a series of Acts in 1945–8 – Family Allowances, the NHS, National Insurance and National Assistance – much of Beveridge's Plan was put into effect. Among the deviations from the original, which the members of the Social Security League were quick to point out, were that levels of provision for children, older people and the unemployed proposed in the Beveridge Report had been scaled down, and the Government's scheme replaced social insurance with emergency assistance as the guarantor of freedom from Want. Along with nine others, including G.D.H. Cole and Seebohm Rowntree, Barbara signed the document putting forward these criticisms.[26] Thereafter, she kept a watchful eye on the way that Beveridge's principles were implemented.

Why, for instance, she asked in 1949, did the new National Health Service treat feet differently from eyes or teeth? Feet were out, but eyes and teeth were in. Three million people had acquired or were acquiring spectacles, and 130,000 were going to the dentist every week. Since neither wearing spectacles nor visiting the dentist were things you would do unless you had to, Barbara took this as firm evidence that state intervention was successfully preventing many bodily inconveniences.[27]

As regards the role of social science in understanding society, Beveridge was a man after Barbara's own heart: 'If, in the Social Sciences, we cannot yet run or fly,' he declared on retiring from his LSE post in 1937, 'we ought to be content to walk, or to creep on all fours as infants ... theorising not based on facts and not controlled by facts assuredly does lead nowhere'.[28] At this time, for some time to come, and in line with Marshall's metaphor of the hesitating lady, social science was still an immature discipline, the child of arguing parents – one passionate about social reform, the other devoted to the scientific study of social facts. The only real chance of the marriage working was if science could be seen as the route to effective social reform. This was how most of the key instigators of social science in Britain, in continental Europe, and in the United States saw it. Comte, Mill, Spencer, Booth, the Webbs, and others whose names are all indissolubly attached to the emergence of social science, had faith in a natural science of society that would yield unassailable facts about the workings of the social system – the here-and-now of how human beings interact with one another and their material environment. Social science offered a way – *the* way – to understand, and thus to control, a society subject to the disruptive and socially unequal effects of rapid change. Barbara's own philosophy was in direct lineal descent from these figures; it was 'positivist' in its belief that the realities of the social world can be described and quantified, and in understanding that such an exercise is key to social progress.[29]

Before the Second World War, the social sciences occupied, outside London 'the smallest, least popular, and least well-endowed position' of all university subjects.[30] Within London, they had the LSE, founded in 1895, as their first institutional base in Britain. The idea of the LSE had been born at a Surrey breakfast in the summer of 1894, when the renowned 'firm' of the Webbs (Beatrice and Sidney) had got up early to discuss what to do about a bequest of money left to benefit Fabian socialism by an eccentric Derby solicitor.[31] The LSE was 'the most successful of all the Webbian experiments',[32] but, until at least the 1920s, it was a small and quite obscure part of the University of London. Britain's first Professor of Sociology, L.T. Hobhouse, had been appointed to the LSE in 1907. Hobhouse was a liberal theorist, trained, like Barbara, in Classics; he taught philosophy, was interested in trade unionism, wrote for *The Manchester Guardian* and had no qualifications we would today recognize as relevant to a professorship in sociology. But sociology was then very much a matter of 'armchair reflection'.[33] Sociology was not the same as social science or empirical research. For many years, social science retained its historical connection with social work; the Department of Social Science which was founded at the LSE in 1912, for example, was intended for the training of social workers, as was the social science that was taught at Westfield College in London where Barbara Wootton cut her own teaching teeth in 1919–20 on the young ladies she remembered as pearls-and-twinset do-gooders.

By 1937, when Beveridge relinquished the directorship, the LSE was the largest centre for the study of social sciences in Britain, with a threefold increase in its premises and a sevenfold increase in its budget since its modest beginnings.[34] The writer, and later *New Statesman* editor, Kingsley Martin, who was also on the staff of the LSE for a time, once paid Beveridge the compliment (subsequently much quoted by Beveridge) of saying that he 'ruled over an empire on which the concrete never set'.[35] This empire, with its mix of theoretical and practical activities, would have been a natural home for Barbara Wootton, but her research scholarship there in 1919 had not been a success. However, a new opportunity to work at the LSE arrived in 1944, with the advertisement of a Professorship in Social Institutions. By this time, Barbara felt she had spent enough years 'in the highways and byways of extra-mural education' and wanted to find a more mainstream academic post. The choice was limited, because she was reluctant to leave London.[36] Another possibility presented itself at the same time, a Readership in Social Studies at Bedford College. Barbara asked Beveridge to write her references for both posts, but she hesitated about the Bedford one, because the place she really wanted to go was the LSE.[37] In his willingly-written testimonials, Beveridge praised Barbara Wootton's combination of 'three things not always found together': 'the capacity to understand and argue about matters of economic theory'; 'knowledge and interest in social problems and the working of social institutions'; and 'clarity and force of expression'.[38]

The LSE rejected Barbara's application. There was already a favoured candidate, the sociologically-minded T.H. Marshall, who had been on the staff there since 1925. So it was Marshall, the inside man, the man with a theoretical disposition, who got the Professorship of Social Institutions at the LSE, and Barbara, the outside woman, the woman whose mind turned on the empirical usefulness of the social sciences, went instead to Bedford College in 1944 as Reader in Social Studies. The Bedford offer 'only partially mitigated' her disappointment at being rejected by the LSE,[39] for in those years the LSE was very much the 'intellectual bastion'[40] of the social sciences, and exclusion from such a bastion could not be taken lightly by anyone with any ambition. Had Barbara got the LSE post, the future of sociology at the LSE might have been quite different, and so might her own.

She made the best of her disappointment. That summer, she wrote to Vera Seal, her long-time student, supporter and colleague, 'I hope you will be pleased that I have got one of the only two jobs in the world I wanted'.[41] The Tutorial Class Department was sad to see her go; in its note to this effect, the Council particularly noted her 'high academic attainments, her wide intellectual sympathies, her administrative skills, and her keen interest in Adult Education which have enabled her to render notable service to this cause'.[42] Barbara certainly left her classes in a healthy state: eight-eight, the largest number ever, in the 1943–4 session: 1,583 students producing the tutorial burden of 9,420 pieces of written work. But she had for some time been weary of the tutorial class problems, which recurred 'in much the same form with monotonous regularity' year after year: variable attendance, poor quality of written work, opinion rather than a thirst for knowledge.[43]

Bedford College presented a different set of challenges, but it was a bit like going home. While working for the Labour Party, Barbara had given a course of lectures in social economics there in 1924. Her mother, Adela, had started her own undergraduate life at Bedford College in 1882, and had later replaced the Greek lecturer at Bedford for a term. Aunt Fanny had held a position as Honorary Secretary to the Council of Bedford College for two years before Emily Davies recruited her for a similar post at Girton College, and from 1909 had also been a long-term Trustee of Bedford College. A student who was at Bedford College in the 1880s recalled the real personal interest and 'gracious kindness' of both Fanny Kensington and 'Mrs Mylne' (Aunt Juliet – though what Aunt Juliet was doing in the corridors of Bedford College is not clear).[44]

Barbara joined Bedford College in October 1944. Her new workplace was in an attractive area of London, in Regent's Park, with its boating ponds and flower gardens, and close to London Zoo. Bedford College, 'the first and last University College for women in England',[45] had started out as the 'Ladies' College, Bedford Square' in 1849, twenty years before Emily Davies and her co-campaigners established the modest beginnings of Girton College. Bedford College was unique among the early women's colleges in providing a full range of teaching for women students within its own walls. It had moved to Regent's Park from Bedford Square and adjacent houses in 1909, as a result of a legacy left by Robert Turle, a wealthy businessman. The Turle bequest enabled the College to take over the Crown Lease of a large Victorian house and eight acres of grounds, and to design and erect a whole new set of buildings incorporating a classical quadrangle and a 'bridge of sighs' as well as science laboratories, a residence for the Principal, rooms for students and a library. The woman whose vision inspired Bedford College, Elizabeth Jesser Reid, was a wealthy social reformer, like many of those who pioneered women's education, and she saw the College as 'a place where by culture of the mind and the acquiring of some knowledge young women might be saved from the dreary futility of the life led by the greater number of those whose parents belonged to the professional and upper middle classes'.[46] When Barbara took up her appointment, Bedford College still admitted only women students: men came as postgraduates two years later and, as undergraduates, only in 1965. She observed a transformation in student habits since she had first been at Bedford twenty years before: hats had disappeared, stockings were on the way out, and students requested leave of absence for such modern reasons as to get divorced and compete in a motor cycle race.[47] But Bedford retained a genteel air of unimpeachable Edwardian respectability, with waxed floors smelling of fresh polish at the start of term.[48]

The duties of her post covered responsibility for students taking the BA Honours Degree in Sociology as well as those preparing for the College Certificate in Social Studies. Like the departments at the LSE and at Westfield, social science at Bedford College inherited the tradition of social-work training. The department Barbara headed there was a reconstituted version of a 'Hygiene Department' which had provided courses for a two-year diploma taken by women public health workers from 1895 to 1919. In 1916, the Charity Organization Society set up an arrangement whereby the College would provide lectures on Social Economics and Social Ethics as part of its Social Work Certificate course. This was the kernel of the Department of Social Studies, whose first Director was the social reformer Eva Hubback – the woman who had in 1927 taken over from Barbara as Principal of Morley College (the world of academic social science was truly a small one in those days).[49] Most of the students who were Barbara's new responsibility at Bedford College were destined for careers in social work. In the years of post-war university expansion, there was such a high level of demand for limited places that Barbara, with her characteristic scepticism of customary but unevidenced methods, proposed they might take all applicants who wore size five shoes, a common size that would yield about the right number of students. 'The suggestion, I need hardly say, was not taken seriously, but I have often wondered whether the results would have been noticeably different if it had been.'[50] Women with different-sized feet enjoyed Barbara Wootton's attention as a teacher. Freda Russell, then Freda Holomstock, recalls Barbara's vibrant figure and wry sense of humour at lectures; when she was interviewed for a place, Barbara interrogated her: 'What do you want to come here for? Why didn't you apply to LSE? We're only women here'.[51] The 'only women' clause had a new meaning in the post-war years, as another of Barbara's students remembers: 'Coping with a diverse group of ex-service women who had carried responsibilities usually confined to men, was a new experience for the "Ladies' College" and quite a challenge for us all'. In a time of 'bankrupt Britain', with rationing and high unemployment and low wages, Barbara's approach to life, teaching and learning was 'both serious and demanding', and it gave her students 'a vision and hopes for the future'.[52] Rachel Pierce, a sociology degree student in 1951–4, retained a strong memory of Barbara for 'her encouragement and almost cajoling of us, a class of young women, to go out and make a contribution to the world. We should not hang back and wait for opportunities, but go out and sell ourselves, demonstrate the, relatively new, skills we would be gaining as sociology graduates.'[53]

In 1948, Bedford College elevated Barbara from a Readership to a Professorship. She was made a Professor of Social Studies, not Sociology – as she argued, social studies rather than social science was the most that could be claimed at this stage of things.[54] She always disliked the word 'sociology', preferring 'social science', because the latter term referred to method rather than any coherent body of knowledge, and the social sciences had a long way to go before they could catch up with the natural ones.[55] Her definition of the social sciences was broad: 'all those studies which seek to explain the behaviour and relationships of human beings and the nature of their customs and institutions through the method of inference from accurate observation which is common to all scientific investigation'.[56] She was excited by the possibility of setting up a programme of empirical research at Bedford College. Social research was lagging even further behind general social science in its fight for academic recognition. Two years after she took up her new post, the Committee on the Provision for Social and Economic Research chaired by Sir John Clapham bemoaned the general lack of appreciation for 'the great practical knowledge' social and economic research could supply to the smooth running of modern industrial communities. The Clapham Committee had been set up at the behest of Clement Attlee, then Deputy Prime Minister, who was sympathetic to the pleas of those social scientists who argued that their skills were needed to understand social change.[57] Its Report showed that spending on social science posts was a mere six per cent of that devoted to science and medicine; among the social science subjects, economics was fairly well represented, but the study of social questions was scarcely at its beginning: 'the idea that provision for research in these fields by way of libraries, calculating machines, computers and research assistants, is as important as provision for laboratories and experimental stations seems still to present an appearance of novelty and paradox'. These aspects of social science university departments consumed less than two per cent of the budgets allocated to science and medicine. Lamentably, social research depended on the 'sporadic and discontinuous subventions of private benefactors' (insecure handouts from private individuals).[58] The Committee recommended an injection of some £250,000–£300,000 a year (between £6.5 million and £7.8 million in 2010 prices) into social and economic research, but it proposed that this should occur as a gradual development. It rejected the idea that a Social and Economic Research Council along the lines of the Medical Research Council should be set up with government money to provide a formal infrastructure for social research. This milestone would happen only in 1965, after Barbara had left the academic world.

The Clapham Report also recommended to the University Grants Committee (UGC) – the body established in 1919 to advise government on the disposition of state grants to support university education in the UK – that a Sub-Committee should be appointed to consider further the position of social science research. Barbara Wootton was invited to be a member of this Sub-Committee. Other familiar names on it were G.D.H. Cole, Margery Fry, Hector Hetherington, T.H. Marshall, Lionel Robbins and R.H. Tawney. *Their* recommendations were for a substantial increase in the earmarked grant for social science research.[59] The increase, which was agreed, was intended to provide for Chairs and other teaching posts, research staff, libraries and equipment. The timing was splendid for the new energetic Head of the Bedford College Sociology, Social Studies and Economics Department. Here was the opportunity to set up a research laboratory, a powerhouse of testable hypotheses and practical projects of field enquiries that would root the contribution of social science in the soil it needed to flourish – detailed investigations of real people's experiences and living conditions. With the new UGC money, Barbara was able to set up a small research unit, and she recruited Margot Jefferys, a social scientist, to head it. Margot had trained in economic history at the LSE and was in the process of transforming herself from a civil servant into an academic.[60] She always got on well with Barbara, although she remembered her as someone who could unwittingly make enemies. 'It was partly, I think, because, if she thought you weren't talking sense, she found it very difficult not to convey that … Her caustic tongue, when she used it, was quite difficult to take.'[61] Barbara and Margot designed a modest study of employment changes in Battersea and Dagenham. This was an attempt to look at industrial mobility among male workers in 1951 in two areas of London, chosen because they were both within easy and cheap reach of central London and they provided contrasting labour patterns. The study addressed the kind of mismatch between economic theory and practice which, in the 1930s, had led Barbara to lament the nature of the contribution economics could make to public policy: if free market capitalism was an efficient method for distributing resources, why did workers move or not move between industrial sectors with different labour demands, opportunities and rewards in ways that did not seem to serve the efficiency of the market very well at all?[62] The book published as a result of the Battersea and Dagenham project was commended as 'an excellent study' which answered a number of employment policy questions.[63]

The labour mobility project was the first output of the first social research unit at Bedford College, but it was also, unhappily the last. Some of the new unit's academic colleagues were hostile to Barbara's initiative. The sabotage campaign was led by Lillian Penson, Professor of Modern History at Bedford, and politically aided by Penson's post as Vice-Chancellor of the University of London. Penson and her colleagues cited the principle of academic freedom as a reason why funds should not be devoted to research.[64] In other words, they were jealous.[65] The details of the campaign against Barbara have been lost to history, but it is clear that she was not alone in being the victim of professional jealousy. Ross McGregor, son of O.R. McGregor (Mac), the sociologist and friend recruited by Barbara to Bedford College in 1947, recalls his father having 'a huge punch up' with Bedford, overtly over Mac's purchase of a primitive computer; the scientists assumed that any piece of expensive mechanical kit was for them and nobody else.[66] Underlying the College's reaction to Barbara's attempt to institute empirical research as a key element in any social science enterprise was the contemptuous attitude towards sociology still held by many in other academic disciplines. There was also what some considered the 'terminal sickness' of Bedford College itself, which, as a result of weak leadership and other problems, would eventually relinquish its status as an independent school of the University in 1985 and merge with 'another unsuccessful college in the outer suburbs'.[67]

The upshot of these wranglings was that Bedford College returned the UGC money and Barbara's research unit was disbanded. Margot Jefferys left Bedford College and went to the London School of Hygiene and Tropical Medicine, although she later returned to Bedford and overcame these early disasters by becoming Director of Social Research there and the first ever Professor of Medical Sociology. Barbara had to soldier on. She was hugely disappointed by these experiences. It was not at all the kind of opportunity she had envisaged when she had decided to become a proper academic. In a letter to Vera Seal, she said that what had happened at Bedford was 'enough to give anyone a persecution mania, mine was really getting very bad. I should have got ill if I had gone on ... If the truth was told I have hated the job there all the eight years I've done it and I think for good reasons.'[68] With that adroit mix of serendipity and careful networking that marks the careers of many successful people, Barbara did manage a creative solution that enabled her to stay in mainstream academia while devoting her time to research. She was successful in obtaining a six-year grant from the Nuffield Foundation to survey the achievements and future needs of social science research – a story told in the next chapter.

She told the College about her grant from the Nuffield Foundation in January 1952. Geraldine Jebb, who had just retired as Principal of the College, and who had in common with Barbara a Cambridge economics background, wrote to say the news was perfectly splendid but 'the fly in the ointment' was her giving up the Bedford post in which she had 'done such magnificent work (even in a state of frustration!)'.[69] Richard Titmuss, two years into his own appointment as Professor of Social Administration in the parallel department to Barbara's at the LSE, and having his own troubles with professional territorialism, wrote to her, too: 'What delights me most is the news that freedom for B.W. really lies ahead. What fun it will be!' He went on to say, 'It is sweet of your students to want me as a "second best" (for I've heard how they adore you) but I too want freedom'.[70] Presumably Barbara was concerned about abandoning her students, and, either seriously or in jest, had suggested to him that he might take her place.

Being Barbara, she was unable to let the whole episode of the stillbirth of social research at Bedford College go without publishing a sustained counter-attack. In her 'Reflections on Resigning a Professorship', she observed that at least some of her negative experiences at Bedford were of 'more than autobiographical interest' – they happened to other people as well.[71] The problem was not only that non-social scientists failed to understand the need for such research, but the universities were suffering from an overgrowth of bureaucracy. The contractual requirement, common to all professorial posts, to advance one's subject through research, could be viewed only as a 'piece of misplaced irony' when the actual conditions of one's job were so overloaded with administrative burdens – committee meetings; decisions about syllabuses and courses, and staff and student problems; appointing staff; writing testimonials; arranging field visits and student placements; advising government departments; participating in professional associations; and so on and so forth. A peculiar aspect of the way universities have developed is that all of this work has accumulated at the top of the status hierarchy. The more important you are, the more of it you have to do. Moreover, the traditional notion that research and teaching must go hand in hand (teachers are good only if they are also researchers and vice versa) was quite without evidence. But where are the research professorships that are needed to solve this dilemma? Before the Nuffield Foundation solved hers, Barbara had been unable to find any for which to apply. (If she had been a man, she would have been eligible for a Fellowship of All Souls College, Oxford.) The sting in the tail of her success in getting the Nuffield Foundation grant was that, although the grant paid her a professorial level salary (plus other expenses), Bedford College saw fit to strip her of her title. This was not technically necessary, and would almost certainly not happen now; one is bound to wonder whether an element of gender discrimination was involved, but Barbara herself did not spot one. Giving up a professorship was not normal academic behaviour, and doing so in order to fulfil one of the most important conditions of its tenure (carrying out research) was to label oneself a deviant from the dominant academic culture. Finding herself at odds with dominant values was something that happened to Barbara all her life. Her resignation, in March 1950, from the UGC after only two years, must have been connected with her disappointment at the fate of her efforts to establish social research at Bedford College.[72]

Fortunately, however, there were other ways of advancing the cause of social science outside the narrow jealousies of particular institutions. Richard Titmuss and Barbara Wootton were both signatories of a letter to *The Times* in May 1951 headed 'Sociological Studies' which reported the recent founding of a new body, the British Sociological Association (BSA).[73] The object of the Association was to promote interest in sociology, advance its study and application, and encourage contact and co-operation between workers in different fields. It would provide opportunities for the discussion of both theoretical and practical problems, and promote good research whose results would be cumulative and lead to the development of a systematic study of society. Within two weeks, the letter had drawn 360 enquiries.[74] The BSA's sponsors thoughtfully decided not to define sociology: 'If a definition of the interests of the Association is needed, it should deliberately be made very broad, embracing such fields as contemporary, historical and comparative studies of social structure, morals and religion; sociological aspects of Law; social philosophy; social psychology; social-biological aspects of mankind; social aspects of urban and rural settlement; human geography; and methodological aspects of social investigations'.[75] One senses the brushstroke of Barbara at the end of the list. Apart from being a founding member of the BSA, she served a term as Chair (1957–59) and was President from 1959 to 1964. During this period, she was one of only five women to be associated with the BSA; the other forty-five activists were all men.[76] Perhaps it was this history which led the BSA to hail the election in 1975 of Sheila Allen as the first woman President. When Allen apologized to Barbara for this error, Barbara expressed no surprise at becoming so invisible so quickly.[77]

A.H. Halsey, later Professor of Social and Administrative Studies at Oxford, was a cheeky young man at the launch of the BSA in 1951. He was reminded of the occasion when it celebrated its 50th year. At this, 'Jo Banks [J.A. Banks, Professor of Sociology at Leicester] gave a reminiscence talk … in which he referred very confidently – and he did have a good memory – to an argument that I had had with

Barbara about whether this thing should be formed or not ... He said it electrified the rest of us because I was very cocky and self-confident. I'd already decided that she, being the Cambridge sort of woman that she was, was automatically in the Establishment and she had just as confidently put me down, so it was sort of honours even, and what the content was I can't remember ... she was interested in some way or other in the formation of the BSA: at the time it was a very important question, it mattered a great deal. There was a small group of people – like Jo Banks and myself and Dahrendorf [Ralf Dahrendorf, later Director of the LSE] and ... Lockwood [David Lockwood, later Professor of Sociology at Essex], who were very, very blatantly and vociferously demanding that it be established and putting ourselves forward as being the first generation of sociologists.'[78] In his Report of the Conference, Barbara's contender for the LSE post, T.H. Marshall, recorded the absence of a sharp line between the academic and the practical: 'There is a place for social scientists among the men of affairs and for men of affairs among the social scientists'.[79] As a woman of affairs and of social science, Barbara chaired a group discussion at the Conference on 'Needs and Standards in the Social Services'.

In 1950 she published her own case for social science. *Testament for Social Science*, a title perhaps modelled on Vera Brittain's *Testament of Youth,* was subtitled *An Essay in the Application of Scientific Method to Human Problems*. Barbara's *Testament* is an intensely serious and somewhat didactic book. It begins with the contrast between 'man's' impressive ability to control his material environment, a control achieved largely through science, and his obvious incompetence at managing the affairs of human society. Poverty, hunger, misgovernment, crime, unhappiness, all cry out for a rational application of the scientific method to social problems. The differences between the natural and the social sciences are those of degree, not kind, and the rewards of applying this perspective are inestimable, not only in curing social distress, but in disposing of the 'clouds of superstition' under which many human beings still live. The book was intended to educate people about the essence of the scientific method, to allay some well-worn concerns about the inapplicability of science to social issues (the problem of the familiar; the obstacle of jargon; the complexity and indeterminacy of human behaviour; the misclassification of social studies as 'arts' not 'sciences'), and to point out the socially damaging effects of what Barbara called 'pre-scientific mental attitudes'. For example, theories of punishment commonly supposed that, if you punish offenders sufficiently, they will see the error of their ways. But there is little evidence to support this. Barbara attacked religion, Marxism ('pseudo-science'), and high-flown social theory in her book. As the last chapter observed, 'The proof of the social science pudding must be in the eating; and that, of course, lies mostly in the future, for the greater part of the pudding is not yet cooked, and ... the public are reluctant to taste the few morsels that are ready'.[80]

Barbara Wootton's view of social science very much echoed that of the Webbs who had, eighteen years earlier in their *Methods of Social Study*, outlined the methods of investigation they themselves used in their various studies of trade unionism and local government. Barbara had reviewed the Webbs' text approvingly: 'Perhaps the reviewer's best comment on the book,' she concluded, 'is to reflect how much human misery might have been avoided had we but on the one hand more investigators willing to practise what the Webbs have both practised and preached with such splendid consistency, and on the other hand administrators with an ear less deaf to the results of investigations conducted in this spirit'.[81] The Webbs and Barbara Wootton shared a sense that insisting on the commonality of all the sciences would help to make sociology respectable. 'The division of our studies into separate sciences is justified only by its convenience in concentrating our attention upon particular ranges of phenomena,' pronounced the Webbs, 'the intellectual method is one and the same.' Where Barbara departed from the Webbs was in her argument that social science, like other sciences, should occupy itself with targeted questions, with hypotheses to test. The Webbs considered this a mistake: the right approach was to choose a particular section of the social environment and sit down patiently in front of it.[82]

Barbara's tract for social science is scarcely remembered today, and at the time it fell mostly on resistant ears. The resistors included the reviewer in *The Manchester Guardian*, who said that he had heard the 'science as saviour of mankind' thesis far too many times before,[83] and the *Scotsman* reviewer who shivered at Professor Wootton's 'cold intellectuality' and disregard for the religious instinct in man.[84] *The Times* was happier: *Testament* was a 'brilliant and fascinating ... highly persuasive and supremely reasonable' book.[85] The professional journals gave it a mixed reception. Despite finding her argument 'eloquent and sustained', *The British Journal of Sociology* was not comfortable with Barbara's stance on science and morals.[86] *The Economist* reviewer thought her 'courteous, incisive, sensible, witty, cool ... a paragon among controversialists', but she claimed too much for science.[87] The methodological pragmatism of *Testament* failed to resonate with fashion among many social scientists in Britain, who were beginning to be captivated by the 'grand' theory emerging from the US and Europe – T.H. Marshall's 'path to the stars'. Empiricism of the kind the book recommended was well on the way to becoming a dirty word.[88] The book's optimism about the promise of a scientific attitude to social problems could be, and was, called 'naïve'; Terry Morris, who wrote Barbara's obituary in *The British Journal of Sociology*, described *Testament* as exemplifying the 'bright-eyed and bushy tailed enthusiasm that one can detect in the photographs of the newly elected Labour ministers in 1945'.[89]

The American journals, perhaps because of the more pronounced scientific tradition of sociology in that country, liked *Testament* better: here was a 'little volume so tightly written, so precisely carved in every sentence, that every page is important';[90] 'a wonderfully clear statement of the nature of scientific thinking and of pre-scientific ways of thought'.[91] One correspondent, H.B. Mayo, Professor of Political Science at the University of Alberta in Canada, wrote to commend Barbara for the craftsmanship, the clear writing, the economy of references and the well organized argument of *Testament*; the reviews he had seen had not done the book justice: 'It has occurred to me that you might get some abuse for some of the plain speaking on matters which millions feel deeply. At any rate I know that people often do get abused, often by anonymous letters, for saying things about cherished ideas and institutions.'[92] He was right, and there is plenty of evidence in Barbara's Girton College Archives of both anonymous and signed statements of abuse, although it was not *Testament for Social Science* that provoked these, but her later work on such obviously controversial topics as prison policy, drugs, euthanasia and the marriage laws.

Among the friends to whom Barbara dispatched copies of the book, two were particularly enthusiastic. William Haley, Director-General of the BBC, took the book very seriously: 'The *Testament* has been a great standby these past ten days. There it was, every evening, to restore one to an air of reason, serenity, and detachment.'[93] Douglas Ritchie, Head of Publicity at the BBC, called *Testament* 'superb'; Barbara had said clearly and effectively many things he himself had been groping for, and he admired her cold logic, especially in the presence of so much 'woolly mindedness'.[94] Ritchie was a fan of hers in other ways: he wrote to her after one of her television appearances in September 1951: 'Sweetie, You were wonderful – a star – you'll be back in Hollywood before you know where you are. There we were looking at that jolly good film ... and then suddenly Professor Barbara Wootton looking beautiful, poised and dignified, talking easily as though it were the most natural thing in the world to take a few minutes out to talk to three million viewers ... I tried to ring you, but didn't get through – I expect you'd taken the receiver off to keep your fans at bay.'[95]

By the post-war years, Barbara had discovered another more populist route for spreading her messages about the values of rationalism and social science. Broadcasting at the time was only a bit younger than social science – the first complete programme broadcast to the public by the Marconi Company was on 23 February 1920. A technology of communication and entertainment that we now entirely take for granted was one of many dramatic social changes that occurred during Barbara's lifetime. In 1947, only a fraction of one per cent of British people owned television sets; fourteen years later, this had risen to seventy-nine per cent.[96] Barbara had begun her broadcasting career in the late 1920s, before Broadcasting House was built, and she had incurred a motoring fine by exceeding the 20 mph speed limit in Regent's Park on her way home to listen to a broadcast.[97] In 1946, she entertained radio audiences with her Forces Educational Broadcast on the Beveridge Report and a talk on 'Liberty and the Individual' for the Midland Home Service; in 1947 she debated the meaning of evil with the Bishop of Bristol, and exhorted the British people to invest in National Savings; in 1948 she took fifteen minutes of the Home Service's airwave time talking about 'The Right Thing to Do' – though we do not now know what this was. We do know that she was a frequent participant in a popular programme with a distinctly non-populist title, 'The Brains Trust'. This ran on the BBC Home Service (later known as Radio 4) from 1942 to 1949 and was listened to by one in three of the UK population.[98] Its format was simple: listeners (later, viewers – the programme was transferred to television in the 1950s) sent in questions for a panel to answer. Barbara's role on the programme had earned her the title 'Brains Trust Analyst' by 1947.[99]

The media world brought Barbara another new challenge in 1950, one which she would later look back on as a source of some of the greatest pleasure she had ever had in her professional life. She was invited to become a Governor of the BBC. 'Prof. Barbara becomes BBC Governor', proclaimed *The Daily Express* headline over a cut-out of Barbara's clear-eyed face: 'Professor Barbara is Mrs George Percival Wright. "My husband was a London taxi-driver" she said last night.'[100] There was just no getting away from the media typecasting – one of the issues with which the governance of the BBC was itself concerned. Barbara was one of seven governors, all appointed initially for two years – though she derived much enjoyment from a misprint in *Who's Who* which extended her governorship for 366 years from 1590 to 1956.[101] The Governors were paid £600 a year and attended, on average, meetings for half a day a fortnight. Their job was a licence to read the newspapers and do as much listening and viewing as possible, and then at Board meetings to consider whatever it was they were asked to consider using this experience and their best judgement. They received over 200 reports from BBC staff every year and were advised by thirty-one separate advisory committees (for example on music, religion, agriculture and so forth); there was also a general advisory council of around fifty eminent people.[102] Heavy reading and hard work were no strangers to Barbara. It was the social side which gave her most pleasure. As she later said, 'I don't think I actually did anything. But everyone there was so nice. It was a very interesting and enjoyable time'.[103] The Governors' lunches, Barbara observed, were always 'excellent in intention' even if slightly ailing in standards of execution. This led her to reflect on a general pattern in types of refreshment offered for media work. The quality on offer was generally tailored to the prestige of the anticipated audience: so, at the bottom of the scale were overseas broadcasts to expatriates or other countries, for which rather an inferior selection of sandwiches and similarly restricted drinks was provided; next came 'Woman's Hour' lunches, with 'a reasonable, but in no way ostentatious', meal: 'Women are apparently ranked a cut above "natives" or "foreigners", but are still not quite first-class citizens'. The apex of the whole business was 'Panorama' or 'The Brains Trust', where one attained the luxury of a 'really slap-up meal'.[104]

She enjoyed the food, and the company, but it was also a rather tense time, although the tensions did not involve Barbara directly. The central question was who was supposed to be running the BBC? Lord Simon of Wythenshawe, the Chairman of the Governors when Barbara joined, did not get on with Sir William Haley, who was Director-General; there was also a general lack of clarity about the responsibilities of the two posts. As Lord Simon put it in his recollections *The BBC from Within*, the three documents that laid down the constitution of the BBC – the 1946 Charter and Licence, and a White Paper – were 'almost bewilderingly vague'[105] on its governance, and the two million words given in evidence to another of William Beveridge's lesser known enquiries on Broadcasting in 1949–50[106] added little illumination. But the constitution did say that the Governors, led by their Chairman, were ultimately responsible for policy and programme content. However, Sir William's view was that *he* ran the BBC, with the Governors acting as 'a reserve of wisdom' – a reserve which Barbara's sharp retaliation noted was most useful when not drawn on, like the gold reserve of the Bank of England.[107] This left the Governors, and especially their Chairman, in an awkward situation, with titles but little power, a situation which Beveridge in the wisdom of his Broadcasting Report had suggested ought to change.

Simon and Haley disagreed about the BBC's function in society. Haley saw the BBC as a vehicle for improving people's taste; according to Francis Williams, another of Barbara's co-governors, Haley wanted the Home and Light (the latter becoming Radio 1 and Radio 2) programmes to wither away entirely so everyone would end up listening to the Third programme (later to become Radio 3). Simon took a more plebeian view.[108] Barbara supported Haley's worry about changing standards; in a piece she wrote on 'The BBC's Duty to Society', she bemoaned its obsession with 'the standards and values of show business and of journalism'.[109] Matters at the BBC eventually came to a head over the appointment of a Director of Television. Radio had three Directors (for talks and news, for general home broadcasting, and for overseas broadcasting), but television was so new it only had a 'Controller'. Simon wanted the existing Controller, the journalist/publisher/novelist Norman Collins, to become Director of Television, but Haley thought Collins (who had previously worked on the Light Programme) would take far too popular a line, and wanted George Barnes, who had been head of the Third programme, instead. Haley enforced his decision and Collins resigned, subsequently taking a lead role in commercial television (which naturally proved Haley's point).

William Haley, the son of a French grocer's daughter and a Yorkshire clerk, was born and educated in Jersey at the same school as some of Barbara's own relations had attended. At various points, he ran, not only the BBC, but Reuters, the Press Association, *The Times, The Manchester Guardian*, and the *Encyclopaedia Britannica*. Barbara and he became close friends. She gave him much support in the struggles that developed between him and Lord Simon. Later, Haley would remember 'the two of us sitting next to each other at Board meetings. Also the little notes you used to jot down for me'.[110] It seems from the correspondence that Barbara took the initiative in expressing support for Haley's position outside the formal meetings, though he did write to her after one such meeting to ask her what she had meant when she had said that, if anything could bring her to doubt the idea of the BBC, it would be the BBC itself. He wanted to come and see her to find out privately what she meant.[111] Francis Williams described Haley as 'an extraordinarily shy man, of strong principles and unbending intellect', a man who found it difficult to display warmth; he was known among his staff as 'the man with two glass eyes'.[112] But there is great warmth in Haley's letters to Barbara. He thanks her for her expression of companionship and for her 'great kindnesses to him'.[113] He sends her poetry and they have lunch. Friendship is a most precious thing. 'And difficult as it is to find the right words to say so I do want you to know how much yours means to me. I am afraid I am not very handy about such things and often become most tongue-tied when I should be the reverse. Then the occasion goes by, and one never says what one should have said.'[114] When Haley leaves the BBC in 1952, Barbara attends his leaving party; she makes a speech in which she recalls something he had said at their first meeting. This causes him to be 'nearer to losing control than ever before'. There are lots of things he wants to say to her, and someday he *will* manage to get out all he feels.[115] But what is not said, or written down, is not known, and is therefore not available for the record. Haley and Barbara would retain their close connection until he died of prostate cancer in 1987, the year before her.

Barbara stopped being a BBC Governor in 1955. That was the year in which a lecturer in Educational Psychology at Aberdeen University, Margaret Knight, gave two BBC radio broadcasts on 'Morals Without Religion'. Her broadcasts sparked a 'hysterically hostile reaction' among some sections of the press and the public, who were unused to having one without the other.[116] Knight was a humanist, and her infiltration of the BBC would not have happened without the support of Barbara Wootton and her BBC connection.[117] Barbara was a leading supporter of the Humanist Broadcasting Council, which was set up as a pressure group by various humanist agencies. Responding to her own case that rational public policy needs the help of social science research, she also agreed to act as advisor for an inquiry into the effects of television on adults. This was sponsored by the BBC's own Audience Research Department, and run by William Belson, who headed the Research Techniques Unit at the LSE. It was intended as a parallel study to a rather better known inquiry looking at the effects of the new medium on children: *Television and the Child* by Hilde Himmelweit and colleagues. Both inquiries responded to alarmist concerns that television might be terrorising children, affecting their moral and physical health, and destroying family life. The study on which Barbara advised focused on the relationship between television-watching and family life and sociability. A detailed survey was conducted of some 8,230 people in London, Birmingham and Wakefield. Some effects were found: for example, television seemed to bring families together more in the evenings, but 14- to 22-year-olds compensated for this by going out more at other times; the pattern of visiting had changed, with television-watching to some extent replacing conversation. However, on balance, Belson was able to report 'hardly any evidence to support the large and sweeping generalizations often made as to [the] effects of television upon family life and social habits. This in itself is a finding of great importance and not less so by reason of its negative character.'[118] This is exactly the kind of comment one might have expected from Barbara, who did not write the report, but who advised on the study's methodology.

Although she was often seen as an inveterately serious person, Barbara did know how to enjoy herself. Someone who helped her to do this during this period of her life was Vladimir Raitz, a young ex-LSE economics student, originally from the Soviet Union, with a flair for spotting unusual business opportunities. While Raitz had been on holiday at Calvi in Corsica in 1949, a local socialite had suggested to him that Calvi would be an ideal place for British holiday-makers, and he guaranteed to arrange a concession of a large piece of land on the beach. Raitz promptly set up Horizon Holidays, which was the beginning of the mass package-holiday industry. He advertised selectively for his first clients in *The Teacher's World*, *The Nursing Mirror* and the *New Statesman*, promising flights, accommodation for two weeks in US Navy tents (which he had bought up cheaply), local wines and meat twice a

day (an attractive proposition for refugees from post-war austerity Britain) – all for
£32.10s (about £650 in 2010).[119] The first holidays were in a camp under the pine
trees by the beach. Barbara visited Calvi many times with George. They often went
with friends, including the McGregors: both Mac and Barbara braved the first Calvi
flight in May 1950. After the holiday season in 1952, Barbara described her stay
in Calvi as 'refreshing, entertaining, and in some respects decidedly "sauvage"';[120]
by 1954, the place had become 'our beloved Corsica'.[121] Her long-lived association
with Horizon Holidays continued into the 1960s, when she contributed to its
publicity material a short piece advertising 'Tour C1 – 15 Days in Calvi from
42 Guineas'. She recommended Calvi because it was not too smart – a holiday
location must be such that the young and shapely '(and perhaps even the not so
young and shapely) must be able to wear sun clothes anywhere anytime without
looking conspicuous or appearing to be exhibitionist'. (Perhaps this was a reference
to the eyebrows raised by George's swimming attire.) Calvi was a place where real
people (fishermen) lived, and there were bars where one could sit and drink in the
evenings 'and watch the colours change and the world go by'.[122] On the tenth
anniversary of Horizon Holidays in 1959, Barbara was delighted to be flown by Raitz
with other faithful clients to lunch at La Pyramide Restaurant near Lyons, although
she complained that no-one had asked her to lunch in London that day to give her
the opportunity to score a 'lifemanship' point by saying she was popping over to
France for lunch.[123] After a further decade of Horizon Holidays, Raitz took 74 friends
and clients on a VC 10 to Istanbul where they consumed 114 bottles of champagne.
None of the party – which included TV stars Barbara Kelly and Bernard Braden as
well as Barbara Wootton – knew where they were going until they got there.[124]

Like many academics, Barbara benefited from the opportunity to combine work
abroad with new horizons. In 1947, she went to Jamaica to take part in a course for
West Indian social workers: the students were 'gay, zestful, keen on their jobs and
above all welcoming and friendly'. However, she felt she was only one step ahead of
them in what she taught, and was sharply aware of the limitations of the idea that
British experiences can automatically be transplanted to such places; she recalled,
with some agony, the British botany teacher who had once lectured in Jamaica on the
English primrose, a flower completely unknown in that country. A Poor Law Officer
from Trinidad acted as Barbara's chauffeur and made her a present of a St Christopher
medal which thereafter accompanied her on all her world travels – though only after
she had removed with a nail file the inscription in the back which insisted that the
bearer was a Catholic and would require a priest in the event of any emergency.[125]

Despite its shortcomings, Bedford College granted her four months' leave of
absence in 1948 for a Visiting Professorship at Columbia University in New York.

During her time there she talked on 'Labor, Economics, and Politics in Great Britain Today' to an audience of 150 economics and government students, many of whom had to stand because the hall was so full. They gave her a rave review in their student publication: 'There are rare, rare occasions at lectures when a harmony of the speaker and the audience takes place', but this was one of them. Dr Wootton was 'charming and witty', turning the complexity of her subject into simplicity, and provoking far more applause than was customary at such meetings.[126] Barbara's most abiding memory of that stay was her astonishment that anyone would *choose* to live in New York if they could live anywhere else. The skyscrapers of Manhattan did not impress her. Now, in her early fifties, it was the Fenland skies of her childhood and her stays in the Surrey countryside that were calling her increasingly back to a rural way of life. But she made good friends in New York. This was where she met Douglas Ritchie and his wife Ev, who became lifelong friends. Ritchie had been temporarily loaned by the BBC to the British Information Services in New York, and one of his duties was to entertain miscellaneous English visitors. After he had a stroke in 1955, Barbara visited Ritchie in the nursing home, and when he wrote a book about his journey to recovery, she added an affectionate Preface.[127]

As Barbara had noted in her paper about resigning her professorship, among the increasingly burdensome duties of senior university staff was that of responding to Government requests for expert help. The *Enquiry into the Closing Hours of Shops*, chaired by Sir Ernest Gowers of *Plain Words* fame, with which she was involved in 1947, was not nearly so demanding as some of these requests. Obviously the task before this Committee was important, since there were at least two million shop assistants whose work was affected by rules about closing hours, and everybody went shopping, although the hours at which they were able to do so had been laid down by a process of historical accretion rather than the kind of rational, evidence-informed decision-making process Barbara would have preferred. Should shops be forced to close, as they were, at 8 p.m. every night (9 p.m. one night a week), always by 1 p.m. on one weekday, and always on Sundays? Why should there be exemptions for sugar confectionery, table waters, ice cream, and cooked or partly cooked tripe? The Committee commissioned a social survey about shopping habits (one senses that Barbara might have had a hand in this). There was an active contingent in favour of 6 o'clock closing, but, 'We asked many advocates of that hour when a woman who worked in a factory or office up to, say, 5.30 p.m., was to do her shopping … some said on her way to work, some in the luncheon hour, and some on the late day. We do not believe there is a satisfactory answer.'[128]

The Gowers Commission resulted in a wide range of recommendations for what would now be called 'occupational health and safety'. Barbara found Gowers to be quite the most skilful and delightful chairman she had ever encountered. She appreciated his ability to seize the essentials of any discussion and 'to deplete windbags without loss of good will and good humour'; and, of course, she very much liked his appreciation of linguistic niceties, which made drafting the report an exhilarating exercise. Taking part in this inquiry expanded her own repertoire of entertainment, since its remit included theatres, restaurants and racecourses; being entertained by the Directors of the Greyhound Racing Association with excellent food and drink might be viewed as corruption, but at least she could report that her own bets were 'uniformly unsuccessful'.[129] She had to miss some meetings because of ill-health, but Gowers reassured her: the meetings were sparsely attended and two very charming representatives of the National Coal Board came prepared to answer all sorts of questions to which Committee members did not want to know the answer and were quite unable to answer any of the questions to which they did.[130]

More important in some ways (though not to the worker-housewife struggling to get her shopping done) was the Royal Commission on the Press, which Barbara joined in 1947. Its object was to 'inquire into the control, management and ownership of the newspaper and periodical Press and the news agencies, including the financial structure and the monopolistic tendencies in control, and to make recommendations thereon'.[131] The instigators of the Commission had been the National Union of Journalists, who, the previous year, had called for a thorough investigation into the British newspaper industry, which would focus on how the freedom of the press could be safeguarded and enlarged. When the Report was published, its length and general obscurity (with respect to finances, particularly) were noted.[132] The Report acknowledged the central dilemma that a free press is essential to a democracy, but a press driven by commercial interests is not really free. The Commission's deliberations allowed them to declare the British press so far more-or-less exempt from the dangers of too much of it belonging to too few hands, and relatively alert to the possibility (which had worried the National Union of Journalists) of undue influence from advertisers. Its main recommendation was the setting up of a General Council of the Press to encourage public responsibility among journalists, a development that would take a further four years, mainly due to wrangles about the balance of lay and press representation on such a body. Barbara Wootton was one of those who held out for a core of lay members and for a lay chairman unconnected with the newspaper industry.

Throughout all this public service, and while fighting to establish social research and dealing with her students at Bedford College, Barbara kept up a stream of interests in a wide range of social issues. In 1944 she wrote a foreword for *A Worker's View of the Wool Textile Industry* by M. Agnes Smith, a first-hand account by an adult education student who had worked in the textile industry from the age of twelve;[133] in 1946, she was exercised about the arrangements being made for British wives in Germany;[134] about the London County Council's School Care Committees, which required men and women to volunteer some of their time (the children's writer Noel Streatfield added her name to this particular Wootton-signed letter to *The Times*);[135] and, with social workers Lady Cynthia Colville, Margery Fry, Eileen Younghusband and others, she campaigned for donations to a hostel for delinquent girls in Hampstead.[136] The same year, she became a member of the governing Committee of the Bureau of Current Affairs sponsored by the Carnegie United Kingdom Trust, and Ellen Wilkinson, the country's first female Minister of Education, appointed her a member of the Central Advisory Council (the new body set up under the 1944 Education Act for whose implementation Wilkinson was responsible). In 1949, the immensely busy Professor Wootton almost made the headlines when she contested the alarmist opinions of the Archbishop of Canterbury about the 'shattering' increase in juvenile crime. Examining the statistics, she pointed out that in 1947, 985 out of a 1,000 14- to 17-year-old boys (the most problematic group) had clean records, but so had 989 in 1937 – hardly a shattering difference.[137]

The year Barbara went to Bedford College was also the year her mother died. Adela Adam's death notice in *The Times* was stark, in contrast to the one Barbara and her brother would later place there for their redoubtable nanny, The Pie. But Adela's own reputation *was* considered notable enough to merit a short obituary in *The Times*; this referred to her brilliance as a student of the man she later married, along with her authorship of works on Plato and Greek ideals of righteousness, on her husband's classical studies, and on the life of her beloved son Arthur. Her sterling service to Girton and other women's colleges was noted, as was her membership of the Cambridge University Musical Society.[138] Adela Adam's desire, to die while singing the Sanctus from Bach's *Mass in B Minor*, was nearly achieved, as the last time she went out it was to a rehearsal of this piece and the fatal heart attack occurred on her way home.[139] Adela Adam had been a Governor of Girton for twenty-six years, retiring at the age of sixty-six, and for the same length of time, from 1918 until her death, had represented Girton on the governing body of the Perse School for Girls, which Barbara had attended; she was also a governor of St Paul's Girls' School, and had taught, not only at Girton, but at Newnham College and Bedford College. In short, she was a woman with a considerable reputation. Her commitment to women's education and civil rights was one her daughter shared, although they disagreed about almost everything else. Once Barbara had left Cambridge, the gulf between them had grown, and Barbara never entirely emancipated herself from the childhood hostility she felt towards her mother. She made no secret of this, telling one interviewer who asked her (when she was seventy-nine) whether she and her mother had mended their relationship in later life, 'No ... I tried to be humane – I mean, I used to go down and see her but I never could do with her. I tried to ... see her point of view, and the sort of unreasoning childhood hatred disappeared: after all, she no longer had power over me.'[140] Writing to Girton about Adela's memorial, Barbara said, 'I do not think one could have wished Mother's life to be much prolonged, she had lost or lost touch with, so many friends that she was beginning to feel very lonely, I fear; and the difficulties of the war mean that the old not only lose the little comforts (though Mother was as independent of these as anyone could be) but they are also much cut off by the fact that everybody is so preoccupied and overworked that little personal attentions become impossible'. On behalf of herself and Neil, she declined the invitation to write an obituary of Adela for the *Girton College Review*,[141] but she provided information for 'J.R.B.' who did write one, especially concerning her mother's travels in the 1930s: starting at the age of sixty-eight, Adela had visited Russia (with a nephew-in-law), 'about a dozen other countries', and 'the near east', and had been on an Amazon cruise (on her own).[142]

Adela's death brought the final break-up of the household in Barton Road, Cambridge. The aunts, those resourceful figures from Barbara's childhood, had died in 1923 (Juliet) and 1931 (Fanny). The Pie, who had continued to live in the Cambridge house with Adela and service the household, as nannies very often did in those days long after their charges had left home, moved back to be near her own family in Somerset. Some of the escalating fame that 'Missie' enjoyed reached The Pie there; she sees photographs of Barbara in the newspapers, including one of her newly abbreviated hair-do, which The Pie decides is acceptable. She knows her 'Own Dear Missie' is now a public figure, an achievement she thoroughly deserves, but she is concerned that Barbara needs new clothes for her elevated status. It is kind of Barbara to visit when she is so busy, and even kinder are the chocolates and the flowers and the new dressing-gown and the cheques which Barbara sends, and the ultimate generosity of Barbara and 'Mr Neil' in paying the expenses of the various nursing homes between which she moves, especially the last, Westwood House, in Taunton, in 'a very nice part of the town'.[143] The Pie's room there is bright and cheerful, and the house has a lovely garden with beautiful shrubs, some of which she has never seen before, and beyond the kitchen garden is a grass field with cows in it that she can see from her window. Again and again in these letters, The Pie thanks Barbara and her brother for making her life easy and comfortable in ways that would never have been possible without their financial help. The Pie has relatives in the town who help her, but the regular visits from Barbara and Neil are clearly much looked forward to.

It was these visits to The Pie in Somerset that also provided Barbara with the closest approximation to family life she was willing to manage. The Pie brought her and her surviving brother, Neil, together in a common interest. In many other respects, brother and sister were worlds apart. Neil was a proper scientist, an expert in quantitative surface chemistry, the author of that 'bible of surface chemistry', *The Physics and Chemistry of Surfaces*, first published in 1930 when he was thirty-nine and working at University College, London, on the payroll of Imperial Chemical Industries Ltd.[144] The topic of his work was 'difficult' even to those who knew about it; it belonged to the general area of surface science, which is the study of physical and chemical phenomena occurring at the interfaces of different materials.[145] Neil Adam's ingenious experiments were of theoretical interest, but they also had practical applications: for example, with respect to the surfactant actions of detergents. A more sinister relevance was to the study of chemical warfare agents. During the Second World War, he had transferred his expertise to the Chemical Defence Experimental Establishment at Porton Down, where he organized work on the vapour pressures of these substances in case they were deployed by the Nazis. Those very skills at glass-blowing he had demonstrated as a child with his sister in the Balfour Laboratory in Cambridge came in useful at Porton Down.[146] Barbara's dislike of warfare is unlikely to have endeared this aspect of Neil's career to her (assuming she knew about it, which she may not have done), but the scientific approach of observation and experiment was one she applied to her own work. Brother and sister had this in common, as well as an impatience with imprecise verbiage, the ability to write lucid economical prose, a talent for engaging student audiences, and the capacity to speak together throughout their adult lives the rapid backwards language they had invented as children.

They were also, claimed Barbara, the first brother and sister in Britain ever to be University professors at the same time.[147] In 1937 Neil had moved to the Chair of Chemistry at Southampton, where he gained a richly-deserved reputation as an eccentric. His red hair and his birthday (5 November) gave him a tendency to explosions. His interest in water and birds resulted in a house full of toy ducks who would sit with him and his family at the dinner table; sometimes he would quack to colleagues or make a silent quack 'by apt movements of thumb and forefinger' in University meetings. His valedictory lecture at Southampton, a masterpiece of caustic wit and surface chemistry, was called 'Water Off The Duck's Back'.[148] The ducks were, according to a relative, a response to the severely disciplined childhood Neil had shared with Barbara, and for the same reason he took up dancing in his sixties, determined to have some fun.[149] His colleagues remembered him wearing cycle clips and gown, and walking with the rolling gait of his favourite duck, or 'sitting in rolled-up shirt sleeves at his cluttered desk, his hair tousled, his temper verging on the irascible, and his labours punctuated with cries of impatience and off-the-cuff scraps of nonsense'.[150] At home, there was equal disarray: tea-time visitors would be greeted with the Professor's long-johns airing on a clothes-horse in front of the fire, piles of books and papers everywhere, and Mrs Adam in her gumboots. The Adams were strict Christian Scientists; Neil believed that the powers of the human intellect developed in higher education were manifestations of divine intelligence: 'We should know" he wrote, 'that in reality we are one with the infinite Mind, whose creation is wholly good and harmonious and spiritual'.[151] It was a curious philosophy for someone whose life's work was devoted to the understanding of material reality, and it would not have made any sense to Barbara. But she was fond of him; she sent him copies of her books, inscribed, mysteriously, 'From Willie to Willie'. Yet her fondness did not extend to keeping in touch with Neil's children and grandchildren. His daughter Jean Adam, born in those troubled days of the First World War in Cambridge, confusedly married a man called John Adams, and they had a daughter, Carolyn, and a son, David, both of whom married and had children of their own. Neil's son was named Arthur Mylne Adam, the 'Arthur' after Neil and Barbara's dead brother Arthur, and the 'Mylne' after Aunt Juliet, and this Arthur followed his father in taking like a duck to water, science and eccentricity. Arthur Adam worked for Marconi's Wireless Telegraph Company Ltd in Chelmsford, Essex, the first purpose-built wireless radio factory in the world. He lived with his wife in another cluttered house near the saltworks in nearby Maldon with ancient outboard motors in the loft, a catamaran at the bottom of the garden, and nothing ever thrown away, including the family papers and photographs inherited from Neil.[152] There are references in Barbara's archives to at least two godchildren – Anna Furth, the daughter of her publisher at Allen & Unwin, Charles Furth, and Jane Brunton, whose father Gordon was a businessman and publisher and a friend of Vladimir Raitz, who had introduced Barbara to package holidays.[153] Gordon Brunton and his wife had adopted Jane through the Agnostics Adoption Society, which Barbara had helped to set up.[154] But, if Barbara had any close contact with these godchildren (a concept which surely must have seemed rather alien to her), she left no record.

Barbara Wootton was not happy about her lack of a successful family life. Her public achievements, of which there were many in these inspiring times of post-war social reconstruction, helped to fill the void. Much had been accomplished, yet there was much more still to be done, including her most substantial and controversial academic work – a review of social science research which would shock the academic and professional world in its demonstration of just how far social studies needed to advance before it could earn the label of science.

12

The Nuffield Years, and Vera

It was originally to be a comprehensive review of all the achievements of all the social sciences. Barbara Wootton's model was historian Arnold Toynbee's mammoth twelve-volume *A Study of History*. She thought the social sciences needed their Toynbee, and she wanted to be him. Like Toynbee, her vision was to include everything in her scope, to ask universal questions and to provide a convincing theoretical and methodological framework for her answers. The whole field of social research would be covered, together with all the social science sub-disciplines: sociology; social anthropology; social psychology; criminology; government, administration and law; and economics. But, while there would be an awareness of disciplinary terrains, the project would differ from Toynbee's in having a highly practical starting point: 'the main social problems of contemporary society, particularly industrial society'.[1] What did the social sciences say about these, and what lines of enquiry ought they to follow in the future?

The eventual product of her vision was one volume and not twelve, as in Toynbee's case. The four hundred pages of *Social Science and Social Pathology*, published in 1959, after six years' hard work, represented a logical next move for the author of *Testament for Social Science*. Two particular sets of personal experiences drove Barbara's commitment to a view of social science as an activity that could, and should, struggle to resemble the natural sciences. Firstly, as an economist, she had laboured to see what useful explanations and predictions could possibly be dug out of the theoretical mud of pre-Keynesian economics; secondly, in her many years as a magistrate in the Juvenile Courts, she had faced the task of treating thousands of children and young people accused of varying degrees of anti-social behaviour. The former had given her a lasting impatience with theory for its own sake, the latter an overriding concern with the need for academic work to have a *practical* focus. Barbara saw contemporary social problems as falling into three groups. The first group were problems related to 'the normal industrial way of life': for example, how do political institutions work, or what are the social functions of the family?

The second group of problems were those of anti-social behaviour: people found guilty of crime, labelled as mentally ill or simply badly behaved; here the challenge was to untangle definitions and to identify causes and cures. The third group of problems resided in the relationships between different cultural groups: dominant and minority 'racial' groups; people of different nationalities; and 'displaced' persons and their host communities. The difficulty with social science work in each of these social problem areas was that, although there were many studies, most of them were small and had been carried out in isolation from one another, using different measures and definitions, and making cumulative knowledge – one of the key criteria for any science – impossible. This vast and repetitive literature needed to be sifted; sadly, she anticipated the likelihood that 'the hard core of reliable knowledge' would be 'much smaller than could be wished'.[2]

It was an ambitious enterprise for one woman a few years short of retirement age. The work that went into *Social Science and Social Pathology* was funded by the Nuffield Foundation, a charitable trust established in 1943 by William Morris (Lord Nuffield), the founder of Morris Motors, to advance social wellbeing through research. In 1950, the Foundation had sponsored an informal conference on the social sciences. Out of this arose the suggestion that the time had come for some kind of survey of the achievements of social research. According to the official record, one of the Foundation's Trustees, Sir Hector Hetherington, aired this idea with Barbara in October 1950. Barbara had worked with Hetherington in the late 1930s and early 1940s on the Royal Commission on Workmen's Compensation. Around the same time, and also with economists Hubert Henderson and Austin Robinson, she had shared with Hetherington membership of the Executive Committee of the National Institute of Economic and Social Research – Britain's longest running independent economic research institute set up in 1938 and still in existence in 2010.[3] Hector Hetherington and Barbara Wootton had also, crucially, both been on the Sub-Committee which had persuaded the University Grants Committee (UGC) to recommend increased investment in social science research. When Hetherington got in touch with Barbara about the social research proposal, she was occupied with a possible visit to the USA, and it was May 1951, before they were able to have 'a good long talk' about it.[4] He found her wonderfully receptive. She laid before him her much more ambitious plan – the *whole* of social science, *all* its accomplishments to date and its potential for the future – and he supported her request for a professorial salary for herself plus salaries for a secretary and a research assistant, and the costs of a base from which to work for five years. At the end of the note Barbara provided for the meeting of the Nuffield Trustees, she admitted, 'I have a very strong urge to tackle this job: in fact, I am determined to find a way of doing it'.[5] It is entirely possible that she had some scheme of this sort in her mind when Hetherington approached her; it is also conceivable that she planted the idea in his.

The response of the Nuffield Trustees was to consider it very likely that something 'good and interesting' would emerge if a grant were made to Professor Wootton, but to decide that she had set herself an impossible task.[6] They asked her to make some selection from within her ambitious programme, and on that basis they would support the expenses of the work. In focusing down on a do-able project, Barbara chose to settle on the second of her groups of social problems – those of social pathology or crime and delinquency or cultural deviation; various terms could be used. This would have a number of advantages: it was an area she herself knew well; it had huge practical importance, since 'All forms of social failure or irresponsibility are a nuisance to somebody – usually *both* to the persons concerned *and* to the community';[7] and it was a specific area of social science work that could stand on its own, but also involved a number of social science disciplines. Most importantly, the study of cultural deviation would meet the requirement of the 'simple ultimate test: how far are we finding out the things that we really want to know, and doing this by the most efficient methods possible?'[8]

The years of the Nuffield Foundation work were some of the most important in Barbara's life, and *Social Science and Social Pathology* is one of her most significant achievements. But she did not do it on her own. The book's authors are listed as 'Barbara Wootton assisted by Vera G. Seal and Rosalind Chambers'. She had accomplices in what would be seen as a major destruction of the myths of value-free social science and of the pretensions to expertise of psychiatrists, doctors, social workers and almost every occupational group which had anything to do with the labelling and treatment of anti-social behaviour. *Social Science and Social Pathology* was not a popular book, but that is a later part of the story. In many ways the story – of the Nuffield project, the book, and key aspects of the last decades of Barbara's life – begins in 1942 with a meeting between Barbara and a barmaid from London's East End at an evening class in economics.

Vera Seal was actually working at the time as a shorthand typist for a firm that made gas mantels in the Farringdon Road when she enrolled in one of the extra-mural classes Barbara Wootton was running in general economics. It was in the evenings and at weekends that Vera helped out in the family pub – The Arundel Arms in Stoke Newington – doing the heavy cellar work and reading books behind the bar when custom was slow. Vera, born in 1916, when Barbara was nineteen, was an only child; her mother had been in service before marrying Vera's father, who died in his twenties during the First World War, not from war wounds but from some condition that failed to be treated because the doctors were at a party and, by the time they saw him, he was dead. As a result, Vera's mother went back into service, this time with her three-year-old daughter. They lived 'below stairs' in a grand house in Regent's Park. Then Vera's mother met and married a window cleaner, and they bought and ran a series of greengrocers' shops, followed by the pub. Vera's father had said to her mother that, if he died, she was to see to it that Vera had a good education. Vera's mother and her stepfather worked hard and bettered themselves and saved, and sent Vera to a cheap private school where she learnt nothing – no English grammar, no history, no Latin (which she particularly wanted to learn) – and then to Clark's College in Stamford Hill to qualify as a shorthand typist. When she worked for the gas mantel firm, Vera bought books at twopence a time from the stalls in Farringdon Road. 'I used to sit with a dictionary on one knee and the book I was reading on the left.' Although she knew nothing of libraries or universities, she had a passion to learn. One of the men in the office said she ought to go to Toynbee Hall, a university settlement where education courses of various kinds were available. She started with a three-year course of evening lectures in psychology. And then she thought, 'Well, I'd learnt a little about what makes men [sic] tick but I didn't know the environment that the ticking went on in … I decided to do economics'.[9]

This was the beginning of Vera's devotion to Barbara: not just the work that went into *Social Science and Social Pathology,* but a role that would extend for more than sixty years as Barbara's research and personal assistant, general helper, and chauffeuse, and then as carer for Barbara in her declining years and for her literary estate after her death. 'I have a vivid memory of her just walking in,' said Vera of that first meeting at the economics class in 1942, 'taking no notice of anybody at all, walking into this class of about fifteen people and saying what she wanted us to do was to tell her our names and what we did. So we went round and did that. And, do you know, she remembered almost everyone without a coach.'[10] Soon Barbara was writing detailed notes in the margins of Vera's essays, encouraging her to speak, lending her books to read, and sending her letters suggesting yet more reading. After each class, a group of students went home on the tube in the same direction as Barbara, and Vera, whose journey home was in the opposite direction, pretended she needed to go the same way, just so she could get more of Barbara. After two exhilarating years thus spent, the blow fell: there would be no third year of the class, since Barbara was leaving adult education and moving to Bedford College. Barbara said she felt 'extraordinarily base' about this, as she knew Vera wanted the class to continue. Perhaps Vera should think about doing a degree? 'Perhaps one should count it as the one and only virtue of the doodlebugs and such like that they slightly break down traditional British reserve,' Barbara noted, with unusual openness, adding that she had made many friends during her years in adult education, and it was a delight to encounter people, such as Vera, who had 'real intellectual quality and appreciation', although probably Vera underestimated these characteristics in herself.[11]

While Barbara immersed herself in the unhappy politics of her new job at Bedford College, Vera took a postal course in order to get a formal qualification to register for a degree. She did a two-year Certificate course in Barbara's new department at Bedford College, and then got a Commonwealth Scholarship for a one-year Certificate in Mental Health at the LSE. In 1948, she went to work at the Maudsley Hospital as a psychiatric social worker. In later years, Barbara would claim that her greatest achievement in life was to turn an East End barmaid into a psychiatric social worker.[12] After a few years in the Maudsley job, at about the same time as Hector Hetherington was raising the subject with Barbara of a project on the achievements of social science, Vera felt it was time to move on, and then there was another letter from Barbara telling her about the Nuffield work, which would allow Barbara to devote herself to thinking and thereafter telling the world 'what, if anything, the social sciences add up to'. 'How do you like that?' she asked Vera, excitedly. 'Myself, I like it a lot.'[13] Vera replied to offer herself as a research assistant. It appears that Barbara's response outlining what the job would require – a mixture of secretarial and research skills – put Vera off, but Barbara sent her a copy of the job advertisement in October, nonetheless. The brief for the job was acting as a private secretary to Barbara as the Nuffield Research Fellow, and typing articles, checking references and preparing material for publication; and, in the other half of the post, 'to assist in research by the preparation of bibliographies and of notes and abstracts on particular subjects'.[14] Having thought about it and having met Barbara to discuss it, Vera decided to apply. At their meeting, they were very honest with each other 'about everything possible … she said to me, "Well, I'm neurotic", and I said, "Yes, well, so am I, so that's alright". And then she said, "If it doesn't work out, you will lose, because I shall sack you". And I said to myself, "If I work with you, you will not sack me. I shall do exactly what you need". And that was what I planned and what I did.'[15] In the letter Vera wrote to Barbara in support of her application (one of ninety applications Barbara received), she boasted about two qualities not recorded formally on it – her good health, and her tea-making abilities. She went on to reassure Barbara that, should she be appointed, 'all the needs you (and I) feel that you have, would be met in full measure, as far as is humanly possible. And of course I would give you as much of a rock to lean on as exists in me. And I think that, in a quiet way, there is quite a bit of rock there.'[16]

Vera was right. Her first day of work was Monday 19 January 1953. Before this (and as a flavour of times to come), Barbara wrote to warn her that her first task would be to help with her forthcoming paper for the Institute for the Study and Treatment of Delinquency on 'Sociological Approaches to the Study of Delinquency', due in March. Then there were various other odd jobs, some connected with Barbara's excursions to the universities of Manchester, Birmingham and Leicester, and Vera would need to arrange for someone to do the routine typing, as there was much of that. The important thing was that they should both feel that they were, 'as the Americans say, "going places". I suspect that, for the first time in my life,' admitted Barbara, 'I am what is called "happy in my work": it will be grand if you are too.'[17] She had shared her excitement at acquiring the Nuffield funding with various friends, including the reserved but romantic William Haley, who wrote to congratulate her: 'You can now look forward to a period of doing fully really what you want to do in life. To know this lights my heart in a way I can't explain, it shows that at least somewhere, in some valuable, vital human sector, all can be right with the world.'[18]

The Nuffield Foundation was paying Barbara and Vera's salaries (the research assistant and the secretary had become one person – Vera), but the two women needed a physical base for the work. The LSE was explored, but had no space. In the end, Bedford College housed the project in a small flat, ex-servants' quarters known as 'The Bothy', consisting of two rooms, kitchen and bathroom, in one of the houses that formed part of the College in Regent's Park. Vera's first task was to get the lavatory seat varnished. After that, they established a routine: Vera would leave home in Barnet, north London, at seven a.m. on her Lambretta and be at The Bothy by seven-thirty. Barbara would arrive about nine, by which time Vera would have opened and dealt with the post. On the occasions when Barbara had been out of London, Vera would have her breakfast waiting: grapefruit, coffee and toast. The routine was quite unvaried. Once a week Barbara would go out for lunch with a friend or friends; she often talked of joining the nearby zoo, as it would be useful to be able to lunch there. Vera loved the work so much that she used very little of her annual holiday entitlement; Barbara took a month or so a year, very often as a visiting lecturer somewhere or other. They worked pretty much in isolation from the rest of the College, reading and writing all day. The work was demanding: searching for relevant studies; getting copies of papers and books (Vera had to spend a fair amount of time in those pre-internet days touring London libraries); reading and assessing these; and trying to work out what social scientists had done and whether what they had done justified any reliable and general conclusions, and particularly the conclusions that the authors of the studies had themselves drawn. Barbara insisted that Vera should read everything *she* read, and at first Vera could not understand why, but then she realized it was important to have two opinions on the merit of any work.

Vera was later to parody the Nuffield project in an eleven-verse limerick entitled 'Barbara's Saga', which began: 'There was an Old Lady of Bedford / Who wondered if criminals were bred for, / Or if the social situation / Was the main precipitation / Of the deviants we get let in for./ So she took her preoccupation / To the lads of the Nuffield Foundation, / Who gave her their blessing / To a plea to end guessing / And substitute facts for prejudication.'[19] Barbara was, apparently, not much impressed by the poetic turn in her researcher. Rosalind Chambers, the third name on the book's cover, played a subsidiary role. Vera's memory of her contribution to *Social Science and Social Pathology* was that at some stage Barbara decided to spend more of the Nuffield grant, and so she asked Rosalind to write an Appendix. According to Vera, Rosalind would come in from time to time and spend half an hour with Barbara, and after one of these occasions Rosalind came into Vera's room and said that Barbara had suggested that Rosalind look at a copy of one of Vera's reports, so she could see how Barbara liked these done. This was a little insensitive to the nuances of academic stratification – Rosalind a senior university lecturer in the Social Science Department at the LSE, and Vera a 'university nobody',[20] although both she and Barbara always protested when people called her Barbara's 'secretary'.[21] The Appendix Rosalind provided on 'Professionalism in Social Work' is certainly professional but it is a little curious, since it seems to have little to do with the rest of the book. Barbara herself acknowledged that, of her two assistants, it was Vera who carried the heavier load, but she did so 'with such skill and devotion as to create the illusion that no burden existed'. Given these very words to type, Vera thought that was not correct. 'I went into her room and I said "But there was no burden, Barbara". She said, "That's what I mean". It took me a year or two to fathom that out.'[22] Should Vera have been an author of the book? Barbara offered this, but Vera declined. She was just doing her job. Although there was rarely a cross word between them, Barbara had exacting standards. One of Vera's tasks was to check the list of Government publications that came in every week: 'If I saw anything I thought we should have I got it, or, if I was in doubt, I would show it to her. And one day – this is typical of Barbara – I said, "Oh, Barbara, what do you think about this?" "Slut!" Walked away. I made a mistake, you see. It was a reprint, we would have had it if it was useful. You had to be a hundred per cent.'[23] On other occasions, Vera scored. 'People used to visit us ... And one day she had an academic from somewhere in America, and I was in my room, the bell rang, I went in and she said, "Vera, do we know about so-and-so?" And I said, "Oh yes, we've got their latest report", and I went over to the bookcase, picked up this report and gave it to her, and I said to her, "It's on your next reading list". I knew she was never going to read it, it was only peripheral to our interests. And she looked at me, "Thank you,

Vera". To think that he had come from America and she knew all about it!'[24] (Of course, the knower was Vera, not Barbara.)

Social Science and Social Pathology was an achievement much ahead of its time in insisting that social science work must respect canons widely accepted in the broader scientific community as to what counts as knowledge. Barbara's starting point was the facts of recorded social pathologies, rather than opinions about them. What she found (as she always tended to do when she took a close look at anything) was a good deal of muddle. Because of bewildering variations in how crimes are defined, recorded and treated, there were only three features of the crime statistics sufficiently marked and persistent to provide reasonable grounds for saying anything definite. The first was the predominance of offences committed by motorists: 'In half a century, the invention of the internal combustion engine has completely revolutionized the business of our criminal courts. The typical criminal of to-day is certainly not the thief, nor the thug who hits an old lady on the head in order to possess himself of her handbag or to ransack her house: the typical criminal of to-day is the motorist.'[25] She worked it out: almost half of those convicted of criminal offences in England and Wales in 1955 were motorists. How striking, then, that this revolution had completely escaped the attention of the public and the professional criminologists. The second consistent feature of crime was age: it is the young who offend most (or who are caught for so doing). Thirdly, crime was mainly a problem of masculine behaviour, with male rates seven times those of women (and eleven times as high for the peak age of fourteen to seventeen years). Like the prevalence of motoring crimes, the gender imbalance had been mostly ignored, the 'habitual reaction' of sociologists and criminologists being simply to eliminate females from their studies on the grounds that numbers were too small to permit any valid conclusions. Clearly, pronounced Barbara, 'In scale and consistency, the sex difference far outweighs any other factor which we have yet been able to associate with delinquent behaviour. No one seems to have any idea why; but hardly anyone seems to have thought it worthwhile to try to find out.'[26] These observations led to her much-quoted statement that, 'if men behaved like women, the courts would be idle and the prisons empty'.[27]

The overview of current crime and delinquency statistics (Part I) in Social Science and Social Pathology is followed by a review of what is known about the socio-economic factors associated with anti-social behaviour, and by a discussion of whether existing work can adequately predict who will engage in it. Part II hosts a penetrating analysis of the relationship between concepts of mental ill-health and criminality, and a tough critique of what would later be called the 'medicalization' of anti-social behaviour. It was this section of the book that earned Barbara the most hostility – from those professional groups whose claims to knowledge she exposed as resting on the doubly insecure base of subjective values and unreliable evidence. In Part III we are returned to the underlying constants: what can we say we *really* know about the causes of misbehaviour; and what *practical* lessons are there for reducing or preventing it? At the core of the book is what today would be called a 'systematic review': an attempt to locate, assess and synthesize as much of the existing literature as possible relating to some clearly defined research, practice or policy question. Unlike conventional literature reviews, which present the results of a selective trawl through studies in an area – the ones the author knows about, can find easily, or particularly likes or dislikes – systematic reviews are more comprehensive: they use transparent and pre-specified criteria for which studies to include and are clear about methods for judging how reliable these are.[28] Such reviews are essentially ways of extracting dependable policy and practice lessons from huge amounts of information – the very task that confronted Barbara and her helpers in the Nuffield project. Systematic reviews of social research were very rarely undertaken when Barbara and Vera began their work in The Bothy, and they did not use that term in the book. They were explicit about the criteria they used to find the studies they looked at, but not about where they had looked for them (a necessary element in systematic reviews today). Despite this qualification, they were methodological pioneers in developing the tools for what would later be called evidence-based public policy.

The question tackled by their systematic review arose from Barbara's concern about the causes of the anti-social behaviour that greeted her in her role as a magistrate in the Juvenile Courts. 'Every day magistrates and judges are obliged to pass sentences, quite unaware whether similar decisions in the past have turned out well or badly.'[29] It troubled her. Her own record of cases (a sample of which was included as Appendix I of the book) showed the kinds of problems on which she was required to pronounce: 'Stole seven bottles of lemonade from a warehouse' (male, aged 10); 'Took and drove car, collided with a bus, which was slightly damaged, and struck a passer-by' (male, aged 15); 'Rail fraud' (female, aged 13).[30] What did social science research have to say about what might be causing these patterns of delinquency? In particular, what light could it throw on popular ideas then current about twelve possibly relevant factors: family size; the presence of other criminals in the family; club membership; church attendance; employment record; social status; poverty; maternal employment; school truancy; broken homes; health; and educational attainment? The criteria used to select studies for the review were that each should have a sample size of at least two hundred; should contain data on 'not less than half, or nearly half'[31] the twelve popular hypotheses; and should present not only findings but methods. They ended up with twenty-one studies spanning the period 1915–1955, relating to a population of some 23,300 adults or young people labelled as having committed some anti-social offence, and a further 3,330 'controls' who had not. Eleven of the studies were British, one was Swedish, and nine were from the USA.

The results of this review were 'strikingly negative', in the sense that they neither proved nor disproved any of the fashionable theories.[32] Offenders tended to come from large families, and sometimes other family members had been in trouble with the law. Church-going was not common and employment patterns tended to be erratic. Many offenders came from poor families, but there was no evidence of any association with maternal employment. Their health seemed average, although many had been labelled as problematic by their teachers and were quite likely to have truanted. Some studies showed an association with 'broken' homes; others not. The reasons for these inconclusive findings were largely methodological: a wide range of ages and definitions of criminality meant that no two studies dealt with similar material, so differences in findings, which were common, could not be resolved. This applied also to many of the factors investigated: even something as apparently simple as family size, for instance, was defined and measured differently (all family members living together? Number of children born alive? Step- or half-siblings included or not?[33]). Tests of this and that, for example of personality characteristics associated with crime, were numerous and inconclusive: a review in 1950 of such tests conducted in the USA over the preceding 25 years found an unbelievable 30 different tests employed 113 times with very little consistency or cross-referencing.[34]

These limitations of research meant that *Social Science and Social Pathology* effectively became 'a treatise on methodology', which was not what Barbara had intended.[35] However, in this, too, it was ahead of its time. Later social scientists would complain about the inability of methodologically flawed social research to make any useful contribution to policy-making.[36] *Social Science and Social Pathology* was also an innovative text in viewing concepts of criminality, delinquency and anti-sociality within a very broad cultural perspective. There are inherent problems of language and moral values in the whole discourse about 'deviation', 'pathology', or 'social problems'; the issue of how crime and other misbehaviours are defined must come first, as the thing to be explained, before we can sensibly understand why some people and not others find themselves thus classified. When people offend, they do so against particular laws or standards of conduct. These are differently set at different times, in different places and among different social groups. For example, the distinction in Britain between 'indictable' and 'non-indictable' offences is not a rational device for distinguishing 'real' crimes from technical or minor offences; it is arbitrary – a 'monument to British tradition or to historical accident'. Thus, for instance, 'The boy who removes a pump from a schoolfellow's bicycle and is unable to establish his intention to put this back figures among the indictable offenders; yet the brothel keeper and the dangerous driver are omitted'.[37] For these reasons, the focus of *Social Science and Social Pathology* was pragmatically on those behaviours *in the prevention of which public money is spent*.[38] At every point, Barbara and her assistants needed to be conscious of the 'difficulty of extracting the social investigator from the shackles imposed by the assumptions and prejudices of his time'.[39]

And it was a time marked by a number of significant shackles. Two in particular get a good deal of attention in the book. The first of these is the idea that anti-social behaviour is primarily caused by a failure of mothering. This notion occupied an enormous amount of academic, policy and political attention at the time, and is one with a long history, reflecting the ways in which women's position and the social construction of mothering have interacted to shape public policy.[40] As the author of *Social Science and Social Pathology* tangentially remarked, 'Even the maternal deprivation hypothesis, it has been whispered, may not be unconnected with the desire to see women safely confined to domestic occupations'.[41] The original architect of 'maternal separation' or 'deprivation' theory was the medically-trained British psychoanalyst John Bowlby, who had a lifelong interest in the effects of early childhood separations from mothers or mother-figures, and in the nature of these early ties. They fascinated and puzzled him; he was 'a man who felt he had a mission' to convince people how important these early relationship experiences were in shaping people's lives.[42] By the time the work for *Social Science and Social Pathology* was under way, Bowlby had become well-known as the expert in the area. He had been commissioned by the World Health Organization to write a report on *Maternal Care and Mental Health*; this report, published in 1951, argued that 'the deprivation of mother-love in early childhood' can have far-reaching effects on children's mental health and personality development. Such deprivation 'almost always' results in retarded physical, intellectual and social development, and these adverse effects include delinquency.[43] The report sold 400,000 copies and was translated into fourteen languages; its popular version, *Child Care and the Growth of Love*, published by Penguin two years later, made Bowlby both famous and notorious. Although he only hinted at it, his concern with deficits in maternal love may have reflected his own childhood in a professional upper-middle-class family where he and his five siblings were largely reared by 'Nanny Friend', a caregiver who was sometimes far from friendly, and by a succession of nursemaids.[44] Bowlby appears to have had a less satisfactory relationship with his mother-substitute than did Barbara with The Pie. But whatever its origins, his work had enormous influence on the policy front. Nurseries and residential homes for children were closed.[45] Policies of placing looked-after children in the care of foster families, and of emphasizing the responsibility of mothers to stay at home with their children, replaced the kind of judicious review of the evidence called for by the author of *Social Science and Social Pathology*.

One of his own children once asked Bowlby's wife whether Daddy was a burglar, since he came home after dark and never talked about his work.[46] Among the studies Bowlby drew on in his World Health Organization report was his own, of *Forty Four Juvenile Thieves,* a study which suffered the ignominy of being excluded from the systematic review in *Social Science and Social Pathology* on methodological grounds (its sample was considered too small). However, because the influence of the 'maternal deprivation' hypothesis was so strong, a separate chapter of the book needed to be given over to discussing it. Barbara was in the habit of handing over major tasks to Vera before going away on one of her lecture tours or holidays. 'One day she said, "I want you to look at the evidence for Bowlby's belief".'[47] Vera was impatient for Barbara to disappear, so she could get absorbed in this task. When Barbara returned, Vera handed her a thick foolscap typescript of the results. This typescript formed the basis of the chapter in the book which identifies many methodological, theoretical and conceptual problems associated with the notion that deprivation of maternal care in childhood causes people to behave badly. The main ones have a resonance with the lessons of other sections of the book: the 'grave breakdown in logic' that underlies investigators' failure to consider how many maternally deprived children do *not* become anti-social; the slippage between mere statistics and meaningful ones; the almost wilfully careless use of terms such as 'separation' and 'deprivation' to cover a multitude of situations, from appalling long-term institutional care to less damaging short-term family separations; the failure to interrogate the notion that it may not be disruption of relationships that damages people so much as conditions such as poverty, unemployment and homelessness; the prevalence of small case-studies with no adequate 'controls' of well-behaved people; and the substitution of dogmatic personal opinions for conclusions based on reliable evidence. Barbara and Vera's own critique is evidenced and thoughtful, and also characteristically pithy: they compare, for example, the problem of deriving conclusions about the deleterious effects of maternal separation from only the badly behaved as 'on a par with trying to calculate the insurance premiums to be charged for fire risks by reference only to those houses which have actually caught fire'.[48] John Bowlby was purportedly very angry about the treatment meted out to his ideas in *Social Science and Social Pathology*.[49] Elsewhere, Barbara noted that presuming the roots of criminal behaviour to lie in some early failure of mothering is spectacularly unhelpful to those such as magistrates, whose public duty is to do something effective about crime. In practice, it is difficult to believe that a tough young man of sixteen years has come before the Court because he was snatched from his mother's breast as an infant.[50] When the World Health Organization published an assessment of Bowlby's *Maternal Care and Mental Health* in 1962, a decade after its original publication, Barbara contributed one of six chapters. Hers, 'A Social Scientist's Approach to Maternal Deprivation', noted that little new research into theories about the effects of maternal separation appeared to have been published since she wrote her own book, and the research that had been done had not advanced the argument at all. Thus, all one could still say was that lifelong, irreversible damage or criminal behaviour as results of 'maternal deprivation' were unproven hypotheses.[51]

The notion of the 'problem family' was a second major shackle imposed on social investigators by the assumptions and prejudices of the time when *Social Science and Social Pathology* was written. Classifying certain kinds of families as 'problem families' is another habit with a lengthy history, this one irretrievably linked to eugenic notions of class and subnormality. The Medical Officer of Health for Bristol, R.C. Wofinden, created a colourful, moralizing and much quoted 'definition' of 'the problem family' in 1944: 'Often it is a large family, some of the children being dull or feeble-minded. From their appearance they are strangers to soap and water, toothbrush and comb; the clothing is dirty and torn and the footgear absent or totally inadequate. Often they are verminous and have scabies and impetigo ... The mother is frequently substandard mentally ... Nauseating odours assail one's nostrils on entry [to the home] ... the amount of housework done by the mother is negligible ... the general standard of hygiene is lower than that of the animal world.'[52] Early in its history, the 'problem family' was viewed as the key to much delinquency and criminality, though evidence for such assertions was always sparse.[53] More realistically, problem families could be seen as those that occupied an undue amount of social work attention without yielding much in the way of results.[54] Of course, the very presence of hierarchy means that anti-sociality is likely to be defined in such a way that the lower classes excel in it: middle-class crimes, like motoring when drunk, are not 'real' crimes, while those associated with poverty, such as stealing food or other material resources, are more likely to be. Careful investigation of the characteristics of families identified as problems (a task carried out for the book by Rosalind Chambers) showed that poverty and size (large) were really the only two that united them. This, in other words, was yet another area where prejudice masqueraded as knowledge.

Throughout her life, Barbara had a sceptical eye for the way in which professionals of many different kinds claim to know what in fact they do not; the critique embedded in *Social Science and Social Pathology* of medicine, psychiatry and social work's colonization of the field of social distress and anti-social behaviour is particularly trenchant, and yet another aspect of the book's pioneering (and hence unpopular) status. Her arguments about the way in which 'science' was deposing traditional morality as the arbiter of the difference between the sinful and the sick were being put by Thomas Szasz, the radical Hungarian-American psychiatrist, at around the same time.[55] Barbara referred to Szasz's views, expounded in his *The Myth of Mental Illness*, that it was a serious mistake to classify many psychological conditions and problems as forms of illness.[56] She paid tribute to his arguments with some cogency as early as 1962 in a House of Lords debate on the working of the Mental Health Act.[57]

Barbara summarized her own case against the medicalization of distress in a lecture she gave to the British Medical Association in 1963: 'In the world in which I grew up,' she observed, 'the child who stole was a problem for the family, the school-master, or the police ... it would have been considered highly eccentric to refer him to a doctor. To-day, personal problems, moral problems, marital problems, problems of deviant behaviour, are constantly brought to the doctor's consulting-room, while social workers, with their "casework" and their "diagnostic" and "therapeutic" techniques, adopt medical poses and express themselves in medical language.'[58] Speaking at a lecture in Canada some years later on the role of psychiatry, she remembered 'a relative of mine' (her brother Neil), in those dark days of the First World War, suffering a totally disabling two-year depression, being cured by a conversion to Christian Science, and living a mentally healthy life thereafter (the point being not the religious salvation but the existence of successful cultural alternatives to medical treatment).[59] The rise of psychiatry, she pointed out, had led more people to be diagnosed as mentally ill; and, while some of this had undoubtedly had a humanitarian effect, it had also detracted from a focus on the *social* causes of mental and social distress. Further, deciding who is mentally ill and who is simply criminal imposes an impossible burden on the penal system. There is no objective definition of mental health; we cannot rely on psychiatrists, doctors or social workers to define the 'good life'.[60] So long as concepts of mental health are entangled with ideas about socially approved behaviour, which they are, it is inevitable that certain kinds of people will find themselves more likely than others both to be seen as mentally ill and to commit crime. Barbara is despairing: so much of the literature dealing with these issues is so confused that the wood and trees are constantly mistaken for one another. The Szasz-Wootton argument against the professional invasion of mental distress was expanded in the 1970s in a substantial literature on medicalization and social control, becoming a key plank in the newly emerging sub-discipline of the sociology of health and illness.[61]

But it was the chapter of *Social Science and Social Pathology* on 'Contemporary Attitudes to Social Work' that got its author into the most trouble. Thinking perhaps of Vera, Barbara opened the chapter with a comment that, according to the latest census, England and Wales now had slightly more than one social worker for every two barmen or barmaids. But, whereas the function of the latter was clear, that of the former was considerably more vague. Many behaved like amateur psychotherapists trying to delve into the backgrounds and personality conflicts of their clients; it is here that we meet Barbara's famous remark that it appears the best way for the social worker to understand her client is to marry him.[62] The copy of *Social Science and Social Pathology* owned by Richard Titmuss, who was running a department training social workers at the LSE when the book came out, is stuffed with notes of indignation inscribed by some of the senior staff in his department at 'Mrs Wootton's' apparent lack of respect for their profession. Staff were particularly upset at her concentration on the American casework literature, whose excesses, they claimed, were not repeated in Britain. British social workers were much more interested in material needs and helping people in the kind of practical way of which Mrs Wootton would have approved.[63] Barbara wrote to Richard Titmuss saying that various people had mentioned the problem of the literature, but no-one had told her what to read instead, so could he please supply some references?[64] (He did, with some help, but Mrs Wootton already knew them all.) As a relatively new and young recruit to the LSE staff when *Social Science and Social Pathology* was published, David Donnison recalls being asked to review Barbara's book for the professional journal *The Almoner*, because his more senior colleagues were reluctant to register their anger in print. Donnison took exception, on their behalf, to the way in which Barbara had aligned the therapeutic intentions of British social workers with the much more strongly psychoanalytically-oriented disposition of the Americans. His review, said Barbara, nicely, was the rudest anyone had ever written of any of her books.[65]

Social Science and Social Pathology fell like a rock causing a tidal wave in what had been a fairly fetid lake of much-loved hypotheses and cherished claims to expertise about the causes and treatment of anti-social behaviour. Criminologist David Downes, then at the start of his own career, recalled his reaction to the book's publication: 'Hot, indeed blistering, from the presses of 1959, it was both an exhilarating and a dismaying experience. It exhilarated because it conveyed a sense of urgency, a biting scorn for waffle, and a clear sense of direction. It dismayed because it laid bare the general poverty of criminology, showing it to be a set of rusty clichés and sloppy generalizations.'[66] 'Criminological research has never looked quite the same since Barbara Wootton's cruelly deflating *Social Science and*

Social Pathology', announced one professional commentator in 1974.[67] Even those who were offended by the book gave in to grudging admiration. Barbara had put the subject of criminology, then a very small affair, on the map, 'even if she was scathing about it'.[68] She had a mastery of the literature: 'Were there things she hadn't read? Well, I don't know,' said Professor Sir Michael Rutter, a leading figure in child psychiatry, in 2009, 'but I doubt that any were key issues she didn't know about. She was very thorough. And it *was* challenging.' The book had changed Rutter's own view of the subject when he first read it, making him think about things that had not occurred to him before.[69]

Some reviews of the book in the press followed Donnison in defensively arguing that Mrs Wootton really did not understand how complex the social worker's job was.[70] The medical profession's response was a long review in the pages of *The Lancet* entitled 'Medicine Versus Morals'. While the tone of the review was generally approving – the book was 'penetrating', 'remarkable', 'a delight to read' – it did note that Lady Wootton's attitude to doctors was rather ambivalent, and perhaps had tilted her impartiality here and there.[71] *The Lancet's* sister publication, the *British Medical Journal*, considered that on the whole she had managed to keep fact and opinion separate, but, 'Although the main purpose of the book is not destructive, the author is not able to conceal her talents in this direction'. Commenting on her dismissal of problem-family studies, this reviewer revealed that Barbara had resigned from the Eugenics Society shortly before the book's publication, after a long membership.[72] The British Eugenics Society, established in 1907, reflected a very widespread interest in the relationship between heredity and environment among middle-class intellectuals and campaigners of varying political persuasions: 'the problem family' was one of the British eugenic movement's signal themes, and its position on this is not one with which Barbara would have had any sympathy.[73]

Many of the more academic reviews of *Social Science and Social Pathology* were complimentary: 'This is a work of great significance',[74] 'a sociological study of exceptional interest and distinction',[75] and a treatise 'entirely free of that peculiarly nauseating jargon which obscures so much of the meaning of social science literature'.[76] People commented on the book's lucidity and wit,[77] and on its 'fine intellectual stimulus';[78] they called it 'forthright' and 'hard-hitting',[79] 'iconoclastic', 'awe-inspiring' 'informative' and 'thought-provoking',[80] though some reiterated the theme of 'excessive partisanship'.[81] Two reviews to which Barbara herself probably paid the most attention were those by the man who pipped her to the post of the LSE job, Tom Marshall, and by her LSE social administration colleague, Richard Titmuss. Marshall thought this 'an important book by an eminent scholar, which should be read by everyone who has a serious interest in the subject', but he considered it not sociological enough; he wanted more of 'the kind of social science which is concerned with quality, and process, rather than with quantity and correlation', and he complained that the whole book was 'deeply coloured by her personal viewpoint'.[82] Perhaps Marshall, like Titmuss, had been talking to the LSE social workers. In his appraisal of her book, Titmuss admired the book's clarity and clear structure, and Lady Wootton's style, which combined 'the smooth perfection of Swift with the limped ease of Trevelyan'. He enjoyed her 'delicious romp with the medical officers and their elephantine attempts to define and classify "problem families"'. But he, too, took sides with the beleaguered social workers, and especially with those in his own department, quotations from whose work in the book he painstakingly corrected.[83] Other friends did her proud: Lord Longford was delighted with 'the flashes of purest alpha on page after page of this, her *magnum opus*. It will long remain,' he predicted, 'an admired if provocative monument of academic study and reflection.'[84] W.J.H. Sprott of Nottingham University opened his salvo with a remark about how Barbara had resigned her Chair at Bedford College in order to write this book, but since its general effects were devastating, some people would doubtless feel that she would have been more safely occupied had she had stayed where she was. He personally found her treatment of social work 'riotously funny', although he also saw that it would cause 'considerable pain'. All in all, she had performed 'a major service to social science' and her book should be read by everyone interested in it and in criminology and social work particularly. 'It is a chastening experience and will bring a blush to many a cheek, as it has done, I confess, to mine. We all claim to welcome a little fresh air, but a blasting wind makes us rather uncomfortable, and yet – there can be no doubt about it – that is just what we need.'[85]

Creators of blasting winds need some time off, and Barbara certainly managed that during the Nuffield years. She spent several holidays in France and Italy (Corsica and Alassio), and visited the USA again for a lecture tour. In 1956, she went to India as a social economist and in 1958 to newly-independent Ghana as an expert on delinquency and the criminal justice system. The Indian trip was made in the company of four (other) economists: Paul Bareau, Roland Bird, Duncan Burn and Andrew Shonfield. Barbara held an informal get-together in her office ('a little obscure to find in the dark,' but 'rather attractive when you actually get there') the month before they went.[86] In her autobiography, she noted that her companions were all much younger than she was, and prone to arguing with one another, so that during their long travels round India she found herself playing the role of a 'conciliatory aunt'. In the process, she grew attached to all of them, but especially to 'the whimsical and charming' Andrew Shonfield.[87] He was thirty-nine to her fifty-nine;

years later she confided to friends that he was the last man she had slept with.[88] The purpose of the Indian expedition is unclear, except that it was at the invitation of the Indian Government, to review its achievements after the completion of its first Five-Year Plan. Barbara was inevitably reminded of her trip to Russia in 1932, which had taken place at about the same stage in that Government's planning process. Like the Russians, the Indians she met were fired with enthusiasm for great enterprises, especially factories, machines, power-stations, and 'all the paraphernalia of industrialism'.[89] Unlike the Russians, however, the Indians were determined to combine centralized economic planning with democracy. This she thought an experiment of unique importance to the British Labour movement – exactly the kind of experiment she would have liked to have been able to draw on when she wrote her *Freedom Under Planning*. Barbara and the four men, and a merchant banker called Macartney-Filgate and his wife, did the rounds of the Ministries and the cocktail parties; they trudged round many factories, shipyards and dams, but were given sufficient time off to see the Taj Mahal and the Southern temples. Barbara rode on an elephant in the jungle and made the acquaintance of an enthusiastic family planning expert who took her to the villages; the sight of rural women going about their daily chores impressed Barbara with its natural beauty and social cohesion. 'To break the link between wealth and ugliness,' she commented, 'would be one of the greatest gifts that India and Africa could offer to mankind.'[90] The awful possibility that India might replicate the horrors of Western capitalism much distressed her, and she sent her thoughts about this to President Nehru. She had met him during her stay in India, and he received her thoughts with great interest.[91]

To Ghana, Barbara went as Visiting Professor at what was then University College, located outside Accra, a place modelled on an outdated vision of Oxbridge with High Tables and gowns and chapels. She was there to lecture to public service workers and to students taking the external University of London sociology degree. In this latter function, she was aided by an academic colleague, Ilya Neustadt, a sociologist from the University of Leicester. Barbara gave three public lectures under the title 'Reflections of a Sociologically-minded Magistrate', building on some of the material gathered for *Social Science and Social Pathology*. According to the newspaper *West Africa*, her lectures were eagerly attended by a large and diverse audience. There were barristers and social workers and 'one dogged police corporal who, at question time, flatly refused to agree with the Chairman's suggestion that he had finished all he wanted to say'.[92] Barbara took great pains to deal sympathetically with the many rather inarticulate questioners who attached great importance to her opinion. The Juvenile Court in Ghana was very like her own back in Chelsea; she met President (then Prime Minister) Nkrumah, whom she considered rather over-impressed by his own success. A feature of the Ghanaian system was the bitter quarrelling engaged in by the political parties, but it was usually unclear what they were actually quarrelling about.[93] 'Ghana spells to me,' she wrote, arrestingly, 'black babies dumped on my lap while their mothers danced; it spells the riotous, colourful gaiety of the markets, the clear cool note of the alarm bird by which I was awakened every morning.'[94]

To Vera, back in The Bothy, she sent mixed notes of instruction about things that needed doing (please tell Hillcroft College that she was willing to serve on the Council, could Vera please find an article in the *Eugenics Review* about the physique of delinquents) with glowing accounts of their various excursions:

> Friday to a highly anthropological festival across the Volta rapids (by canoe). This was quite beyond my powers of description. Would not have missed it for anything, with the chiefs in gorgeous robes, the sacred stools and sundry other sacred objects (incl. tin boxes) carried in procession to the river for purification. Much dancing and drumming and some people in a state of possession. Then on (160 miles) here where Ilya and I are doing a social welfare tour somewhat as in India: two prisons, 1 youth centre ... two villages, one willing to self-help, one not, preferring to drink and bathe in the same filthy stagnant pool. All this is v. strenuous, and Ilya who rashly ate a kipper (!) for breakfast was violently sick in the afternoon and has retired to bed. The climate is unbelievably oppressive – worse even than in Accra. You cannot ever get clean because merely drying after a bath makes you just as sweaty again. Where it all comes from I do not know ... my driver, regarding me as "wise in the world" has poured out a long story of his troubles, for which my casework skills are totally inadequate.[95]

In Kumasi, they attended a meeting of the Asantameni Council ('very gorgeous assembly of chiefs'), where they were not allowed to cross their legs (it would have offended the chiefs), which was surprisingly difficult, and where the programme included 'communal labour, professors participating',[96] but fortunately they arrived too late to do anything.[97]

The experience of advising the United Nations about its pension schemes, the year after Ghana, provided Barbara with another take on cultural diversity: how family dependency is defined differently in the member states and affiliated organizations of the United Nations, which included nearly all the countries of the world. She was taken aback when the Indian representative among them casually acknowledged that he had financial obligations to seventy members of his family; and it was a minor victory on her part to persuade the group that women as well as men have dependants. The United Nations mission allowed her to meet the inspiring Dag Hammarsköld, then UN Secretary-General, and to sit in the monumental glass structure of the UN building, albeit in a windowless basement.[98]

Back in England, Vera had a punt on the Thames, moored in the Paddington arm of the Grand Union Canal. She spent weekends on the river, and she would often come to work in The Bothy on Monday mornings laden with flowers; Barbara would wear one in her lapel, perhaps a yellow water lily, or something else unusual. They gave two parties for College staff, which included the Principal, a rather stiff botanist called Norah Penston (not to be confused with the historian Lillian Penson, whose antipathy to Barbara had led to the disbanding of her research unit), and Vera softened things up by putting her lilies in a vase with the gardener's balsam poplar twigs. Attempts at joint socializing were not so successful. Sometimes Barbara would invite Vera home to tea, but it would be awkward. 'I absolutely worshipped her, I adored her,' said Vera, 'but what do you talk about with your idol? ... I think she had this feeling that she wanted to be closer to me but she didn't know how to do it.'[99] They went to hear Billy Graham together, because Barbara wanted to find out what he was like, and on another occasion Vera and a friend of hers invited Barbara to come to the Players' Theatre under the Charing Cross railway arches. But this was a mistake; Barbara was not amused. She was not a person who wasted time, nor who spent much of it in conventional leisure activities. She played tennis with George sometimes, but otherwise is not recorded for any devotion to exercise; she liked music, and of course she read, all the time. She enjoyed eating and drinking with friends, although was herself not an inspired cook. In her autobiography, she records her passion for modern Venetian glass as being so great that it was a reason for not visiting Venice too often.[100]

The Nuffield work produced many invitations to talk and write. In her report for the Principal of Bedford College on the first year's work, Barbara noted that she had given a paper on social factors in delinquency to a seminar organized by the Institute for the Study and Treatment of Delinquency (the undertaking she had warned Vera about before she started work); and had agreed to give the Josiah Mason Lectures at the University of Birmingham the following year on the theme of 'Social Science and Social Responsibility'. She was reviewing eight reports by European experts on 'Lacunae and Present Trends in Research in the Social Sciences' for the Provisional International Social Science Council, and had been asked to write an introduction for a UNESCO compendium on social science research.[101] In this, as in various other outlets around the same time, she reviewed the progress of social science, measuring its strengths and weaknesses. Strengths included the rise in empirical investigations – even among economists, who were at last asking questions about such topics as people's spending and saving habits – and the development of methodological tools: there had been huge advances since she herself graduated (or would have done, had she been a man): when she left Girton, sample surveys were only beginning to be used, and she had never heard of such things as 'statistical significance' or 'factor analysis'.[102] Other signs of advance were a more delimited role for theory, and the adaptation of social science work to the problems of particular cultures and countries. Among social science's weaknesses were the growth of an obscure technical vocabulary, and the continuing failure for studies to be repeated or for investigators to agree on definitions of key measures and concepts.[103] Values – of the culture, stemming from the social scientist's own personal location in the social world – continued to generate hypotheses which were then fondly clung to 'by people who *want* them to be true'.[104] However, on the benefit side, people *were* beginning to appreciate the value of social science in undermining popular myths – for example, the widely held, but erroneous, idea that floating voters are middle-class, or that watching television saps initiative and corrupts morals.[105] When the journal *New Society* was launched in the autumn of 1962 as a sister publication to *New Scientist* for the social sciences, Barbara contributed a piece to its first issue called, 'Socrates, Science and Social Problems'. She blamed both the Socratic tradition of discussion-for-discussion's-sake and the invention of broadcasting as slowing the pace at which social science could achieve science. Neither Socrates nor broadcasters were interested in facts, only in stirring up opinionated controversy. Barbara, whom the journal introduced in its pages as 'a leading social scientist and reformer', *was* interested in facts, and especially those uncoverable by social science which are 'the raw material of intelligent social policy'.[106]

As the Nuffield work progressed, Barbara developed strands of it in separate papers: the theme of mental illness and anti-social behaviour;[107] the pretentious professional ideology of social workers;[108] and the place of social service in 'the new society' of the post-war welfare state.[109] It was in the latter paper that Barbara advanced another modern argument, that hardly anyone bothers to take into account the views of people who use such services. She noted that the Wolfenden Committee, which had recently pronounced on Homosexual Offences and Prostitution, had not interviewed a single prostitute (it could not really have interviewed homosexuals, since homosexuality was illegal); the less notorious Committee on Public Libraries had not thought to seek the opinions of people who might visit them to read books; the Younghusband Report on Social Workers would like to have undertaken a survey of service-users, but had not done so. In several places, Barbara also expanded on her favourite theme of motorists as criminals. She complained that prosecutions for dangerous or careless driving were rare, and drivers exceeding the speed limit, as happened daily on the

thirty-five-mile stretch of road out of London she knew best, were ignored by
the police.[110] Although there were thousands of convictions annually for illegal
parking (90,000 in 1958), this offence was regarded with the same cynical
disrespect as drinking alcohol during the era of prohibition in the USA.[111] She
applied the theme of *Social Science and Social Pathology* – that notions of health and
adjustment presume a particular cultural framework – to practical problems, such
as the new category of 'maladjusted children' created by the 1944 Education Act.
Just as this legislation referred to the need for every school day to begin with an act
of worship, without specifying *what* should be worshipped, so it talked of the need
for children to be adjusted without being clear what they should be adjusted *to*.[112]
For an understanding of the value-systems of schools we would have to wait for
systematic research, although the reports on individual cases obtained by JP Mrs
Wootton showed how much the premium was on quiet conscientious conformity
rather than anything more exciting: '"Originality" I do not ever recall having seen
mentioned,' she remarked, pointedly.[113]

Looking back twenty years later on the furore caused in the social work world
by that chapter in *Social Science and Social Pathology*, Barbara was unrepentant.
Although the phase of 'psycho-analytic self-deification' had mostly passed, what
social workers had written about themselves during that period had been 'almost
unmitigated rubbish and arrogant rubbish at that'.[114] To underscore her point
about the need for social workers to concern themselves with practical problems,
she gave herself the task of formulating 'a philosophy for the social services',
imagining herself as a woman of about forty with three children, suddenly
widowed by the death of a husband earning between £2,000 and £3,000 a year,
and living in rented accommodation. This was almost exactly the situation that
had confronted her own mother in 1907 when her father died, but Adela Adam
had not had to confront the task of unravelling the mysteries of welfare benefits,
simply because none existed then. In 1974, Barbara takes her imaginary widowed
self on an exhausting round of Social Security and Supplementary Benefit and
Housing Authority offices, concluding that good communication and simplicity
should be the basis of any sound philosophy of the social services. Returning
to her real self, she asks the manager of her local Social Security office to give
her an up-to-date copy of the *Department of Health and Social Security's Handbook
on Family Benefits and Pensions*, together with a set of explanatory leaflets: the
resulting package weighs two pounds. She was always struck, but apparently
hardly anybody else was, by the fact that what is exceptional about the personal
social services is that those who provide them do not normally expect to use
them. This is quite unlike what happens in education and health care: teachers

are taught and doctors seek the attention of their peers when they are ill. The social class gap between social workers and their clients produces a tendency to over-emphasize the importance of professionalism, and to downplay the utility of practical knowledge, particularly about the workings of the services, which 'clients' in the modern world really do need.[115]

It was in July 1958, a few months after her return from Ghana, that the letter from Downing Street arrived suggesting that Barbara Wootton's name might be submitted to the Queen for a life peerage.[116] Once that honour was announced, there was an avalanche of congratulatory letters: from officials at the British Sociological Association, the National Secular Society, the London Probation Service, Hillcroft College, the Ethical Union, the Institute for the Study and Treatment of Delinquency, the National Association for Mental Health, the Medico-legal Society, the Home Office, the Workers' Educational Association; and from many women's organizations celebrating this 'first' for women – the Women's Co-operative Guild, the National Women Citizens Association, the Young Women's Christian Association, the Council of Married Women, the Women's Freedom League, the British Federation of University Women. 'The first sociologist in the House of Lords – and a woman at that,' boasted Moya Woodside, psychiatric social worker and research colleague of Eliot Slater, with whom Vera had worked at the Maudsley, 'The Walls of Jericho may well begin to quake'.[117] The headmistress of Barbara's school in Cambridge wrote to express her pride, as did the Mistress and Fellows of Girton College; cousin Cicely Ford saw Barbara's photograph in the newspaper: 'Never had I realized you had such a strong look of your family in your face. I almost thought I could see aunt Juliet smiling at me and telling me how proud she & aunt Frances would have been, & your parents too .... I hope Lizzie [The Pie] will be well enough to take it all in. I know she is so fond of you, & looks upon you as her own child – as I do too, in some measure. When I think how I used to rush in every day, to see you in your bath on my way to lectures.'[118] Tom Marshall, rescuing himself from that negative review of her book, told her she should enjoy the thought that her name would appear in all future history books on the British Constitution.[119] There were letters from Hugh Gaitskell and Lord Longford, and from Tom and Annie Wootton, Jack's siblings, in Nottingham, with whom Barbara had kept in touch, and from old students, one of whom told Barbara that some of them had prophetically called her Lady Barbara when her back was turned,[120] and another of whom confessed to having illicitly kept Barbara's copy of Keynes' *Monetary Reform* for many years.[121]

On the day of the formal House of Lords proceedings, Sir William Haley wrote affectionately to Barbara from his office at *The Times* in Printing House Square:

Dear Barbara,

I thought the House of Lords ceremony this afternoon very moving. This is the way to make history, and one had all the greater sense of it with Mme Pandit and the Begum Ikramullah in the Ambassadors' Gallery. What thoughts they must have had of how far and how fast women have progressed in their own lands.

But, of course, the chief emotion of the occasion was personal. Seeing you there brought up all kinds of memories, all happy ones, and I was stirred by both past and present ... Exactly what the House of Lords is going to mean in your daily life I do not know. But it will probably be quite demanding. There is much to do there and it really is worthwhile. May it give you a whole range of new interests and some sense of fulfilment, which is surely the truest happiness ...

Yours always, William.[122]

In her letter of congratulations, Albertine Winner, a doctor and influential medical administrator at the Department of Health, recalled several discussions with Barbara at the Titmusses that could have been continued – would Barbara come to dinner?[123] Richard Titmuss and his wife (Ann Oakley's parents) were among the first to express their congratulations. 'Dear Barbara' wrote Kay Titmuss, having just put down either *The News Chronicle*, which she read every day, or *The Times*, which Richard did, 'We are still at the breakfast table – all three of us – so this is an impulsive note sending congratulations to our dear Baroness. Richard, of course, immediately thought of something for you to do – he says he will transfer all his PQs [Parliamentary Questions] for you to handle.'[124]

Barbara's peerage did nothing to change the inhospitable attitude of Bedford College towards her, and the final stages of the Nuffield Foundation work had to be moved elsewhere, to the Foundation's own premises. While Vera laboured on the manuscript of the book, Barbara dealt with a new avalanche of requests to take part in radio and television programmes, to give lectures, write articles, be guest of honour at numerous dinners, and so forth. She found it odd that her reputation should have taken such an abrupt leap. 'The Baroness Wootton of Abinger did not become overnight more knowledgeable, or a more stimulating speaker or in any way more worth hearing than her precursor, Mrs. Barbara Wootton,'[125] she noted with characteristic forthrightness. But this observation did not prevent her from making fulsome use of her new status, achieved at an age (sixty-one) when most people would have been contemplating a quiet withdrawal into retirement. For her, it was just the beginning of a new golden age.

13

High Barn, and the Other Barbara

Throughout the various lives of Barbara Wootton – classicist manqué, lamenting economist, radical social scientist and policy wisewoman – there runs the thread of a person searching for her rightful home. Barbara's disciplinary restlessness was matched by the lack of any physical place that could be called a permanent home. After the devastatingly brief marriage to Jack Wootton when she was twenty, she had gone back to live in her mother's house in Cambridge. Her next two homes were institutions: Girton College in Cambridge and Westfield College in London. After that came a series of cramped rented flats, in Chelsea and St John's Wood, and then a more congenial, but still impermanent, residence with Leonora Simeon on a hill in Hampstead. The marriage to George Wright in 1935, when she was thirty-eight, took her to west London, to a block of flats in Fulham near the river. If the marriage had maintained the happiness of its early years, perhaps she and George would have stayed in Napier Court. But George's serial infidelities became in the end too much for Barbara to bear; it was time to move on.

One of Barbara's most vivid childhood memories was of happy holidays spent with The Pie at the home of Lord Farrer at Abinger Hall in Surrey. An aunt, Jeanie Adam, was governess to the Farrer children, two of whom, Fanny and Kitty, were close to Barbara in age. Abinger Hall was a minor stately home, originally built in 1783 and rebuilt in 1872, with terraces and balustrades, a fountain, glassy slopes for rolling down, a huge kitchen garden and woodlands perfect for childhood games. The whole house was a child's delight for generations of children, as one of Kitty's daughters, remembers: 'an enormous kind of baronial hall, surrounded on the first floor by a gallery, with a swing door to the Nursery quarters, and a long corridor on the second floor where (on wet days) one could play "Rat Trap and Ball" (with the risk of propelling the ball down onto the heads of grown-ups crossing the ground floor hall)'.[1] Lord Farrer was nicknamed 'Railway Tom' because of his obsession with railways: he could reputedly tell you from memory the times of trains between any two points in England and Scotland. Farrer was on the Board of the Midland Railway and the Board of the Underground Electric Railways Company of London, a forerunner of the London Underground. He also displayed a concern with which Barbara Wootton would later empathize, for the preservation of the countryside, and was, for many years, a prominent member of the Commons and Footpaths Preservation Society.

The Farrers and the Adams probably first met in Cambridge. When Lord Farrer's first wife died in 1898, she left three children under six – Fanny and Kitty had an older brother – and their father took them to live for a time with his sister Ida, who was married to Horace Darwin, in Cambridge. The most famous Darwin, Charles, had once used the Abinger Hall site to explore Roman remains; the Roman mosaic floors were apparently an excellent place to observe the work of earthworms. Following Darwin's visit, the first Lord Farrer kept a daily 'Worm Diary' for him, recording the number and weight of each night's worm casts, information that Darwin used for his book on earthworms.[2] After Railway Tom's second marriage in 1903, the Farrers returned to Abinger Hall, and then Barbara's aunt, Jeanie, was the passport to her niece's holiday memories – or perhaps it was the other way round, and the Farrers' sojourn in Cambridge had introduced them to the Adams, and James Adam had perhaps suggested his sister for the post of governess in rural Surrey. At any rate, Jeanie Adam, known to the Farrer children as 'Miss Addy', was an important source of support for them, especially when their new stepmother was busy with committee work and children of her own.[3]

The parish of Abinger lies some thirty miles south-west of London in a green commuter belt bounded on the north by chalk downs 700 feet above sea level, the southern part running into the clay of the Weald. There is Hurtwood Forest, an area of Outstanding Natural Beauty, with its four thousand acres of protected woodland. There is Abinger Hammer, and Sutton Abinger, and Abinger Bottom and Abinger Common, and, most confusingly for this story, a neighbouring village called Wotton. The history of Abinger Common goes back well beyond the Domesday Survey. This is quintessential rural England, much sought after then and now by people who have enough money to buy their way into it. Holmbury Hill, which rises beyond the village of Holmbury St Mary, is reputed to afford the finest view in Surrey,[4] and Abinger Hammer, so-called because it used to be a centre of the iron industry, was voted by *The Independent* in 2008 one of the best picnic spots in England. It has an extraordinary clock, a gift from Railway Tom's stepmother, who put it there in memory of her husband; on it, Jack the Blacksmith strikes the hour.[5] The village of Holmbury St Mary is considered by some to be commemorated as 'Summer Street' in E.M. Forster's *A Room with a View*. Forster lived in Abinger Hammer, at first with his mother in a house designed for his aunt. He produced *Abinger Harvest*, a book of essays and other memorabilia, its title taken from an account of a pageant performed in 1934 to raise money for the local church. The music for the pageant was written by Vaughan Williams, and it included a choral setting, *O How Amiable*, dedicated to Fanny Farrer, who would later, like Barbara Wootton, be 'elevated' to an honour, in her case a damehood acquired through a lifelong service as 'the Queen bee' of the Women's Institutes.[6]

All this history was one reason why Barbara Wootton started her search for a house in the area. There were two other reasons. First, there was her lifelong dislike of cities. 'Towns are ugly,' she wrote in 1946; they are places of 'aesthetic starvation', where one inevitably spends far too much time entangled in the 'machinery of living', for example simply getting from one place to another. In the country, life is simpler, and when you lift your eyes from whatever it is that you are doing they are bound to fall on a pleasing view.[7] Barbara's attachment to the countryside would later translate into a role as the first Chair of the Countryside Commission. In that capacity, she was well aware of the paradox of town-dwellers like herself seeking the peace and aesthetic delights of the country and thereby threatening to alter it.[8] A second reason why Barbara was searching for a new home in Surrey was that a friend of hers owned a cottage in Holmbury St Mary, and she and George regularly went there at weekends to help with the garden. Moves to the country by long-established town-dwellers are often motivated initially by fantasy, and Barbara's was no exception. Several houses were nearly bought, but fear of commitment prevented the purchase going through. Then, in November 1953, she spotted an advertisement in *The Times* for an old barn that could be converted into a home. She motored down to view an almost derelict building overgrown with nettles and brambles, essentially just a stable for horses and bats and bees, with one cold water tap and two naked rooms, and a large open space in the middle for waggons to be driven through. It was the rashest decision she had ever taken in her life.[9] 'High Barn', as she called it, became a major renovation project, and then eventually for more than thirty years exactly the home she wanted. One sign of how much she loved it is that, of the ten photographs reproduced in her autobiography, four are before-and-after shots of High Barn, and two are of the donkeys that came to live with her there.

She could not have done it without her architect, Henry Dalton Clifford. He was an erratic man of ideas who specialized in house conversions, and had very definite views about architecture, and especially home decoration: the ornate fussiness of a late Victorian house, overloaded with awnings, lanterns and the like, resembled, he declared, 'a scarlet woman'.[10] Clifford wrote a number of books – *The Country Life Book of Houses for Today* (1963), *Home Decoration* (1955), and the apposite *New Homes from Old Buildings* (1954). In his *New Houses for Moderate Means*

(1957), he was honest about the risk and tedium involved in building a new house, which was more or less what had to be done with High Barn. However, shortly after agreeing to work on the project, he slipped a disc and gave it all up to run a hotel and become an antique-dealer in Cornwall, much to Barbara's annoyance. He passed the project to his friend 'Philip', who in turn passed it to his friend 'David', but the original Clifford plans were adhered to, more or less.[11] The work took two years. Getting planning permission was not a speedy process, but at least she did get it, whereas other plans to build a house from scratch on a site a mile or two away had been refused, on the grounds that it would spoil the countryside. Barbara quoted this example approvingly in a talk she gave years later called 'More Equality, Less Freedom?' which argued that people must put up with such frustrations in the interests of the principle of planning regulation, which is a matter of ensuring a safe and pleasant environment for everyone, not of restricting individual freedom.[12] What could and could not be done in the parish of Abinger was also determined by an almost medieval system of property ownership: when Barbara's friend Francis Williams built a house in Holmbury St Mary in the 1930s, a large part of the village was still owned by one old lady who made rounds of visits in an open landau, expecting the village children to curtsey as she passed, and whenever a young man in the village wanted to get married, she would refuse him a cottage if she thought he should stay at home and look after his mother instead.[13]

The structure of High Barn had been moved to Abinger from Effingham in Sussex to accompany an Arts and Crafts house built by Edwin Lutyens in 1898–1900. One likes to think that Barbara Wootton knew the purpose of this building, which was to provide 'a Home of Rest to which ladies of small means might repair for holiday'.[14] Goddards, as the Lutyens house was called, was bought in 1953 by Bill and Noeline Hall, who made their money from a haulage business, and who became, along with their two children, friends of Barbara's.[15] Since Goddards and High Barn shared a drive, Barbara had to pay the Halls the token annual rent of a rose on a summer's day.[16] A local builder, Mr Sherlock of Peaslake, had re-erected the barn when it first came from Sussex, and he was still around, so Barbara hired him for her renovations. It must have been a busy time for Mr Sherlock, and his son Denis, since they were enlisted by Francis Williams for *his* building project in Abinger around the same time.[17]

High Barn is set back from the road and backs onto protected woodland. Today it hides behind tall hedges at the back and tall gates at the front, giving it the impression of jealously guarded privacy. The lanes around are lush with vegetation and discrete wealth. In the conversion undertaken by Mr Sherlock, High Barn was not a large house: there was a semi-basement with a large room and its own kitchen and bathroom and a separate entrance; a good-sized high-ceilinged and beamed living space; the usual amenities; a study for Barbara and her bedroom; and then a small guest room with its own bathroom. Visitors who came to interview Barbara in the house called it 'small',[18] and 'charming without quaintness, not large, but comfortable and secluded'.[19] They admired its situation: 'The approach over the west side of Leith Hill is amazing,' observed a journalist from *The Scotsman*, 'a steep climb between high sandy banks with few passing places for cars. The sun winks beguilingly through tall groves of beech, birch, pine, oak and holly. If this is the gin and jaguar belt, there is nothing much wrong with it.'[20] Photographs show a simply furnished house with wooden floors, rugs, plain wooden furniture, not much in the way of decoration or adornment. As one friend of Barbara's noted, 'It was very frugal ... There was no comfort there. No armchairs'.[21] And it was clear, as the journalist from the *Horley Advertiser* remarked, that Lady Wootton took much pleasure in 'having created her own home to her own requirements'.[22] A photograph in her archives shows Barbara's bed, a high white bed positioned at exactly the same height as the bottom of a window, the window casements thrown open wide onto a glowing summer garden. The outside of High Barn was much bigger than the inside, and it needed a great deal of work. At the back was a buttercup meadow, and this was home to the two creatures who would afford Barbara much companionship as she grew older: the donkeys, Miranda and Francesca. Miranda, so named because she was delivered in a tempest, had an 'establishment' nature; Francesca, named after Barbara (whose middle name was 'Frances') was the hippy.[23] Miranda arrived first in 1959, Francesca three years later. They kept the grass in the meadow under control and had peaceable natures, except that Francesca brayed loudly when things were not to her liking, as when her food was delayed by the arrival of a man from the BBC to record an interview with Barbara.[24]

The donkeys inhabited a land of lords and ladies. Abinger gained a Baroness when Barbara Wootton took the title 'Wootton of Abinger' on becoming a life peer in 1958. It acquired a Baron, when Francis Williams joined Barbara as Baron Francis-Williams of Abinger in 1962. Lord Wolfenden, who chaired the 1957 Committee leading to the recommendation that homosexuality should be partially decriminalized, lived in nearby Westcott, and absorbed that village into his title when he added a life peerage to his knighthood in 1974. The banker Lord Catto, from whom Barbara borrowed robes for her initiation in the House of Lords, had a house in Holmbury St Mary. In addition, there was a fair diversity of characters: the pianist William Murdoch had lived and made music in Holmbury St Mary until his death in 1942; his wife, Flossie, was a sister of Ernest Simon, Lord Simon of Wythenshawe, Chairman of the BBC when Barbara joined as a

Governor. Other inhabitants were the journalist and writer Cecil Sprigge; the early Everest mountaineer Frank Smythe; Barbara's relative Sir John Ford, who lived in nearby Guildford; and her old school friend, the neuropathologist Dorothy Russell, who had a little modern house in Westcott. The district could even be considered a minor outpost of the Bloomsberries, with the Forster connection and Beatrice Webb House, just down the hill from High Barn, a large Victorian building, bought in 1947 by the Webb Memorial Trust, suitably with a mortgage from the Transport and General Workers' Union. Beatrice Webb House was run as a meeting place for the 'advancement of education and learning with respect to the history and problems of government and social policy'.[25]

Like Beatrice Webb House, Barbara Wootton was politically not at all representative of the tone of the area. But, as Francis Williams commented, 'even the strong Conservatives who predominated among our neighbours did their best in a neighbourly way to forgive us our socialism'.[26] His son John Melville Williams, who later negotiated the planning regulations to build a house with sweeping views over Holmbury Hill, recalls having a different relationship with Barbara from those with other neighbours: in conversation with her, one could let one's hair down and make comments about what was really happening in the world. He found it quite interesting that she had relationships with people who were rather different from her – comfortably off, middle-class women who lived in the neighbourhood and who were very good neighbours to Barbara, despite not necessarily sharing her political affiliation.[27] One, Audrey Bradley, remembers being a guest at one of her dinner parties: 'Barbara had been up in the House of Lords … and she'd asked everybody what they'd been doing all day with a slightly naughty look in her eye because she got round to me and I said I'd been playing golf'.[28] (The politics of golf, the House of Lords and British political party affiliations were by no means straightforward.) In Barbara's later years when her health declined, these Surrey neighbours were an important source of support and help, and essential in a rural area without much in the way of public transport. In the early 1950s when Barbara found High Barn, a steam train ambled in the morning and back in the evening between Gomshall and London Bridge stations on a line through the chalk hills of the North Downs, and there were also convenient fast trains from Dorking to London. But in the 1960s, a new line removed the convenience of the fast trains.

It was a complicated and quite secretive transition, this one from being George Wright's wife in Fulham to being a Lady of Abinger. By far the most secretive aspect of it was that Barbara was not only moving house and leaving George, but she was also moving a new companion into her life. The cottage in Holmbury St Mary that had provided the base for house-hunting belonged to a woman called Barbara

Ruth Fuessli Kyle. When Barbara Wootton moved into High Barn, Barbara Kyle moved up the hill, to a cottage opposite, and then she moved into High Barn itself. She was known as 'Barbara' Kyle professionally, and to her family as 'Ruth', and sometimes she published under the name 'Ruth Archibald' ('Archibald' was one of her father's forenames). Barbara Wootton called her 'Fuessli' ('my friend Fuessli Kyle'[29]) because having two Barbaras would be too confusing. The Pie, whom Barbara Kyle was taken to meet, and who referred to her affectionately and often in her letters to Barbara Wootton, called her simply 'the Other Barbara'.

Barbara Kyle started out as a librarian. She worked in libraries from the age of sixteen, beginning with the Paddington Public Library in 1929, graduating to public libraries in Fulham (in 1935) and Islington, and then to a senior post in the Library of the Royal Institute of International Affairs (Chatham House) in 1945. She stayed at Chatham House for ten years, creating a classification scheme for the library and reorganizing it so it became one of the main collections in its field.[30] The two Barbaras may have first met in Fulham, when Barbara Wootton was living there, and Barbara Kyle was working in the library: the Preface to *Freedom Under Planning* acknowledges Barbara Wootton's 'perpetual debt' to the staff of Fulham Public Library, as well as to Barbara Kyle for providing criticism and checking details. They may also have encountered each other in the context of Chatham House. In the late 1930s, Barbara Wootton had worked with Lionel Curtis, the founder of Chatham House, at the beginning of the Federal Union movement; she had also been secretary of a Study Group on Reconstruction there, and the Trades Union Congress representative on the Chatham House Council in 1940–1. At any rate, Barbara Wootton and Barbara Kyle knew each other by 1942. In that year, Barbara Wootton acknowledged Barbara Kyle's help with the survey of the social services she had undertaken with one of her university tutorial classes.[31] The Other Barbara's meticulous librarian's eye was also called into service for the texts of *Testament for Social Science* (1950) and *Social Science and Social Pathology* (1959).

Barbara Kyle was twelve years younger than Barbara Wootton. She was a handsome woman with sparkling eyes and a wide smile, and is always smiling in the photographs, whether lounging on the terrace of High Barn, ministering to the donkeys, or at a dinner table with a glass of wine. Her professional colleagues knew her as energetic, loyal, warm-hearted, strong-minded, forthright and passionate.[32] She was born in Richmond, on the western edge of London, in 1909, to a family that was relatively well-off, but afflicted with an unusual amount of premature death. Her grandmother was left with eight dependent children when her husband died early, and Barbara Kyle's own father died when she and her sister Elspeth were young, forcing their mother to take responsibility for their

upkeep.[33] Among the family's accomplishments was the founding of Grindlays
Bank, a major British overseas bank which began life in 1828 as a business
providing travel and financial services for British travellers to India.[34] The bank's
founder, Barbara Kyle's grandfather, Captain Robert Melville Grindlay, was also
a gifted amateur painter. Painting ran in the family. Her third name, 'Fuessli', the
one that Barbara Wootton used, came from a distant relationship through her
father with the Swiss painter Henry Fuseli. (Originally Füssli or Fuessli in English,
he changed his name to Fuseli when he lived in Italy in the 1770s, because it
sounded more Italian.[35]) Henry Füssli's art is intensely Gothic: violent, troubling,
supernatural, some would say frankly pornographic. His most famous painting,
'The Nightmare', purportedly hung alongside Rembrandt's 'The Anatomy Lesson'
in Freud's Viennese consulting room.[36] It is a frightening painting showing a
sleeping girl clothed in virginal white with a brown incubus squatting on her belly,
and a horse peering out between theatrical dark red curtains. Füssli himself was a
short, somewhat ugly man with prematurely whitened hair and trembling hands,
whose views about women would hardly have recommended him to any feminist.
This makes his short affair with the English feminist and author of the powerful
Vindication of the Rights of Woman, Mary Wollstonecraft, all the more extraordinary.[37]

By comparison, Barbara Kyle's life was, at least on the surface, much more rooted
in the ordinary. She wrote a bestseller about librarianship in the yellow-and-black-
covered 'Teach Yourself' series, a text awash with 'quick, clean prose' and 'much
humour', which is still relevant today.[38] She was for a time Assistant Director of the
National Book League, in which capacity she had the foresight to support the then
embryonic scheme for a public lending right through which authors would be able
to benefit financially from public library borrowings of their works.[39] She played a
major role in the Association of Special Libraries and Information Bureaux (ASLIB),
being elected to the ASLIB Council in 1949, serving on many of its committees, and
becoming its Research Librarian in 1962 and editor in 1962 of its journal, *The Journal
of Documentation*. ASLIB was formed in 1924 by a small group of people working in
industry and science who were concerned with the scientific rationalization of society
and with problems of disseminating information and securing equality of access to
it.[40] These were topics that were attracting increasing attention at the time. Barbara
Kyle was also a leading figure in a network called the Classification Research Group
which was set up in 1952 by major figures in library and information science in
the UK, following an initiative sponsored by the Royal Society and led by scientist
J.D. Bernal.[41] Bernal, a molecular physicist based in Cambridge, was a major figure
in the scientific community of the 1930s, and an inspired proponent of the social
uses of science and technology. He remembered as a young scientist going to ask the

curator of the Natural History Museum mineralogy collection for a very, very small crystal to examine, and being told, 'No, I am in charge of this museum. My duty is to preserve the specimens in it. You cannot have it.' Bernal asked what the curator was preserving them for, and was told, 'Some time they may be of use to science'.[42]

Barbara Kyle's own interests went far beyond the parochial stewardship of particular library collections. Librarianship – the art of looking after books – in the modern era is really the science of knowledge management, a discipline which merges with epistemology.[43] Barbara Kyle's work in the 1950s and 1960s influenced the development of library and information science during a period of great technical and intellectual change. Her writings are distinguished for their focus on the theory and practice of classification, on information science and professionalism, and on the public's right to information in what she called the 'intellectual welfare state'. Her paper on 'Privilege and Public Provision in the Intellectual Welfare State', recently republished,[44] and with strong resonances in the twenty-first century,[45] presents a strongly argued case for people's rights to 'adequate intellectual fare', rights which parallel the right to material welfare. Just as is the case for the social services in the material welfare state, library services – both public and private – need to co-operate in clearly identifying and meeting these needs. The efficient and easy retrieval of information is especially important, as Barbara Kyle herself noted, in order to avoid potentially biased dependence on who knows whom and who has heard of what.[46] Among Barbara Kyle's international connections was her membership of the UNESCO International Advisory Committee for Bibliography, Documentation, and Terminology, and her Vice-Presidency of the International Federation for Documentation; she was also a member of the International Committee for Social Sciences Documentation (ICSSD), and represented that body at various European meetings. Unfortunately, her status as a 'pioneering woman'[47] was partly obscured by her early death, which left her work on social science classification unfinished. When she died prematurely of cancer in 1966, ASLIB dedicated a special issue of its journal to her. The topics of the various chapters illustrate the range of the debates to which she contributed: 'Documentation Services and Library Co-operation in the Social Sciences', 'Problems in Analysis and Terminology for Information Retrieval', and 'The Library as an Agency of Social Communication'. There was an annotated bibliography of all her work, a total of fifty-three publications, ranging from the technical ('Merits and Demerits of Various Classification Schemes for the Social Sciences') to the general ('Books for the Holidays'), and even a poem about the Indian librarian S.R. Ranganathan, with whom she participated in a long-drawn out but highly civilized argument about the specialist technical topics of zone analysis and colon classification.[48]

Barbara Wootton was not open about her personal life, so the story of her relationship with Barbara Kyle is hazy. It is clear that the transition from a friendship to a domestic partnership was not a sudden one. When they first met, Barbara Kyle was living with her mother, and Barbara was living with George. But, by 1950, the Kyles had moved to Napier Court, into the block where Barbara and George had their flat: the Kyles lived at number 80, the Wrights at number 84. Around the same time, Barbara Kyle preceded Barbara Wootton to Surrey, acquiring the Holmbury St Mary cottage. In Barbara Wootton's autobiography, her eventual break with George is explained as the wearing out of a relationship between two people, neither of whom is very suited to monogamy: he because of his polygamous nature, she because of her preoccupation with her own affairs and way of life.[49] However, George was obviously shocked to discover that Barbara's intention was to leave him behind in the move to High Barn. He sent several imploring letters to her office at Bedford College, and stayed in the Napier Court flat on a camp bed until she managed to persuade him to leave.[50] She did not find it easy to abandon George, and she did not tell people she had done it. The Pie was certainly kept in the dark. Writing in response to Barbara's news about the finding of High Barn, she warned, 'It will cost some money and take a long time to build and do as you like it. But it will be very nice to have a place and garden for George and yourself of your own'.[51] Writing to her friend William Haley in the summer of 1957, and inviting him and his wife Susan to stay with her at High Barn, Barbara told them: 'To save future embarrassment, I fear I should now say that since I have been living here – over a year now – George and I have not been living together. Perhaps you have heard rumours; perhaps not; but, if you have, they are well-founded, though there have not been any [divorce] proceedings, and we meet occasionally.'[52] She complained that, 'When other people do these things, it all seems very straightforward and matter of fact; but in one's case it is not so at all, as doubtless everybody finds who gets into this situation. However, no doubt daylight, and perhaps even sunshine will appear in time. If only one could manage not to feel guilty.'[53]

By this time, the two Barbaras were living in High Barn together. 'They were very close,' said Barbara Kyle's cousin, Ann Monie.[54] 'They were extremely close,' said Vera Seal, Barbara's colleague and friend, who experienced Barbara Kyle's jealousy when she accompanied Barbara Wootton home to tea after one of their sessions in the Chelsea Juvenile Court.[55] The two Barbaras sometimes wore the same clothes; that was a feature of Barbara Wootton's close relationships with people, she wanted to wear the same. For example, they owned two traditional blue-and-white Norwegian jerseys, purchased on one of their holidays in Norway. The consensus of opinion among those who knew Barbara Wootton well in these years was that she and the Other Barbara had a close and loving, but probably not sexual, relationship. Barbara Kyle was 'mannish' in appearance and Barbara Wootton liked mannish women, but she also liked mannish men.[56] Her Surrey neighbours noted with amusement Barbara's interest in *their* men. Most of Barbara Wootton's London friends were never introduced to Barbara Kyle. According to Frank Field, Barbara Wootton 'deliberately kept her as a mystery and kept her in a sense away from any other life'.[57] Life after the move to High Barn probably did become rather compartmentalized: work in London, domesticity in Surrey. But those who were allowed to meet the Other Barbara recognized her strength and intelligence, and important place in Barbara Wootton's life. Thus, Vera Seal said of her: 'I could quite admire her. I could see why Barbara needed her … I just remember one incident. I was at High Barn and we were having a meal, and Barbara suddenly wanted some butter and she went like this [gesture] … and immediately Ruth Kyle passed it to her … I think she was very good to, and for, Barbara. I think she probably did quite a lot for Barbara … She was an attractive woman, she was very intelligent, I think. You could have a laugh with her. I would have said in a sense that she ran Barbara, but I think that Barbara was glad to be run.'[58]

An aspect of their relationship that may not have been fully appreciated by those who knew them was that the partnership of the two Barbaras was intellectual as well as domestic. They shared a passion for the democratic and socially useful organization of knowledge. Barbara Kyle's concern was with how to define and classify literature so as render it retrievable and useful; Barbara Wootton's was with the chaotic terminology of social science. Without an exact vocabulary of agreed terms, the social sciences were unlikely to get themselves out of their backward state. Their joint paper 'Terminology in the Social Sciences', published in the *International Social Science Bulletin* in 1950, reflects Barbara Wootton's particular irritation with social scientists' sloppy use of language: terms such as 'democracy', 'social class', 'power' and even 'society' varied in meaning according to the intentions of the user, which made genuine communication impossible. One of her illustrations was taken from an economics book by Professor L.M. Fraser, who had given her *Lament for Economics* an unfortunate review some years earlier: Fraser showed that economists were not at all agreed about the definition of key terms such as 'value' or 'capital'. The sociologists were no better, being totally unable to agree what that rather fundamental term 'society' meant, with one esteemed sociologist calling it 'every willed relationship of man to man', a formula so comprehensive that love, hate, robbery, banking, posting letters, and performing a surgical operation would all be covered. Arnold Toynbee, whose monumental *A Study of History* had originally been a model for Barbara Wootton's Nuffield Foundation project, was guilty of extremely imprecise references to manifestations such as 'Hellenic' or 'Islamic' or 'Far Eastern' or even 'Nomadic' society. 'What would happen to, say, genetics, if chromosomes were as elusive as this?' inquired Barbara.[59]

Both Barbara Kyle and Barbara Wootton are mentioned in the records of a group of intellectuals led by Julian Huxley from around 1950 devoted to the search for a unified world-view. The 'Idea-Systems Group' pursued Huxley's vision of evolutionary humanism – his insistence that a new synthesis of knowledge was needed to transcend traditional disciplines and subject boundaries.[60] On a less visionary but nonetheless important level, Barbara Wootton joined Barbara Kyle in her work for ASLIB. She chaired a meeting of ASLIB's London branch in 1951, and was elected President of ASLIB in 1953; after a second term as President, she served on the ASLIB Council. At the Paris meeting of the ICSSD in 1957, the Committee elected Barbara Wootton as one of four new corresponding members. At an ASLIB 'luncheon' at the Trocadero restaurant in Piccadilly in the summer of 1955, William Haley was enlisted as the special guest, Barbara Kyle was there, and Barbara Wootton presided.[61] In the record of the 1954 ASLIB conference held in Church House, Westminster, there is a charming photograph of the two Barbaras during a coffee break, with ASLIB's chairman, Mr B. Agard Evans, standing between them.[62] It can hardly have been an accident that the first International Conference on Classification for Information Retrieval convened in May 1957, with forty participants from seven countries, took place at Beatrice Webb House just down the road from High Barn. Barbara expanded on her irritation with social science terminology in the two keynote addresses she gave to ASLIB's annual conferences in 1953 and 1954 on problems of communication.[63] The sub-title of the second of these was 'The Language of the Social Sciences', and in this paper she made the point that controversies about the meanings of words are often screens for power battles.

The two Barbaras undoubtedly had fun in their various ASLIB activities. Barbara Kyle had a legendary capacity for living, 'a sparkling personality that caught every ear and eye',[64] and it must have infected Barbara Wootton, who, if only in terms of the sheer amount of work she accomplished in her lifetime, appears as an unremittingly serious person; she attributed her inability to play games – with the notable exception of Scrabble – to the fact that work absorbed all her intellectual powers.[65] Barbara Wootton and Barbara Kyle would go to the Proms in London, with free tickets provided through Barbara Wootton's connection to the BBC; they would invite Vera and her friend Eric Glithero, and order glasses of beer in the interval, which they would then leave half-empty balanced in precarious positions. They behaved like 'a couple of minxes', cajoling and provoking others with their own brand of insider humour.[66]

In 1955, Barbara Kyle gave up her Chatham House job, and joined Barbara Wootton as the recipient of a Nuffield Foundation grant. Her application to the Nuffield Foundation argued the need to bring the social sciences into line with the other sciences, which all had efficient indexing and abstracting systems. The social sciences presented special problems of information management, due to the enormous variety and scatter of the literature, and social scientists' insistence on using imprecise and inconsistent terminology. Existing classification systems would not work well on account of their rigid notations and underlying assumption that all types of writing can be analysed in the same way – an assumption that falls down when the terms used vary semantically from one user to another.[67] Barbara Kyle had made a detailed study of the existing standard systems – Dewey, Universal Decimal Classification, Bliss and Library of Congress – but all these had been invented to organize large libraries dealing with the whole field of knowledge, and each suffered to some extent from nationally biased terminology. The plan was to start again and devise a framework for classifying social science literature – not, she stressed, actually to *write* abstracts and bibliographies, but to 'prepare a series of consistent schemes or recipes'. She also planned to carry out a survey of research and library facilities for social scientists. For all this she requested funds for herself and secretarial help over a three- to five-year period, the funds to be administered by the National Book League, which would provide accommodation for the project.[68] In 1955, the Nuffield Foundation Trustees agreed to provide £2,500 a year for three years.[69] This was supplemented by an extension until 1959. By then, Barbara Kyle had successfully drafted an appropriate scheme, and had had some encouraging preliminary reactions: the ICSSD had accepted her draft classification in principle; the Librarian of the British Library of Political and Economic Science had endorsed it; and the editor of the leading information science journal in the USA, *American Documentation*, had offered to publish the final draft.[70]

These were, of course, the days before computers – the possibility of globally accessible internet-based electronic systems for storing and retrieving huge amounts of information was only just beginning to be entertained.[71] Kyle's work was undertaken jointly with the ICSSD, which had identified the need for a new approach appropriate to the social sciences. The ICSSD published annual bibliographies of new work in sociology, economics, political science and social anthropology, but the same article would probably be inconsistently indexed in the different bibliographies and even in the same bibliography from year to year. Kyle and her assistants did much painstaking work classifying and indexing some 14,000 entries in the 1957 versions of the four ICSSD bibliographies according to a new scheme based on an approach called 'facet analysis'. This was a technique for classifying literature which enabled concepts and topics treated in different disciplines (for example, economics and sociology) to be linked together through a complex notational system. The result was claimed to be knowledge maps that provided much more efficient entries into available literature.[72] Kyle and her co-workers went on to choose samples of studies to test whether the new system retrieved relevant titles more effectively than the old, and it did.[73]

What Barbara Kyle had produced became known as the Kyle Classification for social science literature. The Kyle Classification was developed in the same period as Barbara Wootton worked on her disturbing critique of one branch of social science literature, *Social Science and Social Pathology.* Social science *qua* science received an important boost as a result of the two Barbaras' initiatives, although recognition of both accomplishments is sadly almost non-existent today. Both were fertilized by the soil of High Barn and paid for by the Nuffield Foundation. It was a productive and happy period for the two women. One imagines them labouring away in their respective London offices during the day and then repairing to the green sanctuary of Abinger in the evenings, and enjoying a drink on the terrace and perhaps a Kyle-cooked meal with friends. Barbara Kyle did most of the cooking in High Barn, and Barbara Wootton most of the housework; she only dusted the bedrooms, maintaining that nothing else got dusty, and she kept a hoover on each floor. She had two of everything – vacuum cleaners, fridges, cars – in case one of them broke down. One of the cars, unfortunately known as 'Little Black Sambo', was generously lent to a friend in the village twice a year so he could get himself to and from the local dramatic performances, which he helped to manage in Westcott.[74]

By the time Barbara Wootton's autobiography was published in 1967, Kingsley Martin could title his review of it 'Abinger Harvest'.[75] As William Haley remarked in a letter to Barbara in 1978, 'You must now be Abinger's doyenne, much more entitled to its harvest than ever Forster was'.[76] Abinger and the countryside had been kind to her. If Barbara Wootton ever read the original Forster version of *Abinger Harvest*, she might have noted some of the Woodman's remarks in Forster's account of the local pageant:

> Lords and ladies, warriors and priests will pass, but this is not their home, they will
> pass like the leaves in autumn but the trees remain ... Houses, houses, houses! You
> came from them and you must go back to them. Houses and bungalows, hotels,
> restaurants and flats, arterial roads, by-passes, petrol pumps, and pylons – are these
> going to be England? Are these man's final triumph? Or is there another England,
> green and eternal, which will outlast them ... You can make a town, you can make
> a desert, you can even make a garden; but you can never, never make the country,
> because it was made by Time.[77]

14

Crime and Penal Policy

John Bird founded Britain's best-selling street newspaper for the homeless, *The Big Issue*, in 1991. Behind this success lay a different story, of a childhood and youth laced with poverty, violence and criminality. At the age of ten, and newly emerged from an orphanage, John had been charged with shoplifting. He was fined at Chelsea Juvenile Court and put on probation by a 'grey-haired old lady' with half-rim glasses. Later he reappeared for not going to school; he had been at home, minding the younger children: 'Stupid woman. She should try bringing up a handful of children', complained his mother.[1] Then he was back again in front of the grey-haired lady for stealing a banana and five shillings, and then taking some bikes, and then receiving money under false pretences: 'My mate stole his granny's Home and Colonial savings book and I cashed it ... the police officers asked for me to be remanded in custody because they thought I'd do a bunk ... And she turned to me and it was the first time a grown up had ever asked me my own opinion ... she said, "Well, what do you think?"'[2] Lady Wootton, peering over her half-rim glasses, decided to return John to his approved school rather than dispatch him to a borstal. This proved to be a turning point. At school, John Bird learnt practical skills and he started to paint and draw, and he began to see that a life of crime was a life of crime and nothing more than that.

Barbara Wootton had been a magistrate for thirty years when first confronted with the delinquent John Bird, and the conundrum of establishing how best to keep boys like him out of trouble was one of the strongest motivations of her life, both as an academic and as a policy-maker. It led her to research and write her best-known work, *Social Science and Social Pathology*, with its blistering attack on the confusions of criminology and the arrogance of social workers; it drew her beyond the imperfections of economics to those of psychology and sociology as sciences purporting to explain human behaviour; and it led her into a lifelong study of the workings of the penal system. Every crime, she once observed acutely, is committed by a person who might not have committed it.[3] Her quest to answer fundamental questions about the causes and deterrents of crime and the efficacy or otherwise of the penal system took her into all sorts of places that as a young woman she could hardly have imagined. She became a stalwart and uncomfortably radical member of many commissions and committees, most notably of the Royal Commission on the Penal System, set up by a Conservative Government in 1964 and disbanded by a Labour one two years later, the only Royal Commission in history to be dissolved without producing anything. She was responsible for the work of two committees both of which resulted in a 'Wootton Report', on cannabis and on alternatives to prison respectively, the former invoking a tide of media hysteria for its mild evidence-informed suggestion that cannabis was probably not so socially damaging as alcohol, and the latter introducing Community Service Orders, a highly significant change in sentencing policy which is still in place today. Her habit of asking the most basic and simple of questions – what is the point of the criminal justice system? What are magistrates trying to do? How much do we know about the effects of different sentencing policies? – led her to challenge the obscurantism of much academic criminology and criminal law, and generated critical debates about whether criminals are sick or sinful, and how tricky concepts such as 'intention' and 'diminished responsibility' can be operationalized in practice.

Her achievements in transforming penal policy were summed up in the Festschrift *Barbara Wootton: Social Science and Public Policy, Essays in Her Honour*, half of which was devoted to her work in this field. She caused others 'to think furiously about matters which they had previously taken for granted'; in a whole series of reforms limiting the penal enthusiasms of the judiciary and the magistracy, she was one of those who designed, if not a new world of criminal justice, then at least a more rational, utilitarian and less moralizing one; she stood out against foolish theories and for sensible hypotheses about the factors encouraging and deterring anti-social behaviour; and she was the parent of 'the most imaginative and hopeful development in penal practice for half a century'.[4] *Crime and Penal Policy*, her last book, was published in 1978. It was not a book for the experts, but for people like herself, or the kind of person she had been when she had first been made a magistrate fifty-one years earlier. It was a collection of essays, a 'personal document' reflecting her own journey through the penal system, written in a language of compelling logic.[5] What Barbara Wootton wanted was a wholesale realignment of the criminal justice system. What she got was a series of important changes. In a world she helped conspicuously to shape, her voice in the field of crime and penal policy was 'one of constant and consistent sanity'.[6]

The story of Barbara Wootton's influence on penal policy has many chapters, each of which could form a book of its own. The background to the story is one of the most significant social changes of her own lifetime, and one that was bound to grab the attention of any social scientist interested in public policy. The crime rate in Britain had historically been low compared with other European countries; from the start of the twentieth century until the 1930s there was actually a decline in the prison population, and a low rate of reoffending.[7] Rising crime figures slid onto the political agenda in the 1950s. Huge social changes co-existed with a penal system designed for a very different and much more conformist social order. The welfare state made people newly aware of what they had not got, as well as what they had, and the pace of social change accelerated in the 1960s. Full employment replaced austerity; a youth culture emerged with a new form of popular music and much more spending money. People owned more property than ever before, thus enormously increasing opportunities for crime. The 478,349 indictable offences known to the police in 1945 swelled to 3.4 million by 1985.[8] Yet to match all of this, there was a 'criminal literature' but little 'criminal science'.[9] Criminology was dominated by a literature 'of little more than historical interest',[10] and in England by psychoanalysts, psychiatrists and psychologists – those professions whose self-important claims to expertise had been laid bare by Barbara Wootton in her *Social Science and Social Pathology*. When Lord Longford carried out his inquiry into the causes of crime in 1954, she wrote a paper for him enumerating what she saw as the main problems with existing research: treating crime/delinquency as a simple unitary phenomenon; and drawing unjustified conclusions from poorly designed studies or by assuming 'soft' data (personal observations and opinions) to be 'hard'. The most important task, she said, was to discriminate between testable and untestable hypotheses.[11]

Barbara's training in penal policy began when she first became a magistrate on 17 February 1926, at the age of twenty-eight. This immediately brought her into a head-on confrontation with the two most singular aspects of the English justice system: its domination by untrained lay people; and the absence of any thorough base of knowledge about either the causes of crime or the effects of different methods for treating offenders. When she began as a magistrate, over ninety per cent of crimes were handled in Magistrates' Courts.[12] (The figure is even higher today.) Most magistrates were and are lay people: a small proportion are trained lawyers and are paid. This use of untrained amateurs – the juries in jury trials as well as magistrates – is a peculiar feature of the English and Welsh penal systems, and the heavy dependence on what Barbara called 'this vast army of amateurs'[13] meant that sentences of great importance to offenders were handed out by people who had no training in criminal law, and who were not obliged to give any reasons for their sentences. Most JPs were selected, as Barbara herself was, not for competence, but through party political routes as a means of 'bestowing political reward'.[14] An exception was that JPs in London Juvenile Courts were appointed directly by the Lord Chancellor – in Barbara's day, by the Home Secretary, on the recommendation of a small Committee appointed by him. For several years, Barbara chaired this Committee.[15]

In a context dominated by these 'amateurish, hit-and-miss methods',[16] what happened to offenders was largely a matter of luck. Barbara noted that studies of Magistrates' Courts in different areas showed an astonishing variation of between three per cent and fifty-five per cent in the proportion of adult men sentenced to imprisonment for indictable offences. A man arrested for dishonesty, for example, would do well to choose the Court which imprisoned under fifteen per cent of such cases rather than the one that imprisoned fifty per cent;[17] a criminal in Kent had a fifty per cent lower chance of going to prison if he appeared before the West Kent rather than the East Kent Sessions.[18] Barbara knew at first hand how sentences passed by magistrates could be shaped by personal views. On her first day in the Juvenile Courts towards the end of the Second World War, when bombing raids were still regularly driving the Court into the basement, there was the case of an 'exceptionally beautiful' girl of sixteen who was regarded as in need of care or protection because she was sleeping with American airmen. Barbara always had a blind spot about conventional sexual morality: 'I just could not persuade myself that a night or two a week with a personable American was so immensely more degrading than forty hours or more of unskilled and uninteresting work in a factory'.[19]

When she first became a magistrate, all the adult criminal work of the Magistrates' Courts in London was reserved for the stipendiary magistrates, with the lay benches being mainly concerned with juvenile offenders or the licensing of public houses. But had she been appointed outside London, she would have tried criminal cases from the start. It took only one day in Court for her to realize the inefficiency of the system: of her two colleagues in Court on that day, one was blind and the other was deaf and senile.[20] After almost twenty years' service, she was promoted to be Chairman of Chelsea Juvenile Court, a post she held until 1962 and the compulsory age of retirement for Juvenile Court Magistrates of sixty-five – and it was in this capacity that she was presented with the challenge of sentencing the youthful John Bird. The Chelsea Court was one of eight Metropolitan Courts devoted to juvenile justice. It drew its clientele from a wide area of London, including Piccadilly and the West End, and some of the more notoriously 'criminal' districts of Chelsea and Fulham.[21] However, serious cases of violence were rare.

The list of 200 cases in the Juvenile Court presided over by Barbara included in *Social Science and Social Pathology* showed a preponderance of boys (157 of the 200) committing larceny, and girls being caught for 'rail fraud'.[22] In Magistrate Wootton's eyes, the prize for ingenuity went to the boy who canvassed a block of flats for subscriptions to a 'Crusade against Juvenile Delinquency', claiming to be sponsored by a local vicarage, and reaping quite a harvest before anyone thought to investigate his credentials.[23] For pure pathos, there was the case of the eight-week-old baby abandoned in a church in Covent Garden with a brown attaché case of baby clothes and a bottle of milk beside him. His unmarried mother had been turned out of her parents' home, refused help by the N.S.P.C.C., and housed in a London County Council Hostel which ejected her into the streets from 9 a.m. to 5 p.m. every day and then closed its doors to her altogether.[24] Barbara voiced strong views about the harsh treatment of this young woman, as also about other cases which came under her jurisdiction. When a boy of sixteen stood before her charged with punching his girlfriend because she refused to kiss him, Barbara asserted the girl's right to decide whom to kiss.[25] She reprimanded a father for 'coddling' his eleven-year-old daughter to the extent of making her wear dark glasses and keeping her out of school for a week after a simple eye test;[26] and another father for spoiling his nine-year-old son by giving him five shillings a day pocket money (a donation that did not succeed in preventing him from stealing).[27] Some of her magisterial decisions were even starker challenges to convention. The mother of a sixteen-year-old girl found travelling on the railway without a ticket was asked by Magistrate Wootton how often she cuddled her daughter, prompting a discussion in the press about whether teenagers *ought* to be cuddled.[28] In another case, she decreed that a six-year-old girl, a child whose parentage was unknown, and who had been found as a 'waif and stray' and informally adopted by a couple with criminal records for manslaughter, should nonetheless be allowed to stay in the only place she knew as home.[29]

A Magistrate's Court was a standpoint from which one got to see quite a lot of life, much of it otherwise invisible to the middle-class policy-maker. Barbara's work as a magistrate belonged to a new tradition of female magistracy which helped to professionalize the institution of lay magistrates. Women magistrates' insistence, from the early 1920s on, on formal guidelines for practice, criteria for appointment, and compulsory retirement, effected a gentle transformation of the penal system that was closely aligned with the kind of feminist agitation Barbara had witnessed in the drawing room of her childhood home, when Mrs Adam and Mrs Keynes and other indomitable Cambridge ladies had assembled to campaign for equal citizenship.[30]

On her last day in the Juvenile Court, a journalist from *The Guardian* came to observe Barbara at work:

Yesterday was a heavy day at Chelsea Juvenile Court. Most of the cases were petty enough – a little amateurish shoplifting, truancy, unfortunate children in need of care or protection, one case of possession of drugs in which the drugs turned out to be fakes. But the Chairman of the Court, Lady Wootton of Abinger, perhaps better known as Barbara Wootton, dealt with each one with care, never speaking harshly to the children, quick to spot a lie or evasion, and always ready with a sympathetic word for parents.

She appeared to take in all the relevant facts, consider them thoroughly, consult with her two colleagues on the Bench and deliver judgement without any haste. Yet in a few hours she cleared upwards of 30 cases.[31]

After she retired as Chairman of the Chelsea Juvenile Court, Barbara continued as Deputy Chairman of the South Westminster Petty Sessions at Bow Street and Marlborough Street Courts. The degree of magisterial efficiency noted by the journalist from *The Guardian* enabled her to process some 15,000 cases over a total 44 years of service as a JP.[32] But – a point she was at pains to stress on many occasions – while this long experience opened her eyes to many aspects of human behaviour, it provided no data on which she could either improve her own performance or advise others on how they should improve theirs. 'Justice is indeed blind in more senses than one,' she wrote, looking back on all this at the age of eighty-one, 'and in that respect she is peculiar. Doctors generally get to know of, and can learn from, the results of their treatments. Teachers observe what methods hold or fail to hold the attention of their pupils. Business men (or their accountants) read the results of different policies in their profit and loss accounts.'[33] Magistrates, on the other hand, never get to know what happened to the individuals they consign to the different remedies available to them. 'For all I know, I've been doing untold harm for forty-four years.'[34]

Barbara Wootton's work in the arena of crime and justice was driven, above all, by this acute sense of uncertainty, expressed in the moral context of concern for the vulnerability of the young, respect for individual rights and opposition to violence. She took the opportunities presented to her to pursue these issues through the function of official bodies, but she was also proactive in creating them. Her penal committee work began in 1946, when she was appointed to the Probation Advisory Committee, a body set up to advise 'on questions relating to the administration of the probation system and the other social services of the courts'.[35] Then came the Departmental Committee on Criminal Statistics, and the Interdepartmental Committee on the Business of the Criminal Courts. The former – the Perks Committee, named after its Chair, Wilfred Perks, an actuary with a public conscience – was set up in 1963 to look at the collection and presentation of statistics relating to crime.[36] Her appointment to the Committee on the Business of the Criminal Courts (the Streatfeild Committee) happened a few years earlier, in the summer of 1958, shortly before she became a baroness. Its functions were to consider arrangements for bringing people charged with criminal offences to trial, and to provide courts with the information needed to decide the most appropriate treatment. The nine-member Committee was smaller than most such bodies, and it included a broader range of people: apart from 'the well-known sociologist' Barbara Wootton, there was her academic friend W.J.H. Sprott, the forensic psychiatrist Dr T.C.N. Gibbens, and the former head of the Law Department at the LSE, J.E. Hall Williams.[37] The Committee made a number of sensible and practicable suggestions, including altering the rules for cases that could be tried by magistrates rather than at higher courts, and shortening trial waiting periods. One of their recommendations, though not one given much prominence in the Report, exhibited the definite influence of Barbara Wootton. The Committee suggested that the Home Office should produce regularly updated information for all those responsible for passing sentences; sentencers should 'be systematically provided with a booklet giving comprehensive information, for every form of sentence, about what it involves, what it is designed to achieve and what it in fact achieves, together with information about research into the results of sentences'.[38]

It could not be clearer that every day thousands of people arrested for committing crimes were subjected to sentences by people who had very little idea what they were doing. They exercised this ignorance, moreover, in an extraordinarily archaic and unfriendly setting. There is perhaps no place in English society where class divisions are more obtrusive than in the atmosphere of ritual that flourishes in the higher Courts: the formal language, the wigs and robes, and the remoteness of the judge from the lives and temptations of many defendants.[39] The exclusive ritual of the Court was one reason why Barbara held the radical view that the treatment of children committing unlawful acts should not be the business of the Courts at all. Another was that most children who get into trouble with the law are guilty of naughtiness rather than criminality: 'There is no need to make excuses for these children and I think it is a pity when their parents try to do so, as they often do in court, though I must confess that a parent's heated defence of his [sic] erring child can be very endearing'.[40] Unlike many policy-makers, she saw criminality in the young as a failure in the system. You should not punish individuals for such failures.

Commenting on the White Paper *Children in Trouble* in 1968, she remarked that: 'One of the deepest and most persistent class divisions in this country is that between children who have to play in the streets and those who have adequate play-space in their homes, or for whom organized recreation is available in school or elsewhere'.[41] Those who had to play in the streets were more likely than those who did not to be condemned to formal systems of reprimand and punishment for their naughtiness. Children so condemned should be dealt with, she said, by people with whom they were in contact in their normal everyday lives and who they had reason to listen to, not by strangers. A third reason for keeping the treatment of 'delinquent' children out of the penal system was to avoid their initiation into 'a delinquent culture'.[42] 'I am not sure,' she said, in a House of Lords debate on the Children and Young Persons Bill in 1962, 'that more harm is not done in waiting room than anywhere else.' Children awaiting Juvenile Court appearances could wait for hours in the company of 'young men rising seventeen many of whom may be charged with serious offences, and be quite formidable anti-social characters'. The educational system was full of provisions for children with special needs – those with disabilities of a whole range of kinds – so why not take the staff and other resources away from the Juvenile Courts and approved schools, and add these to educational facilities for children with the special need of requiring attention for anti-social behaviour?[43] Barbara's opposition to the 'stigma' of court appearances for children was part of the evidence taken by the Labour Party's Study Group on crime in 1964. Her evidence 'powerfully and decisively influenced the committee' which produced the Longford Report, *Crime: A Challenge To Us All,* recommending the total abolition of Juvenile Courts, and driving forward a whole series of law reforms.[44] One obvious way of keeping children out of the courts was to increase the age of 'criminal responsibility'. In England and Wales, this had been raised from seven to eight by the Children and Young Persons Act of 1933. Barbara supported the proposal of the Children and Young Persons Bill in 1962 to raise the age of criminal responsibility to twelve, pointing out that many countries had set it at fourteen or higher.[45] Although this proposal was carried by one vote, the Government chose to give Baroness Wootton only 'half the cake' she was asking for[46] and in 1963 settled for ten years (the age it still is, the lowest (apart from Scotland, where it is eight) in the European Union).

An integral part of Barbara Wootton's defence of the rights of children and young people to their personal liberty was her attempt to make corporal punishment illegal. In 1973 she introduced into the House of Lords the Protection of Minors Bill which would have done just that, but it did not even achieve a second reading, despite the Baroness's persuasive case that many other countries had abandoned the practice or never engaged in it, and that even in Britain corporal punishment was illegal in approved schools, leaving the paradox, a dire comment on our social values, that 'the only people who are apparently allowed to wield a cane in the exercise of their profession are prostitutes and teachers'.[47] Was it not, she asked, an extraordinary reflection of our social values that the law forbidding us to strike our equals makes an exception for those who are smaller than us?[48] Barbara did not expect her Bill to succeed. She predicted what in fact happened, that 'a great many of their Lordships' would 'get up and say "It never did me any harm".'[49]

In 1964, the Conservative Government had published an 'aggressively titled'[50] White Paper, *The War Against Crime in England and Wales*.[51] This was the response of an insecure administration to the Labour opposition's determination to make the increase in crime a political issue.[52] Existing penal methods were evidently not putting a stop to what was now officially known as 'the crime wave', and the time was ripe for a 'fundamental review of the whole penal system'. This the Government viewed as a task of such importance and magnitude that it could only be carried out, in true British tradition, by a Royal Commission. So they set one up. The Royal Commission on the Penal System's terms of reference were as follows:

> In the light of modern knowledge of crime and its causes and of modern penal practice here and abroad, to re-examine the concepts and purposes which should underlie the punishment and treatment of offenders in England and Wales: to report how far they are realized by the penalties and methods of treatment available to the courts ... to review the work of the services and institutions dealing with offenders and the responsibility for their administration; and to make recommendations.[53]

The extraordinary story of this Commission has never yet been told in full, and it is one that bears particular witness to the keen intelligence and rationalist courage of Baroness Wootton.

It was an astonishingly broad canvas, an impossibly gigantic task. The Commission had fifteen members, aside from Barbara, including Leon Radzinowicz, a professional criminologist, who had doubts about the whole enterprise from the start, describing its terms of reference as 'suicidal'.[54] Barbara listed their fourteen colleagues in the following terms: 'a trade unionist (who, as far as I know, had no contact with our system of criminal justice), seven JPs, two of whom were also MPs (one being a fervent advocate of capital punishment), an English and a Scottish judge, a psychiatrist with much experience of offenders, a Professor of Social Medicine, a Bishop, and the Secretary of a County Council – all under the chairmanship of a former Chancellor of the Exchequer with wide public experience, but no close acquaintance with penal matters'. Such a motley crew were bound to argue, and they did. They argued for eighteen months, making and re-making plans for future work, hearing 'platitudinous evidence' and debating 'the niceties of penal philosophies'.[55] Penologist Nigel Walker was one of those called to give evidence, and his 'bizarre' experience as a witness was probably typical of many: 'As soon as I began to give my views on the proper aims of sentencing, which is what they had asked me to do, they began to argue with each other, unchecked by the Chairman'.

Such a commission, Walker considered, had as much hope of getting anywhere as one on disease and its treatment.[56] Vast amounts of reading material, equivalent to an Open University course on criminal science, were made available to Commission members, with much time being taken up in discussion of which colours should be used for duplicating different types of document.[57] They decided to break up into three Sub-Committees. The most important of these was the 'Concepts and Purposes' Sub-Committee, to which Barbara Wootton belonged. It was allotted the task of examining the principles which should underlie the punishment and treatment of offenders. Unfortunately, the Sub-Committee drowned in hundreds of pages of 'evidence' which produced a 'hopelessly disorienting pseudo-seminar'; notions of 'concepts' and 'purposes' were endlessly taken apart, shuffled around, described in unreal terms, or in 'ponderous pseudo-philosophical language'.[58]

There are various accounts of what happened to bring this sorry business to an end. The Conservative law reformer, Lord Windlesham, blamed Leon Radzinowicz and Barbara Wootton – 'both strong characters unaccustomed to taking no for an answer' – for saying that nothing could be done without years of systematic research.[59] This was a bit of an overstatement, but Barbara Wootton is certainly likely to have emphasized the need for well-done research, and Leon Radzinowicz, as the country's first Professor of Criminology and Director of the first Institute of Criminology, in Cambridge, had a direct interest in turning criminology into something that it clearly was not, namely a research-based science. He was the first to sound the alarm that the Royal Commission was going nowhere. Then Barbara joined him, and so did the Bishop of Exeter and Lady Adrian and Beatrice Serota (later a Baroness), and academic Professor Gibbens (who had served on the Streatfeild Committee with Barbara). On the days the Commission met, the dissenters would assemble in private at nearby Brown's Hotel for lunch or a drink to discuss their dissent. It was agreed that the Bishop of Exeter, aided by Radzinowicz, would prepare a memorandum outlining their views and proposing the dissolution of the Commission.

The document they produced was concise and logical: the idea that a comprehensive solution to the problem of crime lay round the corner just waiting to be discovered was a dangerous illusion; the Commission's existence might delay urgent, practical reforms; the Government was in any case introducing such reforms (for example, majority jury verdicts and suspended sentences) without consulting the Commission at all; and what was needed was not a 'slow deliberate survey of the field', but a 'continuous survey of the penal system by a body in continuous existence'.[60] They therefore recommended the discharge of the Royal Commission and the constitution instead of a permanent Advisory Council to the Home Office on the Penal System. A deep rift in views was revealed when the sixteen members of the Royal Commission voted on this memorandum. Six, including Barbara Wootton, immediately resigned. Two resigned later on the grounds that a reduced commission would not function.[61] At least one of the remaining eight, the Professor of Social Medicine, Jerry Morris, regarded the Royal Commission as the greatest failure of his life.[62] According to the prominent left-wing QC Louis Blom-Cooper, 'Barbara and Radzinowicz went off to Roy Jenkins [then Home Secretary] and said, "Would you please dissolve this bloody silly body?" which he did.'[63] The business of disbanding it took some time, as there were no procedures for doing this, and it had never been done before. The dissidents' alternative, a permanent Advisory Council on the Penal System, was set up in 1966, and Barbara Wootton, Leon Radzinowicz, and Bea Serota transferred their loyalties to it 'with good grace'.[64] For twelve years, the Council's reports formed an important strand in the formulation of policy,[65] with Barbara's powers of intellectual persuasion steering it in the direction of 'controlled liberalism'.[66] The Council provided a framework within which Barbara Wootton could continue to make her case about the treatment of young offenders: for example, that the strategy of confining young people in institutions was at best 'a costly way of achieving very little', and at worst, the cause of more problems than it solved, since it reinforced rejection and anti-social behaviour.[67]

Barbara Wootton's radical thinking about penal policy and practice is outlined most fully in *Crime and Penal Policy*, and in another of her books, *Crime and the Criminal Law*, published fifteen years earlier, in 1963. This was the published version of a series of prestigious lectures, the Hamlyn lectures – so named after a bequest from a wealthy Devon solicitor. Barbara was the first lay person and the first woman to give the Hamlyn lectures. Hers displayed a 'lucidity and intellectual honesty' that ought to appeal to any lawyer who was not completely hidebound and was still capable of thought.[68] *Crime and the Criminal Law* was a 'blend of irreverence, wisdom and wit', 'a remarkable book by a remarkable Englishwoman',[69] pronounced Herbert Hart, the eminent legal philosopher whose wife Jenifer had taken to communism in the 1930s partly as a result of reading Barbara's *Plan or No Plan*. He wrote a long review of the book in a respected legal journal, commending Barbara for having raised to a higher level the whole debate in England about the basic principles of the criminal law. Her views on sentencing policy and procedure were, he noted, still highly controversial, which is why *The Daily Mirror* deemed her book 'a strong attack on Britain's criminal-court system'.[70]

Crime and the Criminal Law began, as Barbara Wootton usually did, with the facts of the matter: 'Penal treatments could be described as cumulative failures. The more anyone experiences them, the greater the probability that he will require further treatment still'.[71] And yet, certain aspects of the statistical picture did stand out: young men and cars were responsible for most crime. Barbara's second husband, George Wright, a delinquent in his own youth, once attempted to console 'his over-anxious magisterial spouse' with the observation that many cases of youth criminality would be cured by maturation: "'Don't worry about what you do in court",' advised George, "'As we grow up, we see it's a mug's game and give it up."'[72] The association with masculinity was more of a puzzle. In 1961, eighty-seven per cent of all those convicted of indictable offences were men, with the biggest gender differences at the younger ages, a picture virtually unchanged over the decades.[73] As Barbara had remarked in her *Social Science and Social Pathology*, gender far outranked all the other characteristics associated with criminality. If the explanation lay in some aspect of cultural conditioning, which she thought likely, 'To identify this would make possible a larger reduction in criminality than is offered by any other line of inquiry'.[74]

The scanty research evidence available when Barbara Wootton gave her Hamlyn lectures showed remarkably few differences in reconviction rates between offenders fined, imprisoned, or put on probation.[75] She might well have quoted, in the later edition of the published version of these lectures, though she did not, a systematic review by Robert Martinson of 231 studies involving thousands of individuals that was so damning about the failure of research reliably to establish any sure way of preventing reoffending that its funder, the New York State Governor's Special Committee on Criminal Offenders, tried to prevent publication.[76] Any consideration of whether sentencing works involves thinking about what the function of the courts is in the first place: to punish or to prevent? 'I do not think that it is our business to punish the wicked', pronounced Barbara. 'Our business is to do what we can to prevent the repetition of crimes.'[77] Punishment does not work in deterring offenders from further offences, although of course it does prevent harm to the public while the offender is actually institutionalized. The word 'punishment' was not in her vocabulary as a magistrate; she never used it.[78] Instead, she held strongly to a view, which was not popular among many of her colleagues in the penal system, that the only justification for depriving someone of their liberty is the utilitarian one of preventing harm to others.[79] The emphasis on prevention rather than punishment means that it is necessary to be very sure, both that not depriving people of liberty *does* risk harm, and that whatever custodial sentence is imposed is likely to prevent reoffending. The difference between punitive and preventive approaches is a real one, and it has real consequences for how courts and magistrates ought to behave.

A key theme of Barbara Wootton's writing, thought and practice in the area of penal policy was the need for a *practical* approach to the treatment of crime. Yet, as noted earlier, hers was also a *moral* view: she wished to conserve the idea that most of us are responsible, in an ordinary sense, for our actions. Here she was up against two traditional aspects of English law: the distinction between intended and not intended actions, and the associated principle that mental incompetence or (in its more modern formulation) 'diminished responsibility' is a reasonable defence. A concept closely cherished by criminal lawyers at the time she entered the penal policy field was that of *mens rea* (Latin for 'guilty mind') as a necessary element in a crime. In order to be guilty, you have to intend, or at least know, what you are doing. The importance of intention was one reason why motoring offences tended to be treated more lightly than others: 'No guilty intention, no crime, is the rule'.[80] It was a rule that derived from the traditional bias of English justice towards the punishment of the wicked: the penal system was a device for rooting out the wicked. Yet, said the sage Baroness, if the object of the criminal law is to prevent socially damaging actions, it is absurd to turn a blind eye to those which are due to carelessness, negligence or accident, since these often cause more damage in the modern world than deliberate wickedness. The question of motivation is strictly irrelevant; the only important matter to be decided is whether harm was done and how to stop it happening again.[81] Barbara Wootton's attack on the sacred concept of *mens rea* was one of her most influential and unsettling contributions to the crime and penal policy field. As Herbert Hart remarked in 1965, her name became synonymous 'with the claim that the whole doctrine of *mens rea* and the conception of responsibility embodied in it is an irrational hindrance to sound social policy'.[82] He took a different view, and the civilized disagreement between them produced what became known in the philosophy of law as the 'Wootton-Hart' debate.[83] Hart believed that a system based on the abolition of *mens rea* would not be a system of punishment. Precisely so, Barbara said.

The irrelevance of mental state in Barbara Wootton's approach to penal treatment had major implications for the notion of diminished responsibility, and thus for the role of psychiatrists in arbitrating who was, and was not, irresponsible. Barbara did not like psychiatrists. She did not like them when she wrote *Social Science and Social Pathology* in 1959 and she certainly did not like them when she understood the full extent of their 'wholly exceptional powers' over people who came into contact with the penal system.[84] Before the 1948 Criminal Justice Act, only offenders who were either insane or mentally defective qualified for medical, rather than penal, treatment. Nine years later, the 1957 Homicide Act restricted the use of capital punishment to specific kinds of murder, and/or repeated murders, and allowed a plea of diminished responsibility for the first time, thus hugely expanding the dependence of the penal system on the opinions of psychiatrists. This development was taken even further when the 1959 Mental Health Act allowed a prison sentence to be replaced with a hospital or 'guardianship' order if certain kinds of mental disorder could be medically certified. In debates about the Act in the House of Lords before it became law, Barbara spoke out trenchantly about the danger of creating, as the Act proposed to do, a new category of psychopathic persons defined, not by the presence of a mental condition, but simply by virtue of anti-social behaviour. She noted that a contemporary textbook on social pathology widely used in the USA had a chapter devoted to radicals and radicalism as examples of psychopathological conditions.[85]

The power of psychiatrists in penal policy would not matter so much, said Barbara, if psychiatry were a science. But psychiatrists disagreed with one another; definitions and concepts of mental disorder were unstable and elusive, and far from socially or ethically neutral.[86] There was the problem of spurious (unevidenced) expertise; and there was the problem of labelling. She was fond of pointing out that 'all the successful reforms in the world' had been instigated by powerful emotional drives, and all reformers have been motivated by emotional disturbances: Florence Nightingale and Emmeline Pankhurst were two examples she liked to quote of individuals who certainly would have qualified as in need of psychiatric treatment.[87] She made her audience laugh at a National Association of Mental Health Conference in London in 1962, when she pointed out that one result of the growth of psychiatry had been to give wives of unfaithful husbands a new excuse: to say the poor man was sick was so much more acceptable than admitting he preferred another woman. Talking about the 'cult' of psychiatry in the USA, she mentioned a friend of hers who taught at an American university and had told her that about fifty per cent of the staff were receiving psychiatric treatment. 'It seems rather a pity that young American students are being taught by such a collection of invalids', said Lady Wootton, getting yet more laughs.[88]

Barbara's best-known attack on the concept of diminished responsibility took the form of an analysis of the 73 cases in which a defence of diminished responsibility had been raised in the 27 months following the 1957 Homicide Act. What these cases showed was that the only stable factor differentiating cases in which diminished responsibility was successfully, as opposed to unsuccessfully, argued, was that the person had a history of mental instability. In many instances, a propensity to commit criminal acts was taken as a sign of mental instability. This created the paradox that those people most likely to re-offend (as judged by this history) were those most likely to be returned to the community: 'The worse your conduct, the better your chance'. It would be interesting, said social scientist Barbara, to know how often psychiatrists would diagnose diminished responsibility if they did not know that the subject was on trial for murder.[89] Dependence on psychiatric judgements to determine who was criminal and who was ill meant that 'the ranks of the blameless will be steadily expanded', and had the further resounding weakness of making an individual's personal guilt completely contingent on the state of medical science at the time.[90] Unsurprisingly, these statements of hers acted as a profound irritant to psychiatrists, lawyers and others.

Central to Barbara Wootton's approach to penal policy was her moral opposition to violence. Capital punishment was a burning question in the 1950s and 1960s; indeed, probably more words had been uttered over the years, in both public and private, on capital punishment than on any other single public policy issue.[91] Barbara was implacably opposed to it, as she was to almost all forms of violence (the exception being 'certain cases of mercy killing'). For one human being deliberately and irrevocably to curtail another human being's life is 'an act of unsurpassable arrogance' and this is so whether the killer is a soldier in battle, an executioner or a murderer. Furthermore, killing degrades those who do it. She found 'the whole monstrous ritual' of judicial execution an offence to civilized values: 'the solicitous care for the condemned man's last days, the elaborate precautions to prevent him from taking his own life (why shouldn't he?). The stealthy introduction of the hangman into the prison the day before an execution in order that he may surreptitiously observe his victim's physique from which to make the calculations necessary for the successful performance of his hideous task.'[92] She published a prose poem in *The Spectator* called 'I am ashamed of my country': 'I am ashamed that men can be found who, for a suitable wage, will build and maintain in good repair an apparatus for strangling their fellow men'. It made her wish she were not British.[93] Her friend Ernest Gowers, with whom she had shared the much less contentious platform of the Commission on Shop Hours, had provided in his little book *A Life for a Life?* a horrendous description of the procedures involved in using the execution chamber.[94] Gowers had chaired the 1949 Royal Commission on Capital Punishment, and, in the course of his four years' work on it, had changed his own mind about the death penalty.[95] He wished Barbara Wootton had been there to help him on the Commission: 'When it comes to a selected trio of prison doctors stoutly maintaining, as they did, that no pleasanter or more humane method of disposing of people than hanging could possibly be devised – Well, Really, as Lloyd George used to say when there was nothing more to be said'.[96]

Barbara contributed a chapter to an 'avowedly abolitionist' symposium on *The Hanging Question* for the Howard League for Penal reform in 1969.[97] She joined the National Campaign for the Abolition of Capital Punishment as a member of its Committee of Honour, renewing the ethical case for abolition in the company of other distinguished members such as Benjamin Britten, E.M. Forster, John

Gielgud, Julian Huxley, R.H. Tawney, Arnold Toynbee and Leonard Woolf.[98] When
the Murder (Abolition of Death Penalty) Act of 1965 finally arrived in Parliament
as a Private Member's Bill, Barbara agreed to be its main sponsor in the House of
Lords. Introducing its second reading there in the summer of 1965, she told their
Lordships that it was an extremely simple Bill, whose main provision was that a
sentence of life imprisonment should follow any conviction for murder. Voting in
its favour would allow their Lordships to recover their (in her view) unfortunate
history of supporting retention of the death penalty, even when a majority in
Another Place (The House of Commons) did not: did they realize, for example,
that between 1800 and 1818 they had rejected no fewer than six times a Bill
abolishing the death penalty for shoplifting? What would they think about that
now?[99] When the Bill was passed on its third reading, she was congratulated for her
success in the face of 'the strongest opposition' – the retentionists had been vocal,
and had given her a hard time,[100] but she was forced to return to the fray four years
later because the provisions of the 1965 Act had been limited to five years. She was
the 'unofficial Whip' in the 1969 debate. Her opening speech prioritized the moral
case – that to take life in cold blood is wrong – but the strongest element in her
case was the evidential one: 'This is not a topic on which opinion has the slightest
value,' she enunciated – and one can just imagine the ringing tones in which she said
it, perhaps peering over the half-rim glasses from behind which she had sentenced
the founder of *The Big Issue*. 'But I have heard noble Lords, one after another,
and many persons of influence outside, simply make the categorical statement,
"I believe that the death penalty is a unique deterrent". My Lords, it makes no
difference what you believe or what I believe: this is a question of fact.' And the fact
was that there was no evidence that hanging people for murder had any deterrent
effect at all.[101] It was a tense debate, with the outcome doubtful until the last
minute; when the result was finally announced, she felt like bursting into tears.[102]

Of all the arenas relating to crime and justice which Barbara Wootton entered
over her long life, the two that gained her most prominence were cannabis and
alternatives to prison. These two issues are, on the surface, opposing cases in the
relationship between evidence and policy: the work of the Sub-Committee she chaired,
which produced the Wootton Report on cannabis in 1968, was entirely disowned by
the Government that had sponsored it, whereas the main recommendations of the
second Wootton Report on alternatives to prison in 1970 led directly to legislation
establishing the radical alternative of Community Service Orders. However, the
picture of what happened is rather more complicated than this.

The Cannabis Report was the work of the Advisory Committee on Drug
Dependence. Barbara chaired its Hallucinogens Sub-Committee, a body set up

when cannabis use by students at Oxford University in 1967 led the Vice-Chancellor to write to the then Home Secretary, Roy Jenkins, asking for a national inquiry into cannabis and Lysergic Acid Diethylamide (LSD).[103] These were the hippie years, the years of flower power, pop festivals, and a general relaxation of mores. The epicentre of the drug scene was in London, in Piccadilly Circus at the notorious open-all-hours pharmacy Boots, but a wide range of drugs was available in a 'poly-drug culture'[104] to a wide range of people. By the mid-1960s, cannabis was firmly planted, not only in the culture of pop music and flower power, but among students and the upper classes, and via respectable routes of migration, including British naval ships and mail delivery to foreign embassies in London.[105] In 1967, when the Hallucinogens Sub-Committee began its work, there were well-publicized drug charges against Keith Richards and Mick Jagger of the Rolling Stones. Jagger's arrest and imprisonment for possessing four Italian amphetamine pills gave rise to a famous editorial in *The Times*, 'Who Breaks a Butterfly on a Wheel?' which compared his offence with the act of an Archbishop of Canterbury who purchased four proprietary airsickness pills at Rome airport after visiting the Pope: the two offences carried exactly the same legal status.[106] In May 1967, the Beatles released their psychedelically-charged 'Sergeant Pepper' album with a cover including marijuana plants, and the summer saw the 'Legalize Pot Rally' in Hyde Park with poets Allen Ginsburg and Adrian Mitchell, political journalist Carolyn Coon, and Black rights activist Stokely Carmichael, among others. The organization 'Release' was founded in that summer of 1967 by Coon, then a nineteen-year-old art student, and an artist friend, Rufus Harris, under the wings of Eros in Piccadilly Circus, and run as the world's first free twenty-four-hour drugs and legal advice telephone line from Coon's basement flat in Shepherds Bush. Release published a report in 1968 about police harassment in relation to drugs, and Coon was summoned to Scotland Yard. Afterwards she rang up Barbara Wootton.[107] Barbara was supportive of the Release venture, and is today listed on Release's website 'Roll of Honour'.[108]

On 24 July 1967, *The Times* carried a whole-page advertisement advocating the reform of cannabis laws. The advertisement was signed by sixty-five people, including scientists, doctors, MPs, Graham Greene, one member of the Hallucinogens Sub-Committee and all four Beatles, who paid for its publication.[109] One aim of the publicity in *The Times* was to persuade the Sub-Committee to drop LSD from its terms of reference and focus on cannabis alone, on the grounds that the two drugs were different, both pharmacologically and in their patterns of use. The task of Barbara Wootton's drugs committee was thus to review the available evidence on the pharmacological, clinical, pathological, social and legal aspects of cannabis. The increased use of drugs had produced a sharp rise in convictions for drug offences: from four convictions and four customs seizures in 1945, the total by 1967 was 2,393 convictions and 87 seizures.[110] Many courts were faced for the first time with the task of how to deal both with drug-users and drug-traffickers. Cannabis was in the same class as heroin as a prohibited drug under the 1965 Dangerous Drugs Act, and the penalties common to all drugs covered by the Act were fairly substantial: on summary conviction (by a Magistrates' Court) a fine of not more than £250 or prison for not more than 12 months or both; and, on conviction on indictment, a fine of not more than £1,000 and prison for not more than ten years, or both. In 1967, a quarter of all cases, mostly involving possession of small quantities of cannabis, attracted prison or other custodial sentences.[111] The same penalties applied both to possession and supply. The questions in front of the Sub-Committee then were: did the dangers of cannabis merit this treatment, and should personal use and trafficking carry the same penalty?

Both public attitudes and the burden on the penal system were factors Baroness Wootton and her eleven colleagues on the Hallucinogens Sub-Committee had to consider. The group included four psychiatrists, a stipendiary magistrate, two pharmacologists, representatives of a drug company and the police, the editor of *New Society* and a sociologist. They went about their business in an unorthodox way, advertising for people to submit written or oral evidence, although the result of this initiative was disappointing.[112] According to the sociologist in the group, Michael Schofield, in the early meetings the weight of the Sub-Committee was against lightening the penalties for cannabis: six members wanted to take a hard line, four were undecided, and only two considered the penalties too severe; one member declared that no research was necessary, as all the Sub-Committee had to do was to work out ways to 'stop the spread of this filthy habit'.[113] They held seventeen meetings, examined a huge body of evidence and commissioned a review of the international clinical literature by the renowned psychiatrist, Sir Aubrey Lewis. Their general conclusions were straightforward: 'There is no evidence that in Western society serious physical dangers are directly associated with the smoking of cannabis'; 'It can clearly be argued on the world picture that cannabis use does not lead to heroin addiction'; 'We believe that the association of cannabis in legislation with heroin and the other opiates is entirely inappropriate … the present penalties for possession and supply are altogether too high'; 'All in all, it is impossible to make out a firm case against cannabis as being potentially a greater personal or social danger than alcohol'.[114] These conclusions were substantially in line with the most comprehensive previous attempt to come to grips with the effects of cannabis: the seven-volume Report of the Indian Hemp Drugs Commission, which was produced in 1894 by four British and three Indian men, based on the testimony of 1,193 witnesses.[115]

Federal Union meeting, 1940 (BW on the extreme right)

Barbara Wootton in the House of Lords on the day she became a baroness, 21 October 1958
(with Lord Longford, left, and Lord Burden, right)

High Barn, Abinger, Surrey,
house and garden

Barbara feeding the donkeys,
Miranda and Francesca

Barbara Wootton inside High Barn

Barbara Kyle

Barbara Kyle (left), Barbara Wootton (far right) and
Ann Monie on the terrace at High Barn, early 1960s

Delegation from British Parliament to Liberia, 1963 (left to right: J.D. Cordle, Ifor Davies, Harold Gurden, BW, Sir Kenneth Thompson, E.J. Milne)

Barbara Wootton at the 20th international training course of the United Nations Asia and Far East Institute for the Prevention of Crime and the Treatment of Offenders, in Tokyo, Japan, 1969

Woman in a Man's World: Barbara Wootton receiving honorary degrees at the universities of Essex, 1975 (top left), Southampton, 1971 (top right), Warwick, 1972 (middle), York, 1966 (bottom left) and Bath, 1968 (bottom right)

Barbara Wootton, aged 67, 1964

Barbara Wootton, aged 80, 1977

'Any Questions?' at Nantyglo Community College and Sports Centre Complex, March 1974
(seated clockwise: Owen Edwards BBC, BW, David Jacobs, Enoch Powell, John Cole and BBC producer;
at rear, June Flower, Les Mitchell and Lyn Mitchell from Nantyglo Youth Centre)

Barbara on the tenth anniversary
of Horizon Holidays, having
lunch in La Pyramide Restaurant
near Lyons, France, 1959

Barbara's eightieth birthday party, 1977: Prime Minister James Callaghan giving a speech (left),
with James Callaghan and Gordon Brunton (right)

Barbara in China, 1972: with a guide (above); in Sian, her hand resting on a tortoise, symbol of longevity (right)

Vera Seal, mid-1980s

The main recommendations of the Wootton Report on cannabis were that possession of a small amount should not normally land the possessor in prison; and that maximum penalties for possession, sale or supply should be lowered on conviction in a Magistrates' Court to a fine of not more than £100, or imprisonment for not more than four months, or both; on conviction on indictment, these penalties should be an unlimited fine or prison for not more than two years, or both. The Sub-Committee did not want to encourage the use of cannabis, but nor did its members advocate legalization. However, legalization would have been logical, and it came as a surprise to some that the report did not recommend it.[116] What the Sub-Committee proposed was a middle way, in which it was recognized that small-scale personal use of the drug was unlikely to harm anyone and certainly did not justify the absorption of police, court or prison resources. This was effectively 'a plea for the use of cannabis to be judged more realistically in our codes of law and social behaviour'.[117] Looking back years later, Barbara conceded that their recommendations had been a 'rather illogical compromise', but they had been right to do as they did; the logic of legalization would have been quite impracticable at the time.[118]

The Report was ready in November 1968, but was not distributed until 7 January 1969. There were enough pre-publication leaks 'to fill a good-sized bathtub'.[119] The leaks predicted that the Home Secretary, James Callaghan, would denounce its findings and recommendations.[120] This Callaghan duly did. His grounds were that reducing the penalties for possession, sale or supply of cannabis would be bound to lead people to think that the Government took a less than serious view of the effects of drug-taking; this was not so.[121] Callaghan's response gave the 'escalation theory' of drugs a new lease of life: the suspicion that all soft-drug uses are inevitable invitations to progression to harder ones was, and remains, the greatest obstacle to clear appraisal of the effects of individual drugs.[122] Callaghan also memorably complained that the Wootton Sub-Committee had been over-influenced by the lobby to legalize cannabis; the existence of this lobby was a fact that had to be combated by the Government and by public opinion. It was an aspect of the permissive society, and the permissive society was wrong.[123] His remarks gained cheers in the House of Commons, but infuriated Barbara Wootton. She and the chairman of the Advisory Committee on Drug Dependence, Sir Edward Wayne, wrote to *The Times* on 5 February, protesting that Callaghan's statement was offensive to their distinguished colleagues and themselves, and that they particularly deprecated the use of the emotive word 'lobby'. They tried to correct his misperception that they favoured legalization, and observed that more than half his speech was devoted to drugs with which their Report was not concerned.[124] However, Barbara's anger at

Callaghan's treatment of the Report did not poison relations between them, which remained sufficiently cordial for him, during his time as Prime Minister, to preside genially over her eightieth birthday party in 1977.[125]

The climate of opinion at the time was not one to appreciate the careful review of the evidence and clarity of thought expressed in the Wootton Report. How many people were willing (i) to agree that the link with violent crime was far stronger for alcohol, a socially acceptable drug, than for cannabis; (ii) to accept the argument that rising prescriptions for so-called 'minor' tranquilizers were a substantial cause for concern; or (iii) to grasp the logic that, although many heroin addicts have a history of cannabis use, it does not follow that most cannabis users will become heroin addicts?[126] Barbara's own publicity for the report singled out the simple message 'Cannabis is Not Heroin',[127] on the grounds that this important distinction was the one most sentencers just did not grasp. Reviews in the British medical press, the *British Medical Journal* and *The Lancet,* were oddly contradictory, with the former, under the emotive title 'Potted Dreams', insisting that cannabis causes mental disorientation and that none of the Report's recommendations would achieve the necessary objective of diminishing its use.[128] The conjunction of the heady topic, an ageing baroness and a rejecting government provided a media opportunity of unparalleled proportions. A consultant psychiatrist's extraordinary description of the Report as a 'junkies' charter' provided several newspapers with heavily quoted headlines.[129] A chief constable from Cambridgeshire who hoped the Home Secretary would file the Report in his wastepaper basket was also newsworthy;[130] and Conservative MP Sir Gerald Nabarro's view that Barbara Wootton should be locked up for downright irresponsibility could hardly be resisted.[131] A County Councillor in Welwyn Garden City decided that the recent 'terrifying increase in cannabis-peddling' in his area was directly due to the Wootton Report.[132] Predictably, several papers ran sensational stories about young people whose lives had supposedly been ruined by cannabis: a nineteen-year-old who started on hash and was then hooked on heroin;[133] and the twenty-two-year-old honours graduate abandoned by her fiancé who tried pot at a party and eight weeks later was on heroin and the streets.[134]

Most of the papers which commented also mentioned Barbara Wootton's age. 'Little Old Lady Talking Pot', was a *Sunday Mirror* headline. *The Sunday Mirror* journalist who interviewed Barbara reported that she sat, 'straight backed and serious, answering each question with precision, her seventy-one-year-old mind showing no trace of its age. Her thumbs don't twiddle. There are no extravagant gestures ... There's a bit of the headmistress in her. You wouldn't like to be caught in the toilets with even a cigarette in your mouth, never mind a reefer.' Lady Wootton was clearly a remarkable woman, but who was she? Her life, the interviewer decided, 'reads like a cross between sensational women's magazine fiction and a chapter from a careers guide for school leavers'. Somehow they even got onto the fact that the donkeys' favourite drug was peppermint creams.[135] Many people wanted to know if Lady Wootton had ever tried pot herself. She apparently came close to admitting this when questioned on television.[136] 'Who is this seventy-one-year-old life peeress,' inquired *Time and Tide*, similarly surprised that anyone of her generation would know anything about drugs, 'who, although she has never been elected to Parliament, sometimes seems to wield more power than any other woman in the country?'[137] The constant references to her age annoyed Barbara, since they implied that the Report was 'the diseased brainchild of her own disordered and senile imagination', whereas a number of distinguished authorities with international reputations had actually shared with her the responsibility for the careful work that had gone into it.[138] She noted that, out of some 600 press notices, no more than half a dozen referred to the existence of any co-signatories, distinguished or otherwise.[139]

'I never actually got letters threatening to kill me,' she observed, 'but several expressed satisfaction that at my age nature would soon take its course.'[140] The negative and/or rude letters in the cannabis file in Barbara's Girton College Archives outnumber the positive ones by more than three to one. 'I never thought I would write to an elderly woman in this strain,' said 'a hard working member of the community' in Manchester, 'but my heart bleeds for the state of this country and for the awful future people like you are preparing for the young folk.'[141] A Mothers' Union in Essex wanted to put on record their protest against the idea that cannabis is not dangerous; they had proof that it was.[142] The worst missives were, naturally, unsigned: 'you MURDERING OLD BITCH';[143] 'you Bloody Stupid OLD FOOL';[144] 'What a *stupid ridiculous interfering meddling* old gas bag you are'.[145] A thoughtful letter came from a Mrs Sonia Argyle in Oxford, a fellow Girtonian and the parent of teenagers, one of whom was 'unstable' and worryingly had access to cannabis. Mrs Argyle felt Barbara Wootton had let her down, and she felt this even more strongly because she herself had been the casualty of a wartime broken home and had been rescued as a teenager by Jack Wootton's family in Nottingham.[146] There were also some who bothered to write to approve of this Wootton Report. Edward Morag in the House of Lords congratulated Barbara and expressed his distress at the 'ill-informed attacks'; she should not despair, as her Report was thirty years ahead of its time in commonsense and forethought.[147] 'A regular cannabis smoker' offered to help her in any way he could.[148] A Mrs Starky in Devon thought it important to warn Barbara that the real danger was not cannabis but 'the dark treacly fluid of the coco-cola'.[149]

At the end of the month in which the Wootton Report on cannabis was published, Barbara opened the 'Camping and Outdoor Life and Travel' Exhibition in London in her capacity as Chair of the Countryside Commission. One would have thought she would have been pleased to leave the whole sorry subject of drugs behind. But she surprised her audience and herself by lashing out at the way the Report had been treated in the press: 'one of the biggest misrepresentations I have ever seen'.[150] Commenting in the House of Lords on the 'hysterical reaction' meted out to the Report from the press, the public and the House of Commons (but not, she noted approvingly, by their Lordships), Barbara offered her diagnosis of the reasons for it. The syndrome was familiar to students of social psychology: people responded with outrage when 'some critical and objective study threatened to block an outlet for indulgence in the pleasures of moral indignation'.[151] In a television interview in 1984, she *still* had to correct the view that her Sub-Committee had recommended the legalization of cannabis.[152] Nonetheless, she did allow her name to appear on the notepaper of the 'Legalise Cannabis Campaign', albeit in very small letters and on the understanding that she would not be pestered to attend meetings.[153]

James Callaghan's shelving of the Wootton Report was not the end of the story, however. 'Drug Law Shock: Jim Changes His Mind' pronounced *The Sunday Mirror* in February 1970.[154] Less than a year later, he introduced legislation which adopted many of the Wootton Report's recommendations and eventually became the 1971 Misuse of Drugs Act. As Barbara Wootton later reflected, it was a considerable irony that, during Callaghan's own spell as Prime Minister later in the 1970s, the four months' sentence her Sub-Committee had proposed as the maximum on summary conviction for a cannabis offence was reduced to three months.[155] During the Committee stage of the Bill, Dr Richard Sharples, then Minister of State at the Home Office, observed that sentences of imprisonment for a first offence of possessing up to 30 grams of cannabis had fallen from 237 out of 1,857 (thirteen per cent) in 1967, to 21 out of 3,179 (less than one per cent) in 1969, a change he ascribed to the impact of the Wootton Report.[156]

One of the headlines that appeared in the aftermath of the first Wootton Report was 'Peeress Who Led "Pot" Inquiry Gets New Drugs Job'.[157] It was not a new job, but part of the old one: an inquiry into amphetamines and LSD. This second drugs report received virtually no press attention. It took the same line as the Cannabis Report in proposing a firm distinction between possession of small quantities for occasional personal use, on the one hand, and habits that could threaten public health or otherwise do significant damage, on the other. Swallowing a few purple hearts was less serious than injecting amphetamines; as regards LSD, the use by psychiatrists then prevalent was not based on any evidence of therapeutic effectiveness, and the grave risks attaching to its unauthorized use placed it 'high on the scale of harmfulness'.[158]

Both Wootton Reports on drugs criticized the absence of reliable research and the weakness of depending on subjective opinion which was liable to conjure up unreal hyperbolic images of drug-takers and drug-taking. '50 Arrested at Pop Festival' was a typical headline during the three-day festival held in Reading in the summer of 1971: 'More than 50 pop music enthusiasts, including girls, were arrested by detectives with long hair and dressed in jeans as they arrived for a three-day festival at Reading ... Hundreds of youths were searched for drugs.'[159] It was a police operation of 'unparalleled magnitude'. As the ever-incisive Lady Wootton pointed out, such an operation was not only an offensive but an inefficient way of doing business: ninety-three per cent of the searches by the duplicitously dressed detectives found nothing.[160] This statistic was completely in line with other evidence about the productivity of 'random' searches.[161] Barbara received a number of letters from people affected by police behaviour at the Reading festival. One man reported what had happened when his twenty-year-old daughter Judith came to visit him during the weekend of the festival:

> On arriving at Reading station, my daughter, who was dressed in a pair of blue linen trousers, blouse, black boots and a nearly new blue mac/coat, which I had just purchased from Harrods for £20 and having sunglasses in her hand, was walking from the train carrying a green plastic Harrods bag. Having left Platform eight she approached the main exit via the sub-way, when, as she was approaching the exit, a "Kinky/Hippy" type of woman, with blonde hair and leather jerkin, stopped her.

The detective asked Judith to go to a room to be searched for drugs, and the search included dropping her trousers and having her bra and pants felt. The young woman was very upset; in order to avoid a repeat event, her father drove her home in the evening.[162]

Barbara wanted to know how such invasions of privacy could possibly be defended.[163] The issue of the police's illiberal use of the 'stop and search' law was one which had come up repeatedly in the enquiries of the Wootton Sub-Committee. Under the 1967 Criminal Law Act, the police had the power to arrest without warrant anyone they suspected of being involved in a dangerous drugs offence. This was a practice which much exercised public feeling, but, as it applied to all drug offences, the Sub-Committee suggested that it should be urgently reviewed by another Sub-Committee of the Advisory Committee on Drug Dependence.[164] Such a group was duly appointed, under the chairmanship of Tory journalist and politician William Deedes. Barbara Wootton was a member of this one as well. The Deedes Report, published in 1970,[165] lacked weight, and was greeted as disappointing by those who wanted a change in the law.[166] It provided yet another occasion for the Baroness to dissent. She and Professor Glanville Williams, a specialist in English law, and the sociologist Michael Schofield, who had been on the Cannabis Sub-Committee, expressed their concern that young people were being searched as drug suspects for no better reason than that they had long hair or wore unconventional clothes. The three dissenters argued that searches should normally only be allowed *after* arrest, and particularly intrusive searches should always only be carried out after arrest, not just casually on the basis of a police officer's suspicion, as appeared to be happening.[167]

Barbara Wootton could imagine a world in which such ineffective and humiliating indignities no longer happened, but it was the imagination she applied to a different aspect of penal policy, alternatives to prison, that earned her a more enduring place in the history books. The second report which became known as a 'Wootton Report' had the uncompromising title of *Non-Custodial and Semi-Custodial Penalties*. In 1966, Home Secretary Roy Jenkins asked the Advisory Council on the Penal System to consider 'what changes might be made in 'non-custodial penalties, disabilities, and other requirements which may be imposed on offenders'.[168] The background to this request was the perceived need to reduce the prison population;[169] concern about the efficacy of existing alternatives to prison;[170] and recognition that imprisonment often had detrimental effects on prisoners and their families and contributed to reoffending: 'Putting men three to a cell with a chamber-pot is unlikely to make them feel that society is just and good and that they want to be part of it'.[171] In the usual manner whereby one committee spawns another, a Sub-Committee was set up to respond to Roy Jenkins' request, and Baroness Wootton was appointed as Chair. They held 39 meetings, solicited much evidence, and investigated schemes in other countries. Sweden had an interesting day-fine system, a formula-based arrangement in which fines imposed for some offences were calculated on the basis of the gravity of the offence and the offender's ability to pay. The Sub-Committee rejected the idea for Britain as not practical because personal incomes were not public knowledge as they were in Sweden. They looked at other fine systems, at deferment of sentences, at attendance centres, at intermittent custody, at probation and at disqualification and forfeiture, finding something in each of these ideas worthy of expansion and evaluation. But the proposal that attracted them the most, that broke new ground, was that of community service.

The idea of Community Service Orders (CSOs), as they became known, 'floated' into Barbara's mind one day 'on the commonsense basis that instead of sending people to prison it would be better to get them to do some useful work'. She vaguely remembered that the Germans had some scheme of this kind.[172] The German in question was 'the Chocolate Judge', Karl Holzschuh of Darmstadt, who acquired a degree of fame in the 1950s for his practical suggestion that a child who had stolen sweets should make reparation for this crime by giving some to a local orphanage. He also enjoined a motor-bike thief to join the local walking club, and a boy who had stolen milk from doorways to wash bottles in a dairy. He was a man after Barbara Wootton's own heart, rejecting the idea of punishment as ineffective retribution. Not only did his policy result in the girl who stole sweets never offending again, but the local delinquency rate was reported to fall by forty per cent.[173] The idea of asking offenders to give back in service what they had illegally taken had also presented itself to Barbara when she went to Australia in 1961. There, in a Juvenile Court in Alice Springs, she saw two boys who had stolen money from a church being ordered to spend their weekends for three months volunteering in an old people's home connected with the church.[174]

The British version of these ideas was Barbara's own, but the other members of the Sub-Committee agreed with it. The kernel of the proposal was that individuals who had committed offences that lay between the trivial and the major – such as theft, some traffic offences, some cases of malicious damage and minor assaults – would be ordered by courts to spend a certain number of hours a week in volunteer service in the community. The scheme was envisaged as committing offenders only to work in the evenings or weekends, during what would otherwise be leisure time. A crucial aspect of the arrangements proposed was that offenders would work alongside non-offenders. The work would be provided by voluntary agencies, but co-ordination would be the task of the Probation and After-Care Service. The Sub-Committee was not trying to make the punishment fit the crime (as the Chocolate Judge did), rather requiring offenders to perform some service of value to the community. CSOs seemed to combine a number of desirable features: the community would benefit; offenders would not be exposed to the malignant effects of prison culture; and they might learn values and practices which would lead them away from crime in future. The scheme appealed to adherents of different penal philosophies; moreover, service to the community was much cheaper than seclusion in prison – perhaps as much as ninety-five per cent cheaper.[175]

The Wootton Report on alternatives to prison is as notable as those on drugs for its careful sifting of the evidence, clarity of expression, and underlying commonsense, but it is also remarkable for the stress it lays on the need for experimental evaluation of all new proposals: 'We would emphasize,' said the Sub-Committee, 'the need for evaluative research in every instance in which an innovation is introduced. We are well aware that every new form of sentence which is not definitely known to be more effective than existing measures increases the risk of a wrong choice on the part of sentencers.'[176] In all untried kinds of treatments it is 'a wise precaution to proceed initially by means of controlled experiments'.[177] It therefore made sense to suggest, as they did, that before CSOs were rolled out nationally they should first be tested in a few pilot schemes in different parts of the country. The argument for pilot testing and for proper evaluation followed the precepts of Barbara Wootton's own *Testament for Social Science* – that the case for social science being useful to public policy must rest on the secure foundation of well-conducted research.

The idea of CSOs, one 'with intuitive appeal'[178] for its combination of novelty and practicality,[179] tumbled into the climate of 'penological optimism allied to the rehabilitative ideal',[180] that prospered in 1960s Britain. There was an enthusiastic policy response. In 1971 the Home Office proposed their introduction, initially in six pilot areas, and this was operationalized once the necessary legislation in the form of the 1972 Criminal Justice Act had been passed. The Act, hailed as 'revolutionary'[181] in the press, did, however, double the Report's suggestions of the number of hours of community service (from 120 to 240) and the length of time over which this could be spread (from six to twelve months). By an astounding stroke of coincidence for the author of the Cannabis Report, the first CSO was imposed on a first-time possessor of cannabis, a 'gentle and inoffensive' man whose ambition was to die on the banks of the Ganges.[182] By the late 1970s, CSOs were being used throughout the UK, and the British scheme served as a model for those elsewhere, in Australia, Belgium, Czechoslovakia, Denmark, Finland, France, Germany, Greece, Italy, Luxembourg, the Netherlands, New Zealand, Poland, Portugal, Norway, Sri Lanka, Sweden, Switzerland, the USA and Yugoslavia.[183] However, in the 2001 Criminal Justice Act, 'community service' was reframed as 'community punishment' in order to increase its attractiveness to sentencers,[184] a change of nomenclature that would have much displeased its originator.[185]

Outside the policy domain, reactions to CSOs at the time were mixed. A senior probation officer in Birmingham championed the recommendations of the Non-Custodial and Semi-Custodial Sentences Report as 'based on humanitarian, economic and commonsense bedrock' and proposing a scheme of keeping people out of prison that would pay for itself.[186] Some academics were more critical: the Wootton Sub-Committee had produced no particular evidence to back up their proposal, which was therefore isolated from the main body of penological and criminological knowledge.[187] Barbara's rejoinder to this was, how else could they fulfil their terms of reference except by thinking up ideas which could then be tested by empirical observation? Moreover, where was the body of criminological knowledge which could be used to predict whether a new idea might work or not?[188] Media discussions distorted the whole idea: 'But surely,' asked one BBC interviewer, 'you are not proposing to have convicts working on the roads?' What might have been a useful discussion was then wholly spent dispelling the image of 'chaingangs in uniforms branded with broad arrows'.[189] The smorgasbord of penal purposes met by CSOs – cost-reduction, retribution plus rehabilitation, benefit to the community – was seen as a weakness rather than a benefit.[190] The relevant paragraph in the Wootton Report which recites the attractions of the scheme to proponents of different penal philosophies was one Barbara later admitted to being 'slightly ashamed' of – it was 'an undisguised attempt to curry favour with everybody'.[191] But that is, perhaps, what you have to do if you want people to agree with you.

'Community Service Works' acclaimed the headline of a report by one Probation and After-Care Service responsible for operating the new scheme in the West Midlands after two years' experience with it. Barbara's smiling face, resting on a hand holding a pen, appeared underneath the headline.[192] But *did* it work? Evaluative research in the six pilot areas sponsored by the Home Office suggested that a sentence of community service was somewhat more likely than other sentences handed out to a comparison group (some of whom went to prison) to be followed by reconviction.[193] But these results were not based on a study in which individuals sentenced to CSOs were randomly chosen from among those considered suitable.[194] The result was 'dubious comparability' between the two groups.[195] The dispute about how to interpret data on the outcomes of the CSO experiment illustrates fundamental points of concern to Barbara Wootton throughout her life about the woolly science in which many important social issues of concern to policy-makers were (and remain) wrapped. Confusion about the purposes to which CSOs ought to be put – a genuine alternative to prison, or a sentence in their own right of quite a different kind – bedevilled their operation, particularly in a context where suspended sentences had been introduced (in 1967) with some of the same aims as the CSO scheme. If both suspended sentences and CSOs are only used in cases where prison would *not* have been seen as appropriate, what is the logic of comparing reoffending rates between the imprisoned and the non-imprisoned? As Barbara noted, even if CSOs yielded only the *same* rate of reoffending as prison, this non-custodial alternative would be counted as a success on the grounds of being much cheaper.[196]

Statistics are notable for misinterpretation, and the issue of those in the pilot evaluation came back to haunt her. Twice in 1977–8 she took up with the BBC its inappropriate and misleading use of figures from the study. On the first occasion a 'Tonight' programme on 10 May 1977 declared it 'a statistical fact' that offenders given CSOs are as likely as ex-prisoners to reoffend. Barbara's contact in the Home Office, who had seen a preview of the programme, told her he had challenged the unreliability of this fact, but the programme-makers chose to keep it in, since many probation officers they had talked to had expressed the view that CSOs did not work.[197] This argument did not impress Barbara. The second occasion for disgruntlement was a 'Panorama' programme on 13 February 1978 on alternatives to prison. Not only were viewers treated to a biased negative view of CSOs – they saw a cross young man whose CSO involved repairing a church, and who refused to do so on allegedly religious grounds – but Barbara's interview was cut up and used as background, rather than in its entirety, resulting in passages acquiring false meanings.[198] She had been on the alert for these devious strategies for some time. Her letter to *The Times* in February 1966 ('A Practice to Watch: Pre-Recording of Broadcasts') had sparked off a mild debate about the distortions clever programme-makers could engineer by stitching together different bits of recorded interviews, thus creating whatever impression they wanted.[199]

The critical Barbara Wootton was opposed to various aspects of the Government's interpretation of her CSO idea. For example, the requirement that CSOs should be limited to persons convicted of offences classified as punishable by imprisonment resulted in the perverse incentive to retain imprisonability as the mark of an offence in order to ensure that offenders might benefit from the scheme.[200] But in 1977, reflecting on the first five years of CSOs, she declared that the idea had caught on much better than she had dared to hope. She was especially pleased that the Home Office had now revamped the crime statistics so that CSOs were shown separately from other non-custodial sentences. She was proud of her invention, admitting to feeling a 'maternal instinct' about it: 'This is about the only thing I've got written down in the book I'm going to show St Peter when I get there,' she told a journalist in 1978. 'I haven't got much, but I will put that down because it is my child.'[201]

She had a lot more than that to show for her time on earth. These years when Barbara rose to fame as the hippie Baroness and the imaginative inventor of a new way of preserving criminals' liberty were also those in which more people knew her name than ever before or since. She was interviewed repeatedly in the press, and had a high profile on radio and television. A journalist who interviewed her for *The New York Times* concluded she was 'one of ablest people in England'. On the day they met, Barbara was wearing 'tweeds of a cheerful purplish color, and her nails were painted pink'. The Earl of Longford, whose opinion the American journalist solicited, passed observation, not on Barbara's clothes, but on her intellect: Barbara simply had 'the most brilliant academic mind of anyone in public life'.[202] An ex-police officer called her 'the Dorothy Parker of criminology', and probably the only person brave enough to observe that the British penal system was 'well stocked with Freemasons'.[203] In 1973, *The Times* placed Baroness Wootton twelfth among the top sixty women then alive – for the qualification of being 'so reasonable' on the Bench, in the Lords and at High Table.[204] Not the least remarkable aspect of

Barbara Wootton's work in this whole area of crime and justice is the one noted by the delinquent John Bird – her age: she was sixty-two when *Social Science and Social Pathology* was published; in her early seventies when she gave up being a magistrate and put her name to the key reports on drugs and alternatives to prison; and eighty-one on the publication of *Crime and Penal Policy*. Throughout her eighties, when she was an active contributor to Parliamentary debates about crime and the criminal law, she was simply the 'Crime Expert of the House of Lords'.[205]

Barbara Wootton's essential ideas on crime and punishment were that the causes of crime are as heterogeneous as the crimes themselves; careful attention to the facts exposes the aridity of many theories: if broken homes create criminals, why are there not as many female as male criminals, since there are as many daughters as sons in such homes?[206] If poverty is the cause of crime, then the typical offender would be an old woman, not a young man.[207] Capital punishment would be the most effective way of preventing re-offending,[208] but the values of a civilized society do not permit such an immoral act. The values of such a society demand that we be rational and humane about crime and punishment, which means that we do what works and what helps, rather than what seems politically expedient or simply a good idea at the time. Penal policy in Britain ought to build on the experience of other countries; mankind's tendency to throw away most of its experience is nowhere more conspicuously true than in relation to penal structures.[209]

In 1981 (aged eighty-four), Barbara wrote postscripts to her four Hamlyn lectures. Among the points she made were the following: why did the Home Office persistently fail to categorize deaths caused by dangerous driving as homicides; changes in the retirement ages of magistrates and judges follow the rule that the risks of senility vary inversely with the elevation of the post occupied; the radical change to majority verdicts in juries accomplished by the 1967 Criminal Justice Act was based on no solid evidence at all; the booklet for magistrates on sentencing recommended by the Streatfeild Committee had now been produced by the Home Office but it was disappointingly slim, and full of imprecise and shifting conclusions about the effects of different policies;[210] saddest of all, the crime rate continued to rise, the clear-up rate to fall, and the prisons were more crowded than ever. While, in 1963, she had been optimistic that better research and the growth of electronic mechanisms for handling complex data would make sentencing more scientific, and hence the penal system more effective in containing and reducing crime, in 1981 she was 'increasingly haunted' by the image of the whole penal system 'as in a sense a gigantic irrelevance – wholly misconceived as a method of controlling phenomena the origins of which are inextricably rooted in the structure of our society'.[211] As she had said in 1963, 'The affluent society is not affluent.

It derives that name rather from its esteem of affluence; and the prizes which it offers, though unequally distributed, are nevertheless not wholly unattainable ... A highly competitive, socially hierarchical, acquisitive society offers in fact an ideal breeding-ground for crimes against property; just as a mechanistic speed-besotted age is a standing invitation to motorized violence.'[212] And in a radio discussion on the subject of drugs in 1972, she remarked: 'If you ask me which I prefer, the values of the Pentagon or the values of the hippies, give me the hippies every time, because life in Western society makes really impossible and extravagant demands on people'.[213] It was spoken from the heart, but also from the mind, from a deep and sustained study of how citizens struggle to be good within the confines of a malignant social system.

15

Madam Speaker

In the autumn of 1958, when Barbara entered the House of Lords as Baroness Wootton of Abinger, she remembered as a small child being driven with her mother in her aunt's horse-carriage on a visit to London almost half a century earlier. Her mother pointed out to her the House of Commons as the place that was busy destroying the British Constitution; it was then engaged in debating a Bill which was designed to restrict the powers of the Lords.[1] But their Lordships survived, and Adela Adam would have been most surprised to find her daughter among them as one of the first four women life peers. Barbara's peerage, accepted when she was sixty-one, marked the beginning of the last distinctive phase of her working life, one that lasted for almost thirty years. Now she was in the world of public policy-making full-time, not as an ordinary MP, but in that much more ambiguous and elastic role as a member of the second chamber, an institution with a long and chequered history and a politically uncertain future. 'I'm in the corridors of the corridors that lead to the corridors of power,' she said.[2] Unlike many of her colleagues in those corridors, she took her new job very seriously; it *was* a job to her.[3] She had an office and a desk, and she attended the House regularly – three days a week when it was sitting – although the environment was not at all like an ordinary office: 'a riot of unrestrained Victorian gothic, with vaulted ceilings, dark elaborate pinnacles of carved wood, extravagant entanglements of brass'.[4]

Despite her youthful proclamations to the effect that no serious democracy would host an institution called the House of Lords, there is no sign that Barbara Wootton hesitated before agreeing to become a peer. She took the view that it was an institution that ought to be abolished, but, if it continued to exist, it should not just be 'the almost exclusive preserve of male Tory Christians'.[5] 'No-one in his senses would invent the present House if it did not already exist,' she declared. 'But there it is, tremendously seductive in its venerable charm.'[6] As a gentleman's club, it offered many advantages. When the social policy activist and entrepreneur Michael Young was offered a life peerage in 1978, he had run out of money for his regular journeys to and from London, and the peerage offered free rail travel as well as attendance allowances; Barbara Wootton advised him to accept, and so he did.[7] To an academic colleague she replied, when asked how she reconciled accepting a peerage with her belief in equality, 'My dear, if *you* are ever offered a peerage, accept it. You will always have a parking place in central London, and when you make a speech it will always be reported.'[8] The *social* advantages of the House of Lords – good conversation in a civilized atmosphere – were greater in Barbara's estimation than the *political* ones: a compact, unitary democracy does not really need two chambers, and the revisions imposed on legislation by a group of supposedly high-minded persons acting in the public interest are often only minor alterations effected by people who are influenced just as much as anyone else by their personal political philosophies.[9]

The consensus of Barbara's friends was that her decision to accept a peerage was a rational move for someone with her gifts. Criminologist Terry Morris considered it an 'absolutely brilliant idea … The institutions of British politics and British society at that time, if not literally a kind of Augean stable, were certainly replete with attitudes of intolerance, illiberalism, and resistance to change. The hereditary peers who turned up from their retreats in the shires to vote for the status quo were openly referred to as the "backwoodsmen". The ever rational Barbara was ready and able to get in there with her broom … I think she was a very powerful member of the Lords. And I also think that she was a very powerful influence on some of the women who joined the House of Lords, like, for example, Bea Serota [Baroness Serota of Hampstead, a life peer from 1967, like Barbara originally an economist, a BBC Governor and interested in crime] who very much took her cues from Barbara … That period of the later sixties and very early seventies there was quite a strong radical movement inside the Lords … particularly over issues like capital punishment and so forth.'[10] According to Nellie McGregor, widow of Professor O.R. McGregor, and their son Ross, Barbara revelled in the House of Lords; it was the pinnacle of the judicial system to which she had devoted all those years of her life as a magistrate and as an academic thinker: 'She would certainly not have been in the House of Lords unless she had a utilitarian reason for being there … Barbara genuinely thought that this was an extension of her attempts to reform society.' She related 'very well' to her fellow members of the House of Lords, including the aristocracy. Perhaps 'there was something atavistic about it – there she was sitting on a bench next to some chap whose ancestor shagged Elizabeth the First's butler'.[11] There was definitely a side to Barbara that enjoyed the status and could even have dubbed her a snob;[12] the 336 letters and 12 telegrams congratulating her on the peerage are carefully preserved in her Girton College Archives.

She was not alone in being seduced by the gentlemen's club. Her friend, the journalist Kingsley Martin, did as Leonard Woolf told him to do and refused a peerage on socialist grounds, but wrote to Woolf to say that he did not necessarily feel contempt for people who did accept. When Barbara Wootton, a woman 'for whom neither of us feels contempt', accepted, it occurred to Kingsley that she might be right and Leonard might be wrong.[13] Barbara wanted Kingsley in the House, because he would look so nice there, but unfortunately no-one she suggested was ever asked.[14] Another of her friends, Francis Williams, who used to regard the House of Lords as the silliest of institutions, changed his mind sufficiently to become Baron Francis-Williams of Abinger in 1962, although he recognized that the charms of the House might lessen if he attended more often, as he would then be unable to escape the feeling that what happened there was an elaborate charade.[15] As one reads the debates in Hansard – the many hundreds of debates in which the name 'Wootton' appears – there is an overwhelming sense of almost obsequious politeness ('the noble Baroness', 'the noble Lord', 'my noble friend'), but there is also the possibility that it is not quite obsequious, that it is merely a very formal mode of address which allows uncompromising things to be said with courtesy so that those who are not asleep are more likely to hear them.

When the Queen opened Parliament in October 1958, that first year when women peers were there, Baroness Wootton arrived early to sit in a chamber crammed with colourfully-robed bodies. The bronze barons of Runnymede between the tall windows looked down on 'a triumph of excess' as the Queen stuck to the traditional formula and addressed them all as 'My Lords', not 'My Lords and Ladies'.[16] It was some time before Barbara found a suitable occasion to treat the noble Lords and Ladies to her maiden speech. Three and a half months after she entered the House, there was a lengthy debate – it ran for more than six and a half hours – on the Youth Services. It was the first time that this topic had received a full discussion in the House, and many of their Lordships were anxious to speak on what they saw as an important and troubling subject. Lord Longford's introduction to the debate signalled their main concern about rising rates of juvenile crime; but he also quoted Macaulay on 'grace and female loveliness, wit and learning' in anticipation of the fact that their Lordships were about to hear the maiden speeches of two lady peers, the Baronesses Ravensdale and Wootton.[17] Two and a half hours later came Barbara's chance to speak. First, and predictably, she put them right on the statistical front: the proportion of indictable offences committed by young people was actually fractionally *less* now than before the War. What had increased were crimes of violence, which were up seven-fold, though most of these were relatively minor in nature. Just as the previous speaker, Baroness Ravensdale, had drawn on her experience of running clubs for young people to lambast parents for their negligence and neglect of moral teaching, so Baroness Wootton referred to her experience as a magistrate as a source of a rather different picture, one in which young people were reacting to a world of unequal life chances and a culture of acquisitiveness. It was, she said, so much easier for the policy response to be the provision of more clubs or clinics, rather than the elimination of slums and extended secondary education, which would address the fundamental material basis of young people's discontent.[18]

Her speech took twenty-two minutes. The Earl of Feversham responded: it was 'a most eloquent speech', testimony to the fact that the noble lady would bring 'wisdom, knowledge and, indeed, humour' to many such debates in future; the House was enriched by her presence.[19] Later in the debate, the Earl of Dundee remarked that, if any of their Lordships were ever guilty of a crime of violence, they would want to be sentenced by Magistrate Lady Wootton. He hoped that they would all hear the Ladies speak much in future, and felt that their contribution put the House a few points ahead of the Other Place (the House of Commons), which had been bi-sexual for so much longer.[20] Lord Longford could not help remarking that Baroness Wootton's speech exceeded in brilliancy even the expectations of those, such as himself, who had sponsored or introduced her to the House, and he, too, picked up on her humour, which proved reassuringly that this was 'not a commodity in which the other sex are behind us'.[21] Flattering though these remarks were, they managed to lay on one side the essence of Barbara's argument, which was that bad behaviour in the young is caused by a bad society. Their Lordships were not used to socialism, even laced with humour.

The overwhelming impression to an observer looking down on their Lordships' Chamber was that most heads were bald, many had shut eyes, and there were plenty of those special hearing aids that looked like miniature telephones.[22] As *The Observer* had noted when the names of the first four women life peers were first announced, the only one of them who was likely to be the 'excited hornet' capable of stirring the 'drowsy flies' of the Lords was Barbara Wootton.[23] She definitely lived up to this promise, and she did so through a period which saw four changes of Government – two transfers of power from the Conservatives to Labour, and two from Labour to the Conservatives. During this time, there were multiple transformations in the British way of life: a decline in Britain's traditional pre-eminence as a world power; new patterns of economic instability; and a supposedly affluent society bringing better living standards for many citizens, and certainly vastly more material consumption, but no diminution of underlying inequalities of wealth. Barbara's performances in the House of Lord throughout these changes of fortune were notoriously spirited and provocative. For example, early in her career as a baroness, she caused the largest division of the 1958–9 session in her unsuccessful attempt to delete the words 'common prostitute' from the Street Offences Bill. She pointed out that this was a term quite without statutory definition. If common prostitutes were defined as people who already had convictions, then this was contrary to the basic principle of English justice, which was that people were innocent until proved guilty.[24] Her trademark cutting edge of witty radicalism was apparent in the speeches and remarks she made in many debates, including those about secondary schools and the training of social workers. The debate on secondary education in 1959, which focused on the selection of children at the age of eleven into different types of schools, provided a ready platform for the airing of many prejudiced views from men who had been selected into a type of education beyond the reach of most British children. After three hours of listening to such attitudes, Barbara was moved to criticize the convenient and habitual assumption that different types of secondary schools (from the secondary modern to the one that 'lies under the shadow of Windsor Castle'[25]) were equally valued and equally valuable. They clearly were not. If they were, ninety per cent of young people attending secondary moderns would not leave at fifteen, whereas forty per cent of those at grammar schools stayed on beyond the age of sixteen. Barbara informed their Lordships that the eleven-plus examination 'broods like a monster' over every home in England with a young child in it. It is 'an extraordinary educational theory' that children should be separated from one another on grounds of measured intelligence. We all have to live together, so what is wrong with comprehensive schools? Barbara's speech was interrupted several times by Viscount Hailsham, who did not agree with her; most graciously, she thanked him for the 'gymnastic exercise' he had given her in constantly rising and sitting, but she was not going to change her mind.[26]

The following year, their Lordships discussed the Report of the Working Party on Social Workers in Local Authority Health and Welfare Services, chaired by Eileen Younghusband, a respected teacher of social work at the LSE. The Earl of Feversham, introducing the discussion, made an early reference to the well-known views of the noble Baroness Wootton on social workers acting improperly as 'the poor man's psychiatrist'.[27] Barbara's riposte observed that criticizing the practice and philosophy of social work was not the same thing as suggesting that social workers were not needed – they were, but they should liberate themselves from the tendency, imported from American social work ideology, to focus on personal disturbance rather than on practical material need. She wanted their Lordships to understand that people could not be counselled out of poverty. Economic matters were a matter of economics. How would their Lordships feel if the accountants they employed to reduce the taxes they paid – a reasonable exercise which she herself engaged in, not wishing to contribute more than she needed to a Government of which she did not approve – subjected them to interrogation about their private lives instead of their financial ones, and proceeded on the assumption that any chaos in the financial arena was due to sexual tension and conflict?[28] There is no record of laughter, but perhaps the question had some impact.

'A fine-looking woman with impressive white hair and stylish spectacles,' noted Lord Longford, of Barbara's physical presence: 'She was a formidable figure but soon much loved in the House'.[29] They loved her caustic and perceptive questions, her unique combination of theoretical and practical knowledge, and her 'remarkable tenderness for the individual human being'.[30] According to Lena Jeger, Barbara gained great respect 'mainly because she tended to concentrate on the subjects she knew best – on sociology and penal reform – and always spoke with authority and concern. More than one old peer had been heard to say that he wished he had been taught by her'[31] – their Lordships do appear to have engaged in several fantasies about the Ladies in their midst. The Labour peer Lord McCarthy, speaking about economic policy in 1976, complained that he was put off by the sudden appearance beside him of the noble Baroness, Lady Wootton, 'because, as noble Lords will know, she has been the doyenne of academic experts on this subject since her path-making publication *The Social Foundations of Incomes* [sic] *Policy* in the early 'fifties. I felt like giving her my notes ... asking her to mark them, and if she did not give me a beta plus, I would not have risen to my feet.'[32]

Barbara Wootton's commitment to the House of Lords included becoming a member of its Offices Committee (in 1959) and its Procedure of the House Committee (in 1965). Just as she had been introduced to the House by two established peers (the Lords Longford and Burden), so she introduced others: Elaine Burton, ex-Labour MP for Coventry South in 1962; Bea Serota in 1967; economist John Vaizey and engineer Paul Wilson in 1976; and O.R. McGregor on his re-recreation as Baron McGregor of Durris in 1978. In between her first speech on 4 February 1959, and her last on 4 July 1985, she is recorded as having made 1,790 'contributions' to House of Lords debates – a surprising total for someone who did not regard herself as a good Parliamentarian. Although people said she was good at it, she disliked public speaking.[33] Her most significant contributions to the House of Lords, discussed in Chapter 14, were in the areas of crime and drugs. Her most participatory years were 1961–2 and 1971–4.

In 1961, most of her time was taken up with penal issues or with mental health and health care, but she also contributed to debates about broadcasting, road traffic, and sickness relief for sub-postmasters. A decade later, the stop-and-search rule and firearms were major preoccupations, but other topics were wage settlements, the proposed abolition of the waterways board, and pensions. Barbara's contributions to these debates reflected concerns she had long held: about the dangers of power; about the need for central economic planning and an equitable income policy; and about the importance of clear thinking in deciding public policy. She was vocal in the debate about the Commonwealth Immigrants Bill in 1962, expressing concern that immigration officers would have the power to exclude people they considered might be mentally disordered without seeking any independent evidence.[34] In her attack in 1979 on the economic policy of Callaghan's Labour government, Barbara declared, 'It has not done very much in particular, and it has done it very badly'. There was no anti-inflation policy. The Government spoke of 'the inflation rate' as though it were a fact of nature 'or what the insurance companies would call an "act of God", which, by the way, is very unflattering to God'. She drew their Lordships' attention to Lord Kaldor's letter putting forward in *The Times* that morning the very system which she herself had proposed years ago – an income gains tax.[35]

In the 1970s, she was appalled to discover that boys (though not girls) learnt how to use guns in cadet forces at school and in borstal institutions: 'It is madness to train young men in borstals in the use of firearms, and then be surprised at the number of crimes involving shooting incidents'.[36] 'Row Over Gun Training for Boys in Borstals', reported *The Daily Mirror*.[37] She pestered the Home Office for information about who was allowed a firearm certificate and why, and about the use of guns in murder and manslaughter cases. Guns had been involved in 23 deaths in England, Wales and Scotland in 1971, and, of the 18 offenders responsible for these deaths, 10 held valid certificates and eight did not. It took the civil servants quite a long time to put this evidence together.[38] Questions about the use of firearms dragged on and on. In 1982, the weary eighty-five-year-old Baroness was driven to remark that, 'The Government takes great trouble to stop people from possessing cannabis, but apparently firearms don't matter'.[39]

Cars fell in rather the same category. Motoring offences were crimes, although the penal system and public attitudes persisted in not treating them as such. For example, men convicted of serious motoring offences were not removed from their posts as magistrates. Shortly after joining the House of Lords, Barbara informed their Lordships that many of them were regular users of 'lethal weapons' – the ones they daily parked in Old Palace Yard.[40] She compared the sentences for 3,000 or so offenders found guilty of drink-driving with a similar number convicted of offences against property without violence: only five per cent of the former but over fifty per cent of the latter got prison sentences.[41] Lords who liked cars did not like Barbara Wootton, who held faithfully to her public anti-car agenda throughout her time in the House. She argued in favour of heavier penalties for most motoring offences, from a baseline position that a driving licence ought not to be regarded as a civic right but rather as a privilege which some capable, qualified people could obtain.[42] Her vehicular disputations were often peppered with graphic statistics. In 1961, more than five times as many people were convicted of causing death by dangerous driving than were convicted of murder; this was a 'recurring slaughter' with its counterpart in all 'developed' countries';[43] a year's victims, if positioned in the gigantic Royal Albert Hall in London, would fill ninety-two per cent of the seats.[44] The Pedestrians' Association was founded as a campaigning group in 1929 (in 2010, it is known as 'Living Streets'), and it counted Barbara Wootton, along with its own Graham Page, as 'by far the most important and influential road safety campaigner' of her day.[45]

The political landscape experienced another earthquake when Barbara Wootton was appointed as the first woman Deputy Speaker of the House of Lords in 1965. The proceedings of the House of Lords are presided over by the Lord Chancellor, but, until the Constitutional Reform Act of 2005, it was the Deputy Chairman of Committees, the role to which Barbara was appointed in December 1965, who took over as Deputy Speaker in his absence.[46] By the time she became Deputy Speaker, Barbara knew thoroughly how the House worked. As Frank Field put it, 'She wasn't somebody who floated along just turning up for the odd vote and all the rest of it. She knew the procedures and how to do things; that's why she was elected as a woman Deputy Speaker.'[47] 'First Woman to Sit on the Woolsack' announced *The Times*;[48] of course it was a splendid thing, observed Lena Jeger in *The Guardian,* to have a woman there, and all the more so because it was Barbara, a woman 'whose wisdom, eloquence, and authority prevail even over the inelegant discomfort of the most unfunctionally designed seat in the Palace of Westminster'.[49] Barbara agreed: the Woolsack, from where the proceedings of the House are directed, was not a very comfortable place.[50] It is a large ceremonial cushion covered with red cloth with no back or arms, and stuffed with wool, a reminder of the trade that once underpinned national prosperity, and it is the focal point of the House, facing the throne. When, in 1973, the House's heating system broke down, the discomfort of the Woolsack escalated as the ventilation grid in the centre of the floor in front of it threw up an Arctic gale; Barbara had to put on trousers in self-defence.[51] But the first time she sat on it, the first time any woman had sat on it, was on 16 February 1966, when she took the place of the Lord Chancellor who had left for dinner.[52] The topic of the debate she had to preside over then was not one she warmed to – road transport and the expansion of the motorway network. As Deputy Speaker, she had to chair debates on an enormous disparity of topics: local government, housing finance, the protection of children, parliamentary pensions, patents, industrial relations, slaughterhouses, rabies, social security, the countryside, water charges, crofting reform, the shipbuilding industry, and race relations.

The year after she was invited to experience the discomfort of the Woolsack, the members of both Houses of Parliament were confronted with a Bill that would change the lives of women in Britain forever. 'Procuring' a miscarriage had been illegal since the Offences Against the Person Act of 1861, although the Act did not prevent the many thousands of abortion-related deaths that occurred every year. The legendary action of the gynaecologist Aleck Bourne in 1938, in inviting police to prosecute him for aborting the fetus of a fourteen-year-old who had been raped, established the preservation of women's health as a legitimate ground for abortion, and opened the doors for what, by the 1960s, had become a lucrative private sector medical industry. Middle-class women could buy their abortions, but working-class women could afford only the cheap services of the illegal practitioners. The abortion law reformer, Diane Munday, recalled with horror doctors telling her in the early 1960s how, in the big London hospitals, wards were put aside every Friday and Saturday night for women, bleeding, often septic and sometimes dying, who were brought in as a result of backstreet abortions – Friday being pay day.[53] The Abortion Law Reform Association (ALRA) was set up in 1936 to campaign for changes which would resolve this appalling situation, but it proved a discouragingly long struggle before Liberal MP David Steel succeeded with his Abortion Law Act of 1967.[54]

Barbara Wootton supported most of the liberalizing initiatives of the period from the 1950s to the 1980s. She had, for example, agreed with the conclusions of her Surrey neighbour Jack Wolfenden's Committee on Homosexual Offences and Prostitution, that private homosexual acts between consenting adults should be decriminalized,[55] and she was a founder member of the Homosexual Law Reform Society in 1958.[56] With this background, and her history of concern for issues relating to women, it was not surprising that she was widely expected to be enthusiastic about abortion law reform. When the ALRA was set up in 1936 to campaign for legal changes, she had, indeed, written a letter of support to the new organization: 'How glad I am to know,' she said, 'that the Association is attempting to put a stop to the enormous damage to women's health and happiness caused by the present state of affairs'.[57] In the House of Lords, she campaigned for the removal of the class barrier which was responsible for dangerous back-street abortions.[58] Her views about abortion came to the attention of abortion law reformers when two pre-Steel versions of an abortion Bill progressed through the House of Lords in 1965–6. Their champion was a seventy-six-year-old solicitor, Baron Silkin of Dulwich, a solid, tactical, but somewhat pedantic, supporter of abortion law reform.[59] At the second reading of the first Silkin Bill in November 1965, when Parliament entered into its first proper debate on abortion – a five-and-a-half-hour marathon – Baroness Wootton voiced her disquiet about a clause in the Bill which was known as the 'inadequate mother' clause. This called on doctors to make decisions on grounds of health and/or social conditions about the suitability of women to continue with, or terminate, their pregnancies. Since this was a provision which made women's access to abortion clearly dependent on the subjective opinions of doctors, Barbara felt it was unsatisfactory; she wanted amendments which would restrict the grounds on which doctors could sanction termination of pregnancy.[60] It was, she said, 'a very profound decision for anybody to make about anybody else'. Among the arguments used to persuade their Lordships, she put to them a 'by no means unlikely case': 'Suppose there is a husband who is selfish – and there are selfish husbands – who does not wish to be bothered with children, who does not wish to have the expense of providing for children. And suppose that, when he finds that his wife has become pregnant, he sees the family doctor and tells him that his wife is extremely neurotic, is not fit to be a mother … The doctor may feel that there are great tensions in the marriage, and that the fact of the pregnancy is going to aggravate those tensions, and that, in the interests of the marriage, it might be better to terminate the pregnancy … This is not an improbable situation. It is perhaps a situation which we have all known in our personal experience.'[61] Was this something she knew about from her own personal experience with George? Frank Field remembers Barbara telling him that George 'forced' her to have an abortion.[62] On many occasions Barbara voiced her regret at not having children: 'It has always been a grief to me'.[63]

The substance of Barbara Wootton's objection to the 'inadequacy' clause in the Abortion Bill had a history. It went back to all those debates about 'problem families' with which she had tangled in *Social Science and Social Pathology*: the middle-class idea that certain kinds of families are inadequate or dysfunctional because they do not meet certain standards of material and social behaviour. Therefore, to suggest, as the 'inadequacy' clause by implication did, that women living in poor circumstances might not be fit to be mothers by virtue of these circumstances was a form of 'pseudo-eugenics'.[64] In a letter to Silkin, Barbara referred to the dangers of 'Nazi racialism'.[65] The problem was not the birth of children to mothers living in slums but the slums themselves. The moral issue was the liberty of the individual: what the Bill proposed to do was 'to say that people of whom we do not approve are not to propagate, and to lay upon the medical profession the responsibility of deciding of whom we do approve and of whom we do not approve … It is not for us, and it is not for the doctors, in the present state of knowledge – perhaps not in any state of knowledge – to say who is to have the right to propagate children and who has not.'[66]

Barbara's wrangle with the 'inadequacy' clause disappointed abortion law reform campaigners, who saw it as undermining the whole of their campaign. As one prominent campaigner, Madeleine Simms, pointed out, Barbara's opposition to this clause lacked rationality, as abortion would only ever be considered if the mother herself asked for it.[67] While the reformers appreciated her reluctance to cede doctors powers over women's lives, Barbara had occupied a position in the abortion debates alongside right-wing religious figures, such as the Archbishop of Canterbury and the Tory Catholic politician Norman St John-Stevas. This suggested that she harboured some underlying objection to abortion, aside from her contentions about abuse of medical power.[68] In a television interview conducted in 1968 with the Canadian journalist Bernard Braden, Barbara did admit a principled opposition to abortion. It followed from her position on killing: nobody had the right to kill anyone else; thus, women had no basic right to abortion. Life begins at conception and life, because there is nothing else, is precious: had she been religious, she told Braden, and had she thus believed that aborted fetuses went straight to heaven, she might be more in favour of abortion.[69] There had, though, to be a few exceptions to these absolute moral stands, so she agreed with abortion after rape and when there was a serious threat to the mother's physical or mental health.

It was the thalidomide disaster in the late 1950s and early 1960s that had reinvigorated the whole campaign for reform of the abortion law; this disaster saw the births in 46 countries of more than 10,000 babies severely deformed because of a drug prescribed for their mothers in pregnancy.[70] In the highest-profile legal case, a Belgian mother had been charged in 1962 with murdering her seven-day-old very severely deformed daughter, and after a sensational trial she had been acquitted.[71] In another television interview with Robin Day for a 'Panorama' programme in January 1962, Barbara was asked what she would have done in the Belgian case; she said she would have agreed with the not-guilty verdict, but would not have gone as far as the Belgian jury in dismissing the case as not one of homicide. It *was* homicide, yet in situations such as that faced by the Belgian mother, when there was no prospect of any quality of life, it was rational to regard death as a humane release.[72] Once the 'inadequate mother' clause in the British legislation had been re-worded, Barbara announced her support for it, and she continued to voice her concern that, whatever legal and medical provision there was for abortion, all women should have equal access to it. For example, in a rather tetchy House of Lords debate in 1972 she argued that women living on supplementary benefit should have the same rights to abortion as any other women, even when this meant that the Supplementary

Benefits Commission itself should pay the costs of abortions arranged by private charities.[73] Still, three years after the 1967 Act was passed, Barbara added her name to St John-Stevas's in a parliamentary delegation calling for an enquiry into the way the Act was working.[74] This anti-reformist move backfired when the results of the enquiry unanimously supported the Act in its original form.[75]

Whatever her real motives and feelings – and abortion *is* a subject that tends to involve deep emotion – the disagreement over abortion legislation had considerable consequences for Barbara. It led to her detachment from the organized humanist movement. She had belonged to this, in one way or another, since the halcyon days of the Federation of Progressive Societies and Individuals with H.G. Wells and others in the 1930s. The separation of moral purposes from religious doctrines in a rationalist humanist philosophy was absolutely central to her approach, both to life and to those domains of public policy she tried to influence. Indeed, she wrote in her Voltaire lectures, given in 1970 under the auspices of the British Humanist Association and published as *Contemporary Britain*, that the loss of a guiding morality, such as could be supplied by a humanist framework, lay behind many contemporary social problems. However, of equal importance to her was another facet of humanism: its reliance on the logic and methodology of science to identify the best route for promoting 'the good life'.[76] She was a member of three organizations – the British Humanist Association (BHA), the Rationalist Press Association (RPA) and the Ethical Union (EU) – which shared the kind of complex conjoined history and overlapping memberships that characterized humanist / ethical / secular activities.[77] In 1950, she had become an Honorary Associate of the RPA, originally created as a book club publishing affordable non-Christian 'liberal' literature; she was Vice-President during Bertrand Russell's term of office as President in 1962–1970, and she took over from him as President in 1970.[78] She was also a Vice-President of the Ethical Union, an umbrella name for a number of small ethical societies, from 1956 to 1969,[79] and she had a close association with the International Humanist and Ethical Union, a worldwide organization set up by the leading humanist Harold Blackman and the Dutch humanist philosopher Jaap van Praag.[80] As a founder member of the BHA, she spoke at its inaugural dinner in the House of Commons in May 1963.[81] In the House of Lords, she belonged to the All-Party Parliamentary Humanist Group. Freethinkers were notoriously promiscuous in their occupation of different committees and associations, and Barbara Wootton was one of the most so.[82] As one of her obituarists put it, she was 'no closet unbeliever. She publicly supported virtually every organisation within the secularist-humanist movement.'[83]

Despite her impressive pedigree as a humanist, the BHA decided at their annual general meeting in April 1966, to remove her as a Vice-President. The reason was their perception of her position vis-à-vis the Abortion Bill: she had been 'instrumental in securing the defeat of the clause relating to abortion in the case of the inadequacy of the mother'. According to Diane Munday, who argued for Barbara's suspension, Barbara had been warned by telegram before the House of Lords debate that her position meant she was not toeing the humanist party line.[84] By no means all the BHA supporters were happy about this, pointing out that Barbara was not opposed to the Abortion Law Reform Bill as a whole, and that 'heresy-hunting' is contrary to the very principles of humanism.[85] The BHA's decision perplexed and upset Barbara. During the House of Lords debates on the Abortion Bill, she found herself at odds with those whose views she normally shared, and she was concerned to spell out why. The first reason was the importance of human life. The second was her concern that the widespread availability of abortion might make people discard contraception as the lesser of two evils, or even not an evil at all.[86] Barbara also parted from the RPA several years later, in 1972, over the issue of what supporting the right to abortion really means, although she did maintain a close and friendly relationship with the organization and was on the Editorial Advisory Board of its journal, *Question*.[87]

In these circles, Barbara was seen as having a more positive view of adoption as an alternative than others in the pro-abortion movement,[88] and there is other evidence to support this. In her disagreement with the BHA, she argued that its members lobbied almost exclusively on abortion, when they ought to develop the Humanist Counselling Service and focus on helping the Agnostics Adoption Society.[89] She left money in her will to an organization called the International Adoption Service. This began life in 1963 as the Agnostics Adoption Bureau through the efforts of the pioneer epidemiologist Richard Doll, and his wife Joan, who wanted to adopt children, but, as agnostics, found themselves shunned by the mainstream adoption agencies. Turning to the BHA for advice, they set up an adoption agency for non-believers in their own home, paying for its first social worker themselves.[90] Barbara was one of this organization's sponsors when it acquired charitable status in 1965, and she made various public appeals on its behalf.[91]

Throughout the decades from 1958 to 1988 when she worked in the House of Lords, the proportion of new life peers who were female remained stable at eleven to twelve per cent.[92] As a bastion of masculinity, their Lordships' House was not severely challenged by the presence of the Ladies. Nonetheless, during her time there, she was part of a marked transformation of the Upper House from an institution that was (almost literally) 'dying in its sleep' – only some 60 peers attending regularly, short sittings on only about 90 days a year – to a much more appropriately modern role as 'something approaching a Council of State – a forum and focus of expert opinions and a dedicated revising assembly'.[93] The House of Lords' transition to a more modern institution gathered momentum when Harold Wilson's 1964 Labour Government used life peerages as a strategy for increasing Labour's representation there. By the mid-1980s, when Barbara was still an active working peer, more than two-thirds of peers were registered as attending, and a substantially higher proportion actually spoke in debates; sittings were longer, and on more days of the year. This greater activity had a measurable effect: by 1989, Prime Minister Margaret Thatcher's Bills had been amended by the House of Lords against her wishes on no fewer than 125 occasions.[94] Many 'lifers' were experienced in public speaking and politics, and they came to dominate debates and committee work, introducing generally more 'liberal' values.[95] Women lifers tended to be more active than their male counterparts; for example, in the 1979–80 session, more than twice as many women life peers as male life peers managed an attendance rate of ninety per cent or higher.[96] As with some other areas of her life, Barbara Wootton held to a degree of ambiguity in relation to her own official political affiliation. She was a cross-bencher,[97] preserving that independence of voice she valued so highly, but she defined herself staunchly as a 'Labour peer';[98] she was very much a member of the left-wing of the Labour Party,[99] a 'democratic socialist without any initial caps'.[100]

She had a sharp tongue for some of the House of Lords' patriarchal customs. The criminologist Philip Bean remembers dining with her at the House one evening: 'We sat at this long table and, at the end, one of the waiters, I don't know what you call them, went past with cigars, and she waited until he'd gone past, and she called him back because he walked past her, you see, without offering her one. And she called him back. "Are you offering me a cigar?" "Oh yes, Madam, of course." "Well, I don't want one," she said. I said to her, "What did you do that for?" "He shouldn't assume." She was a delight really.'[101] Despite being thoroughly entrenched in the furniture and procedures of the House, Barbara continued to argue for its abolition, although with the proviso that, first, the House of Commons needed to do its work properly.[102] She criticized the House of Lords' 'archaic constitution' and the 'ritual dance' of its legislative powers in relation to Government bills,[103] even in the House of Lords itself.[104]

After seven years in the House, she confided to her friend, Shena Simon, that she was rather fed up with it. They had so many new MPs among the Labour Lords that the place was becoming an inferior imitation of the Commons – inferior because the good MP stuck to the Commons. 'It has certainly ceased to be any distinction to be a Lord, especially for a woman,' she muttered, 'all the recent additions – Dora Gaitskell, Norah Phillips, Barbara Brooks, Lady Plummer – are there by virtue of their husbands', not their own, achievements.'[105] The saga of why on earth she and the other Ladies who had earned their titles should be called 'peeresses' like the wives of Lords, who were called 'peeress' as a courtesy title, but had earned nothing themselves, was one that went on and on. Barbara and her disgruntled female colleagues had a meeting with the Lord Chancellor in March 1970, in a further attempt to get the practice corrected. They were evidently seen as rather a nuisance; the Lord Chancellor recorded that he had noted the wishes of 'the militant women peers', and hoped these would be passed onto the lobby correspondent so that the press would reform its habits of nomenclature, although there was 'absolutely no guarantee that it would have the smallest effect'.[106] Barbara never relinquished her objection to the term 'peeress', penning a letter to *The Times* about it as late as 1983, and regretting that the newspaper refused to publish it.[107] One of her last interventions in the House of Lords was during a debate about the Government's ratification of the United Nations Convention on Sex Discrimination in 1984, when she inquired as to whether her husband George might now posthumously be granted the title 'peeress'.[108]

She must have been a constant irritation with her campaign against illogical injustices. In 1970, she provoked a headline in *The Daily Mirror*, 'Row Over Jail Curb Study', when she asked a question in the House about the Home Office's refusal to allow a prisoner, Walter 'Angel Face' Probyn, to be visited by a University of Essex lecturer in order to study sociology.[109] Probyn was serving a twelve-year sentence for shooting at police during one of his many escapes from prison; as Britain's most notorious criminal escapologist, by 1964 he had notched up seventeen escapes from the approved schools and prisons in which he had spent most of his life.[110] Barbara Wootton's interest in Probyn was that she had sentenced him in the Juvenile Courts at the start of his criminal career. Then there was her unexpected defence of the errant Lord Lambton. In 1973, the British press had a field day with the peccadilloes of this fifty-year-old Air Force Minister, whose liaisons with prostitutes had come to light when the husband of one of them had tried to sell to a tabloid a photograph of Lambton and someone else's wife in bed together.[111] Questions were asked about Lambton's possible indiscretions with State secrets during these liaisons, but he protested that he had never taken his red State boxes of Government with him, and it was the futility of his job as a junior minister and wrangles about his title that had caused him to engage in activities such as gardening and debauchery in the first place.[112] Barbara Wootton wrote to *The Times*, as was her wont, noting that, 'If impeccable marital fidelity is to be made a condition of political office, this should be explicitly stated at the time that such office is offered', but, in that case, public life would surely be deprived of the services of many valuable people.[113]

In 1977, Barbara found herself embarking on a new political campaign, one that would leave her ultimately disillusioned. She received a letter from a man called John Dare in Ashford, Kent; twenty-six years earlier, his wife had died, leaving him with two children and a nineteen-year-old-step-daughter. This young woman, Gill, had kept house for all of them, and she and John Dare had fallen in love; the children had since grown up and left home, and John Dare and his step-daughter now wished to marry, as a mark of their mutual devotion, and in order for her to get a pension and inherit his property. The problem was that their relationship fell in the category of proscribed ones according to the marriage laws. Could not – should not – this be changed?[114] A number of other such cases had arrived in Barbara's postbag, and she was sufficiently charged with indignation to sponsor a Marriage Enabling Bill. This aimed to tidy things up, so that the laws determining who could marry whom were based purely on the prohibition of blood relationships.[115] Public opinion, Barbara knew, was in favour of sorting out these anomalies, but she also knew that their Lordships harboured a variety of spurious objections to her proposal, mainly that such a change in the law would threaten the stability of family life by encouraging men to lust after their step-daughters and get rid of their wives. 'While I have lived long enough to know that there are people who will do anything for sex or money,' she said, probably giving her audience one of her famously reprimanding looks, 'a family in which the husband casts lustful eyes upon his step-daughter while he is still married to her mother is not exactly a stable family anyhow'.[116]

The attention of journalists was caught by this spectacle of an eighty-one-year-old Baroness arguing the case of 'Forbidden Love' with all the vigour of a sixth-former.[117] She was right about the objections; she once heard two peers refer to her modest proposal as 'that filthy little bill'.[118] The day the Lords finally threw out her Bill in May 1981, Barbara left the Chamber with a sense of disgust that she had done so badly, and went for a drink with John and Gill Dare, who had become friends, and others of her supporters. She had arranged to stay that night in the Grosvenor Hotel in Victoria, but, once there, found she had nothing to read. She went out and bought Ronnie Biggs' biography, read half of it and felt better.[119] 'We hated leaving you alone at that rather dreary hotel,' wrote John to her later. It had been a valiant battle, they were aware of how much work and nervous strain it had caused her, they marvelled at her courage and stamina, and were tremendously grateful.[120] The Dares put forward a successful personal Bill in March 1982; Barbara introduced it in the House of Lords, expressing great admiration for their patience.[121] They married in the summer, with Barbara in attendance and her name as witness on their marriage certificate. The law was eventually changed (with some restrictions) in 1986.

Barbara Wootton remained uncorrupted by the conformist traditions of her role as a peer. '"Worst Blemish" of Welfare State' said *The Times* of her lecture topic at Columbia University in New York in 1962, which focused on the continuing phenomenon of poverty. She told her audience that, on the morning she received the invitation to give the lecture, she had seen a sad sight at Victoria station: 'an old lady in a paper-thin mackintosh, worn-down house slippers, and no stockings fumbling in an apparently empty purse for the penny necessary for use of the toilet'.[122] In 1965, she devoted herself to the arguments of the Child Poverty Action Group (CPAG), writing a letter, together with Tom Simey, a social scientist at Liverpool University, to Prime Minister Harold Wilson, which pointed out that at least half a million British children still lived in poverty, and the Government needed to take urgent action.[123] When the CPAG's co-founder, Peter Townsend, later published his survey, *Poverty in the United Kingdom*, Barbara wrote to him to observe that, 'William Beveridge would turn in his grave if he knew that nearly forty years after publication of his report you could write 1,200 pages on Poverty in the UK'.[124] Her book *Contemporary Britain* contained an uncompromising analysis of the static nature of inequality and the failure of the Wilson Government to do anything about it. She railed perpetually at the 'appalling tangle' of the benefits system and the unappealing attempts of governments to claw money back from it, these sins adding two new giants to Beveridge's original five – the Giant of Complexity and the Giant of Government Parsimony.[125] In 1975, she published a Fabian pamphlet, *In Pursuit of Equality*, with its opening sentence, 'I seem to have been pursuing an ideal of equality all my life but have been singularly unsuccessful in catching my prey'. It had been suggested to her that, instead of writing a new prolegomenon on inequality, she might simply have republished the 1941 booklet she wrote for Francis Williams' post-war reconstruction series, *End Social Inequality*. Inequality had not ended, and its abolition had been markedly absent from most recent Labour Party programmes.[126] This was a particularly significant comment for one who had co-authored the Labour Party's policy statement, *Towards Equality: Labour's Policy for Social Justice*, back in 1956.[127] *The Guardian* reported Barbara's 1975 pamphlet under the headline 'Inherited Wealth "Should be Taxed Out of Existence"', noting that its author did not shrink from mentioning her anomalous ownership of a life peerage and occupation of the role of Deputy Speaker in the House of Lords.[128]

Three months after her maiden speech in the House of Lords, Barbara Wootton helped to sponsor a public meeting held at the Free Trade Hall in Manchester: 'The Hydrogen Bomb: What is Happening?'[129] The idea of a campaigning organization in favour of unilateral disarmament and tighter global arms regulation was for her a natural progression from the politics of federalism which she had helped to

promote in the 1930s and 1940s, and it was entirely consistent with the values
of pacifism and opposition to violence which had been her constant companions
ever since her personal experiences of death during the First World War. The
Campaign for Nuclear Disarmament (CND) was formed in 1957 in the Amen
Court rooms of Canon John Collins, Canon of St Paul's Cathedral, and a well-
known political crusader. Kingsley Martin, the *New Statesman*'s editor, called the
meeting; Collins was chosen to chair the new organization and Bertrand Russell to
act as its first President. Barbara Wootton was a member of its Executive Group.
Its inaugural public meeting at Central Hall, Westminster, in February 1958, was
attended by some 5,000 people; Barbara was there as a sponsor, in the company of
friends and co-thinkers – Victor Gollancz, Julian Huxley, Francis Meynell, Ernest
Simon – and many other prominent scientists, academics, writers and artists.[130]
In 1960, along with fifty-seven other 'prominent Britons', and on behalf of CND,
she signed an appeal to the United States Government to renew its suspension of
nuclear weapons testing; Joseph Rotblat, the nuclear physicist who had worked
on the atomic bomb project at Los Alamos during the Second World War, was
a co-signatory.[131] On the 26th anniversary of the nuclear bomb on Hiroshima in
the summer of 1971, her name appeared on a large CND advertisement in *The
Guardian* calling on the British Government to renounce unilaterally all nuclear,
chemical and biological weapons.[132] In the 'Ban the Bomb' demonstrations of the
late 1960s in Britain, she was a source of great irritation to the police because
she took the side of the protesters. Philip Bean was a probation officer at the
time: 'What she would do, is she would have these people up before her who'd
committed an affray or something like that, listen to the evidence and say, "I'm
not qualified to deal with this, I'm biased", and withdraw. So the police had to do
it all again … you could see she enjoyed it hugely.'[133]

Barbara's involvement in the politics of nuclear disarmament got her into trouble
with the Labour Party. In 1962, she added her support to that of other prominent
names for the World Congress for General Disarmament and Peace, which was
to be held in Moscow. The Congress was convened by the World Council of Peace
to promote total disarmament, including the destruction of all nuclear weapons,
as 'the most urgent need of our time'.[134] When Barbara's support of the Moscow
Congress became public, she was written to sternly from Transport House by the
General Secretary, A.L. Williams.[135] The World Council for Peace had been on
the Labour Party's list of proscribed organizations since 1953 as an 'instrument of
Communist propaganda'; support of these bodies was regarded by the National
Executive Committee as incompatible with membership of the Labour Party.
Barbara's reply challenged Williams to provide the relevant conference resolutions

or executive minutes. She argued that joining an organization was very different from supporting a proposal sponsored by it, and observed that putting an end to the arms race was far and away the most important issue facing the world.[136] Williams sent the relevant clauses, and stood his ground, inviting her to be interviewed. She refused. In this fracas, she was in the distinguished company of three others – the Lords Chorley and Russell, and Canon Collins. Lord Chorley and Canon Collins both agreed to meet the National Executive; the former said he did not understand what he was doing when he allowed his name to be associated with the Congress, and the latter refused to withdraw his sponsorship or his intention to go to Moscow as a speaker. Lord Russell said his views were well-known and he was not bothered whether the Labour Party expelled him or not.[137] After much to-ing and fro-ing, the National Executive decided to take no action, but to attempt to amend the constitution so that association with, as well as membership of, communist organizations would not be allowed in future.

Barbara did not write much directly about war and her attitudes to it, although her moral opposition to violence is referred to in many of her writings. Her article 'When is a War Not a War?', published in *New Society* in 1981, dissects the notion of a 'proper war' and asks what is different about killing in such a situation from killing in 'non-war hostilities', guerrilla actions, terrorism and crime. The answer is, very little, and certainly not enough to bear 'the profound moral implications ascribed to them in practice'. Exceptionally wicked killings can occur in all these categories, as can mitigating circumstances. Admitting that her personal difficulty in accepting the notion of a 'proper war' was sharpened by being 'the widow of a soldier killed in the first world war, and subsequently of a conscientious objector who served as a London ambulance driver in the second', she argues that continued acceptance of institutionalized warfare means ever-increasing poverty because all our skills and resources are wasted 'in competitive stockpiling of ever more deadly devices in the paradoxical hope that this alone would guarantee that they would never be used'. Such a *reductio ad absurdum* makes a dose of 'naïve morality' – that war, like all violence, is simply wrong – look a much better option.[138]

Contentious in a different way, but linked to the position of non-violence, was Barbara's campaign to protect the environment. In 1966, she became Chairman of the National Parks (later the Countryside) Commission. Moving to Abinger had restored the sense she had enjoyed as a child in the flat Cambridgeshire fens and under their open skies, and in all those family holidays by the sea and at Abinger Hall with its wild woodlands, which were perfect for childhood games, of the rural landscape as an essential tonic for the stressed human spirit. Although her friends teased her about her concern for footpaths and rights of way – 'She never actually *walked* anywhere so far as I know'[139] – Barbara knew what the countryside meant. She very much wanted the Commission to head a new environmental concern for the preservation of rural Britain, particularly once the 1968 Countryside Act had been passed with its rather buried clause requiring every government department and public authority to have due regard for amenity. Her Commission wrote to another Commission convened under Justice Roskill in 1968 to consider where to locate London's third airport – not *whether* there should be one, but *where* it should be – to remind them of their obligation to consider environmental impact.[140] The Roskill Commission's recommendation that the third airport should be at Foulness on the Essex coast was eventually overturned on environmental grounds. The defeat of the Government's air transport plans signalled a new alliance between environmentalists and economists.[141] This was not a period when many people shared Barbara's belief that 'our abject reverence for technological ingenuity' was a 'characteristic menace of our time'.[142] She admired the Labour Government's 1970 White Paper on the Protection of the Environment, a statement of intent which, unfortunately, proved to be one of the Government's dying acts, so, 'it did not live to reap the discredit of opening a motorway that runs on stilts within twenty feet of people's bedrooms. At least we can say that in regard to the prevention of environmental pollution we have not tried and failed,' she observed acerbically, 'We have never yet seriously tried.'[143] She took the Countryside Commission through a difficult transitional phase to become a more socially aware organization, oversaw its drive to create country parks and picnic sites, and was fearless in sticking to conservation principles.[144] But she found it a very heavy assignment, and a frustrating one, as the Government was not prepared to allow the Commission the money, staff and powers it needed, so she resigned at the end of 1969.[145]

The world was changing, and Barbara Wootton felt an obligation to be an active participant in at least some of these changes. The first successful kidney transplant had taken place in 1954 in the USA, with the first in the UK six years later. The use of organs from one human body to preserve the life of another triggered a wave of ethical and practical disputes, familiar to Barbara, about medical power and the public interest. In 1969, Wilson's Government set up a multidisciplinary Advisory Group on Transplantation Problems. The group was chaired by an eminent doctor, Sir Hector MacLennan, and Barbara was one of its other ten members. They produced a Report in June 1969 which established what are now widely accepted rules for organ transplantation: that two doctors independent of the transplant team should determine death in the donor body; that donors should not be transported between hospitals purely to facilitate transplantation; and that the public should be provided with information, but should not be unduly pressured to become donors.[146] The Group was divided as to just how informed consent should be implemented so as to increase the supply of donor organs. Six members, including Barbara, recommended a system of contracting out, which was already in place in Denmark, France, Israel, Italy and Sweden. But their advice suffered the same fate as that of other such exercises with which Barbara had been involved: the Government did not like it and refused to publish it as a White Paper.[147] Nonetheless, the high standards of ethical conduct the Report recommended had an undoubted and enduring impact on medical practice.[148]

Beyond these campaigns and responsibilities inside and outside the House of Lords, these were for Baroness Wootton the years of multiple honours. By 1985, she had acquired no fewer than thirteen honorary degrees: from the universities of Columbia in New York, and in the UK from Aberdeen, Aston, Bath, Cambridge, Essex, Hull, Liverpool, London, Nottingham, Southampton, Warwick and York. The Columbia degree had arrived in 1954, before her entry to the House of Lords; in the ceremonial procession, two of the other Britons similarly honoured were fellow economists with whom she had not always agreed – Lionel Robbins from the LSE and Dennis Robertson from Cambridge. Barbara 'brought up the rear after the Queen Mother and Mr Dulles'.[149] She would, indeed, have had little in common with many of those with whom she processed in whatever colourful assemblage of robes and hats marked that particular university's tradition. At Liverpool, where she became an honorary doctor of laws in 1960, she was in the company of the art historian Sir Kenneth Clark and the writer Sir C.P. Snow, and four male scientists and engineers; at Aberdeen in 1969, her honourable companions were the American political theorist Professor Robert MacIver and the President of Iceland. Barbara signalled the dominance of men in these ceremonies in the speech she made at the Golden Jubilee dinner of the Cambridge branch of the National Council of Women in 1962: 'My very distinguished friend and old school fellow Dorothy Russell,' she observed, 'was going to get an honorary degree across the Atlantic and when the list of graduates was provided, believe it or not, one of the people concerned on the other side looked down the list and said –"I didn't know Dorothy was a man's Christian name"'.[150] The Cambridge honorary degree was the one that meant the most of all to Barbara. 'It is difficult for me to find adequate expression of the value to me of a reward so far outside any legitimate expectation,' she wrote, unusually clumsily for her, to Professor Sir John Butterfield, Vice-Chancellor of the University of Cambridge, before the ceremony there in 1985.[151] This honour, she said, far outdistanced all its predecessors, even including her American example, and there was a 'special delight' in re-establishing links with her original *alma mater* in the city in which she had been born, educated and married – married, of course, only for the first time, but it was *this* time, like *this* honorary degree, that really counted.

'Barbaram Francesam, Baronissam Wootton de Abinger' – Latin was the language of these ceremonies – had truly made it in a man's world. The degree-less Mrs Wootton, who had endured the insult of having to lecture under a male name in Cambridge in 1921, now seemed to have passed beyond the stage of notoriety to a level of widespread public recognition. 'I have never quite got used to the idea that I can have a degree at all,' she admitted at the University of York presentation ceremony in 1966.[152] In 1969, Girton College made her an Honorary Fellow; in 1970, Bedford College, which had not particularly respected her work in the 1950s, made her both an Honorary Fellow and a Governor. The election to the Bedford College fellowship came at the instigation of her protégé and academic colleague, Professor O.R. McGregor, who sent pointed comments to Dame Mary Smieton, Chair of the Bedford College Council, in December 1968, to the effect that the College's failure to confer any recognition on Barbara Wootton as 'its most distinguished retired Professor' might soon become a matter for unfavourable comment in view of all the other honours being piled on her.[153] The psychiatrists whom Barbara had so robustly criticized on so many occasions decided they would recognize her 'outstanding service to psychiatry' and they made her an Honorary Fellow of the Royal College of Psychiatrists in 1979; she was presented with her certificate when she delivered the prestigious Maudsley Lecture on 'Psychiatry, Ethics and the Criminal Law' in December of that year. In 1985 she was asked to be a Patron of the Institute of Psychiatry. Some years before, in 1967, the American Psychopathological Association had presented her with an award and a medal for distinguished services – though not all psychopathologists had thought her services distinguished when she had offered them in her *Social Science and Social Pathology*. Then, in the Queen's Birthday Honours List in June 1977, her name appeared alongside that of Sir John Gielgud under the title 'Companion of Honour', entitling her to put the initials CH after her name. Gielgud became one for services to the theatre; she, simply, for 'public services'.[154] Frank Field had lobbied Prime Minister James Callaghan to set this honour in motion.[155] The Order of the Companions of Honour is a curious distinction, being awarded for outstanding achievements in the arts, music, science, politics, industry or religion, and to a wider range of people than most other such honours. *The London Gazette* list available on Wikipedia of all those so honoured since 1917 has 238 names on it, 215 of them men.[156] Barbara's name is missing. Twenty-one faces were picked by *The Times* to illustrate the 1977 sample of honours: Barbara, and Doris Speed, the landlady of the Rovers Return in 'Coronation Street', and nineteen men.[157]

The Wootton Society was formed in the same year. This was a student initiative based in the Law Faculty at King's College, London, intended to 'encourage a greater understanding of crime, criminality and the treatment of offenders', through a programme of lectures, visits and voluntary work. Barbara agreed to be its Honorary Patron, although she never managed to attend any of its functions.[158] Despite her altercation with the humanists over abortion law reform, she was made a Humanist Laureate by the international humanist movement in 1983, and her work for world peace was recognized in a Diploma of Honour from the International Order of Volunteers for Peace in 1982.[159] Barbara's receipt of a letter from HRH Prince Philip, Duke of Edinburgh, at Buckingham Palace in 1975 was a less conventional honour.[160] She had given a lecture on 'Fair Pay, Relativities and a Policy for Incomes' at the University of Southampton the previous year, one of a series called the Fawley Foundation Lectures. In it, she had updated the arguments of her book *The Social Foundations of Wage Policy* that the distribution and differentials in wages and incomes in Britain were 'the deposits of a long historical process' featuring social conventions and economic pressures rather than any notion of fairness.[161] What was 'fair' could never be defined in a vacuum. Justice was a matter of clear criteria. En route to the reiteration of her earlier proposal for an Income Gains Tax as a fiscal strategy for reducing income inequality, Barbara took what Prince Philip regarded as an 'unfair and inaccurate swipe at The Queen'. As a previous Fawley lecturer himself, he had been sent a copy of her text and he noted on pages six and seven a reference to a survey of take-home pay of a sample of forty people. The biggest earner was the Queen, followed by the chairman of the Green Shield Stamp Company. Prince Philip's point was that the Queen's Civil List income included her expenses as Head of State.

In 1961, Madam Speaker undertook what she thought then would be her last lecturing tour ('I have become somewhat tired of hearing myself'[162]), to Australia. Her sponsor was Sir John Barry, the 'handsome and imposing', but also progressively-minded, judge of Victoria's Supreme Court.[163] Barry had written a nice review of Barbara's *Social Science and Social Pathology*, and sent it to her before he came to London for a conference in the summer of 1960, suggesting that they meet. The meeting never happened because Barbara could not make it, but in her reply she mentioned she had never visited Australia, but would like to do so.[164] Barry informed the Vice-Chancellor of Melbourne University in November 1960 that Lady Wootton of Abinger was willing to consider an invitation to visit Australia.[165] There followed prolonged negotiations between the universities of Melbourne, Adelaide, New South Wales and Sydney, and the Australian National University in Canberra, about the funding of Barbara's visit, on the principle that her time had to be purchased and therefore paid for (and on her side there was the consideration that being a member of the House of Lords was 'not a very remunerative occupation'[166]). She was pleased that Barry himself would meet her off the flight from England, and wrote to advise him that 'for purposes of easy identification I have a lot of rather frothy white hair', and would probably be wearing a green suit with a light overcoat, and no hat, or only a minimal one.[167]

'I am 64,' she told one of her negotiators, Stan Johnston at the Melbourne Criminology Department, 'and I lead a very strenuous life, and though I have so far enjoyed magnificent health I should not wish to work myself to a frazzle.'[168] Unfortunately, some of the Australians did wish to work her to a frazzle, with evening public lectures piled upon daytime seminars and discussions with politicians and civil servants and lawyers and sociologists and visits to judicial institutions. By the time she climbed off the plane at Adelaide on the last lap of her voyage, Barbara looked 'very tired'.[169] She was due to spend the morning in the Juvenile Courts, and give a public lecture that evening: 'A Social Scientist's Reflections on Law and Justice'. She was in Australia for seven weeks altogether, and she went to Canberra, Sydney and Hobart, as well as Adelaide and Melbourne. She found Tasmania particularly exhausting and it was something of a strain to stay at Government House, being waited on by eleven servants.[170] In Canberra she talked to the Research Students' Association about 'The Future of the Social Sciences'; and in Melbourne she gave lectures to criminology students and women's organizations, and was appointed a special magistrate in the Melbourne Children's Court, so she could observe how they handed out juvenile justice in Australia compared with the UK. Both there and in the Juvenile Court at Alice Springs (where she fitted in some sightseeing), she was impressed by the time taken over individual cases: an hour and a quarter per case as against perhaps ten minutes back home. In this respect, Australian justice was advanced, although it was not so in its treatment of aboriginal people, who were regarded as 'wards of the state'; at the time of Barbara's visit, selling alcohol to or having sexual intercourse with a 'ward of the state' were punishable with a prison sentence.[171]

One very definite benefit of Barbara's Australian trip was getting to know Judge Barry and his family. The two criminologists shared many similar beliefs about the role of the law, especially about the insanity of capital punishment and the importance of alternatives to prison – Barry was an expert on the parole system – and the failure of the law to take motoring offences seriously.[172] Although Barbara did not preserve Barry's letters to her, there is a warm correspondence in his Canberra archives. When Barry died prematurely in 1969, Barbara wrote his obituary in *The Times*. She expressed her admiration for this 'maverick judge', picking out especially two characteristics which could also be descriptions of herself: being 'a constant critic of the judicial process which he had to administer' and being 'acutely sensitive to the relations of law and social conditions, on which he lectured and wrote untiringly'.[173]

The Australian journey did not, however, prove to be the last of Barbara's international tours. In 1963, she went to Liberia; in 1969, she spent a longer period in Japan as a visiting lecturer; and the same year she also went to South Africa. The Liberian trip was at the invitation of the Liberian legislature and in the company of five other (male) members of the British Parliament.[174] Her co-travellers were the Welsh Labour Party politician Ifor Davies, the Conservative Party politician Harold Gurden, the British company director and Conservative Party politician Sir Kenneth Thompson, the Labour MP Edward Milne, and John Cordle, the Conservative MP who was later to achieve media fame through his association with the corrupt businessman John Poulson. Cordle was alleged to have profited financially by promoting Poulson's interests in West Africa, and this was an activity that appears to have started some months after the parliamentary visit to Liberia.[175] The point of the trip was to encourage personal contact between Parliamentarians worldwide (an aim that John Cordle may have interpreted quite literally). Barbara found Liberia quite the strangest country she had ever visited: a mixture of Western progressiveness, Soviet-style repression, and reprobate capitalism. Liberia, meaning 'liberty', had been founded by freed American slaves; a large concession had been granted in 1926 to the American-owned Firestone Plantation Company. Barbara decided that work for the company as a rubber tapper might be an agreeable way to pass one's old age. 'The tapper rises at dawn, which is easy enough in the tropics, and proceeds to score his trees in the plantation. About midday, he collects the juice that has dripped into his bucket, hands it in and is paid, and then his day's work is done. For this he gets a free house, subsidized food and the right to medical care in as up-to-date a hospital as I have seen anywhere.'[176] After they returned from Liberia, Kenneth Thompson wrote to thank her for everything she had done to make the trip pleasurable and successful: 'We all owed you a lot for your tolerance of the manners of five men and/or the splendid examples you repeatedly gave of understanding and harmonising our group'.[177]

The purpose of Barbara's South African trip in 1969 was to give a lecture on academic freedom. This was a topic on which she had kept a keen eye over the years. The year of the South Africa visit was also the year of the Guildford School of Art affair: forty teachers had lost their jobs, allegedly for supporting a 1968 sit-in by students protesting at the poor quality of teaching; *The Guardian* ran an advertisement – signed by 330 leading educationalists, artists, authors, and others, including Barbara Wootton – calling for an public inquiry.[178] In a letter to Shena Simon about her South African invitation, Barbara explained that, 'This lecture is the University's retaliation for being forbidden to be multi-racial. I only stayed five days, but saw enough to be much distressed.'[179] In 1958–60, she had been a signatory of various published appeals by the Defence and Aid Fund of Christian Action against the South African Government's policy of apartheid,[180] and she would later also sign public statements supporting the release of Nelson Mandela and all South African political prisoners.[181] Her South African lecture, 'Universities and Their Problems in the Contemporary World', was published in 1969 by the Academic Freedom Committee of the Students' Representative Council at the University of the Witwatersrand. It is a sensitive combination of general commentary on the role of universities in a modern world, with topics of particular urgency in the South African context – for example, 'racial' discrimination in student selection. She also talked about the relationship between universities and the community. There ought to be one – both links with the local community and a responsibility for the broader one. The latter would embrace a concern for the human effects of the 'worship' of technology and 'the ruthless destruction of the natural environment' which was often a consequence of it. Here Barbara inserted a reference to a new menace of recent concern to her: supersonic air travel – 'enormous sums are now being spent on the production of supersonic passenger aircraft, the only advantage of which will be the subtraction of a few hours from the time required to circumnavigate the globe; and for this the price paid includes not only vast sums of money, but also risks to health from radiation, as well as frequent and extensive exposure of both human and animal populations to deafening noises'.[182]

On the subject of both noise and the impact on the balance of trade, Barbara was about to conduct a personal correspondence with Hugh Conway, the Director of Rolls Royce responsible for the development of Concorde.[183] She had already publicized her role as a patron of the Anti-Concorde project. This had been mounted in 1966 by the environmental campaigner Richard Wiggs, and was affiliated to the Citizens' League Against the Sonic Boom in the USA and the delightfully-named Association Nationale Anti-Bangs of France.[184] Full-page advertisements appeared in *The Times* in January 1968 and *The Guardian* in February 1969,[185] both signed by Barbara, among others, arguing that Concorde should be stopped on grounds of cost and environmental, human and animal damage. Sonic booms gave people heart attacks, caused buildings to shake or collapse, and upset sheep and cattle. The costs of developing Concorde were mounting at about £2 million a week, and there were reports of a design fault in the tail unit.[186] The House of Lords was treated to several corrosive interventions by Barbara on the theme of how on earth a sufficient number of 'these machines' would ever be sold to recoup such an astronomical level of expenditure, and whether anyone would seriously be able to afford to travel on them.[187] Some of Concorde's effects may have been exaggerations, and the topic was of doubtful relevance to Barbara's South African audience, but the Anti-Concorde Project which she supported was instrumental in limiting the development of supersonic air travel and bringing about its ultimate demise, and it stands as an early example of the organized promotion of environmental issues.[188]

Barbara's attack on air travel was a little disingenuous in the light of her own use of it. The same comment might be made of her use of cars, but then rationalism and fun are not always congenial bedfellows. Japan Airlines' inaugural flight from London to Tokyo over the North Pole took place on a Douglas DC8 in the summer of 1961, and Barbara Wootton was on it. Her friend William Haley, remembering her long-term ambition to see more of the Far East, had planted in the head of the Japanese Ambassador the purely frivolous idea of inviting Barbara. Her companions on the DC8 were not academics, but travel officers and aeronautical journalists. Barbara was the token woman before they were joined by three beauty queens from Denmark, Iceland and Norway: Barbara liked Miss Denmark the best, because she was the most intelligent.[189] They had a week of the customary tourist exposure to a menu of temples, gardens, tea ceremonies and Geisha girls, before flying over the North Pole again. Then, at the end of 1968, the Japanese Minister of Justice, Kichinosuke Saigo, wrote with an invitation to be a visiting lecturer at the Asia and Far East Institute for the Prevention of Crime and the Treatment of Offenders in Tokyo,[190] an organization that had been set up in 1962 by agreement between the United Nations and the Japanese Government to promote 'the sound development of criminal justice systems' – an aim close to Barbara Wootton's own heart – in Asia and the Pacific Region. Her mission in 1969 was to teach on a training course for twenty women working in 'correctional services'. It was the first such course the Institute had ever run solely for women. The students came from Ceylon, East Pakistan, India, Indonesia, Japan, Korea, Nepal, the Philippines, Thailand and Vietnam. They were all, reported Barbara in a letter to Shena Simon, pioneers in their own penal services 'but not all battle-axes like our feminist pioneers!'.[191] 'Each is more beautiful than the last', she told Vera Seal in a chatty letter, 'and they are all pioneering in destroying the image of the repressed oriental woman'.[192] She was particularly impressed by one from Saigon who had a husband and five children, and was trying to set up a social work service for abandoned children in a war zone. During her month-long stay in Tokyo, Barbara was provided with travel and living expenses, and a small furnished cottage in the Institute's grounds. She was followed everywhere by a shadow who had very little English and would not allow her to walk anywhere unaccompanied. 'So I spend a good deal of ingenuity in trying to give her the slip. I even got to the supermarket on my own and bought her some sweets as she had given me a pair of Japanese slippers. But alas one cannot win; she immediately bought some more chocolates for me. Most conversation seems to consist of exchange of compliments and I find it difficult to keep up.'[193] Barbara looks very stern and wise in the formal photographs of her visit, a redoubtable middle-aged woman (actually she was seventy-two) with pearls and a lifetime of experience. She fitted in some sightseeing to the Old Imperial Palace and the Karyn Ji Temple in Kyoto. There were a few social occasions, but alcohol did not flow freely. She discovered that the Institute's Director served whisky in his private residence, so, 'I plucked up courage to ask where I could buy a bottle. Unfortunately this resulted in his insisting on giving me one. As he gets them duty free at about 25/- and they are nearly £6 in the shops perhaps it was as well, but how will I make it last three weeks?'[194] She also much regretted her inability to accompany the students on their visits to various penal institutions; it was not considered appropriate for her to go, and instead she had to have lunch and go to the theatre with the British Ambassador.

In 1971, she decided that animals would be a nice change from their Lordships – 'at least they wouldn't be able to talk about the Common Market'[195] – and she undertook a safari in East Africa. It was a great success: 'Lying on my bed,' boasted her postcard to Vera Seal, 'I can see elephants and cranes drinking in a nearby pool'.[196] Her month-long tourist trip to China the following year was less restful. The trip was organized by the Society for Anglo-Chinese Understanding; Barbara and her twenty co-travellers paid for themselves. One of her co-travellers was the painter and peace campaigner Vera Delf, who somewhere in China saved her from an episode of serious scalding.[197] Barbara came back with 174 photographs. There are several of her: drinking Jasmine tea (perhaps the source of the scalding?); washing her hands in an enamel bowl ('reception ablutions'); one with a Chinese guide against the splendid panorama of the Great Wall; in another, she reposes on the 'forest of pillars' in Sian with her hands resting on a stone animal – 'tortoise the symbol of longevity' she wrote against this one in the meticulous list she kept. They went to Nanking, Peking, Shanghai, Tsinan and Wusih as well as Sian, seeing all the usual tourist sites: pagodas, monasteries, gardens, markets, tombs; in Peking, the Great Hall of the People, 'Tien an Men' Square, the Ming tombs, the Temple of Heaven, the Summer Palace. But they also fitted in four operas and concerts, nine factories, four educational institutions, two museums, a prison, a hospital, the Shanghai docks, a housing estate, a tree nursery, a Neolithic site, and a number of communes. Barbara saw children learning acupuncture, people doing callisthenics in the parks, and women mending shoes, picking cotton, spinning silk and unloading stones. She thought that most of the Chinese she met were so thoroughly immersed in the ideology of Marxist-Leninism, a phenomenon 'comparable only to a massive religious conversion', that their knowledge of, and interest in, the world outside China was minimal. The key question was whether China's young men and women, nourished on a diet of 'stale opiates', would be able to avoid the excesses of the West: the hideous cities, the choking pollution, and the degrading social and economic inequalities.[198] Barbara took notes on wages and prices, the working conditions, and the retirement ages and relative statuses of men and women. She noted approvingly that the income hierarchy of the West seemed almost totally absent in China; that the University Library in Peking contained a copy of her Hamlyn lectures; that there seemed to be fewer military guards around than in the USSR, and the soldiers were not visibly armed; that the animals (including the donkeys) appeared well-kept, and the people generally well-fed; and that there was very little litter, though there were flies, quite a lot of spitting, and, of course, a multitude of bicycles.[199] Most impressively for someone with her interest in the harms that could be wreaked by patronising experts, there were no professional social workers. 'Street Committees' composed mainly of retired women ran childcare centres, taught domestic hygiene, supported families in trouble, and disciplined the misbehaving young: 'Thus it is the grandmother, rich in experience of life, who replaces the college-trained social worker'.[200]

Few seventy-five-year-olds would have been able to manage such a trip, although she did come back from it very exhausted.[201] Barbara's energy reminds one of the travels of her mother, Adela, and her aunts, Juliet and Fanny, in their old age. Fanny had visited South Africa at the age of seventy-five, travelling 2,000 miles on her own up country. Adela had taken in Russia, a dozen other countries and a solo Amazon cruise, all well beyond the age when women were expected to have settled down to a safely domestic retirement. The concept of retirement was quite alien to Barbara. It was also rather frightening: in 1981, she confessed to a reporter from *The Guardian* her dread of being idle after a long life of influence and action.[202] There was not much chance of that. As well as her travels, and her House of Lords work, and a continued stream of publications and correspondence, she retained her role on the Advisory Council of the Cambridge Institute of Criminology until 1985, when she was eighty-eight; she took on the Vice-Presidency of the Policy Studies Institute, aged eighty-one in 1978; and in the late 1970s, she joined businessman Campbell Adamson in various family policy initiatives. Her lecturing timetable remained full and eclectic in its range: from the normal university and public lectures to attendance at an anachronistic outfit called the Lunchtime Comment Club. The Club, which still exists, is intended to allow 'professional, business and retired people' to talk four or five times a year over 'a congenial meal'; in 1973, when Barbara was a guest speaker, its meetings were held at the

Connaught Rooms in Piccadilly.[203] The list of names on the Club's website leans in the Tory direction, and, although the website declares that 'ladies are especially welcome', Barbara Wootton's name is not on its list of past speakers.[204]

As well as continuing to speak, Barbara went on writing, of course. Aside from the books – *Social Science and Social Pathology* (1959), *Crime and the Criminal Law* (1964), *In a World I Never Made* (1967), *Contemporary Britain* (1971), *Incomes Policy* (1974) and *Crime and Penal Policy* (1978) – there were many articles on crime and justice, economic policy and social welfare. She was a regular contributor to the weekly journal *New Society*, pouring out articles and book reviews, including a long appraisal of a new book by her opponent in the 1930s debate about economic planning, Frederick Hayek.[205] Her favourite topic – the need for a sensible incomes and pay policy – continued to appear in different formats until she was well into her eighties.[206] She wrote introductions to other people's books: to the published version of a doctoral thesis she had been involved in guiding over many years on *Salaries in the Public Services in England and Wales*, the first 'systematic review' of the topic;[207] to Margery Spring-Rice's classic *Working-Class Wives*, first published in 1939: 'Contemporary social reformers' she observed in that new Introduction, 'will reflect whether this book merely portrays the Dark Ages from which we have now happily emerged, or whether ... our descendants will be equally shocked by a corresponding chronicle of a working woman's life today'.[208]

Her media career continued. She took part in a number of 'Panorama' television programmes – on thalidomide, on the death penalty, and in 1978 the one on prison, which had led her to question the use the BBC made of evidence.[209] London Weekend Television interviewed her with Lord Soper for a programme in 1972, 'People with a Purpose', and for another, 'Conscience Without God', in 1975. She had a series of encounters with the broadcaster Robin Day. In 1977, she appeared in one of his 'These Twenty-five Years' programmes, discussing crime with Sir David Napley, the Tory solicitor with an interest in miscarriages of justice; and, in 1980 and 1982, there were two episodes of Day's 'Question Time', the first with William Rees-Mogg, William Waldegrave and Tessa Jowell, the second with Norman Fowler, Ken Livingstone and Becky Tinsley. Audrey Bradley, who worked for the BBC on 'Question Time', remembered Day and Wootton's interaction: 'Robin was very hard to please when it came to women on the programme, but when it came to Barbara, that was absolutely fine ... He had a great deal of respect for her'. Audrey was a neighbour of Barbara's in Surrey: 'When Barbara was coming on the programme I told them I knew her and the first time she came, and the subject of crime obviously came up and money and so forth, and she told the entire nation that she kept money hidden in her books in her quite extensive bookcases, and I remember coming back in the car and saying, "Barbara, I don't think that's a very good idea"'.[210]

Barbara enjoyed her media appearances and she minded when they began to dry up. She had actually solicited the invitation to appear on 'Question Time' by writing to Robin Day and reminding him that she had on several occasions taken part in the radio programme 'Any Questions?'. They had quite an exchange about it. 'Your name was certainly on our list of possible participants,' Day said in answer to Barbara's enquiry, 'but I think it was felt that this programme, which unlike "Any Questions?" includes vigorous audience participation, might involve too much hurly-burly for a person of your eminence.'[211] Barbara's reply was firm: 'I don't think any problems should arise. What you generously called my "eminence" (which I take to be a euphemism for age) is hardly relevant to possible "hurly-burly", as I generally prefer discussion with an audience to my own monologues, and you have already had several people more eminent than myself.'[212]

The last decades of Barbara's life were a time of mixed achievement and loss: not just the loss of old affiliations, but of people she loved. The trio of deaths that had shaken her as a teenager was repeated in the years 1959–1966 when her nanny, the faithful Pie; George; and the Other Barbara all died. Of these three, only The Pie's death was not premature: she died at the age of ninety-one, in Lynchfield Hospital in Somerset, grateful for the plant Barbara had given her, which lasted a long time in flower before new little leaves started shooting up, and for the gift of money: 'I am,' said The Pie in her last letter to Barbara, 'nicely comfortable & do very well. It is better for me.'[213] The Pie was buried the same day as John Foster Dulles, with whom Barbara had ceremonially processed at Columbia University in 1954 – 'a coincidence which provoked much reflection as to the sources of human fame and the quality of human greatness'.[214] Barbara and her brother, Neil, placed a moving announcement of The Pie's death in *The Times*: 'On 22nd May, 1959, Elizabeth Haynes ('the Pie') aged 91, once the nanny and for over 60 years the beloved friend of Neil Adam and Barbara Wootton'.[215] George, whose departure from Barbara's life had been kept a secret from The Pie, developed cancer of the larynx in 1962 and he died, aged sixty, in January 1964. Barbara helped to care for him, and it is her name that appears on the death certificate as the person registering the death. When she told friends of George's illness, she observed that there were practical and emotional complications in the situation because they had not lived together for some years, although they remained close.[216] Terry Morris remembers Barbara coming to dinner one night during the period when George was ill: 'My youngest daughter wanted to sit up to meet her, and George was dying and she had just come straight from the hospital, and I remember her taking Catherine on her knee and just weeping silently … she had a side to her and a gentleness to her which wasn't often on public show'.[217]

Her letter to Shena Simon about George's illness ended on the positive note that in Abinger, 'everything is sunny, calm and beautiful' and that she was glad to be living with her friend and neighbour, Barbara Kyle, whom Shena had met there.[218] But, during the long months of George's dying, Barbara Kyle was herself diagnosed with breast cancer. She had surgery in 1963, when the outlook was considered hopeful. However, further operations proved necessary, and in 1965 she spent two months in hospital twenty miles away, so all Barbara Wootton's spare time was consumed in journeys there and back. 'Now she is home,' wrote Barbara Wootton to Shena Simon in May 1965, 'but wholly confined to a wheelchair, with only one good leg and one good arm, and as we have no help, I am still much tied. Everyone says the outlook for her is "quite unpredictable", but she is rather wretched and depressed – understandably enough! – though in less pain than before her latest (fifth) operation.'[219] According to friends and neighbours, Barbara Wootton looked after Barbara Kyle 'most wonderfully'.[220] For six months during this unhappy time, she journeyed from one hospital – the one in London George was in – to the other, in Surrey, where Barbara Kyle was. When Barbara Kyle died, aged fifty-six, in a private nursing home, Barbara Wootton was the sole executor and inheritor of her will. She had lost someone she cared for deeply, someone who had for nearly a decade been a most congenial companion in the business of daily living. Ironically, she had always supposed that it would be the other way round, and it would be Barbara Kyle who looked after *her* in her declining years. Barbara Wootton's experience as a carer for the dying led to her remarks, at the RPA annual dinner in 1968, about the unwelcome interventions of religion in the whole process. 'I have suffered very much in recent years from seeing people to whom I am deeply attached, very ill, and in fact, dying in hospitals. And I have been infuriated by the intrusions of the clergy. I have been reduced to saying, "Excuse me, but I don't think I know you."'[221]

'For four consecutive years therefore,' wrote the bereaved Barbara in her autobiography, 'I have watched the two people who have meant most to me in the second half of my life fight long-drawn-out, losing battles against incurable disease'.[222] The result of these losses was to thin her attachment to life: she developed a feeling that she was now merely a spectator. The green loneliness of High Barn started to oppress her. She did not like being there on her own. As she confided to her friend William Haley: 'Neither do I now feel that there is anything left that I really want to work for: I don't in fact look forward at all and am still liable to violent depressions. How people survive who are widowed and have nothing but their family life I can't imagine.'[223] She herself had chosen to live without much of a connection to her family of origin. 'She almost never spoke about her family'.[224] The only relatives she saw regularly were her cousin's son Arthur Hetherington, who had been a page at her wedding to Jack Wootton, and his wife Margaret. Arthur was the first chairman of the British Gas Corporation, a man of left-wing views with whom Barbara enjoyed a good argument. The Hetheringtons' flat in Connaught Square was a convenient respite for Baroness Wootton on days when the House of Lords sat late, and it was also sufficiently warm (the gas connection?). Barbara hated the cold. Her brother Neil died in 1973, closely followed by his eccentric wife, Winifred. It was a truncated family – James and Adela's union producing three children but only two grandchildren. Nonetheless, there was a great-niece and a great-nephew and their children whom Barbara Wootton could have claimed as in some sense her own family. She did not: these were people whom, as she confessed to a journalist in 1977, she did not know at all.[225]

Had she known them, she would have discovered at least one story to gladden her heart. Neil's son Arthur had married, late in life, a teacher called Maggie, and they sustained a quietly eccentric life by the coast in Essex. Having no children themselves, they chose to sponsor the education of various African children through the Canon Collins Educational Trust. Since Barbara knew Collins via the CND connection, it seems possible that Arthur consulted her about this. But she apparently did not follow the amazing story of one of Arthur and Maggie's sponsored children, Elliott Lushaba. One of six children, he was the son of a poor Swazi farm worker family. His secondary education and subsequent training in electrical and electronic engineering, including a two-year teaching course in Germany and an advanced course in the UK, was funded by Arthur and Maggie. When Elliott married, Arthur and Maggie sent gifts, and when his first child, Nombulelo, was born, they paid for a family visit to the UK. The two families stayed in touch throughout the births of three more children. In 1991 Arthur and Maggie visited Africa and stayed in the Lushabas' home. When Arthur died in 2006, both the Lushabas and the Canon Collins Educational Trust were left money in his will. 'I was like their beloved son', said Elliott.[226] Why Barbara chose to remove herself from the possibility of knowing this inspiring story is a mystery.

The same year in which she became entitled to put the letters CH (for Companion of Honour) after her name, Barbara's friends held a very grand eightieth birthday party for her. The event was formally given by Gordon Brunton, Director of Times Newspapers – allowing the use of Thomson House in central London. It was orchestrated by 'Mac', Professor McGregor, from his office as Chairman of the Royal Commission on the Press, who by then had become Lord McGregor of Durris, sharing Barbara's lordly robes – the cheap

version, with synthetic ermine.[227] The party was presided over by Prime Minister
James Callaghan, he who had so cavalierly rejected Barbara's words of wisdom
on cannabis in 1968, and was held a few days before her actual birthday,
because Callaghan had to do something with the Queen on that date.[228] In the
photographs of the party which are preserved in a big red book, Callaghan gazes
almost fondly down at Barbara as they grasp their wineglasses and she holds
forth on some important matter. She looks in her element, adorned in a red
and black lace dress, with a choker round her neck, and her white hair well-
coiffed. On the rostrum, with her arms folded, thanking them all, she appears
very serious; cutting the elaborate birthday cake needed a large knife and much
concentration, but in the other photographs she is smiling and animated. Here
is a woman who feels she has got somewhere and has done something, and that
the world which has not always welcomed her with open arms has finally realized
the error of its ways. 'Growing Old Successfully' ran *The Observer* report of the
party.[229] The birthday and the party were announced in *The Times*, and there was
a sizeable tranche of congratulatory letters, cards and telegrams, including from
George Wright's sister-in-law Florrie, and from Richard Titmuss's wife, Kay.

The celebrants at Thomson House were a motley crew, reflecting the breadth
of Barbara's work as a social scientist, magistrate, BBC Governor, writer and
politician. Present were eight Right Honourables and/or Lords, four Sirs or Ladies,
three Professors, one QC and fourteen plain Mr's, Mrs's or Miss's (though one Mrs
was the Prime Minister's wife). Len Murray, the Labour politician and union leader
was there, as was Lord Hunt, who had led the 1953 British expedition to Mount
Everest, but was better known to Barbara as the first Chairman of the Parole Board.
Among the guests were Charles Hill, the doctor and television executive who had
negotiated an independent role for GPs at the start of the NHS in 1948; the Earl
of Listowel, a colourful Labour member of the House of Lords, the first Governor-
General of Ghana at the time of Barbara's visit there; barrister Elwyn Jones, who
prosecuted the Moors murderers and became Harold Wilson's Attorney-General;
the British writer Anthony Sampson, most famous for his *Anatomy of Britain*, a
best-selling exposé of the country's class structure, a man who claimed to have
been pushed by Barbara Wootton in his pram;[230] her publisher, Charles Furth of
Allen & Unwin; Louis Blom-Cooper from the days of her work for the Advisory
Council on the Penal System; Peter Townsend, champion of Barbara's position on
poverty and inequality; and her friend Campbell Adamson and his wife, Mimi.
The young Frank Field came, being notable in the photographs for the quantity
of his hair compared with that of the other male attendees. The women included
Margot Jefferys, by then a professor, who had headed Barbara's shortlived Social

Research Unit at Bedford College in the early 1950s. Reg Hookway, who took over from Barbara as head of the Countryside Commission, was on the list, with his wife Ethel, and, Vera Seal, of course, despite her dislike of social occasions, and two of Barbara's Surrey neighbours, Bridget and David Trotter. We do not know what they all talked about, but there certainly was a lot they *could* have talked about. The talking was helped by the wining and dining: the Puligny-Montrachet and Château Giscours wines, the Moët et Chandon champagne, and the brandy; consommé, coquilles St Jacques, filet de boeuf with courgettes and new potatoes, and a soufflé Grand Marnier to finish. It was a fitting establishment recognition of a woman who never ceased to challenge the establishment both from within – always a solid revolutionary strategy – and from the hinterland of a truly critical life.

16

Incurable Patient

It is said that as people grow older they become more like themselves. In the last years of Barbara Wootton's long life, the focus of her interest and activity, her philosophy of human action, was increasingly on that secular humanism which she had arrived at earlier in her life through a process of self-guided rationalist thought. In her view, reason and the principles of scientific enquiry teach one that this world, and the human beings in it, are all we know we have. It is on this basis that we have to build some system of morality which sets standards for human conduct. She was very clear about this, and about the fundamental principle of any such moral system: that of respect for human life – for the lives of all individual human beings, equally. Rationalism, humanism and socialism were the three 'isms' that she, who so much disliked all 'isms',[1] depended on for the passion that drove her many decades of engagement in the world of knowledge and public policy.

She believed above all in the power of human intelligence, released from the fetters of superstition, magic and religious idolatry. Interviewed for the humanist journal *The Freethinker* in her seventies, and asked which 'ism' she preferred – agnosticism or atheism – she said: 'I don't much mind ... I'm quite prepared to be called an atheist but I suppose that intellectually we *ought* to say agnostic since there is no proof either way as to the existence of the deity'.[2] Barbara had abandoned religion in her early twenties as the result of an 'intellectual transition'.[3] She had been brought up in a 'normal, averagely Christian home': Adela and James Adam had taken their children to church, Barbara had gone through a period of 'considerable religiosity and devoutness' as an adolescent, and the church wedding to Jack Wootton when she was twenty had been at her own wish,[4] although by then, as she saw the terrible cruelties of war around her, faith had begun to be replaced by doubt; and, when Jack was killed a few weeks later, doubt gained the upper hand. As an agnostic (or an atheist), she was more outspoken than many others who shared the same philosophy. It was important, she said at the annual dinner of the National Secular Society in 1967, that humanists in the public eye should stick their necks out. Members of the House of Lords could not be sacked for what they said, so people like her and Lord Willis, another notable humanist, had nothing to lose by sticking their necks out, which is what they had done, and remarkably their heads were still attached to their bodies.[5]

Some of Barbara's debates about religion gave her opponents a hard time. In a Rediffusion Television programme 'Dialogue with Doubt' in 1967, she had confronted the radical clergyman Bruce Kenrick with the impossibility of proving the existence of God. He answered with the example of marriage: marriage was an act of faith; he could not prove he had met his wife and fallen in love with her. No, said Barbara, but you could bring your wife here, and I could see her, and if necessary I could ask her to produce her marriage certificate. 'But you can't bring Christ here and show him to me.' It was not for the individual believer to introduce Christ, responded Kenrick rather weakly; rather, it was for Christ to introduce himself. 'So why hasn't he approached Barbara Wootton?' inquired Peter Snow, who had been charged with the delicate task of arbitrating this debate. Christ is present in every man, tried Kenrick; in that case, said Barbara, 'He conceals himself very well in some men; I think you'd agree'. She was adamant: the Christian narrative is a cosy story people tell themselves and each other to help them with their struggle through life. Cosy stories are not about truthfulness and integrity, and it is these that matter above everything else.[6]

A humanist for Barbara Wootton was someone who does not think that there are any supernatural forces in life. The universe has to be accepted as a 'totally inexplicable mystery'.[7] All we know for certain are those things we can perceive with our senses, those facts that are centred on the existence of human personalities. Thus, humanism greatly respects the sanctity and dignity of individual human life. But – and it is an immensely big but – humanism is not *amoral*: it has its own strong moral codes. An extraordinary feature of human beings, yet one we take for granted, is their innate capacity to experience a sense of moral obligation. While a secular society demands a secular morality, a secular morality also demands an act of faith. In Barbara's case, this involved the Benthamite principle that happiness is better than misery: the greatest happiness of the greatest number. There was no evidence for this, it was just something she had worried her way through to, something she chose to believe.[8] The moral obligation to promote happiness and prevent misery, and a belief in the dignity and worth of human life and social equality were the main pointers that had given her life direction.[9] Crucially, the requirement for social equality actually *derived* from the principle of respect for individual personality, as the latter must always imply 'hatred of the artificial distinction between one human being and another created by a class hierarchy'.[10]

There was, however, she acknowledged, a slight problem with the moral obligation to promote human happiness, one that had been pointed out to her by the political philosopher Bernard Williams: human happiness would sometimes be greatly promoted by assassinating certain people who stood in its path. This made the principle of 'the unique value of human life' even more important.[11] She found it very puzzling that Christians could oppose abortion and euthanasia but defend warfare: 'Either life is sacred, or it is not'.[12] It seemed to other people a paradox, but not to her, that humanism invokes what is actually a *higher* value for human life than the religious alternatives.

In 1980, at the age of eighty-three, Barbara Wootton stuck her neck out again when the Council for Secular Humanism, based in the USA, issued a Secular Humanist Declaration, a five-page document calling for science and reason, and moral standards derived from logic and empirical experience, rather than religion, to solve the problems of human society. This declaration had a long list of sixty-one distinguished signatories, including Isaac Asimov, Francis Crick, Milovan Djilas, Albert Ellis, Dora Russell, B.F. Skinner and Barbara Wootton. It was essentially a response to the rise of religious fundamentalism in its various forms: literalist and doctrinaire Christianity; uncompromising Moslem clericalism in the Middle East and Asia; the reassertion of orthodox authority by the Roman Catholic papal hierarchy; nationalist religious Judaism; and the reversion to obscurantist religions in Asia. Its strident and timely statement made the front page of *The New York Times* and got much media coverage worldwide.[13]

Barbara Wootton's century, the twentieth century, was the one that saw the liberalization of many legal restraints on people's rights to choose and control the manner of their lives. In the West, women were, by the time she died in 1988, if not exactly liberated, then at least allowed their personhood in relation to the suffrage, work in the non-domestic world, ownership of property and of their own bodies, and the right to request equality in personal relationships and duties of care to others. None of these had been the case in the 1890s when she was born. Although the devastations of war continued throughout and beyond the twentieth century, in Britain capital punishment was abolished; suicide lost its status as a crime; adult homosexuality became a personal matter rather than a criminal offence; the restrictions on legal abortion were relaxed; contraception became available outside marriage; and discrimination on grounds of race or sex entered the statute book as unjustifiable actions. In many of these important revolutions Barbara's own rational intelligence played a leading role, but the result fell a long way short of the society she would like to have seen created. Poverty and inequality still existed, and human beings persisted in devoting an inordinate amount of time to idiotically expensive and irrational plans. She would like to resign from the human race, but had not found a way of doing so.[14] Since resignation was not possible, the work had to go on. Perhaps she was increasingly in default mode – after all, what else was there to do *apart* from work? From her late seventies until her death at ninety-one, her mind increasingly followed her body in dwelling on the fact and implications of human illness and mortality; nonetheless, there she was, still working, and still making a difference.

In 1976, the seventy-eight-year-old Baroness Wootton introduced a Private Member's Bill, the Incurable Patients Bill, into the House of Lords. Its main purpose was to protect people with incurable illnesses from avoidable suffering by allowing them to receive whatever quantity of drugs was necessary to relieve their pain and physical distress. Any such patients who brought about their own death by drug overdoses or other intentional actions were to be regarded as having died by 'misadventure'. Barbara defended her Bill not as 'a euthanasia bill', rather as simply providing people with the right to ask for pain-killing drugs even if these caused unconsciousness; the right to refuse intensive care treatment; and the ability to spell out procedures and safeguards for advance declarations of such wishes.[15] The fact that, eleven years into the twenty-first century, we are still debating the moral and legal proprieties of what is now called 'assisted suicide' or, better, 'assisted dying',[16] is one indication of the radical nature of Barbara's last major attempt to have an impact on law-making. Her own chosen term for assisting dying was 'self-deliverance'. In her speech moving that the Bill be read for a second time, Barbara said she was well aware that the unfortunate press publicity accused her of taking the first step towards euthanasia. But rational human beings, having taken one step, consider whether they should take another; if this were not so, every glass of wine taken with their Lordships' lunch would set them on the path to alcoholism.[17] Having outlined for them the Bill's main clauses, she referred to the remarks of one correspondent who had suggested that the origins of the Bill lay in her own emotional reaction to personal and therefore atypical experiences. 'That is not the case,' she answered resolutely. 'Had I been speaking purely from my own personal experience, I should have introduced this Bill at least ten years ago.'[18] During the previous fifteen years, nine of her relatives, friends or former colleagues had all died of various forms of cancer. In seven of these cases certainly, and in all probably, full relief from pain and distress was not obtained. Moreover, in the two cases in which she was most involved (the deaths of George Wright and Barbara Kyle, though of course she did not tell their Lordships this), her encounters with two private nursing homes, six NHS hospitals, four consultants and one dedicated GP informed her that there was enormous variation between different medical practitioners and institutions in the care of the terminally ill. Her Bill would attempt to even out this variation, to give everyone the same right to ensure in advance that in certain circumstances he or she would not be kept alive just because modern medical technology offers that possibility.[19]

'Euthanasia' from the Greek 'eu' and 'thanatos' means 'good death'. The practice of helping people in incurable pain and distress to die has a long history in many civilizations and cultures. Indeed, one of the objections to Barbara's Bill was that, in Britain, new legislation was unnecessary, since doctors already practised, quietly, without making a great fuss about it, what the Bill preached. There had been three previous attempts to introduce a Bill legalizing assisted dying in 1936, 1950 and 1969. The first was the brainchild of a retired public health doctor, C. Killick Millard, a maverick character who championed such causes as temperance, cremation, birth control, and the sterilization of the 'eugenically unfit'.[20] 'A Plea for Legalisation of Euthanasia', a talk given in Leicester in 1931, resulted not only in the first draft Bill but the formation in 1935 of a Voluntary Euthanasia Society (VES). Millard's plea caught the public's attention in a climate spattered with an increasing number of cases of 'mercy killings', both in Europe and the USA, which demonstrated how random the law's response could be. For example, in Michigan, in 1920, Frank Roberts was convicted of murder and sentenced to life imprisonment, solitary confinement and hard labour, because he had helped his wife, who was suffering from multiple sclerosis and had already tried to kill herself, to die by administering a substance called 'Paris Green' containing arsenic. In Britain, fourteen years later, sixty-two-year-old May Brownhill killed her thirty-one-year-old 'imbecile' son with tablets and gas; she was about to have a serious operation and there was no-one else to care for him. She was sentenced to die for 'mercy murder' but, within two days, the Home Secretary had pardoned her; she had her operation and went on holiday with her husband.[21]

It was not until 1969 that a Bill legalizing assisted dying was voted on in the British Parliament. By this time, the British Humanist Association, the National Secular Society and the National Council for Civil Liberties – all organizations with which Barbara Wootton was associated – had come out to join the VES on the side of changing the law. Barbara became a Vice-President of the VES in 1985. During the 1960s, opinions about assisted dying had been severely shaken by the thalidomide scandal, but Lord Raglan's Voluntary Euthanasia Bill of 1969 was rejected, following a big campaign led by the right-wing politician Norman St John-Stevas.[22]

Barbara Wootton's own Incurable Patients Bill was rejected in the House of Lords by 62 votes to 23, a worse result than for Lord Raglan's 1969 Bill. She admitted that her Bill had been poorly drafted, although many such Bills did eventually succeed.[23] What particularly depressed her was that doctors connected with hospices for the dying had actively lobbied against the Bill, arguing that methods of pain relief had improved so much that no dying person need suffer. Maybe so in *your* hospices, she retorted, but in ordinary hospitals up and down the country they do not always do it so well, and the terminal pneumonias which used to be known as 'the old man's friend' are 'thwarted by the administration of the latest antibiotics by enthusiastic young doctors'.[24] When her Bill was rejected, she was inundated with letters from people with distressing stories about 'what they regarded as the cruel prolongation of the lives of their incurably ill friends and relatives by the increasing ingenuity of modern medicine'.[25]

After this failure, she declared she did not have the energy to try again,[26] but she did, in fact, work with a barrister and with the VES two years later to draft a further Bill, which was to be called the Suspension of Medical Treatment Bill. It seems that there was a disagreement about the wording, which in all such legislation was complex, and the Bill never saw the light of day.[27] Attempts to reform the law in Britain on assisted dying were blocked by various episodes of adverse publicity in the late 1970s and early 1980s: the British journalist Derek Humphry published a much-discussed book called *Jean's Way* about his wife's choice to end her life with his help in the terminal stages of breast cancer; in 1981, two of the VES's workers, Nicholas Reed and Mark Lyons, were tried and imprisoned for a number of cases of assisting people to commit suicide (Lyons was also charged with a case of technical murder). Barbara wrote a column in *The Sunday Times* about the Humphry case,[28] and she corresponded with Reed during his two and a half years in prison. He had come to see her in High Barn in 1978 to discuss the wording of a possible new Bill;[29] in prison, he read a couple of her books on penal policy and discussed her ideas with other inmates.[30] The VES, temporarily renamed Exit, had adopted Barbara Wootton's term, and produced a contentious *Guide to Self-Deliverance*. In 1982, the Attorney-General deemed the *Guide* in contravention of the 1961 Suicide Act and ruled that distribution should stop.[31]

To her friend Shena Simon, Barbara had expressed the opinion in 1966 that she did not expect to have a very long life – none of her family had got past eighty, so whatever life remained to her was of the nature of an epilogue, and she would be content if it proved to be a short one.[32] In the event, it was a long one, twenty years of both old and new diversions which continued well into her late eighties. For example, in 1982, she arranged for a group of Andy Croft's WEA students to tour the House of Lords; Croft and she had stayed in touch after he had incorporated her novel *London's Burning* in his review of 1930s utopian fiction. He was still trying to find a publisher who would produce a new edition of her book.[33] She took up the issue of war service and university pensions, challenging the regulation that for war service to count towards a university pension, the job needed to have been started before 30 June 1950 – far too early for some service personnel who might not have completed their undergraduate degrees until then.[34] The same year, she subscribed to a new initiative, to save the Regent's Park site of Bedford College from extinction; the college was merging with Royal Holloway College out in Egham, Surrey, and a campaign was mounted to keep hold of the Regent's Park site as a continuing base for a separate Bedford College identity. Barbara was a member of a forty-strong committee of dons, governors, students, and ex-students, which ultimately failed in holding on to the site.[35] In 1984, she signed a letter to *The Guardian* launching the 'Liberty Campaign' of the National Council for Civil Liberties; it had been fifty years since the formation of that organization, yet the need for a pressure group to defend civil rights remained frighteningly acute.[36] The following year, she acted as a referee for an research grant application to the Economic and Social Research Council by the sociologist and poverty campaigner Peter Townsend (unfortunately, he failed to get it).[37] Around the same time, sociologist Bob Pinker asked her to speak at a big Community Care conference. 'She said, "Oh, I'll do it for you, Bob," but she said they must send a car to Abinger, and "they must take me back and I can only speak for twenty minutes because after that I'll run out of energy".' (She was eighty-eight.) Apparently, she put on an absolutely bravura performance.[38] She was quite herself, too, in the two television interviews she did in 1984, one with MP Ann Clwyd, 'Women of our Century,'[39] and the other a rather gruelling exposure to three journalists in 'Face the Press'.[40] There is no diminution of her radicalism in her last publications, just an accelerated impatience with political resistance to what are obviously (her) sound and sensible ideas. In 1982, criminologist Philip Bean asked Barbara to write a chapter in a book with a title of which she approved, *In Defence of Welfare*. She agreed, and he was very grateful, as other potential authors had backed off with a variety of lame excuses now Mrs Thatcher was in office, afraid of what standing up to her policies might do to them. 'But Lady B didn't care. She was fireproof, wasn't she?'[41] Barbara's chapter, 'The Moral Basis of the Welfare State', returned to the values of altruism and equality celebrated by the welfare state's founders, dismissed some contemporary (mostly economic) alternative proposals as 'utterly contemptible', and ended with the plan she had already put forward many times before that 'the simplest method of establishing a universal standard of civilized living would be to make a regular welfare payment from the tax revenues to every citizen', regardless of personal circumstances. It was a remote dream, but then someone of her age had witnessed many instances of utopian dreams becoming accepted commonplaces.[42]

The Thatcher years were a hostile climate for radical legislation. In the winter of 1985, Lord Jenkins, one of the Vice-Presidents of the VES, sent Barbara a copy of yet another new Bill to amend the Suicide Act.[43] This one tried a different tack, of highlighting the absurdity that aiding suicide was still an offence, whereas suicide itself was not. Introducing the Bill in the House, he justified its relative timidity on the grounds that bolder souls in the past, such as 'my good and noble friend Lady Wootton' had tried something braver and had failed.[44] The eighty-eight-year-old Baroness was present on this occasion, and she voted, though she did not speak. The last time she spoke in the House of Lords was on 4 July 1985, in the debate about the Education (Corporal Punishment) Bill. This aimed to abolish corporal punishment in schools and other institutions, and was a cause she had championed throughout her life. Baroness David, speaking in its support, reminded their Lordships of Barbara Wootton's Protection of Minors Bill in 1973, of which the current Bill was the direct descendant.[45] Barbara was an active supporter of this renewed attempt to stop adults beating children, and she had corresponded with Peter Newell at the Children's Legal Centre about strategies for opposing the Bill which they regarded as deficient in allowing parents to opt out.[46] In her last House of Lords speech, she recalled her visit to Russia all those years ago, when the children had greeted them with the words, 'So you come from Britain, where they beat the children?'. This had, she said, 'remained a stain and a mark of guilt on my mind ever since…I carry this sort of mark of the devil about with me. And so do all of you who are equally to blame!'[47] The Bill was finally passed in the House of Commons in the summer of 1986 by one vote, a result aided by the event of a royal wedding in the capital which caused traffic congestion and delayed several pro-caning Tory MPs.[48]

'Her work was her life.'[49] Although she continued to be busy, by the early 1980s, it was obvious to Barbara that not only the BBC but other people were beginning to drop her from their radars: there were fewer and fewer invitations to speak or write. She was not going to let them get away with it easily. Aged eighty-four, she wrote to Anthony Howard at *The Listener* anticipating his imminent departure for *The Observer* to canvass the possibility of him publishing her in his new journalistic home if she had an idea worth writing about, 'which does still happen now and then'. She complained that the BBC considered her senile: both David Jacobs and Brian Redhead had dropped her from their regular programmes in 'a most discourteous manner'.[50] She took up the cudgels again with Robin Day, writing in late 1981 to express her delight at the return of 'Question Time', and to let him know that 'a wicked thought crossed my mind. I fully appreciate that you do not want to be cluttered up with "regulars" or old stagers; but is there any chance that if you have a vacancy on Thursday April 15, you might give me a birthday treat, as I should reach the age of 85 on the previous day? That would be greatly appreciated.'[51]

Happily, Robin Day was delighted by her 'wicked' thought, although he did recall a TV discussion they had had about fifteen years before in which she had said she did not believe in 'wickedness'.[52] She took part in 'Question Time' on 18 March 1982, a few weeks before her birthday. Audrey Bradley, who worked with Robin Day on the programme, advised her through their mutual neighbour, Bridget Trotter, what to wear. 'She did look absolutely gorgeous in a navy-and-white dress with white hair ... and I said to the floor manager, "Could you please give Baroness Wootton plenty of time because she's quite slow on her feet ..." I took her onto the platform. There were cables everywhere, she came in on my arm and the audience just clapped and she said, "What are they clapping for, dear?" Because she looked so gorgeous... She was sitting next to Ken Livingstone and I said to Ken, "Please look after her", and he did. And in the Green Room afterwards they had some champagne, because it was nearly her birthday. And he said to her across the room in front of everybody, "What are you going to do for your ninetieth birthday, Barbara?" "Oh, I'm going to have a party", she said, and he said, "Well, I hope you'll ask me to your party," and she said, "Well, young man, you have to have done something really important to be asked to my ninetieth birthday".'[53]

The tidal wave of energy that had carried her through so many important spheres and phases of public policy was beginning to dry up. Gradually, work was reduced to attending the House of Lords, dealing with correspondence, a scattering of public events, and a trickle of publications. Abinger was a quiet place, and Barbara Wootton had been lonely there now for more than twenty years without Barbara Kyle. People had expected her to sell High Barn when Barbara Kyle died, but why would she want to do that?[54] She went on living there simply, doing her own housework, sometimes crying despairingly that she was living in a sea of papers.[55] She had no possessions of any material value, just the books and the papers: 'The less you have the less likely you are to be burgled', she would say. 'They can peep in the window and see that I'm not worth burgling.'[56] She had given up driving after a late night car crash sometime in the early 1970s, an incident which demonstrated the neighbourliness that was a positive aspect of living in rural Surrey. She had been on her way back from a dinner party when she crashed into the gateposts outside the house where the Bradleys lived. Her car was on its side. Don Bradley came out and managed to extract her through the window with a stepladder. He walked her gently home, called the doctor and gave her a brandy, so, by the time the police came, the presence of alcohol in her bloodstream would have been quite expected.[57] There had been the donkeys, but, by the late 1970s, these had gone: the old man who fed them had died and Barbara could not manage to feed them every day, so 'they had to go to their eternal rest... It was a great sorrow'.[58]

Yet there were several new friendships, all noticeably attractive men who were considerably younger than her. Campbell Adamson and Barbara Wootton met on the radio programme 'Any Questions?', discussing incomes policy in 1975. He was a New-Labour-style businessman with a background in the steel industry, best known for his directorship of the Confederation of British Industries at a difficult time for the Labour Party and the trade unions in the early 1970s; later, he became Chairman of the Abbey National Building Society, and oversaw its transformation into a bank as a model followed by many others. In the late 1970s, Campbell Adamson set up various initiatives in the field of family policy in which he involved Barbara – a Working Party on the Family, a Study Commission on the Family, and then, in 1980, the Family Policy Studies Centre, an independent body supported by the Leverhulme Trust to study the social effects of marital breakdown.[59] It was Barbara who directed the progression of these initiatives, since Adamson was ignorant about research and social studies, and so relied on her advice.[60] Like Barbara, he had read economics at Cambridge, though not at the same time – he was twenty-five years younger than her; he remembered his father, John Adamson, speaking highly of her when they had both been Governors of the BBC.[61]

The Labour MP Malcolm Wicks first met Barbara when she was co-opted by Campbell to interview candidates for the post of Research Director / Secretary of the Study Commission on the Family in 1978: 'She struck me as a very eminent old lady, if I can use that term ... She was certainly very sharp, intellectually very strong, she asked good questions ... I had put together a cv to attach to my application and I'd totally forgotten to put down that I'd got a degree and she pointed this out, which shows she'd read the papers. "I assume you've got a degree." Oh God, I've left it off, why should they appoint me to run this body? I remember her always – well, she may have missed the odd one – assiduously attending all the meetings.' When Malcolm later introduced his wife Maggie to her, Barbara, who hated Maggie Thatcher, said, 'You can't call her Maggie, call her Margaret'. The only two people Barbara hated (apart from her mother) were Maggie Thatcher and William Beveridge's wife Janet – according to her, they were both bullies.[62] Thatcher's conviction of her own infallibility reminded Barbara of the same infelicitous trait in Beatrice Webb.[63] However, Thatcher did have some admirable characteristics: her mental and physical courage, and her ability to take decisions quickly (although sometimes *too* quickly and without enough consultation).[64] Frank Field pointed out the considerable similarities between the personae of Barbara Wootton and Margaret Thatcher. Both had very secure handbags which they plonked down, and both of them, facing a difficult audience, made it clear that they were not going to give an inch.[65]

In Barbara's handbag was a photograph of Campbell Adamson.[66] Her connection with Campbell was an attraction of like minds, but it was also for her a relationship of some emotional significance. According to Campbell's second wife, Mimi, Barbara regarded Campbell as a son – a son and a boyfriend. He was someone who meant a great deal to her, but he was also a member of the family of friends she had chosen, rather than the one into which she had been born. Mimi understood this perfectly. In Barbara's later years, the Adamsons took Barbara out to dinner every other week. Either Barbara would stay with them, or she would be driven back to Abinger afterwards.[67] Her driver was a handsome young man called Alan Bryant. For more than ten years, Alan drove her three days a week to London when the House was sitting. She stole Alan from Jack (Lord) Wolfenden, who lived in the village of Westcott nearby, after she scared herself with the late night car crash. Alan and his wife Anne lived with their two young children in a modest house in Westcott, and Barbara became very fond of them: she loved being invited to their house, and they took the children up to tea at High Barn.[68] This was the family life from which she had been parted by Jack Wootton's death, and by her estrangement from her own family. One famous winter night, Alan brought Barbara back to Abinger from the House of Lords but was unable to get the car up the hill through the snow, so she stayed the night with the Bryants. Anne Bryant remembers: 'There was no snobbery about it – I kept thinking I ought to turf one of the kids out [of their bedrooms] but she said, "No, no, I'll be quite happy", and she parked herself here [on the sofa]. She was one of the loveliest people… she absolutely adored Alan, no doubt about it.' On a normal day, Alan would get Barbara back to High Barn by about 9 p.m., and then he would make sure she was comfortable before leaving: 'I'd put her tea on. She only wanted simple things. Soup. I'd sit her down and get her eating.' Alan took Barbara shopping every Friday and also took her to have her hair done.[69]

It would have been cheaper to have taken the train from Dorking to London to get to the House, but, as she was developing various infirmities, and she was still Deputy Speaker, Frank Field took her to see the Clerk of the Parliaments, who agreed that Alan driving her was a legitimate expense.[70] It did not help that the fast train service to London had been cut in 1978, and, in the winter, passengers like Barbara had to sit and shiver in the waiting room in front of a gas fire choked with dirt; she had written to Peter Parker, the Chairman of British Rail, about it.[71] She did not see why the travelling public had to shiver, and had once asked a question in the House about the Government's failure to ensure an adequate level of heat on trains when technical difficulties did not prevent travel to the moon, and had got a 'not very warming' answer.[72]

The relationship with Frank Field was another important strand in Barbara's life in these last years. He met Barbara at an LSE lecture in the early 1970s, after which Peter Townsend introduced them to each other properly. Frank and Barbara used to meet every other week for tea in the Lords; she would carefully note down if it were her turn to pay or Frank's. Barbara's concern for monetary equality was reflected in Frank Field's editorship of *The Wealth Report* in 1979, a book he dedicated to Barbara 'with affection and gratitude for a lifetime's service to the cause of greater equality'.[73] She talked to Frank, not necessarily about her innermost feelings, but about some of the things that still concerned her: the tragedy of her brief life with Jack Wootton; her thwarted desire for children; and about politics, of course. She puzzled over what to do about High Barn. Not only was she alone there, but the house was quite remote from its neighbours. 'She said, "I've been thinking very carefully, Frank," – this must be some years before she died – "the only person I could live with is you. Would you come down to High Barn?" And I said, "Barbara it's impossible, I go up to Birkenhead every weekend, I've got this and all the rest of it, but Barbara you can come and share my flat." And she looked at me and she said, "Typically selfish!".' Frank went to see her in High Barn, taking food from Marks & Spencer, partly to save her the trouble of preparing a meal, but partly because her standards of hygiene were falling now her sight was not what it had once been.[74]

Barbara's parsimony over the tea bill convinced Frank that she was not very well off. So he had got her a grant from the Rowntree Trust: 'The opposition spokesman would have an assistant to help them mug up the facts so they'd be more effective against the Government, and I argued that the most distinguished person in public life was Barbara, and that she should have one.'[75] Rowntree gave her £250 a year towards secretarial and research help; in 1983, this was increased to £1,500 a year. It was an unconditional award for any purpose Barbara thought fit, and not subject to any accounting to the Trust in recognition of the 'great work which you have done over so many years'.[76] Barbara was very grateful, especially when in the summer of 1975 she fell on a marble floor in Italy and broke her right wrist. The grant enabled her to consider investing in a tape recorder, and also to make more use of Vera – though in fact Vera was not paid: 'I did it for love. We argued but I won.'[77]

The faithful and most wonderful Vera was becoming increasingly important as the mainstay of Barbara's last years: she who had carried on beyond the time of *Social Science and Social Pathology* to become Barbara's typist, copy editor, friend, and personal assistant. All Barbara's letters in her last years were typed by Vera, who described herself in various different ways – as Barbara's 'personal assistant'[78] or just 'an old friend who helps with letters'.[79] The routine went like this: 'She would ring me up and, say, perhaps she'd just done this review or she'd done this article, and I'd say, "Ok I'll pick it up on my way to work in the morning". I'd go early, about half past six, and get to Abinger, and she'd give me her piece – we never trusted the post, you see – and I would take it home and that evening I would type it and then the next morning I'd go to work again and then at lunchtime I'd go to the House of Lords and she'd be in the guest room waiting.'[80] Barbara had also engaged Vera as a chauffeuse at the beginning and end of holidays: Vera not only had to fill Barbara in when she returned on anything that had happened politically, but she also had to undertake difficult traffic manoeuvres, such as navigating her way in and out of Southampton Docks.[81] And then Vera went to High Barn every other Sunday – the Sundays when Barbara and Dorothy Russell were not playing Scrabble. The purpose was gardening. Vera had to be there on the dot at ten. 'It was always the same. At a quarter to one, she would say "I'm going in now... and you come in at 1 o'clock". It was always exactly the same lunch, chicken and peas.' After a post-lunch session in the garden, Barbara would have a bath upstairs and Vera one downstairs. At six o'clock, the bar opened. Some Sunday evenings, Vera would drive her to see the Adamsons or her friends the Hookways in Twickenham. Otherwise, 'There was a window in her door and I would walk out of the door and she'd stand there, I'd see this serious sad face looking through the window and it wasn't easy'.[82] Vera said she would have done anything for Barbara. But the last thing Barbara wanted was the only thing she felt unable to do. 'When she knew she was failing, before she went into the nursing home, she kept saying she wanted me to go and live there and look after her. I couldn't do it. I knew I couldn't do it.'[83] Vera was close to sixty, and already quite disabled with osteoarthritis – she needed sticks to walk with – and Barbara, who had never been very physically active, and who enjoyed her food and drink, had put on a considerable amount of weight. She would be too heavy for Vera to lift if she fell. Vera had other commitments: two of her close friends were dying. There was also the concern that, with a live-in carer, the help of neighbours would drop away.

On Christmas Day 1982, Barbara wrote to Campbell and Mimi to say that she was awaiting her escort to the first of four local outings to celebrate her eighty-sixth Christmas: 'I am wearing a claret-coloured trouser suit with a multi-coloured blouse, warm and cosy and nice and commodious, for which, after much labour, you are responsible. The effect is, I think, quite smart, but you experts shall judge on a suitable occasion. Meanwhile many thanks indeed for it, and specially to Mimi for her extra trouble.'[84] Barbara was not renowned for her dress sense. O.R. McGregor's son, Ross McGregor, recalls as a young man being exposed to some very entertaining dinners when his father invited Barbara together with W.J.H. (Jack) Sprott from Nottingham, who was a Visiting Lecturer at Bedford College. Jack Sprott was a sociologist, an intimate of Lytton Strachey and of E.M. Forster, and probably Keynes' last male lover, a member of the Bloomsbury group who knew him as 'Sebastian'.[85] Ross remembers Sprott and Barbara together: 'There was a wonderful double act, a pure bit of fun... they had some shared characteristics, one of which, I don't think it was an unfriendly relationship, but the pair of them used to spar. She loved it, so did Jack... And there was one wonderful evening – they both had a profound love of gin – we used to put a bottle of gin and some tonic by each of their beds before dinner... if I had a quid for every time I carried Jack or Barbara or both of them upstairs to bed... They fell to having a row about something one night – I wish I could recall the whole of the conversation – as usual by that time of the night some considerable amount of wine had been taken, but they'd been battling away at something all evening, and Jack had, I think, lost on points, and there was a long pause, and he took a swig of his wine and he just leant across the table, "Barbara, my dear, where *do* you buy your frocks?" Barbara was gobsmacked, absolutely no comeback.'[86]

There was Frank, and there was Campbell, and the dashing Alan with the perfect family, and there was also Tony Gould, the writer who was Reviews Editor of *New Society*, the journal to which Barbara contributed many pieces over the twenty-six years of its life before it merged with the *New Statesman*. Tony and Barbara met through *New Society*, and they found they had a lot to talk about: writing, politics, personal relationships. They took to meeting regularly for lunch in the House of Lords. He was an important confidante, and she probably performed the same role for him. The other side of her meanness with money was her generosity in offering to lend or give him some when he was in difficulty – an offer he refused.[87] She had, he said, a definite eye for younger men. There was a clear quality of sexual flirtatiousness on her side of the relationship. He gave her novels to read, and Philip Larkin's poems: 'I read the two of the latter that you had recommended,' she wrote to him,'and liked the fucking one very much. The aged one I found rather grisly.'[88] Once Tony took his wife and six-year-old son to visit her at High Barn. They had a pleasant time, but the next day Tony had an irate call from Barbara: her alarm clock had gone off in the middle of the night, obviously because his son had fiddled with it when he was sent up to her bedroom to watch television. But she was old, and Tony forgave her.[89]

There was also 'Mac', O.R. McGregor, whose staunch friendship dated back to the 1940s when Barbara had hired him as a young man to teach one of her tutorial classes in Romford.[90] Under her patronage, McGregor proceeded to a professorship at Bedford College and to the House of Lords. Among the many interests they had in common was the freedom of the press: Barbara was a member of the first Royal Commission on the Press in 1947, and McGregor chaired the third in the 1970s. As Barbara aged and acquired various disabilities, Mac assumed a practical role in her life, giving advice and helping to make decisions, and generally acting as a backup to Vera.

She went on holiday until 1983: several times to an old haunt, Malcesine on the eastern shore of Lake Garda in Italy, usually with Margaret Hetherington, her relative Arthur's wife, who had become a regular holiday companion since Barbara Kyle's death. On one occasion, it seemed that Margaret was second choice, replacing Frank Field: Barbara had to change the name on the second ticket at the last minute from 'Frank Field MP' to 'Lady Hetherington'.[91] Margaret's daughter, Ann Ashford, described these holidays the two women took together: one sat and painted, the other (Barbara) sat and read. (Margaret once did a rather good painting of Barbara.) They enjoyed good Italian food, with wine and laughter. Barbara 'thought that taking a nap after lunch was absolutely wicked. She never did it. You did not waste time by doing anything as indolent as having a nap. She never had a nap on holiday with mother. She would go to sleep over the book, and then she woke up and it had never happened.'[92] Barbara's Italian holiday in 1982 was not a successful trip, due to the weather and transport difficulties, as she confided to Lenore Goodings at the feminist publishing house Virago, who invited her to give a lecture to mark the Virago publication of the first Beatrice Webb Diary. Barbara accepted, but then wrote to say she would not be able to do it: she had been very unwell for several months with circulatory problems affecting her legs and feet, problems which were now aggravated by incipient arthritis.[93]

But the illusion that travel would be therapeutic was long-lived. In 1983, she asked Alan, her driver, if he would go on a cruise to Norway with her. Alan declined; she asked her Surrey neighbours, the Trotters. Bridget was a rotten sailor, so David Trotter, who had been in the Merchant Navy and who loved the sea, accompanied Barbara on the coastal voyage from Bergen to Kirkenes: 2,500 miles in eleven days from the south to the north of Norway. They bought drink on the plane to Bergen to reduce costs on the boat. Barbara paid for David's ticket because the Trotters had been victims of the Lloyds insurance fiasco, and she booked a rather classier cabin for herself than for him. They went right round the North Cape, but they missed the aurora borealis because it was the wrong time of year. David did his job well; he cosseted Barbara, always seeing her down to her cabin in the evening.[94]

For most of her life, she had enjoyed splendid health. After the episode of acute tonsillitis that had ended her career as a classical scholar in 1918, there is hardly a trace of her ever being ill in the records that are left. She did have some operation in a Harley Street clinic in 1948; Ernest Gowers, with whom she was working on the Shop Hours Committee, wrote to commiserate.[95] The broken wrist she acquired when she was seventy-eight mended, but she was left with some permanent residual dysfunction in the fingers of her right hand.[96] She was knocked down by a car in London when she was eighty-one, but she picked herself up and was quite alright after resting for a while in a local shop.[97] But from about 1982, when she was eighty-five, references to various infirmities multiply. She complained she was getting tired, though she *was* trying to carry out a programme 'before which many people would quail at 40'.[98] When the Vice-Chancellor of Brunel University, a place with one enormous asset – its location at the end of an underground line – invited her to lunch to discuss war service and the university pension scheme, she objected that she was too old and not mobile enough.[99] To one correspondent, Lee McIntyre, in Portland, Oregon, who was writing a PhD on his own thoughts about social science which were closely modelled on Barbara's *Testament*, she said in the summer of 1983 that she was suffering from 'senile degeneration of this and that' – which accounted for her failure to produce any recent published work. There was no concealing the fact that she had become a grumpy old woman: would he please remember to put his address on every letter if he wanted a reply – she kept her files upstairs but did her correspondence downstairs, and being 'partially disabled' wanted to keep the journeys on the stairs to a minimum?[100] Actually, she had always been quite grumpy – punctilious, attentive to the desirability of correct grammar, spelling, referencing and behaviour, and a keen recorder of any misrepresentations of her position. She wrote many letters about all this, though the habit did intensify in her later years. 'In the various notices about myself which you have produced', she reprimanded the BBC in 1984 when they were preparing material for her contribution to the programme and the book, *Women of Our Century,* 'there is a remarkable collection of untrue statements. You credited me with two extra weeks of effective marriage to Jack Wootton which I could well have done with. You also robbed me of three years in age at the time of that marriage ... You also perpetuated the falsehood that I supported the legalisation of cannabis during the sixties ... It would seem that accuracy is not a virtue highly regarded by the Corporation's employees.'[101] The BBC apologized, and Lee McIntyre was able to recover from the black mark against him. When he inquired about her health in 1985, she informed him that her various organs and limbs did not function as they used to. 'Notably I fear that my brain is inclined to think that it has been over-taxed, and resents my attempting new projects.'[102] She was, simply, 'very old and very tired'.[103] At eighty-eight, she was still going to the House of Lords two or three days a week, though increasingly Alan would get her there in time for lunch and then she would 'totter into the chamber and go to sleep'.[104] In 1984, the House of Lords had presented her with a walking stick carved by a craftsman from wood obtained from Mickelham Downs, near Box Hill in Surrey.[105] Her last recorded attendance at the House was on 21 October 1985.

This was the year, 1985, when her health took an abrupt downward turn. The honorary degree ceremony planned in Cambridge that summer worried her. She wrote to the Vice-Chancellor, saying she was 'rather seriously disabled' and only able to walk a few steps at a time slowly. She could manage steps or stairs if there was a rail, or a friendly arm, but she would not be able to take part in any formal procession. They reassured her that they would cope with her disability, quoting the example of another honorary graduand who had managed to collect his degree earlier in the year despite being both infirm and blind.[106] In the event, her visit to Cambridge was 'in every way thoroughly enjoyable and by no means over-exhausting'.[107] But something in particular happened to her that summer. She told Frank about it in one of their tea encounters: 'She said, "Oh, a funny thing happened to me at the weekend, Frank. I heard part of my brain collapsing and running past my ear as though it was water".'[108] Mac recalled her saying: 'I felt a piece of my mind drop off. Where do you think it went?'[109] His son Ross remembers picking up a telephone call from Barbara: 'I said, "How are you Barbara, long time no see", and she said, "Well, I'm not terribly happy," she said, "The trouble is I'm going mad"... And I said, "Barbara, how terribly tiresome for you". And she said, "Thank God, you said that. You're absolutely right. Everyone else makes these platitudinous statements ... The trouble is that in my lucid periods I know I'm mad, but then I go mad."'[110]

What had happened was probably a small stroke. This was a diagnosis Barbara herself offered in a letter to Tony Gould.[111] A stroke would have caused symptoms similar to those of Alzheimer's or senile dementia. The result was that she was forced to recognize that she was now fighting against the odds. She was 'doing her best', but 'working against great difficulties'; she was 'not at all well, mentally or physically,' and was 'liable to devastating gaps in memory which obstruct progress'.[112] She wrote to Peter Townsend and complained that she was forgetting things, so he and Jean (Baroness Corston) went to see her. Peter made her scrambled eggs and she said his scrambled eggs were wonderful. She said to Jean, 'I wish I could have you to look after me. I need somebody to look after me'.[113] There was something very plaintive and vulnerable about these requests.

She went to the House less and less, and then it got to the point where she hardly went at all. Despite having suggested resignation at least twice in the early 1980s – an offer their Lordships reputedly refused[114] – sometime in the summer of 1985 Barbara did give up her role as Deputy Speaker. According to her, she succeeded in resigning; the other version of events is that their Lordships removed her from office. Frank Field recalls Barbara telephoning him in some distress; he went down to High Barn to spend time with her.[115] The Private Secretary to the Chairman of Committees, Michael Pownall, who was responsible for the rota of Deputy Speakers, arranged with the Chairman of Committees, Lord Aberdare, an informal leaving party. It was a moving and sad occasion which persuaded Barbara it was time to go.[116] At the meeting of Deputies in the House on 14 October 1985, Lord Aberdare announced that Baroness Wootton would be no longer be one of them.[117] He wrote to her afterwards:

Dear Barbara

I informed the weekly meeting of Deputy Speakers and Chairmen of your decision to resign and they all wished me to tell you how very sorry they were to hear the news and to send you their very best wishes.

I am sure that you have made the right decision for health reasons but we shall all miss you very much. You have not only been one of our most efficient members but you have been wonderfully conscientious in attending meetings and carrying out duties on the Woolsack and in the Chair.

Thank you ever so much for all your help over so many years.[118]

In 1981 she had said to a journalist, 'If I was to give up the Lords, what should I do? I should sit here and die'.[119] Living on her own became ever more difficult. She worried about safety. She slept with a knife under her pillow and a rope coiled in her bed in case of fire (so she could climb out of the window).[120] There were repeated episodes of her telephoning the police and complaining there was someone in the house, or ringing friends or neighbours in the middle of the night. Bridget Trotter recalls: 'She'd ring up and forget who she was ringing up and you would hear this heavy breathing, which was slightly alarming, and I suddenly twigged, and I'd say, "Is that you, Barbara?" We were quite bothered about her being on her own.' The Trotters used to ring up every few days to make sure she was alright. Barbara took to phoning Alan first if she needed anything; once it was because she was unable to get herself out of the bath.[121] Tony Gould remembers her phoning and saying, 'I can't remember whether I've had breakfast or not'.[122] In the summer of 1986, she was receiving the help of Meals on Wheels.[123] Friends and neighbours tried to persuade her to accept living-in help. Barbara's GP arranged one day for a 'country cousin' – someone who would live in and help with domestic and personal care –

but Barbara was resistant. Vera, who arrived while this was going on, managed to get Barbara to agree to try it. But in the middle of the night Barbara wandered downstairs, and the country cousin appeared, and Barbara attacked her with her walking stick, and that was the end of that.[124] The stick was called into action on another occasion, when Barbara started accusing Alan of something she said he had done. The police were called. It was, said the criminologist Philip Bean, 'one of the deepest ironies of them all ... the sergeant said she needed a social worker ... she was accusing the chauffeur and trying to hit him with a stick ... and I think they tried to restrain her, and the sergeant said she should have a social worker under the old Section 136 of the Mental Health Act.' But of course calling in a social worker could never be allowed, not after that chapter in *Social Science and Social Pathology*.[125]

In the autumn of 1985, Barbara went into hospital. Neil Kinnock, then Leader of the Opposition, wrote to urge her to find somewhere to live in Dorking when she came out, somewhere where other people could provide meals and see that she was all right. This would mean that she would be able to get back to the Lords. 'Few people have made the contribution you have to improving our country and I look forward to seeing you around again attending to the business of the Other Place.'[126] It was a warm letter, and certainly indicative of Barbara's importance to the political process at a time when Thatcher's second period of office was set on a relentless programme of de-nationalization, attacking the power of the trade unions, and dismantling the health and welfare services. Barbara herself very much wanted to survive Thatcher's ruinous administrations, but in the end she was the one who went first. She never did what Kinnock suggested; instead, she went to convalesce in a nursing home, and in the nursing home she fell and fractured her hip, which meant another hospital stay and surgery for the hip. In December 1985, she wrote to her friends from Dorking Hospital, a shaky handwritten Christmas greeting: 'The scenery is fine, but hospital wards do not compete with HL [the House of Lords]: so hope springs eternal'.[127]

Holmesdale Park residential home in Nutfield, Surrey, was built in the 1880s and had enjoyed a varied career as an adjunct of Guy's Hospital and then a police training establishment before opening its doors in 1980 to people like Barbara who were no longer able to care for themselves. It was a large solid house in wonderful grounds, about nine miles from Abinger. There were thirty-six residents and sixty-two nursing beds. Barbara had a room on the ground floor. The decision to move her into Holmesdale was not one she was party to; Bridget Trotter and Barbara's GP had taken it.[128] At first, it was a temporary arrangement, but quite soon she began reluctantly to accept that it was likely to become her permanent home. She had a set of sticky labels printed with her name and the address and telephone number of the nursing home which she attached to House of Lords notepaper. In April 1986, she wrote to McGregor: 'This is almost certain to become a life sentence ... I am necessarily fixed here for as long as I can afford it and am alive to pay the bills'. As with a Christmas note she wrote to friends, she was effusive in her appreciation of his friendship and urged him to visit as much as possible: seeing him would be 'a wonderful oasis in an otherwise dreary existence'.[129] Barbara, a feisty critic of many institutions over the course of her life, seems to have been relatively satisfied with the physical care provided at Holmesdale. To her friends in New York, the Lekachmans, she reported she was 'reasonably housed and fed'.[130] 'There are some difficulties in the arrangements, but on the whole the system is working reasonably well', she told Florrie Wright; she would stay at Holmesdale largely because she could not think of any accommodation that would suit her better.[131] To Vera Delf, who had saved her from scalding in China, she commented that, 'If one has to be in an institution (which is I think at present my fate) it is better to be in a good one than a bad one'.[132] When she first went to Holmesdale Park, she was sufficiently *compos mentis* to interrogate the other residents, and she was amazed to find that almost everyone except her had been in service. Frank Field explained why: the social security rules had changed, with the result that many people could now get the full cost of residential care covered, so the rich had tipped all their elderly servants out into residential care.[133]

She never returned to live at High Barn again. The house which had meant so much to her was put on the market in August 1986 and sold quickly the same month. Sometime before this, Barbara had asked Vera if she would live there if she left it to her, but Vera had said it would be like living with a ghost.[134] Its contents were given to Bridget Trotter, who had two daughters on the verge of setting up homes. Frank was asked if there was anything he wanted: he chose the dark picture that hung over the mantelshelf. It turned out to be by Henry Lamb, a follower of Augustus John and a relative of Lord Longford, so there might have been something worth burgling the house for, after all.[135]

Even after her removal to Holmesdale Park, the world continued to behave as though the eminent Baroness Wootton would live forever. Janusz Stechley of the Orchestra of the World wanted her as a Patron; so did the International Benthamite Society; and the Bentham Club at University College in London, of which she was a past President, instated her as an Honorary Fellow. The Nuclear Weapons Freeze Campaign asked her to become a Patron; and in 1987 the International Campaign for Peace and Democracy in Iraq and Iran, of which she was already a sponsor, requested Barbara's attendance at a World Congress in Moscow. Vera Seal wrote politely to explain that a ninety-year-old could hardly undertake such expeditions.[136] An invitation with a more colourful background arrived in January 1987 from one Michael Luvaglio. He ran a charity for disabled people called Share, and, like all the others, wanted Barbara on his notepaper as Patron, but he also wished to thank her for all the support she had given him during his long years in prison.[137] In a high-profile case which was commemorated in the film *Get Carter* starring Michael Caine, Luvaglio had been sentenced in 1967 for shooting the one-armed bandit cash collector Angus Shibbert. It was a seamy story set in the shadowy world of gaming machines and night clubs in the north of England, and involving the notorious Kray twins; a number of notable people, including Barbara Wootton, had campaigned to reclassify Luvaglio's sentence as a miscarriage of justice.[138] Her role in the Luvaglio case was typical of her tendency to pay personal attention to the experiences behind public causes.

During her unenviable decline, various of Barbara's colleagues and friends in the House of Lords wrote or visited, or spoke in the House to wish her well. In the summer of 1987, Lord Longford referred to her in a debate about the Criminal Justice Bill: 'No individual has done so much for penal reform in our time in the domain of policy as has the noble Baroness, Lady Wootton ... She has a wonderful record and my thoughts go out to her at this moment because she has not been well for some time'.[139] Baroness Jean Trumpington sent her a postcard from Strasbourg: 'We miss you in the House of Lords, Mother dear'.[140] Baroness Lucy Faithfull wrote warmly to say how much she personally missed her;[141] and Baroness Joan Vickers told her that 'the Ladies Room does not seem the same without you', and to offer to send her a daily Hansard.[142] It was an offer Barbara turned down – she was quite happy to have a rest from Hansard.[143] Lord Harmar Nicholls dispatched a slightly curious note to complain that her 'absence from the "corridors" has taken all the flavour out of my own attendances. Make sure you obey this "whip" in the New Year. I am so happy to hear you are making excellent progress – so until we next meet please accept my love and good wishes for Christmas. Yours ever Harmar (your corridor boyfriend)'.[144] Lord Walston's 'long-smouldering intention' of writing to her was 'fanned into flame by a Bill in their Lordships on Donkeys. Do you still retain a love for them?'[145] Lord Aberdare kept her informed of progress on the attempt, which Barbara had spearheaded, to change the laws about who could marry whom: 'I am in a welter of negotiation on those Marriage Enabling Bills, in which you were so interested. We have Lord Merton's Bill now which has Church support to permit "Step" marriages, but not "In-law" ones. But we have two Personal Bills for the "In-law" sort! ... We miss your wise counsel.'[146]

Although she had given up being Deputy Speaker, she had absolutely not given up the idea of returning to the House. In the spring of 1986, she wrote to Neil

Kinnock to say so,[147] and to Lord Elwyn Jones, Speaker of the House of Lords: 'I cannot accurately forecast when I may be able to contribute help in dealing with the heavy programme of work which you say is now starting. I am afraid I must leave all the burdens on the shoulders of those of our colleagues who are at full strength in both physique and mind, which is slightly more than I can claim as yet. However, I shall certainly make my way back to the Lords when I can be satisfied that it is really safe to do so'.[148] The staff at Holmesdale told Jean Corston that sometimes Barbara became very stressed and disoriented, and she kept saying, 'I've got to be on the Woolsack today, I've got to be on the Woolsack today', and they could only satisfy her by saying, 'the House isn't sitting today, Milady', and then she calmed down.[149]

Barbara Wootton: Social Science and Public Policy, Essays in Her Honour was published in 1986. Barbara was not pleased when the senior editor, Philip Bean, wrote to her to suggest it. She wrote back to him with her grumpy old woman response saying he had absolutely no right to ask people to write chapters about her work. Then two or three weeks later she followed this by apologizing and saying could they please start again.[150] The finished product is a handsome hardback with a smart picture of Barbara – neatly done hair, sparkling spectacles and lipstick – on the cover, and sixteen chapters by people she knew well and less well about her work in economics and social policy, and in crime and penal reform. McGregor wrote the Introduction, called 'Champion of the Impossible'. They decided to present her with the book at a carefully orchestrated party in the House of Lords. Vera took her to have her hair done, and then drove her there. Philip Bean remembered the occasion: 'The plan was that, because she didn't know where she was, though she had a vague idea that she was the centre of it all, we would present her with the book, and, if she started talking inconsequentially, we would all applaud. But we didn't need to, she stood up and said something that was vaguely relevant, mainly about unless you have evidence for it you can't sustain the argument.'[151] According to Vera, Barbara, rising from her wheelchair, gave a very short, witty and to-the-point speech of thanks.[152]

They all trooped out to Nutfield to see Barbara in Holmesdale Park: George Wright's niece, Brenda Collison; Lucy Faithfull; Frank Field; her relative Sir John Ford, who had been an ambassador and who brought her homemade cakes; Tony Gould; the Hetheringtons; Lena Jeger; Lord Longford; Mac (McGregor); Barbara Kyle's cousin and their neighbour in Surrey, Ann Monie; Peter Townsend and Jean Corston; the Trotters; and Vera, of course. Before High Barn was sold, Vera developed a new routine: she would drive from her home in London to Abinger, collect the post, deal with it at the house to make it look as though Barbara were still living there, and then go on to the nursing home – a round trip of some 142 miles via the M25. She would spend the afternoon in the day-room at Holmesdale Park with Barbara, eat supper with her, stay while she was 'got ready' for bed, and leave when she had gone to sleep. One day, Vera arrived at Holmesdale to find a tense atmosphere: the BBC was making a programme about euthanasia and had rung and spoken to Barbara and asked her to be filmed. She had agreed, but the managers of Holmesdale were not happy; there was no way they were having their home on a programme about euthanasia.[153] Vera had to extract Barbara from the arrangement. On another matter, Jean Corston remembers that Barbara missed the availability of alcohol in Holmesdale and asked them to bring some in. They had strict instructions not to let any of the staff know. Barbara also asked them to bring a vase, because she only had two vases. 'So I said that I'd brought it and she told me where to put it. She looked out of the door and when she was satisfied there were no staff around she told me to stand on a chair and reach up into this cupboard and get out the three vases. The staff thought these were vases for flowers but they weren't, they were actually drinking glasses. So we sat there drinking out of the vases ... she was perfectly lucid that day.'[154]

By the summer of 1986, Barbara was mostly confined to her room, and only able to manage short excursions to the outside world with help. Vera was her lifeline. She still brought in Barbara's post and tried to involve her in it, although increasingly the answers that were composed were entirely Vera's creation. Vera took her to visit her own family in the New Forest and to the wedding of one of the Trotters' daughters, whose entry into the medical profession had been partly spurred by Barbara's encouragement and ability to 'pull a few strings';[155] and the following year to another wedding, of John Ford's daughter in Guildford. The Trotters used to take Barbara out once a week, in her wheelchair. Vera tried to think of interesting places to take her in the car. Once they went to look at a causeway: they drove about twenty miles to somewhere in Kent and Barbara refused to even look out of the window, and then half way back she said, 'Well, where is that bloody causeway?' It was an exception to her normal rule of never swearing.[156] Another day they came across a llama in a field. They met a woman who was the mother of the llama-owner, and Vera explained that her friend was rather poorly and she was trying to find things to interest her: was it alright if they got a bit closer to the llama? 'Yes,' she said. 'It likes bourbon biscuits.' So they went back with some bourbon biscuits, and they stopped outside the field, and there was the llama right at the other end of the field; Vera called and called, and eventually its attention was attracted. 'Barbara was sitting in the passenger seat and I'd opened the door so she could have a good sight of it, and I took these chocolate biscuits and I gave it these chocolate biscuits and it went [slurping sound], and I thought, oh, it likes them, it might like another one, so I got another chocolate biscuit out and suddenly it went [huffing sound] all over my blouse and everything. Barbara laughed. It was the only time she laughed in those last two and a half years. She laughed, and during the next few weeks, if I said to her, "Barbara, what about the llama?" She would chortle about it. It was lovely.'[157]

Barbara's friends were careful to ensure that the ritual of birthday celebrations was sustained. In 1986 she had a pleasant lunch orchestrated by Campbell Adamson, and then Vera took her for a scenic drive. There were various celebrations for her ninetieth birthday in April 1987. A telemessage arrived from four Labour peers in the House wishing her a happy birthday.[158] Campbell and Mimi took Barbara, plus the Bryants and the Trotters and John Ford and his wife, and Vera, and Vera took Barbara in her wheelchair, out to a local restaurant. It was only a partial success. Barbara felt that Campbell did not pay her enough attention, and when Vera took her back to Holmesdale afterwards, she suddenly said, "'I've fallen out of love with Campbell" ... This was at a point where many people thought she was not really aware of what was going on.'[159] Holmesdale also hosted a party for her; Lena Jeger, who went, wrote a piece about it for *The House Magazine*: 'Barbara Wootton was 90 on April 14. Friends and colleagues who joined her on that sunny felicitous day were glad to see how well she looked – elegantly coiffed and wearing a cheerful ruby velvet suit – as she held court from her wheel chair. After the sherry and the birthday cake there were gracefully short speeches ... Barbara stood to thank her guests and said bravely that she hoped they would all have as happy a ninety years as her.'[160] Ken Livingstone was not there; and we can only guess whether, had Barbara been in a position to draw up the guest list herself, she would have considered his achievements merited an invitation.

The labels Barbara had made to affix to her letters from Holmesdale Park did not mention its status as a nursing home, which may be why her entry in the Dictionary of National Biography describes it as her own home.[161] Her correspondents may as well have believed it was. By the time Diana Grassie arrived at Holmesdale Park to be Director of Residential and Nursing Care, Barbara already needed quite a lot of nursing attention. Diana perceived Barbara as someone who hated relying on others for her care, to a greater degree, probably, than many people; she would get very impatient at her inability to do things for herself.[162] Although Holmesdale Park was a well-run home with a 'quietly happy feel' about it, it did suffer from some of the dehumanizing rituals of many such institutions. Barbara did not always take kindly to being dressed, undressed and toileted, according to schedule.[163] Right until the end, she cared how she looked: 'She had this wonderful hair, silver-white hair, curly, and she liked her hair to be good. We had a hairdresser who used to do it. She looked radiant. She wore spectacles, it was always important that they were sparkling.' The staff called her 'Lady Barbara'. It helped that she was able to form a particular friendship with a West Indian care assistant called Annie. Barbara had good days and bad days; they had the sense that here was someone who sat and observed all that was going on – all the interaction between staff and patients, relatives and families. 'She was very quiet but she had an enormous presence ... She did not have a very expressive face at that stage but, when she could, her eyes gave quite a smile as you greeted her in the morning ... I can remember this Ward Sister ..."What do you think about this, Lady Barbara, I can see your twinkle?"'[164]

Early in 1986, Barbara was moved to a much better room upstairs, and then to an even larger room, a sunny room at the front of the house, when she got more dependent and needed more space around her for nursing equipment. She had a ceramic donkey in her room, and some of her own furniture, and some photographs, including two by her bed. Frank Field recalled saying to her one day, '"Barbara who *are* these people?" ... "I don't know, Frank," she said, "I don't know, but they are the two people who most loved me." Not that I most loved. Very interesting. They were George, her second husband, and her partner that she went down to live with, whoever she was [Barbara Kyle]. She never told me what the woman's name was.'[165]

'Nobody wants me,' she wrote in a diary, the only fragment that has been preserved, on 27 February 1986.[166] Leaving the Woolsack had been a devastating blow: the work, status and ceremonies had been part of her life for twenty years. The withdrawal of the Rowntree Trust's support in March 1987 on the grounds of her repeated absence from the House of Lords was another rejection.[167] By January 1988, as Vera explained in a letter to Barbara's friends the Lekachmans, her health had declined further; her memory was thin; conversation and correspondence were difficult; she did not want her friends to know about her disablement; she was very unhappy and it was an appalling situation.[168] She was nearly ninety-one, the age at which her beloved nanny The Pie had died. What did death mean to her, she who had been so clear in her life that it was simply the end to everything? 'I think she wasn't very easy about the idea of dying. I don't think she was entirely resigned to it, let's put it that way. I think she was afraid. She didn't believe in any kind of future life ... I'm sure she would have got to a point where her very rationality would have suggested there wasn't much to live for.'[169] She was rational, and she was consistent, and so she had joined Exit; no-one with her history of association with the assisted dying movement could have done anything else. In the 'Face the Press' interview in 1984, when she was eighty-seven, Anthony Howard told her she was a pillar of the euthanasia cause. 'That cliché I will not have,' she replied tersely, 'but I do think that there ought to be some legitimate means by which you could dispose of your life when it is no longer worth living.' Later in the interview, Polly Toynbee had asked her the straightforward question, 'If you were to become very seriously disabled yourself, would you wish to be able to end your own life?' 'Yes,' declared Barbara. 'I hope that I have the means of doing it.'[170]

The subject of Barbara desiring to end her life under such circumstances had come up in a conversation with Vera: Vera had said she would do whatever Barbara wanted. Barbara responded that she could not allow Vera to help, as she would go to prison.[171] Sometime before that summer of 1985 when she had her first small stroke, Frank Field had gone to see her in High Barn and she had told him that she was now a fully paid up member of Exit. He joked with her: how could she possibly want to be put away by a man in a woolly hat who put a plastic bag over her head and then sat there eating banana sandwiches? Such a story had been in the news at the time. No, what she had done is she had secured some knock-out pills from one of her medical friends in the House. After she moved into Holmesdale Park, Frank kept expecting her to ask him to get her the pills, but she never did. Was this evidence of her determination to live, or was it because those parts of her mind which were needed to put the plan into action were now somewhere else? He would have got the pills for her, and he would have assisted her dying, even though he personally disagreed with any form of suicide. He would have risked imprisonment and losing his seat had she asked him, and he believed that this would have been quite proper, because people in Barbara's position need as much protection as possible from abuse by those who pose as close friends but may have something to gain from their death.[172]

She had always expected to 'go out like a light when I die and that will be the end of that'.[173] Sometime in the late spring or early summer, three years after she had first complained that bits of her mind had gone somewhere else, she stopped eating. She lost a lot of weight. She drank water, but that was all. She had made up her mind; that was it.[174] According to Vera, Barbara's relative Sir John Ford had instructed Holmesdale not to resuscitate Barbara in the event of such a decline.[175] Vera had been visiting daily for some time. Barbara was much weaker, and had got a chest infection. Vera stayed at Holmesdale all the time. She got up in the middle of the night to check on Barbara, to make sure that the staff had remembered her medication. As the opponents of Barbara's Incurable Patients Bill had observed, good medical practice would keep patients such as her free of pain, and it seemed to do so, in her case. Everyone thought she would die sooner than she did, but she held on – or life held on to her. When Alan and Anne Bryant went to see her on 13 July, she was in a coma. Vera said they would not get any response. 'Alan put his hand on her face and she said, "Oh, my darling Alan". She was with it just for a second. She heard his voice and opened her eyes. That was the last thing she said.'[176]

Was it Alan, or was it George, or was it even Jack? It was some man with a smiling face and a masculine body, someone who represented that world of comforting intimacy she had scarcely had a chance to know: life, which should be equal, is cruel in its imposition of misfortune; and yet she had resolutely carried on. Behind the bravery was always the loss. As Barbara Frances Wootton, Baroness Wootton of Abinger, lay dying early in the ninety-second year of her life, was it the loss that mattered? Did she see Jack Wootton's tall uniformed figure, and hear the rumble of guns in the polished corridors of Girton with the candles burning and the coal fires lit, and were the strains of 'Sleepers Wake' mingled with the sheaves of corn lying in the harvest sunlight of Haslingfield, as Mr and Mrs Wootton took their truncated honeymoon? As we grow older, it is the far-off past that comes back to haunt or delight us most: the stern Adela; the scholar father; the brothers with whom Barbara shared a secret backwards language full of Latin, so that 'dog' would not be 'god'; The Pie as a young woman, fresh from the household of the errant Maynard Keynes in her starched white apron and cap; the brooding contours of Emmanuel House, the fishpond with its little island and the fertile swans; Miss Ratcliffe's dancing class, and the Perse School for Girls – God's partial response to Barbara Adam's lavatorial prayers.

There in the hygienic bed of Holmesdale Park, Barbara Wootton's fading mind must have entertained many ghosts and shadows: Hugh Dalton admiring her ankles and gossiping about party politics; the becapped and airsick William Beveridge on the plane to Paris in search of world peace; Beatrice Webb and Bertrand Russell arguing about socialism and toilets; the harsh landscapes of Russia through the train window, the fellow-travellers munching on almonds and raisins; all the journeys she had taken everywhere – to India with the charming Andrew Shonfield; to Africa with Ilya Neustadt, who made himself ill by eating kippers; to China, to rest her hand on a tortoise, to walk through the Summer Palace and the Great Hall of the People; to America, evading the Inland Revenue with that other man who loved her, the delightful rogue, George Wright, creeping in from his photograph by her nursing home bed to remind her of Summer Schools and the sea at Mundesley where she taught him some things and he taught her others, and bringing her the remembered laughter of friends at that outrageous bathing costume of his; the ice-blue water of the Norwegian fjords, the little coloured houses, and the fishing boats, and made-up stories about men and women; Vera's lilies gathered in The Bothy in Regent's Park; the wide casement window of her bedroom in High Barn; Miranda and Francesca braying in the field; gin and tonic with the Other Barbara on the terrace; the rhododendron parties at midsummer; and then, of course, because she was the Baroness who had married a taxi-driver, the journey to the corridors that led to the corridors of power – the hushed baroque of the House of Lords, making history by being a woman and wearing fake ermine, and rejecting God; leaping up and sitting down as words poured out of the mouths of noble Lords and Ladies: words, words, words, it was always important to say what you mean and mean what you say.

Vera was in Barbara's room: 'I heard her breathing change so I went straight to the bed, and I looked at her and – I don't think I thought whether she was going to die at that moment – but I sort of crouched down, I can't kneel, I crouched down so I could see her face to face. And, you see, one of the things she used to say to me when I went in, was, "Keep me safe, keep me safe, keep me safe". And I stroked her face and I said, "Barbara, you're quite safe, you know" ... then, at that moment, she looked at me. She looked straight in my eyes and she focused and I was gently stroking her face and saying, "You're quite safe, Barbara, you're quite safe". I don't know whether she recognized me or not.'[177] 'I thought recently, what did she look like? Was she frightened? She wasn't, there was no suggestion that she was fearful, but I thought, well now, could you put a name to it, and I would say she looked puzzled.'[178]

In the World She Never Made

When a person is dead they are dead, she said. What do you do when someone dies? 'Well, you have to dispose of the body. I don't go to the funeral. I don't go to the funeral of anybody, no matter how near to me he was, even "my nearest and dearest". I regard the funeral, or the cremation more probably, as a necessary hygienic measure; you must dispose of bodies. That is the finish.'[1] And so it was. The day after Barbara Wootton died, Vera Seal went to register her death. The deputy registrar, a young woman, exclaimed with joy when she recognized the name – her aunt, the registrar, was a great fan of Barbara's. On Wednesday 20 July 1988, nine days after Barbara died, there was a short non-religious funeral at Golders Green Crematorium in London. The flowers on the coffin were picked from Vera's garden. Vera was chief mourner; Lord Longford came on his bicycle; and there were a few other peers and some of Barbara's loyal friends and neighbours. The husband of Barbara's deceased niece attended with his new wife, as did her second cousins, John Ford and Arthur Hetherington, with their wives. From the nursing home in Surrey came a contingent of five carers, in their uniform, in the matron's car: 'I was really surprised how few people were there ... For a life like that that seemed incredible ... I remember feeling totally deflated. I can remember that feeling now. This isn't right. This isn't good enough; this wasn't what should have happened.'[2] The small band of mourners entered to the music of César Franck's *Violin Sonata*, the last movement, a piece which Barbara's brother Arthur, who had died in the First World War, had particularly loved. Campbell Adamson and O.R. McGregor both talked for a few minutes about Barbara. The coffin slid away accompanied by the first movement of Elgar's *Cello Concerto*. Three days later, Barbara Wootton's ashes were scattered in section I-L of the Crematorium's Garden of Remembrance.

There were plans for a memorial service, but it never happened. Barbara's solicitor, Nicholas Morgan, picked a date that did not work for members of the House of Lords. McGregor rearranged it for another day, but there were problems with that date too.[3] When people die, and their bodies are disposed of, that, as

Barbara said, is the end. But in the case of people who lived lives like hers, the end is usually followed by a flurry of eulogies, and then there comes a phase of reappraisal in which the person's life is reinserted into its social and temporal context, and seen and valued as part of that. Barbara's obituaries certainly celebrated her many accomplishments: her distinguished career of public service, with its membership of four Royal Commissions and four Departmental Committees; her role on the Home Office Penal Advisory Council and the Advisory Committee on Drug Dependence; her Chairmanship of the Committees which produced the famous cannabis and alternatives to prison reports; her Governorship of the BBC; her Chairmanship of the Countryside Commission; her forty years' service as a magistrate; and her peerage, inhabitation of the Woolsack, and thirty years as a debater in the House of Lords. They followed her trajectory through the academic world, from her first lectures in the handmade double skirt as Hubert Henderson in early 1920s Cambridge, through the earnestly cheerful society of the Workers' Educational Association, the principalship of Morley College, and seventeen years running extra-mural classes in London, to the professorship at Bedford College and the Nuffield Foundation grant; they noted her service on the University Grants Committee, and all the books, the lasting legacy of her social scientific mind, her lucid rationality, her no-nonsense, no-jargon approach to the asking of answerable questions about the problems of human society. Her obituary-writers fastened on the fascination of a life which had emerged from conventional origins to carve an extraordinary path; they alluded to the personal discomforts of that life, with its record of loss and thwarted motherhood. George and his taxi-cab did not escape a few mentions. In *The Guardian,* Lena Jeger called Barbara 'An Architect of the Welfare State';[4] for McGregor in *The Times,* Barbara was 'Social Philosopher and Public Servant';[5] in her local newspaper, *The Dorking Advertiser* she appeared as 'A Caring Reformer'.[6] Rob Canton in the *Probation Journal* chose 'Magistrate and Social Scientist',[7] and Philip Bean in *The British Journal of Criminology* played on the title of Barbara's own book, 'Testament for a Social Scientist'.[8] In *New Statesman & Society* she was 'the socialist and social reformer'; Tony Gould, who wrote her obituary there, used as a caption the inscription that Barbara had written inside the copy she had given him of *In a World I Never Made,* 'The Girl Who Never Made It'. This was not modesty, protested Gould, but a reference to the way Americans persistently misread the title of her book.[9]

Barbara's will omitted any arrangements for her considerable literary estate. This is strange, but it does resonate with her decided lack of interest in life after death. It was Vera who one day suggested to her that Girton College might be an appropriate location for her personal papers. During the process of tidying up such a long and productive life, a plan emerged to finance a Barbara Wootton Chair or Research

Fellowship, but, as with the memorial service, nothing happened.[10] What did happen was the publication of four volumes of Barbara's writings in 1992. The editors were Vera Seal and the criminologist Philip Bean, who described in their Preface what a 'labour of joy' it had been to put the collections together: Barbara Wootton's writing remained highly relevant, not least because she was so often ahead of her time, and its fastidious and witty language recalled her often-forgotten talents as a teacher and an orator. Has Macmillan gone mad? asked one reviewer of this labour of joy: 737 pages, or 2 kg of writings and speeches by a charter member of the great and the good. No, he decided: the 2 kg were a lot of use as well as a lot of fun. 'Anyone who wants to be reminded of how to make a civilized society should read Barbara Wootton.'[11]

Her generation was born into a world that exploded around its ears: two world wars; the development of cars and aeroplanes and atomic power; the arrival of mass broadcasting and of men on the moon. When Barbara Wootton was born, Britain had no national health service, no sickness or health insurance, no old age pensions or family allowances, no public system of secondary education and no Labour Party. Victorian Britain was certainly not a world of her choosing. She hated its class structure and the attitudes that went with it, no less because she was a beneficiary of it. She saw the economic and social system of capitalism as inefficient, unjust and destructive of human community. Religion was an excuse for not facing up to reality. Aggression and violence, whether towards individuals, communities or nations, were dismissed as unacceptable in a philosophy that placed the value of human life at the centre of everything – this 'brief flash that illumines the interval between birth and death'.[12] Her passion for social equality, 'the fire at the centre without which great things are never done',[13] burnt undiminished across the many shifting political landscapes of her life. She wore the mantle of what Noel Annan called 'a wonderful old battle-axe of the left'.[14] That was why, although being a deeply political animal and an almost lifelong member of the Labour Party, she was not at home in party politics, and refused many approaches from constituency parties looking for candidates.[15] She could not swing with the wind: if an incomes policy was morally and economically correct, the official Labour Party policy on it was irrelevant; if the Labour ministers of the day did not agree with her efforts, as Chair of the Countryside Commission, to put the principle of conservation first, she would fight the battle and she would win it.[16] She was what sociologist and poverty campaigner Peter Townsend, in his eightieth-birthday tribute, called 'The Unrepentant Democratic Socialist'.[17]

She was many other things too: 'one of the outstanding intellectuals of our time',[18] 'one of the most eminent women of her generation',[19] 'one of the most distinguished social scientists produced by this country',[20] and 'an iconoclast whose formidably critical mind challenged many conventional wisdoms'.[21] She was an example *par excellence* of a 'public intellectual': someone whose powerful mind was devoted to the analytic activities of thought and reasoning in the interests of a wide community, and in an open and accessible way.[22] In the 1960s, Barbara Wootton was 'almost a household name in contemporary Britain';[23] as the writer Rebecca West indelicately phrased it, 'Lady Wootton of Abinger is dear to all of us because we see her so often on TV, and in other places of exposure, among people who look as if they had died long ago and been stuffed by a skilful taxidermist, and she alone seems alive'.[24] When *In a World I Never Made* was published twenty-one years before Barbara's death, a number of reviewers had observed the disingenuity of its title. One of the noble Lords in that place of taxidermy complained that, whatever fresh field he found himself turning to in order to prepare for this debate or that, he found she had been there before him. 'I believe she titled her biography *In a World I Never Made*. She may feel that, but I do not believe I am alone in finding myself in a world that she has greatly influenced.'[25] As *The Birmingham Post* put it: 'Anyone who didn't know better might say that here was a woman with a man's clarity of mind and singleness of purpose who had made an extravagant success in a man's world'.[26]

For more than sixty years, Barbara Wootton provoked and inspired social scientists, politicians, political activists, bureaucrats and professionals of all kinds to think more clearly and act more wisely with respect to economic and social policy. In the 1930s, she was an intellectual leader in international movements for peace and human rights. Through her analysis of one of the great debates of the twentieth century – the dialectic between individual freedom and state planning – and her contribution to the Beveridgean welfare state, she acted as 'fairy godmother' to the post-war Labour Government.[27] 'I seem to be always saying our whole system is wrong,' she observed, with mordant clarity, in 1967.[28] No topic or policy arena or group of experts was ever quite the same once she had turned her critical gaze on it. Criminology never recovered from her allegations that opinion is not the same thing as systematically tested knowledge; penal policy was fundamentally altered by her questions about the role of punishment, the appropriateness of prison, and the kinds of control that need to be imposed on people's freedom to use mind-altering substances; and laws relating to killing and physical violence reflect her particular brand of respect for human life. Economists were so threatened by her rigorous surveillance of their abstract theories and models that all they could do was forget her. When she called sociology 'a lot of waffle' and theoretical sociology 'bunk',[29] she did not expect to endear herself to sociologists, and so she did not; this was a view, pronounced David Martin, Professor of Sociology at the LSE, which definitely limited her accomplishment.[30] In a memorable metaphor, criminologist Nigel Walker called her 'one of those intellectual helicopters who hover over other academics' fields, spraying defoliants'.[31] She never worried about upsetting people. 'Once she had come to a conclusion, she would go for it.'[32] She was a source of perpetual irritation for her ability to ask awkward questions that nobody else had bothered to ask: 'She kicked holes in things that it never occurred to me to kick holes in, and having kicked holes in them, I could see why she did it, and I thought why didn't I think of that?'[33]

What Barbara Wootton did throughout her long life was persistently and successfully to advocate the application of scientific method to the analysis and resolution of social problems. Her work was characterized by a utilitarian commitment to relevance and public service.[34] She wanted policies based on evidence which would serve utilitarian principles: the greatest happiness for the greatest number. Her brand of social science was in direct lineage from that of its early founders (Comte, Mill and Spencer), and from the earnest social accounting of the Webbs: a tradition of meticulous social observation, data-collecting and record-making, driven by practical questions, and based on a view of the social world as observable, quantifiable, and composed of facts. Most importantly for Barbara Wootton, social science was an instrument for increasing the democratic tone of a society because its methods of enquiry gave access to the experiences of ordinary people. She did not herself found a school; there was no completely new model of thinking. What she did was build a newly tight analytic framework onto the scaffold of an existing approach. In her framework, the empiricism and the utilitarianism were tied to the morality of socialism and agnosticism. Rationality was the governing principle, and it was rationality that insisted on an instrumental role for social science in gathering the kind of evidence politicians ought to have before instituting any form of governance over our lives.

Although there is no Barbara Wootton school as such, her approach to a systematic social science makes her a founding mother in Britain of a new tradition: that of evidence-informed public policy. In the early 1990s, in Britain and elsewhere in Europe, the idea that systematically gathered and reliable research evidence should feed directly into policy and practice began to spread from health care into domains of social intervention: education, social welfare, crime and justice, transport, and the environment. Impressed by the need for rationality and resource-efficiency in a climate that was rejecting old-style political ideology, governments voiced the need to know what works before making policy changes.[35] Academics, particularly those who had worked in health care, found numerous examples of well-intentioned social interventions that did more harm than good.[36] This was a message that appeared only once the research evidence had been thoroughly sifted and analysed, an embarrassing process for many social scientists who were used to taking quicker, more selective and hence potentially misleading journeys through research evidence, exactly of the kind Barbara Wootton had uncovered in her *Social Science and Social Pathology*.

One reason why Barbara Wootton's name has not been linked to the establishment of evidence-informed policy is suggested in McGregor's Foreword to the four posthumous volumes of *Selected Writings*. Barbara was a loner: 'It was in the nature of her self-contained and assured method of work that she attracted admirers but no disciples or collaborators for she had no need for the intellectual support of others'.[37] Whether or not she felt the need for such support, its absence is more likely to have been the result of the way her life was lived than a conscious choice. *Her* social science was not in sympathy with the way the social sciences were developing in Britain. Her kind of pragmatism became increasingly unpopular among British social scientists captivated by 'the apparently grand and heady sociological theory' emanating from the USA and from Europe.[38] Barbara regarded theories as only useful if they were based on facts; she wanted factual answers to such questions as: 'How do people live? Are they free to speak their minds? Do they have enough to eat? What sort of houses do they live in? Do they have fun and gaiety in childhood, adventure and opportunity in youth, ease of mind and body in old age?'[39] During the latter period of her work particularly, there was a decided turn away from the idea of the social scientist *qua* scientist, observing and experimenting with the social world like true scientists in their laboratories. This model of social science was overcome by a post-modernist rejection of the whole notion of society – not the catchy Thatcherite dismissal, 'there is no such thing as society', but a more thoughtful recitation of the ways in which society is made up of all the societies each of us thinks we live in. The complex implications of this view were hostile to Barbara Wootton's vision of social science. Her contribution to social science was not just on its practical edge, however: her perspectives on economic structures and systems, and on the place of punishment in crime and justice, for example, could never have been worked out without the kind of analytic and severely logical thinking which underlies the best and most resilient theories. Richard Titmuss, her colleague at the University of London in the 1950s, called it 'controlled passion': 'She passionately believes in social justice, yet she argues on the basis of logic,' he said in an interview about her in 1970. 'She takes up statements or hypotheses and looks at them coldly. If the function of the university is the destruction of myth, then Barbara Wootton has done more than her share.'[40] She tried to shape the form of social science during a period of its own evolution, but her particular mix of the intellectual and the practical was seen by the dominant masculine leadership as old-fashioned, perhaps even too *womanly* – serious academic study meant not muddying your feet with the troubles and puddles of social reform.

Interestingly, the one social scientist who has long respected her for her intellectual prowess and for her method, philosophy and commitment is A.H. Halsey, himself an advocate and practitioner of a rationalist and empirical social science.[41]

It might have been different had she lived and worked in the USA. American sociology had a definite positivist, scientific bent from the start: its founding fathers saw the social world much as Barbara Wootton did, as the laboratory for social science. Social science was *the* method for social reform: and at the heart of it was the need to quantify and to test experimentally different approaches to reform. In the 1930s, when President Roosevelt's New Deal programmes arrived on the policy scene, social science was waiting with the tools to establish their impact.[42] Social scientists in the USA, much more than those in Britain, embraced the vision of *Testament for Social Science* – of social science's capacity to achieve scientific rigour. One of the puzzles of Barbara Wootton's approach to social science and public policy is why she did not make more use of these American examples. She did write papers about the New Deal, but these focused on the Roosevelt Government's drive to unionization and Industrial Recovery programme, rather than 'the welter of experiments' which broke new ground in the interface between evaluation research and policy.[43] There are few references in her writings to American social science. Her *Social Science and Social Pathology* could, for instance, be seen as a direct amplification of a famous challenge by the American social scientist C. Wright Mills in a 1943 paper on 'The Professional Ideology of Social Pathologists'.[44] Wright Mills, like Barbara Wootton (or should it be 'Barbara Wootton, like Wright Mills'), was concerned to remove the value-laden assumptions that masqueraded as knowledge in professional utterances. But if Barbara had read Wright Mills, she does not say so. Her neglect of the American sociological tradition is even more striking in the light of another feature of her own social science: the emphasis she placed on controlled observation of the results of different interventions, and the systematic recording of the results of past experience.[45]

The review of research on the causes of young people's anti-social behaviour contained in *Social Science and Social Pathology* shadowed a developing tradition of systematic research reviews of social topics which avoid the potential biases and gaps of unsystematic ones. Barbara Wootton's advocacy of controlled experiments, especially in the field of penal policy, would have been very much in tune with the disposition of fellow social scientists across the Atlantic. A decade after she published *Social Science and Social Pathology*, and around the time she was arguing that the new invention of Community Service Orders should be tested in controlled experiments, the American behavioural scientist Donald Campbell put forward the idea that all efforts at social reform should be subjected to systematic evaluation before being adopted.[46] In 2000, Campbell's name was remembered in the founding of the Campbell Collaboration, an international organization of people committed to the kind of systematic reviews of the evidence obtainable from well-done studies that Barbara tried her hand at in *Social Science and Social Pathology*. The fifty-eight systematic reviews in the areas of crime and justice, education and social welfare held in the Campbell Collaboration's online library in October 2010,[47] are just the kind of evidence that she argued for in her lifetime, in her roles both as magistrate and social scientist.

Aside from the British rejection of empirical 'positivist' social science, three other features of Barbara Wootton's life and work counted against any enduring recognition of her work. First, she was a polymath: she had 'a remarkable capacity for entry into many worlds'.[48] A character in Barbara's short story 'The Morning After' acts as spokesperson here: 'There are two many octaves on your keyboard,' says Geoffrey to Nora, aka Barbara. 'So you must play complicated tunes, and inharmonious ones, because life has no music for instruments like yours.'[49] The social sciences, declared Barbara, non-fictionally, give one a licence to trespass,[50] and trespass she certainly did. She walked all over the fields of economics and social policy, and sociology and psychiatry, and medicine and criminology, and environmental policy. She not only walked there, but she left a considerable trail of footprints: hers was 'the most powerful mind' in all these fields of endeavour.[51] It has certainly been a challenge for this biographer, to follow her to all these places. Congenital trespassers continually tug at the boundaries of the way we organize our understanding of how knowledge is created, and, with the post-war sharpening of disciplinary boundaries, this mode of travel has become an increasing problem.[52] Barbara Wootton herself realized that, had her activities sprawled over fewer worlds, they might have been more effective; but, for her, the sacrifice of wide-ranging interests was temperamentally impossible.[53] Closely allied to her wandering habit was the facility she had for writing in many different kinds of journals and newspapers. She wrote what was readable, not what was academically acceptable and (like this book) full of footnotes. Peter Townsend remembers reading her *Freedom Under Planning* – a scantily footnoted book 'too readable to attract attention' but nevertheless one which did and does put an extremely well-argued case against the free market.[54] It was Townsend who noted that the particular combination of distinguished social scientist and politician manqué has a disruptive effect on reputation: the academic and Labour Party adviser Brian Abel-Smith, like Barbara Wootton a 'creative genius of post-war social policy', also suffered from it.[55]

A second aspect of Barbara Wootton's life which is woven into her invisibility as an important public figure is that she was a woman. The influence of her gender was both obvious and subtle. Her life was spattered with many absurdities of sexual inequality and discrimination, and many 'firsts' as a woman. She enjoyed telling these personal stories, but they were stories of triumph, not suffering: she got the starred first at Cambridge but could not claim a degree; there she was, a Justice of the Peace before as a woman she could vote; how ridiculous that the American authorities suspected her of nits and George of venereal disease, and only him of earning money, when it was the other way round financially. She could not count the number of times in her life when she had been graciously informed that she had a 'masculine brain'.[56] 'We get awfully tired,' she observed in the debating chamber of the House of Lords, 'of seeing all the pictures of important people signing treaties, conducting debates, forming commissions and all the rest of it, almost always entirely masculine, and certainly with a vast over-representation of the minority sex.'[57] Her personal experiences told her that women were discriminated against, but she also knew this intellectually: it was a matter of evidence. She wrote a chapter in her autobiography called 'Woman' in which she details this pattern of inequality: 'If we have come a long way, we still have far to go'.[58] Barbara herself spoke in the House of Lords on several topics of particular concern to women: the aggregation of their incomes with those of their husbands for tax purposes;[59] the invidious 'cohabitation rule', an issue that much enraged feminists in the 1970s, whereby a woman lost her right to supplementary benefit if she was found to be living with a man;[60] and the ridiculous practice of requiring a husband's consent for a wife's sterilization, but not vice versa.[61] She played a considerable role in debates relating to the Bill which eventually became the 1975 Sex Discrimination Act. She understood – and she was one of the first to do so – that women, a statistical majority, are nevertheless, like non-white men, a cultural minority group. When their noble Lords made speeches about women, she pointed out that they would never dare say that about coloured people.[62] In 1971 she inquired, not very naïvely, why only 14 out of 150 directors of Social Services were women, when most social workers were women, receiving a not very satisfactory answer.[63] 'One reason why women seldom reach senior positions,' she had already concluded in a letter to *The Times*, 'is the curious, but widespread, pretence that they do not exist.'[64] Reviewing a book on *Women in Top Jobs* in 1981, she observed that women had broken down many professional doors, but the stairs inside continued to present a formidable obstacle, which is why most of the women never got further than the ground floor.[65] Equality was a *moral* issue for Barbara Wootton. Equality between men and women involved a simple judgement that women should not be discriminated against.[66] That was the beginning and the end of it. Alone of all the topics with which she tangled during her long life, it is remarkable that what is now called 'gender' was never subjected to her critical analytical gaze. Her analysis of the class system was piercing and unrelenting, but gender as a parallel axis of stratification escaped her attention. Despite arguing that women should not be a special case, they remained a special case to her.

The greater part of her life and work happened before there was public recognition in Britain of gender equality as a moral right and a political goal. Frank Field said that 'a confident Establishment' would have appointed Barbara Wootton as Lord Chief Justice, despite the fact that she was not a barrister and not a man.[67] The problem is that confident establishments tend to be masculine and therefore unfriendly to such reversals of convention. Barbara's attitude towards the politics of feminism was curiously ambivalent. She did not see herself as campaigning for women's causes, although early in her life she had headed a young suffragists' organization.[68] The difference between suffragists who used peaceable means to claim the vote, and the suffragettes who used other means, mattered a good deal to her, as it had to her mother. Many years later, she was asked to join a women's protest against Britain joining the European Economic Community: 'I would never do it as a woman. I would do it as a political person'. Having had ample experience of being a statutory woman, she was totally opposed to this practice, and to any policy of positive discrimination: women should achieve as people, not as women.[69] Rejecting the label 'feminist',[70] she decisively dissociated herself from what she saw as the manifestations of feminism in the 1970s.[71] She abhorred the stridency of Greer's *The Female Eunuch*, although she did enjoy Kate Millett's more intellectual analysis of *Sexual Politics*.[72] The biological differences between the sexes mattered to her. In a speech she gave to the National Council of Women in Cambridge in 1962, she put forward the view that women in their jobs as 'professors, bus conductors, research chemists, or what have you' want to be treated exactly like their opposite numbers, but 'Ladies and gentlemen, when we go home we don't want to be treated like that, we want to be women, and we hope that we may be able to retain our essential femininity'.[73]

She said women had to choose between a career and motherhood,[74] but she had not chosen. Like much of her life, not having children was as much of an accident as, in different circumstances, having them could have been. Motherhood was the most complex area of Barbara Wootton's life. It was associated not only with a sense of blocked fulfilment, but with her own mother's perceived vicarious ambitions for her children, ambitions which were divided between the surviving son who was unquestionably distinguished, and the daughter who only might have been. She carried Adela's hurtful remark – 'My daughter, who might have been distinguished' – with her throughout life.[75] Barbara Wootton's hostility towards her mother never dimmed, and it was accompanied by a reluctance to recognize, not only Adela's own achievements as a scholar and teacher and defender of women's rights, but the difficulties she must have surmounted when widowed on a small income with three children. Perhaps, because she never experienced it herself, motherhood retained for Barbara the conventional aura of romanticism it has for many women before the reality hits home. Her defence of children over her many years as a magistrate and a peer was based on a practical knowledge of their problems, but it also reflected to some extent a distanced and unrealistic view; according to one of her friends, it may have been this attitude that helped to explain her very radical proposal that erring children should not be treated in the criminal justice system at all.[76]

A third factor contributing to the disappearance of Barbara Wootton's reputation is her marginality in the academic world. Women have rarely prospered in that world, which retains a marked ability to treat them differently.[77] A.H. Halsey, one of the few sociologists to take Barbara Wootton's work seriously, sees her as one of the four most important intellectual figures in British sociology during the first half of the twentieth century; the others – Hobhouse, Ginsberg and Marshall – were all LSE men. Strikingly, though, in his 2001 survey of sociology professors' views about the shapers of their subject in the twentieth century, not one mentioned Barbara Wootton. All their significant figures were male, and most were European or American theorists.[78] Although Barbara Wootton moved in and out of academic institutions, she never, unlike male theorists, felt at home in them; she did not particularly cultivate the attention of academics, and she did not devote herself to pedagogy or to fostering post-graduate work. Academia responded by denying her access to many of its opportunity-structures, and by refusing to reward her presence through the usual mechanism of creating groups or departments around her work. Had the situation at Bedford College in the late 1940s and early 1950s been more receptive to Barbara and her programme of social science research, she might have established a stream of work and scholar-researchers who advanced her kind of empirically-based social science. However, the College was hostile, and by the time her *tour de force*, *Social Science and Social Pathology*, was published, she had given up the academic world as a lost cause.

Barbara Wootton took a straightforward view of the relationship between research and policy: you should not have one without the other, and it is dangerous not to rest policy on a secure research base. Yet social facts uncovered by social scientists are rarely used in any direct way to formulate policy, for all sorts of reasons. Towards the end of her life, Barbara was beginning to acknowledge this. For example, of all the hours of her life she had devoted to the work of Royal Commissions and similar organs of enquiry, few produced results, and these were often small in proportion to the hours consumed; legislation rarely followed and, even where it did, government departments tended to do the Commission's work all over again before the relevant Bill was introduced. The best that could be said was that a Commission Report and its assembled evidence 'is one of the factors in the lengthy and mysterious process of modifying the mental climate'.[79] Much of the influence of social science research on policy, especially in Britain, was, and is, achieved through social networking.[80] Barbara was not very interested in this; she was not particularly disposed to take a strategic line towards power structures and relationships in trying to get policy-makers to use what she regarded as the right sort of evidence. For much of the time when she was active in the social science and policy world, Barbara Wootton was perceived as too challenging to the establishment. She once joked that the main Committee Room in the Home Office was 'the cell in which she served a life sentence',[81] but, without her reputation for radicalism, the sentence might have been a good deal longer. The statistician and criminologist Leslie Wilkins remembers in his *Unofficial Aspects of a Life in Policy Research*, how, when he was a Home Office civil servant in the 1960s, a circular came round asking for suggestions for people to be recommended to the Minister as members of a proposed Royal Commission on law reform. Wilkins nominated Barbara, but her name was removed almost immediately by his superior who complained that her radicalism made her a liability.[82] She was a liability, and she knew she was. When she talked about academic freedom in South Africa in 1969, Barbara expressed a concern about the funding of research by governments. She feared especially the fate of social science research, given that it is 'prone to uncover social evils which governments prefer to brush under the carpet or to elicit facts which reveal either the failure of well-intentioned governmental policies or the sinister quality of the ill-intentioned'.[83]

Barbara Wootton did not much favour the examination of deep psychological motives – indeed her distrust of social workers and of psychiatrists for indulging in this habit is spelt out in much of her writing – so she looks over my shoulder as I speculate now about what might have lain behind her extraordinary achievements. It is the line of that Housman poem that comes before 'In a world I never made' in his *Last Poems* which holds the clue: 'I, a stranger and afraid'. Again, Barbara's fiction speaks for her: 'In your heart you're afraid … You're afraid of all the things you think you want. You're afraid ever to let go of anything you've ever had your hands on … But most of all, of course, it's yourself you're afraid of.'[84] The stiff upper lip, the turning one's back on tragedy and just carrying on – a characteristic of her class and generation – came at a price. Strong emotions – love, sexual passion, despair, anger, hatred, frustration – could not easily be felt or named. The intellect was the instrument of control. Barbara revered the power of human intelligence above everything. 'In this astonishing age,' she said, 'we have learnt to fly above the earth and to voyage beneath the deeps of the ocean. Our stockings are made from coal and air, our spectacle frames from milk. We make love without conceiving and have our teeth removed without pain. And all this has been accomplished … by the unfettered exercise of the human intelligence.'[85] Her respect for intelligence stemmed not just from what it could do to transform human society but from its role in providing the steer for her own life. She knew what she had, and what she did not have. 'If I were to be granted the realization of one wish on behalf of the human race,' she wrote movingly in her autobiography, 'that wish would be that the love of two people for one another should always begin and end at the same moment in each case.'[86]

In the 1920s and 30s, and also later, she suffered from 'prolonged periods of great emotional disturbance'.[87] She did not call it depression – the depression which her father and her brother Neil had endured – and one imagines a certain stubborn resistance on her part to any kind of labelling or official diagnosis. But she did admit in a letter to William Haley, written around the time *In a World I Never Made* was published, that she had been 'kept going' for nearly a year 'by some of the modern specific anti-depressant drugs'.[88] Some years later, she confided in a letter to Peter Townsend that, 'I sometimes think my values are all wrong and that I fritter endless time away in trivialities (and unsuccessful activities) when it would be better to give to personal than to public obligations.'[89] Not many people thought of Barbara Wootton as afraid of anything,[90] but there was an intense vulnerability about her, a neediness. Sociologist Jean Floud recalled an occasion when Barbara gave a seminar at Nuffield College, Oxford – a prestigious event on the subject of sociological jurisprudence. It was very well attended, although Jean was the only other woman there apart from Barbara. Some of the men, especially the American academics, gave Barbara a hard time; there was much learned disagreement conducted in the confrontational style of debate usual in Oxbridge circles. As Jean Floud remembers: 'The awful thing was at the break I took her to the, what do you call it, the powder room, and she burst into tears and said, "I can't bear this. They just grill one", and I tried to say, "but it's the sign of the greatest respect here. They take you terribly seriously." She couldn't bear it … she said, "these beastly Oxbridge people".'[91] Barbara's own style of debate was very different: she was good at stimulating discussion, and clear about what she herself thought, but she never put people down.[92]

A sign of a painful inner insecurity was that she much disliked being alone. 'Often she would say to me, do you get lonely, or are you often lonely? … she always wanted someone beside her.' Every week when Barbara went to preside over the Chelsea Juvenile Court, she insisted that Vera go with her. Vera had no official role there, but they gave her a chair and a small table. 'When the Court was about to begin, the three Justices would enter, led by Barbara, who would look immediately at where I would be and give a little bow (which I returned).'[93] In her later years, Barbara's increasing difficulty with walking gave her an excuse to hang off men's arms.[94] Sometimes people who have a reputation for appearing cold, abrupt, caustic, contemptuous of other people's weaknesses – all descriptions offered at various times of Barbara Wootton – are inhibited by shyness from expressing warmth and compassion. Barbara could be warm and compassionate in private, and she is remembered for this by many of her friends. She was 'quite amazingly open to any sort of conversation.

She was both interesting and interested.'[95] 'She was also very tactile. She would put her arm round you and cuddle you and make you feel wanted.'[96] She had a developed 'sense of fun and of the ridiculous'; 'she loved a good flirt'.[97]

But, in her public persona, the veneer of unemotional super-rationality was all-important. Almost everything Barbara Wootton said or wrote was considered very carefully and uttered very precisely; hesitation, uncertainty and self-criticism were not conditions with which she engaged. These traits and behaviours did not make her likeable. 'In public places she could be mistaken for one of those able, independent women who are as tough as old boots.'[98] She was 'an intellectual giant' who ate most men alive.[99] Her likeability decreased as she got older, a fact of which she was well aware. Ageing, she declared, brings a diminution of the will or the power to maintain 'the inhibitions, the poses and the protective masks by which many of us have struggled to present a respectable face to the world'.[100] She was often cantankerous and bad-tempered. In his speech at her funeral, Campbell Adamson recalled how irritating Barbara had been on a holiday five of them had taken on the canals of Burgundy a few years earlier. The anecdote involved Barbara's major pastime, Scrabble. She insisted that Campbell should play it with her every evening, and was determined 'with a seriousness which was almost frightening' to win. Thus, he succeeded on winning on very few occasions, but, when he did, it took more than the usual round of drinks to get rid of her grumpiness for the rest of the evening.[101] She had a reputation for writing to newspapers with sternly worded reprimands about mistakes they had made in reporting her views; she took a hard line with interviewers who put words into her mouth or generalized about her, or used the word 'always' too much; and she got steadily crosser over the years about people's misspellings of her name. One of her latter furies was vented on the author and journalist Angela Neustatter, who inadvertently gave the 'Lady Wooton' in Oscar Wilde's *A Picture of Dorian Gray* an extra 't', thereby suggesting that the unflattering remark about the fictional character's wardrobe being 'designed in a rage and put on in a tempest' applied to the real Lady Wootton. Neustatter was forced to apologize.[102]

She would be irate at the continuance of this tradition today. The digitalized version of Hansard has her as 'Ms Barbara Wooton', an error which goes back to the Lord Chamberlain's omission of the second 'T' in the Parliamentary Papers announcing her peerage in 1958.[103] She appears as Wootten, Wooten, and Wooton in various books and library catalogues – when she appears at all. It is hard not to see as a conspiracy Barbara Wootton's very obvious omission from the websites of so many endeavours with which she was connected: the British Humanist Association, the British Sociological Association, the list of Members of the Order of the Companions of Honour, the exclusive London Lunchtime Comment Club;

and her absence from political dictionaries and dictionaries about women, from histories of the British Left, and economic planning, and sociological thought and method and economics and its methodology; and from accounts of public policy development.[104] Barbara Wootton has largely faded from our assembled narratives about people who shaped the world of social problems and social policy.

This is sad in itself, but also because much of what she said and wrote is still, or newly, relevant today. She had an unnerving capacity to be 'ten steps ahead of anybody else'.[105] Many of the views with which Barbara Wootton shocked conventional opinion at the time have now been woven into the culture: her scepticism about social work; her disappointment in economics; her acceptance of changing sexual relationships and behaviour; her mistrust of the legal system's ability to deliver ethical, effective and equal justice; and her understanding of poverty as a problem of material resources, not of inadequate biology. Her criticisms, in 1984, of the Thatcherite policy of curbing investment and production to promote economic recovery referred to the very different strategy used successfully in the 1930s to boost demand without creating inflation;[106] similar issues confront the British economy in the second decade of the twenty-first century. Social economists would find her *Lament* well worth citing for its incisive critique of the neoclassical theory that is still expounded and practised today.[107] Peter Townsend noted how much her arguments about incomes and about inequality still apply – and how that image of the elephant earning its unfair whack in Whipsnade Zoo compared with hers in Regent's Park retains its capacity to capture the imagination.[108] *The Social Foundations of Wage Policy* is regularly quoted in discussions about the ethics and economics of the wage structure and income distribution, and nobody has seriously disproved Barbara Wootton's contention that the wage structure is simply a socially engineered restrictive practice for better-off members of the community.[109] In the domain of penal policy, the transformation of Community Service Orders into a punitive scheme would incur one of her famous appeals to the (lack of) evidence. Barbara Wootton's famous remark – if men behaved like women, the criminal justice system would be deprived of most of its work – is still true; and explanations for the gender discrepancy in crime have become more elaborate, but not very much more precise, since her trespassing on the criminological literature in the 1950s.[110] Cars and the deaths they cause, another of her signal themes, now constitute 'a major public health crisis', accounting for more than a million deaths and around 50 million injuries every year – some three per cent of the global disease burden – but the war on the roads is almost as neglected now as it was in her lifetime.[111]

Barbara Wootton's other most-quoted work, *Social Science and Social Pathology*, retains its resonance for many contemporary issues.[112] In social work, she anticipated many of the themes at the heart of modern debates on social work practice, and she was often the first to propose questions that have still to be resolved, especially about the social worker-client relationship.[113] Her book provided a rebuttal of eugenic theories of the 'underclass' some thirty years before they were advanced by Charles Murray and others.[114] The essentially pragmatic view she put forward, that deviance is what people define as deviance, ante-dated the sociological literature of the late 1960s in which 'numerous writers in varying degrees of tortuous prolixity' said basically the same thing.[115]

The modesty and pessimism of old age made Barbara answer 'No' to the question, whether she considered herself a successful person. She realized she had acquired a certain public reputation, but what mattered more to her was that the world was about as nasty or even nastier than it had been when she started. 'I set out to make a little dent in it. Well, I have made tiny little dents here and there.'[116] The size of the dents belies Barbara Wootton's own belief in accurate social observation. She had a profound influence on the intellectual and political world, and her reluctance to take ownership of this fact reflects as much the world's treatment of her efforts as the constraints imposed on these by character and circumstance. Future historians are likely to re-evaluate her role as 'the intellectual midwife of a new kind of society'.[117]

McGregor summed up the relationship between her politics and her intellect: she was a revolutionary in ideas, but a democrat in politics.[118] The last paragraph of *In a World I Never Made* is one of Barbara Wootton's most quoted texts. It is about politics not being what it is often said to be, the art of the possible. It was not that to her. 'The limits of the possible constantly shift, and those who ignore them are apt to win in the end. Again and again I have had the satisfaction of seeing the laughable idealism of one generation evolve into the accepted commonplace of the next. But it is from the champions of the impossible rather than the slaves of the possible that evolution draws its creative force.'[119]

Barbara Wootton's life saw many shifts in the boundaries of political and other kinds of possibility. It was habit and insatiable curiosity – about the future of the world, about Britain and its politics – that kept her going. In her optimistic moments, she was amazed at the social progress that had been accomplished in her lifetime, and comforted when she found younger energetic socialists who shared her ideas.[120] Her reputation for being a critical woman was well-deserved. She was a critical woman because criticism and reform go hand in hand. While not all critics are reformers, criticism is the engine of reform. Far from being an abstract, solipsistic activity, it is what causes us to look around at this world we did not make for places, sometimes entire landscapes, where our individual efforts can make a difference.

Notes

Abbreviations used in the notes

BL	British Library
BLPES	British Library of Political and Economic Science
BW	Barbara Wootton
CAC	Churchill Archives Centre, Churchill College, Cambridge
GCAC	Girton College Academic and Library
GCAR	Girton College Administrative Records
GCAS	Girton College Clubs Societies and Associations
GCPP Cam	Girton College, Personal Papers, Helen Maud Cam
GCPP Duke	Girton College, Personal Papers, Alison Duke
GCPP Wootton	Girton College, Personal Papers, Barbara Wootton
GCRF	Girton College Historical Reference
Harrison, TWL	Oral evidence on the suffragette and suffragist movements: the Brian Harrison Interviews, The Women's Library, London Metropolitan University, 8SUF/B/068, Barbara Wootton interview, 1976
HC Deb.	House of Commons Debates
HL Deb.	House of Lords Debates
HLRO	House of Lords Record Office
PA	Parliamentary Archives
Seal Papers	Personal Papers of Vera Seal
Titmuss Papers	Papers of Richard Titmuss held by Ann Oakley
Townsend Papers	Personal Papers of Peter Townsend
UAA	University of Adelaide Archives

Barbara Wootton's books

BWSW	*Barbara Wootton: Selected Writings – Volume 1 Crime and the Penal System 1, Volume 2 Crime and the Penal System II: Social Welfare, Volume 3 Social and Political Thought, Volume 4 Economic and Methodological Thought* (eds V. G. Seal and P. Bean, 1992), London: Macmillan.
CB	*Contemporary Britain* (1971), London: Allen & Unwin.
CCL	*Crime and the Criminal Law: Reflections of a Magistrate and Social Scientist* (1963, 2nd edition 1981) London: Stevens & Sons.
CPP	*Crime and Penal Policy: Reflections on Fifty Years' Experience* (1978), London: Allen & Unwin.
ESI	*End Social Inequality* (1941), London: Kegan Paul Trench Trubner & Co Ltd.
FUP	*Freedom Under Planning* (1945), London: Allen & Unwin.

IP	*Incomes Policy: An Inquest and a Proposal* (1974), London: Davis-Poynter.
IWNM	*In a World I Never Made* (1967), London: Allen & Unwin.
LE	*Lament for Economics* (1938), London: Allen & Unwin.
LB	*London's Burning: A Novel for the Decline and Fall of the Liberal Age* (1936), London: Allen & Unwin.
PNP	*Plan or No Plan* (1934), London: Victor Gollancz.
SFWP	*The Social Foundations of Wage Policy* (1955, 2nd edition 1962) London: Allen & Unwin.
SSSP	*Social Science and Social Pathology* (1959), London: Allen & Unwin.
TT	*Twos and Threes* (1933), London: Gerald Howe Ltd.
TSS	*Testament for Social Science: An Essay in the Application of Scientific Method to Human Problems* (1950), London: Allen & Unwin.

Note on sources for BW writings quoted in the text: The full published citation is given where known, but when the source consulted was in GCPP Wootton, the relevant file number is given in square brackets.

Introduction: Writing a Life of Barbara Wootton

1   There have been several commentaries on aspects of her work: see Dimand, R.W. and Hardeen, I. (2003) 'Barbara Wootton's Lament for Economics and Vision of a Social Economics', *Forum for Social Economics*, 33(1); King, J.E. (2003) 'Lament for Economics, or How Barbara Wootton Gave It All Away and Became a Sociologist', *Research in the History of Economic Thought and Methodology*, 22: 301–321; Jacobs, E. (2007) '"An Organizing Female with a Briefcase": Barbara Wootton, Political Economy and Social Justice, 1920–1950', *Women's History Review*, 16(3): 431–446; Johnson, Y.V. (2008) 'Remembering Barbara Wootton's Contribution to Social Work Education', *Journal of Social Work Education*, 44(1): 23–36. There is also a festschrift: Bean, P. and Whynes, D. (eds) *Barbara Wootton: Social Science and Public Policy, Essays in her Honour*, London: Tavistock; and O. R. McGregor's 'Foreword' to the four posthumous volumes, *BWSW*.

2   Thompson, E.P. (1968) *The Making of the English Working Class*, Harmondsworth: Penguin Books, p. 13.

3   Jefferys, M. (1978) 'Serendipity: An Autobiographical Account of the Career of a Medical Sociologist in Britain', in Elling, R.H. and Sokolowska, M. (eds) *Medical Sociologists at Work*, New Brunswick, New Jersey: Transaction Books: 135–161, p. 144.

4   N. Morgan, Personal communication.

5   'Women of Our Century: Baroness Barbara Wootton', Interview by A. Clwyd, 26 July 1984, BBC Television, transcript, p. 40, GCPP Wootton 3/2/1 (published in L. Caldecott (1984) *Women of Our Century*, London: Ariel Books).

6   Correspondence between T. Gould and T. Lacey, November 1985; thanks to T. Gould.

7   Stanley, L. (1992) *The Auto/biographical I: Theory and Practice of Feminist Autobiography*, Manchester: Manchester University Press, p. 135.

8   See Oakley, A. (2010) 'The Social Science of Biographical Life-Writing: Some Methodological and Ethical Issues', *International Journal of Social Research Methodology*, 10 February 2010 (iFirst) DOI:10.1080/13645571003593583.

9   Gottschalk, L., Kluckhohn, C. and Angell, R. (1945) *The Use of Personal Documents in History, Anthropology and Sociology*, New York: Social Science Research Council.

10   A. Ashford, Interview, 30 July 2008.

11   Wright Mills, C. (1959) *The Sociological Imagination*, New York: Oxford University Press, p. 3.

12   *The Spokesman Review*, 22 October 1958.

13   BW to P. Bean, 16 February 1982, GCPP Wootton 2/2.

14   BW to C. Tomalin, 14 August 1974, *New Statesman* Archives, Correspondence Wootton, Barbara (2) 29.7.74, 14.8.74 and (1) 8.8.74, University of Sussex.

15   R. McGregor and N. McGregor, Interview, 8 August 2008.

1. Ladies of the House

1 Sutherland, D. (2000) 'Peeresses, Parliament and Prejudices – the Admission of Women to the House of Lords, 1918–1963', in Upton, A. F. (ed.) *Parliaments, Estates and Representation* Vol. 20, Aldershot, Hants.: Ashgate Publishing Ltd, pp. 215–231.

2 Cited in Brookes, P. (1967) *Women at Westminster,* London: Peter Davies, p. 208.

3 HL Deb., 31 October 1957, 205: 690.

4 Brookes, *Women at Westminster*, p. 206

5 HC Deb., 13 February 1958, 582: 611.

6 Cited in Hollis, P. (1997) *Jennie Lee: A Life*, Oxford: Oxford University Press, p. 381.

7 BW, *ESI,* p. 35.

8 Brazier, R. (1999) 'The Second Chamber: Paradoxes and Plans' in Carmichael, P. and Dickson, B. (eds) *The House of Lords*, Oxford: Hart Publishing, pp. 53–65.

9 BW, *IWNM,* p. 268.

10 HL Deb., 3 December 1957, 206: 710.

11 HL Deb., 30 October 1957, 205: 590.

12 'A Writ of Summons to Parliament', GCPP Wootton 1/3/7.

13 BW, *IWNM,* p. 130.

14 Stanford, P. (2001) 'Lord Longford', Obituary, *The Guardian,* 6 August.

15 F. Field, Interview, 7 February 2008.

16 'The First List of Life Peers', *The Times,* 24 May 1971.

17 'A Writ of Summons to Parliament'.

18 BW, *IWNM,* p. 133.

19 'Life Peeresses' Room at Westminster: Walls in "Light Neutral Shades"', *The Times,* 20 October 1958.

20 BW, *IWNM,* p. 133.

21 BW to Viscount Hailsham, 30 November 1962, PA, LH/1/74.

22 'Peeresses Will Need Robes, Hire from "Pool" Suggested', *The Times,* 25 July 1958.

23 '4 New Lady Lords Must Wear Robes Costing Great Deal', *The Free-Lance Star,* 25 July 1958.

24 'The Ladies Join the Lords as Though Born to It,' *The Manchester Guardian,* 22 October 1958.

25 'Women First to Join Lords; Keep Hats On', *Chicago Tribune,* 22 October 1958; 'The Ladies Join the Lords as Though Born to It', *The Manchester Guardian,* 22 October 1958.

26 BW, *IWNM,* p. 253.

27 BW, *IWNM,* p. 130.

28 Kamm, J. (1966) *Rapiers and Battleaxes,* London: Allen & Unwin, p. 217.

29 'The Ladies Join the Lords as Though Born to It'.

30 'Women First to Join Lords; Keep Hats On'.

31 'Life Peeresses Take the Oath, First in History of Parliament', *The Times,* 22 October 1958.

32 Longford, Lord (1994) *Avowed Intent,* London: Little, Brown and Company, p. 139.

33 'The Ladies Join the Lords as Though Born to It.'

34 Drewry, G. and Brock, J. (1983) *The Impact of Women on the House of Lords,* University of Strathclyde: Centre for the Study of Public Policy, p. 15.

35 De Courcy, A. (2000) *The Viceroy's Daughters*, London: Weidenfeld and Nicolson, p. 140.

36 See http://www.bbc.co.uk/radio4/history/sceptred_isle [accessed 21 April 2008].

37 Kamm, *Rapiers and Battleaxes*, p. 217.

38 Tennant, E. (1998) *Strangers: A Family Romance,* London: Jonathan Cape.

39 See http://www.bbc.co.uk/radio4/history/sceptred_isle [accessed 21 April 2008].

40 Phillips, M. (1980) *The Divided House: Women at Westminster,* London: Sidgwick and Jackson, p. 136.

41 Arnold, S. 'No Trolling Around on the Woolsack', *The Observer Magazine,* 1 May 1977 [GCPP Wootton 1/2/3].

42 Lundberg, F. and Farnham, M.F. (1947) *Modern Woman: The Lost Sex,* New York: Harper and Row.

43 Riley, D. (1983) *War in the Nursery,* London: Virago.

44 Myrdal, A. and Klein, V. (1956) *Women's Two Roles: Home and Work*, London: Routledge & Kegan Paul.

45 Mitchell, J. (1971) 'Women: The Longest Revolution', *New Left Review*, 40.

46 Greed, C. 'Why UK is Going Down the Pan', *The Times Higher*, 26 July 2002, p. 21.

47 Cited in 'Respectable, But …' *Time*, 4 August 1958.

48 'Dulles, Dulles, Lloyd & Dulles', *The Observer*, 27 July 1958.

49 M. Rees to BW, 24 July 1958, GCPP Wootton 1/3/4.

2. A Cat Called Plato

1   BW, *IWNM*, p. 23.

2   Adam, A.M. (1908) 'Memoir' in A. M. Adam (ed.) *The Religious Teachers of Greece* by J. Adam, Edinburgh: T & T Clark, pp. i–lv, p. i.

3   Adam, 'Memoir', p. iii.

4   D. Bruce to BW, 26 December 1958, GCPP Wootton 1/5/4.

5   Letter from M. Adam to A.M. Kensington, 12 May 1890; thanks to D. Adams.

6   Adam, 'Memoir', p. vi.

7   Ibid., p. ix.

8   Ibid., p. x.

9   Ibid., pp. xviii–xix.

10 Giles, P. (2004) 'Adam, James (1860–1907)', rev. M.J. Schofield, *Oxford Dictionary of National Biography*, Oxford: Oxford University Press. http://0-www.oxford.dnb.com.catalogue.ulrls.lon.ac.uk/view/article/30331 [accessed 24 May 2010].

11 Adam, 'Memoir', p. xxxii.

12 Diary entries; thanks to D. Adams.

13 Record of Speeches Made by Baroness Wootton of Abinger and Mrs C.D. Rackham at Golden Jubilee Dinner of the Cambridge Branch of the National Council of Women on 9 July 1962, GCPP Duke 1/30, p. 1.

14 Adam, 'Memoir', p. xxxv.

15 G. Thomas, Personal communication.

16 BW, *IWNM*, p. 19.

17 [No author given] (1822) *The Stranger's Guide Through Jersey in Three Descriptive Tours Throughout That Island*, Guernsey: T. Dowdney.

18 Hopkins, C. (2005) *Trinity: 450 years of an Oxford College Community*, Oxford: Oxford University Press, pp. 230–231.

19 C.J. Hopkins, Personal communication.

20 Société Jersiaise (1905) *Bulletins* 27–30 1912–5, Jersey: Labey et Blampied, Vol. 5: p. 230; R. Prendergast, Personal communication.

21 W. Haley to BW, 2 June 1981, GCPP Wootton 2/1.

22 Balleine, G.R. (1948) *A Biographical Dictionary of Jersey*, London: Staples Press Ltd.

23 Payne, J.B. (1859–65) *An Armorial of Jersey* [no publisher given].

24 'The Jersey Revolution, 28th September 1769', BBC News, http://www.isthisjersey.com/news.php?item.543.8 [accessed 29 December 2008].

25 'C.W. Le Geyt Esq.', Obituary, *The Gentleman's Magazine*, April 1827, p. 367.

26 Payne, *An Armorial*.

27 [No author given] (1955) Review of *Privileges Loix et Coutumes de l'Isle de Jersey* by Philippe le Geyt. 'Code Le Geyt' (completed in 1698, published by Bigwoods, Ltd., Jersey, for the Jersey law Society, 1953), *International and Comparative Law Quarterly*, 4(4): 574–576.

28 Drake, W.R. (1882) *Heathiana: Notes, Genealogical and Biographical of the Family of Heath Especially of the Descendants of Benjamin Heath*, D.C.L. of Exeter, London: Privately printed for Baron Robert Amadeus Heath.

29 Rose Mary Le Geyt, 1816–1901; R. Prendergast, Personal communication.

30 BW, *IWNM*, p. 19.

31   Adam, A.M. (1931) 'Frances Kensington: A Friend of the College', Obituary, *The Girton Review*, 85&86: 3–4.

32   BW, *IWNM*, p. 27.

33   Willmott, P. (1992) *A Singular Woman: The Life of Geraldine Aves 1898–1986*, London: Whiting & Birch, p. 14.

34   Adam, 'Memoir', pp. xxii–xxiii.

35   BW, *IWNM*, p. 17.

36   A. Ashford, Interview, 30 July 2008.

37   Essex, R. (1977) *Woman in a Man's World*, London: Sheldon Press, p. 2.

38   Postgate, J. and Postgate, M. (1964) *A Stomach for Dissent: The Life of Raymond Postgate 1896–1971*, Keele: Keele University Press, p. 14.

39   Keynes, J.M. cited in Skidelsky, R. (2004) *John Maynard Keynes 1883–1946*, London: Pan Books, pp. 42–43.

40   A.V. Williams to BW, 1 July 1968, GCPP Wootton 3/2/4.

41   Adam, J. (ed. Adam, A.M.) (1911) *The Vitality of Platonism and Other Essays*, Cambridge: Cambridge University Press, pp. 215–216.

42   Giles, 'Adam, James'.

43   BW, *IWNM*, pp. 18–19.

44   Ibid., p. 19.

45   'Mrs James Adam', Obituary, *The Times*, 15 August 1944.

46   BW, *IWNM*, p. 20.

47   Record of Speeches, p. 8.

48   'Women's Suffrage. Cambridge Mass Meeting, Eloquent Addresses', *Cambridge Independent Press*, 7 January 1910.

49   Record of Speeches, p. 7.

50   Tullberg, R.M. (2004) 'Keynes, Florence Ada (1861–1958)', *Oxford Dictionary of National Biography*, Oxford: Oxford University Press, online edn. http://0-www.oxford.dnb.com.catalogue.ulrls.lon.ac.uk/view/article/39171 [accessed 24 May 2010].

51   Harrison, TWL, p.1.

52   Adam, A.M. et al. (1917) 'Women's Suffrage', Letter, *Cambridge Independent Press*, 26 January.

53   A. Ashford, Interview, 30 July 2008.

54   Harrison, TWL, p. 1.

55   Mack, J. (1977) 'Barbara Wootton', *New Society*, 14 April, pp. 58–59.

56   Cunningham, J. (1982) 'Out of Step', *The Guardian*, 4 June.

57   Harrison, TWL, p. 8.

58   'Women of Our Century: Baroness Wootton', Interview by A. Clwyd 26 July 1984, BBC Television, transcript, p. 4, GCPP Wootton 3/2/1 (published in L. Caldecott (1984) *Women of Our Century*, London: Ariel Books).

59   Christmas, L. (1977) 'Situation Wanted: Girton Girl', *The Guardian*, 14 December [GCPP Wootton 1/2/2].

60   Raverat, G. (1952) *Period Piece: A Cambridge Childhood*, London: Faber and Faber, p. 210.

61   BW, *IWNM*, p. 22.

62   Ibid., p. 22.

63   Ibid., pp. 24–25.

64   Wootton, B. (1946) 'John Maynard Keynes', Obituary, *The Highway*, November, pp. 11–12 [GCPP Wootton 3/4/1].

65   'Face the Press', Tyne Tees Television Ltd, recorded 4 January 1984, Baroness Wootton of Abinger interviewed by P. Toynbee, G. Smith and A. Howard, transcript, p. 13, GCPP Wootton 3/2/1.

66   BW (1982) 'Memories of an Edwardian Girlhood', *London Review of Books*, 4(4): 13–14.

67   BW, *IWNM*, p. 26.

68   Ibid., p. 24.

69   Gathorne-Hardy, J. (1974) *The Rise and Fall of the British Nanny*, London: Arrow Books, p. 7.

70   Churchill, W.S. (1973, originally published 1900) *Savrola*, Bath: Cedric Chivers, Ltd, p. 41.

71   Raverat, *Period Piece*, p. 76.

72   Hutchinson, D. (1954) *Family Inheritance: A Life of Eva Hubback,* London: Staples Press.

73   E. Haynes to BW, May 1954, GCPP Wootton 1/1/4.

74   E. Haynes to N.K. Adam, 10 April 1958, GCPP Wootton 1/1/4.

75   Clwyd, 'Women of Our Century'.

76   Postgate, R., cited in Postgate and Postgate, *A Stomach for Dissent*, p. 23.

77   Cole, M. (1949) *Growing Up Into Revolution*, London: Longmans, Green and Co, p. 16.

78   BW, *IWNM*, p. 58.

79   A.M. Adam to W. Chawner, 4 January 1906, COL.9.3./James Adam, Emmanuel College Archives.

80   Clwyd, 'Women of Our Century'.

81   Adam, A.M. (1920) *Arthur Innes Adam 1894–1916: A Record Founded on His Letters,* Cambridge: Bowes and Bowes, pp. 6–7.

82   Adam, *Arthur Innes Adam*, p. 35.

3. Alma Mater

1   Emmanuel College Archives, Col. 9.3./James Adam.

2   BW, *IWNM*, p. 29.

3   Mitchison, N. (1975) *All Change Here: Girlhood and Marriage*, London: The Bodley Head, p. 113.

4   Vicinus, M. (1985) *Independent Women: Work and Community for Single Women,* London: Virago, p. 137.

5   Raverat, G. (1952) *Period Piece: A Cambridge Childhood,* London: Faber and Faber, p. 104.

6   Dyhouse, C. (1981) *Girls Growing up in Late Victorian and Edwardian England,* London: Routledge & Kegan Paul.

7   Raverat, *Period Piece*, p. 61.

8   Cole, M. (1949) *Growing Up Into Revolution,* London: Longmans, Green and Co, p. 17.

9   Mitchison, *All Change Here*, pp. 11–12.

10   Scott, M.A. (1981) *The Perse School for Girls, Cambridge: The First Hundred Years, 1881–1981,* Cambridge: The Governors of the Perse School for Girls, p. 68.

11   Reports from Commissioners: *Schools Inquiry*, 1 (Session 19 November 1867–31 July 1868 pp. 548–549), cited in Burstall, S.A. (1907) *English High Schools for Girls,* London: Longmans, Green & Co, p. 6.

12   Burstall, *English High Schools*; Hunt, F. (1987) 'Divided Aims: The Educational Implications of Opposing Ideologies in Girls' Secondary Schooling, 1850–1940', in Hunt, F. (ed.) *Lessons for Life: The Schooling of Girls and Women 1850–1950,* Oxford: Basil Blackwell, pp. 3–21.

13   Scott, *The Perse School*, p. 14.

14   Raverat, *Period Piece,* p. 61.

15   Scott, *The Perse School*, p. 108.

16   Ibid., pp. 47–48.

17   Ibid., p. 64.

18   BW, *IWNM,* p. 31.

19   Letter from B. L. Kennett, 23 October 1913, GCAC 2/4/1/6.

20   BW to Mrs Cubitt, 22 May 1981, The Stephen Perse Foundation Archives.

21   Geddes, J.F. (1997) 'A Portrait of "The Lady": A Life of Dorothy Russell', *Journal of the Royal Society of Medicine,* 90: 455–461.

22   BW, *IWNM*, pp. 33–34.

23   *The Persean Magazine* (1911), 6(52): 272; *The Persean Magazine* (1912), 6(54): 379; 7(56): 7.

24   Adam, A.M. (1912) *The Need for a Course of Study in Classical & Later Literature Combined.* Paper read before the Cambridge Classical Society, Cambridge: Bowes and Bowes, University of Southampton Library Archives and Manuscripts, MS 102 LF 780 UNI 8/12/551/1.

25   A.M. Adam to 'Miss Clover', 26 March 1920 and 31 May 1931, GCAR 2/5/1/1.

26   A.M. Adam to W. Chawner, 7 September 1909, Emmanuel College Archives, Col. 9.3./James Adam.

27 BW, *IWNM*, p. 35.

28 M. Cole to BW, 20 February [no year given] and 1 March [no year given], GCPP Wootton 1/2/5.

29 Meynell, F. (1971) *My Lives,* London: Bodley Head.

30 Williams, F. (1970) *Nothing So Strange: An Autobiography,* London: Cassell, p. 149.

31 Harte, N.B. (1979) *The Admission of Women to University College London: A Centenary Lecture,* London: University College.

32 Jepson, N.A. (1973) *The Beginnings of English University Adult Education – Policy and Problems,* London: Joseph.

33 Deléphine, S. (1894) 'A Sketch of the Life and Work of Sir Andrew Clark, Bart.,' *Journal of Pathology and Bacteriology,* 2: 255–268.

34 BW, *IWNM,* p. 62.

35 Blunt, A. (1994) *Travel, Gender and Imperialism: Mary Kingsley and West Africa,* New York and London: The Guilford Press, p. 183.

36 Adam, A.M. (1931) 'Frances Kensington: A Friend of the College', Obituary, *The Girton Review,* 85 & 86, Lent and May Terms, pp. 3–4.

37 Green, V. (1985) *Love in a Cold Climate: The Letters of Mark Pattison and Meta Bradley 1879–1884,* Oxford: Clarendon Press, p. 14.

38 Ibid., p. 198.

39 BW, *IWNM,* p. 35.

40 Carrington, A., Hills, G.J. and Webb, K.R. (1974) *Neil Kensington Adam, 1891–1973, Biographical Memoirs of Fellows of the Royal Society,* 20: 1–26.

41 Adam, A.M. (1920) *Arthur Innes Adam 1894–1916: A Record Founded on His Letters,* Cambridge: Bowes and Bowes, p. 140.

42 Ibid., p. 144.

43 Carrington et al., *Neil Kensington Adam.*

44 D. Adams, Interview, 7 August 2009; A. Ashford, Interview, 30 July 2008.

45 BW, *IWNM,* p. 48.

46 Mitchison, *All Change Here,* p. 102.

47 Willmott, P. (1992) *A Singular Woman: The Life of Geraldine Aves 1898–1986,* London: Whiting & Birch Ltd, p. 19.

48 BW, *IWNM,* pp. 38–40.

49 A. Adam to B. Adam 2 November 1915, cited in Adam, *Arthur Innes Adam,* p. 188.

50 Baron, L. (1965) 'Girton in the First World War', *The Girton Review,* Easter Term, 178: 9–11.

51 Bradbrook, M.C. (1969) *'That Infidel Place': A Short History of Girton College 1869–1969,* London: Chatto & Windus, p. 6, p. 12.

52 Tullberg, R.M. (1998) *Women at Cambridge,* Cambridge: Cambridge University Press.

53 *The Girton Review* (1944), Michaelmas Term, 126: 25–27.

54 Adam, 'Frances Kensington,' pp. 3–5.

55 Adam, A.M. (1927) 'Girton in the Eighties', *The Girton Review,* Michaelmas Term, 75: 11–16.

56 Stephen, B. (1929) 'Girton in the Nineties', *The Girton Review,* Lent Term, 79: 3–7.

57 Adam, 'Girton in the Eighties'.

58 Lehmann, R. (1927) *Dusty Answer,* London: Chatto & Windus.

59 Vicinus, *Independent Women,* p. 129, p. 146.

60 See http://www.cuswpc.org/index.php?option=com_frontpage&Itemid=1 [accessed 1 June 2010].

61 Russell, R. (1977) *The Tamarisk Tree: Vol. 1, My Quest for Liberty and Love,* London: Virago, p. 34.

62 Hodgkiss, W. (1987) *Two Lives,* Castleford, West Yorkshire: Yorkshire Art Circus, p. 39.

63 Crane G. (1955) 'A Gyp's Memories 1919–1948', in Lindsay, J. (ed.) *A Cambridge Scrapbook,* Cambridge: W. Heffer & Sons, pp. 107–112.

64 Baron, 'Girton in the First World War'.

65 Tullberg, *Women at Cambridge,* p. 102.

66 Vicinus, *Independent Women,* p. 146.

67 Mitchinson, *All Change Here,* pp. 69–70.

68 BW, *IWNM,* p. 43.

69   Essex, R. (1977) *Woman in a Man's World,* London: Sheldon Press, pp. 16–17.
70   Mitchison, *All Change Here,* p. 40.
71   Cole, *Growing Up Into Revolution,* p. 37.
72   *The Girton Review* (1916), 'Girton College Debating Society', Lent Term, 46: 6–10, p. 9.
73   V. Seal, Interview, 20 February 2008.
74   *The Girton Review* (1917) 'College Notes', Michaelmas Term, 51: 2.
75   *Girton College Fire Brigade 1879–1932,* Girton College Fire Brigade Leaflet, Girton College Archive.
76   Vicinus, *Independent Women,* p. 123.
77   Steegmann, J. (1940) *Cambridge,* London: B.T. Batsford Ltd, p. 41.
78   Mitchison, *All Change Here,* p. 52.
79   *The Girton Review* (1918) 'College Notes', Lent Term, 52: 1.
80   *The Girton Review* (1916) 'College Notes: First Year Entertain Wounded Soldiers', Michaelmas Term, 48: 6.
81   See http://militaryhistory.about.com/od/worldwari/p/somme.htm [accessed 28 September 2009].
82   Adam, *Arthur Innes Adam,* p. 246.
83   'Fallen Officers "The Times" List of Casualties', *The Times,* 28 August 1917.
84   A. Ashford, Interview, 30 July 2008.
85   BW, *IWNM,* p. 46. Her death certificate records the cause of death on 21 September 1916, aged eighty-three, as a heart attack.
86   Adam, *Arthur Innes Adam,* p. 2.

4. Jack

1   BW, *IWNM,* p. 41, p. 44.
2   Ferguson, C.L. (1931) *A History of the Magpie and Stump Debating Society 1866–1926,* Cambridge: W. Heffer & Sons.
3   'Newham Military Wedding', *The Cambridge Chronicle,* 12 September 1917.
4   Englander, D. and Osborne, J. (1978) 'Jack, Tommy, and Henry Dubb: The Armed Forces and the Working Class', *The Historical Journal,* 21(3): 593–601, p. 595.
5   Levsen, S. (2008) 'Constructing Elite Identities: University Students, Military Masculinity and the Consequences of the Great War in Britain and Germany', *Past and Present,* 198: 147–183, p. 154.
6   Levsen, 'Constructing Elite Identities', p. 158.
7   Swinnerton, H.H. (1910) *Nottinghamshire,* Cambridge County Geographies. http://www.nottshistory.org.uk/swinnerton1910/chapter13.htm [accessed 15 September 2009].
8   Jones, D.J. *Dictionary of Perse History,* unpublished ms; thanks to D.J. Jones and to P. Graham for providing access to this.
9   BW, *IWNM,* p. 41.
10   Mack, I.A. (2006) *Letters from France,* Project Gutenberg, EBook etext19521, p. 2.
11   Murphy, C.C.R. (1928) *The History of the Suffolk Regiment 1914–1927,* London: Hutchinson, pp. 150–151.
12   Ibid., p. 151.
13   Ibid., p. 154.
14   'Swavesey and the Great War, The First of July 1916'. http://www.curme.co.uk./somme.htm [accessed 22 September 2009].
15   *The War Diary of the 11th Battalion Suffolk Regiment,* Public Records Office WO95 2458, Pte. W.J. Senescall, p. 2. http://www.curme.co.uk/p2.htm [accessed 24 September 2009] [punctuation added to quote in text].
16   BW, *IWNM,* p. 45.
17   H. Allgood to BW, n.d. GCPP Wootton 1/5/4 [punctuation added to quote in text].
18   'Swavesey and the Great War; '11th Battalion, The Suffolk Regiment, Full List of Casualties'. http://www.curme.co.uk/casualts.htm [accessed 15 September 2009].
19   BW, *IWNM,* p. 45.

20 Ibid., p. 48.
21 Ibid., p. 49.
22 Ibid.
23 Ritchie, A.D. (1923) *Scientific Method: An Inquiry into the Character and Validity of Natural Laws*, London: Kegan Paul Trench Trubner and Co Ltd.
24 'Newnham Military Wedding'.
25 BW, *IWNM*, p. 50.
26 Mack, J. (1977) 'Barbara Wootton', *New Society*, 14 April: 58–59.
27 Mitchison, N. (1975) *All Change Here: Girlhood and Marriage*, London: The Bodley Head, p. 87.
28 BW, *IWNM*, p. 50.
29 Wootton, B. (1983) 'Reflections of a Lifelong Agnostic', *Free Inquiry*, 3(4): 16–17, p. 16.
30 Cole, M. (1949) *Growing Up Into Revolution*, London: Longmans, Green and Co, p. 54.
31 Winter, J. and Baggett, B. (1996) *The Great War and the Shaping of the Twentieth Century*, London: Penguin Studio, p. 101.
32 'Battle of Passchendaele'. http://en.wikipedia.org/wiki/Battle_of_Passchendaele [accessed 28 September 2009].
33 The probate certificate for Jack Wootton's estate, issued on 11 December 1917, said that he died on 11 October 1918 'at France or Belgium on active service' (Nottingham District Probate Registry).
34 'The 11th Battalion, the Suffolk Regiment, Frequently Asked Questions'. http://www.curme. co.uk/faq.htm [accessed 22 September 2009].
35 Winter, J.M. (2003) *The Great War and the British People*, Basingstoke, Hants.: Palgrave Macmillan, pp. 71–72.
36 Robson, S. (2007) *The First World War*, Harlow, Essex: Pearson Education Limited, p. 103.
37 Winter and Baggett, *The Great War*, p. 107.
38 Winter, *The Great War and the British People*, p. 291.
39 BW, *IWNM*, p. 50.
40 Bailey, H. (1987) *Vera Brittain*, Harmondsworth: Penguin Books, p. 31.
41 R. Stevenson to BW, 14 April 1967, GCPP Wootton 1/5/4.
42 C.L. Morgan to BW, 10 December 1958, GCPP Wootton 1/5/4
43 Russell, D. (1977) *The Tamarisk Tree: Vol. 1, My Quest for Liberty and Love*, London: Virago, p. 45.
44 BW, *IWNM*, p. 51.
45 'Women of Our Century: Baroness Barbara Wootton', Interview by A. Clwyd, 26 July 1984, BBC Television, transcript, p. 10, GCPP Wootton 3/2/1 (published in L. Caldecott (1984) *Women of Our Century*, London: Ariel Books).
46 BW, *IWNM*, p. 51.
47 Berry, P. and Bostridge, M. (1995) *Vera Brittain: A Life*, London: Chatto & Windus, p. 2.
48 Ibid., p. 8.
49 Joannou, M. (1995) *'Ladies, Please Don't Smash These Windows': Women's Writing, Feminist Consciousness and Social Change 1918–38*, Oxford: Berg Publishers, Chapter 1.
50 Berry and Bostridge, *Vera Brittain*, p. 2.
51 Trodd, A. (1998) *Women's Writing in English in Britain 1900–1945*, Harlow, Essex: Longman, p. 153.
52 See Winter, *The Great War and the British People*, Chapter 3.
53 Bourke, J. (1999) *An Intimate History of Killing*, London: Granta Books.
54 Brittain, V. (1936, originally published 1923) *The Dark Tide*, New York: Macmillan, p. 204.
55 Nicholson, V. (2008) *Singled Out*, London: Penguin Books, p. 15, p. 22.
56 Winter, *The Great War and the British People*, p. 49.
57 Adam, A.M. to the Mistress of Girton, 15 May 1918, GCAC 2/4/6.
58 Adam, A.M. to the Mistress of Girton, 19 May 1918, GCAC 2/4/6.
59 BW, *IWNM*, p. 54.
60 Baron, L. (1965) 'Girton in the First World War', *The Girton Review*, Easter Term, 178: 9–11.
61 *The Girton Review* (1918), Michaelmas Term, 54: 1–3.
62 *The Girton Register* (1973) GCPP Wootton 1/2/1.

63   'No Robes, Crest for Life Peeress Barbara Wootton', *The Evening Times*, 24 July 1958.
64   V. Seal, Interview, 20 February 2008.

5. Cambridge Distinctions

1   Gilbert, B.R. (1967) *Britain Since 1918*, London: B.T. Batsford, p. 15.
2   Havighurst, A.F. (1979) *Britain in Transition: The Twentieth Century*, Chicago: Chicago University Press, pp. 158–160.
3   Webb, B. (1952) *Beatrice Webb's Diaries 1912–1924* (ed. M. Cole), London: Longmans, Green & Co, p. 153.
4   Graves, R. and Hodge, A. (2006, originally published 1940) *The Long Weekend*, Manchester: Carcanet Press, p. 12.
5   Stephen, B. (1927) *Emily Davies and Girton College*, London: Constable & Co, p. 352.
6   Rathbone, I. (1932) *We That Were Young*, London: Chatto & Windus, p. 430.
7   Graves and Hodge, *The Long Weekend*, p. 9.
8   Pyecroft, S. (1994) 'British Working Women and the First World War', *Historian*, 56(4): 699–710.
9   Nicholson, V. (2008) *Singled Out*, London: Penguin, p. 109.
10   Gilbert, *Britain since 1918*, p. 27.
11   'Professor Dorothy Russell, LHMC Alumna, Pathology Institute Director'. http://www.women.qmul.ac.uk/virtual/women/atoz/Russell.htm [accessed 24 May 2010].
12   BW in 'Any Questions?' 1 November 1957, transcript, p. 5, GCPP Wootton 2/1/3.
13   BW (1982) 'Women's Political Heritage', *New Statesman*, 17/24 December.
14   Cole, M. (1949) *Growing Up Into Revolution*, London: Longmans, Green and Co, p. 41.
15   Bailey, H. (1987) *Vera Brittain*, Harmondsworth: Penguin, p. 45.
16   Cited in Tullberg, R.M. (2005), 'Marshall, Alfred (1842–1924)', *Oxford Dictionary of National Biography*, Oxford University Press, Sept 2004; online edn, May 2005. http://o-www.oxforddnb.com.catalogue.ulrls.lon.ac.uk/view/article/34893 [accessed 8 June 2010].
17   Ibid.
18   Berg, M. (1992) 'The First Women Economic Historians', *The Economic History Review*, New Series, 45(2): 308–329, p. 315.
19   Keynes, J.M. (1944) 'Obituary – Mary Paley Marshall', *The Economic Journal*, 54(214): 268–284, p. 276.
20   Stephen, B. (1933) *Girton College 1869–1932*, Cambridge: Cambridge University Press, p. 111.
21   Cole, *Growing Up Into Revolution*, p. 130.
22   Bradbrook, M.C. (1969) *That Infidel Place: A Short History of Girton College 1869–1969*, London: Chatto & Windus, p. 68.
23   Levsen, S. (2008) 'Constructing Elite Identities: University Students, Military Masculinity and the Consequences of the Great War in Britain and Germany', *Past and Present*, 198: 147–183, p. 176.
24   Postgate, J. and Postgate, M. (1964) *A Stomach for Dissent: The Life of Raymond Postgate, 1896–1971*, Keele: Keele University Press, p. 219.
25   Mannin, E. (1971) *Young in the Twenties*, London: Hutchinson, p. 16.
26   Graves and Hodge, *The Long Weekend*.
27   *The Girton Review* (1919), Lent Term, 55: 14.
28   *The Girton Review* (1919), May Term, 56: 9.
29   Hopkinson, D. (1954) *Family Inheritance: A Life of Eva Hubback*, London: Staples Press, p. 46.
30   *The Girton Review* (1919), May Term, 56: 9.
31   'D.S.R.' [Dorothy Stuart Russell] (1968) Review of *IWNM*, *The Girton Review*, Lent Term, 183: 22–23, p. 22.
32   Berg, 'The First Women Economic Historians'.
33   S. Donnelly, Personal communication.
34   BW, *IWNM*, p. 55.
35   'The Cairnes Scholarship', GCAR 5/3/3/1.

36 Sondheimer, J. (2008) 'Maynard, Constance Louisa (1849–1935), *Oxford Dictionary of National Biography*, Oxford University Press, Sept 2004; online edn, Jan 2008. http://o-www.oxforddnb. com.catalogue.ulrls.lon.ac.uk/article/48459 [accessed 8 June 2010]; Vicinus, M. (1985) *Independent Women: Work and Community for Single Women, 1850–1920,* London: Virago.

37 Sondheimer, J. (1983) *Castle Adamant in Hampstead: A History of Westfield College 1882–1982*, London; Westfield College, p. 33.

38 *The Sphere*, 1 July 1922, Queen Mary, Westfield College Archives, WFD 83.

39 Letters of Hilda Green, Queen Mary, Westfield College Archives, WFD 115.

40 *Ísafold*, 28 August 1909, cited in Gunnell, T. (2008) 'Newall, Dame Bertha Surtees (1877–1932)', *Oxford Dictionary of National Biography*, Oxford University Press, Sept 2004; online ed, May 2008. http://o-www.oxforddnb.com.catalogue.ulrls.lon.ac.uk/view/article/35207 [accessed 8 June 2010].

41 Sondheimer, *Castle Adamant*, p. 92.

42 *Student Register 1917–22*, Queen Mary, Westfield College Archives, 10/1/4.

43 Calendar of Westfield College, July 1920, Queen Mary, Westfield College Archives, WFD 3/37.

44 BW, *IWNM*, p. 56.

45 E. Wicksteed to BW, 27 June 1970, GCPP Wootton 1/2/5.

46 BW, *IWNM*, p. 57.

47 Holden, K. (2005) 'Imaginary Widows: Spinsters, Marriage, and the "Lost Generation" in Britain after the Great War', *Journal of Family History*, 30: 388–409.

48 Hodgkiss, W. (1987) *Two Lives*, Castleford, West Yorkshire: Yorkshire Art Circus, p. 21.

49 Secretary of Girton College to BW, 12 May 1920, GCAR 2/5/1/1.

50 BW, *IWNM*, p. 57.

51 Russell, D. (1977) *The Tamarisk Tree: Vol. 1, My Quest for Liberty and Love,* London: Virago, p. 64.

52 BW to Miss Clover, 12 July 1920, GCAR 2/5/1/1.

53 BW, *IWNM*, pp. 58–59.

54 Record of Speeches Made by Baroness Wootton of Abinger and Mrs C.D. Rackham at Golden Jubilee Dinner of the Cambridge Branch of the National Council of Women on 9 July 1962, GCPP Duke 1/30, p. 3.

55 *Cambridge Reporter*, 12 January 1921, 'Lectures proposed by the Special Board for Economics and Politics, 1920–1921', GCPP Wootton 2/1/9.

56 BW to A. Robinson, 6 July 1985, GCPP Wootton 2/1.

57 Keynes (1982, originally published 1921 in *The Cambridge Review*, 21 February) Letter to the Editor in Moggridge, D. (ed.) *The Collected Writings of John Maynard Keynes, Vol. 28, Social, Political and Literary Writings,* London: Macmillan, pp. 415–416, p. 415.

58 Howson, S. (2004) 'Henderson, Sir Hubert Douglas (1890–1952)', *Oxford Dictionary of National Biography*, Oxford University Press, Sept 2004; online edn, Oct 2009. http://o-www.oxforddnb. com.catalogue.ulrls.lon.ac.uk/view/article/33812 [accessed 9 June 2010].

59 Christmas, L. (1977) 'Situation Wanted: Girton Girl', *The Guardian,* 14 December [GCPP Wootton 1/2/2].

60 A. Robinson to BW, 25 June 1985, GCPP Wootton 2/1.

61 A. Robinson to K. Perry, 2 September 1989, GCPP Wootton 2/1.

62 [No author given] (1986) 'Austin Robinson: A Child of the Times', *The Economist,* 20 December: 39–41.

63 Martin, K. (1967) 'Abinger Harvest', *The Listener,* 26 March [GCPP Wootton 1/2/6].

64 Martin, K. (1966) *Father Figures: A Volume of Autobiography*, London: Hutchinson, p. 115.

65 BW, *IWNM*, p. 60.

66 BW (1920) 'Classical Principles and Modern Views of Labour', *The Economic Journal*, 30(117): 46–60.

67 Peace Treaty of Versailles, Article 427, http://www.cooper.edu/humanities/core/hss3/versailles. html [accessed 2 October 2009].

68 BW, 'Classical Principles', p. 58.

69 Cole, *Growing Up Into Revolution*, p. 89.

70 BW (1921) 'The British Association Meeting at Edinburgh', *The Economic Journal*, December, 31(124): 554–556.

71 See, for example, BW (1921) Review of *Wealth: Its Production and Distribution*, by A. W. Kirkaldy, *The Economic Journal*, 31(121): 105–106; BW (1921) Review of *English Political Theory*, by I. Brown, *The Economic Journal*, 31(121): 108–109.

72 BW (1921) Review of *Economics*, by J. Cunnison, *The Economic Journal*, 31(121): 107–108.

73 BW (1920) 'Is Progress an Illusion?' *The Hibbert Journal*, October 1919–July 1920, 18: 18–26.

74 BW, *IWNM*, p. 57.

75 GCPP Cam 1/17.

76 *The Girton Review* (1921), Lent Term, 61: 1.

77 BW, *IWNM*, p. 57.

78 BW to Miss Clover, 24 February 1922, GCAR 2/5/1/1.

79 Adam, A.M. (1920) 'Women at Cambridge', *The Girton Review*, Michaelmas Term, 60: 2–4.

80 BW, *IWNM*, p. 60.

6. Real Work

1 Montgomery, J. (1957) *The Twenties: An Informal Social History*, London: Allen & Unwin, p. 42.

2 Sayers, R.S. (1967) *A History of Economic Change in England 1880–1939*, London: Oxford University Press, p. 53.

3 Cole, M. (1949) 'Labour Research', in Cole, M. (ed.) *The Webbs and Their Work*, London: Frederick Miller, pp. 147–163, p. 148.

4 Webb, S. (1923) 'Memorandum on the Conditions of Engagement of the Staff of the Joint Departments', TUC Library Collections, London Metropolitan University, JN 1129 LAB.

5 Williams, F. (1970) *Nothing So Strange: An Autobiography*, London: Cassell, p. 111.

6 BW, *IWNM*, p. 61

7 BW to Miss Clover, 24 February 1922, GCAR 2/5/1/1.

8 Record of Speeches Made by Baroness Wootton of Abinger and Mrs C.D. Rackham at Golden Jubilee Dinner of the Cambridge Branch of the National Council of Women on 9 July 1962, GCPP Duke 1/30, p. 7.

9 E. Power to Mr Coulton, 30 January 1921; thanks to M. Berg for access to this correspondence.

10 Lovell, J. and Roberts, B.C. (1968) *A Short History of the T.U.C.*, London: Macmillan, p. 69.

11 BW, *IWNM*, p. 61.

12 Wrigley, C. 'Henderson, Arthur (1863–1935)', *Oxford Dictionary of National Biography*, Oxford University Press, Sept 2004; online edn, Jan 2008. http://www.oxforddnb.com.catalogue.ulrls. lon.ac.uk/view/article/33807 [accessed 18 June 2010].

13 BW, *IWNM*, p. 62.

14 Joint Research and Information Department, *Report for December 1924 and January 1925*, TUC Library Collections, London Metropolitan University, JN 1129 LAB.

15 Note by Anthony Greenwood re BW, PA, LH/1/74.

16 Douglas, C.H. (1924) *Social Credit*, London: Cecil Palmer.

17 Robinson, J. (1978) *Contributions to Modern Economics*, Oxford: Basil Blackwell, p. 10.

18 BW, *IWNM*, p. 61.

19 Christmas, L. (1977) Situation Wanted Girton Girl', *The Guardian*, 14 December [GCPP Wootton 1/2/2].

20 Corthorn, P. (2006) *In the Shadow of the Dictators: The British Left in the 1930s*, London: Tauris Academic Studies, p. 10.

21 Milne-Bailey, W. (1926) *A Nation on Strike*, unpublished ms, TUC Library Collections, London Metropolitan University.

22 BW, *IWNM*, p. 68.

23 Cole, M. to BW, 20 February [no year given], GCPP Wootton 1/2/5.

24 Rolt, L.T.C. (1950) *Horseless Carriage*, London: Constable, p. 98.

25 Koerner, S. (1998) 'Four Wheels Good: Two Wheels Bad: the Motor Cycle Versus the Light Motor Car 1919–39', in Thoms, D., Holden, L. and Claydon, T. (eds) *The Motor Car and Popular Culture in the Twentieth Century*, Aldershot, Hants.: Ashgate Publishing, pp. 151–175, p. 167.

26   Montgomery, *The Twenties*, p. 181.

27   BW, *IWNM*, p. 64.

28   Ibid., pp. 63–64.

29   Rathbone, I. (1932) *We That Were Young*, London: Chatto & Windus, p. 422.

30   Daunton, M. (2002) *Just Taxes: The Politics of Taxation in Britain 1914–1979*, Cambridge: Cambridge University Press, p. 73.

31   BW (1922) 'Where Your Money Goes: What Every Woman Ought to Know', *Good Housekeeping*, 1(2): 49, 106.

32   *The Daily News*, 20 March 1924.

33   *The Northern Daily Telegraph*, 19 March 1924.

34   *The Daily News,* 19 March 1924.

35   'Woman Expert and the Nation's Debt: Her Highest Honour Ever Taken in Economics: Brilliant Career', *The Daily Chronicle*, 20 March 1924.

36   *The Daily News,* 20 March 1924.

37   'Mrs. Wootton, An Important Appointment', *The Manchester Guardian*, 20 March 1924.

38   'Famous Woman Economist: Mrs. Wootton Talks of Her New Appointment: High Finance Expert: Life Work and a Hobby for Nine Years', *The Evening Standard,* 18 March 1924.

39   *The Daily News*, 20 March 1924.

40   'National Debt Inquiry', *The Irish Times*, 19 March 1924.

41   'An Open Letter to the Prime Minister', *The Vote*, 25(758), 2 May 1924.

42   *Report of the Committee on National Debt and Taxation (the Colwyn Committee)* (1927), London: H.M.S.O., p. viii.

43   McDonald, A. (1989) 'The Geddes Committee and the Formulation of Public Expenditure Policy, 1921–1922', *The Historical Journal*, 32(2): 643–674, p. 643.

44   Peden, G. (2000) *The Treasury and British Public Policy, 1906–1959*, Oxford: Oxford University Press, p. 169.

45   Colwyn Committee Report, p. 355.

46   Ibid., p. 357.

47   Ibid., p. 31.

48   Ibid., p. 357.

49   The Labour Party (n.d.) *Labour and the War Debt: A Statement of Policy for the Redemption of War Debt by a Levy on Accumulated Wealth*, London: The Labour Party, p. 4.

50   TUC Library Collections, London Metropolitan University, BW's papers on the Colwyn Committee, HJ 8627, Box 7.

51   Daunton, *Just Taxes*, p. 74. The entry in the *Dictionary of Labour Biography* (Bellamy, J.M. and Saville, J. (eds) (2000) Basingstoke, Hants.: Macmillan) by D. Martin ('Barbara Wootton: Social Scientist, Public Servant and Socialist', pp. 218–221) correctly ascribes the writing of the Report to her.

52   McDonald, 'The Geddes Committee', p. 644.

53   See Erreygers, G. and Di Bartolomeo, G. (2007) 'The Debates on Eugenio Rignano's Inheritance Tax Proposals', *History of Political Economy*, 39(4): 605–638.

54   The Labour Party, *Labour and the War Debt*.

55   Delisle Burns, C. (1922) 'A Capital Levy in Old England', *The Labour Magazine*, 1(8): 350.

56   Churchman, N. (1997) 'Ricardo's Capital Levy Proposal: "By-Product of a Visionary"?' *Journal of the History of Economic Thought*, 19: 93–113.

57   BW to Hugh Dalton, 18 February 1925; BW to Ruth Dalton, 17 March 1925, TUC Library Collections, London Metropolitan University, BW's papers on the Colwyn Committee, HJ 8627, Box 1.

58   Colwyn Committee Report, p. 412.

59   Daunton, *Just Taxes,* p. 68.

60   Colwyn Committee Report, p. 245.

61   Keynes, J.M. (1927) 'The Colwyn Report on National Debt and Taxation', *The Economic Journal*, 37(146): 198–212, p. 198.

62   BW (1931) Review of *The National Debt* by E.L. Hargreaves, *The Economic Journal*, 41(161): 97–98, p. 97.

63   Daunton, *Just Taxes*, p. 73.

64   *Minutes of the 1st Meeting of the Colwyn Committee Held 2 May 1924*, TUC Library Collections, London Metropolitan University, BW's papers on the Colwyn Committee, HJ 8627, Box 7.

65   BW, *IWNM*, p. 65.

66   Ibid., p. 60.

67   Webb, 'Memorandum'.

68   TUC Library Collections, London Metropolitan University, JN1129 LAB, *Minutes of Meeting of the Executive Committee of the Labour Party*, 27 February 1924, p. 7.

69   TUC Library Collections, London Metropolitan University, JN1129 TUC Report 1926, p. 297.

70   BW, *IWNM*, p. 69.

71   T. Gould, Interview, 24 April 2008.

72   BW (1982) Review of *The Diary of Beatrice Webb, Vol. 1 1873–1892* (N. Mackenzie and J. Mackenzie, eds), *London Review of Books*, 21 October, 4(19): 19–20.

73   Webb, 'Memorandum', p. 1.

74   Whitbread, L.G. (1975) 'Tennyson's "In the Garden at Swainston"', *Victorian Poetry*, 13(1): 61–69.

75   Will of Mary Leonora Simeon, 21 March 1969.

76   Holden, K. (2005) 'Imaginary Widows: Spinsters, Marriage, and the "Lost Generation" in Britain after the Great War', *Journal of Family History*, 30: 388–409.

77   BW, *FUP*, Preface, p. 5.

78   Gillard, D. (2009) 'The Hadow Reports: An Introduction,' The Encyclopaedia of Informal Education. http://www.infed.org/schooling/hadow_reports.htm [accessed 24 November 2009].

79   WEA (1928) *The Estimated Cost of the Hadow Committee's Proposals to Raise the School Leaving Age to 15*, London: WEA; WEA (1928) *Adolescent Education: The Next Step*, London: WEA.

80   Consultative Committee on Education for the Adolescent (1926) *Report of the Consultative Committee on the Education of the Adolescent*, London: H.M.S.O.

81   Broadbent, B. (1990) 'A History of Women on the Bench', *The Magistrate*, July/August: 122–124.

82   Hopkinson, D. (1954) *Family Inheritance: A Life of Eva Hubback*, London: Staples Press, p. 111.

83   Richards, D. (1958) *Offspring of the Vic: A History of Morley College*, London: Routledge & Kegan Paul.

84   'Baroness Wootton', *The Surrey County Magazine*, 8(6), December/January/mid-February 1977/8, Surrey Personality Profile No. 35 [GCPP Wootton 1/2/3].

85   Richards, *Offspring of the Vic*, p. 216.

86   'The New Head of Morley College', *The Manchester Guardian*, 15 December 1926.

87   Richards, *Offspring of the Vic*, p. 216.

88   BW, *IWNM*, p. 72.

89   Richards, *Offspring of the Vic*, p. 217.

90   'Nancy Astor, Viscountess Astor'. http://en.wikipedia.ork/wiki/Nancy_Astor_Viscountess_Astor [accessed 18 June 2010].

91   Richards, *Offspring of the Vic*, pp. 218–219.

92   BW, *IWNM*, p. 70.

93   W. Beveridge to BW, 13 January 1926; BW to W. Beveridge, 14 January 1926. Beveridge Papers, Beveridge/2/B/25/3, BLPES.

94   'A Leisure-time University', *The Manchester Guardian*, 2 February 1927.

95   Walters, F.P. (1952) *A History of the League of Nations, Vol. 2*, Oxford: Oxford University Press.

96   Pemberton, J-A. (2002) 'New Worlds for Old: the League of Nations in the Age of Electricity', *Review of International Studies*, 28: 311–336.

97   Northedge, F.S. (1986) *The League of Nations: Its Life and Times 1920–1946*, Leicester: Leicester University Press, p. 171.

98   Salter, A. (1927) 'The Economic Conference: Prospects of Practical Results', *Journal of the Royal Institute of International Affairs*, 6(6): 350–367.

99   Northedge, *The League of Nations*, p. 171.

100   'League of Nations. The Appointment of Women', *The Sydney Morning Herald*, 3 January 1928.

101 'Women at Economic Conference', *The Argus* (Melbourne, Victoria, Australia), 24 June 1927, p. 6. In *IWNM* (p. 73), BW refers to three women attending the conference; Freundlich is listed as a member of the Austrian delegation.

102 BW to the Secretary-General of the League of Nations, 26 April 1927. League of Nations Archives and Historical Collections Section, United Nations Library, Geneva.

103 BW, *IWNM*, pp. 74–75.

104 'The League of Nations. A Woman on Economics', *The Globe*, 1 July 1927; 'City Economic Conference', *The Times,* 24 November 1927.

105 'Again No Woman!' *The Vote*, 26 May 1933, p. 4.

106 Goldman, L. (1999) 'Education as Politics: University Adult Education in England Since 1870', *Oxford Review of Education*, 25(1&2): 89–101.

107 Burrows, J. (1976) *University Adult Education in London: A Century of Achievement*, University of London, pp. 17–18.

108 Fieldhouse, R. (1977) *The Workers' Educational Association: Aims and Achievements 1903–1977*, Syracuse University, Publications in Continuing Education.

109 Cole, M. (1971) *The Life of G.D.H. Cole*, London: Macmillan, p. 106.

110 Burrows, *University Adult Education*, pp. 34–35.

111 Ibid., p. 42, p. 44.

112 Blyth, J.A. (1983) *English University Adult Education 1908–1958*, Manchester: Manchester University Press.

113 *The Girton Review* (1915), Michaelmas Term, 45: 10.

114 Cole, *The Life of G.D.H. Cole*, p. 109.

115 Ibid., p. 111.

116 Ibid., p. 112.

117 Burrows, *University Adult Education*, p. 59.

118 Richards, *Offspring of the Vic*, p. 219.

119 Hopkinson, *Family Inheritance*.

120 *Minutes of the Tutorial Classes Committee of the University Extension and Tutorial Classes Council for the Session 1929–30*, The Archive of the Department of Extra-Mural Studies, University of London, EM 6/1/22.

121 BW, *IWNM*, p. 77.

122 Blyth, *English University Adult Education,* p. 67.

123 Cole, *The Life of G.D.H. Cole,* p. 109.

124 *Minutes of the Tutorial Classes Committee of the University Extension and Tutorial Classes Council for the Session 1930–1*, The Archive of the Department of Extra-Mural Studies, University of London, EM 6/1/23.

125 'Notes on Prospective Tutors Made by Barbara Wootton', The Archive of the Department of Extra-Mural Studies, University of London, EM 6/14.

126 BW (1927) 'The Need for Differentiation,' *Journal of Adult Education*, 11: 55–67.

127 Hill, C. (1964) *Both Sides of the Hill*, London: Heinemann, p. 36.

128 *Minutes of the Tutorial Classes Committee of the University Extension and Tutorial Classes Council for the Session 1929–30*, The Archive of the Department of Extra-Mural Studies, University of London, EM 6/1/22, p. 20.

129 'A Remarkable Young Woman', *Everywoman,* 4 July 1924. On BW's role in the WEA, see Stocks, M. (1953) *The Workers' Educational Association: The First Fifty Years*, London: Allen & Unwin.

130 BW (1929) Review of *The Next Ten Years in British Social and Economic Policy* by G.D.H. Cole, *The Economic Journal*, 39(156): 575–579, p. 577.

131 BW (1929) Review of *The Intelligent Woman's Guide to Socialism and Capitalism* by G.B. Shaw, *The Economic Journal*, 39(153): 71–77, p. 71.

132 'War and Peace, International Democratic Congress', *The Scotsman*, 18 September 1924.

133 BW (1925) 'Banking, Credit, and Currency,' in Tracey, H. (ed.) *The Book of The Labour Party*, London: Caxton Publishing Company, pp. 329–341.

134 BW (1923) 'The Costs of Unemployment', *The Labour Magazine*, 1(10): 446–449.

135 BW (1923–4) 'Unemployment Amongst Women', in Evelyn Gates, G. (ed.) *Woman's Year Book*, National Union of Societies for Equal Citizenship, pp. 350–352.

136 'Young Suffragist Demonstration', *The Manchester Guardian*, 10 November 1926.

137 'Labour Research: The Acland Travelling Scholarships', *The Times*, 9 January 1928.

138 Crick, B. (2006) Review of *Leonard Woolf: A Life*, by V. Glendinning, *The Political Quarterly*, 77(4): 501–520.

139 'Educational Talks for Students: Programme of the BBC', *The Times*, 15 January 1929.

140 'Wireless Notes and Programmes', *The Manchester Guardian*, 2 April 1929.

141 Reynolds, K.D., 'Greville, Frances Evelyn, Countess of Warwick (1861–1938)', *Oxford Dictionary of National Biography*, Oxford University Press, Sept 2004; online edn, Jan 2008. http://0-www.oxforddnb.com./catalogue.ulrls.lon.ac.uk/view/article/33567 [accessed 19 June 2010].

142 Cole, *The Life of G.D.H. Cole*, pp. 158–160.

143 BW (1959) 'Miscellany, Cole and Sullivan,' *The Manchester Guardian*, 22 January.

144 BW, *IWNM*, p. 79.

145 Mackay, T.A. to BW, 12 July 1967, GCPP Wootton 1/2/5. In 1930 BW went to the USA on another Cunard ship, the *Carmania*. She is recorded as travelling on the *Queen Mary* in 1936 (New York Passenger Lists, 1820–1957).

7. Fact and Fiction

1 Pimlott, B. (1977) *Labour and the Left in the 1930s*, Cambridge: Cambridge University Press, p. 1.

2 Corthorn, P. (2006) *In the Shadow of the Dictators: The British Left in the 1930s*, London: Tauris Academic Studies.

3 Fordham, J. (2003) 'The Revolution of the Scots Word: Modernism, Myth and Nationhood in Gibbon and MacDiarmid', in Shuttleworth, A. (ed.) *And in Our Time: Vision, Revision and British Writing of the 1930s*, London: Associated University Presses, pp. 181–203.

4 Ritschel, D. (1997) *The Politics of Planning: The Debate on Economic Planning in Britain in the 1930s*, Oxford: Clarendon Press, p. 114.

5 BW, *IWNM*, p. 78.

6 BW, *TT*, p. 152.

7 N. Adam to BW, 11 March 1967, GCPP Wootton 1/5/3.

8 BW, *IWNM*, p. 78.

9 BW, *TT*, p. 79.

10 Ibid., pp. 85–86.

11 Ibid., p. 98.

12 Ibid., p. 106.

13 Ibid., p. 151.

14 Ibid., p. 170.

15 Ibid., p. 213.

16 Ibid., pp. 224–225.

17 BW, *PNP*, pp. 60–61.

18 Fitzpatrick, S. (1982) *The Russian Revolution*, Oxford: Oxford University Press.

19 Wood, N. (1959) *Communism and British Intellectuals*, London: Gollancz.

20 Northedge, F.S. and Wells, A. (1982) *Britain and Soviet Communism: The Impact of a Revolution*, London and Basingstoke: The Macmillan Press, p. 146.

21 Caute, D. (1973) *The Fellow-Travellers: Intellectual Friends of Communism*, London: Alan Sutton Publishing.

22 Rodden, J. (1990) 'On the Political Sociology of Intellectuals: George Orwell and the London Left Intelligentsia of the 1930s', *The Canadian Journal of Sociology*, 15(3): 251–273.

23 Kershaw, A. (2006) 'French and British Female Intellectuals and the Soviet Union. The Journey to the USSR, 1929–1942', EREA 4.2 (automne), pp. 62–71.

24 Cole, M. (1949) *Growing Up Into Revolution*, London: Longmans, Green and Co, p. 96.

25 Martin, K. (1969) *Editor,* Harmondsworth: Penguin Books, p. 73.
26 Martin, B.K. (1932) *Low's Russian Sketchbook*, London: Victor Gollancz.
27 Caute, *The Fellow-Travellers*, pp. 19–21.
28 Martin, *Editor*, p. 97.
29 Dalton, H. (1957) *The Fateful Years: Memoirs 1931–1945*, London: Frederick Muller Ltd, p. 27.
30 Russell, D. (1975) *The Tamarisk Tree: Vol. 1, My Quest for Liberty and Love*, London: Virago, p. 83.
31 Seymour-Jones, C. (1993) *Beatrice Webb: Woman of Conflict*, London: Pandora, p. 309.
32 Northedge and Wells, *Britain and Soviet Communism,* pp. 170–172.
33 Corthorn, *In the Shadow of the Dictators*, p. 9.
34 Graves, R. and Hodge, A. (1963) *The Long Week-End: A Social History of Great Britain 1918–1939*, New York: W.W. Norton and Company, p. 338.
35 Ibid., p. 340.
36 Webb, B. (1956) *Diaries 1924–1932,* London: Longmans, Green & Co, p. 298.
37 Northedge and Wells, *Britain and Soviet Communism*, p. 165.
38 Webb, S. and Webb, B. (1944, originally published 1935) *Soviet Communism: A New Civilisation*, London: Longmans, Green & Co, p. 971.
39 Morgan, K. (2006) *The Webbs and Soviet Communism*, London: Lawrence and Wishart, p. 11.
40 Webb and Webb, *Soviet Communism*, p. viii, p. x.
41 Ibid., p. 496, p. 539, p. 546.
42 Webb, *Diaries,* p. 298.
43 Northedge and Wells, *Britain and Soviet Communism*, p. 165.
44 Cole, M. (1961) *The Story of Fabian Socialism*, London: Heinemann, p. 229.
45 Pritt, D.N. (1965) *The Autobiography of D.N. Pritt* (7 vols) Basingstoke (duplicated text in British Library), p. 133.
46 BW, *IWNM*, p. 79.
47 BW, *IWNM*, pp. 79–80.
48 Ibid., pp. 80–81.
49 Ibid., p. 82.
50 Allen, W.M. et al. (1932) 'Restoration of Prices. Fresh Money for Spending', Letter, *The Times*, 5 July, p. 10.
51 Ritschel, *The Politics of Planning*, p. 50.
52 Ibid., p. 102.
53 Mannin, E. (1936) *South to Samarkand*, London: The Beacon Library, p. 15.
54 Taylor, A.J.P. (1965) *English History 1914–1945,* Oxford: Clarendon Press, p. 348.
55 Morgan, J. (1933) 'Agriculture', in Cole, M.I. (ed.) (1933) *Twelve Studies in Soviet Russia*, London: Victor Gollancz, pp. 107–121, p. 111.
56 BW, *IWNM*, pp. 81–82.
57 BW (1932) 'The Mind of the Soviets', *The Highway,* 25: 5–7.
58 Hardcastle, E. (1933) 'Marxism and Russia', *Socialist Standard,* Marxists Internet Archive. http://www.marxists.org/archive/hardcastle/marxism_russia.htm [accessed 21 June 2010].
59 BW, *PNP*, pp. 35–36.
60 Ibid., p. 174.
61 Ibid., p. 105.
62 Ibid., p. 166.
63 Ibid., p. 310.
64 Smith, T. (1979) *The Politics of the Corporate Economy,* Oxford: Martin Robertson, p. 69.
65 Hart, J. (1998) *Ask Me No More: An Autobiography*, London: Peter Halban, pp. 64–65.
66 Sargant Florence, P. (1934) Review of *PNP, The Economic Journal,* 44(175): 470–472, p. 470, p. 472, p. 471.
67 Thresher, B.A. (1935) Review of *PNP, The American Economic Review,* 25(3): 497–499, p. 498.
68 Wedgwood, J. (1934) Review of *Reconstruction* by H. Macmillan and *PNP, The Political Quarterly*, 5(2): 284–289, pp. 287–288.
69 Knight, F.H. (1935) Review of *PNP, The Journal of Political Economy*, 43(6): 809–814, p. 814.
70 Halm, G. (1934) Review of *PNP, Economica,* New Series, 1(4): 488–491.

71 BW (1936) Review of *The Russian Financial System* by W.B. Reddaway, *The Economic Journal*, 46(181): 146–147.

72 BW, *IWNM*, p. 83.

73 BW, *LB*, p. 25.

74 Ibid., p. 34.

75 Ibid., p. 38.

76 Ibid., p. 198.

77 BW, *IWNM*, p. 84.

78 BW, *LB*, p. 108.

79 Ibid., p. 58.

80 A. Croft to BW, 24 September 1981, GCPP Wootton 2/1.

81 BW to A. Croft, 27 September 1981, GCPP Wootton 2/1.

82 T. Gould, Interview, 24 April 2008.

83 Gibson, W. (1936) 'Fashion in Fiction', *The Manchester Guardian*, 28 April.

84 'An Incidental Prophecy', *The Sydney Morning Herald*, 3 July 1936.

85 C. Calil to T. Gould, 17 June 1982; thanks to T. Gould.

86 Croft, A. (1990) *Red Letter Days: British Fiction in the 1930s*, London: Lawrence and Wishart.

87 Jacobs, E. (2007) '"An Organizing Female with a Briefcase": Barbara Wootton, Political Economy and Social Justice, 1920–1950', *Women's History Review*, 16(3): 431–446, doi:10.1080/09612029601022329, p. 7.

88 Firchow, P.E. (2007) *Modern Utopian Fictions from H.G. Wells to Iris Murdoch*, Washington, D.C.: The Catholic University of America Press, p. 101.

89 Webb, B. quoted in Lepenies, W. (1988) *Between Literature and Science: The Rise of Sociology*, Cambridge: Cambridge University Press, p. 139.

90 Ibid., p. 140.

91 Joannou, M. (ed.) (1999) *Women Writers of the 1930s: Gender, Politics and History*, Edinburgh: Edinburgh University Press.

92 Schweizer, B. (2001) *Radicals on the Road: The Politics of English Travel Writing in the 1930s*, Charlottesville and London: University Press of Virginia.

93 Haldane, C. (1942) *Russian Newsreel: An Eye Witness Account of the Soviet Union at War*, Harmondsworth: Penguin.

94 Curie, E. (1945) *Journey Among Warriors*, London: The Travel Book Club; thanks to F Cave for drawing my attention to the German version.

95 Mannin, *South to Samarkand*, p. 20.

96 Corthorn, *In the Shadow of the Dictators*.

97 Schweizer, *Radicals on the Road*.

98 Fitzpatrick, S. (1999) *Everyday Stalinism: Ordinary Life in Extraordinary Times: Soviet Russia in the 1930s*, Oxford: Oxford University Press, p. 2.

99 Rosenfielde, S. (1997) 'Documented Homicides and Excess Deaths: New Insights into the Scale of Killing in the USSR during the 1930s', *Communist and Post-Communist Studies*, 30(3): 321–333.

100 BW, *PNP*, p. 301.

101 Ibid., pp. 301–302.

8. George

1 C.M. Rolph, Interview with BW, 19 October 1971, Kingsley Martin Archive, 38/35, University of Sussex.

2 GCPP Wootton 1/1/1.

3 R. McGregor and N. McGregor, Interview, 8 August 2008.

4 Burrows, J. (1976) *University Adult Education in London: A Century of Achievement*, University of London, p. 69.

5 'Alderman G.P. Wright', Obituary, *The Times*, 27 January 1964.

6 University Extension and Tutorial Classes Council (UETCC), Tutorial Classes Committee (TCC) (1935–6), 'Memorandum by the University Secretary Concerning the Suggested Grant to the London District, W.E.A.', The Archive of the Department of Extra-Mural Studies, University of London, EM 6/1/28.

7 BW (1924) 'The Next Twenty-five Years', *The Highway*, 26: 142–144.

8 BW, *IWNM*, p. 85.

9 A. Linton to BW, 18 June 1967, GCPP Wootton 1/2/5.

10 Cole, M. (1949) *Growing Up Into Revolution*, London: Longmans, Green and Co, p. 117.

11 UETCC, TCC (1936–7), 'The Central Joint Advisory Committee on Tutorial Classes, Report of the Summer Schools Movement', The Archive of the Department of Extra-Mural Studies, University of London, EM 6/1/29.

12 Cited in Burrows, *University Adult Education*, p. 68.

13 UETCC, TCC (1933–4), 'Residential Summer School 4 August – 1 September 1934', Brochure, p. 2, The Archive of the Department of Extra-Mural Studies, University of London, EM 6/1/26.

14 Ibid., p. 2.

15 UETCC, TCC (1934–5), 'Residential Summer School 1934, Report of the Director of Studies', The Archive of the Department of Extra-Mural Studies, University of London, EM 6/1/27.

16 Cobbett, W. (1967, originally published 1830) *Rural Rides*, Harmondsworth: Penguin Books, p. 74.

17 'Lost Heritage: Stratton Park'. http://lh.matthewbeckett.com/houses/lh_hampshire_strattonpark.html [accessed 17 June 2010].

18 UETCC, TCC (1931–2), 'Residential Summer School 1931, Report of the Director of Studies', The Archive of the Department of Extra-Mural Studies, University of London, EM 6/1/24.

19 UETCC, TCC (1937–8), 'Report of Tutorial Classes Committee 7 October 1937', The Archive of the Department of Extra-Mural Studies, University of London, EM 6/1/30.

20 UETCC, TCC (1934–5), 'Report on the Conference with Secretaries and Representatives of Classes and W.E.A. Branch Secretaries', The Archive of the Department of Extra-Mural Studies, University of London, EM 6/1/27.

21 UETCC, TCC (1932–3) 'Memorandum on the Finance of Adult Scholarships', The Archive of the Department of Extra-mural Studies, University of London, EM 6/1/25.

22 UETCC, TCC (1936–7), 'Provision of Facilities for Selected Tutorial Class Students to Enter Upon Courses of Study in the University', The Archive of the Department of Extra-Mural Studies, University of London, EM 6/1/25.

23 UETCC, TCC (1929–30) EM 6/1/22, (1930–1) EM 6/1/23, (1932–3) 6/1/25.

24 UETCC, TCC (1934–5), 'Report on the Conference with Secretaries and Representatives of Classes and W.E.A. Branch Secretaries', The Archive of the Department of Extra-Mural Studies, University of London, EM 6/1/27.

25 'J. Lyons & Co, Extended Obituary'. http://www.kzwp.com/lyons.pensioners/obituary2W.htm [accessed 13 January 2009].

26 'The Baroness Who Was Ashamed of Being British', *Time and Tide,* 20–26 February 1969, GCPP Wootton 1/2/2.

27 'When my Husband was a Delinquent, by Baroness', *The Daily Mirror*, 10 August 1964.

28 R. McGregor and N. McGregor, Interview, 8 August 2008.

29 B. Collison, Interview, 18 September 2008.

30 Mansbridge, A. (1920) *An Adventure in Working-Class Education*, London: Longmans, Green and Co.

31 Goldman, L. (1999) 'Education as Politics: University Adult Education in England Since 1870', *Oxford Review of Education,* 25(1&2): 89–101.

32 'The Mezzo-Brows. Problem of Intellectually Middle-Class Adult Education', *The Manchester Guardian*, 12 September 1927.

33 'Address by Lord McGregor at Memorial Meeting for George Wright', Seal Papers.

34 *Minutes of the Tutorial Classes Committee of the University Extension and Tutorial Classes Council for the Session 1936–7*, The Archive of the Department of Extra-Mural Studies, University of London, EM 6/1/29, p. 7.

35   Rose, J. (1989) 'The Workers in the Workers' Educational Association, 1903–1950', *Albion: A Quarterly Journal Concerned with British Studies*, 21(4): 591–608.

36   Worley, M. (2005) *Labour Inside the Gate: A History of the British Labour Party between the Wars*, London: I.B.Tauris.

37   'Report of Conference on the Teaching of Economics in Adult Classes', p. 17, E2/3/1/3, G.D.H. Cole Papers, Nuffield College, Oxford.

38   BW (1937) 'A Plea for Constructive Teaching', *Adult Education*, 10: 99–105.

39   Fieldhouse, R. (1977) *The Workers' Educational Association: Aims and Achievements 1903–1977*, Syracuse University: Publications in Continuing Education, p. 29.

40   'Mrs. Barbara Wootton', Court and Personal, *The Manchester Guardian*, 26 March 1935.

41   'Economist to Wed Taxicab Driver', *The Daily Herald,* 26 March 1935.

42   'Woman Finance Expert to Marry Taxi-Driver', *The Daily Mail*, 26 March 1935.

43   'Woman Chief of Varsity to Wed Taxi-man', *The Daily Mirror*, 26 March 1935.

44   Black, S. (1967) 'Exceptional People', *The Financial Times*, 14 March [GCPP Wootton 1/2/6].

45   'Don who Married Taxi Driver', *The Daily Mail*, 28 April 1967 [GCPP Wootton 1/2/6].

46   BW, *IWNM*, p.86.

47   'Cabbie's Widow', *The Listener*, 5 May 1977 [GCPP Wootton 1/2/2].

48   BW, *IWNM,* p. 86.

49   Hassid, V. (1967) 'Life and Barbara Wootton', *The Ethical Record,* June: 13–15, p. 14 [GCPP Wootton 1/2/6].

50   Davies, A.R. (1937) *The London County Council 1889–1937: A Historical Sketch*, Fabian Society Tract No.243, London: The Fabian Society, p. 34.

51   BW, *IWNM*, p. 87.

52   Fulham, Register of Electors 1935, thanks to Anne Wheeldon, Archivist, London Borough of Hammersmith and Fulham.

53   Saville, J. (2004) 'Phillips, Morgan Walter (1902–1963)', rev. *Oxford Dictionary of National Biography*, Oxford University Press. http://0-www.oxforddnb.com.catalogue.ulrls.lon.ac.uk/view/article/35513 [accessed 30 June 2010].

54   M. Phillips to D, Ginsburg, 30 June 1953, GS/EMRLP/55, Labour History Archive, People's History Museum.

55   L. Blom-Cooper, Interview, 9 February 2009.

56   Williams, F. (1970) *Nothing So Strange: An Autobiography,* London: Cassell, p. 310.

57   Macintyre, S. (1977) 'British Labour, Marxism and Working Class Apathy in the Nineteen Twenties', *The Historical Journal*, 20(2): 479–496.

58   Cohen, M. (2007) '"Cartooning Capitalism": Radical Cartooning and the Making of American Popular Radicalism in the Early Twentieth Century', *International Review of Social History*, 52: 35–58, p. 53.

59   'Henry Goes on a Poll-Day Tour with her Ladyship', *Forward*, 22 February 1957, p. 8.

60   Tawney, R.H. (1953) *The Attack and Other Papers*, London: George Allen & Unwin, p. 163.

61   Ellison, N. (1994) *Egalitarian Thought and Labour Politics: Retreating Visions*, London: Routledge.

62   Davies, *The London County Council*, p. 5.

63   Jackson, W. E. (1965) *Achievement: A Short History of the London County Council*, London: Longmans.

64   Davis, J. (1989) 'The Progressive Council, 1889–1907', in Saint, A. (ed.) *Politics and the People of London*, London: Hambledon Press, pp. 27–48 pp. 30–31.

65   LCC Members' Cards, London Metropolitan University Archives, GLC/DG/MSU/02/55.

66   'Planning a Full Future at Eighty-One', *The Surrey Advertiser,* 13 October 1978 [GCPP Wootton 1/2/3].

67   'Life Peeress's Husband Dies', *The Sunday Telegraph*, 26 January 1964.

68   'Address by Lord McGregor'.

69   'Alderman G.P. Wright', *The Times*.

70   'Planning a Full Future at Eighty-One', *The Surrey Advertiser*.

71   New York Passenger Lists 1820–1957. http://search.ancestry.co.uk/search/db.aspx?dbid=7488 [accessed 14 December 2010].

72   Mallon, W. (1936) '3 War Debt Plans Heard at Institute', *The New York Times*, 9 July.

73   Gull, E.M. (1936) 'Institute of Pacific Relations, This Month's Conference in California', *The Manchester Guardian*, 14 August.

74   *Minutes of the Tutorial Classes Committee*, The Archive of the Department of Extra-Mural Studies, University of London, EM 6/1/28.

75   C.M. Rolph, Interview with BW.

76   BW, *IWNM*, p. 89.

77   Record of Speeches Made by Baroness Wootton of Abinger and Mrs C.D. Rackham at Golden Jubilee Dinner of the Cambridge Branch of the National Council of Women on 9 July 1962, GCPP Duke 1/30, pp. 4–5.

78   *Minutes of the Tutorial Classes Committee of the University Extension and Tutorial Classes Council for the Session 1935–36, and Minutes for the Session 1936–37*, The Archive of the Department of Extra-Mural Studies, University of London, EM 6/1/28; EM 6/1/29.

79   New York Passenger Lists.

80   BW to V. Seal, 25 September 1953, GCPP Wootton 1/7/2.

81   New York Passenger Lists.

82   BW, *IWNM*, p. 140.

83   'Lady Wootton's Husband Dies', *The Daily Herald*, 27 January 1964.

84   'Baroness Wootton's Husband Dies', *The Morning Advertiser*, 27 January 1964.

85   'Life Peeress's Husband Dies', *The Sunday Telegraph*, 26 January 1964.

86   BW, *IWNM*, p. 138.

87   P. Bean, Interview, 18 March 2009.

88   'Frank Field on Barbara Wootton', *The Independent Magazine,* 1 October 1988.

89   See the correspondence in the Lena Jeger Archives, Jeger/1/17, BLPES.

90   V. Seal to the Editor of *The Independent Magazine*, 4 October 1988, GCPP Wootton 1/2/13.

91   McGregor, O.R. (1992) 'Foreword', in *BWSW*, pp. ix–xix, p. xviii.

92   C. Kay to D. Ginsburg, 6 June 1953, GS/EMRLP/55, Labour History Archive, People's History Museum.

93   BW, *IWNM*, p. 138.

94   B. Collison, Interview.

95   BW, *IWNM*, p. 138.

96   'Face the Press', Tyne Tees Television Ltd, recorded 4 January 1984; Baroness Wootton of Abinger interviewed by P. Toynbee, G. Smith and A. Howard, transcript, p. 96, GCPP Wootton 3/2/1.

97   Wootton, B. (1955) 'Holiness or Happiness', *The Twentieth Century*, November, pp. 407–416, p. 410.

98   'Cabbie's Widow', *The Listener*.

99   'The Private Enterprise of Lady Wootton's Husband', *The Daily Mail*, 25 January 1961.

100   B. Collison, Interview, 18 September 2008.

101   R. McGregor and N. McGregor, Interview, 8 August 2008.

102   B. Collison, Interview, 18 September 2008.

103   B. Trotter, Interview, 4 March 2008.

104   Barbara Wootton, 'Curriculum Vitae, Criminology Department, University of Melbourne', UAA Series 200, Registrar's Correspondence, File 1961/553.

105   Morris, T. (1989) 'In Memoriam: Barbara Wootton 1897–1988', Obituary, *The British Journal of Sociology,* 40(2): 310–318, p. 312.

9. Planning for Peace

1   BW (1939) 'Wanted: A New Science of Politics', *The Highway*, 32: 50–22 [reprinted in *BWSW*, Vol. 4, pp. 139–142, p. 141].

2   BW (1941) *Socialism and Federation*, Federal Tracts, 6, London: Macmillan and Co. Ltd [reprinted in *BWSW*, Vol. 3, pp. 132–153].

3   Mayne, R. and Pinder, J. (1990) *Federal Union: The Pioneers, A History of Federal Union*, Basingstoke, Hants.: Macmillan.

4   'Obituary: Sir Charles Kimber, Bt', *The Daily Telegraph*, 22 April 2008.

5   BW, *IWNM*, p. 97.

6   Kimber, C. 'The Birth of Federal Union'. http://www.federalunion.org.uk/about/birth/ [accessed 17 November 2008].

7   King-Hall, S. (1937) *Chatham House: A Brief Account of the Origins, Purposes and Methods of the Royal Institute of International Affairs*, London: Oxford University Press, p. 27.

8   BW, *IWNM*, p. 96.

9   *Federal Union News* (1939), 5, 21 October.

10   Castelli, A. (2002) *Una Pace da Costruire: I Socialisti Britannici e il Federalismo*. Milan: FrancoAngeli, pp. 68–69.

11   'From Our Correspondent, Oxford, September 24', *The Times*, 25 September 1939.

12   Lipgens, W. (1982) *A History of European Integration, Vol. I 1945–1947*, Oxford: Clarendon Press, p. 142.

13   Martin, K. (1969) *Editor*, Harmondsworth: Penguin, p. 292.

14   BW, *IWNM*, p. 98.

15   Minion, M. (2000) 'The Fabian Society and Europe during the 1940s: The Search for a "Socialist Foreign Policy"', *European History Quarterly*, 30: 237–270.

16   W.B. Curry to BW, 25 April 1940, The Dartington Hall Trust Archives, T/AE/4/B; BW to W.B. Curry, 27 April 1940, The Dartington Hall Trust Archives, T/AE/4/B.

17   Caldwell, B. (1997) 'Hayek and Socialism', *Journal of Economic Literature*, 35(4): 1856–1890.

18   'Education for Citizenship: A New Association', *The Manchester Guardian*, 17 May 1934; Heater, D. (2001) 'The History of Citizenship Education in England', *Curriculum Journal*, 12(1): 101–123.

19   HC Deb., 19 November 1941, 376: 354.

20   HC Deb., 20 November 1941, 376: 506.

21   Curry, W.B. (1939) *The Case for Federal Union*, Harmondsworth: Penguin, p. x, p. ix, p. 80.

22   Streit, C.K. (1939) *Union Now*, London: Jonathan Cape, p. 19.

23   Attlee, C.R. (1940) 'The Peace We Are Striving For', in Attlee, C.R., Greenwood, A., Dalton, H., Morrison, H., Noel-Baker, P.J., Gould, B.H., Woolf, L. and Laski, H. *Labour's Aims in War and Peace*, London: Lincolns-Prager, pp. 96–110, p. 106.

24   Angell, N. and Wootton, B. (1940) 'International Co-operation', in Angell, N., Wootton, B., Bentwich, N., Cole, G.D.H., Arthur Lewis, W., Carter, H. and Wood, H.G. *What Kind of Peace?* London: National Peace Council, pp. 65–84, p. 84.

25   BW (1941) 'Do the British Need their Empire?' *Common Sense*, December, 10(12): 367–371, pp. 370–371.

26   BW (1939) 'Economic Problems of Federal Union', *New Commonwealth Quarterly*, 5(2): 150–156 [reprinted in *BWSW*, Vol. 4, pp. 84–89, p. 87].

27   SPGB Library no. 14 (1940) *Should Socialists Support Federal Union? Report of a Debate between Federal Union (Mrs. Barbara Wootton) and Socialist Party of Great Britain (E. Hardy)*, London: SPGB, pp. 4–6.

28   Pritt, D. N. (1940) 'Socialism and Federation, Barbara Wootton', Reply, *Fabian Quarterly*, Summer, 26: 10–17.

29   Minion, 'The Fabian Society'.

30   Gilbert, M. (2009) 'The Sovereign Remedy of European Unity: The Progressive Left and Supranational Government 1935–1945', *International Politics*, 46: 28–47.

31   BW, *Socialism and Federation*, p. 136.

32   Ibid., p.133.

33   Mayne and Pinder, *Federal Union*, p.25.

34   Burt, C. et al. (1939) 'Manifesto by Leading Educationalists', Letter, *The Manchester Guardian*, 15 November.

35   Beveridge, W. (1940) *Peace by Federation*, London: Federal Tract No. 1.

36   BW to W. Beveridge, 8 June 1935, Beveridge Papers, 2/B/33/6, BLPES.

37   BW to W. Beveridge, 10 November 1937, Beveridge Papers, 2/B/37/4, BLPES.

38   BW to W. Beveridge, 14 January 1940, Beveridge Papers, 2/B/39/4, BLPES.

39   Lipgens, *A History of European Integration*, p. 144.

40   Kimber, 'The Birth of Federal Union'.

41   BW (1940) 'Report on First Conference: Economic Aspects of Federation', *First Annual Report 1939–40*, London: Federal Union Research Institute.

42   Mayne and Pinder, *Federal Union,* p. 30.

43   BW (1940) 'A Plea for Long Views', *Adult Education,* 12(3): 107–116.

44   Speech in Newcastle, February 1946, in *Federal Union News,* August 1947, 149: 9.

45   Wilford, R.A. (1980) 'The Federal Union Campaign', *European History Quarterly,* 10: 101–114.

46   Mayne and Pinder, *Federal Union*, p. 214.

47   'The History of Federal Union, Notes of a Discussion at the Federal Union Committee on 27 May 2002'. http://www.federalunion.org.uk/about/history/ [accessed 17 November 2008].

48   Jenkins, L. (1996) 'Godfather of the European Union: Altiero Spinelli', *European Campaigner,* Spring. http://www.brugesgroup.com/mediacentre/index.live?article=104 [accessed 25 February 2009].

49   Pistone, S. (1990) 'Altiero Spinelli and the Strategy for the United States of Europe' in Levi, L. (ed.) *Altiero Spinelli and Federalism in Europe and the World,* Milan: FrancoAngeli, pp. 133–140.

50   Jenkins, 'Godfather of the European Union', p. 2.

51   Delzell, C.F. (1960) 'The European Federalist Movement in Italy: First Phase, 1918–1947', *Journal of Modern History,* 32(3): 241–250.

52   Ibid.

53   BW (1945) *Socialismo e Federazione,* Lugano: Nuove Edizioni di Capolago.

54   BW (1947) *Libertà e Pianificazione,* Torino: Einaudi.

55   Castelli, A. (2004) 'I Socialisti Britannici e l'idea di "Popolo Europeo"', in Malandrino, C. (ed.) *Un Popolo per L'Europa Unità,* Florence: Leo S. Olshcki, pp. 143–155; see also Castelli, *Una Pace da Costruire.*

56   Bosco, A. (1988) 'Lothian, Curtis, Kimber and the Federal Union Movement (1938–1940)', *Journal of Contemporary History,* 23(3): 465–502.

57   Newman, M. (1980) 'British Socialists and the Question of European Unity, 1939–45', *European Studies Review,* 10: 75–100.

58   BW, *ESI,* p. 9.

59   Ibid, p.33.

60   Tribe, D. (1967) *A Hundred Years of Freethought*, London: Elek, p. 50.

61   Joad, C.E.M. (1932) 'Organizing for Progress', Letter, *The Manchester Guardian,* 4 October.

62   Tribe, *A Hundred Years of Freethought*, p. 50.

63   Flugel, J.C. et al. (1933) 'Bringing in Fascism by the Backstairs, The Tom Mann Case', Letter, *The Manchester Guardian,* 18 January.

64   Wilford, R.A. (1976) 'The Federation of Progressive Societies and Individuals', *Journal of Contemporary History,* 11(1): 49–82.

65   Burgers, J.H. (1992) 'The Road to San Francisco: The Revival of the Human Rights Idea in the Twentieth Century', *Human Rights Quarterly,* 14(4): 447–477.

66   Robertson, G. (n.d.) Cornerstones Conference, Speech. http://www.nswtf.org.au/cornerstones/G_Robertson_speech.pdf [accessed 7 April 2009, p. 5].

67   BW, *IWNM*, p. 88.

68   Wells, H.G. (1939) 'War Aims: The Rights of Man', Letter, *The Times,* 25 October.

69   'Rights of Man: World Challenge', *The Daily Herald,* 5 February 1940.

70   'Historic Challenge to Civilisation', *The Observer,* 4 February 1940

71   Whateley, M. (1940) 'Women Put Their Case', *The Daily Herald,* February 28.

72   Burgers, 'The Road to San Francisco'.

73   Robertson G. (2006) Launch of the Human Rights Law Resource Centre, Melbourne, Australia, Speech. http://www.hrlrc.org.au/content/events/robertson-launch/ [accessed 20 April 2009].

74   Robertson, G. (2000) 'Britain's Champions of Liberty', *The Guardian* 2 October. http://www.guardian.co.uk/world/2000/oct/02/humanrights.comment [accessed 1 January 2009].

75   BW, *IWNM*, p. 95.

76 Information from Bill Hetherington, Peace Pledge Union, Archives.

77 BW, *IWNM*, p. 95.

78 Willmott, P. (1992) *A Singular Woman: The Life of Geraldine Aves 1898–1986,* London: Whiting & Birch Ltd, p. 60.

79 Titmuss, R.M. (1950) *Problems of Social Policy,* London: H.M.S.O.

80 Martin, *Editor,* p. 279, p. 280, p. 278.

81 BW (1980) 'Saving the World', Review of *A Life of J.D. Bernal* by M. Goldsmith, *London Review of Books,* 19 June, 2(12): 8–9.

82 Trades Union Congress General Council (n.d.) The Trade Unions and Workmen's Compensation: The Case for Reform. http://www.library.lse.ac.uk/collections/pamphlets/document_service/HD7/00000216/doc.pdf [accessed 21 April 2009].

83 *Report of the Royal Commission on Workmen's Compensation* (1945) London: H.M.S.O.

84 Huxley, A. (1938) *Ends and Means,* London: Chatto & Windus, p. 31.

85 Pemberton, J-A. (2004) '"O Brave New Social Order": The Controversy Over Planning in Australia and Britain in the 1940s', *Journal of Australian Studies,* 83: 44–47.

86 Ritschel, D. (1997) *The Politics of Planning: The Debate on Economic Planning in the 1930s,* Oxford: Clarendon Press.

87 Boettke, P.J. (1995) 'Hayek's *The Road to Serfdom* Revisited: Government Failure in the Argument Against Socialism', *Eastern Economic Journal,* 21(1): 7–26.

88 Hutton, G. (ed.) (1935) *The Burden of Plenty?* London: George Allen & Unwin.

89 BW (1934) 'The Necessity of Planning', *The Listener,* 28 November: 912–913.

90 BW (1932) 'In the Midst of Wealth ...' *The Highway,* Vol. 24: 15–18.

91 Harris, J. (1977) *William Beveridge: A Biography,* Oxford: Clarendon Press, p. 435.

92 Beveridge, W.H. (1944) *Full Employment in a Free Society: A Report,* London: George Allen & Unwin.

93 Dimand, R.W. (1999) 'The Beveridge Retort: Beveridge's Response to the Keynesian Challenge', in Pasinetti, L.L. and Schefold, B. *The Impact of Keynes on Economics in the Twentieth Century,* Cheltenham, UK: Edward Elgar, pp. 221–238.

94 BW (1943) *Full Employment,* Research Series No.74, London: Fabian Publications Ltd, p. 1, p. 2, p. 11, p. 12.

95 Ibid., p. 20.

96 Durbin, E. (1985) *New Jerusalems: The Labour Party and the Economics of Democratic Socialism,* London: Routledge & Kegan Paul.

97 The New Fabian Research Bureau (1934) *Taxation Under Capitalism: Effects on Social Services. A Report of the Taxation Committee of the Bureau Under the Chairmanship of Mrs Barbara Wootton,* London: New Fabian Research Bureau and Victor Gollancz Ltd.

98 Durbin, *New Jerusalems,* p. 184.

99 Leruez, J. (1975) *Economic Planning and Politics in Britain,* London: Martin Robertson.

100 BW, *IWNM,* p. 98.

101 On the Hayek-Wootton debate, see Castelli, A. (2001) 'Pianificazione e Libertà. Il Dibattito tra Hayek e Barbara Wootton', *Il Politico,* 66(3): 402–405.

102 Caldwell, B. (2007) 'Introduction', in Caldwell, B. (ed.) *The Collected Works of F.A. Hayek Vol. 2, The Road to Serfdom: Text and Documents – The Definitive Edition,* Chicago: University of Chicago Press, pp. 1–22.

103 Pemberton, '"O Brave New Social Order"', p. 40.

104 Ranelagh, J. (1991) *Thatcher's People: An Insider's Account of the Politics, the Power and the Personalities,* London: HarperCollins, p. ix.

105 Muller, J.Z. (2003) *The Mind and the Market,* New York: Anchor books.

106 Finer, H. (1945) *The Road to Reaction,* Chicago: Quadrangle Books, p. v.

107 Fisher, A.G.B. (1946) Review of *FUF, International Affairs,* January, 22(1): 123–124, p. 124.

108 Partridge, P.H. (1946) Review of *FUF, The Institute of Public Administration,* 6(3): 162–170, p. 162.

109 Mayer, J. (1947) Review of *FUF, The Annals of the American Academy of Political and Social Science,* July, 252: 151–152, p. 151.

110 Blackwell, G.W. (1946) Review of *FUF, Social Forces,* 24(4): 464–466.

111   Ross, E.J. (1946) Review of *FUP, American Catholic Sociological Review,* 7(1): 66–67.

112   'H.J.L.' (1945) Review of *FUP, The Manchester Guardian,* 7 September.

113   Davy, C. (1945) Review of *FUP, The Observer,* 16 September.

114   Merriam, C.E. (1946) Review of *FUP* and *Road to Reaction* by H. Finer, *American Political Science Review,* 40(1): 133–136, p. 135.

115   BW, *FUP,* p. 9, p. 13.

116   Ibid., pp. 139–140.

117   Ibid., p. 5.

118   Ibid.

119   Kresge, S. and Wenara, L. (eds) (1994) *Hayek on Hayek,* London: Routledge, p. 103.

120   BW, *FUP,* p. 6.

121   Smith, T. (1979) *The Politics of the Corporate Economy,* Oxford: Martin Robertson, p. 142, p. 79.

122   Adams, V. et al. (1934) 'Appeal to Hitler: Release of Torgler', Letter, *The Manchester Guardian,* 19 March.

10. Lament for Economics

1   'Notes on Prospective Tutors Made by Barbara Wootton', The Archive of the Department of Extra-Mural Studies, University of London, EM 6/14.

2   Elias, N. (1994) 'Notes on a Lifetime' (originally published in 1984) in *Reflections on a Life,* Cambridge: Polity Press, p. 81; thanks to G. Crow for drawing my attention to this. Vera Seal comments that BW is unlikely to have shouted (personal communication).

3   'A "Fantastic Economic World"', *The Manchester Guardian* 3 April 1934.

4   BW, *LE,* p. 19.

5   Ibid., p. 35.

6   Ibid., p. 130.

7   Ibid., p. 67.

8   Ibid., pp. 252–253.

9   'Six Economists, Seven Opinions – or More', *The Straits Times,* 28 October 2004.

10   BW, *LE,* p. 14.

11   Dimand, R.W. and Hardeen, I. (2003) 'Barbara Wootton's Lament for Economics and Vision of a Social Economics', *Forum for Social Economics,* 33(1): 23–32, p. 26.

12   BW, *LE,* p. 14.

13   Keynes, J.M. (1936) *The General Theory of Employment, Interest and Money,* New York: Harcourt Brace, p. 16.

14   Robinson, J. (1978) *Contributions to Modern Economics,* Oxford: Basil Blackwell, p. 75.

15   See, for example, Condliffe, J.B. (1938) Review of *LE, Economica,* New Series, 5(18): 238–239.

16   Samuels, W.J. (1995) 'The Present State of Institutional Economics', *Cambridge Journal of Economics,* 19(4): 569–590.

17   Robbins, L (1984, originally published 1932) *An Essay on the Nature and Significance of Economic Science,* New York: New York University Press, p. 16.

18   Ibid., p. 104.

19   BW, *LE,* p. 130.

20   Ibid., p. 189.

21   Ibid., p. 302.

22   See King, J.E. (2003) 'Lament for Economics, or How Barbara Wootton Gave It All Away and Became a Sociologist', *Research in the History of Economic Thought and Methodology,* 22: 301–321; Dimand, M.A., Dimand, R.W. and Forget, E. L. (eds) (1975) *Women of Value: Feminist Essays on the History of Women in Economics,* Aldershot, Hants.: Edward Elgar.

23   There is only one reference to Barbara Wootton in Skidelsky, R. (2003) *John Maynard Keynes 1883–1946,* London: Macmillan (p. 594, referring to her role as an economic adviser to the Labour Party), and in Harris, J. (1977) *William Beveridge: A Biography,* Oxford: Clarendon Press,

there are only three: referring to her work with Beveridge in the Federal Union (p. 367), and to her part in his Full Employment inquiry (p. 435, p. 437).

24   Fraser, L.M. (1938) 'Economists and Their Critics', *The Economic Journal*, 48(190): 196–210.

25   *The Times*, 'Economists Arraigned', 25 January 1938.

26   'A Critic of Economists', Review of *LE*, *The Manchester Guardian*, 25 February 1938.

27   'W.A.B.' (1938) 'A Woman Asks', *The Argus*, 9 April.

28   McCreary, J. (1938) Review of *LE* and *The Theory of Investment Value* by J.B. Williams, *The American Economic Review*, 28(4): 763–768. The reference is to p. 191 of *LE*, and is a little unfair, as the 'I' in question is the consumer.

29   Evans, J.G. (1939) Review of *LE*, *Southern Economic Journal*, 5(4): 556–557, p. 557.

30   Bye, R.T. (1940) Review of *LE*, *The Journal of Political Economy*, 48(1): 122–123.

31   Hewett, W.W. (1940) 'The Use of Economic Principles in the Teaching of Applied Subjects', *The American Economic Review*, 30(2), part 1: 333–338.

32   Fraser, 'Economists and Their Critics', p. 207.

33   Harrod, R.F. (1938) 'Scope and Method of Economics', *The Economic Journal*, 48(191): 383–412, p. 384.

34   Keynes, J.M. (1938) Letter to Roy Harrod, 26 January 1938. Thanks to Tony Atkinson for supplying a copy of this.

35   King, 'Lament for Economics', p. 14.

36   T. Atkinson, Personal communication.

37   Dimand et al., *Women of Value*; Dimand, R.W. (1999) 'Women Economists in the 1890s: Journals, Books and the Old Palgrave', *Journal of the History of Economic Thought*, 21(3): 269–288; Dimand, R.W., Dimand, M.A. and Forget, E.I. (eds) (2000) *A Biographical Dictionary of Women Economists*, Cheltenham, UK: Edward Elgar.

38   Berg, M. (1992) 'The First Woman Economic Historians', *The Economic History Review*, New Series, 45(2): 308–329.

39   Millmow, A. (2003) 'Joan Robinson's Disillusion with Economics', *Review of Political Economy*, 15(4): 561–574.

40   Ormerod, P. (1998) *Butterfly Economics,* London: Faber and Faber, p. 79.

41   Lewis, M. (1990) *Liar's Poker,* London: Coronet Books.

42   Waring, M. (1988) *Counting for Nothing,* Wellington, New Zealand: Port Nicholson Press.

43   McCloskey, D.N. (1985) *The Rhetoric of Economics,* Madison, Wisconsin: University of Wisconsin Press.

44   Ormerod, *Butterfly Economics*.

45   McCloskey, D.N. (1996) *The Vices of Economists and The Virtues of the Bourgeoisie*, Amsterdam: Amsterdam University Press p. 13.

46   King, 'Lament for Economics'.

47   'Open Letter from Economic Students to Professors and Others Responsible for the Teaching of This Discipline'. http://www.paecon.net/PAEtexts/a-e-petition.htm, [accessed 7 December 2009]. The movement started by the French students' letter, 'post-autistic economics', developed into a forum of various groups critical of the mainstream pedagogy in economics. The label 'autistic' was later dropped (as offensive to those with this health condition) and the title changed to 'real-world economics', under which heading the movement continues to thrive.

48   Whynes, D. (1986) 'Is Economics Still Lamentable?' in Bean, P. and Whynes, D. (eds) *Barbara Wootton: Social Science and Public Policy, Essays in Her Honour,* London: Tavistock, pp. 57–73, p. 59.

49   BW, *SFWP*, p. 9.

50   Land, H. (1990) 'What are Wages for?' Inaugural Lecture delivered at Royal Holloway and Bedford New College on 15 March, unpublished ms. Thanks to H. Land.

51   BW, *SFWP*, p. 45.

52   Ibid., p. 28.

53   Titmuss, R.M. (1962) *Income Distribution and Social Change*, London: Allen & Unwin.

54   BW, *SFWP*, pp. 56–58.

55   Ibid., p. 161.

56 Atkinson, A.B. (1997) 'Bringing Income Distribution in from the Cold', *The Economic Journal*, 107(441): 297–321.

57 Parnes, H.S. (1956) Review of *SFWP*, *The American Journal of Sociology*, 61(6): 634.

58 Guillebaud, C.W. (1955) Review of *SFWP*, *The Economic Journal*, 65(259): 506–599, p. 507.

59 Goldberg, J.P. (1957) Review of *SFWP*, *Journal of Political Economy*, 65(1): 87–88, p. 87.

60 Dickinson, H.D. (1958) Review of *SFWP*, *The British Journal of Sociology*, 9(1): 92–97.

61 Hicks, 'Economic Foundations'.

62 Phelps Brown, H. (1996) 'Autobiographical Notes', *Review of Political Economy*, 8(2): 129–139.

63 Phelps Brown, E. H. (1955) 'Wage Policy and Wage Differences', Review of *SFWP*, *Economica*, New Series, 22(38): 349–354, p. 354.

64 Strange, S. (1955) 'Cutting the Cake', Review of *SFWP*, *The Observer*, 20 March.

65 Sargant Florence, P. (1955) Review of *SFWP*, *The Political Quarterly*, 26(3): 309–312.

66 'Equality': No.7, 'Equality of Remuneration' by BW, London Calling Asia, 9 February 1958, transcript, GCPP Wootton 3/2/1.

67 BW (1956) 'The Ethics of the Wage Structure', *The Hibbert Journal*, 54(2): 115–123.

68 BW (1961) *Remuneration in a Welfare State*, Liverpool: Liverpool University Press, p. 7.

69 Routh, G., Wedderburn, D. and Wootton, B. (1980) *The Roots of Pay Inequalities*, Discussion Series No. 1, London: Low Pay Unit.

70 Callaghan, J. (1996) 'The Fabian Society Since 1945', *Contemporary British History*, 10(2): 35–50, p. 45.

71 BW (1975) *In Pursuit of Equality*, Fabian Tract 443, London: Fabian Society.

72 BW (1962) Introduction to the 2nd edn of *The Social Foundations of Wage Policy*, p. 3.

73 Hall, P. (1971) 'A Way Through the Pay Chaos', *New Society*, 20 May.

74 Turner, H.A. (1963) Review of *SFWP*, 2nd edn., and H.R. Kahn, *Salaries in the Public Services in England and Wales*, *The Political Quarterly*, 34(3): 306–307.

75 BW, *IP*, p. 9.

76 Ibid., p. 84.

77 BW (1970) 'Why Not a Tax on Income Rises?' *The Observer*, 13 December.

78 Neale, W.C. (1986) 'Tax-based Incomes Policies: A Commentary for the Future', *Journal of Economic Issues*, 20(4): 969–987.

79 BW, *IP*, p. 162.

80 Wallich, H.C. and Weintraub, S. (1971) 'A Tax-based Incomes Policy', *Journal of Economic Issues*, 5(2): 1–19.

81 BW to P. Townsend, 18 October 1982, Townsend Papers.

82 BW to J. Collins, 22 June 1980, GCPP Wootton 4/8.

83 J.K. Galbraith to BW, 26 February 1975, GCPP Wootton 1/1/6.

84 BW, *LE*, p. 267.

85 BW (1944) 'Am I My Brother's Keeper?' *Agenda*, III(2): 1–13.

86 Royal Commission on the Civil Service, 1953–1955 (1955) *Report*, London: H.M.S.O.

87 Committee on the Pay of Postmen (1964) *Report*, London: H.M.S.O.

88 Royal Commission on Equal Pay, 1944–1946 (1946) *Minutes of Evidence and Appendices*, Appendix IX, London: H.M.S.O.

89 Phelps Brown, E.H. (1949) 'Equal Pay for Equal Work', *The Economic Journal*, 59(235): 384–398.

90 BW (1968) 'The Financial Crisis: Call for Curb on Speculators', Letter, *The Times*, 27 November.

91 BW (1980) 'A New Kind of Incomes Policy', Letter, *The Times*, 11 June.

92 K.V. Roberts to BW, 11 June 1980, GCPP Wootton 4/8.

93 BW to K.V. Roberts, 22 June 1980, GCPP Wootton 4/8.

94 BW (1978) 'The Great Big World Keeps Turning', Review of *The World Economy* by W.W. Rostow, *New Society*, 19 October.

95 BW (1975) Review of *Economics and the Public Purpose*, by J.K. Galbraith and *Against the Stream: Critical Essays on Economics* by G. Myrdal, *Journal of Social Policy*, 4(1): 89–112.

96 BW (1975) 'A Blue Print for Britain's Future,' LSE Lecture, GCPP Wootton 3/4/3, p. 1.

97 Ibid., p. 6.

98 Ibid., p. 20.

11. Testament for Social Science

1   BW, *IWNM*, p. 210.
2   Marshall, T.H. (1963, originally published 1947) *Sociology at the Crossroads,* London: Heinemann, p. 21.
3   Christmas, L. (1977) 'Situation Wanted: Girton Girl', *The Guardian,* 14 December [GCPP Wootton 1/2/2].
4   BW to S.D. Simon, 17 August 1966, GCRF 9/1/40.
5   BW, *IWNM*, p. 96.
6   R. McGregor and N. McGregor, Interview, 8 August 2008.
7   BW (1947) 'The Married Woman's Dilemma', *World Review,* August, pp. 20–23 [GCPP Wootton 3/4/2].
8   UETCC, TCC (1937–8) 'Report of the Tutorial Classes Committee', The Archive of the Department of Extra-Mural Studies, University of London, EM 6/1/30.
9   BW (1940) 'Some Aspects of the Social Structure of England and Wales', *Adult Education,* 13: 97–116.
10   BW (1942) 'Chaos in the Social Services, *The Sociological Review,* 34(142): 1–11.
11   BW (1943) 'The Beveridge Report', *Agenda,* 11(1): 1–10, p. 1.
12   BW (1944) 'Social Security and the Beveridge Plan', *Common Wealth Popular Library* No. 4, London: Common Wealth Publishing Ltd, p. 1.
13   Harris, J. (1977) *William Beveridge: A Biography*, Oxford: Clarendon Press, p. 426.
14   Longford, Lord (1994) *Avowed Intent: An Autobiography,* London: Little Brown and Company, p. 93.
15   Inter-departmental Committee on Social Insurance and Allied Services (1943) *The Beveridge Report in Brief*, London: H.M.S.O., p. 4.
16   Ibid., p. 59.
17   BW, 'The Beveridge Report', pp. 5–6.
18   BW (1946) 'History Backwards 1. Background to Beveridge', Forces Educational Broadcast, Light Programme, 6 August, transcript, p. 8, GCPP Wootton 3/2/1.
19   BW (1943) 'Before and After Beveridge', *The Political Quarterly*, 14(4): 357–363, p. 357.
20   BW to W. Beveridge, 6 May 1944, Beveridge Papers, 2/B/43/2, BLPES.
21   Harris, *William Beveridge*, p. 441.
22   BW et al. (1943) 'Social Security League' Letter, *The Manchester Guardian*, 23 June.
23   'Beveridge Plain, Beveridge Coloured', *The Manchester Guardian*, 22 July 1943.
24   Havighurst, A.F. (1979) *Britain in Transition: The Twentieth Century*, Chicago: University of Chicago Press, p. 377.
25   Ibid., p. 422.
26   'Social Security Plan, Criticisms by League Experts', *The Times*, 2 November 1944.
27   BW (1949) 'Record of the Labour Government in the Social Services', *Political Quarterly*, 20(2): 101–112.
28   Beveridge, W. (1939) 'The Place of the Social Sciences in Human Knowledge: A Farewell Address Given at the LSE, June 1937', *Politica* II(9): 459–479, pp. 467–468.
29   Morris, T. (1989) 'In Memoriam: Barbara Wootton 1897–1988', Obituary, *The British Journal of Sociology,* 40(2): 310–318, p. 312.
30   Burns, E.M. (1935) 'The Social Sciences as Disciplines: Great Britain', *Encyclopaedia of the Social Sciences*, New York: Macmillan and Co, p. 231.
31   Beveridge, Lord (1949) 'The London School of Economics and the University of London', in Cole, M. (ed.) *The Webbs and Their Work,* London: Frederick Muller, pp. 41–53.
32   Martin, K. (1966) *Father Figures: A Volume of Autobiography,* London: Hutchinson, p. 152.
33   Bulmer, M. (1985) 'The Development of Sociology and of Empirical Social Research in Britain', in Bulmer, M. (ed.) *Essays on the History of British Sociological Research*, Cambridge: Cambridge University Press, pp. 3–36 p. 5.
34   Beveridge, J. (1960) *An Epic of Clare Market. Birth and Early Days of the London School of Economics*, London: G. Bell and Sons, pp. 67–68.

35 Martin, *Father Figures*, p. 152.

36 BW, *IWNM*, p. 99.

37 BW to W. Beveridge, 6 May 1944, Beveridge Papers, 2/B/43/2, BLPES.

38 W. Beveridge to the Academic Registrar of the University of London, 6 June 1944, Beveridge Papers, 2/B/43/2, BLPES.

39 BW, *IWNM*, p. 99.

40 Morris, 'In Memoriam', p. 314.

41 BW to V. Seal, 9 July 1944, Seal Papers.

42 *Minutes of the Tutorial Classes Committee of the University Extension and Tutorial Classes Council for the Session 1944–5*, The Archive of the Department of Extra-Mural Studies, University of London, EM 6/1/38.

43 Ibid.

44 Tuke, M.J. (1939) *A History of Bedford College for Women*, London: Oxford University Press, p. 286.

45 Mordaunt Crook, J. (2001) 'Introduction', in Mordaunt Crook, J. (ed.) *Bedford College University of London: Memories of 150 Years,* Egham, Surrey: Royal Holloway and Bedford New College, pp. 1–12.

46 Tuke, *A History of Bedford College*, p. xiii.

47 BW, *IWNM*, p. 101.

48 T. Morris, Personal communication.

49 Drewry, G. and Brock, J. (2001) 'Social Studies and Social Science', in Mordaunt Crook, *Bedford College,* pp. 313–354.

50 BW, *IWNM*, p. 101.

51 F. Russell, Interview, 11 May 2010.

52 D. Runnicles to A. Ingold, Personal communication.

53 R. Pierce to A. Ingold, Personal communication.

54 'Women of Our Century: Baroness Wootton', Interview by A. Clwyd, 26 July 1984, BBC Television, transcript, p. 40, GCPP Wootton 3/2/1 (published in L. Caldecott (1984) *Women of Our Century,* London: Ariel Books).

55 BW, *IWNM*, p. 210.

56 BW (1953) 'Some Problems of Communication', *ASLIB Proceedings,* 5(4): 261–270 [reprinted in *BWSW,* Vol. 4, pp. 100–111, p. 103].

57 Nicol, A. (2001) *The Social Sciences Arrive,* Economic and Social Research Council.

58 *Report of the Committee on the Provision for Social and Economic Research* (1946) London: H.M.S.O., pp. 3–4.

59 Nicol *The Social Sciences Arrive,* Chapter 3.

60 Stacey, M. (1999) 'Obituary: Professor Margot Jefferys', *The Independent,* 12 March.

61 M. Jefferys, Interview, 5 March 1998.

62 Jefferys, M. with the assistance of W. Moss (1954) *Mobility in the Labour Market: Changes in Battersea and Dagenham,* London: Routledge & Kegan Paul.

63 Palmer, G.L. (1955) Review of *Mobility in the Labour Market* by M. Jefferys, *Industrial and Labor Relations Review,* 9(1): 147–148, p. 147.

64 Morris, 'In Memoriam'.

65 BW, *IWNM*, p. 103.

66 R. McGregor and N. McGregor, Interview, 8 August 2008.

67 McGregor, O.R. (1992) 'Foreword', in *BWSW*, pp. ix–xix, p. xii.

68 BW to V. Seal, 17 March 1952, Seal Papers.

69 G. Jebb to BW, 22 January 1952, GCPP Wootton 1/3/2.

70 R.M. Titmuss to BW, 9 March 1952, GCPP Wootton 1/3/2.

71 BW (1952) 'Reflections on Resigning a Professorship', *Universities Quarterly,* 7(1): 36–49, p. 36.

72 'University Grants Committee', *The Times,* 7 March 1950.

73 'Sociological Studies', *The Times,* 16 May 1951.

74 Platt, J. (2003) *The British Sociological Association: A Sociological History,* Durham: Sociologypress, p. 21.

75 Ibid., p. 18.

76   Ibid., Appendix Table A1, 'Members of the Executive Committee'.

77   Allen, S. (2001) 'Peaks and Troughs in British Sociology', *Network*, October, 80: 1.

78   A.H. Halsey, Interview, 11 March 2008.

79   Marshall, T. H. (1953) 'Conference of the British Sociological Association 1953, 1. Impressions of the Conference', *The British Journal of Sociology*, 4(3): 201–209, p. 201.

80   BW, *TSS*, p. 190.

81   BW (1933) Review of *Methods of Social Study* by S. Webb and B. Webb, *The Economic Journal*, 43(169): 152–153.

82   Webb, S., Webb, B. (1932) *Methods of Social Study*, London: Longmans, Green and Co, pp. 16–17.

83   Polanyi, M. (1950) 'Science as Saviour', *The Manchester Guardian*, 28 November.

84   'Physical and Social Sciences', *The Scotsman*, 26 December 1950.

85   Edwards, O. (1950) 'Talking of Books', *The Times*, 10 October.

86   Russell, L.T. (1950) Review of *TSS*, *The British Journal of Sociology*, 2(1): 79.

87   'Very Taking Lecturer', Review of *TSS*, *The Economist*, 11 November 1950, p. 735.

88   Wedderburn, D. (1994) 'Barbara Wootton and Contemporary Social Problems: Fighting for Good Causes', The Fawcett Lecture, Royal Holloway College, 1 March [GCPP Wootton 1/1/12].

89   Morris, 'In Memoriam', p. 315.

90   Hovde, B.J. (1951) Review of *TSS*, *The Annals of the American Academy of Political and Social Science*, 276: 171–172, p. 171.

91   Lasswell, H.D. (1952) Review of *TSS*, *The American Economic Review*, 42(3): 406.

92   H.B. Mayo to BW, 7 November 1950, GCPP Wootton 3/2/2.

93   W. Haley to BW, 21 October 1950, GCPP Wootton 2/1.

94   D. Ritchie to BW, 6 November 1950, GCPP Wootton 3/2/2.

95   D. Ritchie to BW, 19 September 1951, GCPP Wootton 1/1/2.

96   Hole, V. W and Attenburrow, J.J. (1970) 'The Home', in Butterworth, E. and Weir, D. (eds) *The Sociology of Modern Britain*, London: Collins and Sons, pp. 53–57, p. 54.

97   BW, *IWNM*, p. 262.

98   Havighurst, *Britain in Transition*, p. 369.

99   'Barbara Wootton Brains Trust Analyst Finds Pools Not Guilty', *The National Coal Board Magazine*, July 1947, p. 8 [GCPP Wootton 3/4/7].

100   'Prof. Barbara Becomes BBC Governor', *The Daily Express*, 22 December 1949.

101   BW, *IWNM*, p. 258.

102   Simon, Lord of Wythenshaw (1953) *The BBC from Within*, London: Victor Gollancz, p. 67.

103   'A Hard-working Baroness Wants to Take it Easy', *The Sunday Express*, 15 June 1969.

104   BW, *IWNM*, pp. 259–260.

105   Simon, *The BBC from Within*, p. 29.

106   Beveridge, W. H. (1951) *Report of the Broadcasting Committee 1949*, London: H.M.S.O.

107   Williams, F. (1970) *Nothing So Strange: An Autobiography*, London: Cassell, p. 271; BW, *IWNM*, p. 263.

108   Ibid., p. 272.

109   BW (1965) 'The BBC's Duty to Society', *The Listener*, Vol. 74, pp. 121–122 [reprinted in *BWSW*, Vol. 4, pp. 146–151, p. 148].

110   W. Haley to BW, 23 June 1965, GCPP Wootton 2/1.

111   W. Haley to BW, 18 February 1951, GCPP Wootton 2/1.

112   Williams, *Nothing So Strange*, p. 270.

113   W. Haley to BW, 25 February 1951, GCPP Wootton 2/1.

114   W. Haley to BW, 26 December 1951, GCPP Wootton 2/1.

115   W. Haley to BW, 20 July 1952, GCPP Wootton 2/1.

116   Smoker, B. (2008) *Humanism*, London: South Place Ethical Society (5th edition), p. 24.

117   'Into the Second Century, National Secular Society', *The Freethinker*, 5 May 1967: 2–10 [GCPP Wootton 3/4/1].

118   Belson, W.A. (1959) *Television and the Family: An Effects Study*, London: BBC Audience Research Department, p. 127.

119   Bray, R. and Raitz, V. (2001) *Flight to the Sun: The Story of the Holiday Revolution*, London: Continuum.

120 BW to W Haley, 12 August 1952, William Haley Papers, HALY 1/1, CAC.

121 BW to W. Haley, 24 May 1954, William Haley Papers, HALY 1/1, CAC.

122 BW (n.d., probably early 1960s) 'Calvi, Corsica Tour CI – 15 Days from 42 Gns,' GCPP Wootton 3/4/3.

123 BW, *IWNM,* p. 127.

124 'Floating Holiday', *The Times*, 31 October 1969.

125 BW, *IWNM*, p. 105.

126 'Wootton on British Planning', *The General View*, The Student Publication of the School of General Studies, Columbia University, 7 April 1949 [GCPP Wootton 3/4/7].

127 BW (1974) 'Preface', in Ritchie, D., *Stroke: A Diary of Recovery* (2nd edn), London: Faber.

128 *Closing Hours of Shops, Report of a Committee of Enquiry* (1947) Chairman Sir Ernest Gowers, London: H.M.S.O., p. 9.

129 BW, *IWNM*, pp. 253–254.

130 E. A. Gowers to BW, 2 August 1948, GCPP Wootton 1/1/2.

131 HC Deb., 26 March 1947, 435: 1232.

132 HC Deb., 28 July 1949, 467: 2734.

133 Smith, M.A. (1944) *A Worker's View of the Wool Textile Industry*, with a Foreword by BW, Surbiton, Surrey: Hillcroft College.

134 Atoll, K. et al. (1946) 'British Wives in Germany', Letter, *The Times,* 10 October.

135 Latham, I.J. et al. (1946) 'School Care Committees', Letter, *The Times*, 3 December.

136 Colville, C. et al. (1946) 'A Hostel for Girls', Letter, *The Times,* 24 December.

137 'Crime Among Juveniles: Archbishop's View Contested', *The Times*, 8 January 1949.

138 'Mrs. James Adam', Obituary, *The Times*, 15 August 1944.

139 BW, *IWNM*, p. 20.

140 Harrison, TWL.

141 BW to H. McMorran, 17 August 1944, GCAS 1/6/2.

142 BW to H. McMorran, 23 October 1944, GCAS 1/6/2.

143 E. Haynes to BW, 25 May 1951, GCPP Wootton 1/1/3.

144 Carrington, A., Hills, G.J. and Webb, K.R. (1974) 'Neil Kensington Adam 1891–1973', *Biographical Memoirs of Fellows of the Royal Society*, 20: 1–26, p. 7.

145 Ibid., p. 18.

146 Ibid., p. 11.

147 BW, *IWNM*, p. 18.

148 Adamson, A.W. (1974) 'Obituary, Neil Kensington Adam', *Journal of Colloid and Interface Science*, 48(2): 358–360, p. 360.

149 A. Ashford, Interview, 30 July 2008.

150 Adamson, Obituary, p. 359.

151 Adam, N.K. (1964) 'The Utilization of Divine Intelligence in Academic Work', *The Christian Science Journal*, 82(9): 449–450.

152 D. Adams, Interview 7 August 2009; J. Payne, Personal communication.

153 C. Furth to BW, n.d. and G. Brunton to BW, 12 January 1983, GCPP Wootton 1/1/6.

154 G. Brunton, Personal communication.

12. The Nuffield Years, and Vera

1 Minutes of the Meeting of the Trustees of the Nuffield Foundation, 31 October 1951, p. 177.

2 Ibid., p. 184.

3 Advertisement 'The National Institute for Economic and Social Research', *The Economist*, 14 November 1942, p. 608.

4 Minutes of the Meeting of the Trustees of the Nuffield Foundation, 18 March 1951, p. 38.

5 Ibid., p. 140.

6 Minutes of the Meeting of the Trustees of the Nuffield Foundation, 31 October 1951, p. 59.

7 Minutes of the Meeting of the Trustees of the Nuffield Foundation, 10 January 1952, p. 200.

8   Ibid., p. 199.
9   V. Seal, Interview, 20 February 2008.
10 Ibid.
11 BW to V. Seal, 9 July 1944, Seal Papers.
12 V. Seal, Interview, 20 February 2008.
13 BW to V. Seal, 17 March 1952, Seal Papers.
14 'Research Assistant and Secretary to the Nuffield Research Fellow', 7 November 1952, Seal Papers.
15 V. Seal, Interview, 23 October 2007.
16 V. Seal to BW, 14 November 1952, Seal Papers.
17 BW to V. Seal, 16 January 1953, Seal Papers.
18 W. Haley to BW, 4 March 1952, GCPP Wootton 2/1.
19 V. Seal, 'Barbara's Saga', Seal Papers.
20 V. Seal, Personal communication.
21 V. Seal, Personal communication.
22 BW, *SSSP*, p. 7.
23 V. Seal, Interview, 23 October 2007.
24 V. Seal, Interview, 20 February 2008.
25 BW, *SSSP*, p. 23.
26 Ibid., p. 318.
27 Ibid., p. 32.
28 Petticrew, M. and Roberts, H. (2006) *Systematic Reviews in the Social Sciences,* Oxford: Blackwell Publishing.
29 BW, *SSSP*, p. 325.
30 Ibid., Appendix I.
31 Ibid., p. 81.
32 Ibid., p. 83.
33 Ibid., p. 85.
34 Ibid., p. 310.
35 V. Seal, Interview, 16 July 2008.
36 Oakley, A., Gough, D., Oliver, S. and Thomas, J. (2005) 'The Politics of Evidence and Methodology: Lessons from the EPPI-Centre', *Evidence and Policy,* 1(1): 5–31.
37 BW, *SSSP*, p. 24.
38 Ibid., p. 15.
39 Ibid., p. 45.
40 Eyer, D.E. (1992) *Mother-Infant Bonding: A Scientific Fiction,* New Haven, Conn.: Yale University Press; Franzblau, S.H. (1999) II 'Historicizing Attachment Theory: Binding the Ties that Bind', *Feminism and Psychology,* 9: 22–31.
41 BW, *SSSP*, p. 317.
42 Van Dijken, S. (1998) *John Bowlby: His Early Life, a Biographical Journey into the Roots of Attachment Theory,* London and New York: Free Association Books, p. 153.
43 Bowlby, J. (1951) *Maternal Care and Mental Health,* Bulletin of the World Health Organization. Geneva: W.H.O., p. 365.
44 Van Dijken, *John Bowlby*.
45 Riley, D. (1983) *War in the Nursery*, London: Virago.
46 Van Dijken, *John Bowlby*, p. 144.
47 V. Seal, Interview, 23 October 2007.
48 BW, *SSSP*, p. 152.
49 R. Pinker, Interview, 23 March 2010.
50 'Portrait Visiting Professor,' *West Africa*, 29 March 1958 [GCPP Wootton 1/2/2].
51 BW (1966, originally published 1962) 'A Social Scientist's Approach to Maternal Deprivation', in Ainsworth, M.D. et al., *Deprivation of Maternal care: A Reassessment of its Effects,* New York: Schocken Books, pp. 255–265, p. 264.

52 Wofinden, R.C. (1944) 'Problem Families', *Public Health*, 57 (September), p. 136, cited in Wofinden, R.C. (1946) 'Problem Families', pp. 21–30 in Blacker, C.P. and Wofinden, R.C. (1946) 'Social Problem Families: Two Contributions', *Eugenics Review* reprint, 38(3): 22).

53 Phelp, A.D.F. and Timms, N.G. (1957) *The Problem of 'The Problem Family': A Critical Review of the Literature Concerning the 'Problem Family' and its Treatment,* London: Family Service Units.

54 Cavanagh, W.E. (1958) 'The Problem Family in Court', in Institute for the Scientific Treatment of Delinquency, *The Problem Family*, London: I.S.T.D., pp. 3–10, p. 3.

55 Szasz, T.S. (1961) *The Myth of Mental Illness: Foundations of a Theory of Personal Conduct*, New York: Harper and Row.

56 BW (1969) 'British Medical Practice as Seen Through the Eyes of a Layman', *Journal of the Royal College of General Practitioners,* 17(1, suppl.): 15–24.

57 HL Deb., 4 July 1962, 241: 1281.

58 BW (1963) 'The Law, the Doctor, and the Deviant', *British Medical Journal* 27(ii): 197–202, p. 202.

59 BW (1972) 'The Place of Psychiatry and Medical Concepts in the Treatment of Offenders: A Layman's View', *Canadian Psychiatric Association Journal,* 17: 365–375, p. 366.

60 'Doubts on Medical Advice to Courts, "Moral Judgments" Questioned', *The Times*, 8 June 1955.

61 See, for example, Freidson, E. (1970) *Profession of Medicine*, New York: Dodd, Mead & Co; Zola, I. (1972) 'Medicine as an Institution of Social Control', *The Sociological Review*, 20: 287–504.

62 BW, *SSSP*, p. 273.

63 K. McDougall to R.M. Titmuss (n.d. probably February 1960), Titmuss Papers.

64 BW to R.M. Titmuss, 29 December 1959, Titmuss Papers.

65 D. Donnison, Interview, 28 June 2010.

66 Downes, D. (1986) 'Back to Basics: Reflections on Barbara Wootton's "Twelve Criminological Hypotheses"', in Bean, P. and Whynes, D. (eds) *Barbara Wootton: Social Science and Public Policy, Essays in Her Honour,* London: Tavistock, pp. 195–214, p. 196.

67 McLachlan, N. (1974) 'Penal Reform and Penal History: Some Reflections', in Blom-Cooper, L. (ed.) *Progress in Penal Reform*, Oxford: Clarendon Press, pp. 1–24, p. 1.

68 D. Downes, Interview, 3 July 2008.

69 M. Rutter, Interview, 26 January 2009.

70 Irvine, E.E. (1960) Review of BW, *SSSP, Child Psychology and Psychiatry,* Vol. 1, pp. 244–247.

71 Fox, R. (1959) 'Medicine Versus Morals', *The Lancet,* 4 June: 1238–1242, p. 1238.

72 Kennedy, A. (1960) 'Sick Society', *British Medical Journal*, 12 March: 785.

73 Welshman, J. (1999) 'The Social History of Social Work: The Issue of the "Problem Family", 1947–70', *The British Journal of Social Work*, 29: 457–476.

74 Barry, J.J.V. (1960) 'The Study of Social Pathology – Science or Scientology', *Adelaide Law Review*, 1(2): 123–137, p. 137.

75 Ramsbotham, M. (1959) 'Strong Medicine', *New Statesman,* 30 May: 764–765, p. 764.

76 'Medicine and Morals', *The Economist*, 11 July 1959, p. 89.

77 Barry, 'The Study of Social Pathology', p. 123.

78 'Counting the Cost of Bad Behaviour', *The Times*, 21 May 1959.

79 'Medicine and Morals', p. 89.

80 Young, R.M. 'Review of Criminological Texts', p. 1, p. 4. http://human-nature.com/rmyoung/papers/paper73h.html [accessed 11 January 2005].

81 Rapoport, L. (1960) Review of *SSSP, Social Service Review*, 34(2): 237–239, p. 238.

82 Marshall, T.H. (1960) Review of *SSSP, The British Journal of Sociology*, 11(1): 82–86, p. 86, p. 83.

83 Titmuss, R.M. 'Perfectionism and Pessimism: A Review Article', *Case Conference*, 6(5): 119–124, pp. 119–120.

84 Pakenham, Lord (1959) 'Magnum Opus', *The Observer*, 24 May.

85 Sprott, W.J.H. (1959) 'Spring Cleaning', *The Listener,* 28 May, p. 947.

86 BW to D. Burn, 19 October 1956, Burn Papers, BURN//2/16, BLPES.

87 BW, *IWNM,* pp. 117–118.

88 F. Field, Interview, 7 February 2008; T. Gould, Interview, 24 April 2008.

89 BW (1957) 'The Worry of Five Million Extra Mouths to Feed Each Year', *Forward*, 1 February, p. 3, and 'I Could Have Sat Down and Cried ...', *Forward*, 8 February, p. 4.

90 BW, *IWNM*, p. 119.

91 Nehru, J. (1972–1982) *Selected Works of Jawaharlal Nehru*, New Delhi: Orient Longman, pp. 98–99.

92 'Portrait Visiting Professor.'

93 BW (1958) 'The Puzzling Politics of Ghana', *The Twentieth Century*, May, 163: 416–426 [GCPP Wootton 3/4/1].

94 BW, *IWNM*, p. 113.

95 BW to V. Seal, 9 February 1958, GCPP Wootton 1/7/1.

96 BW to V. Seal 20 February 1958, GCPP Wootton 1/7/1.

97 BW, *IWNM*, p. 111.

98 Ibid., pp. 119–120.

99 V. Seal, Interview, 23 October 2007.

100 BW, *IWNM*, p. 36.

101 BW (1955) 'Preface', in *International Register of Current Team Research in the Social Sciences 1950–52*, Paris: UNESCO, pp. 17–27 [GCPP Wootton 3/4/2].

102 BW (1962) *The Future of the Social Sciences* (Lecture delivered 18 October 1961), Canberra: The Australian National University [reprinted in *BWSW*, Vol. 3, pp. 49–60].

103 BW, 'Preface'.

104 BW (1959) 'Lions and Water Wagtails', *The Listener*, 17 September, pp. 437–438.

105 BW *The Future of the Social Sciences*.

106 BW (1962) 'Socrates, Science and Social Problems', *New Society*, 4 October, pp. 16–17.

107 BW (1956) 'Sickness or Sin?' *Twentieth Century,* May: 433–442.

108 BW (1959) 'Daddy Knows Best', *Twentieth Century,* October: 248–261.

109 BW (1952) 'Social Service in the New Society', *Social Service*, 25(4): 167–170.

110 BW (1957) 'Who are the Criminals?', *Twentieth Century*, August: 138–148.

111 BW (1960) 'Parkers and Drinkers', *Family Doctor,* 10(8): 502–503.

112 BW (1953) 'Adjustment to What? A Sociological Approach to Maladjustment', Talk given to National Association for Mental Health Inter-clinic Conference, GCPP Wootton 3/4/3.

113 BW (1956) 'Why Not Change the Schools?' *The Highway*, 47: 132–136, p. 133.

114 BW (1978) 'The Social Work Task Today', *Community Care*, 4 October: 13–16, p. 13.

115 BW (1975) 'A Philosophy for the Social Services', *Socialist Commentary*, January, pp. ii–vii [reprinted in *BWSW*, Vol. 2, pp. 142–155].

116 H. Macmillan to BW, 10 July 1968, GCPP Wootton 1/3/7.

117 M. Woodside to BW, 24 July 1958, GCPP Wootton 1/3/4.

118 C. Ford to BW, 24 July 1958, GCPP Wootton 1/3/4.

119 T. Marshall to BW, 31 July 1958, GCPP Wootton 1/3/4.

120 M. Breed to BW, 24 July 1958, GCPP Wootton 1/3/4.

121 V. Taverner to BW, 15 December 1958, GCPP Wootton 1/3/4.

122 W. Haley to BW, 21 October 1958, GCPP Wootton 2/1.

123 A. Winner to BW, 4 August 1958, GCPP Wootton 1/3/4.

124 K. Titmuss to BW, 24 July 1958, GCPP Wootton 1/3/4.

125 BW, *IWNM*, p. 134.

13. High Barn, and the Other Barbara

1 S. Corke, Personal communication. Abinger Hall was pulled down in 1958.

2 See http://www.british-history.ac.uk/report.aspx?compid=42944 [accessed 2 January 2009]; S. Corke, Personal communication.

3 S. Corke, Personal communication.

4 See http://www.british-history.ac.uk/report.aspx?compid=42944 [accessed 2 January 2008].

5 'The 50 Best Picnic Spots – Rural', *The Independent*, 26 July 2008; Corke, S. (n.d.) *Abinger Hammer, Surrey: A Short History and Guide to the Village* [no publisher given].

6 See http://www.rvwsociety.com/workschoral.html [accessed 5 January 2009].

7 BW (1946) 'Does the Country Want You?' *Countryman: A Quarterly Non-Party Review and Miscellany of Rural Life and Work for the English-Speaking World*, 34(1): 95–96.

8 BW (1968) 'Retaining Rural Peace Without Regimentation', *The Birmingham Post*, 28 December.

9 BW, *IWNM*, p. 137.

10 Samuel, R. (1994) *Theatres of Memory Vol. 1: Past and Present in Contemporary Culture*, London: Verso, p. 80.

11 BW, *IWNM*, p. 137.

12 BW (1978) 'More Equality Less Freedom?' unpublished ms, GCPP Wootton 3/4/3.

13 Williams, F. (1970) *Nothing so Strange: An Autobiography*, London: Cassell, p. 127.

14 See http://www.landmarktrust.org.uk/featured/goddards.htm [accessed 30 December 2009].

15 Following the death of their architect son, Lee, in 1988, the Halls gave Goddards to the Lutyens Trust; it is now leased to the Landmark Trust.

16 B. Trotter, Interview 4 March 2008.

17 Williams, *Nothing So Strange*, p. 287.

18 Mack J. (1977) 'Barbara Wootton', *New Society*, 14 April: 58–59, p. 59.

19 Rothwell, B.K. (1967) 'A Strong-minded Woman Who Has Made her Mark in Many Spheres', *Horley Advertiser*, 15 September 1967.

20 Foster, W. (1981) 'Following a Radical Road: William Foster meets Barbara Wootton', *The Scotsman*, 2 September 1981.

21 R. McGregor and N. McGregor, Interview, 8 August 2008; V. Seal said there was one small armchair.

22 Rothwell, 'A Strong-minded Woman'.

23 Hill, F. (1973) 'Baroness Wootton – "Keep Children Out of Courts"', *The Times Educational Supplement*, 12 January.

24 BW (1968) 'Donkeys with Famous Owners – the Baroness Wootton of Abinger', *The Donkey Magazine*: 24–25 .

25 See http://www.webbmemorialtrust.org.uk [accessed 23 June 2008]. Beatrice Webb House later became a Further Education College, Hurtwood House.

26 Williams, *Nothing So Strange*, p. 129.

27 J.M. Williams, Interview, 1 May 2008.

28 A. Bradley, Interview, 9 May 2008.

29 BW, *IWNM*, p. 135.

30 Kyle, B.R.F. (1953) *A Classification for a Library of International Affairs*, London Chatham House. Information on B.R.F. Kyle's work is taken from: Miksa, S.D. (2008) 'Barbara R.F. Kyle: Lessons Learned'. Draft unpublished paper; Hamerton, D. (1966) 'Barbara Kyle,' *The Library Association Record*, June, p. 239; Wilson, L. (1965) 'Barbara Kyle', in *The Journal of Documentation, Essays Presented to Barbara Kyle*, 21(4): 227–235.

31 BW (1942) 'Chaos in the Social Services', *The Sociological Review*, 34(1&2): 1–11.

32 Miksa, 'Barbara R.F. Kyle'.

33 A. Monie, Interview, 19 March 2008.

34 Tyson, G. (1963) *100 Years of Banking in Asia and Africa, 1863–1963*, London: National and Grindlays Bank.

35 See http://en.wikipedia.org/wiki/Henry_Fuseli [accessed 2 January 2010].

36 Powell, N. (1973) *Fuseli: The Nightmare*, London: Allen Lane, p. 15.

37 Tomalin, C. (1992) *The Life and Death of Mary Wollstonecraft*, London: Penguin Books.

38 Sturt, R. (1965) Review of *Teach Yourself Librarianship* by B.R.F. Kyle, *The Index*, 4(3): 93–94, p. 93.

39 Kyle, B. (1960 'Authors on Loan', Letter, *The Times*, 19 March 1960.

40 Muddiman, D. (2005) 'A New History of ASLIB, 1924–1950', *The Journal of Documentation*, 61(3): 402–429.

41   Justice, A. (2004) 'Information Science as a Facet of the History of British Science: The Origins
      of the Classification Research Group', in Rayward, W.B. and Bowden, M.E. (eds) *The History and
      Heritage of Scientific and Technological Information Systems*, Medford, N.J.: Information Today, Inc,
      pp. 267–280, p. 271.

42   Bernal, J.D. (1960) 'Information and its Users', *ASLIB Proceedings*, 12(12): 432–438,
      p. 432.

43   Shera, J.H. and Perry, J.W. (1965) 'Changing Concepts of Classification: Philosophical and
      Educational Implications', in Kaula, P.N. (ed.) *Library Science Today*, London: Asia Publishing
      House, pp. 37–48, p. 45.

44   Kyle, B. (2005, originally published 1956) 'Privilege and Public Provision in the Intellectual
      Welfare State', *The Journal of Documentation*, 61(4): 463–471.

45   Sturges, P. (2005) 'Clear Thinking on the "Unity" of the Information Professions', *The Journal of
      Documentation*, 61(4): 471–476.

46   Our Special Correspondent (1959) '25% of Scientific Knowledge Passed on Personally', *The Times*,
      20 April, p. 6.

47   Bonnici, L.J., Furner, J., Justice, A., La Barre, K., Miksa, S.D. and Plant, H. (2005) 'Pioneering
      Women in Information Science', *Proceedings of the American Society for Information Science and
      Technology*, 40(1): 425–426.

48   (1965) *The Journal of Documentation: Essays presented to Barbara Kyle*, 21(4). The total of
      B. Kyle's publications is expanded to 92 in Miksa, 'Barbara R.F. Kyle'.

49   BW, *IWNM*, pp. 138–139.

50   V. Seal, Interview, 23 October 2007.

51   E. Haynes to BW, 22 November 1953, GCPP Wootton 1/1/3.

52   BW to W. Haley, 11 June 1957, CAC, William Haley Papers, HALY 1/5, CAC.

53   BW to W. Haley, 20 June 1957, CAC, William Haley Papers, HALY 1/5, CAC.

54   A. Monie, Interview, 19 March 2008.

55   V. Seal, Interview, 20 February 2008.

56   B. Trotter, Interview, 4 March 2008.

57   F. Field, Interview, 7 February 2008.

58   V. Seal, Interview, 20 February 2008.

59   BW in collaboration with Kyle, B. (1950) 'Terminology in the Social Sciences', *International Social
      Science Bulletin*, II(I): 47–55, p. 50.

60   Dronamraju, K. R. (1993) *If I Am to be Remembered: The Life and Work of Julian Huxley, with Selected
      Correspondence*, Singapore: World Scientific Publishing Co, pp. 143–144.

61   'Luncheon Chatham House', *The Times*, 28 June 1941.

62   Collison, R. (1954) 'Documentation at Westminster: A Report on the 29th Annual Conference of
      the Association of Special Libraries and Information Bureaux', *Special Libraries: Official Journal of
      the Special Libraries Association*, 45(9): 386–387.

63   BW (1953) 'Some Problems of Communication', *ASLIB Proceedings*, 5(4): 261–270 [reprinted
      in *BWSW*, Vol. 4, pp. 100–111]; BW (1954) 'Further Problems of Communication: The
      Language of the Social Sciences', *ASLIB Proceedings*, 6(4): 215–225 [reprinted in *BWSW*, Vol.
      4: 112–123].

64   Wilson, 'Barbara Kyle, p. 227.

65   V. Seal, Personal communication.

66   Ibid.

67   Kyle, B. and Vickery, B.C. (1961) 'The Universal Decimal Classification: Present Position and
      Future Developments', *UNESCO Bulletin for Libraries*, Vol. 15, no.2, March–April (items 96 and
      181).

68   Nuffield Foundation Papers, Paper F. 57/10, 'International Committee for Social Sciences
      Documentation, Application from Miss Barbara Kyle', Minutes of 57th Meeting held on 4 January
      1955.

69   Ibid., Minute III. 215.

70   Ibid., Paper F. 74/4, 'Social Sciences Documentation: Note by Miss Barbara Kyle', Minutes of
      74th Meeting held on 22 March 1957; Kyle, B. (1958) 'Towards a Classification for Social Science

Literature', *American Documentation,* 9(3): 168–183; 'Guide to the Use of the Kyle Social Science Classification', *American Documentation,* 9: 320–321.

71 Shera, J.H. (1957) 'Pattern, Structure and Conceptualization in Classification for Information Retrieval', in *The Journal of Documentation, Essays Presented to Barbara Kyle,* 21(4): 15–27.

72 Broughton, V. (2010) 'Facet Analytical Theory in Managing Knowledge Structure for Humanities'. http://www.ucl.ac.uk.fatks/fat.htm [accessed 5 January 2010].

73 Kyle, B. (1964) *Final Report on the Trial Application of the Kyle Classification for Arranging of Entries and Indexing of the Contents of the Annual Bibliographies of the International Committee for Social Sciences Documentation, carried out under National Science Foundation Grant G9176.*

74 B. Trotter, Interview, 4 March 2008.

75 Martin, K. (1967) 'Abinger Harvest', *The Listener,* 26 March [GCCP Wootton 1/2/6].

76 W. Haley to BW, 9 June 1978, GCPP Wootton 3/4/9.

77 Forster, E.M. (1967, originally published 1936) *Abinger Harvest,* Harmondsworth: Penguin Books, pp. 370–371, p. 384.

14. Crime and Penal Policy

1 Bird, J. (2002) *Some Luck,* London: Hamish Hamilton, p. 136, p. 108.

2 J. Bird, Interview, 9 February 2010.

3 BW, *CCL,* p. 21.

4 Bean, P. and Whynes, D. (eds) *Barbara Wootton: Social Science and Public Policy, Essays in Her Honour,* London: Tavistock, p. 141, p. 191, p. 216, p. 243.

5 BW, *CPP,* p. 1.

6 Blom-Cooper, L. (1978) 'The Voice of Sanity', Review of *CPP, The Observer,* 27 August.

7 Radzinowicz, L. (1999) *Adventures in Criminology,* London: Routledge, pp. 86–97.

8 Morris, T. (1989) *Crime and Criminal Justice Since 1945,* Oxford: Basil Blackwell, p. 35, p. 89.

9 Radzinowicz, *Adventures,* p. 81.

10 Walker, N. (2003) *A Man Without Loyalties,* Chichester: Barry Rose Law Publishers, p. 97.

11 BW, 'Summary of Evidence to Lord Pakenham's Committee', March 1954, GCPP Wootton 3/4/3.

12 BW, *CPP,* p. 67.

13 BW (1978) 'Reflections on Crime and Penal Policy in Contemporary England', *Current Legal Problems* [GCPP Wootton 3/4/1 p. 2].

14 BW, *CPP,* p. 43.

15 Ibid., p. 16.

16 BW, *CCL,* p. 107.

17 Ibid., p. 16.

18 BW (1959) *Contemporary Trends in Crime and its Treatment,* The Nineteenth Clarke Hall Lecture, London: Clarke Hall Fellowship, p. 18.

19 BW, *CPP,* pp. 157–158.

20 BW, *IWNM,* p. 218.

21 Ibid., p. 219.

22 BW, *SSSP,* Appendix I.

23 BW, *IWNM,* p. 221.

24 'The Lonely Mother Who No One Would Help', *The Daily Mirror,* 4 August 1955.

25 'A Girl's Right Not to Kiss', *The Daily Mirror,* 22 December 1951.

26 'Girl, 11, is "Coddled," Court Told', *The Daily Mirror,* 19 October 1950.

27 'Mirror Brief', *The Daily Mirror,* 20 August 1959.

28 'Cuddling? Don't Stop It', *The Daily Express,* 1 September 1953; 'Should a Mother Cuddle Her Sixteen-year-old Daughter?' *The Daily Mirror,* 27 August 1953.

29 'The Little Waif Who Brought Love to Couple With Past', *The Daily Mirror,* 16 September 1954.

30 Logan, A. (2006) 'Professionalism and the Impact of England's First Women Justices, 1920–1950', *The Historical Journal,* 49(3): 833–850.

31 'Juvenile Reliquent', *The Guardian,* 22 March 1962.

32   BW, *CPP*, p. 16.

33   BW, 'Reflections on Crime', p. 9.

34   'Baroness Wootton', *The Surrey County Magazine,* 8(6), December/January/mid-February 1977/8, Surrey Personality Profile No. 35 [GCPP Wootton 1/2/3].

35   'Probation Advisory Committee', *Probation Journal,* March–April 1946, 5: 14.

36   The Perks Committee (1967) *Report of the Departmental Committee on Criminal Statistics,* London: H.M.S.O.

37   Hall Williams, J.E. (1961) 'Report of the Interdepartmental Committee on the Business of the Criminal Courts', *The Modern Law Review,* 24(3): 360–365.

38   The Streatfeild Committee (1961) *Report of the Interdepartmental Committee on the Business of the Criminal Courts,* London: H.M.S.O., p. 123.

39   BW, *CPP*, pp. 20–21.

40   BW (n.d. 1960–1?) 'Five Thousand Children', unpublished ms, GCPP Wootton 3/4/6, p. 2.

41   BW (1968) 'The White Paper on Children in Trouble', *The Criminal Law Review,* September: 463–518, p. 468.

42   BW, *CB*, p. 83.

43   HL Deb., 10 December 1962, 245: 400–402.

44   Bottoms, A. (2002) 'On the Decriminalisation of English Juvenile Courts', in Muncie, J., Hughes, G. and McLaughlin, E. (eds) *Youth Justice: Critical Readings,* London: Sage, pp. 216–227, p. 220.

45   BW (1961) 'The Juvenile Courts', *The Criminal Law Review,* October, pp. 669–677.

46   'Parliament: Age of Criminal Responsibility', *The Glasgow Herald,* 25 January 1963.

47   BW (1974) 'Spare the Rod and Civilise the Child', *Teachers World,* 13 December, p. 5.

48   HL Deb., 10 December 1973, 347: 883.

49   Fairhall, J. (1973) 'Baroness Will Present School Cane Bill', *The Guardian,* 5 January.

50   Radzinowicz, *Adventures*, p. 333.

51   *The War Against Crime in England and Wales 1959–1964* (1964) London: H.M.S.O.

52   Walker, *A Man Without Loyalties*, p. 112.

53   *The War Against Crime in England and Wales*, p. 15.

54   Radzinowicz, *Adventures*, p. 346.

55   BW (1977) 'Official Advisory Bodies,' in Walker, N. (ed.) *Penal Policy-making in England. Papers Presented to the Cropwood Round-table Conference December 1976,* Cambridge: University of Cambridge Institute of Criminology, pp. 13–24, pp. 15–16.

56   Walker, *A Man Without Loyalties,* pp. 112–3.

57   Radzinowicz, *Adventures*, p. 345.

58   Ibid., p. 338.

59   Windlesham, Lord (1993) *Responses to Crime. Vol. 2, Penal Policy in the Making.* Oxford: Clarendon Press, p. 101.

60   Radzinowicz, *Adventures*, p. 349.

61   Ibid., p. 350.

62   J.N. Morris, Personal communication.

63   L. Blom-Cooper, Interview, 9 February 2009.

64   Windlesham, *Responses to Crime*, p. 104.

65   Morgan, R. and Smith, B. (1979) 'Advising the Minister on Crime and Punishment', *The Political Quarterly,* 50(3): 326–335.

66   L. Blom-Cooper, Personal communication.

67   Advisory Council on the Penal System (1974) *Young Adult Offenders: Report of the Advisory Council on the Penal System,* London: H.M.S.O., pp. 158–159.

68   J.V. Barry to BW, 10 December 1963, Papers of Sir John V. Barry, MS 2505, National Library of Australia.

69   Hart, H. (1965) Review of *CCL*, *The Yale Law Journal,* 74(7): 1325–1331, p. 1325, p. 1331.

70   'Do Britain's Courts Need a New Look?' *The Daily Mirror,* 13 November 1963.

71   BW, *CCL*, p. 3.

72   BW, 'Reflections on Crime', p. 10.

73   BW, *CCL*, p. 5.

74   Ibid., p. 7.

75   BW, *CCL*, pp. 92–93.

76   Martinson, R. (1974) 'What Works? – Questions and Answers about Prison Reform', *Public Interest*, 35: 22–54.

77   BW, *IWNM*, p. 242.

78   BW (1965) 'Crime and Its Rewards', *New Society*, 6: 17–19, p. 19.

79   BW, *CCL*, p. 95.

80   Ibid., p. 52.

81   BW (1960) 'Diminished Responsibility: A Layman's View', *Law Quarterly Review*, 76(302): 224–239 [reprinted in *BWSW*, Vol. 2, pp. 111–125].

82   Hart, 'Review', p. 1325.

83   Bayles, M.D. (1982) 'Character, Purpose, and Criminal Responsibility', *Law and Philosophy*, 1(1): 5–20. Unfortunately, Bayles misspells 'Wootton-Hart' as 'Wooton-Hart'.

84   BW (1980) 'Psychiatry, Ethics and the Criminal Law', *The British Journal of Psychiatry*, 136: 525–532, p. 525 [reprinted in *BWSW*, Vol. 2, pp. 1–12].

85   HL Deb., 4 June 1959, 216: 717–719.

86   BW, 'Psychiatry, Ethics and the Criminal Law'.

87   BW, *CB*, p. 72.

88   'Unfaithful? – No, He Is Sick,' *The Daily Mirror*, 9 March 1962.

89   BW, 'Diminished Responsibility', p. 120.

90   BW (1968) Review of *The Insanity Defense* by A. S. Goldstein , *The Yale Law Journal*, 77(5): 1019–1032, p. 1032.

91   Blom-Cooper, L. (1969) 'Introduction', in Blom-Cooper, L. (ed.) *The Hanging Question*, London: Duckworth, pp. 1–4, p. 1.

92   BW (1969) 'Morality and Mistakes', in Blom-Cooper, L. (ed.) *The Hanging Question*, London: Duckworth [reprinted in *BWSW*, Vol. 3, pp. 126–130].

93   'The Baroness Who Was Ashamed of Being British', *Time and Tide*, 20–26 February 1969 [GCPP Wootton 1/2/2].

94   Gowers, E. (1956) *A Life for a Life? The Problem of Capital Punishment*, London: Chatto & Windus, pp. 14–25.

95   Ibid, p. 8.

96   E. Gowers to BW, 23 November 1949, GCPP Wootton 1/1/2.

97   BW (1969) 'Morality and Mistakes', in *The Hanging Question*, pp. 13–19.

98   Harewood et al. 'The Death Penalty', Letter, *The Times*, 22 January 1962.

99   HL Deb., 19 July 1965, 268: 458.

100   L. Blom–Cooper, Interview, 9 February 2009.

101   HL Deb., 17 December 1969, 306: 1142.

102   BW to S. Simon, 7 January 1970, GCRF 9/1/40.

103   Abrams, S (2008) 'Soma, the Wootton Report and Cannabis Law Reform in Britain During the 1960s and 1970s', in European Monitoring Centre for Drugs and Drug Addiction, *A Cannabis Reader: Global Issues and Local Experiences*, Monograph Series 8, 1: 41–49, Lisbon: EMCDDA.

104   Davis, J. (2006) 'The London Drug Scene and the Making of Drug Policy, 1965–73', *Twentieth Century British History*, 17(1): 26–49, p. 44.

105   McCabe, J. (2010) *Hemp: What the World Needs Now*, Carmania Books, p. 210.

106   'Who Breaks a Butterfly on a Wheel?, Editorial *The Times*, 1 July 1967.

107   'It was Twenty-five Years Ago Today – Release', *The Times*, 24 July 1992. http://www.release.org.uk/about/history-of-release [accessed 13 August 2010].

108   See http://www.release.org.uk/about/ourpeople/roll-of-honour [accessed 28 June 2010].

109   McCabe, 'Hemp: What the World Needs Now'.

110   The Wootton Report on Cannabis (1968) *Cannabis: Report by the Advisory Committee on Drug Dependence*, London: H.M.S.O., p. 8.

111   Ibid., p. 20.

112   Ibid., p. 2.

113   Schofield, M. (1971) *The Strange Case of Pot*, Harmondsworth: Penguin, p. 93.

114   Cannabis Report, p. 7, p. 13, pp. 20–21, p. 15.

115   Indian Hemp Drugs Commission (1894) *Report of the Commission* 1893/4. http://www.druglibrary.
      org/schaffer/library/studies/inhemp/ihmenu.htm [accessed 18 August 2010].

116   Editorial (1969) 'The Problem of Cannabis', *The Times,* 8 January.

117   Cannabis Report, p. v.

118   Cavadino, P. (1978) 'Abolish Juvenile Courts', *Inside Out*, October, p. 5.

119   Steele, J. (1969) 'Legalising Pot', *The Guardian,* 2 December.

120   Abrams, 'Soma, the Wootton Report and Cannabis Law Reform', p. 9.

121   Butt, R. (1977) 'Cannabis and the Law: The Narrow Escape', *The Times,* 17 March

122   Davis, 'The London Drug Scene', p. 45.

123   HC Deb., 27 January 1969, 776: 959.

124   Wayne, E., and BW (1969) 'Drugs Report: Answer to Minister', Letter, *The Times,* 5 February.

125   BW (1978) 'Crossman Confused Over Cannabis', Letter, *The Guardian*, 15 July.

126   Cannabis Report, p. 13, p. 14, p. 16, p. 12.

127   BW (1969) 'Cannabis is Not Heroin', *Science Journal,* September, 5A(3): 3.

128   'Potted Dreams', Editorial, *British Medical Journal*, 18 January, pp. 133–134.

129   *The Yorkshire Morning Telegraph,* 9 January 1969.

130   'Ignore Drugs Report Urges Police Chief', *Cambridge Independent Press,* 17 January 1969.

131   'Sir Gerald Hits Out at the Barbaras', *Gloucestershire Echo,* 18 January 1969.

132   Lees, J.M. (1969) 'Government Rejects British Panel's Call for Reduced Marijuana Penalties', *The
      New York Times*, 24 January.

133   'Remember Carole Gibbens', *News of the World,* 1 December 1968.

134   'A Letter from a Girl Who Went on Drugs', *The Evening Times,* 20 January 1969.

135   'Little Old Lady Talking Pot', *The Sunday Mirror,* 12 January 1969.

136   R.M. Helsdon to BW, 18 March 1971, GCPP Wootton 3/3/3.

137   'The Baroness Who is Ashamed of Being British.'

138   'Cool Lady Wootton', *The Times,* 27 March 1969.

139   BW (1970) 'The Relation of Law and Morality in Contemporary Britain', lecture delivered at
      Bedford College, University of London [reprinted in *BWSW*, Vol. 1, pp. 80–94, p. 85].

140   'That's Why the Lady is a Fighter', *Lancashire Evening Post,* 16 December 1970.

141   E.C. Somerville to BW, 5 December 1969, GCPP Wootton 3/3/3.

142   D.M. Harris to BW, 10 February 1969, GCPP Wootton 3/3/3.

143   Anon., n.d., GCPP Wootton 3/3/3.

144   Anon., n.d., GCPP Wootton 3/3/3.

145   Anon., n.d., GCPP Wootton 3/3/3.

146   S. Argyle to BW, 20 January 1969, GCPP Wootton 3/3/3.

147   E. Morag to BW, n.d., GCPP Wootton 3/3/3.

148   M. Palmer to BW, n.d., GCPP Wootton 3/3/3.

149   G. Starky to BW, 8 January 1969, GCPP Wootton 3/3/3.

150   'Lady Wootton Hits Back at "Pot" Critics', *The Daily Express,* 30 January 1969.

151   'Cannabis Law Change Undesirable – Minister', *The Times,* 27 March 1969.

152   'Face the Press', Tyne Tees Television Ltd, recorded 4 January 1984; Baroness Wootton of Abinger
      interviewed by P. Toynbee, G. Smith and A. Howard, 4 January 1984, transcript, p. 20, GCPP
      Wootton 3/2/1.

153   Cunningham, J. (1982) 'Out of Step', *The Guardian,* 4 June.

154   'Drug Law Shock: Jim Changes His Mind', *The Sunday Mirror,* 1 February 1970.

155   BW (1977) 'Cannabis and the Law', Letter, *The Times,* 21 March.

156   Cited in BW (1973) 'The British Cannabis Report and After', unpublished ms, GCPP Wootton
      3/4/6, p. 5.

157   'Peeress Who Led "Pot" Inquiry Gets New Drugs Job', *The Daily Express,* 10 January 1979.

158   Advisory Council on Drug Dependence (1970) *The Amphetamines and Lysergic Acid Diethylamide:
      Report by the Advisory Council on Drug Dependence*, London: H.M.S.O., p. 48.

159   '50 Arrested at Pop Festival', *The Times,* 26 June 1971.

160   BW (1971) 'Measures to Control Crime', Letter, *The Times,* 1 September.

161 BW (1971) 'Stop and Search: A Critical View of the Law', *SHE,* July.

162 W.T. Duncan Vincent to BW, 6 July 1971, GCPP Wootton 3/3/3.

163 HL Deb., 14 July 1971, 322: 341–342.

164 Cannabis Report, p. 31.

165 Advisory Committee on Drug Dependence (the Deedes Report) (1970) *Powers of Arrest and Search in Relation to Drug Offences: Report by the Advisory Committee on Drug Dependence,* London: H.M.S.O.

166 Schofield, *The Strange Case of Pot,* p. 84.

167 'Unfair to Use Long Hair as an Excuse for Drug Search', *The Times,* 8 March 1970.

168 Advisory Council on the Penal System (the Wootton Report) (1970) *Non-Custodial and Semi-Custodial Penalties: Report of the Advisory Council on the Penal System,* London: H.M.S.O., p. v.

169 Walker, N. (1977) 'Preface', in Walker, *Penal Policy-making in England.*

170 Pease, K. (1985) 'Community Service Orders', *Crime and Justice,* 6: 51–94, p. 58.

171 Wright, M. (1971) 'Alternatives to Prison', Letter, *The Times,* 3 August.

172 BW to M. Wright, 8 April 1984, GCPP Wootton 4/1.

173 'Education: The Chocolate Judge', *Time Magazine,* 19 April 1954. http://www.time.com/time/magazine/article/0,9171,860573,00.html [accessed 3 November 2008].

174 BW, *IWNM,* pp. 116–117.

175 Non-Custodial and Semi-Custodial Penalties Report, p. 3.

176 Ibid., p. 2.

177 Ibid., p. 66.

178 Pease, 'Community Service Orders', p. 59.

179 Windlesham, *Responses to Crime,* p. 122.

180 McIvor, G. (1997) 'Evaluative Research in Probation: Progress and Prospects', in Mair, G. (ed.) *Evaluating the Effectiveness of Community Penalties,* Aldershot, Hants.: Avebury, pp. 1–18, p. 2.

181 MacManus, J. (1972) 'Hard Labour by Court', *The Guardian,* 27 October 1972.

182 Pease, 'Community Service Orders', p. 63.

183 Ibid., p. 58; McGagh, M. (2007) *Community Service: An Exploration of the Views of Community Service Supervisors in the Irish Probation Service.* Dissertation submitted to the National University of Ireland, Dublin, in part fulfilment of the degree of Master of Social Science, p. 22.

184 Ibid., p. 23.

185 Canton, R. (1988) 'Barbara Wootton, Magistrate and Social Scientist', Obituary, *Probation Journal,* 35: 152.

186 Mouzer, B. (1970) 'Wootton on Probation', *Social Work Today,* 1(7): 20–22, pp. 20–21.

187 Hood, R. (1974) 'Criminology and Penal Change: A Case Study of the Nature and Impact of Some Recent Advice to Governments,' in Hood, R. (ed.) *Crime, Criminology and Public Policy,* London: Heinemann, pp. 375–417.

188 BW, 'Official Advisory Bodies', pp. 17–18.

189 BW (1973) 'Community Service', *The Criminal Law Review,* January: 16–20, p. 18.

190 Pease, 'Community Service Orders'.

191 BW, *CPP,* p. 128.

192 BW (c.1980) 'Preface', in West Midlands Probation and Aftercare Service, *Community Service Works,* p. 1.

193 Pease, K., Billingham, S. and Earnshaw, I. (1977) *Community Service Assessed in 1976,* Home Office Research Study, No. 39, London: H.M.S.O.

194 BW (1977) 'Some Reflections on the First Five Years of Community Service', *Probation Journal,* 24(4): 110–112, p. 112.

195 BW, *CPP,* p. 129.

196 BW, 'Some Reflections', p. 112.

197 BW to M. Swann, 15 May 1977; M. Swann to BW, 1 June 1977, GCPP Wootton 2/1.

198 BW to I. Trethowan, 19 February 1978 and 27 March 1978; I. Trethowan to BW, 15 March 1978 and 24 April 1978, GCPP Wootton 2/1.

199 BW (1966) 'A Practice to Watch, Pre-recording of Broadcasts', Letter, *The Times,* 7 February.

200 BW, 'Some Reflections'.

201 Cavadino, 'Abolish Juvenile Courts', p. 5.

202 Cleave, M. (1970) 'The Hip Baroness Wootton of Abinger', *The New York Times*, 10 May.

203 Rolph, C.H. (1978) Review of *CPP*, *Police Review*, 29 September, pp. 1444–1445.

204 'For Posterity: Top of the Pops People of 1973', *The Times*, 23 April 1973.

205 'Crime Expert of the House of Lords', *The Age*, 20 October 1961.

206 BW (1959) *Contemporary Trends in Crime*, p. 14.

207 Ibid., p. 9.

208 Ibid., p. 23.

209 BW (1972) 'The Changing Face of British Justice', in Morris, N. and Perlman, N. (eds) *Law and Crime: Essays in Honor of Sir John Barry*, New York: Gordon and Breach, pp. 103–119, pp. 118–119.

210 Ann Ashford's experiences working in the USA were that Barbara's scepticism about the magistrates' booklet was not shared by sentencers there, who regarded it as a model to be adopted elsewhere (A. Ashford, Personal communication).

211 BW, *CCL*, 2nd edition [reprinted in *BWSW*, Vol. 1, pp. 1–79 p. 76].

212 Ibid., p. 30.

213 'Out of the Air: "Taking Something"', *The Listener*, 23 March 1972.

15. Madam Speaker

1 BW, *IWNM*, p. 267.

2 Cunningham, J. (1982) 'Out of Step', *The Guardian*, 4 June.

3 V. Seal, Personal communication.

4 Pendennis (1968) 'Gothic Glories and Tea', *The Observer*, 23 June.

5 BW (1977) 'The End of the Peers', *New Society*, 42: 232–233 [reprinted in *BWSW*, Vol. 3, pp. 172–176, p. 174].

6 BW, *IWNM*, p. 274.

7 Dean, M. (2002) 'Lord Young of Dartington', Obituary, *The Guardian*, 16 January.

8 Wedderburn, D. (1994) 'Barbara Wootton and Contemporary Social Problems: Fighting for Good Causes', The Fawcett Lecture, Royal Holloway College, 1 March, pp. 5–6 [GCPP Wootton 1/1/12].

9 BW, *IWNM*, p. 267, pp. 271–2; BW (1962) 'A Life Peeress Looks at the Lords', *The Observer*, 10 June.

10 T. Morris, Interview, 29 April 2008; Personal communication.

11 R. McGregor and N. McGregor, Interview, 8 August 2008.

12 T. Gould, Interview, 24 April 2008.

13 Rolph, C.H. (1978) *Kingsley: The Life, Letters and Diaries of Kingsley Martin*, Harmondsworth: Penguin, p. 424.

14 C.M. Rolph, Interview with BW, 19 October 1971, Kingsley Martin Archive, 38/35, University of Sussex.; BW to K. Martin, 11 December 1960, Kingsley Martin Archive, University of Sussex.

15 Williams, F. (1970) *Nothing so Strange: An Autobiography*, London: Cassell, p. 334.

16 'A Magnificent Masque, The Queen Opens Parliament', *The Manchester Guardian*, 29 October 1958.

17 HL Deb., 4 February 1959, 213: 1053.

18 Ibid., 213: 1100–1105.

19 Ibid., 213: 1105.

20 Ibid., 213: 1166–1167.

21 Ibid., 213: 1173.

22 Pendennis, 'Gothic Glories'.

23 *The Observer*, 27 July 1958, quoted in Sutherland, D.P. (2000) *Peeresses, Parliament, and Prejudice: The Admission of Women to the House of Lords, 1900–1963*, PhD Thesis, University of Cambridge, p. 307.

24 HL Deb., 9 June 1959, 216: 777–857, 820–822.

25 HL Deb., 26 February 1959, 214: 602.

26   Ibid., 214: 607.

27   HL Deb., 17 February 1960, 221: 77.

28   Ibid., 221: 105–106.

29   Longford, Lord (1988) *A History of the House of Lords*, London: Collins, p. 195.

30   HL Deb., 3 November 1964, 261: 33.

31   Jeger, L., Notes for Obituary of BW, Lena Jeger Archives, JEGER/1/17, BLPES.

32   HL Deb., 3 March 1976, 368: 1051–1052.

33   Cunningham, 'Out of Step'.

34   HL Deb., 19 March 1962, 238: 440.

35   HL Deb., 5 December 1979, 403: 765–770.

36   'Borstal Training to be Reviewed', *The Times*, 18 November 1970.

37   'Row Over Gun Training for Boys in Borstals', *The Daily Mirror*, 18 November 1970.

38   M. Carlisle to BW, 28 April 1972, GCPP Wootton 4/5.

39   BW, note on back of letter to BW from N.S. Conrad, 23 March 1982, GCPP Wootton 4/5.

40   HL Deb., 8 April 1959, 215: 483.

41   HL Deb., 10 June 1959, 216: 960–961.

42   HL Deb., 13 April 1961, 230: 388–389.

43   BW, *IWNM*, p. 212.

44   HL Deb., 13 January 1971, 314: 190.

45   B. Luckin, Personal communication; Luckin, B. (2010) 'A Kind of Consensus on the Roads? Drink Driving Policy in Britain 1945–70', *Twentieth Century British History*, 21(3): 350–374.

46   The Constitutional Reform Act of 2005 Act brought the House of Lords into line with the House of Commons in creating the role of Lord Speaker as an elected office.

47   F. Field, Interview, 7 February 2008.

48   'First Woman to Sit on the Woolsack', *The Times*, 18 December 1965.

49   Jeger, L. (1966) 'Not Made for Woman', *The Guardian*, February 18.

50   A. Bradley, Interview, 9 May 2008.

51   'Hot Stuff', *The Observer*, 2 December 1973.

52   'Woman Peer Presides', *The New York Times*, 17 February 1966.

53   Munday, D. (2007) Interview, in Furedi, A. and Hume, M. (eds) *Abortion Law Reformers, Pioneers of Change: Interviews with People Who Made the 1967 Abortion Act Possible*, London: British Pregnancy Advisory Service, pp. 8–14.

54   Hindell, K. and Simms, M. (1971) *Abortion Law Reformed*, London: Owen.

55   Annan, N. G. et al., 'Homosexual Acts, Call to Reform Law', Letter, *The Times*, 7 March 1958.

56   See   http://www.nationmaster.com/encylopedia/Homosexual-Law-Reform-Society   [accessed 18 February 2009].

57   Abortion Law Reform Association Archives, SA/ALR/A.2/1 Pre-1949 Material, 1930–1937.

58   HL Deb., 22 February 1966, 273: 103.

59   Hindell and Simms, *Abortion Law Reformed*, pp. 132–133.

60   BW (1966) 'Abortion Bill in Lords Committee and in Commons', *British Medical Journal*, 4 June: 1430.

61   HL Deb., 22 February 1966, 273: 103–104.

62   F. Field, Personal communication; A. Bryant (Interview, 23 April 2008) suggested that BW may have had a miscarriage during her marriage to George Wright.

63   Mack J. (1977) 'Barbara Wootton', *New Society*, 14 April: 58–59.

64   HL Deb., 26 July 1967, 285: 1012.

65   Hindell and Simms, *Abortion Law Reformed*, p. 149.

66   HL Deb., 22 February 1966, 273: 106–107.

67   M. Simms, Interview, 20 October 2010.

68   D. Munday, Interview, 29 April 2010.

69   'Lady Barbara Wootton 1968', 'Now and Then'. http://www.bfi.org.uk/inview/collection/now-and–then [accessed 28 September 2010] (This series was never shown on British television.)

70   Kemp, N.D.A. (2002) *'Merciful Release': The History of the British Euthanasia Movement*, Manchester: Manchester University Press, p. 179; Bren, L. (2001) 'Frances Oldham Kelsey: FDA Medical Reviewer Leaves Her Mark on History', *FDA Consumer*, 28 February.

71 Kemp, 'Merciful Release', pp. 178–179.

72 'Panorama', 'Thalidomide', recorded from transmission 12 November 1962, transcript, BBC Written Archives Centre.

73 HL Deb., 21 March 1972, 329: 589.

74 Hindell and Simms, *Abortion Law Reformed*, p. 153, p. 149.

75 Wivel, A. (1998) 'Abortion Policy and Politics on the Lane Committee of Enquiry, 1971–1974', *Social History of Medicine,* 11(1): 109–135.

76 BW (1961) 'Humanism and Social Pathology', in Huxley, J. (ed.) *The Humanist Frame*, London: George Allen & Unwin, pp. 347–356.

77 Smoker, B. (2008) *Humanism,* London: South Place Ethical Society.

78 Cooke, B. (2003) *Blasphemy Depot: A Hundred Years of the Rationalist Press Association*, London: Rationalist Press Association.

79 Ibid., p. 158.

80 See http://www.iheu.org/in-memoriam-harold-blackman-an-iheu-founder [accessed 23 March 2010].

81 Tribe, D. (1967) *A Hundred Years of Freethought*, London: Elek, p. 55.

82 Ibid., p. 236.

83 McIlroy, W. (1988) 'Baroness Wootton of Abinger', Letter, *The Independent*, 18 July.

84 'Afternoon: EU AGM', *Humanist News*, May/June 1966: 2.

85 Smoker, B. (1966) 'Baroness Wootton', Letter, *Humanist News*, September: 8.

86 HL Deb., 26 July 1967, 285: 1066–1067.

87 Cooke, *Blasphemy Depot,* p. 246.

88 Ibid.

89 'Barbara Wootton, Resignation of Vice-President', *Humanist News*, December 1967; 'Barbara Wootton', Letter, *Humanist*, October 1967: 317.

90 Keating. C. (2009) *Smoking Kills: The Revolutionary Life of Sir Richard Doll*, Oxford: Signal Books, pp. 201–202.

91 See, for example, 'BBC Appeal on Behalf of the Agnostics Adoption Society', 1969, GCPP Wootton 3/4/6.

92 'Life Peerages Created Under the Life Peerages Act 1958'. http://www.election.demon.co.uk/lifepeers.html [accessed 29 August 2010].

93 Adonis, A. (1988) 'The House of Lords Since 1945', *Contemporary British History*, 2(3): 6–9.

94 Brazier, R. (1999) 'The Second Chamber: Paradoxes and Plans', in Carmichael, P. and Dickson, B. (eds) *The House of Lords: Its Parliamentary and Judicial Roles*, Oxford: Hart Publishing, pp. 53–65, p. 57.

95 Rusbridger, A. (1988) 'Lords Leap into Focus', *The Guardian,* 30 April.

96 Drewry, G. and Brock, J. (1983) *The Impact of Women on the House of Lords,* University of Strathclyde: Centre for the Study of Public Policy, p. 15.

97 'Outstanding Life Peers'. http://lordsoftheblog.net/2008/05/29/outstanding-life-peers/ [accessed 5 January 2009].

98 BW, 'The End of the Peers', pp. 232–233.

99 'Bruce Kenrick and Baroness Wootton of Abinger talk with Peter Snow' (1967) Central Rediffusion Services Ltd, *Dialogue with Doubt: Last Programmes from Rediffusion Television*, London: SCM Press, pp. 73–97, p. 94.

100 BW (1981) 'The Sad Defection of Our Shirley', *New Society*, 16 April: 109–110, p. 110.

101 P. Bean, Interview, 18 March 2009.

102 'Women of Our Century: Baroness Wootton' Interview by A. Clwyd, 26 July 1984, BBC Television, transcript, p. 28, GCPP Wootton 3/2/1 (published in L. Caldecott (1984) *Women of Our Century,* London: Ariel Books).

103 BW, *CB*, p. 39.

104 HL Deb., 20 November 1968, 297: 942.

105 BW to S. Simon, 28 May 1965, GCRF 9/1/40.

106 D. Stephens to Mr Wheeler-Booth, 9 March 1970, HL/PO/CP/1/6/42.

107 Unpublished letter from BW to *The Times* 8 May 1983, Lena Jeger Archives, JEGER/1/17, BLPES.

108 HL Deb., 31 July 1984, 455: 649.

109 'Row Over Jail Curb Study', *The Daily Mirror*, 14 November 1970.

110 'Prisoner Runs off into Dartmoor Fog, Dogs Join Hunt for "Houdini", Eighteenth Escape', *The Times*, 25 August 1964.

111 'Interview with Norma Levy', *The Daily Mail*, 26 January 2007.

112 'Antony Lambton'. http://en.wikipedia.org./wiki/Antony_Lambton [accessed 3 March 2010].

113 BW (1973) 'The Changing Ethic of British Public Life', Letter, *The Times*, 26 May.

114 J. Dare to BW, 2 December 1977, GCPP Wootton 4/9.

115 HL Deb., 13 February 1979, 398: 1108. This was the second reading of the first version of the Bill. BW's speech at the second reading of the second version is reprinted in *BWSW*, Vol. 3, pp. 154–159.

116 Ibid., 398: 1112–1113.

117 'Forbidden Love', *The Daily Express*, 15 February 1979.

118 Cunningham, 'Out of Step'.

119 Ibid.

120 J. Dare to BW, 20 May 1981, GCPP Wootton 4/9.

121 HL Deb., 4 March 1982, 427: 1377.

122 '"Worst Blemish" of Welfare State', *The Times*, 1 May 1962.

123 Philp, A.F. on behalf of The Rt. Hon. Baroness Wootton of Abinger, Professor the Rt. Hon. Lord Simey of Toxteth, and others (1965) 'Letter to the Prime Minister', 22 December. http://www.cpag.org.uk/about/history/letter-to-PM./htm [accessed 10 January 2009].

124 BW to P. Townsend, 23 December 1981, Townsend Papers.

125 BW (1983) 'Reflections on the Welfare State', in Bean, P. and MacPherson, S. (eds) *Approaches to Welfare*, London: Routledge & Kegan Paul, pp. 280–293, pp. 285–286.

126 BW (1975) *In Pursuit of Equality*, Fabian Tract 443, London: Fabian Society, p. 1; BW (1963) 'Is There a Welfare State? A Review of Recent Social Change in Britain', *Political Science Quarterly*, 78(2): 179–197.

127 *Towards Equality: Labour's Policy for Social Justice* (1956) London: The Labour Party; 'Labour's Plans for a "More Just" Division of Wealth', *The Times*, 9 July 1956.

128 'Inherited Wealth "Should be Taxed Out of Existence"', *The Guardian*, 26 July 1976.

129 'The Hydrogen Bomb: What is Happening?' Display, *The Manchester Guardian*, 17 April 1959.

130 Comerford, P. '50 Years Later, CND is Still on the March in a Nuclear World'. http://revpatrickcomerford.blogspot.com/2008_02_23_archive.html [accessed 30 September 2009].

131 'Britons in Plea to U.S., 58 of Prominence Urge No Nuclear Weapons Tests', *The New York Times*, 7 January 1960.

132 'Advertisement, What's a Hiroshima?', *The Guardian*, 6 August 1971.

133 P. Bean, Interview, 18 March 2009.

134 'World Congress for General Disarmament and Peace, Moscow 9–14 July 1962', *The New York Times*, 8 June 1962.

135 A.L. Williams to BW, 21 May 1962, GCPP Wootton 2/1.

136 BW to A.L. Williams, 24 May 1962, GCP Wootton 2/1.

137 'Labour Party to Expel Lord Russell: Leaders See Canon Collins', *The Times*, 20 June 1962.

138 BW (1981) 'When is a War Not a War?' *New Society*, 27 August: 339–341, p. 341.

139 A. Bradley, Interview, 9 May 2008.

140 Bendixson, T. (1969) 'Country Act Offers Chance for Design – and Fewer Pylons', *The Guardian*, 6 August.

141 Patterson, W. (1973) 'London Report: Airports, Concorde in Trouble', *Environment: Science and Policy for Sustainable Development*, 15(3): 2–3.

142 BW, *CB*, p. 25.

143 Ibid., p. 26.

144 Phillips, A. (1988) 'Baroness Wootton of Abinger', Obituary, *Countryside Commission News*, September/October, 33.

145 BW to S. Simon, 7 January 1970, GCRF 9/1/40.

146   MacLennan, H. (Chair), Advisory Group on Transplantation Problems (1969) *Advice on the Question of Amending the Human Tissue Act*, London: H.M.S.O.

147   Richards, H. (2010) 'It was 30 Years Ago Today', *Times Higher Education*, 30 April.

148   Sells, R.A. (1979) 'Live Organs from Dead People', *Journal of the Royal Society of Medicine*, February, 72: 109–117.

149   BW to S. Simon, 22 January 1960, GCRF 9/1/40.

150   Record of Speeches Made by Baroness Wootton of Abinger and Mrs C.D. Rackham at Golden Jubilee Dinner of the Cambridge Branch of the National Council of Women on 9 July 1962, p. 4, GCPP Duke 1/30.

151   BW to J. Butterfield, 16 June 1985, GCPP Wootton 2/1.

152   BW Speech, University of York, June 1966, GCPP Wootton 1/3/3.

153   O.R. McGregor to M. Smieton, 16 December 1968, RHC AR 130/1 Archives, Royal Holloway, University of London.

154   'Jubilee and Birthday Honours,' *The Times*, 11 June 1977.

155   F. Field, Personal communication.

156   See   http://en.wikipedia.org/wiki/List_of_Members_of_the_Order_of_the_Companions_of_ Honour [accessed 27 August 2010].

157   'Jubilee and Birthday Honours'.

158   J. Hutchins to BW, 21 September 1977; J. Freeman to K. Perry, 24 August 1990, GCPP Wootton 1/3/16.

159   P. Kurtz to BW, 30 June 1983, and International Order of Volunteers for Peace, 2 June 1982, GCPP Wootton 1/3/11.

160   Prince Philip to BW, 27 March 1975, GCPP Wootton 3/1/4.

161   BW (1974) *Fair Pay, Relativities and a Policy for Incomes*, The Twentieth Fawley Foundation Lecture [reprinted in *BWSW*, Vol. 4, pp. 16–32, p. 20].

162   BW, *IWNM*, p. 117.

163   Sir John Vincent William Barry 1903–1969, *Australian Dictionary of Biography*, online edn. http:// adbonline.anu.edu.au/biogs/A130146b.htm [accessed 8 March 2010].

164   J.V. Barry to BW, 20 June 1960; BW to J.V. Barry, 24 August 1960, Papers of Sir John V. Barry, MS 2505, National Library of Australia.

165   G.W. Paton to the Vice-Chancellor, University of Melbourne, 23 November 1960, UAA Series 200, Registrar's Correspondence, File 1961/553.

166   BW to G.W. Paton, 14 February 1961, Papers of Sir John V. Barry, MS 2505, National Library of Australia.

167   BW to J.V. Barry, 7 September 1961, Papers of Sir John V. Barry, MS 2505, National Library of Australia.

168   BW quoted in letter from S.W. Johnstone to N. R. Morris, 28 February 1961, UAA Series 200, Registrar's Correspondence, File 1961/553.

169   'Crime is Her Study', *The Advertiser*, 8 November 1961.

170   BW to J.V. Barry, 17 October 1961, Papers of Sir John V. Barry, MS 2505, National Library of Australia.

171   BW, *IWNM*, p. 116.

172   BW to J.V. Barry, 24 August 1960, Papers of Sir John V. Barry, MS 2505, National Library of Australia.

173   BW (1969) 'Sir John Barry, Social Conditions and the Law', Obituary, *The Times*, 15 November.

174   In *IWNM* (p. 123), BW states she went with four male MPs, but a note on the back of an official photograph of the delegation in GCPP Wootton 1/4/7 lists five.

175   Barnes, J. (2004) 'John Cordle: Moralistic MP Brought Down by the Poulson Affair', *The Independent*, 9 December.

176   BW, *IWNM*, p. 125.

177   K. Thompson to BW, 26 March 1963, GCPP Wootton 4/2.

178   'Students Geared for Battle', *The Observer*, 14 September 1969.

179   BW to S. Simon, 7 January 1970, GCRF 9/1/40.

180   'The South African Treason Trial', Display, *The Observer*, 31 August 1958; 'A Most Urgent Appeal,' Display, *The Manchester Guardian*, 11 March 1959; 'South Africa: A Most Urgent Appeal,' Display, *The Observer*, 17 April 1960.

181   'British Defence and Aid Fund', *The Times*, 13 and 25 October 1980.

182   BW (1969) 'Universities and Their Problems in the Contemporary World', The Sixth Richard Feetham Lecture delivered on 2 October 1969 at the University of the Witwatersrand, Johannesburg [reprinted in *BWSW*, Vol. 3, pp. 61–75, p. 72].

183   GCPP Wootton 2/2.

184   'Anti-bangs', *The Irish Times*, 11 February 1969.

185   'Stop the Concorde', Display, *The Times*, 15 January 1968; 'Should the Concorde be Cancelled?', Display, *The Guardian*, 10 February 1969.

186   'Anti-bangs'.

187   HL Deb., 16 July 1969, 304: 258–262.

188   Edwards, A.W.F. (1993) 'Concorde Campaign', Letter, *New Scientist*, 2 October; 'Richard Wiggs', Obituary, *The Daily Telegraph*, 19 July 2001.

189   BW, *IWNM*, p. 121.

190   K. Saigo to BW, 24 December 1968, GCPP Wootton 4/2.

191   BW to S. Simon, 7 January 1970, GCRF 9/1/40.

192   BW to V. Seal, 8 March 1969, GCPP Wootton 1/7/7.

193   Ibid.

194   Ibid.

195   BW to S. Simon, 26 December 1971, GCRF 9/1/40.

196   BW to V. Seal, 11 August 1971, GCPP Wootton 1/7/1.

197   'Vera Delf', Obituary, *The Independent*, 30 March 1999.

198   BW (1973) 'Journey to China', *Encounter*, June: 21–27, pp. 21–22.

199   BW China notebook, GCPP Wootton 4/2.

200   BW, 'Journey to China'.

201   B. Trotter, Interview, 4 March 2008.

202   Cunningham, 'Out of Step'.

203   'Lunchtime Comment Club', *The Times*, 21 May 1975.

204   http://www.lunchtimecomment.com/past_events.htm [accessed 5 March 2010]. BW also spoke in 1973 to the Manchester Luncheon Club, which lists her among its distinguished past speakers. http://www.manchesterluncheonclub.org.uk/Speakers.htm [accessed 18 October 2009].

205   BW (1979) 'Two Cheers – or Less – for Democracy', Review of *Law Legislation and Liberty, Volume 3*, by F. A. Hayek, *New Society*, 24 May: 464–465.

206   BW (1963) 'Stopping the Pay Smash and Grab', *The Observer*, 21 April; (1978) 'A Proposal for the Next Pay Phase', *New Statesman*, 30 April, pp. 557–558; (1979) 'Towards a Rational Pay Policy', *New Society*, 29 March, pp. 735–737; (1980) 'Asking for More Money: How the Methods Have Changed ...', *The Times*, 10 April.

207   BW (1962) 'Introduction', in Kahn, H. *Salaries in the Public Services in England and Wales*, London: Allen & Unwin, pp. 19–21, p. 19.

208   BW (1981) 'New Introduction,' in Spring-Rice, M. *Working-Class Wives* London: Virago (originally published 1939), pp. iii–iv, p. iii.

209   'Panorama' on thalidomide, 12 November 1964; on the death penalty, 21 December 1964; and on prison, 5 February 1978 (see Chapter 14).

210   A. Bradley, Interview, 9 May 2008.

211   R. Day to BW, 6 November 1979, GCPP Wootton 2/1.

212   BW to R. Day, 11 November 1979, GCPP Wootton 2/1.

213   E. Haynes to BW, n.d., GCPP Wootton 1/1/44.

214   BW, *IWNM*, p. 26.

215   *The Times*, 25 May 1959.

216   BW to J.V. Barry, 30 August 1962, Papers of Sir John V. Barry, MS 2505, National Library of Australia.

217   T. Morris, Interview, 29 April 2008.

218   BW to S. Simon, 22 December 1962, GCRF 9/1/40.

219   BW to S. Simon, 28 May 1965, GCRF 9/1/40.

220   B. Trotter, Interview, 4 March 2008.

221   BW (1969) 'The Role of the RPA Today: Four Speeches from the Recent RPA Dinner', pp. 262–264, BW Speech pp. 262–263, *Humanist*, September [GCPP Wootton 3/4/3].

222   BW, *IWNM*, p. 143.

223   BW to W. Haley, 6 October 1967, William Haley Papers, HALY 1/1, CAC.

224   V. Seal, Personal communication.

225   Mack, 'Barbara Wootton'.

226   D. Adams and E. Lushaba and N. Lushaba, Personal communication.

227   R. McGregor and N. McGregor, Interview, 8 August 2008.

228   'Growing Old Successfully,' *The Observer*, 3 April 1977.

229   Ibid.

230   Ibid.

16. Incurable Patient

1   BW (1942) 'A Plague on All Your Isms', *The Political Quarterly*, 13: 44–56.

2   'Baroness Wootton interviewed by David Reynolds', *The Freethinker*, 7 February 1970.

3   Mack, J. (1977) 'Barbara Wootton', *New Society*, 14 April: 58–59.

4   'Bruce Kenrick and Baroness Wootton of Abinger talk with Peter Snow' (1967) Central Rediffusion Services Ltd, *Dialogue with Doubt: Last Programmes from Rediffusion Television*, London: SCM Press, pp. 73–97, p. 74.

5   Knight, M., Malleson, M., Tribe, D., Willis, L. and Wootton, B. (1967) 'Into the Second Century', *The Freethinker* 5 May [GCPP Wootton 3/4/1, 57/16, p. 9].

6   Central Rediffusion, *Dialogue with Doubt*, pp. 76–83.

7   BW (1966) in A. J. Ayer et al., *What I Believe*, London: Allen & Unwin, pp. 205–218, p. 205.

8   Central Rediffusion, *Dialogue with Doubt*, p. 77; BW (1963) 'The Philosophy of a Social Scientist,' Talk given to the Oxford University Humanist Group, GCPP Wootton 3/1/1; *What I Believe*, p. 207, p. 210.

9   BW, 'The Philosophy of a Social Scientist', p. 1.

10   BW, *What I Believe*, p. 213.

11   'Face the Press', Tyne Tees Television Ltd, recorded 4 January 1984, Baroness Wootton of Abinger interviewed by P. Toynbee, G. Smith and A. Howard, transcript, p. 21, GCPP Wootton 3/2/1.

12   BW, *IWNM*, p. 175.

13   Kurtz, P. 'Progress Report: The Continuing Growth of Our Movement, Council for Secular Humanism'. http://www.secularhumanism.org [accessed 5 March 2010].

14   'Face the Press,' p. 17.

15   'Patients' Rights to Die in Bill', *The Guardian*, 5 December 1975.

16   Booth, R. (2010) 'Law on Assisted Dying is Inhuman, Says GP with Cancer', *The Guardian*, 25 February.

17   HL Deb., 12 February 1976, 368: 200–201.

18   Ibid., 368: 198.

19   Ibid.

20   Dowbiggin, I. (2005) *A Concise History of Euthanasia*, Lanham, Maryland: Rowman & Littlefield Publishers Inc, p. 80.

21   Humphry, D. and Wickett, A. (1986) *The Right to Die: Understanding Euthanasia*, London: The Bodley Head, pp. 14–15.

22   *What I Believe*, pp. 211–212.

23   BW (1980) 'Death – Whose Right to Choose?' *Midwife, Health Visitor and Community Nurse*, 16(5): 205–206, p. 205.

24   Ibid.

25   BW (1979) 'The Right to Die', *New Society*, 26 October: 202–203, p. 202.

26 'Face the Press', p. 18.
27 Correspondence between BW and M. Rose, GCPP Wootton 4/7.
28 BW (1978) 'The Right Way to Die', *The Sunday Times,* 12 March.
29 N. Reed to BW, 13 October 1978, GCPP Wootton 4/7.
30 N. Reed to BW, 'January 1983', GCPP Wootton 4/7.
31 Kemp, 'Merciful Release', p. 215.
32 BW to S. Simon, 17 August 1966, GCRF 9/1/40.
33 A. Croft to BW, 17 December 1982, thanks to A. Croft.
34 HL Deb., 6 April 1982, 429: 114–117.
35 GCPP Wootton 2/1.
36 Avebury, Lord et al. (1984) 'The Golden Age of Liberty', Letter, *The Guardian,* 22 February.
37 P. Townsend and J. Corston, Interview, 6 February 2008.
38 R. Pinker, Interview, 23 March 2010.
39 'Women of Our Century: Baroness Barbara Wootton', Interview by Ann Clwyd, 26 July 1984, BBC Television, transcript, GCCP Wootton 3/2/1 (published in L. Caldecott (1984) *Women of Our Century,* London: Ariel Books).
40 'Face the Press'.
41 P. Bean, Interview, 18 March 2009.
42 BW (1985) 'The Moral Basis of the Welfare State', in Bean, P., Ferris, J. and Whynes, D. (eds). *In Defence of Welfare,* London: Tavistock, pp. 31–45, p. 34, p. 40.
43 Lord Jenkins to BW, 20 November 1985, GCPP Wootton 4/7.
44 HL Deb., 11 December, 469: 289.
45 HL Deb., 4 July 1985, 465: 1315.
46 GCPP Wootton 4/4.
47 HL Deb., 4 July 1985, 465: 1324.
48 Gould, M. (2007) 'Sparing the Rod', *The Guardian,* 9 January.
49 A. Bryant and A. Bryant, Interview, 23 April 2008.
50 BW to A. Howard, 27 September 1981, GCPP Wootton 2/2.
51 BW to R. Day, 25 October 1981, GCPP Wootton 2/1.
52 R. Day to BW, 9 November 1981, GCPP Wootton 2/1.
53 A. Bradley, Interview, 9 May 2008.
54 'A Hard-working Baroness Wants to Take it Easy', *The Sunday Express,* 15 June 1969.
55 V. Seal to L. Jeger, 4 October 1992, Lena Jeger Archives, JEGER/1/17, BLPES.
56 A. Bryant and A. Bryant, Interview, 23 April 2008.
57 A. Bradley, Interview, 9 May 2008.
58 Mack, 'Barbara Wootton'.
59 Faith, N. (2000) 'Obituary, Sir Campbell Adamson', *The Independent,* 29 August.
60 Adamson, C. (1989) 'Sir Campbell Adamson Remembers Barbara Wootton', *Family Policy Bulletin,* Winter, 6: 3.
61 C. Adamson to BW, 24 June 1975, GCPP Wootton 2/1.
62 M. Wicks, Interview, 2 April 2009.
63 BW (1983) 'Honeymoon', Review of *The Diary of Beatrice Webb Vol. II, London Review of Books,* 1 December, 5(22/23).
64 BW (1980) 'Mrs Thatcher's Instincts', *London Review of Books,* 7 August.
65 F. Field, Interview, 7 February 2008.
66 V. Seal, Interview, 20 February 2008.
67 M. Adamson, Interview, 14 April 2008.
68 A. Bryant and A. Bryant, Interview, 23 April 2008
69 Ibid.
70 F. Field, Interview, 7 February 2008.
71 BW to P. Parker, 12 March 1978, thanks to G. Thomas.
72 HL Deb., 20 January 1965, 262: 920–924.
73 Field, F. (1979) 'Introduction' in Field, F. (ed.) *The Wealth Report,* London: Routledge & Kegan Paul, pp. 1–9, p. 9.

74   F. Field, Interview, 7 February 2008.

75   Ibid.

76   P. Chitnis to BW, 19 December 1975, GCPP Wootton 1/3/12.

77   BW to P. Chitnis, 29 December 1975, GCPP Wootton 1/3/12; V. Seal, Personal communication.

78   J. Chanter to BW, 10 February 1987, GCPP Wootton 2/1.

79   BW to Lady Haley, 16 September 1987, GCPP Wootton 2/1.

80   V. Seal, Interview, 20 February 2008.

81   V. Seal, Personal communication.

82   V. Seal, Interview, 20 February 2008.

83   V. Seal, Interview, 23 October 2007.

84   BW to C. Adamson and M. Adamson, 25 December 1982, GCPP Wootton 2/1.

85   Halsey, A.H. (2004) 'Sprott, Walter John Herbert [Sebastian] (1897–1971)', *Oxford Dictionary of National Biography*, Oxford University Press, September. http://0-www.oxforddnb.com.catalogue.ulrls.lon.ac.uk/view/article/62699 [accessed 13 August 2010].

86   R. McGregor and N. McGregor, Interview, 8 August 2008.

87   BW to T. Gould, 12 July 1984; thanks to T. Gould.

88   BW to T. Gould, 29 October 1979; thanks to T. Gould.

89   T. Gould, Interview, 24 April 2008.

90   *Minutes of the Tutorial Classes Committee of the University Extension and Tutorial Classes Council for the Session 1944–5*, The Archive of the Department of Extra-Mural Studies, University of London, EM 6/1/38.

91   BW to M. Hetherington, (n.d., 1979?); thanks to A. Ashford.

92   A. Ashford, Interview, 30 July 2008.

93   BW to L. Goodings, 13 August 1982, GCPP Wootton 2/2.

94   B. Trotter, Interview, 4 March 2008.

95   E. Gowers to BW, 2 August 1948, GCPP Wootton 1/1/2.

96   BW to P. Chitnis, 29 December 1975, GCPP Wootton 1/3/12.

97   BW (1978) 'My Relations with the Police', unpublished ms, GCPP Wootton 3/4/6.

98   BW to A. Croft, 10 May 1982; thanks to A. Croft.

99   R.E.D. Bishop to BW, 20 April 1982, and BW to R.E.D. Bishop, 25 April 1982, GCPP Wootton 4/4.

100   BW to L. McIntyre, 3 July 1983, GCPP Wootton 2/2.

101   BW to J. Dawson 18 September, GCPP Wootton 2/1.

102   BW to L. McIntyre, 25 August 1985, GCPP Wootton 2/2.

103   BW to G. Trasler, 21 April 1986, GCPP Wootton 2/2.

104   B. Trotter, Interview, 4 March 2008.

105   GCPP Wootton 1/1/10.

106   G.B. Skelsey to BW, 28 December 1984, GCPP Wootton 1/3/11.

107   BW to A. Duke, 22 August 1985, GCPP Duke 2/1/7.

108   F. Field, Interview, 7 February 2008.

109   O.R. McGregor (1992) 'Foreword', in *BWSW*, pp. ix–xix, p. xiii.

110   R. McGregor and N. McGregor, Interview, 8 August 2008.

111   BW to T. Gould, 5 May 1984; thanks to T. Gould.

112   BW to M-K. Wilmers, 17 August 1985, GCPP Wootton 2/2.

113   P. Townsend and J. Corston, Interview, 6 February 2008.

114   BW to R. Day, 25 October 1981, GCPP Wootton 2/1.

115   F. Field, Personal communication.

116   Hayman, H. (2007) 'Women in the Lords: The Life Peerages Act – Women and Change in the House of Lords since 1958', 6 December. http://www.meg.qmul.ac.uk/pastevents/Women1Hayman/index.html [accessed 29 August 2010]; F. Field, Interview; C. Clarke, Personal communication.

117   Earl and Countess of Listowel to BW, 14 October 1985, GCPP Wootton 1/1/6.

118   Lord Aberdare to BW, 15 October 1985, GCPP Wootton 1/1/6.

119   Cunningham, J. (1982) 'Out of Step', *The Guardian*, 4 June.

120   V. Seal, Interview, 16 July 2008; K.C. Titmuss, Personal communication.

121   B. Trotter, Interview, 4 March 2008.

122   T. Gould, Interview, 24 April 2008.

123   V. Seal, Personal communication.

124   V. Seal, Interview, 13 December 2008.

125   P. Bean, Interview, 18 March 2009.

126   N. Kinnock to BW, 12 November 1985, GCPP Wootton 1/1/11.

127   BW to 'Very Dear Friends', Christmas 1985; thanks to R. McGregor.

128   V. Seal, Personal communication.

129   BW to O.R. McGregor, 6 April 1986; thanks to R. McGregor.

130   BW to E. Lekachman and R. Lekachman, 24 August 1986, GCPP Wootton 2/2.

131   BW to F. Wright, 8 January 1986, GCPP Wootton 1/1/6.

132   BW to V. Delf, 8 August 1986, GCPP Wootton 1/1/6.

133   F. Field, Interview, 7 February 2008.

134   V. Seal, Personal communication.

135   F. Field, Interview, 7 February 2008.

136   L. Rushford to BW, 1 May 1987; V. Seal to L. Rushford, n.d., GCPP Wootton 1/3/11.

137   M. Luvaglio to BW, 20 January 1987, GCPP Wootton 1/3/11.

138   'Get Carter Murder Duo Insist We're Innocent', *The Guardian,* 3 February 2002.

139   HL Deb., 14 July 1987, 488: 968–969.

140   J. Trumpington to BW, n.d. (April/May 1986), GCPP Wootton 1/1/6.

141   L. Faithfull to BW, 11 February 1986, GCPP Wootton 1/1/6.

142   J. Vickers to BW, 29 November 1985, GCPP Wootton 1/1/6.

143   BW to J Vickers, 26 August 1986, GCPP Wootton 1/1/6.

144   H. Nicholls to BW, 20 December 1985, GCPP Wootton 1/1/6.

145   H. Walston to BW, 14 June 1985, GCPP Wootton 1/1/6.

146   Lord Aberdare to BW, 17 February 1986, GCPP Wootton 4/9.

147   BW to N. Kinnock, 6 January 1986, GCPP Wootton 1/1/12.

148   BW to Lord Elwyn Jones, 8 May 1986, GCPP Wootton 1/1/6.

149   P. Townsend and J. Corston, Interview, 6 February 2008.

150   P. Bean, Interview, 18 March 2009; Bean, P. and Whynes, D. (eds) *Barbara Wootton: Social Science and Social Policy, Essays in Her Honour*, London: Tavistock.

151   Ibid.

152   V. Seal to G. Davies 16 February 1986, GCPP Wootton 2/2.

153   V. Seal, Interview, 20 February 2008.

154   P. Townsend and J. Corston, Interview, 6 February 2008.

155   A. Bradley, Interview, 9 May 2008.

156   V. Seal, Interview, 20 February 2008.

157   V Seal, Interview, 23 October 2007.

158   Telemessage to BW, 13 April 1987, GCPP Wootton 1/1/6.

159   V. Seal, Interview, 23 October 2007.

160   Handwritten notes, Lena Jeger Archives, JEGER/1/17, BLPES.

161   A. H. Halsey, 'Wootton, Barbara Frances, Baroness Wootton of Abinger (1897–1988)', *Oxford Dictionary of National Biography*, Oxford University Press, 2004; online edn, Oct 2009. http://0-www.oxforddnb.com.catalogue.ulrls.lon.ac.uk/view/article/39876 [accessed 28 October 2010].

162   D. Grassie, Interview, 9 October 2008.

163   V. Seal, Personal communication.

164   D. Grassie, Interview, 9 October 2008.

165   F. Field, Interview, 7 February 2008.

166   Page from BW diary, thanks to V. Seal.

167   P. Chitnis to BW 16 March 1987, GCPP Wootton 1/3/12.

168   V. Seal to E. Lekachman and R. Lekachman, 20 January 1988, thanks to V. Seal.

169   T. Gould, Interview, 24 April 2008.

170   'Face the Press,' p. 17, p. 19.

171 V. Seal, Personal communication.

172 Frank Field's account of Barbara's own career as an incurable patient was first told during a House of Commons debate in 1995 (HC Deb., 19 April 1995, 258: 158–159); it was repeated in 2005 in another debate he sponsored there on 'End-of-life' Care following the death of his own mother (Westminster Hall debates, 19 July 2005, http://www.theyworkforyou.com/whall/?id=2005-07-19a.365.1) [accessed 2 September 2010]) and then reported in *The Liverpool Daily Post* (22 July 2005) with the headline: 'MP: I Was Prepared to Help My Friend to Die'. The story was resurrected again by the *News of the World* in July 2009, and appeared at that time on 'Frankly Speaking', Field's Westminster blog. (http://www.frankfield.co.uk/~ff-resources/rss.php) [accessed 12 December 2010].

173 'Woman of Action: Lady Wootton', Radio 4, 17 May 1975; transcript, BBC Written Archives Centre, p. 6.

174 B. Trotter, Interview, 4 March 2008.

175 V. Seal, Personal communication.

176 A. Bryant and A. Bryant, Interview, 23 April 2008.

177 V. Seal, Interview, 23 October 2007.

178 V. Seal, Personal communication.

17. In the World She Never Made

1 'Bruce Kenrick and Baroness Wootton of Abinger talk with Peter Snow' (1967) Central Rediffusion Services Ltd, *Dialogue with Doubt: Last Programmes from Rediffusion Television*, London: SCM Press, pp. 73–97, p. 96.

2 D. Grassie, Interview, 9 October 2008.

3 V. Seal, Personal communication.

4 Jeger, L. (1988) 'Barbara Wootton, An Architect of the Welfare State', Obituary, *The Guardian*, 13 July.

5 'Baroness Wootton of Abinger, Social Philosopher and Public Servant', Obituary, *The Times*, 13 July 1988.

6 'Baroness Wootton Dies at 91, A Caring Reformer', Obituary, *The Dorking Advertiser*, 14 July 1988.

7 Canton, R. (1988) 'Barbara Wootton, Magistrate and Social Scientist', Obituary, *Probation Journal*, 35: 152.

8 Bean, P. (1989) 'Barbara Wootton, Testament for a Social Scientist', Obituary, *The British Journal of Criminology*, 29(1): 71–75.

9 Gould, T. (1988) 'The Girl Who Never Made It', *New Statesman & Society*, 22 July.

10 V. Seal to N. Morgan, 15 December 1988; Seal Papers.

11 Burgess, T. (1994) Review of *Selected Writings, Royal Society of Arts Journal*, 142(5447): 76–77.

12 BW, *IWNM*, p. 190.

13 O.R. McGregor (1977) Speech at BW's Eightieth Birthday Party, GCPP Wootton 1/1/7.

14 N. Annan to R. Silvers, 15 February 1973, Noel Annan Papers, King's College, Cambridge, NGA/5/1/1059.

15 'Face the Press', Tyne Tees Television Ltd, recorded 4 January 1984; Baroness Wootton of Abinger interviewed by P. Toynbee, G. Smith and A. Howard, transcript, pp. 4–5, GCPP Wootton 3/2/1.

16 Phillips, A. (1988) 'Baroness Wootton of Abinger', Obituary, *Countryside Commission News*, September/October.

17 Townsend, P. (1977) 'The Unrepentant Democratic Socialist', *New Statesman*, 15 April: 487–488.

18 Longford, Lord, HL Deb., 3 November 1964, 261: 33.

19 'Baroness Wootton of Abinger', Obituary, *The Daily Telegraph*, 13 July 1988.

20 Field, F. (1988) 'Frank Field on Barbara Wootton', *The Independent Magazine*, 1 October, p. 62.

21 'Baroness Wootton of Abinger, Social Philosopher and Public Servant', Obituary, *The Times*, 13 July.

22 Stina Lyon, E. (2009) 'What Influence? Public Intellectuals, the State and Civil Society', in Fleck, C., Hess, A. and Stina Lyon, E. (eds) *Intellectuals and Their Publics: Perspectives from the Social Sciences*, Farnham, Surrey: Ashgate Publishing Ltd, pp. 69–88, p. 70.

23 Mays, J. B. (1967) 'Lady with Briefcase', Review of *IWNM*, *New Society*, 23 March.

24 West, R. (1967) 'From Bench to Box', Review of *IWNM*, *The Sunday Telegraph*, 5 March.

25 HL Deb., 14 January 1971, 314: 226.

26 Ashdown, P. (1967) 'Baroness Wootton: A Long Way to Go After Coming a Long Way', *The Birmingham Post*, 4 March.

27 Barker, P. (1993) 'Rebel With a Cause', Review of *Selected Writings*, *The Times Literary Supplement*, 28 May, p. 4.

28 'Changing Society No. 78, Interview with Baroness Wootton by A. Symonds', European Service General News Talk, 1 January 1967, GCPP Wootton 3/2/1.

29 'Women of Our Century: Baroness Wootton', Interview by A. Clwyd, 26 July 1984, BBC Television, transcript, p. 26, GCPP Wootton 3/2/1 (published in L. Caldecott (1984) *Women of Our Century*, London: Ariel Books).

30 'Homage to Wootton', *The Listener*, 28 August 1986, p. 1.

31 Walker, N. (2003) *A Man Without Loyalties*, Chichester: Barry Rose Law Publishers, p. 98.

32 A. Ashford, Interview, 30 July 2008.

33 P. Bean, Interview, 18 March 2009.

34 Pinker, R. (1988) 'Baroness Wootton of Abinger', Obituary, *The Independent*, 13 July.

35 Oakley, A., Gough, D. Oliver, S. and Thomas, J. (2005) 'The Politics of Evidence and Methodology: Lessons from the EPPI-Centre', *Evidence and Policy*, 1(1): 5–31.

36 Chalmers, I. (2003) 'Trying to do More Good Than Harm in Policy and Practice: The Role of Rigorous, Transparent, Up-to-Date Evaluations', in *The Annals of the American Academy of Political and Social Science*, 589 (Special Issue, Sherman, L.W. (ed.) 'Misleading Evidence and Evidence-led Policy: Making Social Science More Experimental'): 22–40.

37 O.R. McGregor (1992) 'Foreword', in *BWSW*, pp. ix–xix, p. xvi.

38 Wedderburn, D. (1994) 'Barbara Wootton and Contemporary Social Problems: Fighting for Good Causes', The Fawcett Lecture, Royal Holloway College, 1 March, p. 8 [GCPP Wootton 1/1/12].

39 BW (1942) 'A Plague on All Your Isms', *The Political Quarterly*, 13: 44–56.

40 Cleave, M. (1970) 'The Hip Baroness Wootton of Abinger', *The New York Times Magazine*, 10 May.

41 Halsey, A.H. (1996) *No Discouragement: An Autobiography*, Basingstoke, Hants.: Macmillan, pp. 104–105, pp. 205–202.

42 See Oakley, A. (2000) *Experiments in Knowing: Gender and Method in the Social Sciences*, Chapter 10 'Lessons from America', Cambridge: Polity Press.

43 BW (1935) 'The New Deal at the Crossroads', *The Highway*, 27: 119–122; BW (1937) 'The Outlook for American Labour', *The Highway*, 29: 6–8, p. 7.

44 Wright Mills, C. (1943) 'The Professional Ideology of Social Pathologists', *American Journal of Sociology*, 49: 165–180.

45 BW (1961) 'Humanism and Social Pathology', in Huxley, J. (ed.) *The Humanist Frame*, London: George Allen & Unwin, pp 347–356, p. 353.

46 Campbell, D. T. (1969) 'Reforms as Experiments', *American Psychologist*, Vol. 24, pp. 409–29.

47 See http://www.campbellcollaboration.org/.

48 Younghusband, E. (1967) Review of *IWNM*, *Magistrate*, April: 58.

49 BW (1933), 'The Morning After', in *TT*, pp. 86–87.

50 BW, *IWNM*, p. 210.

51 O.R. McGregor, Speech at BW's Eightieth Birthday Party, GCPP Wootton 1/1/7.

52 Stina Lyon, E. (2004) 'The Use of Biographical Material in Intellectual History: Writing about Alva and Gunnar Myrdal's Contribution to Sociology', *International Journal of Social Research Methodology*, 7(4): 323–343.

53 BW, *IWNM*, p. 278.

54 P. Townsend, Interview, 6 February 2008.

55 Townsend, P. (2004) 'Smith, Brian Abel- (1926–1996)', *Oxford Dictionary of National Biography*, Oxford University Press; online edn, Oct 2006. http://0-www.oxforddnb.com.catalogue.ulrls.lon.ac.uk/view/article/60482 [accessed 15 Oct 2010].

56 BW, *IWNM*, p. 153.

57 HL Deb., 14 March 1972, 329: 398.

58 BW, *IWNM*, p. 147.

59 HL Deb., 20 January 1965, 262: 917–920.

60 Harrison, TWL.

61 HL Deb., 13 February 1973, 338: 1400.

62 HL Deb., 14 March 1972, 329: 398–400.

63 HL Deb., 3 March 1971, 315: 1335–1338.

64 BW (1962) 'Senior Posts for Women', Letter, *The Times*, 26 March.

65 BW (1981) 'Ground Floor', Review of *Women In Top Jobs* by M. Fogarty et al., *London Review of Books*, 15 October, 3(19): 11.

66 HL Deb., 14 May 1973, 342: 625–626.

67 Field, F. (1988) *The Guardian*, 13 July.

68 Crawford, E. (1999) *The Women's Suffrage Movement: A Reference Guide 1866–1926*, London: UCL Press, p. 765.

69 BW Interview with B. Harrison, TWL. 17 February 1976. The Women's Library 8SUF/B/068).

70 Bean, 'Barbara Wootton'; Clwyd, 'Women of Our Century'.

71 Harrison, TWL.

72 R. McGregor, Personal communication.

73 Record of Speeches Made by Baroness Wootton of Abinger and Mrs C.D. Rackham at Golden Jubilee Dinner of the Cambridge Branch of the National Council of Women on 9 July 1962, GCPP Duke 1/30, p. 6.

74 BW (1947) 'The Married Woman's Dilemma', *World Review,* August, pp. 20–23 [GCPP Wootton 3/4/2].

75 Stott, C. (1968) 'The Daughter Who Became Distinguished', *The Guardian*, 5 December.

76 P. Bean, Interview, 18 March 2009.

77 Newman, M. (2008) 'Academe Still Male Bastion, Assert Female Scholars', *The Times Higher Education*, 10 July.

78 Halsey, A.H. (2004) *A History of Sociology in Britain*, Oxford: Oxford University Press, p. 171.

79 BW (1978) 'Uses of Sociology', *New Society* 44: 553–554 [reprinted in *BWSW*, Vol. 3, pp. 117–121].

80 Bulmer, M. (1986) *Social Science and Social Policy*, London: Allen & Unwin.

81 'Baroness Wootton of Abinger, Social Philosopher and Public Servant'.

82 Wilkins, L. (1999) *Unofficial Aspects of a Life in Policy Research*. http://www.essex.ac.uk/psychology/overlays/policyresearch.htm [accessed 4 March 2009], p. 124.

83 BW (1969) 'Universities and Their Problems in the Contemporary World', The Sixth Richard Feetham Lecture, delivered on 2 October at the University of the Witwatersrand, Johannesburg [reprinted in *BWSW*, Vol. 3, pp. 61–75, p. 69].

84 BW (1933), 'The Morning After', p. 87.

85 BW (1942) 'A Plague on All Your Isms', *The Political Quarterly*, 13: 44–56, p. 56.

86 BW, *IWNM*, p. 185.

87 BW, *IWNM*, p. 63.

88 BW to W. Haley, 22 January 1967, William Haley Papers, HALY 1/6, CAC.

89 BW to P. Townsend, 29 May 1976, Townsend Papers.

90 Jeger, 'Barbara Wootton'.

91 J. Floud, Interview, 27 January 2009.

92 M. Rutter, Interview, 26 January 2009.

93 V. Seal, Personal communication.

94 P. Bean, Interview, 18 March 2009.

95 T. Gould, Interview, 24 April 2008.

96 T. Morris, Interview, 29 April 2008.

97 Field, 'Frank Field on Barbara Wootton'.

98 Morris, T. (1989) 'In Memoriam: Barbara Wootton 1897–1988', Obituary, *The British Journal of Sociology*, 40(2): 310–318, p. 313.

99 L. Blom-Cooper, Interview, 9 February 2009.

100 BW (1979) 'The Old Are Just Like Us – But Older', Review of *The View in Winter* by R. Blythe, *New Society*, 1 November: 269–270.

101 Adamson, C. (1988) 'Baroness Wootton of Abinger', Funeral Address; thanks to V. Seal.

102 Neustatter, A. (1976) 'Why Top Form Girls Are Joining the Bottom Class', *The Guardian*, 10 November.

103 '2 Women Join House of Lords', *The Spokesman-Review,* 22 October 1958.

104 On economics, see King, J.E. (2003) 'Lament for Economics, or How Barbara Wootton Gave It All Away and Became a Sociologist', *Research in the History of Economic Thought and Methodology*, 22: 301–321. For omission, see, for example, Feiner, S., Kuiper, E. and Notburga, O. (eds) (1995) *Out of the Margin: Feminist Perspectives on Economic Theory*, London: Routledge. Among the dictionaries that omit BW, see Law, C. (2000) *Women: A Modern Political Dictionary*, London: I.B. Tauris. On omissions from texts about planning, see, for example, Budd, A. (1978) *The Politics of Economic Planning*, London: Fontana, and O'Hara, G. (2007) *From Dreams to Disillusionment: Economic and Social Planning in 1960s Britain,* Basingstoke: Palgrave Macmillan. On omissions from histories of left-wing politics, see, for example, Pimlott, B. (1977) *Labour and the Left in the 1930s*, Cambridge: Cambridge University Press; Corthorn, P. (2006) *In the Shadow of the Dictators: The British Left in the 1930s*, London: Tauris Academic Studies; and Beech, M. and Hickson K. (2007) *Labour's Thinkers: The Intellectual Roots of Labour From Tawney to Gordon Brown*, London: Tauris Academic Studies. On omissions from histories of social policy and social theory, see, for example, Glennerster, H. (2000) *British Social Policy Since 1945,* Oxford: Blackwell, and Inglis, F. (1982) *Radical Earnestness: English Social Theory 1880–1980*, Oxford: Martin Robertson.

105 M. Adamson, Interview, 14 April 2008.

106 'Clwyd, 'Women of Our Century'.

107 Dimand, R.W. and Hardeen, I. (2003) 'Barbara Wootton's Lament for Economics and Vision of a Social Economics', *Forum for Social Economics*, 33(1): 23–32.

108 P. Townsend, Interview, 6 February 2008.

109 Appleton, D. (1983) 'A Job Today Does Not Mean Work Tomorrow', *The Guardian*, 19 October.

110 Heidensohn, F.M. and Gelsthorpe, L. (2007) 'Gender and Crime', in Maguire, M., Morgan, R. and Reiner, R. (eds) *The Oxford Handbook of Criminology*, 4th edn, Oxford: Oxford University Press: 381–420.

111 Dyer, O. (2004) 'One Million People Die on World's Roads Every Year', *British Medical Journal*, 328: 851.

112 M. Rutter, Interview, 26 January 2009.

113 Johnson, Y.V. (2008) 'Remembering Barbara Wootton's Contribution to Social Work Education', *Journal of Social Work Education*, 44(1): 23–36.

114 Walker, A. (1996) 'Blaming the Victims', in Lister, R. (ed.) (1996) 'Charles Murray and the Underclass: The Developing Debate', *Choice in Welfare No. 33*, London: IEA Health and Welfare Unit: 66–74, p. 68.

115 Morris, 'In Memoriam: Barbara Wootton', p. 316.

116 De-la-Noy, M. (1971) 'Making Dents in a Nasty World', *Illustrated London News*, 13 February: 17–18.

117 Harris, J. (1994) 'Last Victorian', Review of *BWSW*, *London Review of Books*, 10 November, 16(21): 12.

118 'Baroness Wootton of Abinger, Social Philosopher and Public Servant'.

119 BW, *IWNM*, p. 279.

120 BW (1982) 'Public Tasks', *The House Magazine*, 12 February: 8.

Select Bibliography

Note: The following books have been referred to in the text but not detailed in the Notes section.

Adam, N.K. (1930) *The Physics and Chemistry of Surfaces*, Oxford: Oxford University Press.

Atwood, M. (1985) *The Handmaid's Tale*, Toronto: McClelland and Stewart.

Beauvoir, S. de (1953) *The Second Sex*, London: Cape.

Bowlby, J. (1946) *Forty-Four Juvenile Thieves: Their Characters and Home Life*, London: Baillière, Tindall & Cox.

Brandt, B. (1995) *Whole Life Economics*, Philadelphia, PA: New Society Publishers.

Burdekin, K. (under the pseudonym Murray Constantine) (1937) *Swastika Night*, London: Victor Gollancz.

Clifford, H.D. (1955) *Home Decoration*, London: Country Life.

Clifford, H.D. (1957) *New Houses for Moderate Means*, London: Country Life.

Clifford, H.D. (1963) *The Country Life Book of Houses for Today*, London: Country Life.

Clifford, H.D. and Enthoven, R.E. (1954) *New Homes from Old Buildings*, London: Country Life.

Cole, G.D.H. (1913) *World of Labour*, London: Bell.

Cook, J., Roberts, J. and Waylen, G. (eds) (2000) *Towards a Gendered Political Economy*, Basingstoke, Hants.: Macmillan.

Elias, N. (1969 and 1982, originally published in German 1939) *The Civilizing Process, Vol. 1 The History of Manners*, and *The Civilizing Process, Vol.11 State Formation and Civilization*, Oxford: Blackwell.

Ferber, M.A. and Nelson, J. A. (eds) *Beyond Economic Man: Feminist Theory and Economics*, Chicago: University of Chicago Press.

Friedan, B. (1963) *The Feminine Mystique*, London: Victor Gollancz.

Galbraith, J. K. (1973) *Economics and the Public Purpose*, Boston: Houghton Mifflin.

Gowers, E. (1948) *Plain Words: A Guide to the Use of English*, London: H.M.S.O.

Greenidge, T.L. (1938) *Philip and the Dictator*, London: Fortune Press,

Greer, G. (1970) *The Female Eunuch*, London: MacGibbon & Kee.

Hancock, W.K. (1943) *Argument of Empire*, Harmondsworth: Penguin.

Harrod, R. (1951) *The Life of John Maynard Keynes*, London: Macmillan.

Hayek, F.A. (1944) *The Road to Serfdom*, London: George Routledge & Sons.

Henderson, H.D. (1922) *Supply and Demand*, London: Nisbet.

Hicks, J.R. (1932) The Theory of Wages, London: Macmillan.

Himmelweit, H.T, Oppenheim, A. N. and Vince, P. (1958) *Television and the Child: An Empirical Study of the Effects of Television on the Young*, London: Nuffield Foundation.

Humphry, D. with Wickett, A. (1978) *Jean's Way*, London: Quartet Books.

Hutchinson, T.W. (1938) *The Significance and Basic Postulates of Economic Theory*, London: Macmillan.

Jameson, S. (1936) *In the Second Year*, London: Cassell & Co.

Keen, S. (2001) *Debunking Economics,* London: Zed Books.

Kyle, B.R.F. (1964) *Teach Yourself Librarianship,* London: The English Universities Press Ltd.

Macmillan, H. (1934) *Reconstruction*, London: Macmillan and Co Ltd.

Marshall, A. and Marshall, M.P. (1879) *The Economics of Industry*, London: Macmillan & Co.

Marshall, A. (1910, originally published 1890) *Principles of Economics*, 6th edition, London: Macmillan.

Millett, K. (1971) *Sexual Politics,* London: Hart-Davis.

Mitchison, N. (1935) *We Have been Warned*, London: Constable & Co.

Muggeridge, M. (1934) *Winter in Moscow*, London: Eyre and Spottiswoode.

Myrdal, G. (1974) *Against the Stream: Critical Essays on Economics,* London: Macmillan.

Ormerod, P. (1994) *The Death of Economics*, London: Faber and Faber.

Orwell, G. (1946) *Animal Farm*, New York: Harcourt, Brace and Co.

Pedersen, S. (2004) *Eleanor Rathbone and the Politics of Conscience*, New Haven and London: Yale University Press.

Price, M.P. (1921) *My Reminiscences of the Russian Revolution*, London: Allen & Unwin.

Ransome, A. (1919) *Six Weeks in Russia in 1919*, London: Allen & Unwin.

Reddaway, W.B. (1935) *The Russian Financial System*, London: Macmillan.

Russell, B. (1920) *The Practice and Theory of Bolshevism*, London: Allen and Unwin.

Schumacher, E.F. (1973) *Small is Beautiful*, London: Blond and Briggs.

Skidelsky, R. (2004) *John Maynard Keynes 1883-1946,* London: Pan Books.

Slater, M. (1934) *Haunting Europe*, London: Wishart and Co.

Stocks, M.D. (1949) *Eleanor Rathbone*, London: Victor Gollancz.

Titmuss, R.M. (1938) *Poverty and Population*, London: Macmillan and Co.

Toynbee, A.J. (1934–1961) *A Study of History*, Vols 1-12, Oxford: Oxford University Press.

Upward, E. (1977) *The Spiral Ascent: A Trilogy of Novels*, London: Heinemann.

Wells, H.G. (1920) *Russia in the Shadows*, London: Hodder and Stoughton.

Wells, H.G. (1940) *The Rights of Man*, Harmondsworth: Penguin.

Wollstonecraft, M. (1792) *A Vindication of the Rights of Woman*, Vol. 1, London.

Woolf, V. (1992, originally published 1938) *Three Guineas*, Oxford: Oxford University Press.

Index

Page numbers with 'pl' are plates. BW is Barbara Wootton; GW is George Wright.